PARENTHOOD
IN AMERICA

An Encyclopedia

THE AMERICAN FAMILY

The six titles that make up **The American Family** offer a revitalizing new take on U.S. history, surveying current culture from the perspective of the family and incorporating insights from psychology, sociology, and medicine. Each two-volume, A-to-Z encyclopedia features its own advisory board, editorial slant, and apparatus, including illustrations, bibliography, and index.

Parenthood in America

EDITED BY Lawrence Balter, New York University

Adolescence in America

EDITED BY Jacqueline V. Lerner, Boston College,
and Richard M. Lerner, Tufts University;
Jordan W. Finkelstein, Pennsylvania State University,
Advisory Editor

Girlhood in America

EDITED BY Miriam Formanek-Brunell,
University of Missouri, Kansas City

Boyhood in America

EDITED BY Priscilla Ferguson Clement, Pennsylvania State
University, Delaware County, and Jacqueline S. Reinier, Emerita,
California State University, Sacramento

Infancy in America

EDITED BY Alice Sterling Honig, Emerita, Syracuse University;
Hiram E. Fitzgerald, Michigan State University;
and Holly Brophy-Herb, Michigan State University

The Family in America

EDITED BY Joseph M. Hawes, University of Memphis,
and Elizabeth F. Shores, Little Rock, Arkansas

PARENTHOOD IN AMERICA

An Encyclopedia

Volume 1
A–M

Lawrence Balter, EDITOR
Professor of Applied Psychology
New York University
New York, New York

FOREWORD BY **Robert B. McCall**
Director, Office of Child Development
University of Pittsburgh
Pittsburgh, Pennsylvania

A B C ☯ C L I O

Santa Barbara, California
Denver, Colorado
Oxford, England

Library of Congress Cataloging-in-Publication Data

Parenthood in America : an encyclopedia / Lawrence Balter, editor ; foreword by Robert B. McCall.
    p. cm. — (The American family)
Includes bibliographical references and index.
   ISBN 1-57607-213-4 (hardcover : alk. paper) — ISBN 1-57607-387-4 (e-book)
1. Parenting—United States—Encyclopedias. 2. Family—United States—Encyclopedias. I. Balter, Lawrence. II. American family (Santa Barbara, Calif.)
 HQ755.8 .P3783 2000
 306.85--dc21

00-011782

06 05 04 03 02 01 00   10 9 8 7 6 5 4 3 2 1 (cloth)

ABC-CLIO, Inc.
130 Cremona Drive, P.O. Box 1911
Santa Barbara, California 93116-1911

This book is also available on the World Wide Web as an e-book. Visit www.abc-clio.com for details.

This book is printed on acid-free paper ∞
Manufactured in the United States of America

CONTENTS

A-to-Z List of Entries   *ix*

Contributors and Their Entries   *xiii*

Foreword   *xxv*

Preface   *xxxi*

Acknowledgments   *xxxiii*

Volume 1: Entries A to M   *1*

Volume 2: Entries N to Z   *389*

Bibliography   *689*

Index   *731*

A-to-Z List of Entries

VOLUME 1, A–M

A

Abandonment
Abortion, History of
Academic Achievement
Acculturation
Adolescents, Parenting of
Adoption
Adoptive Family
Adoptive Fathers
African American Parenting
AIDS Education for Children and
    Adolescents
AIDS, HIV, Pregnancy and Childbearing
Ainsworth, Mary (1913–1999)
Alcohol Abuse
Alienation, Student
Altricial and Precocial
Ames, Louise Bates (1908–1996)
Anorexia
Apgar Scoring System
Asian American Parenting
Assisted Reproduction, Children of
Attachment
Attention Deficit Hyperactivity Disorder
    (ADHD)
Attractiveness, Physical
Autism

B

Baby Talk, by Adults
Baby Talk, by Children
Baumrind, Diana Blumberg (1927–)
Bed-Wetting
Behavioral and Emotional Problems:
    Assessment and Evaluation
Benedek, Therese F. (1892–1974)
Bilingualism
Birth Order
Bonding
Bowlby, John (1907–1990)
Brain, Development of
Breast-Feeding
Bulimia
Bullies and Victims

C

Chaos
Child Care
Chronic Illness, Parenting a Child with
Circumcision
Communication, Parent-Child
Communication, Parent-Teen
Contraception, History of
Contraception, Methods of
Coparenting
Corporal Punishment
Cultural Influences on Parenting
Custody Conflicts

D

Deafness and Parenting
Death of a Child
Death of a Parent
Demographic Transition
Development,
    Parental Beliefs about
Development,
    Parental Knowledge about
Disabilities,
    Parenting a Child with
Discipline in the Home
Divorce
Doula
Dual-Career Families

E

Emotion,
    Infants' Facial Expression of
Emotional Development
Employment, Maternal
Employment, Parental,
    Children's Views of
Erikson, Erik (1902–1994)
Ethnic Identity

F

Failure to Thrive
Family Leave
Family Rituals
Father-Adolescent Relationships
Father-Child Relationships
Fatherhood, Transition to
Fathering
Fathers, Stay-at-Home
Father's Day
Feeding Problems, Prevention of
Fetal Alcohol Syndrome (FAS)
Foster Parents
Freud, Anna (1895–1982)
Friendship, Adolescent
Froebel, Frederick (1782–1852)

G

Gay and Lesbian Children
Gay Fathers
Geisel, Theodor Seuss (1904–1991)
Gender Stereotyping
Generativity
Genetic Counseling
Genetic Disorders
Gesell, Arnold L. (1880–1961)
Gifted Children
Ginott, Haim (1922–1973)
Grandfatherhood
Grandparenthood
Grandparents as
    Primary Caregivers
Growth, Patterns of

H

Hall, G. Stanley (1844–1924)
Head Start, Early
Home Schooling

I

Immigrant Families
In Vitro Fertilization (IVF)
Incarcerated Parents
Infanticide
Infants, Parenting of
Infertility
Intelligence Testing
Interracial Families

L

Labor, Division of
Labor and Delivery,
    Complications of
Labor and Delivery, Stages of
Language Acquisition
Latino Parenting
Lesbian Mothers, Children of
Literacy

Locomotor Development
Low Birth Weight Infants

M

Malnutrition
Maternal Depression and Parenting
Maternal Guilt
Memory in Infancy
Menopause
Mental Retardation, Parenting a Child
    with
Montessori, Maria (1870–1952)
Moral Development
Mother's Day
Munchausen Syndrome by Proxy

VOLUME 2, N–Z

N

Naming Children
Native American Parenting
Neglect
Neglect, Child, Prevention of
Neonatal Behavioral Assessment Scale
Newborn Behavior
Night Terrors
Nightmares

P

Parent Education
Parental Authority, Children's Concepts
    of
Parental Conflict
Parental Control
Parental Investment
Parental Sensitivity
Parent-Child Interaction:
    Sex Differences
Parenthood, Decision about
Parenthood, Stages of

Parenthood, Transition to
Parenthood as a Developmental Stage
Parenting, Urban versus Rural
Parenting and Adolescent Substance Use
    and Abuse
Parenting Competence
Parenting in Colonial America
Parenting in Later Adulthood
Parenting Styles
Peer Relationships
Physical Abuse
Physical Abuse, Prevention of
Piaget, Jean (1896–1980)
Planned Parenthood, History of
Play, Parent-Child
Play, Pretend
Postpartum Depression
Post-Traumatic Stress Disorder
Poverty and Children
Pregnancy, Complications of
Pregnancy, Prenatal Care
Pregnancy, Stages of
Prenatal Development
Preschoolers, Parenting of
Privacy
Pro-Life
Psychological Abuse

R

Relocation
Resiliency
Roe v. Wade
Rogers, Fred McFeely (1928–)

S

Sanger, Margaret (1879–1966)
School Involvement, Parental
School Readiness:
    Competencies
School Readiness: Parental Role
School-Aged Children, Parenting of
Security Objects
Self-Confidence, Parental
Self-Esteem

xii   A-to-Z List of Entries

Separation Anxiety
Sesame Street
Sexual Abuse
Sexual Abuse, Prevention of
Shyness
Sibling Relationships
Single Parents
Single-Sex Education
Sleep Deprivation, Parental
Sleep Patterns and Arrangements
Social Development in Childhood
Social Support
Socialization
Spacing of Children
Spock, Benjamin (1903–1998)
Sport Participation
Steiner, Rudolf (1861–1925)
Stepfamilies
Storytelling by Children
Stress, Early Childhood
Substance Abuse, Parental
Substance Abuse, Prevention of
Substance Abuse, Progression of
Sudden Infant Death Syndrome (SIDS)

T

Teenage Fathers
Teenage Mothers
Television, Educational

Television, Parental Depictions on
Television and Children
Temperament
Time-Out
Toddlers, Parenting of
Trends in Child Rearing
Twins and Multiples

V

Values, Child-Rearing
Video and Computer Games
Violence, Community
Violence, Domestic
Violence, Media
Violence among Children

W

Watson, John B. (1878–1958)
Winnicott, Donald Woods (1896–1971)

Z

Zygote

CONTRIBUTORS AND THEIR ENTRIES

Thomas M. Achenbach
University of Vermont
Burlington, Vermont
  Behavioral and Emotional Problems:
    Assessment and Evaluation

Ressa Adamek-Griggs
Washington, DC
  Parenting in Later Adulthood

Karen E. Adolph
New York University
New York, New York
  Locomotor Development

Julie Agresta
Temple University
Philadelphia, Pennsylvania
  Gay and Lesbian Children

Poonam Ahuja
WestEd, Center for Child and
  Family Studies
Sausalito, California
  Parental Sensitivity

David E. Barrett
Clemson University
Clemson, South Carolina
  Friendship, Adolescent
  School Readiness: Competencies

Lisa Baumwell
New York University
New York, New York
  Separation Anxiety
  Sibling Relationships

Martha Ann Bell
Virginia Polytechnic Institute
  and State University
Blacksburg, Virginia
  Brain, Development of

Gretchen Biesecker
Tufts University
Medford, Massachusetts
  Social Support

M. Antonia Biggs
University of California,
  San Francisco
San Francisco, California
  Ethnic Identity

Maureen M. Black
University of Maryland School of Medicine
Baltimore, Maryland
  Feeding Problems, Prevention of
  Growth, Patterns of
  Neglect
  Neglect, Child, Prevention of
  Physical Abuse
  Physical Abuse, Prevention of

John Bock
California State University, Fullerton
Fullerton, California
  Demographic Transition
  Parental Investment

William Borden
University of Chicago
Chicago, Illinois
  Winnicott, Donald Woods
    (1896–1971)

Lea Bornstein
Bethesda, Maryland
    Naming Children

Marc H. Bornstein
National Institute of Child Health and
    Human Development
National Institutes of Health
Bethesda, Maryland
    Acculturation
    Adoptive Family
    Communication, Parent-Child
    Cultural Influences on Parenting
    Deafness and Parenting
    Labor, Division of
    Language Acquisition
    Naming Children
    Parenting, Urban versus Rural
    Parenting Competence
    Parenting in Later Adulthood

Preston A. Britner
University of Connecticut
Storrs, Connecticut
    Bowlby, John (1907–1990)
    Family Leave

David W. Brook
Mount Sinai School of Medicine
New York, New York
    Parenting and Adolescent
        Substance Use and Abuse

Judith S. Brook
Mount Sinai School of Medicine
New York, New York
    Parenting and Adolescent
        Substance Use and Abuse

Matthew S. Broudy
St. John's University
Jamaica, New York
    Freud, Anna (1895–1982)
    Hall, G. Stanley (1844–1924)

N. Elizabeth Bryant
University of Florida
Gainesville, Florida
    African American Parenting
    Violence among Children

Ester Schaler Buchholz
New York University
New York, New York
    Apgar Scoring System
    Father's Day
    Mother's Day
    Parenthood as a
        Developmental Stage
    Privacy

Lorissa Byely
St. John's University
Jamaica, New York
    Montessori, Maria (1870–1952)
    Spock, Benjamin (1903–1998)

Elizabeth Callaghan
Ithaca College
Ithaca, New York
    Custody Conflicts

Joanne Cantor
University of Wisconsin, Madison
Madison, Wisconsin
    Violence, Media

Martha P. Carlton
Southern Illinois University,
    Edwardsville
Edwardsville, Illinois
    Self-Esteem

Peter Yuichi Clark
Emory University
Atlanta, Georgia
    Grandfatherhood

Annemarie F. Clarke
Temple University
Philadelphia, Pennsylvania
    Gifted Children
    Intelligence Testing

Priscilla K. Coleman
University of the South
Sewanee, Tennessee
    Attachment
    Pro-Life
    Self-Confidence, Parental
    Temperament
    Toddlers, Parenting of

Cynthia García Coll
Brown University
Providence, Rhode Island
  Incarcerated Parents

Linda R. Cote
National Institute of Child Health
  and Human Development
National Institutes of Health
Bethesda, Maryland
  Acculturation
  Foster Parents

Lesley Epperly Cottrell
West Virginia University
Morgantown, West Virginia
  Sleep Deprivation, Parental

Marvin W. Daehler
University of Massachusetts
Amherst, Massachusetts
  Failure to Thrive
  Prenatal Development
  Sudden Infant Death Syndrome (SIDS)

Donna J. Dahlgren
Indiana University Southeast
New Albany, Indiana
  Video and Computer Games

Martin Daly
McMaster University
Hamilton, Canada
  Infanticide

Amy Melstein Damast
Mathematica Policy Research
Springfield, New Jersey
  Separation Anxiety
  Sibling Relationships

Patrick T. Davies
University of Rochester
Rochester, New York
  Parental Conflict

Jack Demick
Center for Adoption Research
University of Massachusetts
Worcester, Massachusetts
  In Vitro Fertilization (IVF)
  Infertility
  Parenthood, Stages of
  Parenthood, Transition to

Susanne A. Denham
George Mason University
Fairfax, Virginia
  Preschoolers, Parenting of

Shelley Mae Drazen
State University of New York,
  Binghamton
Binghamton, New York
  Fetal Alcohol Syndrome (FAS)
  Parent Education

M. Ann Easterbrooks
Tufts University
Medford, Massachusetts
  Maternal Depression and
    Parenting
  Social Support

David Elkind
Tufts University
Medford, Massachusetts
  Froebel, Frederick (1782–1852)
  Steiner, Rudolf (1861–1925)

Eugene K. Emory
Emory University
Atlanta, Georgia
  Adoptive Fathers

Susan Engel
Williams College
Williamstown, Massachusetts
  Storytelling by Children

Martha Farrell Erickson
University of Minnesota
Minneapolis, Minnesota
  Abandonment

Garret D. Evans
University of Florida
Gainesville, Florida
  African American Parenting
  Violence among Children

Robert S. Feldman
University of Massachusetts
Amherst, Massachusetts
  Bilingualism
  Breast-Feeding
  Genetic Counseling

Catherine A. Fiorello
Temple University
Philadelphia, Pennsylvania
   Gay and Lesbian Children
   Gifted Children
   Home Schooling
   Intelligence Testing

Celia B. Fisher
Fordham University
Bronx, New York
   Sexual Abuse
   Sexual Abuse, Prevention of

Robert Frank
Oakton Community College
Des Plaines, Illinois
   Fathers, Stay-at-Home

Andrew Fuligni
New York University
New York, New York
   Immigrant Families

Alice Ginott
New York, New York
   Ginott, Haim (1922–1973)

Ellen Galinsky
Families and Work Institute
New York, New York
   Employment, Parental,
     Children's Views of

Jean Berko Gleason
Boston University
Boston, Massachusetts
   Baby Talk, by Adults
   Baby Talk, by Children

Carla Gober
Emory University
Atlanta, Georgia
   Father-Adolescent Relationships
   Father-Child Relationships

Susan Golombok
City University
London, England
   Assisted Reproduction, Children of
   Lesbian Mothers, Children of

Benjamin J. Gorvine
University of Michigan
Ann Arbor, Michigan
   Fathering

Christine A. Graham
Tufts University
Medford, Massachusetts
   Maternal Depression and Parenting

Sherryl Browne Graves
Hunter College,
   City University of New York
New York, New York
   Television, Educational
   Television, Parental Depictions on

Wendy S. Grolnick
Clark University
Worcester, Massachusetts
   Parental Control

Jennifer J. Grubba
George Mason University
Fairfax, Virginia
   Native American Parenting

Gwen E. Gustafson
University of Connecticut, Storrs
Storrs, Connecticut
   Altricial and Precocial

Leslie Morrison Gutman
University of Michigan
Ann Arbor, Michigan
   Academic Achievement
   School Involvement, Parental

Perry N. Halkitis
New York University
New York, New York
   AIDS Education for Children and
     Adolescents
   AIDS, HIV, Pregnancy, and Childbearing

Tara M. Hall
Fairleigh Dickinson University
Teaneck, New Jersey
   Bed-Wetting
   Nightmares
   Night Terrors

Bonnie L. Halpern-Felsher
University of California, San Francisco
San Francisco, California
    Adolescents, Parenting of

Gerald Handel
The City College and The Graduate Center
City University of New York
New York, New York
    Socialization

Penny Hauser-Cram
Boston College
Chestnut Hill, Massachusetts
    Mental Retardation, Parenting a
        Child with

Christine Reiner Hess
University of Maryland
Baltimore, Maryland
    Physical Abuse, Prevention of

E. Mavis Hetherington
University of Virginia, Charlottesville
Charlottesville, Virginia
    Divorce
    Stepfamilies

Carol H. Hoare
The George Washington University
Washington, DC
    Erikson, Erik (1902–1994)
    Generativity

John D. Hogan
St. John's University
Jamaica, New York
    Ainsworth, Mary (1913–1999)
    Ames, Louise Bates (1908–1996)
    Freud, Anna (1895–1982)
    Gesell, Arnold L. (1880–1961)
    Hall, G. Stanley (1844–1924)
    Montessori, Maria (1870–1952)
    Parenting in Colonial America
    Spock, Benjamin (1903–1998)
    Watson, John B. (1878–1958)

Grayson N. Holmbeck
Loyola University of Chicago
Chicago, Illinois
    Chronic Illness, Parenting a
        Child with
    Parenting Styles

Irwin A. Hyman
Temple University
Philadelphia, Pennsylvania
    Alienation, Student
    Corporal Punishment
    Discipline in the Home
    Post-Traumatic Stress Disorder

Linda R. Jeffrey
Rowan University
Glassboro, New Jersey
    Violence, Domestic

Helen L. Johnson
Queens College of the
    City University of New York
Flushing, New York
    Substance Abuse, Parental

Sharon Z. Johnson
Prospect Heights, Illinois
    Chronic Illness,
        Parenting a Child with

Sandra Jordan
Public Health Institute
Washington, DC
    Abortion, History of
    Contraception, History of
    Contraception, Methods of
    Planned Parenthood, History of
    Roe v. Wade
    Sanger, Margaret (1879–1966)

Theresa J. Jordan
New York University
New York, New York
    Adoption

Kimberly J. Josephs
Syracuse University
Syracuse, New York
    Family Rituals

Michele V. Karpathian
Waynesburg College
Waynesburg, Pennsylvania
    Low Birth Weight Infants
    Menopause

Katherine Hildebrandt Karraker
West Virginia University
Morgantown, West Virginia
  Attractiveness, Physical
  Gender Stereotyping
  Sleep Deprivation, Parental
  Stress, Early Childhood

Robert D. Kavanaugh
Williams College
Williamstown, Massachusetts
  Play, Pretend
  Storytelling by Children

Melanie Killen
University of Maryland, College Park
College Park, Maryland
  Peer Relationships

Su Yeong Kim
University of California, Davis
Davis, California
  Asian American Parenting

Bruce G. Klonsky
State University of New York,
  College at Fredonia
Fredonia, New York
  Shyness
  Sport Participation

Dafna E. Kohen
University of British Columbia
Vancouver, British Columbia, Canada
  Relocation

Janet P. Kremenitzer
Yale University
New Haven, Connecticut
  School Readiness: Parental Role

Esther Kresh
Head Start Bureau
Washington, DC
  Head Start, Early

Regina Kuersten-Hogan
Brown University School of Medicine
Marlboro, Massachusetts
  Coparenting

Sharon F. Lambert
University of Maryland
Baltimore, Maryland
  Neglect, Child, Prevention of

Jarlette E. Lampard
Johns Hopkins University
Baltimore, Maryland
  Parenting, Urban versus Rural

Sarah Landy
University of Windsor
Windsor, Canada
  Infants, Parenting of
  Time-Out

Marta Laupa
University of Nevada, Las Vegas
Las Vegas, Nevada
  Parental Authority,
    Children's Concepts of

Allison Lauretti
Clark University
Worcester, Massachusetts
  Coparenting

Chung-Yol Lee
University of California, San Francisco
San Francisco, California
  Adolescents, Parenting of

Elyse Brauch Lehman
George Mason University
Fairfax, Virginia
  Security Objects

Robert M. Lembo
New York University School of Medicine
New York, New York
  Circumcision

Michael Lewis
University of Medicine and
  Dentistry of New Jersey
New Brunswick, New Jersey
  Emotional Development
  Social Development in Childhoood

Judith Lieberstein
Westport, Connecticut
    Postpartum Depression

L. Oriana Linares
New York University School of Medicine,
    Child Study Center
New York, New York
    Violence, Community

Eric W. Lindsey
Texas Tech University
Lubbock, Texas
    Parent-Child Interaction:
        Sex Differences
    Play, Parent-Child

Deborah L. Linebarger
University of Kansas
Kansas City, Kansas
    Poverty and Children
    Television and Children

Kathryn E. Livingston
Parenting Partners
Bogota, New Jersey
    Fathers, Stay-at-Home

Amy MacConnell
University of Massachusetts, Amherst
Amherst, Massachusetts
    Failure to Thrive
    Prenatal Development
    Sudden Infant Death Syndrome (SIDS)

Louis Manfra
George Mason University
Fairfax, Virginia
    Birth Order
    Spacing of Children

Mary Beth Mann
Southwest Missouri State University
Springfield, Missouri
    Maternal Guilt

José Antonio Maradiaga
George Mason University
Falls Church, Virginia
    Geisel, Theodor Suess (1904–1991)
    Rogers, Fred McFeely (1928–)

Ludovic Marin
New York University
New York, New York
    Locomotor Development

Robert S. Marvin
University of Virginia
Charlottesville, Virginia
    Bowlby, John (1907–1990)

Sandee Graham McClowry
New York University
New York, New York
    Resiliency

James P. McHale
Clark University
Worcester, Massachusetts
    Coparenting

Kristen McNamara
Temple University
Philadelphia, Pennsylvania
    Post-Traumatic Stress Disorder

Stacey Mellinger
Temple University
Philadelphia, Pennsylvania
    Alienation, Student

Alan L. Mendelsohn
New York University School of Medicine
New York, New York
    Circumcision

Rosanne Menna
University of Windsor
Windsor, Ontario, Canada
    Infants, Parenting of
    Time-Out

Rachael B. Millstein
Loyola University Chicago
Chicago, Illinois
    Parenting Styles

Anne S. Mitchell
University of Virginia, Charlottesville
Charlottesville, Virginia
    Divorce
    Stepfamilies

Tanya M. Morrel
University of Maryland
*   School of Medicine*
Baltimore, Maryland
    Feeding Problems, Prevention of

Barbara J. Myers
Virginia Commonwealth University
Richmond, Virginia
    Disabilities, Parenting a Child with

Cheryl A. Nolte
George Mason University
Fairfax, Virginia
    Genetic Disorders

Barbara M. Ostfeld
St. Peter's University Hospital
New Brunswick, New Jersey
    Munchausen Syndrome by Proxy

Anthony Papa
Teacher's College, Columbia University
New York, New York
    Death of a Child

Peggy Tuter Pearl
Southwest Missouri State University
Springfield, Missouri
    Grandparents as Primary Caregivers
    Psychological Abuse

Colleen Pilgrim
University of Michigan
Ann Arbor, Michigan
    Substance Abuse, Prevention of

Christopher R. Poirier
University of Massachusetts, Amherst
Amherst, Massachusetts
    Bilingualism
    Breast-Feeding
    Genetic Counseling

Angelo Ponirakis
University of Maryland
Baltimore, Maryland
    Growth, Patterns of

Mary A. Pressman
Mt. Sinai School of Medicine
New York, New York
    Parenting and Adolescent
        Substance Use and Abuse

Joyce Prigot
St. John's University
Jamaica, New York
    Grandparenthood
    Memory in Infancy
    Parenthood, Decision about
    Sleep Patterns and Arrangements

Leslie Reese
California State University,
*   Long Beach*
Long Beach, California
    Latino Parenting

Marilyn L. Riese
University of Louisville
Louisville, Kentucky
    Newborn Behavior

Joanne Roberts
New York University
New York, New York
    Head Start, Early

Neena Roumell
St. Joseph's Mercy Hospital
Mt. Clemens, Michigan
    Doula
    Emotion, Infants'
        Facial Expression of

Yana Rusanova-Vaknin
New York University
New York, New York
    AIDS Education for Children and
        Adolescents

Sara J. Salkind
University of Delaware
Newark, Delaware
    Deafness and Parenting

Herbert D. Saltzstein
Graduate Center of the
*   City University of New York*
New York, New York
    Moral Development

Carolyn E. Sartor
Pacific Graduate School of Psychology
Palo Alto, California
    Communication, Parent-Teen
    Death of a Child

Charles E. Schaefer
Fairleigh Dickinson University
Teaneck, New Jersey
    Bed-Wetting
    Night Terrors
    Nightmares

Erika S. Schmidt
Institute for Clinical Social Work
Chicago, Illinois
    Benedek, Therese F. (1892–1977)

Nancy L. Segal
California State University, Fullerton
Fullerton, California
    Twins and Multiples

Jacqueline D. Shannon
New York University
New York, New York
    Development,
        Parental Knowledge about

Wendy E. Shapera
Loyola University of Chicago
Chicago, Illinois
    Parenting Styles

Jerrold Lee Shapiro
Santa Clara University
Santa Clara, California
    Fatherhood, Transition to

Edmond D. Shenassa
Brown University Medical School
Center for Behavioral and Preventative
    Medicine
Providence, Rhode Island
    Substance Use, Progression of

Myrna B. Shure
MCP Hahnemann University
Philadelphia, Pennsylvania
    Bullies and Victims

Margaret L. Signorella
Penn State McKeesport
McKeesport, Pennsylvania
    Single-Sex Education

Rebecca B. Silver
Brown University
Providence, Rhode Island
    Incarcerated Parents

M. Trika Smith-Burke
New York University
New York, New York
    Literacy

John Snarey
Emory University
Atlanta, Georgia
    Adoptive Fathers
    Father-Adolescent Relationships
    Father-Child Relationships
    Grandfatherhood

Susan Sonnenschein
University of Maryland,
    Baltimore County
Baltimore, Maryland
    Development, Parental Beliefs about

Ann Steele
Boston College
Chestnut Hill, Massachusetts
    Mental Retardation,
        Parenting a Child with

Marie-Anne Suizzo
National Institute of Child Health and
    Human Development
National Institutes of Health
Bethesda, Maryland
    Death of a Parent
    Single Parents
    Trends in Child Rearing

Patricia Sullivan
Fordham University
Bronx, New York
    Sexual Abuse
    Sexual Abuse, Prevention of

Joan T. D. Suwalsky
National Institute of Child Health and
    Human Development
National Institutes of Health
Bethesda, Maryland
    Adoptive Family

Shannon Taich
Temple University
Philadelphia, Pennsylvania
 Corporal Punishment

Jean Talbot
Clark University
Worcester, Massachusetts
 Coparenting

Catherine S. Tamis-LeMonda
New York University
New York, New York
 Communication, Parent-Child
 Development,
  Parental Knowledge about
 Head Start, Early
 Language Acquisition
 Parental Sensitivity
 Values, Child-Rearing

Fiona Tasker
Birbeck College,
 University of London
London, England
 Gay Fathers

Dennis Thompson
Georgia State University
Atlanta, Georgia
 Anorexia
 Bulimia

Eirikur Thorvardarson
George Mason University
Fairfax, Virginia
 Dual-Career Families

Caroline Monforte Tisot
Temple University
Philadelphia, Pennsylvania
 Discipline in the Home

Rosemarie T. Truglio
Sesame Workshop
New York, New York
 Sesame Street

Anastasia Tryphon
Archives Jean Piaget
University of Geneva
Geneva, Switzerland
 Piaget, Jean (1896–1980)

Marion K. Underwood
University of Texas at Dallas
Dallas, Texas
 School-Aged Children, Parenting of

Hendrika Vande Kemp
Fuller Theological Seminary
Pasadena, California
 Baumrind, Diana Blumberg (1927–)

Sandra L. Vedovato
Fredonia, New York
 Shyness

Mary D. Voigt
National Institute of Child Health and
 Human Development
Bethesda, Maryland
 Parenting, Urban versus Rural
 Parenting in Later Adulthood

Theodore D. Wachs
Purdue University
West Lafayette, Indiana
 Chaos
 Malnutrition

Beverly Wallace
Mansfield University
Mansfield, Pennsylvania
 Attention Deficit Hyperactivity
  Disorder (ADHD)

Gregory L. Wallace
George Mason University
Fairfax, Virginia
 Autism
 Genetic Disorders

Shuyuan Wang
New York University
New York, New York
 Values, Child-Rearing

Niobe Way
New York University
New York, New York
 Teenage Mothers

Evelyn H. Wei
University of Pittsburgh Western Psychiatric
 Institute and Clinic
Pittsburgh, Pennsylvania
 Teenage Fathers

Idell B. Weise
New York University
New York, New York
  Locomotor Development

Kathleen Whitten
University of Virginia
Charlottesville, Virginia
  Interracial Families

Diane E. Wille
Indiana University Southeast
New Albany, Indiana
  Child Care
  Employment, Maternal

Melvin N. Wilson
University of Virginia
Charlottesville, Virginia
  Interracial Families

Margo Wilson
McMaster University
Hamilton, Canada
  Infanticide

Michael Windle
University of Alabama, Birmingham
Birmingham, Alabama
  Alcohol Abuse

Adam Winsler
George Mason University
Fairfax, Virginia
  Attention Deficit Hyperactivity
    Disorder (ADHD)
  Autism
  Birth Order
  Dual-Career Families
  Native American Parenting
  Self-Esteem
  Spacing of Children

Steven K. Wisensale
University of Connecticut
Storrs, Connecticut
  Family Leave

Leonard Wolf
New York University School of Medicine
New York, New York
  Labor and Delivery, Complications of
  Labor and Delivery, Stages of
  Pregnancy, Complications of
  Pregnancy, Prenatal Care
  Pregnancy, Stages of
  Zygote

John Worobey
Rutgers University
New Brunswick, New Jersey
  Bonding
  Neonatal Behavioral Assessment Scale

Elena Zaretsky
Boston University
Boston, Massachusetts
  Baby Talk, By Children

FOREWORD

Child and family advocates are fond of screaming that it takes more to qualify for a driver's license than to qualify to be a parent, and that society pays more to people who park our cars and collect our garbage than to those who care for our children. These assertions are factually correct but, more importantly, advocates cite them as symbols of the low status that parenting, child rearing, and child-care are accorded in modern America.

As a society, we require utterly nothing in the way of education, knowledge, or demonstrated competence to rear children, although children are often touted as our most precious national resource. Presumably, this is out of deference to the sanctity and privacy of the family and the political belief that government should not interfere with the rights and responsibilities of parents. But, of course, society violates these principles in other contexts when it sees fit. For example, the schools have a long history of progressively being asked to teach topics that have historically been parental responsibilities but which society feels parents are no longer shouldering adequately. These include driver's and reproductive education, more recently drug and alcohol education, and currently the teaching of values. Indeed, some have lamented that these topics now occupy such a large segment of the school curriculum that American children spend disproportionately less time on academic subjects than do children in the schools of the remaining industrial world. Conversely, even when one would assume society has an obligation to train and qualify parents, such as in the foster care system and adoption, it often does not do so. Further, most children who are left in the care of adults other than their parents on a regular basis to allow parents to work are looked after in the home of an adult who cares for up to six children and, although that individual may be asked to register with the state, little more than knowing first aid and CPR is typically required.

The American education system also reflects the lack of societal attention to parenthood. While high schools often offer courses in child development, such material is typically not required of all students and, while helpful, is likely to be far different from a course in parenting. For example, it is one thing to know the ages and stages of child development; it is another to know what to do when a child writhes in a tantrum on the floor of the supermarket because you correctly refuse to buy junk food, or what you should do with a child who refuses on every occasion to obey instructions, or how to encourage responsibility in human and sexual relationships.

American universities are no better—perhaps worse—given their role in society. Universities are society's paid critics and exist, in part, to promote revisions in society's thinking and actions. Ironically, however, many colleges and universities seem to be the slowest institutions to revise themselves. A course in parenting, at least until recently, was a rarity even in universities having catalogues of several hundreds of pages of courses and that offer applied degrees in child development and childcare, social work, education, and pediatrics. Even social workers and other professionals who provide education to parents typically have no formal educational training in parenting and cannot find continuing education courses to help prepare them. And, when parenting course are offered, they tend to be more conceptual and theoretical rather than focusing on the practical issues and decisions that nearly every parent will be called upon to make.

Some would argue that we do not have such courses in parenting at any level because we simply do not know enough to be able to tell parents what to do. There is a grain of truth to this, but I regard it as a lame excuse. It is true that academics have been, well, "academic" in their study of parenting, preferring to study child development and describing how parents and children behave rather than investigating the consequences of different decisions that parents make or the strategies they use to guide the development of their children. We desperately need several "parental consumer research centers" at American research universities that would study not products and services, but parental choices and actions and their effectiveness and consequences for children's development. But even without such centers, it is not the case that we are so ignorant that we could not offer an academically substantive and eminently practical course in parenting that would at least describe alternatives available to parents, how they can be implemented and executed, what is known or is not known about their effectiveness and consequences, and other background information that is helpful to parents in making the myriad decisions they face every week.

The consequence of this general inattention to parenting is that while families often go through prenatal training in clinics, hospitals, and other venues, they are offered almost nothing except basic feeding, changing, and nutritional information about how to care for their infant and child once it arrives. A new mother lamented, "They just hand you your baby, as if to say 'good luck'. I'm panicked. What do I do with it—I mean her? Don't they know there is life after birth?"

Fortunately, interest in parenting is on the rise in society, in politics, and in the academy. Parenting courses in high schools and colleges are now more common, new academic journals concerned with parenting are being published, and there is a sociopolitical emphasis on parents assuming their responsibilities and society providing some educational and social support to do so. Why is parenting suddenly becoming popular? After a few decades of the "me" generation, perhaps the pendulum is swinging back and people are recognizing that "me" is less fulfilling without "us." Perhaps as both parents leave the home for work, there is a greater compensatory concern with family and parenting because of the limited time now available for those activities. Perhaps faced with mounting child and family problems across the country, the nation has elevated on the public agenda the treatment and prevention of such problems and recognized that their roots are often in inadequate parenting. And business, after cost-cutting produced increased stress in employees, has recognized that employees are more productive when their lives outside the workplace—that is, in their families—have less stress and are more fulfilling.

This two-volume encyclopedia represents a cutting-edge compendium of information on parenting and parenthood for professionals, paraprofessionals, and parents. Not only does it provide the knowledge tools to understand, interpret, and decide courses of action for professionals and parents, but it is a symbol of the new value placed on parenting and on informational supports for parenthood. Even its organization in the form of an encyclopedia is apt, because precisely at the time when parents need more training and information they have less time to acquire it. Studies show that parents tend to seek information when they have a problem, and the topical organization and concise statements contained in these volumes fit that prescription well.

There are several wonderful features of these volumes. First, the authors are typically prominent and sometimes world authorities on the material they report. This means not only have they successfully selected what professionals and parents need to know and distilled the important kernels, sometimes from volumes into a few pages, but they make wise judgments about what parents need not worry about as well as what signs should prompt additional exploration and perhaps professional attention.

Second, the range of topics covered in these volumes is indeed encyclopedic. For one thing, the editor has covered the entire age range of parenting, from the decision whether to have children and even alternative methods to conceive them (e.g., in vitro fertilization) and prenatal care, through parenting in later adulthood and grandparenting. Parenting, as well as development, is indeed lifelong, and these volumes cover the major issues along the entire trek. Moreover, each segment concludes with references that provide additional information for readers who need to go beyond the succinct presentations offered here.

Third, many topics are covered with a historical perspective, which frequently helps the reader understand how we have arrived at current policies and practices.

Themes in child rearing change dramatically from one decade to the next, sometimes even flip-flop, and, like art, what is currently in vogue often represents a reaction to what has previously dominated thought and practice, perhaps in the extreme. For example, it is useful to know that in 1985, when the first family leave bill was introduced in the U.S. Congress by Patricia Schroeder (D-CO), 135 countries had already established maternity leave benefits, and, of those, all but 10 nations mandated paid maternity leave. Notice that it took until 1993 to pass the Family and Medical Leave Act. Also, the United States provides only for unpaid leave, and finances is the most frequent reason American parents do not take the leave or do not take all of the twelve weeks that is permitted. Historically, the United States is still behind.

Fourth, the volume contains a wonderful mix of theoretical/conceptual/ background entries on the one hand and practical and problem-focused topics on the other. The background pieces help us understand parents, children, and parenting, and although they do not tell us what to do, they do provide information that helps us make those how-to decisions. For example, background sections on abandonment and neglect tell us the scope of this public problem as well as common consequences to children who have been abandoned or neglected. The brain development section provides valuable information about the course of early brain development, currently a hot media topic, and how behavior is influenced by that neurological development. It also shows the role of experience in the neurological development of the brain, lest we assume that everything is prewired. On the other hand, a variety of entries deal with problems and practical issues, such as bedwetting, attention deficit hyperactivity disorder (ADHD), baby talk, circumcision, and family rituals.

Fifth, these volumes provide substantial information, not only on children as the object of parenting, but on the parents and the factors that are likely to influence their behavior and parenting practices. For example, maternal depression, maternal guilt, parental self-confidence, and even parental sleep deprivation are likely to be major influences on how parents treat their children, and improving parenting is likely to require dealing with these parent factors before dealing with the actual parent-child behaviors.

Sixth, this encyclopedia has not shied away from very contemporary as well as controversial issues. There is material on fathers, including teenage fathers as well as grandfathers. Gay and lesbian parents and children are discussed, as well as parents who are incarcerated and those who may wish to school their children at home. No parental stone has been left unturned.

Seventh, some of those stones I especially appreciated are the segments on social and political policies that affect parents. These include a wide range of issues, such as family leave, *Roe v. Wade*, preventing neglect and abuse, poverty and its effects, abandonment, preventing substance abuse, and so forth. When I was a contributing editor and columnist for *Parents* magazine, I once suggested that the publication should have a regular feature that dealt with family social and political policies. Parents, despite their numbers in society, are not a cohesive political force, in contrast to senior citizens, for example. Now that family issues seem to be rising on the social and political agenda, this volume is taking one of the leads in providing background information on these issues that might contribute to increasing the awareness of parents and, I hope, galvanizing parents into a meaningful political force.

Eighth, a unique feature of this encyclopedia is the biographical profiles of leading academic and public figures in the field of child development and parenting. In a sense, these profiles represent integrated, life span examples of many of the themes that are presented in separate segments of the encyclopedia. Particularly fascinating to me personally was the profile of Theodor "Dr. Seuss" Geisel. Major life trajectories often hinge on the background of skills and experiences of the person on the one hand, and relatively minor opportunities and seemingly inconsequential events, on the other. For example, Geisel wanted a doctorate in English literature, and went to Lincoln College at Oxford University in England to pursue it. He became disenchanted with the teaching at Lincoln College and abandoned his plans for a doctorate. But he had a history of drawing cartoons in college, so upon returning to the United States he submitted cartoons to *Life*, the *New Yorker*, and the *Saturday Evening Post*. He received $25 from the *Post* for one of his cartoons, which inspired him to move to New York and pursue this career. He signed his cartoons with his middle name (his mother's maiden name), which was simply Seuss, and later added "Dr." to poke fun at himself and Lincoln College for the doctorate he had decided not to pursue. On a European vacation, he was struck by the unique cadence of the engines on the ship, which inspired him to write rhyming prose, especially for a children's book. Twenty-seven publishers rejected the manuscript. It took persistence and dedication to be rejected twenty-seven times, but enough is enough and Geisel decided to burn the manuscript. But shortly before it went up in smoke, he showed it to a college friend who helped him get it published, which resulted in *And to Think That I Saw It on Mulberry Street*. Finally, two of Dr. Seuss's most famous books were the result of unique challenges: first, to write a children's book using the 225 words that were essential to the vocabulary of first grade children, which became *The Cat in the Hat*; and then

Bennett Cerf's wager that Geisel could not write a book using only fifty different words, which became *Green Eggs and Ham*. I will need to reread these two books in view of those criteria.

One of the things I hope readers will derive from these volumes is that, like Dr. Seuss's work, development is a symphony of environmental events and themes, many provided by parents, which often match in wonderful harmony the biological dispositions of the child. For example, parents who naturally talk baby talk to their infants are probably matching the infant's predisposition toward being maximally attentive to sounds in the range of the human voice, repetition, and hearing only a few words. These circumstances, in turn, promote learning in the infant that may not occur if parents speak to their infant in the manner in which they speak to other adults. Good parenting often involves parents who are responsive, rather than primarily stimulating, to their infant's and child's behaviors, and thereby match their own actions to the dispositions of their child to create a parent-child duet. Chances are, if parents are having a good time with their children, they are doing "the right thing."

At the same time, there is an underlying theme in these volumes that I hope readers will discern. While a good deal of parenting is common sense and doing what comes naturally, common sense actually is not so common, and there are instances in which one's natural dispositions are not necessarily effective or even appropriate. It is natural to be mad at a disobedient and defiant child, but it is not good discipline or child rearing to follow that frustration with the natural urge to spank or hit. More benignly, we are all prone to wanting to correct the grammatical errors of our children, but in fact such corrections do little to improve their grammar and may serve to irritate the parent-child relationship.

Finally, I hope this volume will communicate to professionals, paraprofessionals, and parents that child rearing is not just a potentially emotionally fulfilling (albeit with some frustrations) but also an intellectually fascinating endeavor. Nature has created a spectacular and often amazing product. For example, nature overproduces neural connections in the brain during the prenatal and early infancy period, only to prune them by having those that are exercised by experience live on, while those that are not literally die off in a "use it or lose it" strategy. For example, infants are capable of initially hearing and producing all of the sounds of all of the world's languages, but eventually they lose the ability to produce certain sounds that do not occur in the language that they hear, which acquired deficit may later be manifested as an accent when that person learns a foreign language. Similarly, although a child may correctly use the verb "went," sometime later the child may appear to regress to using "goed" or "wented." This is not a sign of language regression, but of the fact that the child is learning the grammatical rule that the past tense is often produced by adding "-ed" to verbs. Don't worry, everyone gets it straight eventually!

Nature has created a wondrous phenomenon, not only insofar as the development of a human being is concerned, but also with respect to the shepherding of that development by parents. This compendium provides numerous glimpses of this miracle, as well as information and guidance that will be useful to the participants in this miraculous drama and to those who seek to guide them.

—*Robert B. McCall, Ph.D.*
Director, Office of Child Development,
University of Pittsburgh

PREFACE

Parenthood in America: An Encyclopedia represents the contribution of scores of outstanding social scientists, researchers, and health professionals who specialize in parenthood, parenting, and child development. One need only glance at the list of entries to immediately realize that parenthood refers to a great deal more than just child rearing concerns. Any serious investigation of parenthood must include consideration of numerous fascinating and relevant topics such as the psychological transition to parenthood, bereavement and loss, parental sleep deprivation, adoption, circumcision, home schooling, assisted reproduction, grandparents, contraception, menopause, postpartum depression, stages of parenthood, and community violence, to mention only several. The two volumes that make up this work provide the reader with a compendium of terms that cover the enormous range of subjects that pertain to the area of parenthood.

Intended for an audience comprised of parents, professionals, and students, the volumes are user-friendly and high quality. Indeed, readers will find references to virtually everything that pertains to the vast subject of parenthood. *Parenthood in America* includes more than 200 A-to-Z entries. Overall, it consists of more than 300,000 words plus illustrations. The book is not meant to be a "how-to" manual, but rather a reference work on parenthood that an intelligent layperson will wish to read. Accordingly, it is written in clear, jargon-free, and concise language. Suggested references for further reading accompany each entry for readers who are interested in delving more deeply into a given topic.

In a very real sense, the selection of topics evolved as this vast project advanced. Initially, a review of the leading professional journals, textbooks, and the programs of scientific meetings led to the selection of concepts that I deemed appropriate as encyclopedia entries. The advisory board reviewed these and, in turn, suggested additional entries. I contacted potential contributors for the preliminary group of entries and, in the course of many ongoing discussions, additional entries and contributors were recommended. It was truly a work-in-progress throughout each phase of its preparation. An effort was made to include all significant concepts that bear on parenthood. Advisory board members periodically reviewed the growing list of entries and provided advice and guidance.

The purpose of this book is to provide the latest information on a wealth of topics within a prescribed area of study—parenthood. Consequently, there are entries on the role of parenthood, the development of children, the social and cultural factors impinging on parenthood, and a number of biographies of individuals from the fields of psychology, education, and entertainment who are noteworthy for their impact on the way we think about parenthood and children.

In an overall sense, the entries are uniform in that each defines the topic, provides an empirically supported treatise about the subject, and is limited in its length. Beyond that, however, individual entries reflect the various authors' approaches to their subject matter, their selection of salient information, and their prioritization of what amounts to, in some cases, mountains of material. Furthermore, the entries in these volumes go beyond anecdotal and personal arguments and, instead, rely on research-based information that can guide a discerning reader who wishes to apply the material found within these pages to practical matters. It is hoped that this reference book proves to be rewarding, accessible, and useful to as wide a readership as possible.

—*Lawrence Balter, Ph.D.*
Professor of Applied Psychology
New York University

Acknowledgments

First and foremost, my deepest gratitude goes to Karen M. Adams for her unflagging support, flawless judgment and taste, and tireless devotion. Her help was inestimable in every way imaginable. Without her, there would be no encyclopedia.

I thank Joanne Hwang, a School Psychology doctoral student at New York University, who worked as my graduate assistant during the development and early stages. Her methodical, timely, and conscientious help during the launching of this project made the lift-off smooth and steady.

I extend my appreciation to the members of the Advisory Board: Marc Bornstein, David Elkind, Ellen Galinsky, and Barry Zuckerman, each of whom managed to find time in their already overburdened schedules to lend their wisdom and support to this endeavor.

At ABC-CLIO there are several people I wish to thank. Marie Ellen Larcada, for inviting me to this project. Her optimism and diplomacy kept the whole team on an even keel. Jennifer Loehr, for her sensible and organized approach and good-natured encouragement during the beginning stages of the project. Martha Whitt, for her efforts during the production phase, which required attending to innumerable and often-thankless tasks under severe time pressures. Mary Kay Jezzini and Vincent Duggan, crack marketing team, for their know-how and enthusiasm.

At New York University, I thank Dr. LaRue Allen, Chairperson of the Department of Applied Psychology and Rosalie and Raymond Weiss Professor, for her encouragement and constructive guidance at the outset. Thanks to Charles Sprague, at the Office of Sponsored Research Development, who walked me through the process of applying for financial support for the essential, but hidden, nuts and bolts costs entailed in such a project. I want to thank Dean Ann Marcus and the members of the New York University School of Education Challenge Fund committee for granting support.

—*Lawrence Balter, Ph.D.*
Professor of Applied Psychology
New York University

Abandonment

To give up by leaving. In the context of parenthood in America, child abandonment is relevant because of the prevalence of physical desertion of children, particularly during certain periods in American history. The concept of abandonment also is relevant because of the documented impact of emotional abandonment on children's lifelong development, as well as the fear of abandonment, a normal phenomenon in human development.

The stark reality of child abandonment has been with us since antiquity, as evidenced in literature from *Oedipus* to *Oliver Twist* to *Little Orphan Annie*. Even today, high rates of child abandonment are a fact of life in many parts of the world, usually driven by dire poverty, war, or natural disasters. In some cases, abandonment stems from cultural attitudes that characterize children as a burden—or at least some children, such as girls (in recent Chinese history) or children with serious illnesses or disabilities. Over the course of American history, rates of child abandonment have risen and fallen with the economy. In recent years, an upsurge in abandonment has been linked to parental substance abuse, illustrated most dramatically by the phenomenon of "boarder babies," left in the hospital by their mothers and often suffering from disease (including HIV infection) and/or prenatal substance exposure. Today, as throughout American history, infants are discarded—dead or alive—most often by very young, unmarried mothers unable to care for them and/or trying to conceal the birth because of shame or fear. The American response to abandoned children has changed over time, reflecting changing conceptualizations of children (e.g., from resources for the labor market to vulnerable beings in need of special protection and nurture), as well as changing societal views of parents unable to care for the children they bear.

Certainly, physical desertion of a child is the most sensational manifestation of abandonment. However, recent studies document the devastating effects of "psychologically unavailable" parenting—emotional abandonment, if you will—particularly when it occurs in the earliest years of a child's life. Children need reliable care and love in order to thrive. Indeed, human behavior is motivated by a fear of losing that love, a basic fear that has been the theme of psychological theorists and writers of classic fairy tales. But for many children, that fear becomes reality because of actual physical desertion or emotional abandonment by the parents who gave them life.

Abandoned Children in the United States: Historical Perspectives

Throughout American history, children have been abandoned when their parents lacked the resources to care for them. Up through the 1700s, abandoned children who were strong enough to work typically were indentured as servants or sold at auction. Infants and the infirm were left to die. Although the practice of selling children ended around 1800, the next century continued to see countless children abandoned, particularly in major urban areas. Before the advent of orphanages, older abandoned children fended for themselves on the streets. Some were "rescued" and placed in industrial schools or apprentice programs, where the boys were taught a trade and girls learned domestic arts. Demand for child labor was high. However, employers were reluctant to accept responsibility for the children's welfare.

At this same time baby desertion was epidemic in cities, where it was relatively easy to discard an infant without being caught. Some parents left babies on the doorsteps of churches or hospitals, trusting that someone would provide for them. But many babies were left to die in trash cans, rivers, or culverts. In the mid-nineteenth century, 100 to 150 bodies of discarded infants were found each month in New York City alone. (Ashby, 1997) Abortion was illegal or expensive, and there were neither insurance policies nor relief programs to help poor families care for their children. Abandonment became the solution for parents who saw no other way.

By 1850, abandonment had begun to capture the attention of the American public, triggering the emergence of both private and public orphanages or asylums. The term *orphanage* is most often used to describe these facilities; however, the majority of children placed there had at least one parent living and 20 percent had two. In 1890, an estimated 50,000 children were living in orphanages in American cities. (Ashby, 1997) Struggling to survive in the face of extreme poverty, many parents technically had not abandoned their children, with the sense of permanency

that term implies. Rather, they had left their children in what they believed to be a safe place, maintaining contact through letters or visits, desperate to find a way to reclaim their children when they had the necessary resources to care for them. These facilities came to be known as the "poor man's boarding schools."

Although the development of asylums was seen as a step forward for children who otherwise would be living on the streets, too often the care was far from adequate. Children lacked adequate food, heat, clothing, and sanitation. Disease was rampant. The youngest of these children died at astounding rates. For example, in the nineteenth-century almshouses of Massachusetts, 97 percent of infants died. (Ashby, 1997)

After the mid-1800s, a new view of child and family began to emerge, with an emphasis on children as vulnerable individuals in need of care and protection, particularly within the nurturing bonds of family. This view led to new developments in society's response to abandoned children. First was the practice of "placing out," relocating children from urban orphanages or industrial schools to rural areas, where they were expected to be embraced by the farm families who took them in (albeit with an expectation that the children would contribute significantly to the productivity of the farm). In this same period the first adoption laws were developed, based on the new assumption that children need parents, not owners. Children whose parents were still living and had hopes of reclaiming them were put into temporary foster care rather than adoptive homes. The assumption was that the foster parents would use the children for labor, but also would allow them a place at the family table.

A significant modification of foster care occurred in the 1890s when some states instituted paid foster care—that is, the state provided funds to foster parents to enable them to support the child without the payback of child labor. One striking result of this was a dramatic decrease in infant mortality, as compared to the rates in institutional care. In the twentieth century, most orphanages disappeared as foster care and/or adoption became the primary ways of responding to abandoned children.

Adoption was not without controversy, particularly when it involved the baby of an unwed mother. As adoption agencies proliferated across the country, debates ensued as to whether "rescuing" the baby of an unwed mother was encouraging her sinful behavior. On the other side, child advocates questioned why the baby should be punished for his or her parents' wrongdoing. Some agencies found a middle ground: placing illegitimate children only when the mother was too poor to care for them.

Child Abandonment Today

Child abandonment is rampant today in many parts of the world, particularly areas devastated by war, governmental collapse, or natural disaster. But in the United States, most child abandonment cases involve one of two situations: very young parents trying to conceal the birth of the baby from family and friends, or substance-abusing parents too incapacitated to care for their child. In the first situation, the baby sometimes is left to be found by someone who will care for him or her. But in too many cases, the baby is discarded and left to die. Although the underlying reasons are not clear, some American cities have experienced an increase in discarded babies in recent years, leading several states to pass legislation and launch public awareness campaigns offering young parents safe alternatives for giving up their babies in secrecy without fear of prosecution.

In the second situation, substance-addicted parents leave their newborn babies in the hospital and never return. These so-called boarder babies often are medically fragile or developmentally disabled due to the mother's substance use and poor nutrition during pregnancy. In other cases, addicted parents abandon older children—if not forever, then for too long to be safe or healthy. These cases typically show up in child neglect statistics and, depending on the ages of the children and the severity of the consequences, may lead to placement of the children and termination of the parents' rights.

Overall, there are no official data that capture the scope of child abandonment in the United States today. Numerous newspaper articles quote figures in the range of 22,000 babies abandoned each year, but a search of federal and state databases revealed no official count.

Fear of Abandonment: Role in Human Development

Certainly most human beings never experience real abandonment by their parents. Yet fear of abandonment shows up as a core psychological theme both in theories of human development and in classic myths and fairy tales. Most experts in child development see fear of abandonment as an important motivator in the socialization of young children. In other words, a child cooperates with his or her parent in order to prevent the parent from turning away. Or stated more positively, the child usually tries to please the parent to maintain that important, loving connection.

In the earliest stages of development, a child is establishing a sense of trust, learning that his or her caregivers will provide love and protection. The infant feels most secure in the presence of a loving parent (or other special caregiver) and usually protests loudly when that parent abandons him or her, even for just a few minutes. But as the child matures and learns to count on the parent as a reliable source of comfort and care, fear of separation becomes less consuming, allowing the growing child to develop a healthy sense of independence.

For the child who does experience real abandonment (as opposed to the fleeting separations all children must endure), that important foundation of trust is sabotaged. Consequently, later stages of development are likely to be more difficult for the child. From a child's perspective, abandonment can happen in many ways—not just the dramatic kind of physical desertion discussed so far. For example, children often feel abandoned when they are separated from a parent by divorce or death. And, as described below, a child may bear the burden of abandonment when his or her parent is physically present, but emotionally unavailable.

Emotional Abandonment
Since the 1960s, when the emotional consequences of child maltreatment first were documented, researchers have examined the various ways children are affected by different kinds of abuse and neglect. Studies in the 1980s first demonstrated the lasting consequences of emotional neglect, as, for example, when parents chronically failed to respond to a baby's cries and other signals, even though they were physically present and providing other basic care, such as food and clothing. Over time, these children learned to keep other people at a distance, either through aggressive uncooperative behavior or withdrawn self-isolating behavior. Not surprisingly, they often failed to develop empathy and the capacity to care for others. Although their parents had not physically deserted them, they had abandoned them emotionally at a time when children most need sensitive, predictable responses to their cues and signals. Children learn about their own value, power, and their place in a social world through interactions with those who are supposed to care for them. Abandonment, either physical or emotional, teaches a harsh lesson with lasting consequences.

Martha Farrell Erickson

See also Adoption; Foster Parents; Neglect, Child, Prevention of

References and further reading
Ashby, LeRoy. 1997. *Endangered Children: Dependency, Neglect and Abuse in American History.* New York: Twayne Publishing.
Briere, John, Lucy Berliner, Josephine Bulkley, Carole Jenny, and Theresa Reid, eds. 2000. *APSAC Handbook on Child Maltreatment.* Los Angeles: Sage Publications.
Dubowitz, Howard, ed. 1999. *Neglected Children: Research, Practice and Policy.* Thousand Oaks, CA: Sage Publications.

Abortion, History of

Abortion can be simply defined as a medical or surgical termination of a pregnancy. But the ways Americans have come to terms with this procedure have profoundly affected discourse in U.S. society and impacted the nation's politics. The Supreme Court decision *Roe v. Wade,* which legalized abortion in the United States in 1973, did not create abortion. But it did intensify the heated rhetoric and fierce ethical debates that divide those who support women's constitutional right to access to abortion and those who oppose it. This battle has neither prevented women from seeking abortions nor stopped politicians from working to enact laws restricting access and attempting to recriminalize the procedure.

The history of abortion is as ancient as women's struggle to control their fertility and limit the size of their families. No consistent laws governing abortion in the ancient world existed; some cultures permitted it, some did not. A document from 3000 B.C. China makes reference to abor-

Actresses Morgan Fairchild, Glenn Close, and Jane Fonda rally support as they lead protesters to the Capitol in support of a woman's right to have an abortion (Reuters/Terry Bochatey/ Archive Photos)

tion as does an Egyptian medical papyrus from 1550 B.C. Plato and Aristotle both argued for abortion, and the Greeks, Romans, and Egyptians produced documents describing abortion techniques that ranged from irritating the uterus with laurel and peppers to using drugs that caused the uterus to contract. Many of these remedies are still in use. For example, modern Egyptians still employ ergot, a fungus found on rye, as an abortifacient, even though it can cause death. In Thailand, women use a deep massage technique that was practiced by their ancestors.

Roman law did not criminalize abortion, and early Christians only opposed it after "quickening," that is, the stage of gestation at which fetal motion is felt. Medieval clerics allowed abortion during the first forty days after conception, although Sir Thomas More went a step further, asserting that the soul entered a male fetus after forty days, a female fetus after eighty days. And not until 1869 did the Catholic Church, under Pope Pius IX, ban abortion both prior to quickening and after.

U.S. laws governing abortion came from England, where the practice was commonplace throughout the seventeenth, eighteenth, and early nineteenth centuries. English jurisprudence tolerated the practice prior to quickening, viewing the fetus as part of the mother's body, and not as an independent being. After quickening, authorities disputed whether obtaining an abortion should be a felony or a misdemeanor. In 1803, Britain passed its first abortion statute making post-quickening abortion a capital crime and assigning lesser penalties to pre-quickening abortion. With the removal of the death penalty in 1837, there was no distinction in punishment until 1929, when English statute centered on destroying "the life of a child capable of being born alive" as the major element of the crime and made it a felony except those abortions done "in good faith for the purpose

only of preserving the life of the mother." England liberalized its abortion laws in 1967, authorizing abortions if the physical or mental health of the mother would be affected or if the child would be born with deformities.

Abortion came to America with the colonists, who implemented the common law inherited from England—there were no penalties for pre-quickening abortion and only minor penalties for post-quickening abortion. This common law formed one of the platforms on which the 1973 *Roe v. Wade* Supreme Court decision rested. After 1830, as married women in the United States moved to lower their fertility rates, abortion became a widespread practice in this country. Indeed, abortion rates in the 1860s and 1870s were very similar to the rates of the 1960s and 1970s.

Abortion was not outlawed in any state until 1821, when Connecticut passed the first restrictions, banning the use of poison to bring on miscarriage after quickening. Next to enact a law was Missouri (1825), Illinois (1827), and New York (1828). New York's law served as the model for those in many other states: pre-quickening abortion was a misdemeanor; post-quickening abortion was considered second-degree manslaughter, with an exception for abortions necessary to save the mother's life. By 1841, ten states and one federal territory had enacted laws similar to Connecticut's. In 1860, pre-quickening abortion was outlawed in Connecticut, but most mid-century abortion laws were lenient toward pre-quickening abortion.

With the Civil War and the huge death toll that was its legacy, an increasing number of states passed abortion laws as lawmakers sought to rebuild their populations. In addition, the distinction between pre- and post-quickening abortions lessened, and most abortions became a felony offense, although many states continued to keep the exception for the life of the mother.

Another impetus leading to increased restrictions on abortion—and the advent of abortion laws—came from the American Medical Association (AMA), founded in 1847, which applied great pressure to make abortion illegal because of its professional aspiration to upgrade and regulate American medical practice. Led by physician Horatio Robinson Storer of Boston, the AMA worked to outlaw abortion at any stage of gestation, except when physicians decreed it necessary. These harsher laws drove the practice of abortion underground, but the practice was not ended. Studies conducted by the AMA and the federal government showed that abortion was still widespread through the 1930s.

Abortion has always been a divisive social issue. Early advocates of women's rights argued at opposite ends. Susan B. Anthony and Elizabeth Cady Stanton shared the view that the discipline and self-control required by noncontraceptive birth control was in itself liberating and by the 1870s, the feminist movement transformed this tradition of thought into a new political demand, with the slogan, "voluntary motherhood." Nineteenth-century feminists continued to oppose contraception and abortion, which, they feared, would further license predatory male sexual aggression. Instead, they recommended abstinence.

However, not all early feminists shared their views. In the first decade of the twentieth century, a renewed birth-control movement arose among feminists, among them, Margaret Sanger, the founder of Planned Parenthood Federation of America. Along with others, Sanger advocated for the legalization of contraception, believing that women's control over their own reproductive processes should be one of the fundamental demands of feminism. Sanger wrote: "I believe that woman is enslaved by the world machine, by sex conventions, by middle-class morality, by customs, laws and superstitions."

Along with the increasing independence of women in the 1960s came greater public acceptance of both birth control and abortion. By 1967, a national survey of American doctors showed they favored liberalization of the abortion laws—a sharp reversal of their colleagues' work one hundred years previously. By the 1970s, several states had modified or repealed their restrictive abortion laws, although these efforts gave rise to a strong anti-abortion movement that was initially launched by the Catholic Church but was quickly adopted by evangelical Protestants and those who felt threatened by women's advances in society. Those opposing abortion viewed the procedure as murder, no matter what the stage of gestation, and focused on what they viewed as degenerating moral standards in America. At the same time, many groups that favored a woman's right to self-determination sprang up, and even the more mainstream groups, such as Planned Parenthood, accepted abortion as part of the reproductive health services that should be available to women. This belief that a woman should be able to choose whether and when to have a child, and that she should have a full array of safe medical services to support her decision, is the basic premise of the pro-choice movement.

One battle culminated and another was launched with the 1973 Supreme Court decision *Roe v. Wade* that ruled that women, as part of their constitutional right to privacy, could choose to terminate a pregnancy to the point of viability. This ruling struck all anti-abortion laws from the state books and returned the United States to a close approximation of the common law that governed abortion in colonial times. It also launched a major social war over a woman's right to determine whether and when to have children, a controversy that continues to this day. Anti-choice forces, who were initially galvanized by President Ronald Reagan, have successfully forced several appointments of anti-choice justices to the Supreme Court. The result has been a narrowing of the Court's opinion on abortion, with the more conservative view affecting subsequent rulings on access to abortion services by the high Court.

The controversy also continues to play out in the court of public opinion. Polls show a majority of Americans support abortion under certain circumstances, including rape, incest, unmarried minor children, fetal anomalies, or health of the woman. Roughly 20 percent consistently favors outlawing all abortions while another 20 plus percent consistently favors free choice for all women.

Anti-choice violence has also increased in recent years. Clinics have had to fight against an increasingly violent surge of domestic terrorism that is targeted against women's health professionals associated with the provision of abortion. Health centers have been bombed and burned, clients have been stalked and threatened, and staff have been assassinated at work and in their homes. In addition, anti-choice organizations across the country provide a haven for individuals sought for these crimes and have launched highly funded misinformation campaigns to discredit abortion providers.

Sandra Jordan

See also *Roe v. Wade;* Sanger, Margaret

References and further reading
Bullough, Vern L., and Bonnie Bullough, eds. 1994. *Human Sexuality: An Encyclopedia.* New York & London: Garland Publishing.
Foner, Eric, and John A. Garraty, eds. 1991. *The Reader's Companion to American History.* Sponsored by the Society of American Historians. Boston: Houghton Mifflin.
Hartmann, Betsy. 1995. "Sterilization and Abortion." Chapter 13 of *Reproductive Rights and Wrongs: The Global Politics of Population Control.* Cambridge, MA: South End Press.
Leonard, Arthur S. 1993. *Sexuality and the Law: An Encyclopedia of Major Legal Cases.* New York and London: Garland Publishing.
75 Years of Family Planning in America: A Chronology of Major Events. April 1991. Planned Parenthood of America, copyright revised version.

Abuse
See Alcohol Abuse; Parenting and Adolescent Substance Use and Abuse; Physical Abuse; Physical Abuse, Prevention of; Psychological Abuse; Sexual Abuse; Sexual Abuse, Prevention of; Substance Abuse, Parental; Substance Abuse, Prevention of; Substance Abuse, Progression of.

Academic Achievement
Parents are the first, and often the most important, influence on children's learning and achievement. Although the specific strategies they use may differ from infancy to adolescence, parents have the most enduring impact on their children's educational settings, opportunities, and choices. To examine the influence of parenting on children's academic achievement, researchers have taken a variety of approaches, from focusing on overall parenting styles to parents' specific behaviors and beliefs.

Parenting style has been found to influence a variety of children's outcomes, including academic achievement. According to this perspective, authoritative parenting (that is, high behavioral expectations, high parental warmth, and high use of democratic parenting strategies) is more successful in promoting the academic achievement of European-American, middle-class children than authoritarian parenting (high behavioral expectations, low parental warmth, and low use of democratic parenting strate-

Parental involvement in academic activities fosters good school performance. (Elizabeth Crews)

gies) or permissive parenting (low behavioral expectations, high parental warmth, and high use of democratic parenting strategies).

However, the success of authoritative parenting in different contexts is less certain. For instance, several studies suggest that the effectiveness of authoritative parenting on achievement may vary according to ethnicity. Community and demographic factors may also influence the effectiveness of various parenting styles. For example, parents living in dangerous, risky neighborhoods may have to adopt very different practices than parents living in resource-rich, stable neighborhoods. High levels of parental control that would seem excessively strict in other contexts may be more advantageous in dangerous environments. Some researchers have also

questioned the usefulness of considering the influence of parenting style on children's development. Because the dimensions of the parenting styles are not mutually exclusive (for example, both authoritarian and authoritative parents place high behavioral expectations on their children), it is difficult to know with any certainty which particular aspects of parenting are most important for children's academic achievement. For these reasons, many researchers have focused on specific parenting behaviors (e.g., parental control) rather than overall parenting styles (e.g., authoritarian parenting). These studies have examined behaviors such as parental involvement, parental support for autonomy, parental warmth and acceptance, and parental structure, as well as parents' expectations for success and beliefs about the general abilities of males and females.

Parental involvement is the extent to which parents are interested in, knowledgeable about, and take an active part in their children's lives. Parental involvement includes participating in children's school and other activities, providing stimulation for additional development (for example, encouraging children to develop special talents), and monitoring routine organized learning activities both within and outside of the home. Parental involvement has been found to be positively related to a number of school-related outcomes such as teacher-rated competence and grades. Research has also shown that parental involvement varies widely by ethnicity and income and thus may help explain different achievement levels. For example, evidence indicates that for families living in poverty, parents of high achievers are more involved in their children's school than are parents of low achievers.

Parents who support their children's autonomy encourage self-determined behaviors, or behaviors initiated and regulated through choice, and participation in family decision making. Central to autonomy-supportive parenting is a willingness to take the child's frame of reference into consideration when motivating or regulating behavior. Numerous studies have found that parental support of autonomy has a positive influence on children's academic achievement. For instance, parental autonomy support has been positively related to perceived competence, teacher-rated competence, and grades. Children of autonomy-supportive parents are also more likely to report a willingness and interest in school-related tasks.

The influence of parental autonomy support on achievement may also vary according to the children's developmental stages. Optimal levels of parental autonomy support undoubtedly change as chil-

dren grow older. Adolescents, in particular, have a greater desire for autonomy, and thus, parents often need to renegotiate the power and authority relationships within the family for successful achievement. In fact, researchers have found that a mismatch between adolescents' desire for autonomy and the amount of adult control exercised may have a negative impact on adolescents' school motivation. Moreover, other studies have demonstrated that parents' support for adolescents' needs for autonomy and greater decision making is associated with such positive school-related outcomes as better school coping skills, greater self-reliance and perceived competence, greater satisfaction with school and student-teacher relations, and a stronger mastery orientation toward problem solving in the classroom. Therefore, it seems that children's academic achievement may be enhanced in environments that respond to their changing needs for autonomy.

Parental warmth and acceptance refers to the degree to which children feel loved, valued, and supported by their parents. It also involves the amount of closeness and intimacy in the parent-child relationship. Positive parent-child relationships have been associated with better academic outcomes for children and adolescents. Children who feel close to their parents may be more likely to confide in, and rely on them in times of stress. As a result, parents may be better able to intervene before children make decisions that could have negative effects on their academic achievement. Moreover, parents who provide a positive emotional climate are also more likely to raise children who internalize the parents' values and goals and imitate the behaviors they model. Finally, children with supportive parents may also be more likely to follow their parents' rules, such as homework schedules.

Parental structure is the extent to which parents provide clear and consistent guidelines, expectations, and rules for behaviors. The consistent provision of structure by parents enhances predictability and thus facilitates an understanding of what controls outcomes. A lack of structure, on the other hand, results in a sense of helplessness and unpredictability about events and control over events. Parental provision of structure has been linked to a variety of positive academic outcomes including higher grades and less frequent school absences. Researchers suggest that parents who provide more structured and consistent discipline may be more supportive and conscious of their children's school achievement and attendance than parents who provide inconsistent discipline.

In addition to parenting behaviors, parents' beliefs may also influence their children's academic achievement. In particular, parents' expectations for their children's success have been shown to have an important impact on children's academic achievement. Parents who have higher expectations for their children to succeed in school are likely to treat their children differently than parents who have lower expectations for their children's success. For example, parents who have high expectations may provide their children with plenty of educational opportunities and extracurricular activities, encourage them to take educational risks such as more demanding course work, and provide them with educational support such as help with homework. Parents' beliefs about the general abilities of males and females may also influence their beliefs about their children's abilities and, in turn, affect their children's future academic endeavors and successes. For example, parents with stereotypical views of gender tend to believe that their daughters are below average in math and that their academic successes are due to hard work. Conversely, they tend to believe that

their sons are above average in math and that their academic successes are due to high ability. These parental beliefs have a direct effect on children's perceptions of their own math abilities and, in turn, affect the amount of time and effort children spend on math.

Although these parenting practices have been associated with positive academic outcomes for children and adolescents, there is no single formula that supports children's academic achievement. Certain parenting practices, such as those that emphasize autonomy, may be more suitable for children from low-risk environments, whereas they may be inappropriate for, or even detrimental to, youth living in more risky environments. Indeed, children and adolescents who live in more dangerous environments may benefit from levels of parental control that may appear excessively strict in other environments. For these reasons, it is not possible to separate the influence of parenting behaviors on children's academic outcomes from the larger context in which families live.

Leslie Morrison Gutman

References and further reading
Alexander, Karl L., and Doris R. Entwisle. 1988. "Achievement in the First Two Years of School: Patterns and Processes." *Monographs for the Society for Research in Child Development* 53, no. 2.
Clark, Reginald. 1983. *Family Life and School Achievement: Why Poor Black Children Succeed or Fail.* Chicago: University of Chicago Press.
Dornbusch, Sanford M., Phillip L. Ritter, P. Herbert Leidermann, Donald F. Roberts, and M. J. Fraleigh. 1987. "The Relation of Parenting Style to Adolescent School Performance." *Child Development* 58:1244–1257.
Marjoribanks, K. 1979. *Families and Their Learning Environments.* New York: Routledge and Kegan Paul.

Acculturation

Acculturation is the dynamic bidirectional process by which an individual or group

First/second grade bilingual class in Oakland, California. One of every five U.S. children under age eighteen is either an immigrant or the child of immigrant parents. (Elizabeth Crews)

retains beliefs and practices of an ethnic heritage and adopts those of an ethnic group with which there is repeated or prolonged contact, regardless of the reason for this contact (for example, migration, trade). Acculturation is relevant to the study of American parenting for several reasons. First, the United States is by and large an immigrant nation. Statistics indicate that one out of every five children under the age of eighteen, or 14 million children, are either immigrants themselves or the children of immigrant parents. (Committee on the Health . . ., 1998) Thus, large numbers of families consistently come into contact with American culture, and parents face the psychological task of acculturation for themselves and for their children (for example, decid-

ing whether to enroll their child in a bilingual education program).

Second, though America has historically been considered a "melting pot," wherein all individuals eventually fully adopt American beliefs and practices, growing evidence indicates that many Americans are in fact bicultural to some degree; that is, the individual or family group simultaneously adopts values and practices of the new culture while retaining aspects of the old (for example, celebrating American holidays, such as Thanksgiving, and holidays unique to their culture of origin, such as Japanese Children's Day).

Third, little is known about the parenting beliefs and practices of ethnic minority groups, and what is known suggests that ethnic differences in mother-infant interaction have consequences for children's development. Moreover, patterns of parent-child interaction that lead to cognitive and social competence for ethnic minority children may be influenced by parental acculturation and may not necessarily be the same as those that lead to competence for ethnic majority children. Furthermore, studies of non-European immigrants to the United States suggest that immigrant children perform equally well or superior to children of American-born parents on measures of health, well-being, and educational achievement, but that, over time and across generations, these advantages disappear. An understanding of acculturation processes may help to explain and prevent this disappearance.

Rates of acculturation vary within and among ethnic groups. For example, if two ethnic groups share a number of values prior to contact (for example, academic achievement orientation), then these groups may more readily acculturate than groups who hold very different beliefs and values. But rarely, if ever, do two ethnic groups share all parenting goals and practices, and these differences may create tensions between parents from minority ethnic groups and the dominant ethnic community. For example, parents from ethnic groups that typically discipline their children harshly or fail to supervise their children closely may find themselves in conflict with American social service or law enforcement agencies. Individuals within an ethnic group or within a family may also differ with respect to acculturation. Typically, individuals with the most contact with the dominant culture, by virtue of participation in the larger community through work, schooling, or other activities, will acculturate more rapidly than individuals with less contact. This differing rate of acculturation can be a source of conflict within the family. Finally, individuals do not acculturate all facets of their lives in a uniform fashion. For example, an individual may acculturate quickly in one aspect of his or her life (e.g., becoming proficient in and only using the new language) but not in others (e.g., using traditional parenting practices such as sleeping in a bed with the children rather than using a crib).

Research suggests that parents' behaviors acculturate more quickly than parents' beliefs, even when the same aspect of parenting is assessed (e.g., social behavior). Because research on acculturation is still in its infancy and is very complex, it remains to be seen what effect, if any, this discordance has on children's development. As American society becomes increasingly ethnically diverse, it is imperative that researchers recognize that immigrants do not immediately and forever relinquish the beliefs and behaviors of their cultures of origin and adopt those of the dominant ethnic group. Rather, it would be more fruitful to study how parents and families reconcile and implement child-rearing goals, values, and strategies from both ethnic groups and to examine the effects of this reconciliation on children's development.

Linda R. Cote
Marc H. Bornstein

References and further reading
Berry, John W. 1990. "Psychology of Acculturation: Understanding Individuals Moving between Cultures." Pp. 232–253 in *Applied Cross-Cultural Psychology: Cross-Cultural Research and Methodology Series.* Edited by Richard W. Brislin. Newbury Park, CA: Sage Publications.
Committee on the Health and Adjustment of Immigrant Children and Families: Board on Children, Youth, and Families, National Research Council and Institute of Medicine. 1998. *From Generation to Generation: The Health and Well-Being of Children in Immigrant Families.* Washington, DC: National Academy Press.
Garcia Coll, Cynthia T., Elaine C. Meyer, and Lisa Brillon. 1995. "Ethnic and Minority Parenting." Pp. 189–209 in vol. 2 of *Handbook of Parenting.* Edited by Marc

H. Bornstein. Mahwah, NJ: Lawrence Erlbaum Associates, Inc.

Olmedo, Esteban L. 1979. "Acculturation: A Psychometric Perspective." *American Psychologist* 34, no. 11:1061–1070.

Szapocznik, José, Mercedes Arca Scopetta, and William Kurtines. 1978. "Theory and Measurement of Acculturation." *Interamerican Journal of Psychology* 12:113–130.

Adolescents, Parenting of

Parent-child relations go through significant adjustments during adolescence due to the rapid and pronounced physical, cognitive, and social changes that characterize this transitional period from childhood to adulthood. Once thought to be a transitional period full of "storm and stress," research has shown that most adolescents mature through this period without major difficulties. When parent-adolescent conflicts do arise, they are mostly over trivial daily issues and serve to redefine parent-adolescent relationships. However, major disturbances, including high levels of parent-adolescent conflict, should be taken seriously rather than discounted as a temporary adolescent phenomenon. High levels of parent-adolescent conflict are related to adolescents' moving or running away, joining religious cults, marrying or becoming pregnant early, dropping out of school, developing psychiatric disorders, attempting suicide, and abusing drugs.

Although there are multiple influences in adolescents' lives that determine their developmental course, parents are the single most important external influence on the outcome of the adolescent. Further, despite the view of adolescence as a life stage, there is continuity in many aspects of parenting and parent-child relationships from childhood through adolescence and into adulthood. As children grow into adolescence, and as adjustments in parenting become necessary, the efforts of parenting can build on previously established positive child-parent rela-

tionships. As a consequence, the effects of successful parenting, as measured by such criteria as responsible independence, behavioral competence, and psychological well-being, continue over time. In fact, being well connected to parents is protective against multiple problems during adolescence, such as emotional distress, suicidal tendencies, violence, and cigarette, drug, and alcohol use.

Three major areas of adolescent development that have important implications for parenting are as follows.

Physical Development

The onset of adolescence is signaled by the early manifestations of puberty, the biological process that transforms the child into a reproductively mature adult. The visible changes that characterize puberty, such as the development of breasts and rapid growth, have been associated with increased emotional distance between parents and their adolescent. Mothers and fathers experience changes in relationships with their daughters and sons differently. Mothers have interactions with their sons and daughters that are characterized by high levels of discord, and they report high levels of closeness with their daughters. In contrast, fathers become less affectionate with their daughters and sons compared to mothers; and they share fewer activities with their daughters. In particular, there is a marked distancing, emotionally and physically, between fathers and daughters. Fathers often initiate this distancing, despite daughters' desire for continued closeness. This is most likely a more pronounced expression of fathers' gender role socialization, as well as their seeing the physical changes of puberty as representing a sexually maturing woman, who is off limits to them. In addition, fathers generally take on the role of the more demanding parent, focusing on problem solving and encouraging separation, while mothers

Fathers often initiate distancing, despite adolescent daughters' desire for continued closeness. (Laura Dwight)

tend to emphasize connectedness and nurturance. However, with increasing egalitarian views of male and female roles, as well as increasing numbers of children in nontraditional families, such as single-parent, same-sex, and stepparent families, these relationships are likely to change over generations. It is important to realize, though, that the emotional distancing is usually not great enough and not permanent to cause serious perturbations in parent-adolescent relations.

In addition to social distancing, puberty often signals changes in parents' expectations for their adolescents. Although the direction of influence is unclear, parental expectations depend largely on their perception of the maturity of the adolescent. For example, taller and more mature-looking adolescents are often expected to take on adult roles and behaviors earlier than less physically mature peers of the

same age group. Such expectations from parents (as well as peers) do not always translate positively to the adolescents' self-perceptions. For example, early-maturing girls tend to show increased dissatisfaction with their body image, have lower self-esteem, show problem behavior in school, and engage in smoking and early sexual behavior as compared to late-maturing girls. In contrast, late-maturing boys express more dissatisfaction with their body image, tend to be less popular and less athletic, and perform less well academically than early-maturing boys. The psychological and behavioral difficulties resulting from puberty can be ameliorated through parental involvement, communication, and support.

Cognitive Development
During adolescence, thinking becomes more abstract rather than concrete. The

adolescent begins to be able to think about more than one concept at a time, and the adolescent becomes more self-conscious. With these changes comes the ability to consider another person's view, the consequences of one's own behavior and that of others, behavioral options, and the future. These cognitive changes are accompanied by adolescents' questioning of parental control and rules and their need to be autonomous, which often translates into their desire to participate in, and eventually to dictate, their own decision making. Several other simultaneous changes during adolescence serve to increase adolescents' desire for autonomy. First, physical changes of puberty result in the adolescent seeing himself or herself as more deserving of privileges. Second, increased time spent with peers leads to more experiences and comparison of others' authority, power, and privileges. Finally, cultural and societal beliefs indicate that adolescence is a time to practice adult roles. The expectation that adolescents become increasingly competent to make decisions is evidenced by societal willingness to allow them to make a wide range of decisions in areas such as friendship, academics, extracurricular involvement, and consumer choices.

Learning to make decisions, to live with their consequences, and to learn from them is an important developmental task. However, all too often, just when the adolescent is maturing cognitively and seeking more autonomy, parents and other adults in their lives (e.g., teachers) place more rules and regulations upon the adolescent, thus increasing conflict. One of the most critical and difficult tasks for parents during this period is to find the right balance between granting autonomy and setting limits, between granting freedom while providing appropriate supervision, and not getting confused over the

adolescents' contradictory and volatile behavior and feelings.

Social Development
Parallel with physical and cognitive maturation, important social changes take place that influence the interaction between parents and adolescents. Increasing autonomy shifts the adolescent's focus of affiliation gradually from parents to peers and from group relations to intimate relations with individuals outside of the family. Adolescents in the United States spend approximately twice as much time with peers as they spend with parents or other adults. (Brown, 1990) Accordingly, peers become a major source of socialization and development for adolescents. In contrast to previous views that peers are detrimental to an adolescent's development, it is currently believed that peers can have a positive influence on adolescents. Peer influences may, however, depend on the quality of the parent-child relationship. Adolescents who have positive relationships with their parents may be more likely to have friends who engage in socially valued activities than adolescents with less positive parental interactions. Similarly, more involved parents oversee and monitor their adolescents' peer relationships more than do less involved parents, thereby reducing adolescents' engagement in undesired behaviors.

These expanding social relationships broaden adolescents' sense of extrafamilial reality and reinforce their increasing sense of individuality and need for autonomy. Their newly acquired ability to think abstractly and to empathize are important prerequisites for adolescents' desire to make their own decisions about school, dress, relationships, and risk behaviors. It is here that parents continue to provide adolescents with values, reinforce rules and conventions, and serve as consistent role models. Conflicts are bound to arise in a context of shifting expectations, but in an environment of expressed and perceived cohesion and trust, conflicts can serve constructive purposes, such as providing opportunities to learn how to understand and respect the needs of others, while simultaneously communicating clearly and openly one's own needs. Effective parent-adolescent communication fosters adolescent development, including identity formation and mature role-taking ability.

Contrary to earlier theories, adolescents do not need to detach themselves from their parents in order to become autonomous. Assuming they have had the opportunity to become securely attached to their parents earlier in their childhood, adolescents will continue to have positive relationships with their parents, while simultaneously redefining their relationship from one of unilateral authority to one of cooperative negotiation. One has to be careful not to mistake attachment and connectedness for dependence. Similarly, granting of autonomy should not be mistaken for negligence. While being connected to parents is beneficial to adolescent development, dependence, as opposed to independence or autonomy, is detrimental to healthy growth into mature adulthood. However, the acquisition of autonomy must be age appropriate and needs to happen gradually. There is evidence that premature autonomy can be just as harmful as no autonomy. For example, single parents encourage early autonomy among their adolescent children, and this is associated with poorer grades in school and higher rates of deviance. Moreover, the development of autonomy must be closely linked to taking responsibility for one's own actions in order to be meaningful for interdependent and mutually satisfactory relationships. Being able to express differing points of view without being rejected, judged, or devalued furthers identity

development and interpersonal skills. This newly defined interdependent relationship is crucial to healthy development and serves as a basic model for future successful intimate relationships. Adolescents' realization of parental imperfection, on the other hand, does not by itself lead to a rejection of parental authority and values, as long as there is a relationship of mutual understanding and trust.

Chung-Yol Lee
Bonnie L. Halpern-Felsher

References and further reading
Brown, B. B. 1990. "Peer Groups and Peer Cultures." In *At the Threshold: The Developing Adolescent.* Edited by S. S. Feldman and G. R. Elliott. Cambridge, MA: Harvard University Press.
Feldman, S. Shirley, and Glen R. Elliott, eds. 1990. *At the Threshold: The Developing Adolescent.* Cambridge, MA: Harvard University Press.
Greydanus, Donald E., William A. Daniel, Jr., Marianne E. Felice, Iris F. Litt, Robert B. Shearin, and Victor C. Strasburger, eds. 1991. *The American Academy of Pediatrics. Caring for your Adolescent: Ages 12 to 21.* New York: Bantam Books.
Males, Mike A. 1996. *The Scapegoat Generation: America's War on Adolescents.* Monroe, ME: Common Courage Press.
Muuss, Rolf E. 1996. *Theories of Adolescence.* 6th ed. New York: McGraw-Hill.
Steinberg, Laurence, and Wendy Steinberg. 1994. *Crossing Paths: How Your Child's Adolescence Triggers Your Own Crisis.* New York: Simon & Schuster.

Adoption

Adoption typically refers to the process through which an adult who wishes to parent a child is matched with a child who needs parenting. In contemporary society, adoption is a heavily legalized process, one that requires a great deal of paperwork in addition to a great deal of emotional work. In contrast to foster parenting, adoption is an arrangement by which adoptive parents obtain permanent custody of a child.

Traditionally, adoption has been viewed as the final recourse of individuals who are unable to produce a child biologically. Increasingly, this view of adoption as a last resort is changing, as some individuals elect adoption rather than biological procreation and as families that already contain biologically produced children elect to expand through adoption.

The process of adoption differs widely depending on the route taken by the prospective parent(s). Many individuals begin by contacting a social worker or similar professional who specializes in adoption work in order to learn about options. Available options may include "going it alone" by hiring a lawyer who assists in the process of locating a child and legalizing the connection between child and parent. Another option is using an adoption agency that matches children with prospective adoptive parents and assists in finalizing the adoption through whichever court system is involved.

Individuals who wish to become adoptive parents are confronted with many questions and processes that are not typically encountered in biological parenting. First, the adoptive parents select either an adoption agency or an adoption attorney. Early in the process, the adoptive parents undergo a series of what are called home studies. A professional, usually a social worker, who is licensed to conduct home studies visits the adoptive parents' residence for the purposes of determining whether an adequate home exists for a prospective child and to discuss values and beliefs about child rearing. These discussions typically include questions about the prospective parents' own histories, beliefs about discipline, and plans for education and religious orientation. Several home studies occur prior to adoption, and one or more after adoption, depending on the state in which the adoptive parents reside and the time it takes for an adoption to be finalized.

When prospective parents begin the adoption process, they complete an application that inquires about their financial status, education, occupation, health status, past and present marital status, and the kind of child they are seeking. This latter point refers to the desired age of the child (e.g., neonate, infant, toddler), gender preference, and the kinds of health limitations they are willing or unwilling to accept. Unless the application is specific to the target population of available children, prospective parents will also be asked about their views of parenting a child from a range of ethnic and racial groups. Many of the statements made by the prospective parents must be supported by letters from relevant professionals, such as physicians, and must be notarized. Letters of recommendation supporting the prospective parents' potential parenting abilities are often required. In some states, prospective parents are required to take a battery of psychological tests in order to qualify for adoption.

By the time prospective parents are involved in this level of paperwork, they will have made a decision to adopt a child from their home country or a child from a different nation. When prospective parents are U.S. citizens, adoption within the home country means that all legal activities associated with the adoption will occur within the United States. When adoption occurs across nations, the regulations set by the child's country of origin must be adhered to, as well as the regulations set by the adoptive parents' country. In cross-nation adoptions, the legal finalization often occurs in the child's country of origin; the parent-child dyad immigrates together as a family. If the prospective parent has elected not to travel to the child's country, the adoption agency may bring the child home, with the understanding that finalization will occur through the U.S. legal system. The finalization of an adoption means that all necessary requirements have been met, often including home studies conducted after the child has been living with the adoptive parents for a few months. At the point of finalization, the adoptive family is no longer subject to evaluation and the child is permanently placed.

The time from the point of submitting an application to receiving a child varies from a few months to over a year, depending on the country and circumstances involved in the adoption. Typically, longest wait times are for healthy infants, while older children with disabilities may be immediately available, having waited years for adoptive parents. Adoptive parents may receive their child immediately after the infant is born. In other cases, children will have resided in orphanages or foster homes until they are matched with adoptive parents.

At the time when the court creates a new parent-child relationship through adoption, ties with biological parents typically are considered dissolved. In a sealed record adoption, all information regarding biological ties are kept from the adopted child. This confidentiality is maintained unless an overwhelming necessity emerges to open the records. One reason for sealed record adoptions is the preference of the biological parents to remain anonymous. In these instances, the adopted child receives all new identifying information, which may include a new birth certificate that reads as though the child were born to the adoptive parents.

Sealed record adoptions became feasible in the United States only in the late nineteenth century, when the courts first became involved in adoption. Prior to this point, adoptions in the United States, as well as in many other countries up through the present, have been rather informal, and without court jurisdiction. Under these more informal adoption arrangements, children often knew both biological and adoptive parents. Presently, there is a trend in the United States toward making adoption information, including information regarding biological parents, available to the adoptive child. These open adoptions also permit the birth mother to be involved in the placement of her child, even to assist in selecting an adoptive family. In many other countries, record keeping of this sort may be difficult, if not impossible, meaning that "open" adoptions are not feasible. The pros and cons of open and closed adoptions continually are under debate in the United States.

Cross-nation adoptions are done by many Western European and Scandinavian countries, as well as the United States. Children are most readily available from Eastern European countries, South America, and the People's Republic of China. A child's country of origin will have regulations in place regarding adoptive parents; these regulations typically refer to parents' ages, marital status, and sexual orientation. Currently, it is possible for single women to adopt children from some countries, and for couples married several years to adopt from most countries. Most countries restrict adoptions to heterosexual singles and couples. When U.S. parents adopt children from other nations, the adopted children do not automatically become U.S. citizens. After an adoption is finalized, a U.S. parent can pursue the process by which the child becomes a naturalized citizen.

After adoption has occurred, adoptive parents confront issues regarding how and when to tell their children about adoption, and how to deal with some of the special problems adoptive children may experience (such as a sense of loss of biological ties). As adoption has become more prevalent, as well as more open, resources are more readily available on the topic of parenting adopted children.

Theresa J. Jordan

References and further reading
Bartholet, E. 1993. *Family Bonds: Adoption and the Politics of Parenting.* Boston: Houghton Mifflin.
Melina, L. R. 1986. *Raising Adopted Children: A Manual for Adoptive Parents.* New York: Harper & Row.

Adoptive Family

An adoptive family is formed when an adult voluntarily and legally accepts responsibility for parenting a child not born to him or her. Approximately 100,000 domestic adoptions are believed to occur in the United States annually, about half of them by relatives. In addition, in 1997, approximately 13,000 children born in foreign countries were adopted by Americans. (National Council for Adoption, 1999) Although adoptees constitute only about 2 percent of U.S. children, it has been estimated that one out of five Americans has a close connection with adoption; that is, they have a relative or good friend who has adopted, have adopted a child themselves, or have themselves been adopted. (Kirk, 1964) Although traditionally most nonrelative adoptions involved married couples adopting a child of the same race, adoptive families today are increasingly assuming diverse forms, including single-parent households and multicultural family groupings.

Adoptive families are confronted with unique issues and challenges, all of which influence the context in which children grow and develop. These issues vary in degree for different individuals and families, but they exist throughout the lives of all. Starting before the adopted child arrives home, parents confront a constellation of stresses. These can include resolving issues of infertility; identifying and negotiating the constantly changing labyrinth of adoption sources; evaluating their own willingness or ability to accept a child who may be of a different race or culture, older, or handicapped physically or emotionally; dealing with institutions and paperwork that are often confusing and perceived as threatening; coping with the delays and uncertainties about the child's arrival; dealing with a lack of personal and societal support for adoption as a form of family building, as well as with the psychological process of "claiming" the child as one's own; coming to terms with the ambiguity surrounding the rights of all members of the adoption triangle (i.e., birth parents, adoptive parents, and adopted child) and the concomitant fear of "losing" the child's love; and learning how to talk with the child about birth, adoption, and family building.

Adopted children also confront unique issues. These include dealing with the grieving associated with separation from or loss of biological parents, one's biological heritage, and possibly the culture of origin; dealing with emotional or physical scars left by experiences of poverty, abuse, neglect, institutional settings, or multiple changes in caregivers; negotiating the developmental challenge of understanding the legal and psychological dimensions of adoption as a process; dealing with differences between one's self and one's nonbiological relatives; and learning how to cope with the questions and perceptions of peers, teachers, and other adults.

There is general agreement in the research literature that the majority of adopted children and families adjust well and do not suffer serious consequences as a result of their adoptive status. However, there is also consistent evidence that the proportion of adopted children referred for various problems is higher than would be expected, given the incidence of juvenile adoptees in the general population: 5 percent involved in outpatient therapy, 10 to 15 percent in residential centers and psychiatric hospitals, 6 to 9 percent identified by school systems as perceptually, neurologically, or emotionally impaired. Some types of difficulties are more likely than others to be diagnosed in adopted

Mothers and children at the Asian American Festival in St. Paul, Minnesota. Most children adopted by parents of a different race or culture fare as well as other adopted children (Skjold Photographs)

children. (Brodzinsky and Steiger, 1991) Commonly reported problems include acting-out (e.g., aggression, stealing, lying, oppositional behavior, running away, hyperactivity), low self-esteem, and a variety of learning/academic problems. In general, older children and those with prior experiences with social or environmental disruption are at greater risk for developing problems. However, it appears that adoptive status per se confers an increased risk for the development of problems even for children placed under optimal conditions (e.g., as healthy infants to intact families). Frequently, difficulties do not manifest themselves until middle childhood, and boys tend to be overrepresented among those affected. At the same time, a number of studies have reported that, by adulthood, the problems experienced by many adoptees have abated or disappeared. In general, children

adopted by parents of a different race or culture tend to fare as well as other adopted children.

Until recently, research conducted with adoptive families has been of two types: investigations designed to "parse" the contributions of genes and environmental influences on, principally, intelligence and cognitive functioning; and studies of adoptees referred for psychiatric or educational difficulties. A new focus is on studying the characteristics and dynamics of nonclinical populations of adopted children and their families in an attempt to identify and understand the factors that contribute to favorable, as well as more problematic, adoption outcomes. There is interest in characteristics of the child (e.g., temperament, the developmental changes in the child's cognitive understanding of adoption), of parents (e.g., individual and marital adjustment, perceptions of parental entitlement), and of the family (e.g., levels of communication and cohesiveness, patterns of interaction, perceptions of and beliefs about the nature of an adoptive family, sources of social support, extent of and attitudes about contact with the child's biological relatives, acceptance of the child's cultural heritage). There is recognition of individual differences in vulnerability to adoption-related stressors, as well as appreciation of the extent to which multiple factors interact to put a child or family at risk or enhance their adjustment and resilience. Increasingly, theoretical models are guiding research.

Attitudes about adoption are currently in a state of flux in the United States. Issues such as the role of birth parents in making adoption plans for their children, the degree of contact ("openness") among members of the adoption triad before and after placement, the rights of birth parents versus adoptive parents when a relinquishment is challenged, and the rights of adoptees and birth parents to search for information and direct contact are being widely debated at this time. All these issues present difficult ethical dilemmas and are generating vigorous, often rancorous debate. At the same time, there is a trend toward increasing recognition of, and respect for, the legitimate needs of all parties to the adoption.

Joan T. D. Suwalsky
Marc H. Bornstein

See also Adoption; Adoptive Fathers

References and further reading
Brodzinsky, David M., and Marshall D. Schechter, eds. 1990. *The Psychology of Adoption.* New York: New York University Press.
Brodzinsky, David M., Daniel W. Smith, and Anne B. Brodzinsky. 1998. *Children's Adjustment to Adoption: Developmental and Clinical Issues.* Vol. 38 of *Developmental Clinical Psychology and Psychiatry.* Thousand Oaks: Sage Publications, Inc.
Brodzinsky, David M., and C. Steiger. 1991. "Prevalence of Adoptees among Special Education Populations." *Journal of Learning Disabilities* 24:484–489.
Coll, Cynthia García, et al., eds. 1998. *Mothering against the Odds: Diverse Voices of Contemporary Mothers.* New York: Guilford Press.
Grotevant, Harold D., and Ruth G. McRoy. 1998. *Openness in Adoption: Exploring Family Connections.* Thousand Oaks: Sage Publications.
Hibbs, Euthymia D. et al., eds. 1991. *Adoption: International Perspectives.* Madison: International Universities Press.
Kirk, D. H. 1964. *Shared Fate.* New York: Free Press.
National Council for Adoption. 1999. *Adoption Factbook III.* Washington, DC: National Council for Adoption.
Robins, Lee N., et al., eds. 1990. *Straight and Devious Pathways from Childhood to Adulthood.* Cambridge, New York: Cambridge University Press.

Adoptive Fathers

An adoptive father is a man who becomes the paternal parent of a child for whom he is not the birth father through the social-legal process of adoption, which transfers parental rights and obligations to him from the biological parents. The adoptive father is sometimes referred to as a child's psychological father or sociological father, to distinguish him from the biological or birth father.

According to the National Center for Health Statistics, there are presently about 2.25 million adoptive parents in the United States. Most of the joys and challenges of parenthood are the same for both adoptive and biological fathers. Nevertheless, adoptive fatherhood includes added significant challenges that make parenting a little more complex—but equally rewarding—during each of the major periods of an adoptive family's life cycle.

Confronting Frustrated Fatherhood

Men can become fathers in a variety of ways. Most choose to become birth parents. Some couples, particularly if they

Like biological fathers, adoptive fathers assume the responsibility of caring for the next generation. (Skjold Photographs)

already have had one or two children, may decide to satisfy their need for more children and contribute to the common welfare by adopting children who are also in need of parents. Divorced and remarried men also may adopt their spouse's children from a prior marriage. Infertility, however, is the major genesis of adoptive parenthood. Approximately one out of every six couples of childbearing age experiences difficulty achieving their first live birth, and only about half of these couples eventually find a medical solution to their infertility, according to the National Center for Health Statistics.

Involuntary childlessness is typically experienced by an aspiring young father as a painful threat to his desire to contribute a link to the chain that connects his family's name across the generations. While men, in contrast to women, tend to pub-

licly downplay the intense personal anxiety that accompanies infertility, research reveals that their initial shock is typically followed by feelings of disbelief, confusion, and helplessness. Regardless of whether the wife or husband has the major fertility problem, nearly every man who confronts infertility can identify some aspect of his life that is negatively affected (e.g., lowered self-confidence, diminished masculine body image, lowered self-image). Some men resolve their dilemma through adoption.

Choosing Adoptive Fatherhood
Not all men are equally suited for adoptive fatherhood. Studies have shown, for instance, that poor candidates include men who have difficulty accepting others who are different from themselves or who have known little educational or occupa-

tional success. But among apparently qualified men who have confronted infertility, why do some choose fatherhood by adoption? Research has identified two major factors.

The first is the level of medical hope for natural conception by the couple. Those given a good chance of conception usually waited for a successful pregnancy, while couples who were given virtually no hope of a successful pregnancy more commonly chose to remain childless. But couples who were given uncertain hope of conception were more likely to adopt. Apparently, the lack of clarity empowered them to create their own solution, and adoption was more in their control.

The second major predictor was how the husbands adapted to diminished hopes for pregnancy. Most men chose a primary parenting substitute to cope with the years of stress while they tried to achieve a pregnancy. Men who *primarily* chose self-focused substitutes, such as becoming preoccupied with bodybuilding, were the least likely to become adoptive fathers; men who *primarily* used object substitutes, such as treating their house or car as their "baby," were somewhat more likely to chose adoption; and men who *primarily* used parentlike substitute activities with the children of others, such as serving as a "Big Brother," were the most likely to eventually adopt. Men who are able to use sublimation and altruism to cope with stress appear to find adoptive fatherhood attractive and satisfying.

Adoptive Fathers as Expectant Parents
Anticipation of fatherhood by adoption differs dramatically from that of the more traditional avenue to becoming a father. The psychological and emotional differences between birth and adoptive fatherhood are most acute during the prenatal period. For instance, the reciprocal roles of expectant parents, involving a pregnant wife's need for emotional support and her husband's concern to provide for her physical welfare, are diminished or nonexistent for adoptive fathers. They do not have the experience of seeing their wife's abdomen enlarge, of feeling the movement of their offspring in the womb, or of feeling the emotional high that comes with witnessing the birth. Couples who adopt through an agency, however, often do report that the waiting period between approval and placement of a child feels like a "sociological" pregnancy, although of uncertain duration.

The adoptive father-to-be is confronted with a set of cognitive and emotional challenges that must be solved, and for the most part are dealt with in unique ways, depending on the father's temperament. To an extent, the adoptive father-to-be must undergo a transformation of his worldview of fatherhood. Men who primarily hold a biological-continuity worldview, which at least implicitly assumes that our destiny is in our genes, must reconsider the issue of genealogical discontinuity by mourning the loss of bloodline and the fantasized biological child. This emotional burden is mitigated, however, among men who primarily subscribe to a sociological- and cultural-continuity belief system. Adherence to a social-continuity worldview renders the role of biological destiny less important, while simultaneously emphasizing the social reality that, through child rearing, the adoptive father's values are passed on to the next generation. What adoptive and biologic fathers share is the responsibility of caring for the next generation.

Adoptive Fathers and Infants
The differences in experience between adoptive and biological fathers begin to drastically diminish with the arrival of a newborn or very young infant. One reason is the process of bonding. The task of forming a bond with the new baby and assuming the role of "protector and

provider" for his family are virtually identical for both types of fathers. Young infants have certain universal physical and behavioral characteristics (e.g., helplessness, ability to make eye contact, unique bodily proportions) that solicit caregiving behaviors from new parents regardless of how they became parents.

Secondly, although biological fatherhood is most directly indicated by the birth of his child, it also involves the initial nursing and nurturing of the infant. Adoptive fathers of newborns and very young infants, therefore, also contribute directly to the infant's physical viability because their care is absolutely necessary to ensure the child's biological survival. Now the adoptive father finds that he shares the same concerns and challenges as do biological fathers. In this way the adoptive father can relinquish some of his emotional investment in his own immortality and focus instead on providing a safe and nurturing environment for his family.

Adoptive Fathers and Children
Studies have shown that adoptive fathers are typically highly motivated and very adaptable in terms of providing the quality of care necessary for their children to make a good adjustment. Adoptive fathers, for instance, tend to take the time to read about child-rearing practices and child development. One study found that adoptive fathers were more highly involved in all measured types of child care activities than other fathers. Thus, perhaps it is not surprising that other studies have demonstrated that the academic success of adopted children is generally similar to, or better than, that of birth children growing up in the same social class.

Kyle Pruett, in his helpful book *Fatherneed*, emphasizes that the major task of adoptive parents is to progressively educate their children about their adop-

tion in ways that are fitting in terms of the child's growing maturity. The ability of fathers and mothers to openly acknowledge and discuss adoption issues as they arise greatly aids their children's ability to accept adoption as just another way to build a family. Fathers should never leave this responsibility to their wives alone; both parents should discuss new information with a child so that neither parent is missing from the child's adoption story. Fathers who avoid discussions of adoption may convey a sense of shame to their children. It is also possible, however, to overacknowledge adoption and to overemphasize parent-child differences. All children are separate individuals who are distinct from their parents, whether the child and parents became a family through birth or adoption.

Adoptive Fathers and Adolescents
Studies have shown that fathers in adoptive families tend to remain well involved in the lives of their adolescent children. Adolescents in adoptive families report that they are emotionally closer to their fathers, compared to adolescents in nonadoptive families. Adopted adolescents also have more open and less problematic communication with their fathers compared to their nonadopted peers. Both adoptive and birth parents, however, experience a decline in their influence upon their adolescents, who are hard at work constructing their own separate identities and preparing to leave home. And, for adolescents in adoptive families, their adopted status can provide a convenient mechanism by which to claim their differences.

Adoptive parents themselves also tend to become more aware of qualities their adolescent has possibly inherited from his or her birth parents. Such awareness may remind adoptive fathers of the ghostlike birth father who is typically the least-known person in the adoption story. The adolescent may test an adoptive father's worldview that, in terms of social and cultural continuity across the generations, he could contribute a link by passing on his values, interests, and traditions to his adopted children. Adoptive fathers do their adolescents a service if they are able to model confidence and a relaxed attitude toward emerging differences, keeping in mind that values that their children reject during adolescence may be reclaimed during adulthood.

Adoptive Fathers and Young Adults

Research has shown that young adult adoptees being launched from the family nest are generally indistinguishable from similarly aged and similarly advantaged nonadopted youth in terms of autonomy, identity formation, and developmental maturity. Yet, adoptive fathers are likely to be emotionally challenged when their adoptive children are ready to leave home. At this juncture the adoptive father is being tested more than ever before regarding his permanent and enduring influence on the adoptive child's success as an adult. The adoptive father is likely to ask, "Will my influence overshadow whatever biological propensity existed?" Or, "Will he/she remember me as his/her adoptive father or as his/her real father?" When the inevitable challenges of autonomy confront the now-independent adoptive child, the adoptive father and child are likely to gain perspective on the lasting bond that has been developed. The adoptive father is likely to find that no matter what the biology, the child still views him as the real father.

Adoptive families vary in the degree to which they have contact with the birth parents, but, whatever the arrangement, Rosenberg observes that the degree of contact is likely to increase when adopted children enter adulthood. When such contact occurs, it is usually with the birth mother. However, as openness between birth and adoptive families becomes more common, contact with the birth father and birth grandparents is also increasing.

Adoptive Fathers and Grandchildren

A father can become an adoptive grandfather by a variety of avenues: his adopted child becomes a biologic parent, his birth child becomes an adoptive parent, or his adopted child also adopts. In none of these arrangements does the second generation offspring share any genetic connection with the grandfather. Yet most of the developmental tasks of adoptive grandfathers and biologic grandfathers are virtually identical. Adoptive fathers as grandfathers see themselves shifting generational roles just as other fathers do. They may see themselves in more of an advisory and consultative role in the parenting process, and more than likely they become indulgent grandparents as most other grandparents do.

There are, however, some unique elements in becoming an adoptive grandfather. During the transition from fatherhood to expectant grandfatherhood, issues that first appeared when the adoptive father was an expectant parent may reemerge, such as concerns with biological discontinuity and the loss of the fantasized biologic offspring. If the adoptive grandfather subscribes to a biological-continuity worldview, and thus tends to ignore the influence of sociological and cultural factors in child development, he is likely to experience heightened anxiety regarding his place as his child moves into parenthood. In contrast, most adoptive fathers, as grandfathers, are not focused on the lack of a genetic contribution, but are more concerned with how their lives have been a model for the next generation. While numerous exceptions exist, the wisdom of maturity is likely to lead to greater endorsement of the social-continuity worldview because the adoptive grandfather now has witnessed firsthand the cross-generational effects of his child-rearing practices.

John Snarey
Eugene K. Emory

See also Adoption; Adoptive Family; Grandfatherhood

References and further reading
Kelly, Mary, Elizabeth Towner-Thyrum, Andrea Rigby, and Betty Martin. 1998. "Adjustment and Identity Formation in Adopted and Nonadopted Young Adults." *American Journal of Orthopsychiatry* 68:497–500.
Pruett, Kyle. 2000. *Fatherneed.* New York: Free Press.
Rosenberg, Elinor. 1992. *The Adoption Life Cycle.* New York: Free Press.
Rosnati, Rosa, and Elena Marta. 1997. "Parent-Child Relationships as a Protective Factor in Preventing Adolescents' Psychosocial Risk in Inter-Racial Adoptive and Non-Adoptive Families." *Journal of Adolescence* 20:617–631.
Scarr, Sandra, and Richard Weinberg. 1976. "IQ Test Performance of Black Children Adopted by White Families." *American Psychologist* 31:726–739.
Snarey, John. 1993. *How Fathers Care for the Next Generation: A Four-Decade Study.* Cambridge, MA: Harvard University Press.
Sobol, Michael, Sharon Delaney, and Brian Earn. 1994. "Adoptees' Portrayal of the Development of Family Structure." *Journal of Youth and Adolescence* 2:385–401.

African American Parenting

It is estimated that African Americans represent America's largest ethnic minority group, composing roughly 12 percent of the American population, and that the majority of African Americans are descended from those brought to the United States during the time of slavery. (McCubbin et al., 1998) African American culture produces specific parenting beliefs and practices that are worthy of study. With careful research over time, the most commonly occurring parenting beliefs and practices of a group can be identified. However, when studying parenting practices, it is very important to keep in mind the great diversity that exists within any group and to be very careful not to overgeneralize (i.e., to assume that the identified practices represent the beliefs and behaviors of all members of the larger group). Early research compared African American parenting practices to that of middle-class, Caucasian parents, using the Caucasian parenting as the "norm" ("cultural ethnocentrism"). This research reported African Americans as using authoritarian, parent-centered discipline practices, and also using physical punishment more frequently than Caucasian parents. More recently, researchers have begun to study parenting of African Americans in the context of their own culture ("cultural relativism") by linking these practices to their ethnic heritage and looking for the practices that develop resilience in African American children. Some findings from this research include the importance of extended family networks, strong religious beliefs, and the need for parents to instill in their children a sense of racial pride and resilience against discrimination. Researchers have also become more aware of the impact of socioeconomic status on parenting, and how this can confuse many specific findings regarding parenting among African Americans.

Two primary research approaches have been used to study the parenting practices of African Americans. Initially, researchers took the cultural ethnocentric approach. For this type of study, researchers compared African American parenting practices to those of other ethnicities, predominantly middle-class, Caucasian Americans. Any differences identified were seen as "deviant," and therefore, problematic, yielding an emphasis on intervening and changing these behaviors. Within this research approach, African American families were characterized as disorganized, unstable, and unskilled in adequate parenting methods.

Family working with clay at San Diego's Children's Museum. African American parents must prepare their children to live in a society that, in spite of gains made in the past several decades, still exhibits prejudice toward ethnic minorities. (Elizabeth Crews)

In addition, generally only lower-class minorities were studied, but their parenting beliefs and practices were considered representative of all African Americans. In this research, African Americans were seen as restrictive, authoritarian parents, requiring strict obedience from their children. They were also shown to rely primarily on parent-focused discipline methods, such as giving commands or applying punishment, as opposed to more child-focused methods, such as reasoning or negotiation. African American parents were also shown to be more likely to use physical punishment than were Caucasian parents (e.g., spanking), and to believe that this is the appropriate punishment for disobedience.

Over time, researchers have become more sensitive to ethnic and cultural vari-ations in parenting beliefs and practices and more likely to acknowledge the usefulness and validity of diverse parenting practices. This research approach, termed cultural relativism, strives to study parenting beliefs and practices within a specific cultural group while avoiding any evaluative comparisons with any other particular culture. This viewpoint allows researchers to trace parenting beliefs and practices to African American cultural origins, and to identify the specific strengths and resilience of African American families. Cultural values of African American families that descend from their ethnic origins include: interdependence and an emphasis on the community over individual autonomy; strong affectional ties to both nuclear and extended family, with these relationships providing both emotional and instrumental support; strong emphasis on spirituality and organized religiosity; positive self- and racial identity and esteem; strong connection and integration with community; high emphasis and expectations of achievement and a strong work ethic; and the mental toughness and skills necessary for coping with discrimination or oppression. Within this approach, the strict, authoritarian parenting style identified among African American parents can be seen as useful in teaching their children that they must follow rules in society in order to survive and find success in life. This approach to parenting may also reflect the cultural values of respect for elders and authority figures, and the common religious fundamental beliefs of child obedience. Additionally, research has revealed that this strict discipline does not come at the expense of the parent-child relationship, in that African American parents widely demonstrate high levels of warmth and nurturing behaviors toward their children.

Several factors that are generally related to resilience in children are frequently found in African American families. These include having a warm, supportive relationship with at least one caregiving figure, receiving social support from extended family, and being integrated and involved in the activities of one's community. African American parents must also prepare their children to live in a society that, for all the gains made in the past several decades, still exhibits prejudice toward ethnic minorities. The job of African American parents is great, in that they must simultaneously instill in their children a pride in their race and knowledge of their cultural heritage, as well as skills to cope with subtle and overt racism. African American parents take on the task of building in their children the strength of character to "turn the other cheek" when appropriate, and to stand against unfair treatment when necessary.

Extended family networks are a very important part of African American parenting. Extended family members may live within the household, and nonrelated adults may be incorporated into the family unit. These extended family members are often directly involved in providing care and discipline for children in the family. Many African American children are raised by single parents, or by grandparents (frequently grandmothers). It is estimated that African American children are twice as likely to be raised at some point by a single parent than are Caucasian children, due not only to a higher rate of births to unwed adolescent and adult mothers, but also to high rates of divorce among African Americans. (McCubbin et al., 1998) Early studies suggested that the frequent parenting of children by their grandmothers indicated the disorganization and dysfunction of African American families. However, more culturally sensitive views have allowed current researchers to see that the presence of grandparents as caregivers can provide a greater stability and a more nurturing environment for African American children than if they were not involved. Research has revealed that African American parents and children demonstrate a greater valuing of a grandparent's authority and guidance, financial, and parenting support than Caucasian parents and children. (Hunter and Taylor, 1998) In this context, grandparents are nurturing caregivers and valuable teachers for their grandchildren.

Another factor that must be considered when studying the parenting beliefs and practices of African American families is that of socioeconomic status (SES). SES refers to an individual's educational, occupational, and/or economic attainment. African Americans are disproportionally represented among lower SES levels. As a group they are undereducated, underemployed, and underpaid in comparison to the larger population. Lower-income families face the stresses of inadequate or transient living arrangements, financial stresses, and crowded or unsafe neighborhoods. This high level of stress can negatively affect a parent's ability to provide consistent, nurturing parenting, as his or her effort and concentration is needed merely to cope with everyday living. When SES is taken into account, the strict, authoritarian parenting found within African American families is again shown to be adaptive, and a necessary means for keeping children safe in dangerous neighborhoods, or for preventing children from participating in antisocial behaviors modeled for them in such neighborhoods.

N. Elizabeth Bryant
Garret D. Evans

References and further reading
Garcia Coll, Cynthia T., Elaine C. Meyer, and Lisa Brillon. 1995. "Ethnicity and Minority Parenting." Pp. 189–210 in vol. 2 of *Handbook of Parenting.* Edited by Marc H. Bornstein. Mahwah, NJ: Lawrence Erlbaum Associates.
Hunter, Andrea G., and Robert J. Taylor. 1998. "Grandparenthood in African American Families." Pp. 70–86 in *Handbook on Grandparenthood.* Edited by Maximiliane E. Szinovacz. Westport, CT: Greenwood Press.
McAdoo, Harriette P. 1993. *Family Ethnicity: Strength in Diversity.* Newbury Park, CA: Sage Publications.
———. 1997. *Black Families.* 3d ed. Thousand Oaks, CA: Sage Publications.
McCubbin, Hamilton I., Elizabeth A. Thompson, Anne I. Thompson, and Jo A. Futrell. 1998. *Resiliency in African-American Families.* Thousand Oaks, CA: Sage Publications.
McDade, Katherine. 1995. "How We Parent: Race and Ethnic Differences." Pp. 283–300 in *American Families: Issues in Race and Ethnicity.* Edited by Cardell K. Jacobson. New York: Garland Publishing.

AIDS Education for Children and Adolescents

The need for practical and theoretically grounded pedagogical programs to combat the spread of acquired immune deficiency syndrome (AIDS) among adolescents and young adults has gained increased importance in the last decade. This idea is supported by the fact that the number of adolescents infected with the human immunodeficiency virus (HIV) that causes AIDS has increased significantly in the last few years, and AIDS has become labeled a disease of the young in the United States. In fact, the Centers for Disease Control and Prevention (CDC) reports that of the 40,000 new infections annually, one-quarter occur among young people under the age of twenty-two. (CDC, 1999a) Because there is no cure for AIDS, some believe that the only measures to control the epidemic are prevention-oriented educational programs.

A major goal of AIDS education for children and adolescents is to provide knowledge and promote risk reduction strategies about sex and drug injection that may in turn alter the attitudes and behavior of youth at risk for HIV infection. AIDS education programs aim to prepare young people to make responsible decisions, taking into consideration their own well-being as well as the good and health of others. In some cases, these programs emphasize the role of abstinence, as sexual intercourse represents the major transmission mode of the HIV virus in this population. Several HIV education-related research studies have indicated the ineffectiveness of such programs in improving adolescents' knowledge and attitudes about HIV/AIDS.

Throughout the last two decades the implementation of such curricula has met with resistance in some sectors of the country, where many educators have neglected the subject of AIDS out of lack of familiarity with the resources available, as well as fear of the disease and associated stigma, and the belief that communities have the right to reject AIDS education because such programs may compromise

Alice Carey of the Gay Men's Health Crisis hands out condoms to commuters at New York's World Trade Center (Reuters/Mark Cardwell/Archive Photos)

community values. Historically, the need for AIDS education in schools has been debated since the CDC published the "Guidelines for Effective Health Education to Prevent the Spread of AIDS" in 1988. At that time, former Surgeon General C. Everett Koop insisted that this type of education was the greatest weapon we had to combat the spread of HIV. More recently, the Office of National AIDS Policy has recommended that programs and preventive messages be developed and delivered by parents, teachers, religious leaders, youth leaders, and professionals in regard to HIV, and that educational messages must extend beyond the classroom and should begin at an early age. The effectiveness of comprehensive sexu-

ality education has been demonstrated by the CDC. In the Youth Risk Behavior Surveillance system, it was found that the number of high school students engaging in sexual activity decreased from 54.1 percent in 1991 to 48.4 percent in 1997, and that condom use increased from 46.2 percent to 56.8 percent among students when they were enrolled in comprehensive sexuality education that included information about safe sex, as well as abstinence. (Kann et al., 1997)

In response to the AIDS crisis, numerous programs have been developed by community and state agencies for implementation in schools. Others have been developed on a national level by organizations such as Planned Parenthood, the

American Red Cross, and the Names Project, a nonprofit organization that memorializes those who have died of the disease through the sewing of quilts that are displayed nationally. Although these programs differ in their techniques, the main goal of all of them is the same: to reduce the spread of HIV. Currently, in most school curricula the topic of AIDS is incorporated into health education courses for students. The discussion topics in such classes emphasize prevention of violence, suicide, and pregnancy, stressing the use of alternative conflict resolution methods. AIDS is thus treated as one aspect of general health education.

AIDS education programs for young people may be implemented in a variety of settings other than schools, such as community-based organizations, in group meetings, street outreach programs, and other places where adolescents can be reached. Small group settings have been shown to be effective in improving adolescents' attitudes toward safer sex and reducing risky sexual and drug-use behaviors. Peer education also has been documented as a successful pedagogical tool in AIDS prevention. Because adolescents often turn to their peers for advice and support, information they receive from them often influences their choices relating to risky behaviors. Moreover, peer educators are perceived by many young people as more credible and empathetic than school authorities or other adults. Therefore, trained peer educators play a crucial role in delivering AIDS prevention messages to the target populations and have been shown to enhance learning and improve AIDS-related knowledge and attitudes of students.

Finally, counseling is another useful method of educating young people about AIDS and developing and maintaining strategies to lower high-risk sexual and drug-use behaviors. Professionals in a variety of occupations can serve as AIDS edu-cation counselors, such as social workers, psychologists, health care professionals, and individuals without formal training but with significant relevant work experience. Other AIDS prevention strategies, such as distribution of brochures, videos, books, and posters, providing lectures for large groups, and condom distribution, have all been shown to be effective in altering knowledge and attitudes about AIDS and have sometimes resulted in behavior change.

In 1999, the CDC published recommendations for AIDS education on all levels. (CDC 1999) These guidelines considered the developmental levels of children and adolescents and suggested how programs might be tailored to children in various age groups. For children at an early elementary school level, the delivery of age-appropriate programs is crucial. It has further been suggested that at this level a successful AIDS education program should begin at home, with parents encouraging broad AIDS-related questions from their children and providing accurate and honest information about human sexuality. It has been recommended that school-based AIDS education programs for young children focus on action-oriented activities, such as puppet character shows, and less on lecture-based educational formats because young children have a short attention span.

As young people begin to reach puberty, they enter a stressful time in their lives, when they often feel awkward and uncomfortable with their body image and increasingly rely on their peers for support. This is the time when AIDS education becomes crucially important because this is the age of experimentation with sex and drugs. It has been suggested that programs for this group should include warnings of the consequences of having unprotected sex and using drugs, including death. Because many children at this age may feel uncomfortable with asking sex-related questions, anonymous question notes should be encouraged to facilitate participation and free discussion of sensitive topics. Role-playing scenarios and group projects are also recommended because they lead to communication and discussion of AIDS-related topics with peers under the supervision of qualified educators.

Young people at the high school level seek autonomy from parents and often rebel against adult authority. In learning to belong to a peer group, teenagers are faced with many pressures that may include risky sexual and drug-taking behaviors. Thus, AIDS educators must be prepared to offer effective interventions that will broaden the young peoples' knowledge of HIV-prevention strategies. Although abstinence is the most effective measure to prevent the spread of HIV infection, other means of protection against the virus, such as proper latex condom use, should be introduced to sexually active teenagers.

Since the onset of the AIDS epidemic in the 1980s, AIDS education programs have been fraught with political controversies. Politics often play a big role in limiting access to AIDS education materials as well. In 1999, Congress approved a $250 million funding grant for abstinence education, which would concentrate exclusively on teaching students to avoid sex. However, some have argued that such policies and programs are meaningless because a majority of young people are already sexually active. Some suggest that such an approach to sex education is an avoidance of critical issues for the modern youth. Alternatively, several groups argue that teaching children and adolescents about sex and AIDS will increase their sexual activity.

Perry N. Halkitis
Yana Rusanova-Vaknin

See also AIDS, HIV, Pregnancy, and Childbearing

References and further reading
CDC. 1999a. "Young People at Risk: HIV/AIDS among America's Youth."
CDC. 1999b. "Be a Force for Change: Talk with Young People about HIV."
Hedgepeth, Evonne, and Joan Helmich. 1996. *Teaching about Sexuality and HIV: Principles and Methods for Effective Education.* New York: New York University Press.
Kann, Laura, et al. 1997. "Youth Risk Surveillance—United States." (CDC report, August 14.)
Tonks, Douglas. 1997. *Teaching AIDS.* London: Routledge.

AIDS, HIV, Pregnancy, and Childbearing

The transmission of the human immunodeficiency virus (HIV) from mothers to their newborn children, perinatally or through breast milk, continues to pose a serious public heath threat around the world. HIV, which is believed to lead to the development of acquired immunodeficiency syndrome (AIDS), has affected all segments of the population in the United Sates and throughout the world.

Early in the epidemic, HIV infection was primarily concentrated in the population of gay and bisexual men in the United States. However, throughout the rest of the world, especially in Africa and in the developing countries, AIDS has been a phenomenon that has primarily affected the heterosexual population and children. More recently in the United States, the landscape of AIDS has also shifted. While gay and bisexual men still represent a large portion of those affected by AIDS, HIV increasingly has become a disease of the young and one that has affected women, especially African Americans and Latinas. A direct impact of the spread of the AIDS epidemic to women has been the increased incidence of HIV transmission from mothers to their newborn children. As of 1996, 7,472 cases of AIDS had been reported among children thirteen years old or younger. It is estimated that 1 to 2 percent of all AIDS cases in the United States are found in children, and that almost all of these children were infected by their mothers. The remainder contracted the virus through other means including contaminated blood transfusions or contaminated blood products used for coagulation disorders. Further, about one-third of all children born from HIV-positive mothers also contract the virus. The phenomenon is most prevalent in New York, Florida, New Jersey, California, Texas, and Puerto Rico. Children of ethnic minority groups have been disproportionately infected with HIV perinatally in the United States, with the most cases being among African Americans and Latinos.

The survival time for children born with HIV is still a matter of study. However, among a cohort of 127 children longitudinally followed for a nine-year period, 26 percent died during that time. (Papova et al., 1999) More pointedly, it was found that among infants born with the HIV virus, the development of AIDS can occur within the first year of life and may be related to a difficult pregnancy as well as the development of AIDS-related disease by the mother while she is carrying the child. More recent treatment advances are sure to prolong the lives of children born with HIV infection as they have in the general population, where the implementation of highly active antiretroviral therapy (HAART) has resulted in a 47 percent decrease in AIDS-related deaths between 1996 and 1997 and the decline of AIDS from the eighth to the fourteenth most common cause of death among adults in the United States. HAART represents the current standard and recommended treatment for HIV and uses several types of medication in combination to suppress the virus.

In 1981, the first cases of AIDS were reported in children. While AIDS was of unrecognized etiology at that time, the circumstances of the disease were peculiar, as the children suffering from the pediatric syndrome had mothers who were similarly affected. The earliest reports of AIDS in children were among infants whose mothers were either intravenous drug users or had multiple sexual partners. Initially, these cases were concentrated in New York and New Jersey. Of all the pediatric AIDS cases reported in 1981, 61 percent were due to prenatal transmission of the virus to the children. Today, that number has risen to 90 percent.

Transmission of HIV from mother to child during pregnancy has been labeled *vertical transmission*. However, in addition to vertical transmission, infection with HIV can occur through the breastfeeding of an infant by an HIV-positive mother.

Vertical transmission represents a significant public health concern throughout the world, but especially in developing countries where HIV detection, monitoring, and treatment is much more limited than it is in the United States or Western Europe. Reports from the late 1990s indicate that transmission of HIV prenatally is more likely to occur during the intrapartum or very late prenatal periods of pregnancy. Further, other effects of HIV infection in the mother during pregnancy include fetal wastage, premature birth, low birth weight, still birth, and neonatal death. Worldwide estimates suggest that each day approximately 6,000 women of childbearing age become infected with HIV. Because of this phenomenon, vertical transmission rates are sure to escalate. Without access to treatment, an estimated 15 to 30 percent of HIV-positive mothers will bear a child born with HIV infection. In Europe and the United States the estimate is 15 to 20 percent, and in sub-Saharan Africa the incidence of vertical transmission is 30 percent. (Campbell 1997)

For those children who do not contract the viral infection during incubation, the risk for becoming HIV-positive continues to exist postnatally if breast-feeding is used as a form of nourishment for the child. Recent studies have suggested that the likelihood of becoming HIV-positive in this manner increases greatly as the period of breast-feeding increases. In a recent study of women in both industrialized and developing countries, it was found that children born without HIV infection were less likely to seroconvert if they were breast-fed by their infected mothers for a period of less than four months than those children who had been breast-fed for a period of six months or longer. (Tess et al., 1998)

Since 1995, advances in treatment have been utilized to decrease the possibility of vertical transmission. Numerous investigators have shown that treating the mother with the antiviral drug zidovudine, also known as AZT, during pregnancy substantially decreases the probability that the child will be born infected with HIV. Some researchers have demonstrated that this treatment alone can reduce the transmissibility of the virus by up to 20 percent. However, the optimal dosing of AZT during pregnancy is unclear and is complicated by a variety of factors, including the implications of this therapy on the mother's own health. Because AZT monotherapy is an ineffective way to treat HIV disease compared with HAART, researchers are currently assessing the impact of HAART on perinatal transmission.

In addition, transmission during the intrapartum period of pregnancy is decreased if delivery of the child is undertaken via Caesarian section because transmission of the virus from mother to child may be heightened during vaginal delivery because of increased exposure to infected fluids. In a comparison of vaginal delivery to Caesarian section delivery, rates for transmission of HIV were found to be substantially less when the latter form of delivery was used (10.2 percent as compared to 3.4 percent). More recently it has been documented that the likelihood of prenatal transmission increases when the HIV-positive mother also suffers from a severe vitamin A deficiency.

The issue of vertical transmission is a matter that crosses medical, ethical, and legal domains. Some states require screening for HIV of women who have positive pregnancy results. In addition, treatment with AZT is highly recommended in those situations in which a positive result for HIV is determined. For some women who test HIV-positive, the decision to carry the child to full term is a difficult one and encompasses both the fate of the mother in relation to pregnancy-induced effects as well as the fate of the child.

The issue of an HIV-positive mother breast-feeding her newborn seronegative child has recently been tested in the courts of the United States. In 1999, parents in Eugene, Oregon, lost custody of their newborn son when the mother refused to stop breast-feeding him, believing that HIV could not be spread in this manner. A court ruling on the matter resulted in the state gaining legal custody of the child, although he was allowed to live with his parents under the condition that he be fed with formula. To ensure that this practice was upheld, a caseworker was assigned to visit the family regularly.

The social matters related to mother-to-child transmission of HIV are complex. Some have suggested that the best approach to preventing perinatal transmission is to prevent HIV infection in women of childbearing age, including sex education and the promotion of both male and female condom use at a very young age.

Perry N. Halkitis

See also AIDS Education for Children and Adolescents

References and further reading

Campbell, Tomas. 1997. "A Review of the Psychological Effects of Vertically Acquired HIV Infection in Infants and Children." *British Journal of Health Psychology* 2:1–13.

Faden, Ruth R., and Nancy E. Kass, eds. 1996. *HIV, AIDS, and Childbearing: Public Policy, Private Lives.* London: Oxford University Press.

Shepard, Caroline M. 1994. *HIV Infection in Pregnancy.* Portland, OR: Butterworth-Heinemann.

Tess, Beatriz H., et al. 1998. "Breastfeeding, Genetic, Obstetric, and Other Risk Factors Associated with Mother-to-Child Transmission of HIV-1 in São Paulo State, Brazil." *AIDS* 12, no. 5:513–520.

Ainsworth, Mary (1913–1999)

Mary D. Salter Ainsworth is best known for research she conducted on the attachment between infants and their mothers. She designed a laboratory method called "the strange situation" that enabled her to investigate different patterns of attachment. Although her work was largely directed to an academic audience, it has had many practical implications. In general, Ainsworth found that parents who were sensitive and responsive to their children's needs had children who were more securely attached to them. She also maintained that feeding infants on a demand schedule or picking them up when they cried did not spoil them. Instead, it helped them learn that the world was a secure place. Ainsworth's work has been the foundation for hundreds of studies of child-parent interactions, a topic of increasing interest as more mothers work outside of the home. Her research has also been extended to investigate the effects of early attachment on adult development.

Ainsworth was born in Glendale, Ohio, on 1 December 1913. The family moved to Toronto, Canada, in 1918, when her father was transferred to a Canadian branch of his company. She spent the remainder of her childhood in Toronto

Mary Ainsworth (Vickie Hensley/University of Virginia)

and in 1939 received a Ph.D. degree in psychology from the University of Toronto. While there she was strongly influenced by psychologist William E. Blatz, who introduced her to his security theory, a topic on which she later wrote her doctoral dissertation. Security theory maintained that children needed to establish certain dependent relationships in the home before they could move successfully into the world. The theory had many roots in psychoanalysis, but Blatz was careful not to advertise that fact because of the strong antipsychoanalytic bias that existed at the university. Parts of the theory, particularly the "secure base" aspect, anticipated Ainsworth's later work in attachment theory.

As for many people of her generation, World War II interrupted Ainsworth's career. She joined the Canadian Women's Army Corps in 1942 and was decommissioned in 1945 with the rank of Major. After her military service, Ainsworth returned to a faculty position at the University of Toronto. She married Leonard Ainsworth in 1950 and the couple moved to London in order for him to complete his doctoral degree. In London, Ainsworth answered a newspaper advertisement to conduct research on personality development in children, and was hired to work at the Tavistock Clinic, a pyschiatric clinic. There she assisted John Bowlby, a child psychiatrist, who had been investigating the results of separation and loss in childhood. She stayed at the clinic for four years. Both her career and that of Bowlby were immeasurably affected by the relationship. Although Ainsworth and Bowlby conducted the bulk of their work independently, they are considered cofounders of attachment theory.

Attachment theory contains some elements of psychoanalysis, but its strongest influence comes from ethology—the study of animal and human behavior from an evolutionary point of view. Several prominent researchers, notably Konrad Lorenz, had shown how survival among certain animals is linked to the establishment of bonds between adult animals and their young. In a phenomenon known as imprinting, young animals may even learn to follow an adult animal if the opportunity appears during a specific period. If the opportunity is not available, this type of bonding may never occur. Bowlby argued that many parallel opportunities for attachment occur in the human infant. Further, he believed that children are not infinitely adaptable, and that in order for optimal development to take place there must be a match between the environment and inborn evolutionary mechanisms. At first, Ainsworth was reluctant to accept such an interpretation of mother-infant relationships, but eventually, the experimental evidence convinced her.

In early 1954, the Ainsworths left for Kampala, Uganda, where Leonard had obtained a position with the East African Institute of Social Research. Mary was able to secure funds from the institute to conduct an observational study of local children that tested some aspects of attachment theory, the first study of its kind. She made extensive observations of infants in twenty-six families over a period of many months, with a particular focus on the nature of the mother-child interaction. The couple left Uganda for Baltimore late in 1955. Mary took a position at a hospital where she conducted diagnostic assessments of children. She also became a lecturer in developmental and clinical psychology at Johns Hopkins University. Over the next ten years she published several papers based on her research in Uganda, and the papers were enriched by the later work of Bowlby with whom she had reestablished an association. Her work demonstrated that normal development could be affected by variations in attachment, and, for the first time, she discussed different patterns of attachment. Additionally, she showed that children use parents as a secure base from which to explore. This was an important addition to Bowlby's research.

Ainsworth's next research project was conducted in Baltimore, where she and her assistants observed the behavior of infants in twenty-six homes during their first year of life, with particular emphasis on the context in which the behavior occurred. The depth, detail, and extent of these observations remain unsurpassed. Characteristic patterns of mother-infant interactions began to emerge by three months of age, with striking differences among the mother-child pairs. At the end of the year, the infants were brought to a playroom at Johns Hopkins University to observe their exploratory behavior and to note their reaction to stress. The "strange situation" was devised to evaluate these aspects of the child's behavior. The methodology involved careful observation of the child under several conditions, including when the mother left the playroom, when the child was left in the presence of a stranger, when the mother returned, and when the child was left alone.

The infants exhibited distinct patterns in reaction to the situation. Securely attached infants used the mother as a secure base to explore the room. When she left the room, they often became visibly upset. But when she returned, they reestablished their exploratory behavior. Insecure-avoidant infants displayed an independent attitude throughout most of the "strange situation." They did not become upset when the mother left the room, and they were not particularly interested in her when she returned. Insecure-ambivalent infants remained dependent and clingy throughout most of the "strange situation," to such an extent that they did very little exploring. They were ambivalent toward the mother, clinging one moment, avoiding her the next.

According to Ainsworth, these patterns were a reflection of child-care practices. Securely attached infants came from homes in which their mothers were attentive to their needs and responded promptly and accurately to their signals. These children had learned that they could depend on their mothers. Ainsworth thought they were the best adjusted of the three groups. Insecure-avoidant infants came from homes in which the mothers were rated as relatively insensitive and rejecting. These children had learned not to trust their mothers and, consequently, acted in a defensive way, thus avoiding further pain. Insecure-ambivalent infants came from homes in which the mothers were inconsistent in their child-rearing practices. Their children's behavior reflected that ambivalence.

Several criticisms of attachment research have arisen. Ainsworth focused on the mother-infant bond and showed little interest in potential father-infant bonding. This is not surprising given the time in which her research was conducted, beginning in the 1950s. Fathers were rarely discussed in studies conducted until the 1970s. Later, some of Ainsworth's associates, notably Michael Lamb, conducted research in father-infant attachment. Ainsworth did not take into account temperamental differences in children that may explain, at least partially, some of the differences found in the mother-infant bond. (The temperamental qualities of the child, presumably biologically based, have a potential impact on all bonds of attachment, including that with both father and mother.) Finally, there have been questions raised about the relationship of early attachment to adult personality development. Nonetheless, her work has generated an enormous amount of interest and research, and pediatricians have used her work as the foundation for much practical advice to parents.

Ainsworth and her husband were divorced in 1960. She accepted a professorship at the University of Virginia in Charlottesville in 1975, where she remained until her retirement in 1984. She received many honors during her lifetime and continued to be professionally active until 1992. She died on 21 March 1999 in Charlottesville at the age of eighty-five.

John D. Hogan

See also Attachment; Bowlby, John

References and further reading
Ainsworth, Mary D. Salter. 1983. "A Sketch of a Career." Pp. 200–219 in *Models of Achievement: Reflections of Eminent Women in Psychology*. Edited by Agnes N. O'Connell and Nancy F. Russo. New York: Columbia University Press.
Bretherton, Inge. 1992. "The Origins of Attachment Theory: John Bowlby and

Mary Ainsworth." *Developmental Psychology* 28:759–775.

Ravo, Nick. 1999. "Mary Ainsworth, 85, Theorist on Mother-Infant Attachment." *New York Times*, 7 April, C22.

Alcohol Abuse

Parental alcohol abuse has multiple adverse influences on successful parenting that may undermine healthy parent-child relations and child development. The consumption of high levels of alcohol by parents may impair parents' fundamental cognitive processes such as decision making and judgment, may disinhibit aggressive and violent responses, and may reduce psychomotor coordination and behavioral functioning. These impairments, in turn, may contribute to compromised parenting in several ways. For example, parental alcohol abuse has been associated with more inconsistency (or less predictability) in parenting practices. Similarly, parental alcohol abuse has been associated with poorer parenting styles—either overly permissive parenting that enables children to engage in risky behaviors (e.g., alcohol use, deviant peer affiliation, poor academic performance) or authoritarian parenting characterized by harsh discipline and poor parent-child communication. The abuse of alcohol by parents may also contribute to the emotional unavailability of parents to their children because the alcohol-abusing parent may be self-absorbed with his or her own alcohol use and associated difficulties, and hence have neither the time nor energy to interact constructively with his or her children. Finally, parental alcohol abuse may influence parenting practices by contributing to an overall lower level of family harmony and higher levels of family stress due to more frequent marital conflict, financial setbacks (e.g., loss of employment due to drinking), and legal encounters (e.g., arrests for drunk driving). Collectively, these increased family stressors may reduce levels of family cohesion and adaptability that, in turn, may spill over into poorer parenting practices.

A parent's alcohol abuse may adversely influence the consistency and predictability of responses to requests by, and interactions with, his or her children. For example, on some occasions a child's request to have a friend visit after school to play may be met with parental consideration and approval, whereas on other occasions the same request may be met with parental verbal or physical abuse. Similarly, the failure of a child to perform assigned household tasks (e.g., to make a bed, to take out the trash) may be tolerated sometimes by the alcohol-abusing parent, whereas other times such behavior is met with severe punishment. The parental response to the child may be largely influenced by the amount of alcohol the parent has consumed, family stress levels, and events influenced by heavy alcohol use, or by mood-influenced behaviors associated with alcohol abuse (e.g., hangovers). Whatever the cause, inconsistency and unpredictability of parenting associated with parental alcohol abuse damages a child's sense of order, control, and stability in the family environment. Damage in these family domains, in turn, weakens a child's self-esteem and perceptions of self-competence.

Three alternative parenting styles are useful for illustrating problems caused by a parent's alcohol abuse. A *permissive parenting style* is one in which the rules for appropriate child conduct are relatively lax and contain few explicit contingencies (i.e., conditional "if-then" statements such as "If you are not home by nine o'clock, then you will be grounded Saturday night.") for violations. By contrast, an *authoritarian parenting style* is one in which rules are quite rigid and strict and are imposed by parents without any contribution by, or constructive

Parents' abuse of alcohol contributes to emotional unavailability and an inability to interact constructively with their children. (Laura Dwight)

communicative exchange with, children. An *authoritative parenting style* is one in which clear guidelines (contingent rules) for child behavior are established via parent-child communication, as the perspectives and opinions of children are taken into consideration, and the rationale for child conduct rules are openly discussed. This latter parenting style has been most frequently associated with better child outcomes (e.g., higher academic performance, greater social competence, fewer mental health problems).

However, alcohol-abusing parents are much more likely to be characterized by either permissive or authoritarian parenting styles. Permissive alcohol-abusing parents are more likely to tolerate child/adolescent substance use and deviant behaviors, and less likely to establish appropriate rules of childhood conduct (e.g., for curfew, for household

responsibilities) or to supervise the activities of their children. Low parental monitoring has been associated with a child's earlier initiation into deviant peer groups, which, in turn, has been associated with multiple problems in adolescence.

In the authoritarian model adopted by many alcohol-abusing parents, harsh or severe parental discipline may be associated with relatively mild child transgressions. The judgment of parents under the influence of alcohol may become impaired in meting out punishment to children, with the consequence of overly aggressive (even physically abusive) behavior by parents. The frequent use of harsh disciplinary practices by parents is associated with poor childhood outcomes, including greater emotional distance between parents and their children, higher levels of aggression expressed by children, poorer academic performance, and earlier deviant peer affiliation.

Another very important parenting dimension that may be substantially weakened by parental alcohol abuse is the level of emotional sharing and nurturance between parents and their children. It is evident that the strength of the parent-child emotional bond can greatly facilitate healthy development of the child in all areas (e.g., biological, cognitive, and social). Unfortunately, many alcohol-abusing parents are often emotionally unavailable to their children because of drinking-related consequences such as hangovers, irritability, and negative mood states, or because they are very self-focused on their own drinking problems and are unable to extend themselves to meet the social and emotional needs of their children. Lower levels of parental warmth and nurturance have been consistently associated with poorer outcomes for children, including the earlier onset of substance use, earlier deviant peer affiliation, and higher levels of deviant behaviors.

In addition to the more direct effects of parental alcohol abuse on parenting skills, several other detrimental influences of drinking on broader family functioning may impact the quality of parenting. Parental alcohol abuse is associated with lower levels of marital satisfaction and higher levels of marital conflict, including spouse physical abuse. Such high levels of marital conflict in alcoholic families may reduce levels of parental tolerance, influence negative mood states among family members, and induce fears in children (of family breakup or of personal danger) that intensely stress parent-child relations and the use of constructive parenting skills. Parents who abuse alcohol are also much more likely to miss work (and thereby lose income) and to lose jobs due to their drinking habits. These events introduce additional financial stressors on the family unit. Similar to the stress produced by marital conflict, financial stressors may alter family dynamics and undercut opportunities for constructive parenting, family cohesiveness, and optimal child development.

Michael Windle

See also Fetal Alcohol Syndrome (FAS); Parenting Styles; Substance Abuse, Parental; Violence, Domestic

References and further reading

Barnes, Grace M., Michael P. Farrell, and Alan Cairns. 1986. "Parental Socialization Factors and Adolescent Drinking Behaviors." *Journal of Marriage and the Family* 48:27–36.

Baumrind, Diana, and Kenneth A. Moselle. 1987. "A Developmental Perspective on Adolescent Drug Use." *Advances in Alcohol and Substance Use* 5:41–67.

Collins, R. Lorraine, Kenneth E. Leonard, and John S. Searles, eds. 1990. *Alcohol and the Family: Research and Clinical Perspectives.* New York: Guilford Press.

Windle, Michael, and John S. Searles, eds. 1990. *Children of Alcoholics: Critical Perspectives.* New York: Guilford Press.

Alienation, Student

One common definition of alienation describes it as a feeling of estrangement from others, one's environment, and society at large. When that environment is the school and the alienated individual is a student in that school, the results can be disastrous. Though schools are not the vicious battlefields that the media often portray, they can be a frightening and lonely place for many students. Closer inspection of those youth who commit the most violent of crimes in schools often reveals that those students have been alienated from peers, teachers, and the school in general. Whether subtly or obviously, individuals, groups, or the school itself ostracized these students in a number of ways. This common thread of evidence regarding alienation demonstrates a basis for explaining acts of violence against students and teachers; once recognized, this basis of alienation can be

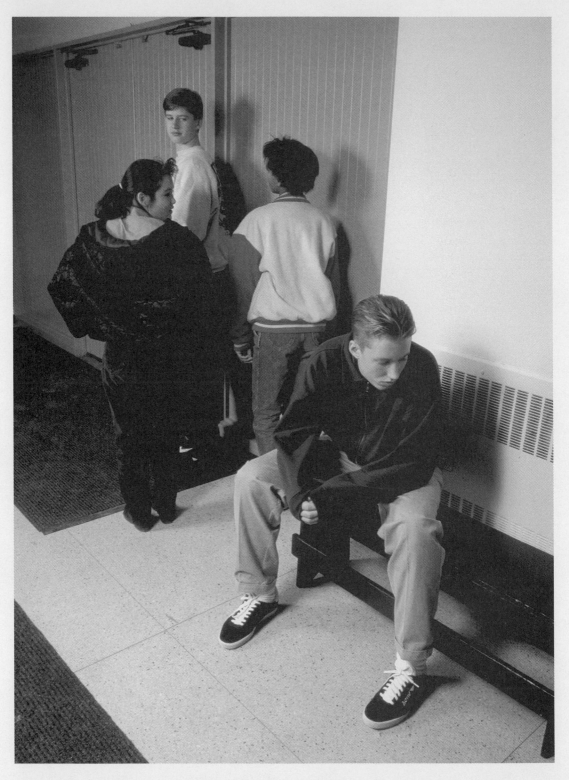

The forming of cliques among adolescents at school is inevitable. (Skjold Photographs)

remedied by caring and competent school personnel.

Feelings of alienation are formed in a very real and large way by the climate of the school in which students find themselves. A positive school climate yields students who describe themselves as treated fairly, as well as being both valued and respected as individuals. These schools are not devoid of rules or certain constraints. Rather, the necessary rules and regulations are viewed as fairly enforced and beneficial to all students. Verbal assaults, in the form of sarcasm, ridicule, and other put-downs, are nonexistent. Teachers recognize the potential harm of bullying and do not allow it to occur unchecked. The forming of cliques is inevitable among adolescents; in the best of situations, those students left outside of the groups are recognized and offered support by school staff. Given the academic requirements of today's students, school is still difficult; however, students in these positive climates generally are eager participants in the school system.

In contrast, when teachers do not recognize students and their families as clients who should be valued, nurtured, and encouraged, the tragic result is an extremely negative school climate. Such schools produce high rates of alienated students and are characterized by a number of misbehaviors. Discipline may be applied unfairly and inconsistently by seemingly uncaring educators. Verbal assaults—both by teachers and student peers—within the classroom flourish in such a harsh, rule-bound environment. Scapegoating, name-calling, and put-downs are common and used by both staff and peers. Both staff and students can form cliques, leaving no one to support those left on the outside. Whether it is created consciously or not, a negative school climate either perpetuates or ignores both physical and psychological assaults on students.

Misbehavior can be seen as a function of the interaction between individuals and the environment. Surely, a student struggling to fit in and become connected socially to others in such a negative school climate would face a tremendous battle. Although schools are not the only cause of youth violence, the activities that go on within their walls may likely trigger aggression by alienating these already vulnerable children.

A child who feels alienated at school often exhibits certain characteristic behaviors. Young children may develop a fear of attending school, which manifests itself as a variety of avoidance symptoms. These behaviors may range from psychosomatic or feigned illnesses to outright refusal and temper tantrums.

In addition to physical complaints, older children—after the age of eight or nine—show a variety of behavioral and personality changes. They may distrust adults, have poor peer relationships, or engage in aggressive outbursts. These factors inevitably affect their school performance in a negative manner. Such children, who are at the same time struggling for independence, may further manifest their feelings of alienation in terms of refusal to do schoolwork, bullying, experimentation with drugs, stealing, vandalism of school property, and covert attacks on teachers' property—especially cars in the school parking lot.

Adolescents who feel alienated from their peers and school may express their frustration in increasingly destructive acts, as they express physical and verbal aggression along with a constant hostility toward adults. The adolescent may rebel, withdraw, or even physically attack those whom he or she sees as the victimizer. The resulting pain from these harmful school experiences may further express itself in substance abuse, delinquency, precocious sexual behavior, and school truancy.

These children perceive that they are victims of an unrelenting negative school climate. They see both staff and peers as the perpetrators of their alienation. If not recognized and helped, these students may engage in vengeful ideation against the enemy, which is what the school environment has become to them. Fortunately, when school personnel are properly trained about the characteristic symptoms of alienated students, they can intervene and provide assistance and guidance. As they become further educated, teachers may also learn what attitudes and behaviors to eliminate in their own classrooms.

Students, teachers, and parents can work together to change the climate of a school that leads to student alienation and contributes to violence. First, students can extend their friendships to include people who are different from them. Students learn and grow by having friends with varying interests and of different genders, socioeconomic classes, races, or sexual orientations. Young people need to adopt a "zero tolerance" policy of their own, in that they will not allow others to insult them or their classmates with demeaning and bigoted remarks, in or out of the classroom.

The majority of teachers are hardworking individuals who truly want to serve their students in the best ways possible. They can further their skills by learning to intervene—without blaming or punishing—to reduce the harassment, insults, and exclusiveness that are prevalent in some schools. Teachers can form networks among themselves to exchange the emotional support and positive reinforcement they need to face the daily challenges of nurturing young students. In addition, educators should take the opportunity to engage students in discussions about the importance of mutual respect. If a crisis does occur, teachers must be sensitive to the needs of their respective students, possibly allowing class time to have students talk or write about their views and experiences.

As children grow older, their peers often become more influential over their actions; however, parents must recognize that they can still play a part in shaping their children's choices. Parents must spend time playing with their children when they are young and continually listening to them as they grow. By treating others with respect, parents can serve as role models for their children through their own actions. Finally, parents need to give unconditional attention to their children, while trying to reserve judgment as their children express frustration or fear. Children must feel free to talk with their parents without the fear of harsh punishment or ridicule.

Schools may create negative climates where educators are viewed as adversaries, and the emphasis is on punishment rather than prevention. Interpersonal alienation runs high, as students develop hostile and angry feelings toward the school, teachers, and peer groups. Many media accounts of school violence suggest that such acts were carried out by alienated students seeking revenge against individuals or groups within the school. When certain students perceive themselves as mistreated by those connected to the school, they may seek retribution. Schools need not be the battlefields that some children experience them to be. Vigilant and caring parents, teachers, and students have within their power the ability to create positive school climates where individuals can be nurtured and supported.

Irwin A. Hyman
Stacey Mellinger

References and further reading
Garbarino, James. 1999. *Lost Boys: Why Our Sons Turn Violent and How We Can Save Them*. New York: Free Press.

Pipher, Mary. 1994. *Reviving Ophelia: Saving the Selves of Adolescent Girls.* New York: Putnam Publishing Group.

Altricial and Precocial

The terms *altricial* and *precocial* describe the immaturity or maturity, respectively, of a species's offspring at birth; more generally, they refer to reproductive strategies that have profound implications for the extent, nature, and consequences of parenting behavior. The young of an *altricial* species come into the world in a primitive state: very small, often naked, with eyes and ears still closed, and unable to fend for themselves. Mammalian examples include opossums, rats, and mice. Despite their immaturity, they require and receive little individualized parental care, in part because they reach maturity very rapidly, and in part because they tend to arrive in large litters that are cached in nests. Life spans in such species are brief, and social organization tends to be minimal. The altricial reproductive strategy appears characteristic of species that evolved in environments where resources were unstable; large numbers of organisms are produced quickly on the chance that some will survive to perpetuate the species.

The young of a *precocial* species, on the other hand, are born well developed and competent. Paradoxically, they receive elaborate and individualized parental care. Each offspring, thus, represents a great investment of time, energy, and resources. Precocial reproductive strategies are thought to have evolved in relatively rich and stable environments, wherein longer periods of gestation and development and complex social structures not only could be supported, but in which they could be advantageous. In precocial species, litter size is small (often only one), gestation takes a long time, sexual maturity is delayed, and life spans are long. Brain size is large relative to body size. Social organ-

Mothers in precocial species tend to take their infants with them as they travel through the environment. (Renee Lynn)

ization tends to be complex, and it often includes parent-offspring attachment. The young tend to travel about the environment with the mother rather than to wait behind in nests. Through their travels and social experiences, the young acquire key skills and information, such as how to locate and exploit their environment's food sources, how to interact with other members of their species, and even how to care for their own young. Precocial species include guinea pigs, sheep, and the primates. Parental care has become particularly elaborate in the primates, where the evolutionary trend "has clearly been toward quality rather than quantity. Fewer offspring are produced, but the few that are born are well cared for and are likely to live for a long time." (Martin, 1975, 50–51)

Our own species is unique, in that an otherwise precocial reproductive strategy produces an infant that is in many respects as immature and helpless as the most altricial creatures. This immaturity appears to have been added on to the precocial strategy of our most recent ancestors; thus, we are sometimes described as "secondarily altricial." The selection pressures that might have favored this *heterochrony* (here, an alteration in the relative timing of developmental events in comparison with other precocial species) have long been debated. Predictably, some of the arguments have been based in a view of evolution as an inevitable progression toward intellectual (and perhaps spiritual) perfection, but this view of evolutionary process is misguided. In a charming essay titled "Human Infants as Embryos," author, scholar, and Harvard professor of zoology Stephen Jay Gould reviews some of these arguments and sides with those who favor a pragmatic explanation. He notes that our nearest relatives, the primates, are the "archetypical precocial mammals" (Gould, 1977, 71): their gestation times are long, most litters are singletons, life spans are long, brains are large relative to body size, and newborns are physically mature and behaviorally competent. Human beings share all of these precocial traits except the last.

The explanation may be that evolution has favored the large, well-developed brains of primates, but the advantage turns to disadvantage as fetal head size begins to exceed the limits of the maternal pelvis. This problem may have been particularly relevant in human evolution, because of the narrower pelvis required for upright locomotion. Being born a bit earlier (and, thus, smaller) may have become advantageous, and more and more of development was gradually shifted to the postnatal period. Human infants are born essentially as embryos, Gould argues, still small enough to escape the maternal pelvis, quite immature in comparison with the developmental status of other primates, but able to survive given the elaborate parental care of our otherwise precocial species. Our infants are seven to nine months old before they reach the overall level of development and behavioral competence that other primates show at birth. The demands on human parents are thus intensified and greatly protracted.

In our species, an extreme period of dependency on caregivers is imposed upon a young organism whose brain and sensory-perceptual systems are highly precocial. This arrangement has interesting implications, three of which will receive brief mention here. First, as more of early development is shifted to the postnatal period, parental behavior assumes greater potential as a cause of development in the offspring. Human caregivers provide extensive social interaction, and they mediate experiences with the nonsocial environment, thus providing predictable forms of input to the process of development. The "developmental psychobiological systems model" (Gottlieb, Wahlsten, and Lickliter, 1998) is a useful framework for considering how these inputs may contribute to physical, behavioral, and perceptual development. Second, because young human infants can neither follow their caregivers nor cling to them, proximity must be achieved by other means. Much of the burden, of course, is borne by the parents. Human infants, nonetheless, are quite competent in some respects. The eminent attachment theorist John Bowlby proposed that evolution had prepared infants with behaviors such as making eye contact, crying, and smiling so that they could initiate proximity to, and interaction with, caregivers. He further proposed that psychological attachment, for many writers the sine qua non of normal social-personality development, came about in the course of these interactions. (Bowlby 1969)

Finally, modifications in the timing of gestation and the events of infancy are just the beginning. Human beings also have a much-protracted period of immaturity after infancy (that is, a childhood). In a provocative book titled *The Descent of the Child* (1995), zoologist Elaine Morgan speculates on the evolutionary forces that favored these modifications and offers a sociological perspective on the implications for parenting.

Whatever its causes and theoretical implications, the helplessness of our young poses an interesting practical problem for parents. Mothers in precocial species tend to take their infants with them as they travel through the environment, and the infants help—lambs follow, for example, and baby monkeys are lightweight and able to cling to their mothers' fur. Human parents, however, must actively carry their infants, for many months, supporting their relatively great and increasing weight, and also keep them from falling off. A look across human history reveals a fascinating array of slings, carriers, and wheeled devices invented to ease this burden.

Gwen E. Gustafson

See also Bowlby, John

References and further reading
Bowlby, John. 1969. *Attachment.* Vol. 1 in *Attachment and Loss.* New York: Basic Books.
Gottlieb, Gilbert, Douglas Wahlsten, and Robert Lickliter. 1998. "The Significance of Biology for Human Development: A Developmental Psychobiological Systems View." Pp. 233–273 in vol. 1 of *Handbook of Child Psychology.* Edited by William Damon and Richard M. Lerner. New York: John Wiley and Sons.
Gould, Stephen J. 1977. *Ever Since Darwin: Reflections in Natural History.* New York: Norton.
Martin, Robert D. 1975. "Strategies of Reproduction." *Natural History* (November):48–57.
Morgan, Elaine. 1995. *The Descent of the Child: Human Evolution from a New Perspective.* New York: Oxford University Press.

Ames, Louise Bates (1908–1996)

Louise Bates Ames was a psychologist who conducted pioneering research on child development. She maintained that development in childhood proceeds in predictable patterns that are often related to specific chronological ages. Ames was a prolific writer who believed that knowledge about development could be of great value to parents and educators. Ames and her associates were criticized for their apparent belief that development was largely genetically based, and that all children develop in the same way. Ames argued that this was a misinterpretation of their position. In fact, she said, they believed strongly in the importance of environment. She further maintained that patterns of development could be used to understand individual differences.

From 1933 to 1950, Ames worked at the Yale Clinic of Child Development as a research assistant to Arnold Gesell, a psychologist and pediatrician. After his retirement, she was instrumental in founding the Gesell Institute in New Haven, Connecticut. Her work was closely associated with Gesell, but she was more of a popularizer than he. She was the coauthor of many books and also became an early media psychologist, conducting one of the first television shows on child development, broadcasting from WBZ in Boston a program in which she answered audience questions; between 1971 and 1974, she was a contributing editor to *Family Circle* magazine. Her work stressed the natural timetable of the child in development. In a departure from her other developmental work, she also conducted research and wrote dozens of articles on the use of projective tests with children.

Louise Bates Ames (Gesell Institute)

Louise Bates was born in 1908, in Portland, Maine, the oldest of three children. Her home environment was an intellectual one, and she was expected to go to college. At first, Louise decided she would be an attorney. Her father was a judge, and she thought she would enter his law practice. She studied at Wheaton College in Massachusetts for two years (1926–1928) but decided that the college was not a good fit for her. She transferred to the University of Maine, where she became interested in psychology. Her studies were interrupted when she eloped in 1930 with Smith Whittier Ames, in her senior year in 1930. She returned to the college to complete her undergraduate degree and to obtain a master's degree as well. Her marriage to Ames, who became a physician, produced a daughter, Joan. The couple divorced in the 1930s.

In 1933, Ames was accepted into the doctoral program in psychology at Yale University where she hoped to study child development under Dr. Arnold Gesell. However, the university did not offer graduate courses in child development or clinical psychology, and so it was impossible to obtain a degree in those areas. The dominant influence at Yale at the time was the learning theory approach of Clark Hull and his followers, a system in strong opposition to the biological approach of Gesell. The learning theory approach holds that behavior is primarily a product of interaction with the environment and that biological differences are largely irrelevant. Ames also believed that child development was held in contempt at Yale because it was not an "experimental" science. She worked as an assistant to Gesell and in 1936 was awarded a doctorate in experimental psychology.

Her doctoral research, conducted at the Yale Clinic of Child Development, used the method of "cinemanalysis." Gesell had been a pioneer in the use of film to study children. The results of Ames's dissertation supported the views of Gesell, notably that development proceeded in predicable patterns. However, to their surprise, they found that behavior did not develop in a straight line. Rather, it gave evidence of frequent regression. Ames and her associates compiled hundreds of hours of film of children playing or engaging in specific tasks. The film was then analyzed in great detail. Along with Dr. Frances L. Ilg, also on the staff of the Yale Clinic, and Gesell, Ames began to formulate a view of child development that leaned heavily on the importance of age in understanding children.

Central to their system was the belief that each age has its own individuality. For instance, they believed that children at age two and one-half were characterized by rigidity and inflexibility, hence the designation "the terrible twos," a phrase they helped to popularize. A three-year-old is not simply a more mature two-and-one-half-year-old, they argued. Rather, age three has its own unique behaviors and potentials. These views resulted in the publication of several books for parents, including *Infant and Child in the Culture of Today* (Gesell, Ilg, Ames, and Learned, 1943), *The Child from Five to Ten* (Gesell, Ilg, Ames, and Bullis, 1946), and *Youth: The Years from Ten to Sixteen* (Gesell, Ilg, and Ames, 1956). Other books followed. Beginning in 1938, Ames also edited a series of films on child development to illustrate the behaviors she had been describing in print.

After Gesell's retirement in 1948, his associates found they were no longer welcome at Yale. This was a shock to them all, including Gesell. Psychoanalytic influences were being more strongly felt in academic psychology, and the approach of Gesell was viewed by some as old-fashioned. Ames, with two associates, then founded the Gesell Institute, located near Yale but not affiliated with it, to continue their work. The institute remains in operation today. For its first two decades, Ames was director of research at the institute. She was also a member of the institute's board of directors from its beginning, and served as president of the board from 1971 to 1987.

Although Ames readily acknowledged her debt to Gesell, largely in terms of the subject matter of her work, she also did some research that departed from his. One of those areas was her work in projective testing, particularly in the use of the Rorschach Ink Blot Test with children. The Rorschach test, which has declined in popularity in recent decades, presents the subject with ambiguous stimuli to which the subject responds; the responses are presumed to provide clues to the subject's personality and other characteristics. She believed that just as children display particular patterns of motor behavior at certain ages, they also display patterns on the Rorschach. In

effect, what some might interpret as pathological responses were simply immature responses that would change as the child matured. Her research supported this view. Children's responses to the Rorschach changed with age, and children who gave so-called abnormal responses early in development gave more mature and "normal" responses later on. Ames and her associates also investigated Rorschach responses in the aged. Although she had been criticized earlier for her research with the Rorschach, she eventually was elected president of the Society for Projective Techniques.

Ames may have made her greatest impact with her work on school readiness. Gesell had first introduced the idea of school readiness in 1919, suggesting that every child should be given a psychophysical exam before entering school. The idea was largely ignored until the 1950s, when Ames and her associate Frances Ilg revived it. Ames and Ilg found that many of the children who were referred to them for learning disabilities and other developmental disabilities were normal children, perhaps developmentally young for their ages, who had been "overplaced" in the school system. They received a research grant to study the problem, and eventually wrote a book on the subject, *School Readiness* (1964). Their premise was that children should be admitted to school based on their behavioral age, not their chronological age or IQ score. They believed that parents must be discouraged from starting children too early in school; rather, starting children at the appropriate time was probably the single most important thing parents could do to encourage their children's scholastic success. They wrote that as many as a third of all school failures could be avoided by proper placement. They further maintained that behavioral age could easily be evaluated through such measures as the Gesell Developmental Scale.

Ames also had a great impact as an early media psychologist. Although she was in demand as a lecturer to both parent and professional groups while she was at Yale, neither the university nor Gesell encouraged her in this kind of activity. After the Gesell Institute was founded, however, she was no longer under such constraints. In 1952, with Frances Ilg, she began writing a daily column that was syndicated in sixty-five large newspapers nationwide. The column not only provided funds for the Institute, it also gave Ames and Ilg an opportunity to promote their non-Freudian view of development.

As an outgrowth of her column, Ames was invited to give a series of lectures in Boston on child development. When those were successful, she was approached to conduct a weekly television show on child behavior. Live and unrehearsed, the show consisted of members of the audience asking Ames questions about child development. The show began in 1953 and ran for two years. For much of that time it was followed by a weekly radio show on the same subject. Ames continued to participate in radio and television long after her initial series had come to an end. She also appeared on many popular talk shows such as *The Mike Douglas Show*, *Sally Jesse Raphael*, and *The Oprah Winfrey Show*. She considered these appearances to be important opportunities to get her message to a large audience. She created a stir in the mid-1980s when she cautioned parents against taking young children to see the movie *Bambi* in which the young deer's mother is killed by hunters. Despite criticism, she stood by her position, explaining how the movie embodied the greatest fears of a young child.

Before Ames's death there had been a successful attempt to establish links between the Yale Child Study Center and the Gesell Institute. Among other things, a Yale professorship and two fellowships were established in the names of Gesell and Ames. Louise Bates Ames died of cancer at the age of eighty-eight at the home of her granddaughter in Cincinnati, Ohio. She remained active until shortly before her death.

John D. Hogan

See also Gesell, Arnold L.; School Readiness: Competencies; School Readiness: Parental Role

References and further reading

Ames, Louise Bates. 1996. "Louise Bates Ames." Pp. 1–23 in *A History of Developmental Psychology in Autobiography*. Edited by Dennis Thompson and John D. Hogan. Boulder, CO: Westview Press.
Fountain, Henry. 1996. "Louise Ames, 88, A Child Psychologist Dies." *New York Times*, 7 November, D27.

Anorexia

Anorexia nervosa is an eating disorder characterized by a strong desire for a thinner body and an intense fear of becoming fat. Individuals who are affected literally starve themselves. Other medical conditions, such as depression and paranoia, may produce anorexic symptoms, but in these conditions excessive concern about weight is not present.

Once considered to be quite rare, the incidence of anorexia has increased dramatically over the past two decades. While it is difficult to pinpoint its exact frequency, the general understanding is that approximately ten in every one thousand young people aged twelve to eighteen may have the disorder at some point in time. The peak periods for onset for anorexia are in early adolescence, and again around age eighteen, as young people prepare to leave home and go off to college. It appears primarily in females, who make up approximately 90 percent of all cases. Relatively little is known about the development of anorexia in males, and authorities disagree on the causes of male anorexia. Caucasian American girls

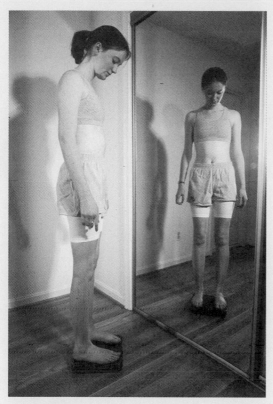

Anorexia may begin as an ordinary attempt at dieting that gradually develops into a more serious obsession with losing weight. (Richard T. Nowitz)

are at greater risk than African American girls, who tend to be more satisfied with their body image.

Diagnosis can be difficult because the anorexic denies she has a problem and rationalizes her behavior. Anorexia is relatively rare in women over thirty, but when this disorder does occur in older women, it is often very serious because of their resistance to treatment.

With respect to body image, people with anorexia sincerely believe they look the way they should. They regard themselves as being in good health, despite severe weight loss that is apparent to everyone else. They ignore or misinterpret bodily sensations that could tell them they are hungry and consequently have little appetite. What they want most

from other people is not to be helped, but to be left alone.

Anorexics may lose between 25 and 50 percent of body weight. Medically, weight loss of more than 35 percent for normal age and height is considered life threatening. As a consequence, the malnutrition associated with anorexia can cause physical symptoms, including dry skin and brittle, discolored nails. The anorexic feels cold and even in warm weather may wear heavy clothes. As the condition advances, a fine silky hair called lanugo covers the body in an attempt to preserve body heat. Potassium deficiency from laxative abuse may throw the digestive system out of balance. Anorexics may suffer from stomach cramps and constipation. Long-term anorexia may lead to kidney failure and shrinking of the heart muscle. Cardiac arrest is one of the leading causes of death among anorexics.

Much of the anorexic's behavior revolves around concern for appearance, control, and thoughts of food. Concern about weight and appearance is normal in adolescent girls and many adolescent girls go on diets. Anorexia may begin as an ordinary attempt at dieting, but gradually develops into a more serious obsession with losing weight. An intense fear of becoming fat continues as the person becomes increasingly undernourished and even appears emaciated. However, because the anorexic is often secretive about her eating patterns, determining the point at which the normal diet ends and the anorexic eating pattern begins is often difficult.

At the same time, the anorexic often displays seemingly contradictory attitudes toward food. On one hand, anorexics often show obsessive concern with the caloric content of food. They may make regular use of caloric counters, collect diet books, and check their weight frequently, including both before and after meals. On the other hand, the anorexic may insist on doing the food shopping and prepare elaborate meals, while she herself does not eat. She may develop strange eating habits, such as cutting her food into tiny pieces or moving the food around on the plate in an attempt to give the impression she is eating. Others collect recipes and in some cases even hoard food.

No clear consensus about the nature and causes of anorexia exists, but several explanations have been advanced. One position asserts that the individual is unwilling to accept her role as a developing woman and her feminine sexuality. Because a normal menstrual cycle requires about 15 percent body fat, either menarche does not occur or menstrual periods stop. Here, anorexia is seen as a defense against the process of sexual maturation. Breast development reverses and may even return to prepubertal development. Interest in the opposite sex and intimacy are reduced.

Another view emphasizes that in Western culture slenderness is desirable and pressure is placed on women to stay fit and slim. Some young women are much more vulnerable than others to such messages and may aspire to exaggerated ideals of attractiveness. The mass media, it is argued, all too frequently reinforces this message. Fashion magazines present the adolescent girl with idealized, but often unobtainable, models of feminine beauty. In advertisements for feminine beauty products, women are presented with messages about the inadequacy of their bodies, their weight, and their appearance. As the adolescent identifies with these social ideals of attractiveness, young girls may come to believe that they are overweight even when they are in fact quite normal. Adding to the problem is the growth spurt during which young adolescent girls accumulate large quantities of fat in subcutaneous tissue. Early maturers seem to be at greater risk for eating problems. Some think that this may be because they are likely to be heavier

than their coeval, but late-maturing peers. These forces may create for the individual the desire to become thinner in an attempt to reach unobtainable ideals.

In this regard, white and African American young women view their bodies in dramatically different ways. While the majority of white junior high and high school girls voice dissatisfaction with their weight, the majority of African American girls are satisfied with their bodies. It seems that many African American teenagers equate a full figure with health and believe that women become more beautiful as they age. Significantly, anorexia is a relatively minor problem among African American young women.

A third explanation behind the development of anorexia maintains that the problem lies more with the anorexic family than with the anorexic individual. Families of anorexics are often rigid and overprotective. While family members may appear to be close, parents may have difficulty with their adolescent daughter's growing need for independence. Interactions between parents and anorexic daughters reveal problems related to adolescent autonomy that may trigger compulsive dieting. Parents in many of these families have high expectations for achievement and are overprotective and controlling. As a result, many anorexic females are perfectionists who have high standards for their own behavior and performance. Although the daughter attempts to meet the demands of the family, she approaches the challenges of adolescence with depression and lack of self-confidence. In this sense, starving herself is a way of gaining control over something in her life, at least the control that she has over her own body.

Some researchers have suggested that a subgroup of male athletes, sometimes called obligatory runners, resemble anorexic women. These are men who devote their lives to running and are obsessed with the distance they run, their diets, and their daily routines. Both anorexics and obligatory runners are concerned about their health, are hardworking, and are high achievers. Like anorexics, obligatory runners are highly concerned about their weight and feel compelled to maintain a lean body mass. It is also now recognized that female runners and other female athletes such as gymnasts and dancers are also susceptible to anorexic behavior. More specifically, these are women and girls participating in activities in which leanness is particularly emphasized.

Most authorities now recognize that anorexia has multiple causes and that it requires a combination of treatment strategies adjusted to the individual needs of the patient. Because anorexic girls often deny that a problem exists, treatment may be difficult. Family therapy aimed at changing the interaction patterns between parent and child is viewed by many sources as the most successful treatment. The aim of family therapy for these patients is to change the structure of the family by establishing clear intergenerational boundaries and by helping the adolescent develop a sense of personal identity, independence, and autonomy. In some cases, hospitalization may be necessary to prevent life-threatening malnutrition. During hospitalization, applied behavior analysis may be used. Here the anorexic is rewarded with additional privileges for gaining weight. Approximately two-thirds of anorexic victims recover or improve. Others may remain chronically ill, and as many as 10 percent die of the disorder.

Dennis Thompson

See also Bulimia

References and further reading

Anderson, Arnold, ed. 1990. *Males with Eating Disorders.* New York: Brunner Mazel.

Costin, Carolyn. 1997. *Your Dieting Daughter: Is She Dying for Attention?* New York: Brunner Mazel.

Field, Howard L., and Barbara Domangue, eds. 1987. *Eating Disorders throughout the Life Span.* New York: Praeger.

Immell, Myra, ed. 1999. *Eating Disorders.* San Diego, CA: Greenhaven Press.

Lemberg, Raymond, ed. 1999. *Eating Disorders: A Reference Sourcebook.* Phoenix, AZ: Oryx Press.

Nasser, Mervat. 1997. *Culture and Weight Consciousness.* London: Routledge.

Sours, John. 1980. *Starving to Death in a Sea of Objects: The Anorexia Nervosa Syndrome.* New York: Aronson.

Apgar Scoring System

The Apgar scoring system is a method of evaluating the health of newborns at birth. The system is named for the physician who introduced it in 1953, Virginia Apgar (1909–1974). Apgar was director of anesthesiology at the New York Presbyterian Hospital and professor at Columbia University's College of Physicians and Surgeons.

The Apgar score assigns a numerical index to the degree to which an infant appears physiologically depressed or not at birth and helps doctors determine whether newborns need medical attention. A first reading is taken within one minute of birth and a second at five minutes after birth. The infant is evaluated on each of the fifteen squares of the Apgar chart as seen below.

	Sign	0 Points	1 Point	2 Points
A	Appearance (skin color)	Blue-gray, pale all over	Normal, except for extremities	Normal over entire body
P	Pulse	Absent	Below 100 bpm	Above 100 bpm
G	Grimace (reflex irritability)	No response	Grimace	Sneezes, coughs, pulls away
A	Acitivity (muscle tone)	Absent	Arms and legs flexed	Active movement
R	Respiration	Absent	Slow, irregular	Good, crying

Virginia Apgar (Collections of the Library of Congress)

If the score is ten, the infant is considered in optimal condition. If the score is five or more, infants usually need no special resuscitative measures, although they probably require clearance of the respiratory passages, warmth, and perhaps a small amount of additional oxygen. A score of four or less may suggest a serious potential problem requiring immediate attention. In fact, resuscitative measures, if indicated, should under no conditions be delayed until the one-minute Apgar score is obtained. The Apgar score is also used to measure the effectiveness of resuscitation efforts.

Typically, delivery or nursery personnel score the babies. Zero, one, or two points are awarded for each category. The higher the score, the better. Although the name

of this pioneering medical researcher has been used as an acronym, as seen in the chart, these are not the true elements of the scoring system. However, that way of setting up the scoring system is the most likely form of the Apgar scale parents may encounter in the popular literature.

Most hospitals continue to use the Apgar system, yet there are a number of precautions taken that are part of standard practice. For example, because the timing of the scoring is critical in order to be useful, an automatic timing device is particularly valuable. Personal bias, especially toward the doctor delivering the baby, influences the scores. Midwives have been found to give higher scores than physicians. Obstetricians allow for higher scores than do anesthesiologists, nurses, and pediatricians. The one-minute Apgar score gives the best impression of the neonate's condition at birth and correlates with acid/base status (the relation of carbon dioxide in the blood to acid and base levels). The most practical use of the Apgar score has been for those not present at delivery to reconstruct a picture of what the baby was like. The change in the score from the one-minute score to the five-minute score could provide an index of the success of resuscitative measures.

If the Apgar score is less than five at fifteen to twenty minutes after delivery, there is an increased likelihood for the baby to have a permanent handicapping condition. Parents, now aware of this score, often request it and find the information comforting.

Ester Schaler Buchholz

References and further reading
Apgar, Virginia, and Joan Beck. 1972. *Is My Baby All Right?* New York: Trident Press.
Calmes, Selma. 1984. "Virginia Apgar: A Woman Physician's Career in a Developing Specialty." *Journal of the American Medical Women's Association* (November/December):184–188.

Asian American Parenting

Asian American parents socialize their children through parenting practices that reflect their cultural values. Asian Americans are authoritarian in their parenting style, with parenting goals and values emphasizing interdependence. An essential element of Asian American parenting is "training," which can facilitate positive outcomes such as high academic achievement. The role of migration and acculturation in changing Asian American parenting practices is important to consider in light of the many immigrant Asian Americans in the United States.

Parenting Concepts and Outcomes

Parenting Goals and Values. Scholars note the importance of considering parenting goals and values, as these can influence parenting style and practices, which in turn relate to child outcomes. Asian American parenting goals and values are expressed in a manner consistent with an interdependent and collectivistic orientation of Asian culture. Asian American parents value education as their parenting goal, a value that emphasizes interdependence whereby high academic achievement can bring honor to the family. This contrasts with European American parenting goals and values that are more likely to emphasize an independent and individualistic orientation. Research has shown that European American parents value a sense of self-esteem for their children as their parenting goal, stressing the personal well-being of the individual.

Parenting Styles and Practices. Parenting studies focus on the authoritative and authoritarian parenting styles. Authoritative parents are warm, democratic, and firm with their children. Authoritarian parents control their children through a set of standards, emphasize respect for

Asian American parents socialize their children through parenting practices that reflect their cultural values. (Laura Dwight)

authority and order, and discourage democratic exchanges between the parent and child. Asian Americans are described as authoritarian in their parenting style, emphasizing practices that are strict in discipline and restrictive in control. Strict discipline may involve physical punishment. One aspect of restrictive control is children's lack of autonomy in making their own decisions.

Parenting Outcomes. Parenting and academic achievement relate in different ways for Asian Americans and European Americans. For European Americans, using an authoritative parenting style results in higher academic performance, while using an authoritarian style results in lower academic performance. For Asian Americans, however, the authoritative parenting style does not relate to higher academic performance. It is surprising that Asian American students perform well academically, even though Asian American parenting is described as authoritarian in style. Despite this characterization, some studies find that Asian American parents are democratic and encourage independence and maturity in their children. This suggests that the authoritarian style may not capture the essence of Asian American parenting.

Reconceptualizing Asian American Parenting. A critical element of Asian American parenting is "training" or teaching, as described by Ruth Chao. This culturally derived concept is endorsed more often by Asian American parents than European American parents. The concept resembles the authoritarian style of parenting since children are expected to follow a standard of conduct. However, Chao contends that it is distinct from the authoritarian concept in its motivation and meaning. This training concept stresses the role of parents as teachers of appropriate behavior for children in general, while emphasizing academic success to reflect positively on the family. Training is accomplished through parental involvement, particularly through parents' devotion and sacrifice for the child.

Parenting Changes

Parenting and Migration/Acculturation. Asian Americans account for a large percentage of the immigrant population in the United States. While the amount of parental warmth is unlikely to change, the level of parental control and involvement are likely to change with migration. There is no consistent pattern of findings showing more parental control or less parental control after migration. A clearer distinction among the various dimensions of parental control (e.g., monitoring versus dominating control) is necessary to untangle the effect of migration on Asian American parenting.

To understand Asian American parenting, researchers have relied heavily on mothers. Parenting is traditionally a mothers' domain in Asian American families, with fathers taking more of a disciplinarian and a breadwinner role. With acculturation, there is evidence that Asian American fathers become more engaged and involved in parenting their children.

Parent-Child Relationship. In Asian immigrant families, family members acculturate to the mainstream U.S. culture at different rates. Children of immigrants, especially girls, acculturate much faster than their immigrant parents. This increases the cultural gap between the two generations, a noted source of parent-child conflict in Asian American families.

Children's school attendance can greatly facilitate their acculturation process. At school, they are expected to learn and speak English and adapt to American institutions. Compared to their children, adult immigrant parents have more difficulty acquiring English as a second language. Lack of fluency in English often leads many immigrant parents to occupations requiring minimal English skills, further hindering their acculturation to American culture.

The Growth and Diversity of Asian Americans
The U.S. Census Bureau reports that Asian Americans constituted about 4 percent of the U.S. population in the year 2000. By the year 2060, Asian Americans are projected to constitute approximately 10 percent of the U.S. population. (U.S. Census Bureau, 2000) Asian Americans are represented by over twenty-five ethnicities, languages, and cultures. Unfortunately, most

studies on Asian American parenting are conducted on Chinese, Japanese, or Vietnamese Americans. The continued focus on a few ethnic groups will limit our understanding of how a range of premigration context and history can impact Asian American parenting. For example, the Hmong are from a rural society with a history of oral language, while the Taiwanese, Japanese, and Koreans are likely to come from an urban society with a history of written languages. Studies also focus on first-generation immigrants, resulting in very little knowledge of parenting for later generations of Asian Americans. It is therefore critical to consider the diversity of Asian Americans. Not all Asian Americans internalize Asian cultural values in the same manner or to the same extent. This in turn can be a source of variability in Asian American parenting goals and values. To further the understanding of Asian American parenting, more research is needed on this growing and diverse population.

Su Yeong Kim

See also Baumrind, Diana Blumberg; Cultural Influences on Parenting; Latino Parenting; Native American Parenting; Parenting Styles

References and further reading
Chao, Ruth K. 1994. "Beyond Parental Control and Authoritarian Parenting Style: Understanding Chinese Parenting through the Cultural Notion of Training." *Child Development* 65, no. 4:1111–1119.
———. 1995. "Chinese and European American Cultural Models of the Self Reflected in Mothers' Childrearing Beliefs." *Ethos* 23, no. 3:328–354.
Dornbusch, Sanford M., Philip L. Ritter, P. Herbert Leiderman, Donald F. Roberts and Michael J. Fraleigh. 1987. "The Relation of Parenting Style to Adolescent School Performance." *Child Development* 58, no. 5:1244–1257.
Jain, Anju, and Jay Belsky. 1997. "Fathering and Acculturation: Immigrant Indian Families with Young Children." *Journal of Marriage and the Family* 59, no. 4:873–883.
Lin, Chin-Yau C., and Victoria R. Fu. 1990. "A Comparison of Child-Rearing Practices among Chinese, Immigrant Chinese, and Caucasian-American Parents." *Child Development* 61, no. 2:429–433.
U.S. Census Bureau. 2000. Projections of the Resident Population by Race, Hispanic Origin, and Nativity: Middle Series, 2050 to 2070. Population Projections Program, Population Division, U.S. Census Bureau, Washington, D.C., January 13. http://www.census.gov/population/projections/nation/summary/np-t5-g.txt.

Assisted Reproduction, Children of

Since the birth of the first "test-tube" baby in 1978, advances in assisted reproduction have led to the creation of family types that would not otherwise have existed.

In vitro fertilization (IVF) uses the father's sperm and the mother's egg, and the child is genetically related to both parents. This procedure involves the fertilization of the egg with sperm in the laboratory, followed by the transfer of the resulting embryo to the mother's uterus. When a donated egg is used, the child is genetically related to the father but not the mother, and when donated sperm are used, the child is genetically related to the mother but not the father. Donor insemination (DI) is a relatively simple procedure when used without IVF and has been widely practiced for many years. When both egg and sperm are donated, the child is genetically unrelated to both parents, a situation that is like adoption, except that the parents experience the pregnancy and the child's birth. In the case of surrogacy, the child may be genetically related to neither, one, or both parents, depending on the use of a donated egg and/or sperm. Thus, it is now possible for a child to have five parents: an egg donor, a sperm donor, a surrogate mother who hosts the pregnancy, and the two social parents whom the child knows as Mom and Dad.

Of the various concerns that have been expressed regarding the potential negative consequences of assisted reproduction for children's psychological well-being, the

Louise Joy Brown, the first test-tube baby, with her parents, England, 1979 (Express Newspapers/Archive Photos)

effects of keeping information about their genetic origins secret from children conceived by egg or sperm donation has been the subject of greatest debate. As few children are told that a donated sperm or egg had been used in their conception, the majority grow up not knowing that their father or their mother is genetically unrelated to them. It is increasingly being argued that parents should be open with their children on the grounds that they have a right to know and because it is believed that secrecy will result in psychological problems for the child. It has also been suggested that the stress of infertility that precedes the birth of a child conceived by assisted reproduction may lead to dysfunctional patterns of parenting that may result in negative outcomes for the child, and that the parents will be overprotective of their children, or have unrealistic expectations of them, due to the difficulties they experienced in their attempt to give birth.

Empirical research on the consequences for children who result from assisted reproduction is beginning to be reported. With respect to cognitive development, there is no evidence that assisted reproduction, in itself, results in impaired cognitive ability, although the increased risk of premature or multiple births from procedures involving IVF techniques is associated with adverse effects. Regarding the children's socioemotional development and the quality of parent-child relationships, studies of families created by IVF, donor insemination, and egg donation point to well-adjusted children and highly committed parents. Nevertheless, research on the consequences for children of growing up in these new family forms is in its infancy and many questions remain unanswered. It is not known, for example, how these children will fare as they reach adolescence, a time when issues of identity become important, or whether keeping the method of conception secret from children conceived by egg or sperm donation will lead to difficulties as they grow up.

Susan Golombok

See also In Vitro Fertilization (IVF); Infertility

References and further reading
Golombok, Susan, Rachel Cook, Allison Bish, and Claire Murray. 1995. "Families Created by the New Reproductive Technologies: Quality of Parenting and Social and Emotional Development of the Children." *Child Development* 66:285–298.
Saunders, K., J. Spensley, J. Munro, and G. Halasz. 1996. "Growth and Physical Outcome of Children Conceived by In Vitro Fertilization." *Pediatrics* 97:688–692.
Van Balen, Frank. 1998. "Development of IVF Children." *Developmental Review* 18:30–46.

Attachment

Attachment between a child and a caregiver is most frequently defined as an active, affectional, enduring, and reciprocal bond that is established through repeated interaction over time. Attachment is also conceptualized as a biologically based emotional tie to the primary caregiver with well-defined motivational properties directing the child to seek proximity to the caregiver during stressful times. From a secure relationship, a child develops confidence in the caregiver's physical and psychological availability, and this awareness forms the foundation for independent environmental exploration. In unscientific circles, attachment is analogous to love. When an attachment relationship is broken for an extended period of time, severe emotional and behavioral problems typically result.

Parent-child attachment relationships provide a fundamental foundation for early social and emotional development. Further, a large body of literature indicates that emotional events occurring early in life are very influential in terms of shaping later development. Secure attachment is associated with the development of a positive concept of self, in addition to confidence pertaining to the responsivity of others. Conversely, insecure attachment results in beliefs that one is undeserving of love and affection. Insecurely attached children, due to their chronic experiences with negative emotions, are especially vulnerable to difficulty regulating their emotions and behavior, which can result in emotional and behavioral problems as well as heightened sensitivity to stress. When compared to their insecurely attached peers, securely attached children tend to have the following qualities: higher sociability with unfamiliar adults, more cooperative behavior relative to their parents, more positive peer relations, longer attention spans, less frequent impulsive behavior, lower levels of aggressiveness, greater competence with problem solving, and happier, more content outlooks on life.

The work of John Bowlby (1969) and Mary D. S. Ainsworth, Mary C. Blehar, Everett Waters, and Sally Wall (1978) has resulted in the delineation of four phases in the development of attachment during early childhood. Phase one, referred to as preattachment, extends from birth to approximately eight to twelve weeks of age. During this phase the infant can direct his or her attention to others and is able to reach out to others. Young infants in this phase, however, cannot identify their mothers and are unable to exhibit differential emotional responses to them. During the early months of life, the infant and the primary caregiver establish means of communicating through vocalizations, facial expressions, and gestures. In phase two, described as attachment in the making, the intensity of the infant's social behavior increases substantially, and friendliness and delight are clearly directed toward particular individuals. During this phase, which lasts from the end of phase one until approximately seven months of age, the infant can distinguish the primary caregiver from all others and tends to engage in more active efforts directed toward promoting contact with this person. Phase three, which lasts from the end of phase two until the second or third year of life, is identified as the phase of clear-cut attachments. Three specific behavioral tendencies characterize phase three: separation distress or crying when the caregiver leaves; greeting reactions in which the infant shows immediate joy and pleasure when the caregiver appears, often by smiling, bouncing, and extending the arms; and secure-base behavior involving a pattern of environmental exploration centered around the caregiver. The

Parent-child attachments provide a foundation for early social and emotional development (Elizabeth Crews)

infant is capable of crawling and walking, which facilitates the infant's ability to seek proximity with the caregiver and explore independently. Confidence in exploring the environment is enhanced when the caregiver is present. Toddlers continuously check back to make sure the caregiver is available, with frightening encounters resulting in rapid movement back to the vicinity of the caregiver. After they are reassured, children typically venture back out again to explore.

The three primary functions of the attachment system are clearly evident during phase three and include the following: keeping children close to their caregivers who provide safety from environmental dangers; enabling children to explore the inanimate world within a safe context; and affording an opportunity for the attachment figure to provide stimulation through play. Toddlers in this phase often interact with attachment figures by showing them objects, pointing to things of interest, giving things to the caregiver, and manipulating an object with the aid of the caregiver.

Finally, phase four, which is termed the goal-corrected partnership, begins at the end of phase three and extends onward into childhood. It is characterized by the child beginning to understand the caregiver's goals, feelings, and point of view. At this point in the child's development a richly communicative relationship with the caregiver is possible.

Individual differences in the quality of attachment are studied experimentally with the "strange situation" test developed by the late Mary Ainsworth (1913–1999) from the University of Virginia. The toddler and the caregiver enter a playroom where the baby is free to explore. In a series of steps the baby is exposed to a strange adult, left alone briefly, and is reunited with the caregiver. The child's behavior is believed to indicate the quality of attachment. In all except the most extreme of cases, infants become attached to caregivers. Only when there is no opportunity for ongoing interaction with a specific person is a failure to attach likely to result. Nevertheless, there are individual differences in the quality of attachment, and four different attachment styles have been identified in the literature using the strange situation test. Most toddlers (66 percent) are securely attached. (Ainsworth, Blehar, Waters, and Wall, 1978; Main and Solomon, 1990) These children show a healthy balance between exploratory, play behavior, and the need for proximity with the caregiver. Mothers of securely attached infants and toddlers are sensitive and responsive to the child's needs and interactive signals (smiles, cries, and other social behaviors), which requires being attentive, affectionate, and warm. These mothers tend not to be anxious or depressed, have generally positive orientations to life, and express confidence in their parenting abilities. Insecure-avoidant children represent approximately 20 percent of the child population. (Ainsworth, Blehar, Waters, and Wall, 1978; Main and Solomon, 1970) These children rarely cry when the mother leaves, ignore the mother when she returns, or actively avoid her. Oftentimes these children will push the caregiver away and avoid eye contact with her. Mothers of insecure-avoidant children tend to be either indifferent and emotion-ally unavailable (often due to depression) or they actively reject the child when he or she seeks closeness or comfort.

An insecure-resistant or ambivalent style characterizes the attachment behavior of 12 percent of children. (Ainsworth, Blehar, Waters, and Wall, 1978; Main and Solomon, 1990) Insecure-resistant children become anxious even before the mother leaves and become extremely upset when she actually goes. When the caregiver returns, children with this attachment style show their ambivalence by seeking contact, while at the same time resisting it by kicking or squirming. They are hard to comfort and do little exploration in the mother's absence. This form of attachment is associated with inconsistent maternal care, exaggerated behaviors, overstimulation, and ineffective soothing.

Finally, disorganized-disoriented attachment is experienced by 2 percent or less of all children. (Main and Solomon, 1990) This category was identified by Mary Main from the University of California at Berkeley and is characterized by dazed, disoriented, and contradictory behavior. Movements are often incomplete or very slow, and these children may appear depressed. The disorganized-disoriented style is not associated with any consistent way of relating to the caregiver when stressed. Mothers of disorganized-disoriented children tend to be very mentally ill, severely abusive, or neglectful.

According to attachment theory, secure attachment will naturally result from a parent-child interactional history based on sensitive and appropriate responsivity by the primary caregiver. Sensitive care does not mean perfect care, and in most cases, care is adequately sensitive to foster secure attachment. More sensitive mothers accurately perceive their children's needs and respond to their signals appropriately, whereas insensitive mothers interact on their own schedules and according to their own needs. Sensitive mothers willingly accept the problems and limitations imposed by the responsibility of having an infant. Although they sometimes become irritated with their babies, they generally enjoy the good moods and accept the bad ones. Less sensitive mothers, on the other hand, are inclined to be rejecting and may feel so angry and resentful that these negative feelings outweigh their affection for their babies. Such feelings are often expressed through complaints about the baby's irritating behaviors, frequent opposition to the infant's wishes, or scolding. Highly sensitive mothers also tend to be cooperative mothers, allowing their babies autonomy, while less sensitive mothers impose their own wills, often abruptly, on their babies with little concern for their children's moods or preferred activities. Sensitive mothers are also accessible mothers, paying attention to their infants' signals even when distracted. In contrast, less sensitive mothers frequently ignore their children and are preoccupied with their own activities and thoughts. Insensitive caregivers usually do not notice their infants' signals and tend to them only during scheduled times or when the infants adamantly demand it.

Maternal behavior is not the whole story in attachment, and security of attachment is based on numerous parental, child, and situational factors interacting in a complex manner. For example, temperamentally difficult children who are very active, frequently irritable, and display more negative emotion are more likely to develop insecure attachments. The quality of parents' social and marital support systems is also likely to influence the nature of the attachment bond, as is the number of children in the family, with the presence of more children being associated with less positive attachments.

Priscilla K. Coleman

See also Ainsworth, Mary; Bowlby, John

References and further reading
Ainsworth, Mary D. S., Mary C. Blehar, Everett Waters, and Sally Wall. 1978. *Patterns of Attachment: A Psychological Study of the Strange Situation.* Hillsdale, NJ: Lawrence Erlbaum Associates.
Bowlby, John. 1969. *Attachment.* Vol. 1 of *Attachment and Loss.* New York: Basic Books.
Cassidy, Jude, and Phillip R. Shaver. 1999. *Handbook of Attachment: Theory, Research, and Clinical Applications.* New York: Guilford Press.
Isabella, Russell A., Jay Belsky, and Alexander von Eye. 1989. "Origins of Infant-Mother Attachment: An Examination of Interactional Synchrony during the Infant's First Year." *Developmental Psychology* 25:12–21.
Lewis, Michael, and Candice Feiring. 1989. "Infant, Mother, and Mother-Infant Interaction Behavior and Subsequent Attachment." *Child Development* 60:831–837.
Lyons-Ruth, Karen, David B. Connell, David Zoll, and Julie Stahl. 1987. "Infants at Social Risk: Relations among Infant Maltreatment, Maternal Behavior, and Infant Attachment Behavior." *Developmental Psychology* 23:223–232.
Main, Mary, and Judith Solomon. 1990. "Procedures for Identifying Infants as Disorganized/Disoriented during the Ainsworth Strange Situation." Pp. 121–160 in *Attachment in the Preschool Years: Theory, Research and Intervention.* Edited by Mark Greenberg, Dante Cicchetti, and Marc Cummings. Chicago: University of Chicago Press.
Matras, Leah, Richard A. Arend, and Alan L. Sroufe. 1978. "Continuity of Adaptation in the Second Year: The Relationship between Quality of Attachment and Later Competence." *Child Development* 49:547–556.
Rosen, Karen Schneider, and Fred Rothbaum. 1993. "Quality of Parental Caregiving and Security of Attachment." *Developmental Psychology* 29:358–367.
Smith, Peter B., and David R. Pederson. 1988. "Maternal Sensitivity and Patterns of Infant-Mother Attachment." *Child Development* 59:1097–1101.

van den Boom, Dymphna. 1994. "The Influence of Temperament and Mothering on Attachment and Exploration: An Experimental Manipulation of Sensitive Responsiveness among Lower-Class Mothers and Irritable Infants." *Child Development* 65:1457–1477.

Attention Deficit Hyperactivity Disorder (ADHD)

Attention deficit hyperactivity disorder is the current diagnostic label given to a large number of children and adults who show difficulties in the areas of impulsivity, hyperactivity, and/or inattention that are serious and persistent enough to prevent them from functioning well in a wide variety of settings. Formerly known as attention deficit disorder (ADD), and before that as hyperactivity, ADHD is currently the most common reason why children are referred by parents and teachers for testing and intervention. It is important for parents to understand the cluster of behavior problems known as ADHD for at least three reasons: to help prevent its emergence in children in the first place; to know when and if a child should be assessed for the diagnosis; and to cope effectively with the stress involved with having a child who has the diagnosis.

Overactivity, inattention, and impulsiveness are the three primary symptoms of ADHD. However, not all children with ADHD show all of these symptoms. As cataloged in *Diagnostic and Statistical Manual of Mental Disorders—Fourth Edition* (DSM-IV), there are three subtypes of the disorder, each with its own identifying characteristics. The first subtype, ADHD, predominantly inattentive type, is usually diagnosed when a child's problems are only with inattention (i.e., excessive daydreaming instead of paying attention to teachers at school and to parents at home). Children with this type of ADHD tend to have difficulties with learning in school. Girls who are diag-

Children diagnosed with one type of ADHD tend to have discipline problems in school and at home and have difficulty getting along with others (Laura Dwight)

nosed with ADHD are most likely to be of this subtype.

The second diagnostic subtype, ADHD, predominantly hyperactive/impulsive type, is given when a child's difficulties are primarily with controlling his or her behavior (i.e., very often unable to stay still, does things quickly without thinking first, can't wait). Children diagnosed with this type of ADHD tend to have discipline problems in school and at home and have difficulty getting along with others.

The third subtype, ADHD, combined type, is the most common of the three and it is diagnosed when a child has serious problems in multiple settings with all of the above—inattention, impulsivity, and motor activity. Children with this subtype of ADHD are at the most risk for extensive difficulties at school, with friends, and at home.

ADHD is a very complex disorder. Although overactivity, inattention, and impulsiveness are the three primary symptoms, this cluster of problems often leads to a whole host of other difficulties, such as poor interpersonal relationships, low self-esteem, negative/coercive interactions with teachers and parents, peer rejection, low academic achievement, oppositional/antisocial behavior, and alcohol/drug use and abuse. It is important for parents to understand that ADHD is a disorder that is defined and diagnosed behaviorally. That is, there is no medical or scientific test to determine whether or not a person definitely has the disorder.

ADHD is a label used to describe a particular and similar pattern of behavioral difficulties seen in many children across the country by many different mental health professionals. The primary instruments used to diagnose ADHD in children are behavioral checklists—questionnaires through which parents and teachers rate the child in question on, say, a one-to-five scale for how much or how often the child exhibits various problematic behaviors compared to other children of the same age (e.g., interrupts others, acts before thinking, can't sit still, doesn't follow directions, has difficulty following directions, can't or doesn't pay attention, no self-control). Sometimes, the child being assessed may receive psychoeducational testing to rule out other possibilities (brain damage, mental retardation, learning disabilities), or the child may be observed by a professional in either a structured (e.g., computerized attention task) or unstructured (free play) setting to confirm or disconfirm the observational impressions of the parents or teachers. Often, parents may be interviewed or surveyed about the child's family history.

Another important point about diagnosis is that ADHD is a developmental problem. Hyperactivity, inattention, and impulsivity are normal for young children such as toddlers and preschoolers, and can be normal even for older children in certain settings and for relatively short periods of time. For this reason, ADHD is typically not (and probably should not be) diagnosed until after the child reaches elementary school. Thus, the defining characteristics for a diagnosis of ADHD are that the child demonstrates developmentally inappropriate levels of activity, impulsivity, and inattention (e.g., significantly more problematic than other children of the same age) that are persistent (have been problems for longer than six months), consistent (symptoms appear in two or more settings, that is, problems are not just at school), present early on (the problems began before the age of seven), and so serious that she or he cannot function well in a variety of settings (e.g., is not learning in school, is having considerable interpersonal problems with peers and adults). It is only when there is evidence of all of the above that a child should be considered for a possible diagnosis of ADHD.

A final point about ADHD and its diagnosis is that the symptoms of inattention, impulsivity, and hyperactivity do not necessarily appear all the time. Such problems are much more likely to appear when the child is in a situation that requires self-control or is attentionally challenging. When tasks are interesting, fun, and exciting (e.g., video games), or there are no constraints or rules for one's behavior (e.g., outside recess time), it is easy to behave like the rest of the children. However, when a task requires active cognitive effort, internally driven sustained attention, and conforming to strict behavioral standards, children diagnosed with ADHD have a hard time. Thus, the fact that a child can sit in front of the television to play a video game for three hours at a time does not rule out ADHD as a diagnosis because in this situation the child's attention and behavior are being controlled from the exciting and external stimuli coming from the television. It is when the child must rely on his or her own tools for regulating attention and behavior that problems emerge. Researchers currently see this lack in the self-regulation of behavior and attention as the key deficit in children diagnosed with ADHD.

The causes of ADHD are multiple and likely represent a complex interaction between both biological/genetic and environmental/family factors. Lead poisoning, birth complications, and exposure to other toxic substances during prenatal development and childhood have been associated with ADHD. Using brain imaging technology, researchers have observed slight differences between ADHD and comparison individuals in the functioning of certain parts of the brain, but because brain functioning and growth are largely determined by a person's experiences, it is unclear if the neurological differences that have been observed were present originally or whether they emerged as a result of either the child's experiences, history of social interactions, or long-term treatment with psychoactive medication. As is the case with all human psychological and physical characteristics, ADHD is at least partly due to genetic factors. Identical twins (who share exactly the same genetic material) are more likely to (but are not destined to) share the disorder than fraternal twins or regular siblings, and parents who themselves were diagnosed with ADHD as a child or who have histories of other mental illness are more likely to have children with ADHD than parents without such histories. Parenting styles, attitudes, and child-rearing practices, however, also run in families. A variety of family/parenting variables have also been linked with ADHD and ADHD-like behavior in children, including lack of discipline, structure, and behavioral expectations in the home; ineffective

and/or inconsistent disciplinary practices; parental negativity, intrusiveness, and overcontrol; lack of parental responsiveness; and insecure parent-child attachment.

Treatment for ADHD typically consists of medication and/or behavioral-psychosocial intervention. About 90 percent of all children diagnosed with ADHD receive psychostimulant medication such as methylphenidate (brand name Ritalin), dexadrine (brand name Aderall), and others for at least some period of time. These medications appear to temporarily assist certain brain systems in transporting information more effectively, which translates into better short-term behavioral control by the child. For about 70 percent of children diagnosed with ADHD, these medications are effective in producing noticeable short-term changes in the child's behavior, such as increased attention span and reductions in disruptive/impulsive/motor behavior. These medications, however, often have mild to moderate side effects for the children, such as growth retardation, loss of appetite, insomnia, tics, stomachaches, and personality changes, which are sources of some concern for many children and parents. Also, the other 30 percent or so of children diagnosed with ADHD either do not respond or respond negatively to such medications.

Although short-term behavioral gains from medication are often impressive (the reason medication for children diagnosed with ADHD is extremely popular among parents and teachers), there do not appear to be clear long-term benefits of medication treatment alone. Studies typically do not show significant differences in adolescent outcomes between children who did and did not take medication for ADHD during childhood. Thus, as would be expected given the complex nature of ADHD and the secondary difficulties it creates, medication alone does not seem to be the answer. Common behavioral and psychosocial interventions for ADHD include: (1) parent training, in which parents are taught strategies for limit setting, effective disciplining, improving parent-child communication, reducing parent-child conflict, providing rewards and consequences for the child's behavior, providing additional structure in the home, and developing general coping skills for dealing with their difficult child; (2) behavior modification programs at home or at school, in which the child's behavior is gradually shaped with clear and consistent rewards and consequences for particular behaviors; and (3) individual cognitive-behavioral therapy for the child in which self-control and social skills training may occur. Psychosocial interventions such as these have been found to be just as effective as medication for improving the behavior of children diagnosed with ADHD. These interventions require increased effort, financial resources, time, and adult personal responsibility, however, and therefore are currently not as popular as medication alone.

There is some evidence that a combination of medication and the above psychosocial interventions is best for long-term positive outcomes for children diagnosed with ADHD. In terms of long-term outcomes, about 50 percent of children diagnosed with ADHD during childhood eventually go through adolescence and adulthood without experiencing noticeable behavioral disturbances or adaptation problems. Approximately 25 percent of individuals diagnosed with ADHD in childhood, however, experience minor to moderate levels of maladaptive behavior, such as impulsivity, extreme risk taking, restlessness, rapid job transitions, and difficulties maintaining stable relationships. These difficulties, however, typically do not require medical or psychological treatment. The other 25 percent or so of children diagnosed with ADHD appear to be on a negative developmental trajectory characterized by increasingly serious behavior problems, oppositionality (that is, a stance toward authority figures that is marked by noncompliance, arguing, and resisting direction), conduct disorder, substance abuse, school failure and dropout, and antisocial or criminal behavior, which puts them at significant risk for poor adaptive functioning in late adolescence and adulthood.

Predictors for positive long-term outcomes for children diagnosed with ADHD include a stable, supportive, high-quality home life; warm, positive (noncoercive) parent-child interactions; family social support and economic resources; and high child intelligence. Children who exhibit ADHD-type behavior present parents with significant stressors and daily challenges. It is important for parents of children diagnosed with ADHD to seek help and social support to assist them in coping with the behavioral challenges their child brings. Children who exhibit ADHD-type behavior tend to elicit negative, directive, controlling, and conflictual reactions from parents and teachers. It is important for adults dealing with such children to be patient and to try to avoid escalating negative and controlling behavior. Finding ways to provide consistency, clear behavioral expectations, effective discipline, and an appropriate degree of structure in the home are important. Parents of such children should also try to get their children engaged in tasks and activities that require attention, self-control, and mental effort on the part of the child, and to offer sensitive "scaffolding" or assistance during these activities—just enough assistance to keep the child working productively on the task and to allow the child to complete the tasks by him- or herself as much as possible. It is through repeated experiences such as these that children improve their skills at controlling and regulating their attention and behavior.

Beverly Wallace
Adam Winsler

References and further reading
Armstrong, Thomas. 1995. *The Myth of the A.D.D. Child: 50 Ways to Improve Your Child's Behavior and Attention Span without Drugs, Labels, or Coercion.* New York: Dutton.
Barkley, Russell A. 1997. *ADHD and the Nature of Self-Control.* New York: Guilford Press.
Campbell, Susan B. 1990. *Behavioral Problems in Preschool Children: Clinical and Developmental Issues.* New York: Guilford Press.
Healy, Jane M. 1990. *Endangered Minds: Why Children Don't Think and What We Can Do about It.* New York: Touchstone.
Hinshaw, Stephen P. 1994. *Attention Deficits and Hyperactivity in Children.* Thousand Oaks, CA: Sage Publications.
National Institutes of Health. 1998. *NIH Consensus Statement: Diagnosis and Treatment of Attention Deficit Hyperactivity Disorder* 16, no. 2:1–37. (Available at: http://odp.od.nih.gov/consensus/cons/110/110_intro.htm.)

Attractiveness, Physical

Physically attractive children are perceived and treated favorably by their peers and adults, and as a result these children often acquire desirable personality traits, skills, and behaviors. Beginning as early as infancy, children are able to discriminate among people who differ in attractiveness. By middle childhood, children acquire a physical attractiveness stereotype that can best be described as a belief that "what is beautiful is good." Children prefer physically attractive peers as friends, and both children and adults believe that physically attractive children have desirable personal and social characteristics. These beliefs can instigate a self-fulfilling prophecy process in which children and adults behave toward attractive children in ways that elicit and reinforce desirable outcomes, and attractive children then come to behave in ways that support the stereotype. The operation of these stereotyping and self-fulfilling prophecy processes also can have deleterious consequences for unattractive children. Fortunately, other information about children often eliminates the effects of physical attractiveness stereotyping, and awareness of the stereotype may help people avoid its manifestations.

In general, people agree about who is more or less attractive. Even young infants look longer at faces that adults have selected as attractive than at faces that adults have selected as unattractive. Children usually agree among themselves and with adults about which other children are more attractive, although preschool children sometimes have difficulty making consistent discriminations. Adults typically show high levels of agreement in their perceptions of the attractiveness of infants, children, and other adults. Studies that compare attractive and unattractive children normally use adults' or other children's ratings to determine attractiveness.

Several characteristics are consistently associated with higher attractiveness ratings. Infants with large eyes placed in the middle of their face are rated as cuter, whereas infants who were born prematurely or who experienced head molding during the birth process are considered less cute. Children's and adults' attractiveness is rated lower when they wear eyeglasses, are obese, have facial deformities, are unclean, have unkempt hair, or have dental problems. Individuals are judged more attractive when they are smiling than when they are showing negative facial expressions, although the effect of facial expression cannot completely negate the effects of more general attractiveness. More familiar individuals are typically rated as more attractive than unfamiliar individuals.

Both adults and children have positive perceptions of physically attractive individuals, in line with the "what is beautiful is good" stereotype. For example, numerous studies have demonstrated that teachers expect higher academic achievement and better social skills from attractive than from unattractive students. In these studies, teachers are typically asked to evaluate a child's potential based on a school folder that contains a variety of information. The folders given to the teachers are all the same, with the exception that some folders contain a photograph of an attractive child and others contain a photograph of an unattractive child. Although physical attractiveness stereotyping is found in most of these studies, in some cases the stereotyping is eliminated by providing detailed behavioral information about the student. In general, it appears that physical attractiveness stereotyping is strongest when other information upon which someone can base an impression is either vague or absent.

Adults' perceptions of infants presented in photographs also are influenced by physical attractiveness. Cuter babies are rated as smarter, more likable, more sociable, easier to care for, more active, and more competent. Adults report that they think the cuter babies cause their parents fewer problems and that they function better overall. The adults also report that they are more interested in interacting with the cuter infants.

Children also attend to physical attractiveness when forming impressions. Preschool children expect attractive children to be more sociable and nice than unattractive children, and older children rate attractive children presented in photographs as smarter, friendlier, and nicer. When asked to select which children they

would like as friends, children select photographs of more attractive children. Finally, children selected photographs of attractive adults from a set of photographs of adults described as potential teachers when asked who they thought would be nicest, happiest, better able to teach them, and less inclined to punish misbehaving students.

Do adults and children behave differently toward attractive and unattractive children? Some evidence suggests that they do. For example, mothers of more attractive newborn infants were found to be more attentive, affectionate, playful, and responsive toward their infants than were mothers of less attractive newborns. In another study, adult women playing with two unfamiliar infants were observed to look and smile more at the cuter infant. Caregivers in a program for toddlers paid more attention to the cuter toddlers at the beginning of the program. However, after the program had gone on for a while, more adult attention was directed toward the behaviorally difficult children, independent of cuteness. In children's peer interactions, attractive preschool girls were found to receive more pro-social and less antisocial behavior from their peers. Girls rated as attractive by their peers prior to the start of kindergarten, when the children didn't know each other, ended up being more popular. These studies, as well as some (but not all) others, suggest that girls' physical attractiveness may be more important in peer relations than boys' physical attractiveness.

If attractive children are treated more positively by adults and peers, do they eventually behave differently and perceive themselves differently? Some differences have been observed. For example, cuter infants smile more when interacting with an unfamiliar adult. Attractive preschool children engage in less aggression and are less active than unattractive children when playing with peers. More attractive children get better grades and perform better on achievement tests, have higher self-esteem, and show better overall adjustment. These findings suggest that a self-fulfilling prophecy process takes place, whereby biased perceptions of attractive and unattractive children cause people to treat children differently on the basis of appearance, eventually leading to differences in those children.

Despite this evidence that attractive children are perceived and treated more positively than unattractive children, and that attractive children are more likely to acquire desirable behaviors and personality characteristics than unattractive children, other studies and histories of individual children amply illustrate that beauty is not necessarily destiny. Physical attractiveness effects are strongest when children interact with unfamiliar persons, when children are in group settings where appearance comparisons are easily made, and when little other information about a child besides physical appearance is available. Physical attractiveness is less likely to influence behavior in interactions with familiar people, in one-on-one interactions, and when a child's behavior or personality is clearly evident. A child's perception of his or her own physical attractiveness also may be a more important determinant of behavior and personality than others' perceptions.

Parents can influence the effects of physical attractiveness stereotyping on their children. In particular, they can help their children learn that "beauty is only skin deep" and that "beauty is in the eye of the beholder." One study found that parents subtly conveyed information consistent with the physical attractiveness stereotype when telling a story to their preschool and elementary school-aged children. Parents need to confront, monitor, and minimize their own stereotyping on the basis of attractiveness. In addition, parents should actively discourage their children from judging others according to their appearance. On the other hand, because physical attractiveness stereotyping is unlikely to ever be completely eliminated, parents should encourage and assist their children in looking as good as possible through good grooming, particularly in group settings and during first encounters. Parents also can help their children acquire a positive self-perception of their own attractiveness, which may be particularly important for pre-adolescent and adolescent girls, most of whom have very negative perceptions of their own attractiveness. Through vigilance and active socialization, parents can help prevent some of the potential negative impact of physical attractiveness stereotyping on their own and other children's development.

Katherine Hildebrandt Karraker

References and further reading
Bull, Ray, and Nichola Rumsey. 1988. *The Social Psychology of Facial Appearance.* New York: Springer-Verlag.
Hatfield, Elaine, and Susan Sprecher. 1986. *Mirror, Mirror . . . the Importance of Looks in Everyday Life.* Albany: State University of New York Press.

Autism

Since the widespread release of the motion picture *Rain Man* in 1988, awareness and knowledge of autism has steadily grown. Autism is a developmental disorder primarily affecting the areas of communication, social interaction, and flexibility of behavior. Current theory dictates that autism is one condition that occurs along a spectrum of disorders, sometimes referred to as autistic-spectrum disorders or pervasive developmental disorders. The pervasive developmental disorders include Asperger's syndrome; high, moderate, and low functioning autism; childhood disintegrative disorder; Rett syndrome; and pervasive developmental

An autistic youth communicates with a staff member of his group home by pointing to a picture (Nancy Pierce)

disorder—not otherwise specified (a category for individuals who meet only a portion of the criteria for autism).

Estimates of the prevalence of autism range from 1 to 15 out of every 10,000 individuals, and this figure continues to escalate as time passes. From infancy to adulthood, persons with this unusual disorder present a variety of challenges to parents and caregivers. Indeed, parents may experience frustration when trying to communicate and form an emotional connection with their child. Parents may feel ignored as their child endlessly engages in repetitive behavior (e.g., flapping hands or repeatedly lining up cars) and exasperated by the strange ways these individuals express themselves. Once parents have come to accept their child's condition, they may feel disappointment, as if hopes and dreams for their children

have been dashed. Such thinking is neither necessary nor warranted, as children with autism display a wide range of functioning, with some responding positively to established treatment methods. This essay aims to provide an overview of autism, including a description of the disorder, a brief discussion of the few known causes, and an introduction to potential treatments.

Autism is a disorder defined behaviorally. That is, children are typically diagnosed through adult identification of behaviors on a diagnostic checklist. This checklist is based on criteria for autism published in the *Diagnostic and Statistical Manual of Mental Disorders—Fourth Edition* (DSM-IV). The criteria are organized into three categories of symptoms: impairment in social interactions; impairment in communication; and restricted, repetitive, and stereotyped patterns of behavior, interests, and activities.

Impairment in the social arena (e.g., social skills and social cognition), such as lack of reciprocity during a social interaction, is considered the hallmark of this disorder. Individuals with autism often prefer isolation to the presence of others, fail to seek comfort at times of distress, demonstrate an indifference to others, and show a deficit in their ability to understand social rules and conventions.

Communicative impairments can range from lack of speech, to limited use of gestures and eye contact, to problems with the melody and rate of speech. About 50 percent of autistic individuals do not develop meaningful communicative language and most others have difficulties with other forms of communication. Many of the more verbal individuals with the disorder also exhibit a speech pattern known as echolalia, meaning they often repeat all or portions of what has just been said to them. Nonverbal autistic children have difficulty understanding others or being understood, causing further retreat from social interactions.

The play patterns of children with autism are often restricted and repetitive (for example, continually lining up cars in a row and a general lack of pretend play). Autistic persons with higher-level abilities may focus on narrow and rather mundane bits of knowledge or topics, such as bus schedules, maps and routes, numbers, etc.

Other characteristics are commonly associated with this disorder. Three out of every four persons with autism are males, about seven out of ten have mental retardation, and approximately 20 percent develop seizures at some point in their lives. Additionally, females with autism are more likely to have a more severe form of the disorder. Autistic individuals sometimes exhibit unusual motor movements such as arm flapping, facial grimacing, and odd walking styles, as well as self-injurious behaviors like head banging and finger or hand biting. In addition, they sometimes demonstrate over- or under-arousal associated with sensory stimulation (for example, resistance to being touched or ignoring sensations such as pain). Additionally, individuals with autism often exhibit an odd mixture of strengths and weaknesses. A particular individual may demonstrate limited ability to express or understand speech, but be able to fluently navigate a driver's route without looking at a map. In even more extreme and rare cases, islands of ability are considered savant skills. Raymond, played by Dustin Hoffman in the movie *Rain Man*, would qualify as a savant as he mentally calculated multi-digit arithmetic problems but ultimately had great difficulty in applying this knowledge to the everyday use of money.

Perhaps the most intriguing aspect of this disorder is that individuals with autism are very different from one another. Individuals with autism run the gamut with respect to range of functioning. For example, educational placements may range from special schools, to special education classrooms in regular schools, to inclusion in regular classrooms, and adult outcomes may range from independent vocational and daily living to required lifelong residential care.

The cause of autism is still a mystery. Perhaps 10 percent or so of cases have a known cause. A very small portion of autistic individuals had infectious diseases (e.g., rubella), metabolic disorders (e.g., phenylketonuria), and/or structural abnormalities (e.g., hydrocephalus) that may have contributed to the disorder. Currently, researchers are focusing their efforts on elucidating the likely multiple causes of this unique disorder, concentrating efforts in the areas of interactions between genetics, brain development and function, environmental toxins, and other determinants.

As yet, there is no cure for autism. Two major treatment approaches for individuals with autism are medical and behavioral. Medical/biological interventions have included drug and vitamin therapies. Behavioral interventions have emphasized the positive reinforcement of appropriate behavior and the elimination of inappropriate behavior. The behavioral approach has been utilized frequently in school settings to help develop academic skills among individuals with autism.

Individuals with autism are idiosyncratic responders to drug therapies and biological treatments. Most do not benefit sufficiently from pharmacotherapy to outweigh the side effects (e.g., seizures, aggression, insomnia, constipation, sedation, agiation, and weight gain), but a small percentage (about 15 to 20 percent) do. This figure does not include the 30 to 40 percent who are helped by anticonvulsant medication. Amphetamines, lithium, antidepressants, and antianxiety medications have all been utilized with varying degrees of success depending upon the individual. Megavitamins and secretin, a neurotransmitter or chemical messenger, have also been administered to children with autism based on claims of small but notable symptomatic improvement. Quite recently, secretin has garnered a great deal of attention as a therapuetic option. Secretin is actually a hormone that assists in controlling digestion. Unfortunately, the one published study involving treatment applications of secretin in a population of individuals with a pervasive developmental disorder and utilizing a significant sample size has resulted in equivocal findings, at best. Future research should continue to address the utility and efficacy of this and other alternative therapies in striving to improve the lives of these remarkable people.

Behavioral interventions have been effective in improving the behavior of people with autism. Based on learning theory, these techniques continue to influence programs for people with autism and other developmental disabilities. Three major behavioral approaches have been applied to treatment: operant, cognitive, and social learning approaches. Operant techniques utilize the straightforward application of the principles of learning theory: clear and direct reward and punishment. Desirable behaviors are paired with positive events, while undesirable behaviors are paired with negative consequences. Although this approach has generally been effective and is still common practice, it has lost favor with many professionals, who instead opt for more positive techniques.

One of the most effective ways of assisting children with autism to maximize their abilities and to minimize their inappropriate behaviors is through structured teaching. This approach emphasizes how well a person with autism can understand the environment and expectations for behavior. Positive reinforcers and consequences are then used to clarify this understanding. Other ideas remain central to the structured teaching technique: organizing the physical environment, using schedules, assessing individual strengths and weaknesses, and establishing positive routines. Relaxation training is another approach that has been utilized for some individuals with autism. Because anxiety frequently occurs with autism, assisting these persons to stay calm and in control is an obvious priority.

Social learning approaches emphasize social skills training. Deficient social skills are targeted and practiced in a naturalistic setting, often in the context of a social skills training group. Specific techniques for teaching more appropriate behaviors include modeling, role playing, and rehearsal.

Behavioral interventions for autistic children have traditionally been used in special education settings. Those that develop specific individualized goals, and strategies to achieve them, have been particularly effective. Community-based instruction is especially popular in the training of daily living skills for adolescents and adults with autism. These techniques involve instruction outside of the classroom in community settings to prepare for effective adult functioning. For example, to learn how to get around his or her community, an autistic individual would be taught how to use the local public transportation system. Emphasis may be placed on learning how to read a bus schedule or utilizing appropriate behavior in a public venue.

Opportunities for the exposure of autistic children to their typical peers are increasingly pursued. Contact with typical children has been shown to benefit the development and acquisition of appropriate social and play skills in children with autism. However, the effectiveness of programs emphasizing exposure to typical children is limited by how well the classrooms and curricula are organized and planned. Generally, the benefit of autistic children's exposure to typical peers is undisputed, but how much and with which method of implementation are hotly debated. Some argue for special classes in regular public schools while others believe in mainstreaming (placement of children with autism in regular classrooms) for part or all of the school day—for example, during lunch, recess, physical education, and even academic subjects where appropriate. With the increased awareness of autism as a lifelong developmental disability, vocational training has more recently received attention. When given adequate support and training, many individuals with autism who are special education graduates obtain competitive jobs and lead fulfilling, productive lives.

Gregory L. Wallace
Adam Winsler

References and further reading
Autism Society of America, Inc. (ASA). http://www.autism-society.org.
Cure Autism Now (CAN). http://canfoundation.org.
Happe, Francesca, and Uta Frith. 1996. "The Neuropsychology of Autism." *Brain* 119:1377–1400.
Howlin, Patricia. 1998. *Autism: Preparing for Adulthood.* London: Routledge.
National Alliance of Autism Research (NAAR). http://www.naar.org.
Rapin, Isabelle. 1997. "Autism." *New England Journal of Medicine* 337:97–104.
Siegel, Bryna. 1996. *The World of the Autistic Child: Understanding and Treating Autistic Spectrum Disorders.* New York: Oxford University Press.
Sigman, Marian, and Lisa Capps. 1997. *Children with Autism: A Developmental Perspective.* Cambridge, MA: Harvard University Press.
Towbin, Kenneth E. 1997. "Autism and Asperger's Syndrome." *Current Opinion in Pediatrics* 9:361–366.

B

Baby Talk, by Adults

The specially modified speech that adults use when addressing very young children is called baby talk, no doubt because of its supposed resemblance to the way that babies talk. Baby talk is simpler and clearer than speech to adults, and it also has some characteristics that convey affection. Because of this affectionate quality, variations of baby talk are also used by some people when talking to their pets, to their lovers, and even to their houseplants. Simplified speech that is not particularly affectionate is used in some various situations, such as when talking to foreigners or to individuals whose ability to comprehend language is limited. Baby talk contains some special words, like "bunny," and in our culture may be produced in a distinctive high-pitched and melodic voice. Even those adults who assiduously avoid using special baby talk vocabulary speak differently to babies and young children than they do to their more mature acquaintances; developmental psychologists refer to this kind of language to young children as child-directed speech and they point out that it is always necessary to take into account the cognitive and linguistic level of the person one is addressing. Young children must hear language that is interesting and comprehensible to them if they are to develop linguistically and intellectually. Most adults are remarkably sensitive to children's developmental stages, and typically tailor their language in an appropriate fashion. They are able to do this at least in part because children, like adults, provide little signals of comprehension or non-comprehension that help the adults adjust their language so that they are neither talking down to the child nor talking over the child's head. When a child is developing atypically, however, it may not be so easy for adults to provide the best language input based on the child's reactions; some children, for instance, have motor impairments that limit their expressive ability, even though their comprehension is excellent. Assessment of atypically developing children by developmental specialists can help parents provide an optimally enriching environment.

Baby Talk Words

In our culture, there is a stereotypical view of what adults say when talking to babies, which probably does not represent what even a tiny fraction of the populace actually says; only in the media and in the comic pages do adults say "kitchy kitchy koo" while bending over a baby carriage. Adults do, however, use some special words in English and in just about every other language that has been studied by anthropologists and linguists. Baby talk words have been reported in diverse languages, including Arabic, Comanche, Romani, Gilyak, Berber, Marathi, and Latvian, as well as in Japanese and the standard European languages. About a

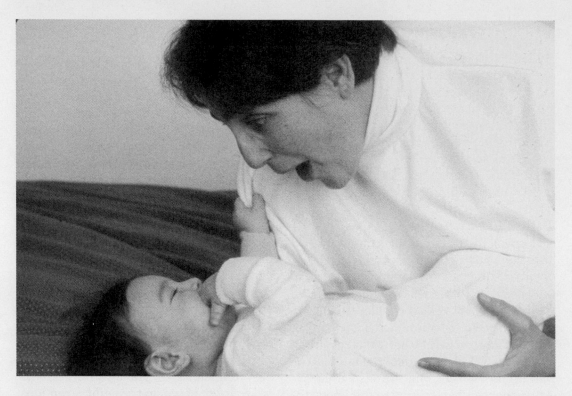

Most adults are remarkably sensitive and typically tailor their language to a child's developmental stage. (Laura Dwight)

half dozen categories of words are particularly likely to have baby talk equivalents. These include: body parts ("tummy"); games ("pat-a-cake"); kinship terms ("daddy"); routines ("night night"); qualities ("icky"); food ("din din"); body functions ("poo poo"); and animals ("bunny"). Linguists who have studied the structure of baby talk words have pointed out that there are some typical sound change rules that relate the baby talk word to its adult equivalent. For instance, reduction of the word to a shorter form is common, as is reduplication of the short form, hence, words such as "din din" and "bye bye." It is not clear, however, how some baby talk words were derived: no simple rule explains how rabbits turned into bunnies.

Although there is a traditional baby talk vocabulary, almost any word in English can be turned into a baby talk word by the addition of a diminutive ending, "-ie": foot becomes "footie," shirt becomes "shirtie," and so forth. These diminutive endings convey affectionate as well as size connotations. In general, they are used by parents to call the child's attention to things of which the parent approves and finds of interest. Parents point out "doggies" and "kitties" to children, but not "ratties" and "roachies," except perhaps in those cases when the rats are actually pets. In using diminutives in this selective way, parents are passing on their own worldview to their young children. Researchers have also found that parents use a wider range of diminutive words when speaking to girls, and they use them to girls at older ages than they do with boys. This appears to correlate with gentler and more affectionate treatment of girls in general.

The Structure of Child-Directed Speech

Whether parents use special baby talk words or not, they modify their speech to children in other typical ways that appear to suit the tastes or preferences of young children. Speech to very young babies is typically melodic, even singsong, and it is produced at a much higher pitch, or fundamental frequency, than speech to adults. A number of studies have shown that babies, when given the choice between listening to this typical kind of baby talk intonation or a more monotonous delivery, will choose the baby talk sound. The musical voice appears to get and hold the baby's attention. Other vocal features of baby talk or child-directed speech that serve similar purposes include extra stress on words that convey meaning, the use of a questionlike intonation on many sentences, and even whispering.

Child-directed speech also has many qualities that help the child who is learning language to segment the stream of speech into comprehensible words, and its slow pace gives the child extra time to process what she has heard. Adults speak very clearly to young children, tend to pause between sentences, and frequently repeat themselves. Speech to young children is delivered at half the rate of speech to adults. Child-directed speech also employs a very limited set of sentence types, and rarely contains long utterances or dependent clauses. This clarity and simplicity has convinced many developmental psychologists that child-directed speech is important, or even necessary, for children to acquire language. This is a matter of some controversy, however, since the extent to which the features just described can be said to be universal is not known. It is known, however, that all healthy children who grow up surrounded by language acquire that language. Most researchers now believe that this remarkable feat is accomplished only because children have both a strong biological potential for language and important social and interactional experiences that make language possible.

Reasons for Baby Talk

Why do parents use baby talk? In part, baby talk is a matter of tradition; we tend to talk to babies in the same way our parents spoke to us—for instance special baby talk words may remain in a family for generations. Baby talk is also a way of conveying affection to children. As children grow older and begin to learn the language, some of the features of baby talk help parents communicate more clearly with their children. Even though all adults may not use the specialized vocabulary of traditional baby talk, we all talk to babies and young children in ways that are different from the ways we talk to other adults, because we are attempting to communicate with them and we need to make some adjustments to their own level. For instance, we all talk more slowly to young children, and we talk about things that are of interest to them, rather than about the events in our world, such as politics or the theater.

Adults sometimes worry about the appropriateness of baby talk, and whether it might be harmful to a child. Baby talk words can be disadvantageous if they are used rather than regular vocabulary at ages when the child should know the adult word: for example, a child who begins kindergarten believing that he has "piggy toes" is in for a rude awakening. Most children, however, quickly learn the adult forms of baby talk words and are unlikely to have trouble of this sort. The use of special vocabulary is completely optional, however, and many parents choose to limit their use to just a few words when their children are babies. The many other features of child-directed speech, such as clarity and simplicity, change as children gain expertise in the language, and adults are usually unaware of the modifications that they are making. Parents tend to provide children with the kind of speech that is most helpful to them almost automatically. Typically, developing children help parents adjust their language to the right level by the way they indicate their understanding. When children are developing atypically, some professional help may be needed to enable parents to provide the kind of optimal linguistic input that will enhance their children's linguistic and cognitive development.

Jean Berko Gleason

See also Baby Talk, by Children

References and further reading

Ferguson, Charles A. 1977. "Baby Talk as a Simplified Register." Pp. 209–235 in *Talking to Children.* Edited by Catherine E. Snow and Charles A. Ferguson. Cambridge, UK: Cambridge University Press.

Fernald, Ann, and H. Morikawa. 1993. "Common Themes and Cultural Variation in Japanese and American Mothers' Speech to Infants." *Child Development* 64:637–656.

Sachs, Jacqueline. 1997. "Communication Development in Infancy." Pp. 40–68 in *The Development of Language.* 4th ed. Edited by Jean Berko Gleason. Boston: Allyn & Bacon.

Baby Talk, by Children

The speech of very young children is often referred to as baby talk. The term baby talk is also used to describe a special kind of speech directed to children. It is important for the adults around them to know that all children speak in a relatively simplified way as they acquire full use of adult language; this is a normal part of language development. Attempts to correct the speech of young children are typically not successful and not needed. Parents also need not be alarmed or surprised if a child who has been talking in a fairly mature way reverts to baby talk on some occasions, particularly stressful ones, such as when a baby brother or sister comes into the family. Even though there are some common characteristics in young children's language, they do not necessarily use the features that adults sometimes think of as baby talk, such as calling a rabbit a "wabbit" or saying "pisghetti" when referring to spaghetti. These are part of a cultural stereotype that is shared by members of our society, and that writers and the media use when attempting to represent the speech of young children.

The Speech of Babies and Young Children

By the time children are four or five years old, most of them are speaking very much like the adults around them, using complex language structures, such as relative clauses. They also have a sophisticated vocabulary, and can typically pronounce all of the sounds of the language, although some children may still not produce a few sounds in adultlike fashion.

On the way to acquiring these advanced skills, children progress through some typical stages that may be thought of as baby talk. Around the age of six months, babies begin to babble. Babbling is a kind of play with sounds that only human beings engage in. Early babbling tends to consist of reduplicated syllables, such as mamama or bababa. Although adults often think that this early babbling is meaningful, it may not be. Babbling becomes more complex over time, and by the time children reach their first birthdays, many of them are producing a kind of varied babbling (e.g., babidaboo) in long sequences and with intonation patterns that resemble sentences in adult speech. Many children have favorite sound combinations that they begin to use in meaningful ways even before they have real words. A baby may say "da" quite consistently, for instance, when she points at something she wants.

Very young children may use the same word to convey a variety of meanings. (Laura Dwight)

Around their first birthdays, children produce their first real words, often embedded in babbling. Children's pronunciations of their first words have very familiar baby talk qualities. For instance, they may produce only the accented part of a word, saying "nana" for banana. They simplify consonant clusters, saying "tee" for tree. They may also substitute sounds, using ones that are easier for them to pronounce, or in order to make all the consonants in a word similar. Thus, they may say "tat," "gog," and "guck" when they mean cat, dog, and duck. In English, babies also learn early on to use the diminutive forms that their parents use when talking to them; in fact, "blankie" and "binky" may be the only words they know for familiar objects like their blanket and pacifier. At the stage when children are producing only one word at a time, they may use their individual words to convey a variety of different meanings. For instance, the child who says "cookie!" may want a cookie, may be noticing a cookie, or may be indicating some other intent. Adults sometimes have difficulty interpreting the intentions behind these early utterances, and have to rely on the context for clues.

Young children continue to have special ways of pronouncing individual words as they begin to produce longer utterances or sentences, which have additional baby talk characteristics. Babies go from babbling in the first year to short sentences with simplified sounds and grammar in early childhood. For example, a two-year-old might say, "No want 'pinach," instead of "I don't want any spinach." These early sentences may not have articles or appropriate verb endings. This, too, is a normal part of language development, and children at this stage will not benefit from explicit attempts to correct their grammar. At the same time, adults help children acquire language by talking to them in a clear, simple, and grammatical way, because children learn the complexities of language by hearing it from older speakers. The parent who replies to the child who says, "Doggie eat," by saying, "Yes, the doggie is eating her dinner," is providing the child with valuable information about the world and about the English language. Between the ages of about two and five children gradually add in the grammatical features of adult language. During this period, children often say things in an imperfect way that adults find amusing or charming, but laughing at a young child's attempts to communicate, or repeating them to others, are not conducive to the child's linguistic or psychological development.

Regression to Baby Talk

Children's language sometimes appears to regress to an earlier baby talk stage: The child who previously said "I fell down and hurt myself," now says "I falled down and hurted myself." Although this may appear to be a step back, it is actually a sign that the child is learning the regular forms of the language—that, for instance, the past tense is usually formed by adding an "ed." Even children in the early grades may say "ringed" and "teached" as part of their normal development of language. Another kind of regression may occur for psychological rather than linguistic reasons: a child who is in a stressful situation may try to talk like a much younger child. This can happen if the child is hospitalized, for instance, or if a baby brother or sister comes into the family. In these cases, children may use baby talk words, long since abandoned, or use an infantile tone of voice, or try to talk the way they think babies talk: "Me wants din din." This is usually a sign that the child needs more attention, reassurance, or comforting.

Stereotypes

In our culture, adults, and even children, think that babies talk a particular way. There is a stereotypical baby talk, often seen in the media, in which babies say "ga ga goo goo" and children say "aminal" rather than "animal." The cartoon character Tweety Bird who says "I tought I taw a puddy tat" is using stereotypical baby talk. Real children acquiring language may sometimes use language like this, but they may not. Not all children use special baby talk words like "tummy" and "bunny," because not all families use such words when talking to their children. The baby talk that children produce as they acquire language varies from child to child. However, all children go through some similar stages as they acquire language, and the immature language that they produce can be considered baby talk, even if it does not match the stereotypical expectations of their parents.

Jean Berko Gleason
Elena Zaretsky

See also Baby Talk, by Adults; Language Acquisition

References and further reading
Golinkoff, Roberta Michnick, and Kathy Hirsh-Pasek. 1999. *How Babies Talk.* New York: Dutton.
Locke, John. 1995. *The Child's Path to Spoken Language.* Cambridge, MA: Harvard University Press.
Menn, Lise, and Jean Berko Gleason. 1986. "Babytalk as a Stereotype and Register: Adult Reports of Children's Speech Patterns." Pp. 111–124 in vol. 1 of *The Fergusonian Impact: In Honor of Charles A. Ferguson.* Edited by Joshua A. Fishman et al. Berlin: Mouton de Gruyter.

Baumrind, Diana Blumberg (1927–)

Diana Baumrind is best known in the parenting and socialization literature for identifying and describing four basic parenting styles: permissive, authoritarian, rejecting-neglecting, and authoritative. The differences among these styles are

Diana Baumrind (Courtesy of Hendrika Vande Kemp)

based on the degree to which each combines *demandingness* (confrontation, monitoring, consistent discipline, and corporal punishment) and *responsiveness* (warmth, friendly discourse, reciprocity, and attachment). The goal of parenting is to rear a child or adolescent who has an identity grounded in both *agency* and *communion*, "validating *simultaneously* the interests of personal emancipation and individuation, and the claims of other individuals and mutually shared social norms." (Baumrind, 1991, 747) Baumrind focuses much of her own research on the structured (authoritative) parenting style that couples directive elements of the authoritarian style with responsive elements of the democratic style.

Baumrind is also a well-known critic of Lawrence Kohlberg's moral development theory, and of the Ethical Principles and Code of Conduct of the American Psychological Association (APA), especially as these govern the treatment of research participants. Her philosophically grounded ethical analyses have earned her a reputation as a major ethical theorist.

Diana Blumberg was the first of two daughters born to Hyman and Mollie Blumberg, a lower-middle-class couple residing in one of New York's Jewish enclaves. Hyman and his brother, Isadore, were Eastern European immigrants who were both educated at the City College of New York. Diana enjoyed a strong intellectual friendship with her father, an atheist with a strong sense of Jewish cultural tradition, and she soon embraced the anti-Zionist and pro-Soviet philosophies of the Blumberg brothers. The young Hyman was a poet and journalist who struggled for the recognition of unions and equal rights for minorities. Isadore was an organizer first for the Transport Worker's Union and later for the Teacher's Union, but was expelled from the unions by the McCarthy inquisition of the 1950s. In 1990, he was the recipient of a special citation from Governor Mario Cuomo for outstanding service to New York State for his later extensive efforts on behalf of the mentally ill. Isadore schooled his niece in the principles of dialectical materialism. Through the modeling of political activism, he and his wife, Hannah Levine, imprinted Diana with their concern to empower the disenfranchised and underrepresented.

Diana, who was the eldest in an extended family of female cousins, inherited the role of eldest son, which allowed her to participate in serious conversations about philosophy, ethics, literature, and politics. In her teens, Diana supplemented her personal education in Marxist philosophy and economics by attending night classes at *The Catholic Worker* newspaper office and the House of Hospitality in New York's slums. The Catholic Workers modeled a life of community and voluntary poverty and embraced a doctrine of equality. Diana joined the Communist Party, and at the *Worker*'s School she met such celebrities as Pete Seeger and Paul Robeson, whose left-wing political activism also subjected them to McCarthy-era investigations.

In 1948, Diana earned an A.B. degree in philosophy and psychology at Hunter College. Many of Diana's teachers were closet Marxists who reinforced her social consciousness and strengthened her philosophical grounding in dialectical materialism. Diana was influenced by the philosopher John Somerville, who edited *Soviet Studies in Philosophy*; the experimental social psychologist, Bernard Frank Riess, who studied issues of social class and the relationship between workers and the intellectual elite; and the social psychologist Otto Klineberg, whose careful research on selective migration and racial stereotypes challenged American racism and eugenics programs. Klinebergian cross-cultural sensitivity permeates Baumrind's writings on ethical theory and moral development.

Newly married, Baumrind began graduate school in 1948 at the University of California's Berkeley campus, which was about to withstand the turmoil of the loyalty oath controversy of 1948–1949 that led to the legal battle of *Tolman v. Underhill*. Baumrind studied developmental, clinical, and social psychology, earning a master's degree in 1951 and a doctorate degree in 1955. Many Berkeley professors modeled personal convictions and professional interests that strengthened Baumrind's Marxist and humanitarian convictions. Baumrind was influenced by the research of Theodor Adorno, Else Frenkel-Brunswik, Daniel J. Levinson, and Nevit Sanford on anti-Semitism and the authoritarian personality; by the teaching of Egon Brunswik, who

impressed upon her the importance of idiographic research; and by the conformity research of David Krech (himself a persecuted Jewish Marxist) and Richard S. Crutchfield.

In 1955, Baumrind completed her doctoral dissertation on structured and unstructured discussion groups under Hubert Coffey, who also refused to sign Berkeley's loyalty oath. Coffey was both an influential teacher and a close personal friend, who served as Baumrind's mentor, protector, and role model of humanity. From 1955 to 1958, Baumrind completed a clinical residency at the Cowell Hospital/Kaiser Permanente, participating as a fellow in the group therapy research project directed by Coffey (and later by Timothy Leary) and funded by the National Institute of Mental Health (NIMH) for the purpose of studying therapeutic change. Here Baumrind extended her leadership research to families and therapy groups. By 1960, Baumrind affiliated with Berkeley's Institute of Human Development, where she still directs the Family Socialization and Developmental Competence Project.

Baumrind, who eventually divorced, chose the research focus over teaching or clinical work because it provided the flexible hours required for the mothering of her three daughters. She also believed that a deep relationship with clients would diminish her emotional involvement with her children. And she chose to live in Berkeley so that her daughters could have a close relationship with their father.

Baumrind's research from 1960 through 1966 was funded by an NIMH grant. Further grants of nearly $3.5 million have funded her research, resulting in the publication of more than three dozen articles and book chapters on family socialization and parenting styles, developmental competence, adolescent risk taking, and ethics. Baumrind is a recipient of the G. Stanley Hall Award (APA Division 7,

1988), and an NIMH Research Scientist Award (1984–1988).

Baumrind's work on research design, socialization, moral development, and professional ethics is "unified" by her belief that individual rights and responsibilities cannot be separated, her conviction that moral actions are determined "volitionally and consciously," and her assertion that "impartiality is not superior morally to *enlightened partiality*." (Baumrind, 1992) She applies these principles in her critiques of Stanley Milgram's research on obedience to authority (her most widely cited work) and APA's principles for research ethics.

Baumrind's early criticism of the NIMH group therapy research focuses on what she perceives as the unjustified leap "from test scores" to "traits, to constructs,"and she pleads for better construct and content validation. (Baumrind, 1959) She identifies the problems inherent in evaluating *change* scores in tests designed specifically to measure *stable* traits, and criticizes researchers who use the concept of causality in a manner differing greatly from that of the public and of social policy planners, who understand causality as a connection that is part of nature or reality itself.

Responsible relatedness undergirds all the more specific principles in Baumrind's writing. In her moral development theory and metaethics, she rejects approaches that value rationalization over personal involvement and those that favor individual human existence over the communal good. In her family socialization and adolescent risk-taking research, she rejects the stance of humanists who see socialization as detrimental to self-actualization; affirms a balance between the feminist values of nurturance, intimacy, and interconnectedness and the masculine values of agency and self-assertion; and refutes the child liberation movement by challenging parents to take an authorative

nurturing stance that includes the inculcation of societal values. In her critique of research ethics, she summons social psychologists to an ethical posture that recognizes the dignity and intentionality of persons and takes responsibility for any violation of what we affirm as inalienable human rights. In her criticism of research design and statistical procedures, she abhors self-deception in researchers who pretend to unwarranted certainty and deceive the public and their colleagues with misleading statements. Throughout, she is unwavering in her commitment to what she understands as humanism, and courageous in her challenge to those who prematurely commit themselves to theoretical or political positions, whether these be represented by McCarthy-era politics, noncritical forms of feminism, or excuses for mistreating research participants in order to promote the sanctity of the scientific method.

Hendrika Vande Kemp

See also Parenting Styles

References and further reading

American Psychological Association Ethics Committee. 1992. "Ethical Principles of Psychologists and Code of Conduct." *American Psychologist* 47:1597–1611.

Baumrind, Diana B. 1959. "Conceptual Issues Involved in Evaluation Improvement Due to Psychotherapy." *Psychiatry* 22: 341–348.

———. 1991. "Parenting Styles and Adolescent Development." Pp. 746–758 in *The Encyclopedia of Adolescence*. Edited by Richard M. Lerner, Anne C. Peterson, and Jeanne Brooks-Gunn. New York: Garland Publishing.

———. 1992. "Leading an Examined Life: The Moral Dimension of Daily Conduct." Pp. 256–280 in *The Role of Values in Psychology and Human Development*. Edited by William M. Kurtines, Margarita Axmitia, and Jacob L. Gewirtz. New York: John Wiley and Sons.

Cornell, Thomas C., Robert Ellsberg, and Jim Forest, eds. 1995. *A Penny a Copy: Readings from* The Catholic Worker. Maryknoll, NY: Orbis Books.

Milgram, Stanley. 1974. *Obedience to Authority: An Experimental View*. New York: Harper & Row.

Moss, Don, ed. 1999. *Humanistic and Transpersonal Psychology: Historical and Biographical Sourcebook*. New York: Greenwood.

Bed-Wetting

Bed-wetting occurs when a child is unable to hold his or her urine for the entire night and as a result urinates in the bed. The average age at which children attain nighttime bladder control is thirty-three months. However, for children between the ages of three and a half and five, nighttime bladder control is often sporadic at best. Frequently, the reason for this is not training per se, but rather an immature bladder. When a child's bladder matures to the point at which it can hold urine for eight hours, the child will stay dry at night.

Nighttime bed-wetting after the age of five is called nocturnal enuresis. Children with primary enuresis have never attained a substantial period of dryness, and those with secondary enuresis had achieved nighttime control of their bladder for at least one year, but then relapsed and resumed bed-wetting. Because mildly delayed nighttime bladder control is not uncommon or abnormal, many parents choose to wait until their child outgrows it, which happens by adolescence in 98 percent of the population. Parents with bed-wetting children may find some comfort in the following statistics: about 5 million school-age children persistently wet their beds. Twenty to 25 percent of all five-year-olds wet their beds, and boys wet their beds twice as often as girls. Ten percent of six- to ten-year-olds wet their beds. (Schaefer and DiGeronimo, 1997)

Although, as previously mentioned, enuresis often resolves itself over time, there are many valid reasons to treat the problem. Some of them include bed-wetting as a source of ongoing parent-child conflict, as a cause of constant embarrassment to the child, and as a source of low self-esteem. Additionally, children who wet their beds do not usually want to go to sleep-away camps or enjoy a night at a friend's house, and there is a 50-50 chance that a five-year-old who has nocturnal enuresis will still be wetting his or her bed at the age of twelve. The following section offers tips for parents who decide to wait out nocturnal enuresis and it describes the various treatments that are currently available for actively treating nocturnal enuresis.

Parents who have decided to wait out the problem may find the following tips helpful for both themselves and their children. First, remember to remain calm at all times. Parental anger and disapproval will only shame and embarrass a child about something over which he or she has little or no control.

Explore family history. Bed-wetting is frequently a family trait. Did either parent or someone else in the family ever have this problem? If so, tell the child about it; it will help the child realize that the problem is not his or her fault and that people do outgrow it.

Limit the child's intake of fluids in the late evening (not in the late afternoon because children need fluids in their bodies), especially of drinks that can irritate the bladder, such as orange juice, colas, coffee, or tea. Make sure that the child urinates just before going to sleep and again immediately upon waking. Wake the child and bring him or her to the bathroom before the parent goes to bed. This will assure an empty bladder and reduce the length of time the child must retain urine.

Keep the child's room at a comfortably warm temperature at night (65–70°). Children urinate more often when they are cold. Adapt the environment to make it easy for the child to get up and use the bathroom. Put night-lights in the child's room and in the bathroom, make sure the path to the bathroom is lit, and give the child pajamas that are easily managed during nighttime toileting.

Protect the child's mattress. One way to do so is to buy rubberized flannel sheets or plastic mattress covers, or put down a plastic sheet (e.g., a shower curtain or plastic tablecloth). Another idea is to place a thick towel across the center of the bed. If the child wets, the towel can be removed and the child placed on the dry sheet beneath. Another plan is to keep a sleeping bag on the floor next to the child's bed so that if he or she wets, he or she can jump in there for the rest of the night instead of disturbing a parent. Always keep dry pajamas nearby and leave a plastic bag in the room for easy deposit of wet clothing. Finally, express confidence that the child will one day stop wetting the bed.

Parents who have decided to actively treat their children's nocturnal enuresis should first make sure that the problem is not caused by physical or emotional difficulties. Medical conditions, such as urinary tract infections, sickle-cell anemia, diabetes, or chronic constipation (which enlarges the child's colon, causing it to press on the bladder) can cause bed-wetting. Also, food allergies can contribute to enuresis, and a deficiency of the antidiuretic hormone (ADH), which decreases urine output during sleep, can cause a child to wet at night. Before starting any treatment, parents should check with their children's pediatrician to rule out any physical cause for the child's enuresis.

Stress Management

Stress is a part of everyday life for both children and adults, so it will take a bit of work on the parent's part to determine if the child's enuresis is triggered by stress. This is especially important to investigate if the child used to sleep dry throughout the night, but then reverted back to wetting. Stress can come from exciting events like a relative visiting, traveling, the beginning of school, or the birth of a new sibling. It can also be the result of frightening events such as seeing scary movies, being the target of a class bully, experiencing parents' divorce, or a death in the family. Parents who suspect that stress may be the root of their children's problem should treat the stress first, rather than the symptom of bed-wetting. Parents should talk with all of the adults who are in contact with the child, such as his or her teacher or day-care provider. Most importantly, parents should talk to their children in a nonthreatening way about what is bothering them. If the parents can identify the problem and deal with it directly, in many cases the bed-wetting will cease. If a parent knows that the child is upset about something, but is unable to pinpoint the source of the stress, or if the parent has difficulty dealing with whatever is bothering the child, he or she should seek professional counseling. The counselor may be able to help the child manage the stress and stop bed-wetting.

Urine Alarm

Once a parent has determined that the child's enuresis is not caused by stress or by a physical or emotional problem, he or she should consider trying a new approach that employs an alarm to awaken the child. Before beginning this remedial training, a parent should discuss the program with all of the adult caretakers in the home; it is vital that everyone is in agreement about the treatment and offers support and encouragement to the child. The parent should remind the child that bed-wetting is not his or her fault, and that the parent knows that he or she is not being disobedient, lazy, or stubborn. Also, the parent should discuss the program with the child. Its success depends in large part on the child's inner motivation to stop wetting, on the child's belief that he or she can control the wetting, and on the child's ability to take personal responsibility for the wetting. The following approach has been shown to have a high success rate. It is a method based on behavioral conditioning that also utilizes an electronic urine alarm.

The process is really quite simple. A metal strip that is attached to an alarm is placed in the child's underwear. When the strip becomes wet, it triggers the ringing of an alarm, which is attached to the shoulder of the child's pajamas. This wakes the child, who then gets up immediately and turns off the alarm. The child then proceeds to the bathroom to finish urinating. Next, the child puts dry bedding on his or her mattress. Finally, the child marks the time of the wetting and the approximate size of the wet spot on a chart so that he or she will be able to see his or her daily progress. The procedure is direct and easy, and if it is consistently followed without deviation, most children learn to stay dry throughout the night. Initially, the program is considered successful when a child is able to stay completely dry for fourteen consecutive nights. At this point the parent should ask the child to drink a cup of water at bedtime and see if he or she can stay dry for another two weeks. The average length of training time is between eight to twelve weeks.

Parents should prepare their children in advance for the use of the urine alarm, explaining to them how the device works and assuring them that it cannot hurt them or give them an electric shock. Then parents should describe to the child his or her role in turning off the alarm, going to the bathroom, changing the wet bedding, resetting the alarm, and keeping an accurate record of wettings on the progress chart. Next, the parent should practice the procedure with the child at least six times daily for about two weeks. This is necessary because the management of the device is usually done in a state of sleepiness.

With this method, a child's progress usually advances in four stages. In the first stage, the frequency of urination remains the same or perhaps even increases. In the second stage, the frequency of wetting decreases; the alarm rings at a later hour as the child learns to hold back longer; and the average size of the wet spot on the bed becomes smaller as the child learns to wake and stop urinating immediately at the sound of the alarm. In the third stage, the child awakens before wetting the bed with increased frequency. He or she finally attains dry nights, but should continue to sleep with the urine alarm. In the fourth stage, the child sleeps without the alarm. He or she may still awaken after increasingly longer periods, but eventually sleeps through the night without waking or wetting. This stage can last a few weeks to several months.

Two major alternatives to the above method are available for the treatment of nighttime enuresis. One alternative is hypnosis. Although some studies have demonstrated that bed-wetting children can attain night dryness through this method, the overall effectiveness of hypnosis for bed-wetting remains inconclusive. The second alternative is drug therapy. Drugs can be an effective treatment for enuresis, but only in special circumstances and always with caution. Although drugs offer quick results, once they are discontinued, a large percentage of children return to bed-wetting. Desmopressin acetate (DDAVP) is now available in a nasal spray for the treatment of enuresis. DDAVP suppresses the flow of urine from the kidneys, thus decreasing the likelihood of bed-wetting. The most common side effects of DDAVP are an occasional headache, nosebleed, or nasal irritation. Children with cystic fibrosis, nasal polyps, epilepsy, or heart or kidney disease should never use DDAVP. This drug is very expensive, relapse rates after discontinued use are high, and it cannot be recommended for long-term therapy. In some cases, drug therapy can be used successfully on a short-term basis or to suppress bed-wetting while the child is at camp, or on a sleepover, or on a vacation. However, in the long run, drugs alone are not the solution to bed-wetting for most children.

Tara M. Hall
Charles E. Schaefer

References and further reading
Maizels, Max, Diane Rosenbaum, and Barbara Keating. 1999. *Getting to Dry: How to Help Your Child Overcome Bedwetting.* Cambridge, MA: Harvard Common Press.
Schaefer, Charles E. 1986. *Childhood Encopresis and Enuresis.* Northvale, NJ: Aronson.
Schaefer, Charles E., and Theresa Foy DiGeronimo. 1997. *Toilet Training without Tears.* New York: Penguin Putnam Inc.

Behavioral and Emotional Problems: Assessment and Evaluation

Most parents become concerned about their children's behavioral or emotional problems at some time in the children's lives. For example, children may have trouble sleeping, become unduly fearful, or have conflicts with peers or family members. Or they may seem unable to pay attention or feel sick with no identifiable medical causes. Some of these problems may be temporary reactions to particular events, to developmental transitions, or to conditions in the child's family, school, or other important arenas. However, other problems may be more persistent and may hinder children's development. What should parents do when concerns arise about possible behavioral or emotional problems?

Identify the Contexts in Which Problems Occur
When parents become concerned about possible behavioral or emotional problems, a first step is to carefully observe the contexts in which the problems occur. For example, perhaps the problems tend to occur only at certain times of day, such as mealtimes or bedtime. They may occur only in relation to particular people, such as the child's mother, father, a sibling, playmate, or others. Or, they may tend to occur in certain situations, such as when the child is being asked to do something or when the child is bored or tired.

In addition to observing whether problems occur primarily in certain contexts, parents can ask for feedback from teachers, relatives, and others who see the child when the parents are not present. Feedback from others can help parents judge whether their children's problems occur mainly in the parents' presence or whether they occur elsewhere as well.

If parents determine that a child's problems occur primarily in relation to a particular family member, teacher, playmate, or other person, they can consider some possible explanations. For example, there may be something about the person's behavior that negatively affects the child. Or, the person may communicate expectations that are hard for the child to meet. If there seems to be nothing in the person's behavior that explains the child's problems, perhaps the child's reactions stem from previous experiences with similar people. As an example, children who have conflicts with their kindergarten teachers may then find it hard to feel comfortable with their first-grade teachers. Today's complex family situations also present many children with changes in relationships and roles that can be stressful and confusing. One consequence is that attitudes stemming from experiences with biological parents and siblings may shape attitudes toward stepparents and stepsiblings.

Are the Problems Getting Better, Worse, or Remaining Stable?
Once parents have determined whether their child's problems occur only in

If a serious behavioral problem is suspected, parents should consider consulting professionals who are trained to help children and their families. (Skjold Photographs)

certain contexts or are pervasive, they can observe whether the problems are getting better, worse, or remaining stable. Many childhood problems are temporary. They may be brought on by factors such as stressful experiences, developmental changes, or a lack of support and understanding from important adults. When stressors abate, or the child advances developmentally, or adults become more supportive and understanding, children may adapt more effectively. However, if problems persist for more than a few months or grow worse, parents should consider obtaining evaluations from appropriate professionals.

Obtaining Professional Help
Schools are required to provide services for a broad range of problems that may interfere with learning. Thus, if problems occur mainly in school or interfere with learning, parents can request their child's school to provide an evaluation.

On the other hand, if the problems are not limited to school or if parents are uncomfortable about seeking help from the school, they should consider consulting professionals who are trained to help children and their families. Some pediatricians, for example, are skilled in evaluating children's behavioral and emotional problems, especially during infancy and the early school years. Under some managed health plans, pediatricians are the primary providers who must be consulted before the services of specialists such as psychologists and psychiatrists can be covered by the plans. In other cases, parents may go directly to psychologists, psychiatrists, and other professionals who work with children and their families.

Importance of Assessment from Multiple Perspectives

Most professionals initially interview the parents and/or the child. However, interviews yield only a limited picture of a child's functioning. Competent professionals therefore request assessment reports from people who are familiar with the child's functioning in everyday contexts. Because people often differ in their observations and judgments of a child's functioning, it is helpful to obtain assessment reports from multiple people. These people would typically include parents, other adults who live in the child's home, teachers, and the children themselves, if they are old enough to provide self-reports.

Standardized assessment forms are often used to describe children's functioning from multiple perspectives. An example of such a form is the Child Behavior Checklist (CBCL), which is widely used to obtain parents' reports of their children's competencies and problems. By completing the CBCL, parents provide information about their child's involvement in sports, activities, organizations, and friendships; how their child gets along with family members and with other children; and their child's functioning in school. Parents are also asked to respond to descriptions of possible problems by indicating for each problem whether it is "not true," "somewhat or sometimes true," or "very true or often true" of their child. Examples include: "Acts too young for age"; "Argues a lot"; "Can't concentrate, can't pay attention for long"; "Disobedient at home"; "Lying or cheating"; "Unhappy, sad, or depressed"; and "Worries." In addition, the CBCL asks parents what concerns them most about their child, and the best things about their child.

Similar assessment forms are available for completion by teachers to describe children's functioning in school and for completion by eleven- to eighteen-year-olds to describe their own functioning. The reference list at the end of this entry contains publications that describe how pediatricians, mental health workers, school-based practitioners, and other professionals use these assessment forms. The typical procedure is for the practitioner to have separate forms completed by relevant people, such as the child's mother, father, and teacher(s). The information from each form is scored on a profile that compares what the particular respondent (e.g., the child's mother) reports about the child with what similar respondents report about typical children of the same age and gender. The practitioner can then easily see the areas in which the respondent's report indicates similarities and differences between the child and typical children of the same age and gender. By examining profiles scored from reports by all the relevant respondents (e.g., both parents and the child's teacher[s]), the practitioner can identify areas in which all respondents agree and areas in which their reports differ. The practitioner can use this information as a basis for further evaluation of the child, for feedback to parents, and for deciding how to help the child and family.

After obtaining documentation from multiple perspectives, practitioners discuss with families their overall evaluation of the situation. Various options may then be considered, such as modifications of certain aspects of the child's environment, changes in the behavior of people who may be affecting the child, treatment of the child, or treatment that involves other family members.

To determine whether recommendations and treatment are effective, it is important that reassessments be done later. Because the initial assessment forms completed by parents and others document the child's functioning prior to interventions, these forms should subsequently be completed by the same people in order to evaluate outcomes. If the outcomes are not favorable, then new recommendations or further interventions may be needed.

Thomas M. Achenbach

References and further reading
Achenbach, Thomas M., and Stephanie H. McConaughy. 1997. *Empirically Based Assessment of Child and Adolescent Psychopathology: Practical Applications.* 2d ed. Thousand Oaks, CA: Sage Publications.
———. 1998. *School-Based Practitioners' Guide for the Child Behavior Checklist and Related Forms.* Burlington, VT: University of Vermont, Department of Psychiatry.
Achenbach, Thomas M., and Leslie A. Rescorla. 1999. *Mental Health Practitioners' Guide for the Achenbach System of Empirically Based Assessment (ASEBA).* Burlington, VT: University of Vermont, Department of Psychiatry.
Achenbach, Thomas M., and Thomas M. Ruffle. 1998. *Medical Practitioners' Guide for the Child Behavior Checklist and Related Forms.* Burlington, VT: University of Vermont, Department of Psychiatry.

Benedek, Therese F. (1892–1977)

In the course of her psychoanalytic career, spanning the years from 1921 to 1977, Therese Benedek worked as a clinical analyst, researcher, and teacher, first in Leipzig, Germany, and then, from 1936 until her death in 1977, as a staff member of the Chicago Institute for Psychoanalysis. She was a pioneer in numerous ways: as a psychoanalyst when it was an emerging profession; in her extensive study of women and families; and most importantly, in her theorizing about the developmental process in adulthood. Originally trained as a pediatrician, she began practicing as a psychoanalyst after emigrating from Hungary to Germany. The political situation in Germany forced her and her family to emigrate a second time and she continued to pursue clinical work, research, and teaching in the United States, becoming prominent for her ideas about female development, family life, and parenthood. In 1959, she published a seminal paper, titled "Parenthood as a Developmental Phase," in which she proposed that the developmental process continues into adulthood, propelled by the biological and psychological forces of parenthood. The ideas in this paper represent her lifelong interest in the correlation between psychology and biology, the application of psychoanalytic theory to understanding developmental aspects of experience, psychoanalytic research, and the transactional nature of parent-child relationships.

Born in Eger, Hungary, in 1892, Therese Friedmann Benedek was the third of four children of Ignatz Friedmann, a businessman, and Charlotte Link Friedmann, a homemaker. Their oldest child and only son died of the flu after serving in World War I. Therese's younger sister died in a concentration camp near the end of World War II. She was very close throughout her life to her older sister, Elisabeth Hoffman, who also emigrated to Chicago. The family moved to Budapest when Therese was six and she completed all her education there. An excellent student, Therese was the first in her family to pursue a scientific career. Though her family valued intellectual achievement, for women of that time and culture, attending medical school was reserved only for exceptional students. During her schooling, she attended lectures about psychoanalysis given by eminent figures in the new and growing field. This exposure led to her commitment to pursue a psychoanalytic career. Asked by fellow students about the reasons for this choice, Therese replied, "Because I want to know why I am living." (Benedek, 1973, 7) This direct and uncompromising stance was characteristic of her.

Therese Friedmann graduated from medical school in 1916 and then did an internship and residencies in pediatrics in Budapest hospitals. In 1919, she married Tibor Benedek, a medical school classmate and dermatologist. Shortly after her marriage, she began her own psychoanalysis with Sandor Ferenczi, a member of the Hungarian Psychoanalytic Society and colleague of Freud's. By today's standards this was a brief analysis that lasted about five months. Despite the brevity, she writes, "It was a meaningful experience, which carried with it the conviction of knowing something that was unknown and unknowable before." (Benedek, 1973, 479) In 1920, the Benedeks emigrated to Germany because of political instability in Hungary and settled in Leipzig, about 100 miles from Berlin. Benedek became an assistant physician in a psychiatric clinic and when she felt fluent in German, in 1921, she began to practice as a psychoanalyst.

Benedek entered the profession of psychoanalysis during a time of transition, which enabled her to quickly establish herself in the field with little formal training. At that time, an experience of personal psychoanalysis and some instruction in theory qualified both lay and medical people to become practitioners. As the first analyst in Leipzig, Benedek had others turn to her as a source for knowledge about psychoanalysis, and she headed a study group throughout her stay there. Benedek was introduced to the psychoanalytic community through Ferenczi and applied for membership in the Berlin Psychoanalytic Association, into which she was admitted in 1924. In her application letter, she explained her career change from pediatrics to psychiatry, stating that she quickly discovered she was solely interested in children's psychological functioning. This membership served as a sufficient credential to practice as a psychoanalyst. Later Benedek became a faculty member there, teaching and conducting training analyses. Her early involvement in teaching and training analysts was renewed much later in her career, when she researched and wrote about psychoanalytic education. Benedek's two children were born during these Leipzig years, Thomas in 1926 and Judith in 1929. Benedek maintained an active professional career as well as being wife and mother.

Because of the increasingly repressive and dangerous political situation in Germany, the Benedeks again decided to emigrate. Franz Alexander, director of the Institute for Psychoanalysis in Chicago, which he helped found in 1932, offered her a position as a staff member. Benedek and her family arrived in Chicago in 1936.

The intellectual camaraderie within the Chicago Institute contrasted greatly with Benedek's sense of isolation in Leipzig, and she found the atmosphere supportive of her own scholarly and clinical ambitions. She immediately plunged into a heavy schedule of teaching, supervising, and seeing patients. In these circumstances, she became fluent in English quickly, but always retained a heavy Hungarian accent. Under Alexander's leadership, a major function of the Institute was its research activity, particularly in the area of psychosomatic medicine. In collaboration with Boris Rubenstein, an endocrinologist, Benedek began a pioneering investigation into the sexual cycle of women. They monitored their subjects' hormonal levels through the menstrual cycle and correlated them with the dreams and verbal content of psychoanalytic sessions. In their findings, which were published in 1942, they linked estrogen activity with an active, outward-directed tendency that gave way, during the production of progesterone, to a passive, receptive, narcissistic attitude in which the woman turns away from the outer world. Benedek theorized that both positions contribute to a woman's capacity for childbearing and child rearing and provide the motivational force for her to do the psychological work necessary for these tasks. In her subsequent writing about development, Benedek would use the results from this study to anchor her ideas about developmental processes. This research confirmed Benedek's conviction about the interrelation between physiology and psychology and is a hallmark of all her work.

In her theoretical and clinical work, Benedek continually emphasized the transactional nature of relationships, the developmental process throughout life, and interpersonal experience. This was an unusual focus in psychoanalytic theory at that time, and gives some of her writing a contemporary quality. In 1935, she wrote a paper, "Adaptation to Reality in Infancy," that drew upon her experience in pediatric clinics, as a mother with her own children, and her psychoanalytic practice. She introduced the idea that the mother's ability to regularly and predictably satisfy the infant's physiological needs creates a sense of confidence in the infant that provides the basis for subsequent positive relationships.

Later, in "Parenthood as a Developmental Phase," Benedek elaborated on this and added a crucial dimension, that of the ways in which the mother, in the process of satisfying the infant's needs, acquires a sense of confidence in her motherliness. She carefully outlines the ongoing, reciprocal nature of the interaction in which the thriving infant reinforces the mother's ability to nurture, and the mother's confidence in this ability enables her to meet the ongoing developmental challenges that the infant presents to her. When this does not happen, Benedek calls the outcome the ambivalent core. If these ambivalent experiences predominate, the relationship acquires a negative cast in which mother and child have difficulty meeting developmental goals.

In this article Benedek introduced a significant revision of psychoanalytic theory, proposing that parenthood, for both fathers and mothers, is a source of continuing psychological development that provides opportunities for consolidation and resolution of developmental conflicts and a further integration of the personality. Whereas traditional theory viewed adolescence as the closure of development, she suggested that the demands for adaptation during adult life, from experiences such as parenthood, menopause, or senescence, require the same kind of psychological work that creates developmental change during childhood and adolescence. In the course of parenthood, as the child grows and changes and moves through developmental periods, conscious and unconscious memories, fantasies, and anxieties from their own childhood are evoked in the parent. Parents are confronted with a revival of their own past, represented by the child's current stage of development. By reviewing past experience from the double perspective of an identification with their own children and an investment in their roles as parents, parents have the potential to revise conflicted areas of development and to reinforce earlier positive adaptations. In this way, the experience of parenthood continues the developmental process into adulthood, enabling parents to grow and change as they nurture and provide for their own children.

Developmental experience and the psychology of women were fundamental concerns of Benedek's throughout her career, but her interests were varied and often reflected social issues, such as refugees or war-related stress on families. Her final writing project, never completed, was in part a response to feminist ideas of the 1970s and attempted to synthesize mythology and anthropology with psychoanalysis. She was active in psychoanalytic organizations on a national and international level and was an influential, though behind-the-scenes, figure within the Chicago Institute. She was much in demand as a speaker, commentator, and reviewer. As an analyst and teacher, Benedek had a reputation of being forthright, perceptive, independent minded, intuitive, and empathic. As she aged, a gradual hearing loss affected her ability to function in public, although one-on-one conversation was not as severely impaired. Despite this and other infirmities, Benedek continued her writing and clinical practice until she died, after a brief illness, at the age of eighty-four.

Erika S. Schmidt

References and further reading
Benedek, Therese. 1973. *Psychoanalytic Investigations, Selected Papers.* New York: Quadrangle/The New York Times Book Company.
Benedek, Therese, and E. James Anthony, eds. 1970. *Parenthood, Its Psychology and Psychopathology.* Boston: Little, Brown.
Benedek, Thomas. 1979. "A Psychoanalytic Career Begins: Therese F. Benedek, M.D., A Documentary Biography." *The Annual of Psychoanalysis* 7:3–15.

Bilingualism

Bilingualism is the ability to use two languages. It offers several benefits, particularly in the realm of cognitive skills. For instance, speakers of two languages show greater cognitive flexibility. Because they have a wider range of linguistic possibilities to choose from as they assess a situation, they can solve problems with greater creativity and versatility. Furthermore, bilingual students often have greater metalinguistic awareness, which means that they understand the rules of language more explicitly. They even may score higher on tests of intelligence, according to some research. For example, one survey of French- and English-speaking schoolchildren in Canada found that bilingual students scored significantly higher on both verbal and nonverbal tests of intelligence than those who spoke only one language.

Many linguists contend that universal processes underlie language acquisition, so that instruction in a native language also may enhance instruction in a second language. Consequently, students who enter school speaking no English may be successfully taught in their native languages, while at the same time learning English. There is no evidence that children will be overwhelmed cognitively by simultaneous instruction in their native languages and in English. In fact, many educators believe that second-language training should be a regular part of elementary schooling.

One form of second-language training is language immersion programs. In language immersion programs, the school teaches all of its subjects in a foreign language. Students enrolled in such immersion programs, which are designed to capitalize on younger children's ability to learn second languages with relative ease, find the experience quite different from traditional language instruction.

Young children in bilingual programs, such as the program mentioned above, make rapid advances in the foreign language in which they are being taught, for several reasons. One reason is that, unlike older children, they have not learned to be frightened by the task of learning a language. Furthermore, they feel relatively little embarrassment if they mispronounce words or make grammatical errors.

In addition, children enrolled in bilingual programs gain benefits beyond command of the language. Learning a second language can raise self-esteem due to the sense of mastery that comes from achieving proficiency in a difficult subject. Moreover, becoming bilingual can make students more sensitive to other cultures. Furthermore, although parents sometimes worry that their children's progress in their first language will be limited by their concentration in a second language,

Student in a bilingual Spanish-English preschool. Children in bilingual programs receive benefits beyond command of languages. (Elizabeth Crews)

such concerns seem unfounded. Research suggests that children who are exposed to two languages at once perform as well as their peers, and sometimes even better, in English grammar, reading comprehension, and tests of English vocabulary.

On the other hand, not all bilingual programs are successful. The most positive results have come from programs in which majority group children are learning languages that are not spoken by the dominant culture. In contrast, when minority group children who enter school knowing only a language other than English are immersed in English-only programs, the results are less positive. In fact, children from minority-language backgrounds enrolled in English-only programs sometimes perform worse in both English and their native languages than same-age peers.

The effectiveness of bilingual programs varies widely. Furthermore, such programs are difficult to operate administratively. Finding an adequate number of bilingual teachers can be difficult, and teacher and student attrition can be a problem. Still, the results of participation in bilingual programs can be impressive, particularly as knowledge of multiple languages becomes less of a luxury and more of a necessity in today's multicultural world.

Robert S. Feldman
Christopher R. Poirier

References and further reading
Hakuta, Kenji. 1999. "The Debate on Bilingual Education." *Journal of Developmental and Behavioral Pediatrics* 20 (February):36–37.
Ritchie, William C., and Tej K. Bhatia, eds. 1996. *Handbook of Second Language Acquisition.* San Diego: Academic Press.

Birth Order
The ordinal position in which a child is born into a family denotes his or her birth order. Many believe that birth order strongly affects one's general personality characteristics. Birth order effects, as they are called, are thought to play at least some role in the development of intellectual, behavioral, and personality characteristics. Interestingly, many commonly held beliefs about birth order effects are not supported by empirical research. Birth order is a very salient issue for many parents. Indeed, most parents have particular notions about how first-born children are systematically different from later-borns, and parenting behavior is indeed different depending on children's ordinal position in the family.

Many of the commonly held opinions about birth order stem from ideas about interactions between both parents and children and between siblings (or lack thereof, in the case of only children). For example, first-born children are thought by many to be high in attention seeking and more academically competent than later-borns. This is possibly because parents spend more time intellectually stimulating the first-born child or because, with the birth of the second child, parental love and attention is perceived to shift from the first-born to the new baby, and first-borns try to make up for this by achievements. Similarly, last-born children are often thought of as hard workers, possibly because they have spent their youth always looking up to the older children, but never able to match their performance. Other commonly held public opinions regarding birth order include: only children are spoiled, lonely, less accepted by peers, and more prone to psychopathology because of their lack of sibling relationships; second-borns are sometimes said to strive for perfection in response to their feelings of inadequacy in the shadow of the first-born; third-borns (in a family of four) are resilient, generally happy, independent, and robust by necessity in order to deal with very little attention from other family members;

Family size and age spacing of children may play a role in birth order effects; the dynamics of families change with the number of children in the family. (Laura Dwight)

and last-born children are often thought to be more sociable, likable, popular with peers, creative, spoiled, and even rebellious due to high interaction with siblings and lack of parental attention and authority. It is clear that there is no shortage of personal theories about the personality characteristics of children in different serial family positions.

Although many opinions about birth order effects are not supported by scientific research, several are. For example, firstborns, on average, have been found to be more academically competent when compared to other siblings, and later-born children have been found to be more popular

with their peers, on average, compared to earlier-born children. Interestingly, research has also shown that parental expectations tend to decrease with the addition of more children in the household, that parents do have preconceived notions about birth order effects, and that parents often treat children of different birth orders differently. Thus, when birth order differences are found among siblings, it is very unclear whether these differences are due to their serial position in the family per se, to differential experiences and expectations for the children, or to other associated factors, such as overall family size, the children's gender, and the amount of age spacing between the siblings.

Parents typically hold different behavioral expectations for children of different positions. Research suggests that parents learn and internalize stereotypes of how children should act based on their ordinal position and then treat children accordingly. Interestingly, these stereotypes are found not only in parents, but among nonparents as well. It is not uncommon to hear adults in general comment on a child's behavior by saying, for example, "You're the oldest, you should be more responsible than that."

Another way parenting can play a role in birth order effects is by changing child-rearing practices over time. Many parents-to-be are very enthusiastic and tend to have high expectations for their first-born child. Often, however, by the time a second or third child enters the family, parents feel more comfortable raising children and they hold different expectations for their children. Parents tend to become more relaxed in structure and discipline in the home, creating a different environment for later-born children to grow up in. Thus, birth order effects can be seen not simply as occurring because of different sibling interactions but also because of changes in parental expectations, structure, and disciplinary practices.

Family size and age spacing of children may also play a role in birth order effects. Siblings respond differently to each other when more children are in the home, just as parents respond differently to their children as more are born. It is not easy to generalize trends found in two- or three-children homes to homes with four or five children because the dynamics of the family change with the number of children in the family. Similarly, the number of years separating the siblings, or sibling age spacing, also plays a role in the effects found in birth order research. Siblings who are five or six years apart interact differently with each other than children who are spaced within two years of each other. Thus, when one considers birth order trends, other factors should be taken into consideration as well.

When considering ordinal position in a family, it is interesting to look first at children who do not have any siblings— only children. Only children, who are often thought to be spoiled and relatively rejected by peers, have instead been found to act in much the same way as first-borns. Research does not support common perceptions that because only children do not have siblings to interact with, they lack social skills. Although only children are not generally the most popular children in school, they do tend to have relatively high levels of achievement, maturity, and independence.

Much like only children, first-borns have been shown to have relatively high intellectual and academic ability compared to later-borns. It has been found that first-born children tend to conform more to adult standards of behavior and achievement than do later-born children. Another finding for first-borns is higher activity levels compared to later-borns. Research suggests that with increasing numbers of children in the family, parents structure the environment to facilitate lower activity levels for children due to increasing demands placed on them by the additional children.

Middle-born children have generally not been found in research studies to behave according to common stereotypes. Some research suggests that they have better within-family sibling relationships than earlier and later siblings. Also, middle children tend to feel closer to their siblings than to their parents. They appear to develop additional social/relationship skills, possibly due to their having to deal with both a dominating older sibling and either an ally or a dependent younger sibling.

Last-born children have been found to be more popular among peers compared to older siblings in the family. Research has shown that the youngest child, on average, is generally more outgoing, open, agreeable, and liked by peers. Two explanations have been offered for this finding. The first is that sibling interaction plays a very important role in developing social skills, and last-born children engage in the most sibling interaction. The second is that differential parental treatment toward children results in different personality features for the youngest child in the family.

One theory of birth order effects on intelligence considers family size. This theory, known as the resource depletion process, suggests that a family has a set amount of resources. As more children are born into the family, the existing resources have to be spread out among the children. This theory suggests that only children would be the most intellectually competent, followed by first-borns who have had the same resources at least for a few years, followed by the subsequent children who get less and less of the resource pool. Research, however, has pointed out obvious holes in the theory. First, only children do not score highest, on average, on intelligence tests compared to other children. Second, families with lower income (and thus less resources) show similar birth order effects as families with higher incomes (and thus less resource depletion relative to other families). Third, relations between intelligence and birth order appear to change depending on the age children are tested. In many studies comparing first- and second-born children, a particular pattern relating the biological age of the children in the study and intelligence test scores is found. Second-born children generally outperform first-borns at ages six and seven, but at ages eight and nine or so, the two are typically equal in intelligence

scores. It is only after age nine or so that first-borns tend to outscore the second-borns. The reason offered for this age-related pattern tends to revolve around a "teaching effect" caused by the older sibling tutoring the younger. The tutoring not only helps create a more intellectually stimulating environment for younger siblings, but it also helps the older sibling's intellectual development by reinforcing habits of learning material well enough to teach. The effect does not typically occur until the older child is between nine and thirteen because it is not until the younger sibling is old enough that they engage in this type of interaction with their older siblings.

Another theory, the confluence model, has been posited to account for birth order effects on IQ scores. This theory suggests that the intelligence of children is affected by the family circumstances and the environment in which the child grows up. Basically, it suggests that as the family dynamics change, the environment is more or less intellectually stimulating. For example, first-born children come into a world of adults that contains a very rich vocabulary and complex language, while the last-born child comes into an environment with more siblings speaking simply and using a limited vocabulary. Later-born children, thus, get less stimulating verbal input than earlier-born children. The theory accounts for the changing environment by creating a mathematical equation describing the intellectual resources available to each child. An example of this is seen by using age as an approximation for intellectual resources. So, when comparing a first-born to a second-born, the amount of resources will change drastically. At birth, the first-born has $(30+30+0)/3$ (where 30 represents each parent and 0 the newborn), or 20 units of intellectual resources; second-borns have $(30+30+4+0)/4$ (where 4 represents the first-born), or 16 units of intellectual resources at birth. However, when looking at the second-born child at age four, (30+30+8+4)/4, or 18, the second-born has more intellectual resources at age four (when there are only two children in the house) than the first-born did at age four.

Though there is empirical research to support this theory, it is not without its complications. One problem with the theory is that when ages are used for intellectual resources, research does not support it. Though research has shown that there is a difference in the environments of first- and last-born children, it is hard to say that the differences are directly due to changing levels of intellectual resources. As discussed earlier, parents change the environments and their expectations between children, which likely affects children's intellectual development in ways unrelated to the direct provision of intellectual resources.

Louis Manfra
Adam Winsler

References and further reading

Baskett, Linda M. (1985). "Sibling Status Effects: Adult Expectations." *Developmental Psychology* 21:441–445.

Eaton, Warren O., Judith G. Chipperfield, and Colleen E. Singbeil. 1989. "Birth Order and Activity Level in Children." *Developmental Psychology* 25:668–672.

Falbo, Toni, and Denise F. Polit. 1986. "Quantitative Review of the Only Child Literature: Research Evidence and Theory Development." *Psychological Bulletin* 100:176–186.

Miller, Norman, and Geoffrey Maruyama. 1976. "Ordinal Position and Peer Popularity." *Journal of Personality and Social Psychology* 33:123–131.

Sulloway, Frank J. 1996. *Born to Rebel: Birth Order, Family Dynamics, and Creative Lives.* New York: Pantheon Books.

Wallace, Meri. 1999. *Birth Order Blues: How Parents Can Help Their Children Meet the Challenges of Birth Order.* New York: Henry Holt.

Zajonc, Robert B., and Patricia R. Mullally. 1997. "Birth Order: Reconciling Conflicting Effects." *American Psychologist* 52:685–699.

Bonding

Bonding is the term used to describe the emotional process by which the parent and child grow in their feelings of closeness toward each other, especially during the first days and weeks after the birth of the newborn. Although the terms *bonding* and *attachment* are often used interchangeably, in the child development literature the word *bonding* has come to more accurately refer to the feelings by the parent toward the infant, with attachment reserved for the infant's increasing affection for the primary caregiver.

Much of the credit for popularizing the modern use of the term is given to a pair of pediatricians, Drs. Marshall Klaus and John Kennell. In the mid-1970s, these two physicians suggested that a "sensitive period" might exist in the first hours following childbirth, during which the mother was psychologically—and hormonally—primed to bond to her newborn. Drawing from research in comparative psychology that indicated maternal behavior to be predictable and routinized in mammals, but disrupted if the mother and her offspring were separated, they proposed that separating human mothers and their newborn infants was similarly maladaptive. Encouraged by work that showed mothers of low birth weight infants to benefit from the opportunity to handle their newborns a few days after delivery (a practice unheard of in the early 1970s), they tested their hypothesis by providing mothers of full-term infants with the opportunity for skin-to-skin contact immediately after birth. Providing this extra contact in the early postpartum period, they reasoned, would serve to promote mother-infant bonding. Their initial papers, in which they reported more sensitive mothering, and not incidentally, better outcomes on infant tests, were met with much enthusiasm in the scientific community.

However, when a number of attempts by other investigators to replicate their

Bonding *has come to refer to feelings of the parent toward the infant (Laura Dwight)*

results were unsuccessful, it became apparent that the original Klaus and Kennell studies were fraught with problems. For example, the early contact that they provided immediately after birth was confounded with the extended contact that was also arranged through allowing the mothers to room-in with their newborns. Other explanations for conflicting results were ventured, with most theorists, Klaus and Kennell among them, acknowledging that the simple provision of skin-to-skin contact to ensure bonding was likely a gross oversimplification.

Despite a lack of empirical support for their hypothesis, maternity practices were irreversibly changed by the attention now paid to the circumstances surrounding birthing procedures in this country. Mothers, nurses, and other medical staff recognized that improvements could be made to "humanize" hospital deliveries, and it is now standard practice to allow mothers immediate contact, rooming-in, and even encouraging fathers to assist with the process of childbirth. Despite their flaws, as a result of the studies on parent-infant bonding, the care of low birth weight infants has also improved with respect to facilitating parental contact in Neonatal Intensive Care Units.

With respect to bonding itself, research has continued to support the validity of this psychological phenomenon, but the process is now viewed as being more developmental than instantaneous. For some couples, the bonding process may begin prior to conception, when the idea of having a baby is thought about or discussed. Shortly after conception, the expectant mother especially becomes increasingly aware that a baby is growing within her, and through her imagination and attributions she gradually forms a relationship with the fetus. To the degree that a name for the infant is chosen or a nursery is prepared, the couple becomes more and more emotionally involved with the baby whose birth may still be months away. As the heartbeat is detected, kicking is felt, or the parents through an ultrasound observe the more human-like fetus, the couple has further opportunities to become attached. For some parents, the appearance of the newborn following birth may not correspond exactly to the romanticized image of a baby that they held in their mind. Nonetheless, the inevitable fussing and crying that the baby exhibits are social signals that demand attention, and success in calming the newborn serves to reinforce the caregiver to maintain proximity. For the nursing mother, the array of sensations experienced while breast-feeding does much to facilitate the bonding process; however, a nonnursing mother and father can derive similar satisfaction while bottle-feeding.

The newborn's responses to a sensitively ministered feed, such as quieting, reflexive grasping, and contented sighs, are likely outcomes regardless of feeding method. As the parents continue to meet with success in holding, feeding, diapering, and playing, their feelings of confidence contribute to their ability to emotionally invest more in their infant. Of greater importance, however, is the infant's increasing ability to establish eye contact, quiet to parental behaviors other than feeding, and exhibit a true social smile. By four months postpartum, when parent-infant interactions are stable and reciprocal, bonding is firmly established. At this time the mother is likely to view the infant as a person, without whom life would be intolerable and unimaginable. Once achieved, the parental bond resembles altruistic love, where the adult provides nurture, comfort, and affection to the infant. Bonding thus serves as the initial stage of what is to become the parents' lifelong commitment to their offspring.

John Worobey

See also Attachment

References and further reading
Brazelton, T. Berry. 1981. *On Becoming a Family.* New York: Dell Publishing Co.
Eyer, Diane E. 1992. *Mother-Infant Bonding: A Scientific Fiction.* New Haven: Yale University Press.
Klaus, Marshall H., and John H. Kennell. 1982. *Parent-Infant Bonding.* St. Louis: C. V. Mosby.

Bowlby, John (1907–1990)

John Bowlby founded attachment theory and is one of the most influential developmentalists and psychiatrists of the twentieth century. His ethological approach to personality development turned the attention of researchers, clinicians, and other practitioners to the essential role of early child-parent interactions. Drawing upon many scientific areas of inquiry and employing a life-span approach to socio-emotional development, Bowlby's trilogy on *Attachment and Loss* (*Attachment,* 1969; *Separation,* 1973; and *Loss,* 1980) remains to this day the most influential work in the field.

One can argue that Bowlby's theory of personality development has had greater impact on contemporary American developmental psychology than any except that of Freud. In contrast to Freud's work, Bowlby's research established a tradition of scientifically testable theories of socioemotional development and has received extensive empirical support.

Edward John Mostyn Bowlby was born in 1907, the fourth of six children of May Mostyn Bowlby and noted London surgeon Major-General Sir Anthony Bowlby. Growing up in a regimented household in which lofty expectations were held for the children, John Bowlby displayed a strong intellect and competitive streak, but also an impressive sense of compassion. Setting out to follow in his father's footsteps, Bowlby majored in natural sciences and psychology at Cambridge University and then enrolled in medical school at University College, London. Bowlby decided that his ambition was to become a child psychiatrist, so he also entered the Institute of Psycho-Analysis. Upon completion of his medical studies, he completed psychiatric training with adults at the Maudsley Hospital in London and with children at the London Child Guidance Clinic.

It was at the Child Guidance Clinic that Bowlby worked with James Robertson and other social workers who shared his evolving ideas about the importance of early family experiences on children's personality. Bowlby's early scholarly publications reflect this interest. In a 1944 paper, for example, Bowlby reported on a study of "Forty-Four Juvenile Thieves: Their Characters and Home Life." He found early disruptions in the child-mother relationship to be a common precursor of later delinquency, psychopathology, and especially an "affectionless" personality.

In 1945, after returning from service in the army during World War II, Bowlby headed the Children's Department at London's Tavistock Clinic, the institution that would be the primary setting for his work for the duration of his prolific career. Notably, he renamed it the Department for Children and Parents to emphasize the importance of the child-parent relationship. Much of the clinical work in the department was, however, driven by the psychoanalytic approaches of the time, especially the orientation of Melanie Klein and her adherents. Their clear disregard for Bowlby's focus on actual family interaction patterns prompted him to establish his own research unit to continue his own work on child-parent separation.

Bowlby first gained worldwide recognition when the World Health Organization (WHO) released his 1951 report on *Maternal Care and Mental Health.* Based upon extensive data he gathered from a vast array of sources, Bowlby reported on the effects of maternal separation, deprivation, and frequent changes of "mother figures" in children's first several years of life. The accumulating research suggested that young children, when separated from their mothers for a considerable period of time, proceed through a series of reactions: protest, despair, and detachment. Starting in 1948, Bowlby and Robertson had also conducted observations of institutionalized or hospitalized children. Their research with—and several important 1950s films of—children enduring long-term separations from their parents illustrated these devastating reactions. Collectively, the work was instrumental in leading to worldwide changes in hospital and residential care facility policies for young children.

Bowlby departed from his contemporaries to conclude that it was the loss of the specific mother figure that was the most important factor in these reaction phases. He realized that current psychoanalytic theory was not compatible with this conclusion, and recognized that a new theory was needed to explain such effects. Bowlby believed that if he could understand the normal course of the development of the child-parent relationship, he would be better able to understand the effects of its disruption. He went on to develop his ethological and eventually ethological-control systems theory of the infant's tie, or attachment, to its mother or primary caregiver. For Bowlby, the formation of an attachment—defined as an enduring affective bond characterized by a tendency to seek and maintain proximity to a specific person, especially under conditions of threat—was vital to the child's protection and development.

As Bowlby was formulating his attachment theory, he was influenced by a number of outstanding scholars from varied fields. His theory represents an integration and elaboration of general systems theory, cognitive science, evolutionary theory, ethology and the study of primate behavior, and descriptive studies of young children interacting with their caregivers. Robert Hinde, among others, encouraged Bowlby's adoption of the constructs and methods of ethology, in which scientists learn about behavioral organization and function through naturalistic observation and experimentation. Specific animal studies by Konrad Lorenz, who observed imprinting in geese, and Harry Harlow, whose experiments with rhesus monkeys countered the "drive" theories of the era, were particularly important to Bowlby.

From 1950 to 1954, Mary Ainsworth worked with Bowlby at Tavistock, beginning the lifelong partnership between the two of them in which Bowlby contributed the overall theory and Ainsworth the midlevel theory and data that supported and refined the overall theory. Her observational studies in Uganda in the early 1950s and in Baltimore in the 1960s provided clear, empirical support for many tenets of attachment theory.

Bowlby's first formal statements of his theory came in a series of papers published from 1957 to 1963. The theoretical constructs of these papers would later be expanded upon in his trilogy on Attachment and Loss (1969, 1973, 1980). In these influential volumes, Bowlby differentiated attachment from other aspects of relationships; emphasized the role of attachment in promoting security and self-reliance; argued for attachment's biological universality; presented a mechanism by which cognitions (internal working models) about early relationships are carried into subsequent close relationships; and proposed developmental pathways from attachment insecurity to psychopathology.

When it was first presented, Bowlby's work was met with initial skepticism from developmentalists from other schools of thought, such as behaviorists and social learning theorists. Reactions from psychoanalysts were much more negative. Many found Bowlby's emphasis on ethological methods and real parent-child interactions to be foreign to their adult-focused, introspective techniques, and they rejected his work out of hand. Nonetheless, Bowlby's theory has slowly gained acceptance, along with accumulating empirical support and an understanding of its clinical utility. His focus on child-parent dyads as a subset of family and extended family relationships led him to write one of the first formal papers on family therapy. This attempt to understand patterns of interaction across multiple generations is consistent with literature on complex animal societies in which knowledge is passed down over generations.

John Bowlby's greatest legacy may be his contribution to the shift that took place during the 1960s through 1980s from theory-based and qualitative analysis-based study of socioemotional relationship development to a truly empirical, scientific approach. Prior to Bowlby's work, the "richest" approach to the study of socioemotional development was psychoanalytic theory. Unfortunately, that theory seemed not to be empirically testable. During the 1940s through 1960s, proponents of social learning theory made gallant efforts to translate many psychoanalytic developmental constructs into empirically testable hypotheses. While many of these efforts did not stand the test of time, Bowlby's attachment theory has remained influential. It also opened the door for many other related theories of social development. At this time, the study of socioemotional development is as rigorous and scientific as the study of cognitive development. Another legacy, only just now being realized, is that his theory is leading directly to empirically testable, programmatic interventions for problematic child-caregiver relationships.

Preston A. Britner
Robert S. Marvin

See also Ainsworth, Mary

References and further reading
Bowlby, John. 1944. "Forty-Four Juvenile Thieves: Their Characters and Home Life." International Journal of Psycho-Analysis 25:19–52, 107–127.
———. 1951. Maternal Care and Mental Health. Geneva: World Health Organization.
———. 1969. Attachment. Vol. 1 of Attachment and Loss. New York: Basic Books.
———. 1973. Separation: Anxiety and Anger. Vol. 2 of Attachment and Loss. New York: Basic Books.
———. 1980. Loss: Sadness and Depression. Vol. 3 of Attachment and Loss. New York: Basic Books.
Holmes, Jeremy. 1993. John Bowlby and Attachment Theory. New York: Routledge.
Karen, Robert. 1994. Becoming Attached: First Relationships and How They Shape Our Capacity to Love. New York: Warner Books.

Brain, Development of

The development of the child's brain is a complex process influenced by multiple factors. From the time the brain starts to form around the third week of prenatal development until the infant is born, billions of neurons, or brain cells, are produced. These neurons are programmed to move to specific locations in the developing prenatal brain and later perform specialized functions associated with their particular location in the brain. While prenatal brain development appears to be mainly determined by biological programs, brain development after birth seems to be greatly influenced by environmental experiences. Postnatal brain development consists of the establishment of interconnections among the billions of neurons. The stimulation that the infant and child receives from the environment determines which connections are formed and which potential connections are lost. Thus, the environment provided by the parents is crucial to the child's current brain development and later behavioral functioning.

About two weeks after conception, the rudimentary beginnings of the brain and spinal cord are formed with the development of the neural tube. The ends of this hollow, open-ended structure begin to close between the third and fourth weeks of pregnancy. Failure of the neural tube to close leads to a class of birth defects called neural tube defects. If the neural tube fails to close at the brain end, a condition known as anencephaly occurs. In this brain defect the cortex of the brain fails to develop, which will either result in a pregnancy not carried to term or an infant who can survive only a matter of days or weeks after birth. Failure of the neural tube to close on the spinal cord end results in a condition known as spina bifida. An infant born with this condition has spinal cord nerves that develop outside the protection of the vertebrae, or backbone. Depending on the severity of the condition, the infant may be born paralyzed or without sensation in the lower extremities. In extreme cases, the development of the brain may also be affected, leading to deficits in cognitive and emotional functioning.

While the timing of the closing of the neural tube appears to be determined by human biological codes, the event is nevertheless greatly influenced by maternal diet. Scientists have discovered that adequate amounts of folic acid, one of the B vitamins, are essential for proper closing of the neural tube. Folic acid occurs naturally in dark green leafy vegetables, orange and grapefruit juice, and fortified cereals. Because the closing of the neural tube occurs so early in prenatal development, it is essential for women to have adequate amounts of folic acid in their diets prior to conception.

After the neural tube closes, brain development proceeds with the mass production of neurons. This proliferation of neurons may occur at a rate of thousands per minute and is more pronounced during the first half of pregnancy. After production, the neurons undergo a process of migration in which they appear to be programmed to move to the various regions within the developing brain. Neurons function with respect to the location to which they migrate, however—not with respect to some prespecified function code. For example, scientists have discovered that if neurons that usually migrate to one brain area in a newborn rat are transplanted into a different brain area of the same newborn rat, the neurons will function as do neurons that normally migrate to that area. While the information for this neuron migration appears to be basic biological code, substances ingested by the mother, such as alcohol, can interfere with neuron movement.

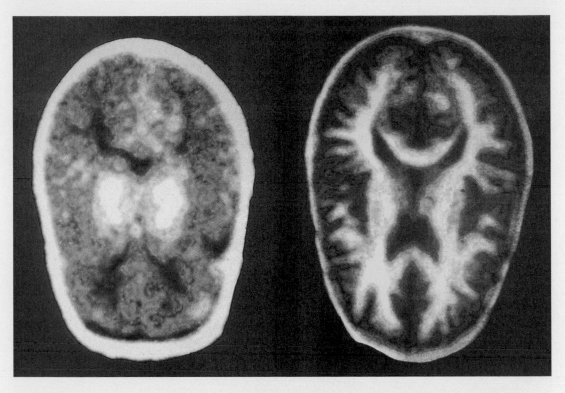

The human brain at six weeks (left) and at nine years (right) (Petit-Format/Science Source)

Thus, health professionals advise women to abstain from alcohol consumption during pregnancy.

Neuron production and migration are mainly prenatal events, with most neurons formed by the seventh month of pregnancy. The process of neuronal differentiation tends to occur after birth. During this process the neurons form connections with other neurons and begin to function. Of course, this process begins on some level prior to birth. Scientists know that fetuses startle to loud noises and respond with movement to some stimuli, such as light and sound. Immediately after birth, newborns recognize the sound of their mother's voice, having heard her voice during the last months of prenatal development. Each of these responses requires a functioning brain, so the neurons do begin the foundation for interconnections during prenatal development.

After birth, brain development is known as a time of "blooming and pruning." During this process, neurons grow in size and in the means to make potential connections with other neurons. Blooming occurs when the infant's brain produces many more connections between neurons than can ever be used. It is as if the brain readies itself for any possible pattern of interconnections and functioning. Pruning occurs to the neuronal connections that are rarely or never used and is essential to the development of an efficiently functioning brain. Most child development experts agree that the infant's environment plays a major role in the formation and strengthening of

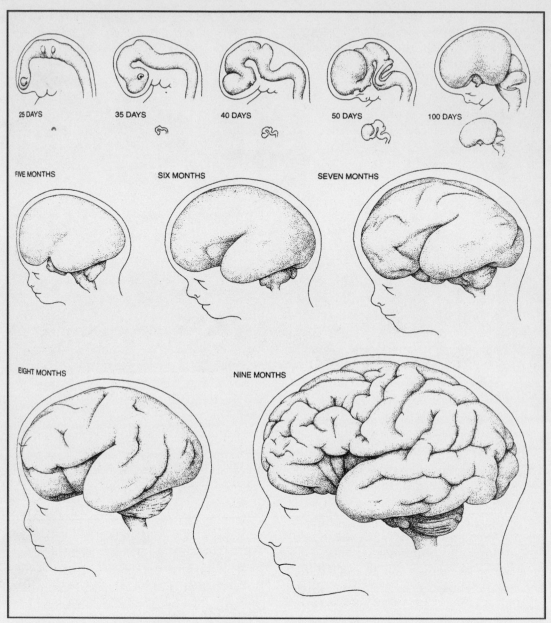

Illustrations of the human brain during prenatal development. Drawings are on a common scale, with the first five enlarged on a common scale for detail. During prenatal development most of the neurons in the brain are formed, although the connections among neurons are only beginning to occur. (From W. Maxwell Cowan, "The Development of the Brain," in The Brain: A Scientific American Book. *New York: W. H. Freeman, 1979, p. 59)*

connections among neurons after birth. Thus, sights, sounds, touches, smells, and tastes experienced immediately after birth and throughout infancy and childhood contribute to the interconnections among neurons. The result is a brain that rapidly increases in size and weight and processing efficiency.

Advances in the study of brain development in laboratory animals have given great insights into the postnatal brain development in human infants and young children. Much of what is known, or speculated, concerning human brain development has its roots in basic scientific research on kittens and rats. For example, from classic research with kittens, scientists know that there is a sensitive period when the part of the brain involved with vision develops its neuronal interconnections. Thus, when kittens are deprived of specific visual input during the time period when the kitten brain "expects" to receive this input, the kittens show deficits in processing visual information. The blooming occurs with the expectation that interconnections will be formed. When that doesn't occur within the specified time period, pruning takes place. These research effects are reversible if the visual deprivation is not prolonged. In cases of long-term deprivation, however, brain differences are reported to persist in adult animals.

Classic research with rats also has given scientists great insight into the effects of environmental stimulation on brain development. Rats raised in impoverished laboratory environments (housed individually in laboratory cages) are behaviorally and physiologically different from rats raised in enriched laboratory environments (housed in complex environments with litter mates and periodic toy changes). Behaviorally, the impoverished rats are more aggressive, take longer to adapt to testing situations, and perform more poorly on learning and memory tasks than the enriched rats. After testing, the rats are sacrificed and the brains examined. Rats raised in enriched environments display greater numbers of connections between neurons than rats raised in impoverished environments. As with the research with kittens, there appears to be a sensitive period for these effects. It

was only for preweaned rat pups that scientists observed differences in brain development with exposure to enriched and impoverished environments. After weaning, exposure to the enriched environment has little effect on brain structure.

Child development experts have used this classic animal research to speculate concerning the effects of the environment on human infants and children. Most agree that the environment provided by the parents is crucial for development and that intervention is important for children not exposed to optimal environments. This is the crux of the federally funded Head Start program for children between the ages of three and five. This program, however, has been greatly criticized since its inception in the mid-1960s. The purpose of the program is to provide enrichment experiences for low-income children prior to school entrance, with the goal of decreasing the gap in academic performance between children from lower-income and middle- to higher-income families. Based on research with children in Head Start, these effects appear to be erratic and temporary, however.

It may be that research on sensitive periods for brain development can explain these inconsistent research results for the Head Start program. In the classic research with kittens and rat pups, scientists discovered that the timing of the stimulation determined whether or not there was an effect on brain development. Obviously, these types of studies cannot be accomplished on human infants and children. There are some infants and children from extremely low-income families, however, who experience these types of impoverished environments on a daily basis from birth. Recent research with these impoverished children has led to exciting implications for early intervention with low-income families.

The Carolina Abecedarian Project was begun by Craig T. Ramey and Sharon L. Ramey in the 1970s at the Frank Porter Graham Child Development Center, at the University of North Carolina at Chapel Hill. This scientific study was designed to examine the benefits of very early intervention for children from low-income families. The children came from high-risk families who were characterized by poor, single, teenage mothers who had low IQ scores and little education themselves. The children from these impoverished environments received full-time, high-quality educational intervention (in the form of games) in a group child-care environment from early infancy until the children entered kindergarten. Progress in school was monitored periodically until the children were twenty-one years old.

Children in this early intervention program had higher reading and math scores from elementary school to age twenty-one relative to children from comparable home environments who were not involved in the intervention. The children completed more years of education and were more likely to attend a four-year college. Of course, it cannot be known if there were specific effects on the neuronal connections of these children. The implication, however, is that the early intervention of the Abecedarian Project influenced brain development at a sensitive period for neuronal connections. Thus, "early intervention" appears to mean infancy and not preschool.

The implications from these scientific studies are great with respect to early development and later functioning. The stimulation the infant and young child receives from the home environment is crucial for brain development. Many well-educated parents listen to media reports concerning these types of scientific studies and play Mozart for their infants in an attempt to enhance future math scores. They also enthusiastically purchase books and videos advertised to create brain connections needed for future learning. Although these efforts are admirable, they appear to be unnecessary. The scientific data with kittens, rat pups, and the Abecedarian Project with human infants and children have demonstrated that it is the organism in the impoverished environment, compared to the organism in the enriched environment, that is at risk for deficits in brain development. There is no scientific evidence to suggest any value to increasing the amount of enrichment to children already in an enriched environment. On the contrary, the timing of environmental stimulation appears crucial. Parents who arrange safe, nurturing, and stimulating environments for their children from birth are providing the very enrichment that is essential for optimal brain development.

Martha Ann Bell

See also Head Start, Early

References and further reading
Bukatko, Danuta, and Marvin W. Daehler. 1998. *Child Development: A Thematic Approach.* 3d ed. Boston: Houghton Mifflin.
The Carolina Abecedarian Project. 1999. http://www.fpg.unc.edu/~abc/.
Johnson, Mark H. 1997. *Developmental Cognitive Neuroscience.* Cambridge, MA: Blackwell.
Ramey, Craig T., and Sharon L. Ramey. 1999. *Right from Birth: Building Your Child's Foundation for Life.* New York: Goddard Press.

Brazelton Scale
See Neonatal Behavioral Assessment Scale

Breast-Feeding
The evidence is clear: breast-feeding is more beneficial for infants during the first four to six months of life than bottle-feeding. Some forty years ago, if a mother asked her pediatrician whether breast-

The level of stress hormones is lower in mothers who breast-feed their infants than those who bottle-feed them. (Elizabeth Crews)

feeding or bottle-feeding was better, she would have received a simple and clear-cut answer: bottle-feeding was the preferred method. Today, however, child-care authorities agree that for the first four to six months of life, there is no better food for an infant than breast milk.

Breast milk is more easily digested than cow's milk or formula, and it is sterile, warm, and convenient for mothers to dispense. Breast milk not only contains all the nutrients necessary for growth, but it also seems to offer some degree of immunity to a variety of childhood diseases, such as respiratory infections and diarrhea. Furthermore, some research suggests that breast-feeding enhances the brain development of children.

In addition, an epidermal growth factor present in breast milk may advance the development of the digestive and respiratory systems in infants. There is also evidence that preterm infants ultimately may do better cognitively as a result of being fed breast milk during infancy.

Breast-feeding is beneficial for mothers as well as infants. For instance, women who breast-feed seem to have lower rates of ovarian cancer and breast cancer prior to menopause. Furthermore, the hormones produced during breast-feeding help shrink the uteruses of women following birth, enabling their bodies to return more quickly to a prepregnancy state. These hormones also may inhibit ovulation, potentially preventing pregnancy and helping to space the birth of additional children. Breast-feeding even helps mothers react to stress better: research shows that the level of stress hormones is lower in mothers who breast-feed their infants than those who bottle-feed them.

Breast-feeding also holds significant emotional advantages for both mother and child. Most mothers report that the experience of breast-feeding brings about feelings of intimacy and closeness that are incomparable to any other experiences with their infants. At the same time, infants, whose rooting and sucking reflexes are genetically well designed to find nourishment and satisfaction from breast-feeding, seem to be calmed and soothed by the experience.

If authorities are in agreement about the benefits of breast-feeding, the question arises as to why in so many cases do women not breast-feed. In some cases, they are unable to do so. Some women have difficulties producing milk, while others are taking some type of medicine or have an infectious disease such as AIDS that could be passed on to their infants through breast milk. Sometimes, infants are too ill to nurse successfully. And in most cases of adoption, when the birth mother is unavailable after giving birth, the adoptive mother has no choice but to bottle-feed.

In other cases, the decision not to breast-feed is based on practical considerations. Women who hold jobs outside the home may not have sufficiently flexible schedules to breast-feed their infants. This problem is particularly true with less affluent women who may have less control over their schedules. Such problems also may account for the lower rate of breast-feeding among mothers of lower socioeconomic status.

The mother's education is also an issue: many women simply do not receive adequate information and advice regarding the advantages of breast-feeding and choose to use formula because it seems an appropriate choice. Indeed, some hospitals may inadvertently encourage the use of formula by including it in the gift packets new mothers receive as they leave the hospital, although this trend has decreased.

In developing countries, the use of formula is particularly problematic. Because formula often comes in powdered form that must be mixed with water, local pollution of the water supply can make formula particularly dangerous. Yet until the early 1980s, manufacturers aggressively sold formula in such countries, touting it as the "modern" choice. It took a massive, worldwide boycott of products manufactured by the Nestle Company, a major manufacturer of formula, to end their promotion of bottle-feeding. Formula containers now include labels that advertise the benefits of breast-feeding and the dangers associated with bottle-feeding, and free samples are no longer supplied to mothers.

Christopher R. Poirier
Robert S. Feldman

References and further reading
Dermer, Alicia. 1998. "Breastfeeding and Women's Health." *Journal of Women's Health* 7 (May):427–433.

Bulimia

Bulimia is an eating disorder in which individuals engage in binge eating, often making use of high-caloric foods. The binge is followed by an attempt to reverse the potential weight-augmenting effects of the food and calories that have been consumed. Medically speaking, there are two types of bulimia. In the purging type, the bulimic makes use of self-induced vomiting, laxatives, diuretics, or enemas on a regular basis. In the nonpurging type, the binging episodes are followed by compensatory behaviors such as fasting or excessive exercise. Like anorexics, bulimics have an obsessive fear of becoming fat, and are extremely concerned about the shape, size, and weight of their body. About half of anorexics are also bulimic and alternate their food avoidance with episodes of binge eating. Bulimics, however, are typically within normal weight range and have healthy appearances. The majority of reported bulimia cases range in age from the teens to the mid-thirties. Although young women are the primary victims of the binge-purge syndrome, approximately 5 to 10 percent of bulimics are male. (Muuss, 1990) In terms of male bulimics, young male athletes are most vulnerable, especially those for whom weight is an important factor.

The American Psychiatric Association's criteria for diagnosing bulimia include the presence of recurrent episodes of binge eating, an awareness that eating patterns are abnormal, and the fear of not being able to stop bulimic behavior. Bulimics are aware of their unusual eating habits, feel depressed about them, and are often desperate to get help. Because bulimics are aware that they have a problem, bulimia is usually easier to treat than anorexia. Treatment generally consists of family therapy, support groups, and nutritional education. Some researchers believe that a hereditary form of depression may underlie bulimia, and some

The binge-purge episode ultimately results in shame, guilt, and depression. (Oscar Burriel/Latin Stock/Science Photo Library)

patients respond to antidepressant medication.

Different figures regarding the frequency of bulimia have been reported. Generally, most sources report about 1 to 3 percent of young females are affected, although some estimates range as high as 20 percent, particularly in the case of college women. (Muuss, 1990) Unlike anorexia nervosa, which is more common during early and middle adolescence, the onset of bulimia typically occurs in late adolescence. Bulimia is primarily a middle- and upper-class disorder and is more common in industrialized societies than in developing countries.

Significant variations exist in the degree of the severity of the disorder. Some persons binge and purge occasionally, while for others this becomes a repetitive obsession. In general, bulimia starts as normal dieting behavior that only gradually becomes compulsive. A binge may continue for a considerable period of time, long after feelings of hunger have been satisfied. It may stop only after all of the food on which the individual has been binging has been consumed. Bulimics regard their gorging as abnormal, and are usually highly upset with themselves for not being able to stop. Vomiting after the binge brings a sense of relief, but in the long run, these feelings may be replaced by feelings of guilt and shame.

Prolonged bulimic eating patterns can produce a variety of health problems, depending on the purging method. Frequent and repeated vomiting can lead to erosion of the enamel of the teeth, an inflamed esophagus, and hiatal hernia. Laxative and diuretic abuse contributes to damage to the colon and urinary tract infection. Vomiting following frequent binging may also affect personal appearance including bloodshot eyes and facial puffiness. In addition, regular bingers frequently report feeling tired and lethargic. Because they generally alternate their eating binges with periods of normal eating, bulimics tend to maintain fairly normal weight and avoid becoming obese.

The binge itself is usually surrounded by great deal of secretiveness. Bulimics are often closet eaters, and parents and loved ones often remain unaware of the bulimic's eating patterns. The feeling that they cannot stop eating when they should has a significant impact on their self-esteem. Depression may become the presenting symptom for women who seek help. Bulimics often have a very low opinion of themselves, and the final outcome of the binge-purge episode is shame, guilt, and depression.

Although bulimics share with anorexics a pathological fear of getting fat and a family background with high expectations, parents of bulimics tend to be disengaged and emotionally unavailable, rather than overcontrolling as in the case of anorexics.

One position is that bulimics tend to turn to food to compensate for a feeling of emptiness resulting from lack of parental involvement. Nourishment becomes a substitute for tenderness, affection, and love, which are just the things that the bulimic feels that she or he needs and deserves. While bulimics may appear to be more extraverted than anorexics, their relationships are often superficial and lacking in genuine intimacy. Although they are liked by peers, many report having few close friends. In this sense, it is argued, their preoccupation with food may become a way of shutting out and compensating for loneliness.

Typically, bulimics are not just compulsive eaters, they also lack self-control in other aspects of their lives. Although they tend to be good students, many engage in alcohol abuse. Others may abuse marijuana, barbiturates, and other drugs, and this tends to further lower self-esteem. The use of these substances may provide relief from the feelings of guilt and depression, but they may also set off future binge-eating episodes.

Most sources argue that treatment for bulimia calls for a broadly based multifaceted approach. This often combines individual, group, and family therapies. Applied behavior analysis may be used, in which the individual is rewarded for appropriate eating behaviors. As has been mentioned, antidepressant medications have also proved useful in relieving the urge to binge. Bulimia, however, is often a chronic condition in which recovery proceeds slowly. Because individuals in therapy may experience relapses, treatment should be of sufficient frequency and duration to provide effective intervention.

Dennis Thompson

See also Anorexia

References and further reading
Burby, Liza N. 1998. *Bulimia Nervosa: The Secret Cycle of Binging and Purging.* New York: Rosen Publishing Group.

Goldstein, David J., ed. 1999. *The Management of Eating Disorders and Obesity.* Totowa, NJ: Humana Press.

Muuss, Rolf E. 1990. "Adolescent Eating Disorders." Pp. 320–333 in *Adolescent Behavior and Society: A Book of Readings,* 4th ed. Edited by Rolf E. Muuss. New York: McGraw-Hill.

Nottridge, Rhoda. 1997. *We're Talking about Eating Disorders.* Hove, East Sussex, UK: Wayland.

Steinhausen, Hans Christoph. 1995. *Eating Disorders in Adolescence: Anorexia and Bulimia Nervosa.* New York: W. De Gruyter.

Bullies and Victims
Bullies
A bully is someone who has a constant need to overpower weaker peers who cannot, or do not, defend themselves, through means of physical, verbal, or emotional abuse with intent to harm. These kinds of behaviors are distinguished from occasional teasing, pushing, shoving, and/or fighting, although even relatively mild teasing, pushing, and so on, can become bullying if a more powerful youngster picks on a weaker one over and over until he is distraught. Researchers have identified two types of bullies. Reactive bullies are emotional, have poor impulse control, react to accidental trespasses as deliberate acts of provocation, and believe that aggressive behavior is a justified response to external threats. Proactive bullies exercise deliberate aggression in nonemotional, controlled ways to achieve a goal. Sensitivity and awareness of who bullies are and why, as well as the consequences of their behaviors, can help parents nip bullying in the bud and seek professional help if necessary. Bullying is not just a phase that will go away without notice, and belief that, for example, "boys will be boys" can be harmful because bullies not only hurt others—they hurt themselves. Parents must also be alert to their child being the victim of a bully, because in time the victim can become the bully.

In general, boys bully both other boys and girls, while girls usually bully other girls. (Skjold Photographs)

Research varies on exact figures, but on the average approximately one in four children in every classroom are bullies, and American schools harbor approximately 2.1 million bullies. Girls as well as boys engage in bullying tactics, with the sex ratio varying with age. Researchers report that in grades one to three, more bullies are girls, but by grade four, more bullies are boys. One study reports that more popular boys bully to establish their place, but by third or fourth grade, bullying behavior becomes unacceptable, and it is the boys who are less popular who become the bullies. On average, boys bully both boys and girls, while girls bully mostly other girls. Bullies are found across racial, ethnic, and geographical location (urban, rural, suburban).

Depending upon the needs of an individual child, one or a combination of motivations may result in bullying behav-ior. A child may have a need to make friends, or to feed upon peers who admire, or imitate their behavior; bullies believe they will gain respect through the only way they know: intimidation. Or, a child may need to regain control taken away from them, perhaps by extreme and harsh discipline at home. Bullies take out their frustration on safer objects: less powerful peers at school. Bullying may also arise from a perception of the world as hostile. Bullies may feel a genuine need to defend themselves. Finally, bullies may be acting on a need to release bottled-up emotions from having been victimized themselves.

A survey of fifth- and sixth-graders revealed important insights by the children themselves into possible motivations of bullies: fear of being left out; doing what they see at home; fear of someone stronger, so they pick on someone weaker; needing attention; their parents bully them; they're jealous and want revenge.

Research shows that the bullying tactics of boys typically include physical aggression, such as tripping a peer, beating someone up, or threatening to hurt them. Girls use more manipulative and psychological methods, such as threatening to leave others out, spreading malicious rumors, sending intimidating notes, teasing about someone's clothing or appearance, saying bad things about their parents, belittling someone in front of others, or joining in on a cruel prank. Boys, as well as girls, may extort possessions or money by threats of ostracism or the opposite, promises of inclusion if the victim complies.

One or more of the following characteristics can be clues to identifying bullies: those who cannot, or do not, show awareness or concern for the feelings of themselves or others; those who have difficulty accepting adult authority, do not want to talk to adults, and do not respond to adult questions; those who have difficulty controlling their impulses, are angry, and who behave with physical, verbal, or emotional aggression toward others; those who display an insatiable desire to win at sports and games, at any cost.

Some bullies are more difficult to identify, as they may appear more compliant and say what adults want to hear. Bursts of temper, or multiple reports of bullying at school, are important indications that compliant behavior at home should be suspicious.

One or more of the following consequences of bullying are predicted: dropping out of school; difficulty in holding a job; failure to sustain close, intimate relationships.

Approaching high school with behaviors acceptable only to others who behave like them, bullies harbor a hostile outlook on life that can lead to growing contempt for the values of others, and can spin them into the life of an outcast, and possible drug abuse and crime.

Research suggests that without help, bullies identified in second grade are still identified as bullies throughout the elementary years, and that 60 percent of those identified in the second grade had one or more felony convictions by age twenty-four.

A child beginning to engage in bullying behaviors can be redirected by engaging the child in sports, science projects, or any other activity for which he or she takes an interest; employing positive, rather than negative, forms of discipline; teaching the child empathy and social skills; and encouraging the child's school to implement a conflict resolution program to help children learn other ways to manage their anger, frustrations, and resolve their conflicts.

Victims
The recipient of another's intent to harm, physically or emotionally, victims must be noticed because they are likely to carry unhappy memories of school with them for a lifetime, and potentially become bullies themselves.

Almost 2.7 million Americans, or 78 percent of those surveyed in one study in the Midwest, say they have been bullied, and 14 percent say they have had severe reactions. Interviews with one hundred eight- to twelve-year-olds of various ethnic and income groups suggest that bullying is the single most important issue on their minds. Passive, whiny, anxious, excitable youngsters who do not attempt to defend themselves when attacked, give in to demands, withdraw from confrontation, cry when attacked, or show fear are the likely victims of bullies. Also likely victims are provocative youngsters who are hot-tempered and restless, who create tension by irritating and teasing others, usually stronger bullies to whom they inevitably lose. Importantly, and contrary to popular belief, children who are different—for example, who are overweight, wear glasses, are too tall or too short, too smart or too dumb—are victimized only if they exude a lack of self-confidence and assertiveness. It is possible that insecure and anxious posture may be the result of these differences, making children who possess them a target, but similar children who exude confidence and assertiveness are not bullied.

Boys are likely to be victimized more with physical aggression, girls more by social intimidation and/or isolation, verbal teasing, spreading of rumors, and other verbal or emotional torment.

One or more of the following characteristics can be clues to identifying victims: change in posture, tone of voice, or facial expressions; loss of interest in, or avoiding, school or other activities; complaints of stomachaches or headaches; whiny or clingy behaviors. One or more of the following consequences of being victimized are predicted: fear of, and/or lack of interest in, school; difficulty establishing and sustaining friendships; hindered academic progress; total withdrawal, or lack of trust in peers and adults who do not help; anxiety, low self-esteem, or depression, which if severe could mean potential suicide; transformation into a bully as a result of developing a need to control from having been controlled by others.

Just as bullies identified by second grade remain so throughout the elementary years, so too do their victims, unless help is forthcoming.

Parents, teachers, and other concerned adults can help children who are victimized in several ways. They can teach the child assertiveness strategies, such as telling the bully, "I don't like it when you do that." Or, teach him or her to use humor responses, such as, "You're the winner of the bragging contest." Show the child that acting upset or giving in to demands only adds fuel to the bully's fire. Concerned adults can encourage the child to band together with other children at school. Children in groups are rarely singled out and victimized. Adults can also teach the child to think about why a child has the need to bully others. Encourage the child to think of many possible reasons. Children who think this way may reach out to help the bully and change the bully's behavior. Finally, adults can help by encouraging the child not to be afraid to ask an adult for help. Adults should never ignore a child's report of bullying, either of him- or herself or another child. If the school is not supportive, parents should consider placing the child in another school.

Myrna B. Shure

References and further reading
Fried, SuEllen, and Paula Fried. 1996. *Bullies and Victims.* New York: M. Evans.
Garrity, Carla, and Mitchell A. Baris. "Bullies and Victims: A Guide for Pediatricians." *Contemporary Pediatrics* 13:90–97, 102–114.
McCoy, Elin. 1997. *What to Do When Kids Are Mean to Your Child: Reader's Digest Parenting Guides, Ages 5 to 13.* Pleasantville, NY: Pen and Pencil Books.
Shure, Myrna B. 2000. *Raising a Thinking Preteen: The I Can Problem Solve Program for 8- to 12-Year-Olds.* New York: Henry Holt.

C

Chaos

A high degree of disorder (or low degree of order) in the physical environment of a family is termed chaos, and is one of the factors being studied for its effect on parenting practices and outcomes. Identifying the factors that influence the nature and quality of parents' behavior toward their offspring has been of long-standing interest to family researchers. For the most part, discussions of this question have focused either around the contributions of higher-order societal influences, such as the level of economic stress on the family or cultural value systems, or upon the contributions of individual child characteristics, such as temperament. Far less attention has been given to the role played by physical characteristics of the family environment as an influence upon parenting behavior. If the family environment is viewed as a theatrical drama, the parents are the actors and the physical environment is the stage upon which the actors perform. As in theater, the characteristics of the stage can influence what the actors (parents) do.

One aspect of the physical family environment that is a particularly important influence upon parenting behavior is the level of chaos in the environment. Family environments can range from nonchaotic to highly chaotic. Highly chaotic environments are those that are noisy, crowded, disorganized, and unstructured (little is scheduled, nothing has its place). Non-chaotic family environments are relatively quiet, uncrowded, and well structured. The level of chaos in the environment can be measured either by direct observation of the family environment or by use of questionnaires that ask parents to assess the degree of chaos in their environment (e.g., "Do you agree or disagree with the statement that "our house is like a zoo"?). Regardless of how it is measured, research has consistently shown that the higher the level of chaos in the family environment, the greater the likelihood of inadequate or inappropriate parenting behavior. Specifically, when environmental chaos is high, parents are typically less responsive, less involved, less verbally stimulating, less likely to show or demonstrate objects to their children, and less likely to monitor their children's ongoing activities. When environmental chaos is high, parents also are more likely to interfere with their children's exploratory behaviors and more likely to use physical punishment with their children.

While higher levels of environmental chaos are more likely to be found in economically disadvantaged families, the relation between environmental chaos and parenting behavior patterns occurs across all social classes and in both Western and non-Western cultures.

Research indicates that the disruption of parenting behavior may be a major reason why higher levels of environmental chaos predispose to less adequate children's development across a variety of areas. Although the evidence is not yet conclusive, research currently suggests that the links between environmental chaos and patterns of inadequate or inappropriate parental behavior may be the result of chaos leading to greater levels of family conflict, poor marital relations, higher levels of parental fatigue, greater parental sensitivity to daily stress, or lower levels of perceived social support by parents.

Theodore D. Wachs

References and further reading
Evans, Gary, Lorraine Maxwell, and Betty Hart. 1999. "Parental Language and Verbal Responsiveness to Children in Crowded Homes." *Developmental Psychology* 35:1020–1024.
Wachs, Theodore D. 1992. *The Nature of Nurture.* Newbury Park, CA: Sage Publications.

Child Care

Since the early 1970s, the need for child care, particularly for infants under one year of age, has increased. In the United States, almost 60 percent of women with children under six years of age and 76 percent of women with school-aged children are employed outside the home. (National Child Care Information Center, 1999) Approximately 55 percent of women now return to work during their infants' first year. Unlike the United States, other industrial countries provide parents with a choice to remain at home for a period after the birth of their children. For example, Norway provides parents with a full year of paid leave following the birth of their infant; one month of this leave is for the use of the father only.

In the United States parents use a wide variety of child care. The type of care chosen depends upon many different factors. The most important factors seem to be the child's age and the cost and availability of child care. Other factors that influence the type of care chosen by the par-

ents include the location of child care, flexibility of hours, number of hours of operation, relationship of the caregiver to the family, curriculum, number and ages of children, mother's and father's income, hours of maternal employment, parental education, and the parent's own experiences in day care.

The 1990 U.S. Census (U.S. Census Bureau, 1990) reports that 57 percent of infants younger than one year of age were cared for by relatives, 20 percent were in home-based day-care, and 14 percent were in day care centers. Parents of young infants are less likely to use day-care centers due to the high cost of infant care in these centers and because many centers will not enroll children who are not toilet trained. As children grow older they are more likely to attend day-care centers. For example, day-care centers provide care for 42 percent of five-year-olds. (National Center for Educational Statistics, 1996) At all ages relatives provide a large percentage of child care.

For single-parent families with preschool children the child care usage is very similar. However, fathers provide less child care: 2 percent in single-family households compared to 19 percent in two-parent households. (Hayes, Palmer, and Zaslow, 1990) Grandparents are providing more child care in single-parent families: 16 percent compared with 3 percent in two-parent households. (Hayes, Palmer, and Zaslow, 1990)

Parents face many problems when deciding about child care. One of their first problems is acquiring adequate information to make a good decision about quality care. A majority of parents report that they have received conflicting information about whether, how often, or with whom to leave their children.

The availability of quality child care is another hurdle faced by many parents. Though the number of day-care centers and licensed day-care homes has increased

Positive outcomes are noted for children when there is a closeness between the child and caregiver and the caregiver encourages the child's interaction with others. (Skjold Photographs)

rapidly, this increase has not kept pace with the demand. Families report that finding care for their children is difficult. Low-income parents may pay 20 to 25 percent of their income for child care. (Hofferth, 1992) The cost of high-quality child care may be prohibitive for many parents.

The quality of child care is a very important factor in the parents' choice. Currently, there are no systematic guidelines for quality of care in the United States. Each state does regulate the licensed care providers, but standards vary from state to state. The regulated quality of care indicators include child-staff ratio, group size (i.e., the number of children in a classroom or home-based day care), caregiver training, space (i.e., square footage available per child both indoors and outdoors), and equipment. Other factors that may have an impact on

quality of child care include staff stability, licensure, and the age mix of the children attending.

Quality of child care is enhanced by the education and training of the caregivers, small child-to-staff ratios, small group size, and staff stability. Each of these factors influences the interaction between the child and care provider. Group size appears to have a major impact on this interaction. The smaller the group, the greater the interaction between each child and the caregiver. The American Public Health Association and the American Academy of Pediatrics (1992) recommend the following standards: (1) child to staff ratios of three children to one staff member from six to fifteen months of age, four children to one staff person at twenty-four months of age, and seven children to one staff person at thirty-six months of age; (2) group sizes (classroom or home-based day care) of six from six to fifteen months of age, eight at twenty-four months of age, and fourteen at thirty-six months of age; and, (3) formal, post–high school training in child development, early childhood education, or a related field for the caregivers.

Other aspects of child care are difficult to regulate, but are nonetheless important in determining the quality of child care. These include the child's relationship and day-to-day interaction with the caregiver. It is in this area that research has noted the largest effect on the child's development. For example, positive outcomes are noted for children when there is a closeness between the child and caregiver and the caregiver is socially competent and encourages the child's interactions with others. Researchers have also found that the largest predictor of development was the caregiver's speech to the child. The National Institute of Child Health and Human Development (NICHD) found that other important positive caregiving behaviors include positive affect, positive physical contact, responsiveness to the child's distress, responsiveness to the child's vocalization, positive talk, asking questions of the child, and stimulating cognitive and social development. (NICHD, 1997) The caregivers' education and training in early childhood education and child development have been found to have a positive influence on the interaction between child and caregiver.

Child care for school-aged children is another area of concern for parents. Due to the parents' work schedule, a child may require supervision both before and after school. Home-based day care and after-school programs appear to be the predominate care arrangement for school-aged children. However, the use of day-care centers is increasing. With approximately 28 million children of working parents in the United States, it is no surprise that the demand for after-school programs is twice the supply. The quality of care for school-aged children is influenced by the continuity between school and after-school care. When the after-school care reinforces what the child is learning in school and occurs within the school setting, development is enhanced. After-school care has also been found to decrease juvenile crime.

Self-care by children (latchkey children) is a major concern because of the potential problems (e.g., drug usage and violence) created by lack of supervision. Approximately 35 percent of twelve-year-olds are left by themselves regularly while their parents are working. (U.S. Depts. of Education and Justice, 1998) Problems are less likely to occur if parents provide some form of supervision, for example, a neighbor who is home and available in case of emergency or parents who are accessible by phone. This supervision should also include rules provided by the parents on appropriate activities after school and whether friends are allowed to visit.

Child-care quality does not influence only the child; parents are also affected. The parents' satisfaction with child care has a positive relationship to work satisfaction, and the fewer types of child care arrangements the parents must rely on (the more "hassle-free" the care arrangements), the greater their satisfaction with work and parenting.

The need for nonparental child care will continue to grow. This is but one of the many changes and challenges facing parents today.

Diane E. Wille

References and further reading
American Public Health Association and American Academy of Pediatrics. 1992. *Caring for Our Children. National Health and Performance Standards: Guidelines for Out-of-Home Child Care Programs.* Ann Arbor MI: APHA and AAP.
Burchinal, Margaret. 1999. "Child Care Experiences and Developmental Outcomes." *Annals of the American Academy of Political & Social Sciences* 563:73–98.

Hayes, Cheryl D., John L. Palmer, and Martha J. Zaslow, eds. 1990. *Who Cares for America's Children? Child Care Policy for the 1990s.* Washington, DC: National Academy Press.

Hofferth, Sandra. 1992. "The Demand for and Supply of Child Care in the 1990s." Pp. 3–25 in *Child Care in the 1990s: Trends and Consequences.* Edited by Alan Booth. Hillsdale, NJ: Lawrence Erlbaum Associates.

National Center for Educational Statistics. 1996. *1996 National Household Education Survey.* Washington, DC: Department of Education, Office of Educational Research and Improvement.

National Child Care Information Center. 1999. www.NCCIC.org.

NICHD Early Child Care Research Network. 1997. "Infant Child Care and Attachment Security: Results of the NICHD Study of Early Child Care." *Child Development* 68:860–879.

U.S. Census Bureau. 1990. "Who's Minding the Kids? Child Care Arrangements" in *Current Population Reports Series P-20,* No. 452, p. 10. Washington, DC: Government Printing Office.

U.S. Depts. of Education and Justice. 1998. "Safe and Smart: Making After-School Hours Work for Kids." June. http://www.ed.gob/pubs/SafeandSmart/chapter1.html.

Chronic Illness, Parenting a Child with

Parents of chronically ill children experience a myriad of emotions related to caring for their child, and many of these feelings exist on a continuum (e.g., from appropriate, healthy emotional responses to distorted, pathological levels of expression). Parental overprotectiveness is one parental reaction to childhood chronic illness that is frequently mentioned in the pediatric literature. Overprotection, defined as parental behaviors (e.g., infantilization, prevention of independent behavior, excessive control) that hinder the development of a child's independence, can lead to difficulties within the parent-child relationship, and subsequent maladjustment (e.g., behavioral, social, and academic problems, as well as more severe forms of psychopathology, such as depression and anxiety) for children living with a chronic illness. Overprotectiveness may be particularly detrimental during key childhood developmental transition periods, such as adolescence, when such strivings for independence are most pronounced.

The importance of considering parent-child relationships within the context of families caring for a chronically ill child has been emphasized by many researchers. As most families face enormous challenges in the event of chronic illness, it is important to understand the multiple impacts of the illness on all family members, the parent-child relationship, and the family system. Most chronic illnesses and physical disabilities require intensive medical management and place considerable physical, psychological, and social demands on the individuals and families involved.

Recent research in the area of developmental psychopathology suggests that the quality of a child's family relationships can be a protective factor or a risk factor for adjustment difficulties. Adaptive family relationships may enhance the psychosocial well-being of a well-adjusted child or protect children at risk for maladjustment from exhibiting increasing levels of problem behaviors. Similarly, less adaptive family relations may make a well-adjusted child more vulnerable to psychosocial maladjustment or exacerbate the level of maladaption already present in an at-risk child.

Although families caring for a chronically ill child are faced with a burden of care far greater than parents caring for healthy children, many are able to manage the illness and maintain healthy parent-child relationships. Preliminary research on long-term parental adjustment to childhood chronic illness suggests that mothers and fathers are competent in caring for their chronically ill child, despite the identification of several illness-related stressors (e.g., financial concerns, uncertainty about the child's prognosis). Research comparing families caring for a chronically ill child to those caring for an able-bodied child has often led researchers to find more dysfunction among families caring for a chronically ill child. However, these studies have been criticized due to the tendency to interpret parental adaptation to child chronic illness in pathological terms. Some have suggested that research should focus more on positive aspects, examining the resilience and competency displayed by families facing chronic illness. Indeed, most families of children with chronic physical conditions tend to be typical families dealing with an atypical stressor.

Parental Overprotectiveness

Several researchers have described the affective responses that have been associated with caring for a child with a chronic illness. These include: shock upon initial diagnosis, anger, denial and rejection, blame, guilt, and overprotection. Indeed, the concept of overprotection has frequently been mentioned within the pediatric chronic illness literature as a common parental response to caring for a child with chronic illness.

The theory of overprotection was first introduced in 1931 in a published report of several selected case studies of mothers who overprotect and their children. The theory describes four behaviors that are characteristic of parental overprotection: excessive contact with the child, infantilization, prevention of independent behavior, and parental control. According to the theory, parents who are caring for chronically ill children are more likely to overprotect than parents of able-bodied children. Research examining parental reactions to pediatric injury suggests that many parents of children with chronic illness behave in an overly controlling manner. It has been suggested that parents caring for ill or disabled children often experience adjustment difficulties, prima-

rily due to the impact of an illness and the profound devastation experienced by families who have experienced this type of loss. Often parents do not have the opportunity to prepare for the tasks of caring for an ill child, and often compensate for the loss of their otherwise healthy child by striving to take control of the situation. This parental control may be especially pronounced in situations in which the parent feels responsible for the illness. Thus, overprotective parents behave in a highly diligent manner, overly controlling the child in an effort to protect the child from further injury, improve the child's medical condition, or satisfy any uncertainties over the child's prognosis. Moreover, a parent that overprotects is likely to be intrusive and use psychological methods of controlling a child. Such parental behaviors prevent the child from developing the appropriate skills necessary for later independence.

Several researchers have explained overprotection in the context of families caring for children who are chronically ill. For example, the relationship can be described from an interactional perspective in which efforts to be helpful can become "miscarried." Miscarried helping in a parent-child relationship is a process by which a parent's efforts to be helpful to the child paradoxically lead over time to unsupportive relationships that become detrimental to the child. Whereas the original theory of parental overprotection suggests that overprotection is largely the result of maternal character flaws (e.g., aggression) or psychopathology (e.g., maternal anxiety), miscarried helping theory differs in that it speculates about a normative process that often occurs in response to an illness or injury. As such, miscarried helping refers to a process in which a parent intends to be helpful, but in which this helpfulness becomes miscarried over time.

"Miscarried helping" is likely to occur in close relationships, especially between family members. A parent's emotional investment in the relationship in terms of wanting to be helpful and create a positive outcome for the child have been identified as components to the process of miscarried helping. The process of overinvolvement is more likely to occur when there is some ambiguity about the reasons for medical setbacks, or a lack of progress in the ill child. In these situations, the caretaker may believe that progress was prevented due to the ill person's lack of motivation. Parents often struggle to help their child with the acquisition of skills that will aid in the development of independence, but become frustrated when the child is unable to master the skills due to his or her limitations related to the illness or a lack of motivation. As a result, the caretaker becomes overprotective in an attempt to increase task-related performance and subsequent recovery.

Examples of the unhealthy interactions that might occur within a miscarried relationship have been documented. For example, the ill person may become uncomfortable in the role of being helped due to feelings of dependency, guilt, or shame, or of feeling little control over whether and when certain things are done for him or her. Support from a caretaker may threaten an ill person's self-esteem, furthering feelings of inadequacy and dependency. As a result, resentment and conflict is likely to occur within the relationship, and may lead to a rejection of the caretaker's efforts as the ill person attempts to maintain self-respect and a sense of control. A child is likely to encounter several problems as a result of maternal overprotection, including difficulties in social adjustment, school problems, sexual problems, restriction of outside interests, and sleep problems. Additionally, many studies have suggested that overprotectiveness may be a risk factor for psychopathology, including depression, anxiety, and adolescent eating disorders. Although these difficulties may not become evident until a child is older, they typically begin to emerge when a child begins to develop a more autonomous relationship with his or her parents.

Chronic Illness and Adolescence

Adolescence is a developmental transition period that is characterized by dramatic biological, psychological, and social changes. Given such changes, it is not surprising that for some adolescents it is a period of satisfactory adjustment and healthy family relationships, but for others it is a period of increasing levels of distress and maladjustment.

For most, adolescence is a time of increased independence and self-reliance. The onset of chronic illness during childhood may challenge the child's autonomy striving just prior to the onset of adolescence—a developmental period during which such strivings are a normal developmental task. Appropriate parental acknowledgment of the importance of adolescent independence and decision making is likely to facilitate the psychosocial development of chronically ill adolescents. Adolescents with chronic illness have the same desires for behavioral autonomy as nonimpaired adolescents, and as a consequence, they may begin to question and challenge their parents' authority during this developmental period. Some have suggested that, given their dependence on medical and familial assistance, strivings for autonomy may be more prominent among adolescents with chronic illness than healthy children.

Parents of children with chronic illness who respond to the developmental changes of adolescence by encouraging gradually increasing levels of responsibility and decision making are likely to have more well-adjusted offspring. It has been observed that some families with chronically ill children respond to the developmental needs of their adolescent child in different ways from what has typically been observed in families caring for a healthy adolescent. For example, prior to adolescence, children with some chronic illnesses may be less behaviorally autonomous (i.e., less likely to make their own decisions over matters of relevance to the family) than are nonimpaired adolescents. They may also gain such autonomy at slower rates, have less influence in the family prior to adolescence, and require more parental supervision. Some parents with chronically ill offspring may also be less likely to change their behaviors toward their child in response to developmental change. Failure to grant autonomy to children may lead many chronically ill children to become noncompliant with prescribed medical regimens, behaviors that (although dangerous) may be manifestations of developmentally appropriate autonomy strivings (see earlier discussion on miscarried helping). This is an important issue because the manner in which the family responds to their child's developmental changes has implications for long-term well-being. Therefore, it is important to identify factors that provide for a successful relationship, particularly during key developmental transition periods such as adolescence, and specifically within the context of caring for a child with a chronic illness. Moreover, difficulties that begin in adolescence are likely to result in a maladaptive developmental trajectory that continues into adulthood, potentially leading to detrimental outcomes.

In order to facilitate healthy functioning for both parents and their chronically ill child, it is important for families to be flexible to meet the demands of the illness.

Some guidelines for parents are as follows. First, understanding the child's strengths and vulnerabilities when implementing a plan for care, and reviewing this with medical personnel involved in the child's care, allows for appropriate parental expectations of the child. Encouraging the child to perform tasks for him- or herself, while at the same time challenging him or her to acquire new skills that will foster independence, is a necessary task related to the care of a chronically ill child.

Second, the importance of shared parental responsibility for the care of the chronically ill child is often overlooked. Often, in two-parent families, one parent is employed while the other is responsible for the medical management of the ill child. When responsibility is shared, parental overprotectiveness is less likely.

Third, sharing parenting experiences and practices with other parents of chronically ill children may ease the increased burden of caring for a child with a chronic illness. Community support groups or networks provided by state and local nonprofit organizations are sources of this type of support.

Fourth, recognition of the impact of the illness and medical management on family routines allows families to prepare in advance, and allows caretaking to become less burdensome and disruptive to normal family routines. Awareness of what areas are not influenced by the illness (e.g., sibling participation in sporting activities, or family events such as vacations) also aids in maintaining a sense of normalcy for the family as a whole.

Sharon Z. Johnson
Grayson N. Holmbeck

References and further reading
Coyne, James C., Camille B. Wortman, and Darrin R. Lehman. 1988. "The Other Side of Support: Emotional Overinvolvement and Miscarried Helping." Pp. 305–330 in *Marshalling Social Support: Formats, Processes, and Effects.* Edited by Benjamin H. Gottlib. Newbury Park, CA: Sage Publications.
Holmbeck, Grayson N. 1994. "Adolescence." Pp. 17–28 in *Encyclopedia of Human Behavior.* Edited by V. S. Ramachandran. Orlando, FL: Academic Press.
Kazak, Anne E., Abbie M. Segal-Andrews, and Kelly Johnson. 1995. "Pediatric

Psychology Research and Practice: A Family/Systems Approach." Pp. 84–104 in *Handbook of Pediatric Psychology.* Edited by Michael C. Roberts. New York: Guilford Press.

Levy, David M. 1931. "Maternal Overprotection and Rejection." *Archives of Neurology and Psychiatry* 25:886–8889.
———. 1943. *Maternal Overprotection.* New York: Columbia University Press.

Parker, Gordon. 1983. *Parental Overprotection: A Risk Factor in Psychosocial Development.* New York: Grune & Stratton.

Parker, Gordon, Leslie Kiloh, and Linda Hayward. 1987. "Parental Representations of Neurotic and Endogenous Depressives." *Journal of Affective Disorders* 13:75–82.

Rolland, John S. 1994. *Families, Illness, and Disability: An Integrative Treatment Model.* New York: Basic Books.

Seligman, Milton, and Rosalyn B. Darling. 1989. *Ordinary Families, Special Children: A Systems Approach to Childhood Disability.* New York: Guilford Press.

Steinberg, Lawrence. 1994. "Autonomy, Conflict, and Harmony in the Family Relationship." Pp. 225–226 in *At the Threshold: The Developing Adolescent.* Edited by Shirley S. Feldman and Glen R. Elliott. Cambridge, MA: Harvard University Press.

Circumcision

Biologic Perspective

Circumcision (literally: to cut around) is the process by which part or the entire foreskin, also known as the prepuce, a natural part of the male genital anatomy that covers the head, or glans, of the penis, is removed. The foreskin consists of an outer layer, which is a continuation of the skin located on the shaft of the penis, and an inner layer, which bears resemblance to the mucus coated tissue of the mouth. The foreskin contains nerves and blood vessels along with specialized glands located in the inner layer that secretes a lubricant known as smegma. The foreskin functions primarily to protect the glans both from injury and desiccation, but its role may extend beyond that of an anatomic barrier and moisturizer to include both sexual arousal and pleasure.

Among the vast majority of adult males, the foreskin retracts over the glans when penile erection occurs, functioning like a hood or sheath. The ability of the foreskin to retract is not present in the newborn male infant because of the tight attachment of the inner layer of the foreskin to the glans. The anatomic attachment of the inner layer to the glans naturally and gradually lessens over the first several years of life, but must be artificially broken during the process of neonatal circumcision. Occasionally, failure of the inner layer to detach spontaneously in part or in whole from the glans during childhood may produce a condition called phimosis, in which the foreskin not only cannot be retracted, but may actually obstruct or impede the outflow of urine from the penis. Often, circumcision is performed to treat cases of phimosis.

When the foreskin is removed, the surface of the glans becomes thickened (keratinized). This adaptation of the glans to environmental exposure provides some protection akin to that of a condom. Debate continues whether keratinization of the glans works to protect the penis against infection more effectively than does the intact foreskin. Even less clear is the effect of the absence of the foreskin on sensation. Some reports by men circumcised later in life indicate a significant decrease in perceived sensation to touch over the glans after the procedure, compared with the level of sensation to touch perceived before the procedure. However, researchers Masters and Johnson in their 1966 book, The Human Sexual Response, noted no differences between circumcised and uncircumcised adults in perception of light touch on the upper or lower surfaces of the penis.

Historical Perspective

Hieroglyphics and works of art from ancient Egypt indicate that circumcision was a practice among the nobility, including the pharaoh and those wealthy enough to afford this procedure. Speculation about the origins and purpose of this practice among the Egyptians continues to this date, but at least one medical author suggests that, apart from facilitating male genital cleanliness in the dry, sandy desert environment, circumcision may also have been employed as a curative or preventive procedure for urinary tract infections.

Clearly, the practice of circumcision was not applied to all males under the pharaoh's rule. However, the biblical covenant between God and Abraham as recounted in Genesis 17:10 put circumcision on the level of a surgical mandate for all males. Despite the clear linkage with religious practice in traditional Judaism, the medical benefits of circumcision as a sustaining force is also hinted at in the Bible. For example, the story of Abraham at age ninety-nine circumcising himself and then fathering Isaac after he and his wife Sarah had been childless for many years raises speculation about an underlying medical condition, perhaps phimosis, relieved by circumcision that promoted fertility.

Despite the propagation of ritual infant circumcision amongst the Israelites in the cradle of civilization, the procedure did not transport well to male members of other societies, religions, or cultures. Despite their roots in Judaism, early Christians did not retain circumcision as a ritual practice and did not elevate the procedure to the level of a sacrament. The pagan Roman government subsequently forbade the practice of circumcision amongst the Jews. Men of the Islamic faith practiced ritual circumcision, but at variable times after the newborn period.

Certainly, circumcision was not a common practice amongst the original American colonists, despite their considerable fundamental religious beliefs. Circumcision was not widely practiced among our European ancestors, with the exception of the nobility or the wealthy, who viewed the practice as a mark of elevated social status. In the late 1800s, infant circumcision began to gain favor in the United States, when it was promoted as a preventive cure for masturbation, a practice then believed to be unhealthy. Beginning in 1933, rates of neonatal circumcision in the United States rose significantly, coincident with the increasing prevalence of in-hospital births and the introduction of the Gomco clamp technique for circumcision (see below), and peaked in the mid-1960s. Since 1976, the percentage of males circumcised in the United States has declined, perhaps in part due to medical reappraisal of the risks and benefits of the procedure. The National Health and Social Life Survey (NHSLS) conducted in 1992 revealed that 77 percent of American-born men were circumcised, compared with 42 percent of non-American-born men living in the United States. Worldwide, the proportion of men who are circumcised is estimated to be only 20 percent.

The proportion of newborn American males circumcised approximated 80 percent after World War II. Today, circumcision is performed on approximately 60 percent of the 1.9 to 2 million male infants born in the United States, although considerable variation in the rate of neonatal circumcision is noted by geographic area. For example, in 1992, 78 percent of male infants were circumcised prior to hospital discharge in the midwestern United States compared to 38 percent in the western United States. The 1992 NHSLS revealed high rates of circumcision for all major American religious groups. However, important racial and ethnic differences were noted, with white males more likely to be circumcised than black or Hispanic males (81 percent, 65 percent, and 54 percent, respectively). In addition, the NHSLS demonstrated significant differences in circumcision rates associated with the level of education of the mother. The rate of circumcision among infants born to mothers who did not complete high school was lower than rates among infants born to mothers with more education (62 percent versus 84–87 percent).

The biblical technique of circumcision may have been quite different than that practiced currently. One medical historian notes that until approximately A.D. 140 circumcision was accomplished by placing a slotted metal shield near the tip of the foreskin after the foreskin was pulled forward by the operator. Subsequently, the small amount of skin at the tip of the foreskin was incised above the shield, swiftly and relatively painlessly with a sharp knife and removed, leaving virtually the entire inner layer of the prepuce intact over the glans. This process was referred to as Bris Milah, and is thought by some to be accurately depicted by Michelangelo Buonarroti's sculpture of King David, who appears on casual inspection to be uncircumcised. Over time, however, the amount of foreskin removed during ritual neonatal circumcision increased, possibly in response to confusion regarding the circumcision status of the infant, child, or adolescent by religious or secular authorities, when ascertained by casual visual inspection, in order to distinguish Jews from Gentiles. The removal of larger amounts of foreskin during circumcision, referred to as Bris Periah, leaves the glans fully exposed and very little of the inner layer of the prepuce intact.

The more radical approach to removal of foreskin during neonatal circumcision is the current surgical standard of practice in the United States. Beginning with the introduction of the Gomco clamp in 1934, a simple mechanical device employed by the surgeon to protect the glans from injury while allowing relatively bloodless removal of the foreskin down to the shaft of the penis during circumcision, the procedure now involves crushing the tissues of the entire circumference of the prepuce and removing the nerve-containing structures of the inner layer of the foreskin. Importantly, the procedure induces pain of variable intensity and duration if performed without an anaesthetic.

Benefits of Circumcision
Claims of benefits of circumcision include improved genital hygiene, reduced risk of sexual dysfunction, protection against infection of the glans, reduction in risk of urinary tract infection and sexually transmitted diseases including human immunodeficiency virus infection, reduced risk of carcinoma of the penis, and elimination of problems related to the intact foreskin, such as phimosis or paraphimosis. These benefits will be examined individually.

Improved Hygiene. Skin cells from the inner layer of the foreskin and the glans are normally shed throughout life. Because shedding takes place in the closed space between the intact foreskin and the glans, these cells escape by eventually moving to the tip of the foreskin. Accumulated cells produce a whitish secretion that can sometimes coalesce into larger particles termed infant smegma. At the time of puberty, the glands of Tyson located in the inner layer of the foreskin produce an oily substance that mixes with shed cells. This combination is termed adult smegma. If allowed to accumulate in the foreskin cavity, adult smegma becomes an unpleasant and foul-smelling substance due to the actions of harmless skin bacteria on the oils secreted by Tyson's glands. In addition, foreign material may gain access to the smegma deposit in the form of dirt, urine, and semen.

Normally, in older children, a healthy foreskin can be retracted for cleansing and smegma can be removed by washing.

Failure to regularly cleanse the glans after retracting the foreskin, or conditions such as phimosis in which the foreskin cannot be retracted, leads to significant accumulations of smegma. In the absence of the foreskin, production of both infant and adult smegma is curtailed and routine hygiene facilitated.

The medical literature contains much speculation about the relationship between poor penile hygiene and the development of diseases of the penis, including cancer. At least one study reports an association between appropriate penile hygiene and a decreased frequency of inflammation of the glans (balanitis) or the foreskin. However, appropriate hygiene did not eliminate all penile problems in this study. Currently, there is no convincing direct scientific evidence that smegma acts as a carcinogen.

Less Sexual Dysfunction.   During sexual intercourse, the foreskin usually rolls back and forth over the glans. This motion of the foreskin stimulates sensitive penile nerve endings and is a source of intense pleasure. The foreskin also acts to reduce friction and chaffing of the penis during intercourse and to contact and stimulate the female partner. However, anecdotal reports suggest that the presence of the foreskin may actually lead to sexual dysfunction by promoting premature ejaculation and preventing maximal stimulation of the clitoris and labia minora by the exposed head of the penis. Indeed, the 1992 NHSLS found that circumcised men older than age forty-five had a significantly reduced risk of sexual dysfunction, including problems achieving and maintaining erection and anxiety about sexual performance, and a consistent trend toward lesser risk of premature ejaculation and greater sexual satisfaction, compared with uncircumcised men.

Protection against Infection.   Local infection of the glans or the foreskin may occur and is associated with inadequate basic hygienic practices and/or phimosis. A report in the British medical literature noted a rate of inflammation or infection of the glans and/or the foreskin (balanoposthitis) to be 4 percent among males, peaking in preschool-aged boys. In another study from the United States, balanitis and irritation were two to three times more commonly found among uncircumcised males than circumcised males (6 percent versus 3 percent, and 3.6 percent versus 1.1 percent, respectively). These conditions were neither serious nor life threatening and easily treatable. However, recurrent bouts of balanoposthitis may occur and can result in complications that require circumcision as treatment.

Sexually transmitted diseases (STDs) continue to account for significant morbidity in the United States, despite considerable efforts of public health officials to promote safer sexual practices. Speculation continues in the medical literature that circumcision status is related to the risk of acquiring a variety of sexually transmitted diseases. A study conducted at an STD clinic in Australia found a statistically significant increase in cases of genital herpes, gonorrhea, syphilis, and yeast infection among uncircumcised men. Several recently published studies indicate that the risk of HIV infection is increased among uncircumcised men, even when other factors known to facilitate transmission of the virus, such as genital ulcers, are taken into account.

These studies are far from conclusive because of limitations in the methods by which the studies were conducted. They cannot exclude differences in sexual behavior or practices accounting for the differences in observed rates of STDs. In addition, other studies report contradictory findings. For example, one study found a higher incidence of infection of the urethra due to microorganisms other than gonorrhea among circumcised men, and no increased risk of common sexually transmitted diseases among uncircumcised males. Importantly, the NHSLS demonstrated no differences between uncircumcised and circumcised men in the risk of ever having had gonorrhea, syphilis, urethral infection with microorganisms other than gonorrhea, or genital herpes. Indeed, circumcised men were actually found to have an increased risk of infection with the microorganism *Chlamydia trachomatis*, a frequent cause of urethral inflammation. Of special note in this study was the finding that, when compared with circumcised men, the risk of acquiring any sexually transmitted disease by uncircumcised men actually decreased as the number of lifetime sexual partners increased in number. This finding actually suggests, but does not establish, some protection against the acquisition of STDs by the presence of the foreskin.

Urinary Tract Infections.   In the early 1980s, pediatricians noted that infants who developed bacterial infections of the bladder or kidney during the first eight months of life were more likely to be boys. Ninety-five percent of these boys with urinary tract infections due to bacteria were uncircumcised. Subsequently, a study conducted on male infants of U.S. military personnel found that urinary tract infections were ten times more likely to occur among uncircumcised, as opposed to circumcised, boys. Importantly, urinary tract infections in these young infants were associated with important complications including bacterial invasion of the blood stream, meningitis, and death from overwhelming infection. Approximately 2 percent of male

infants with urinary tract infections eventually developed kidney failure. Additional research found that uncircumcised boys had increased numbers of bacteria known to cause urinary tract infection around the opening of the urethra during the first six months of life when compared with circumcised infants. Experimental studies found that bacteria known to cause urinary tract infections adhered to and readily colonized the inner layer of the foreskin, but did not adhere to the outer layer of the foreskin.

More recent studies of male infants demonstrate a four- to sevenfold increased risk of urinary tract infection among uncircumcised boys, but a lower risk of complications than had been reported in earlier studies. Based on information from these more recent studies, the American Academy of Pediatrics (AAP) estimates that between 7 and 14 of every 1,000 uncircumcised infant boys will develop a urinary tract infection, compared with 1 to 2 of every 1,000 circumcised infant boys during the first year of life. Unanswered, however, are questions related to the long-term outlook for infants developing urinary tract infections. There may be a causative relationship between young age at the time of an initial bacterial infection of the kidney and either the formation of scars or impairment of kidney function.

Cancer.   Cancer of the penis is a rare disease in the United States. Taking age into account, the annual rate of new cases of penile cancer is approximately 1 per 100,000 men per year. Rates of penile cancer vary considerably in other countries where the percentage of circumcised men is lower than in the United States. The rate of cancer in Denmark approximates 0.8 cases per 100,000 men per year while in India the rate ranges from 2 to 10.5 cases per 100,000 men per year.

Currently, uncircumcised men are believed to be at least three times more likely to develop penile carcinoma than are circumcised men. The presence of phimosis increases the risk of penile cancer beyond that associated with the uncircumcised state. One study suggests that neonatal circumcision, but not circumcision after infancy, confers some protection against the development of penile carcinoma. Because other factors that might be related to the development of penile cancer, such as multiple sexual partners, genital warts (due to human papilloma virus), or smoking, cannot be accounted for in these studies, the true role of the foreskin in the pathogenesis of cancer remains uncertain. Despite this uncertainty, the absolute magnitude of the risk of carcinoma of the penis among uncircumcised males in the United States is extremely low, of the order of nine to ten cases per 1 million men per year. This incidence is far lower than the rate of important complications noted to occur with neonatal circumcision (see below).

Penile Problems. In virtually all uncircumcised male infants the foreskin is normally not retractable. Separation of the inner layer of the foreskin from the glans, thus allowing the foreskin to retract is a slowly progressive developmental process. By the age of four years, approximately 90 percent of uncircumcised boys can retract their foreskin over the glans, and by age seventeen approximately 99 percent of uncircumcised men can retract their foreskin. The inability to retract the foreskin over the glans due to abnormalities in the pliability of the foreskin or acquired adhesions to the glans constitutes the condition termed phimosis, and the inability to return a retracted foreskin back over the glans to its resting state constitutes the condition termed paraphimosis. These penile problems, along with irritation of the glans, are encountered 2.4 times more frequently among uncircumcised infants compared with circumcised infants between the ages of four and twelve months. Of these penile problems, minor irritation of the glans is most often diagnosed.

In the absence of the foreskin, the risk of both phimosis and paraphimosis is eliminated, but irritation of the glans may still occur. Indeed, both inflammation and ulceration of the urethral opening at the tip of the glans occur almost exclusively in circumcised boys. Approximately 1 percent of circumcised infants presented to a general pediatric practice for evaluation of penile problems are diagnosed with these conditions.

Because phimosis has been implicated as a risk factor for penile carcinoma, treatment of this condition is of importance to parents and physicians. Circumcision had been considered the preferred treatment.

Risks of Circumcision

Like all surgical procedures, circumcision is associated with risk of complications. The true incidence of complications is unknown but estimated to range between 0.2 and 2 percent of procedures. The major complications include bleeding, injury to the penis including excessive removal of foreskin or mechanical injury of the glans, and infection. Bleeding is the most common complication, noted in approximately 0.1 percent of procedures, and is usually controlled by local measures that may include the placement of sutures. Bleeding may be severe in infants who have unrecognized blood disorders such as hemophilia or who did not receive vitamin K immediately after birth, and transfusion may be required in these situations. Local infection is the most common infectious complication, but rapidly spreading infection, termed cellulitis, and bacterial invasion of the bloodstream requiring treatment with intravenous antibiotic drugs may occur. Very rare complications documented in the medical literature include amputation of part of the glans, narrowing of the urethral opening causing obstruction to the outflow of urine from the bladder, and a nonviable penis. The Australasian Association of Paediatric Surgeons recommends that circumcision be avoided in circumstances in which a deformity of the penis is identified at birth such as hypospadias, when the infant is ill or judged to be medically unstable, or when a family history of a bleeding disorder is identified. Some surgeons prefer to defer circumcision on small, prematurely born infants or term infants who have a short penile shaft. Deaths can occur during or as a result of complications of circumcision. Approximately one death occurs for every 500,000 procedures performed.

Circumcision may cause intense pain, and many studies document the physiologic correlates of pain noted in adults when the procedure is performed on infants without analgesia. Additionally, at least one study reports discernable short-term alterations in the feeding patterns as well as the sleeping and crying and fussing behaviors of baby boys after circumcision performed without analgesia. A common belief is that infants tolerate these acute episodes of pain well, recover quickly, and have no lasting memory of the event. Recent evidence suggests otherwise. A study published in the British medical literature reports that infants circumcised without analgesia exhibited more intense pain responses to routine immunization at four months of age when compared with either uncircumcised infants or infants circumcised with analgesia. This accentuated pain response subsequent to painful circumcision is analogous to post-traumatic stress disorder in adults. As such, both the American Academy of Pediatrics and the Canadian Pediatric Society concur that neonatal circumcision should be pain free. Currently,

several methods of pain reduction, including topical or injectable analgesics, are available and should be provided by an experienced operator skilled in their application before the procedure is performed.

Conclusions
While currently available information of variable scientific quality indicates potential medical benefits of this procedure when performed by skilled operators, no professional medical organization, including the American Academy of Pediatrics and the Canadian Pediatric Society, recommends routine circumcision of neonates.

General medical ethics dictate that unless the benefits of a medical procedure clearly outweigh the risks and the costs of the procedure, then that procedure should not be recommended for the routine care of infants and children. Several studies have attempted to weigh the issues of benefits, risks, and costs of neonatal circumcision, but none was able to demonstrate a benefit from routine neonatal circumcision that outweighed any of the risks. Thus, the Canadian Pediatric Society concludes that because the overall evidence of the benefits and harms of circumcision are so evenly balanced, there is no compelling medical rationale for recommending the procedure routinely as part of newborn care.

The American Academy of Pediatrics (AAP) concurs with this judgment. In their most recent analysis of neonatal circumcision published in 1999, they concluded that the existing scientific evidence was not sufficient to recommend routine neonatal circumcision on medical grounds. The AAP recommended, therefore, that parents should determine what is in the best interest of their child based on accurate and unbiased information. However, given the variable quality of the scientific information currently available, this recommendation of the AAP is much more easily made than carried out in actual clinical practice.

In reality, decisions regarding circumcision of the newborn male infant usually are not made on the basis of medical information, nor do physicians influence to a great extent the process of parental decision making. Research demonstrates that when parents make decisions about performing circumcision on their newborn sons, they rely primarily on social factors and nonmedical concerns. In one study, the strongest factors associated with decisions to perform or withhold the procedure were the circumcision status of the father, and parental concerns about the self-concept of the child and the attitudes of peers regarding the circumcised or uncircumcised penis. Evidence that mothers in the United States are more likely to be the primary decision makers regarding circumcision in the immediate newborn period, and that their decisions are often made before the birth of the baby and may be related to the aesthetics and/or future sexual connotations of the appearance of their son's penis, are provocative, controversial, and as yet unsubstantiated. The AAP clearly endorses the primacy of parents in this decision-making process. Their 1999 policy statement emphasizes the legitimacy of parents to take into account cultural, religious, and ethnic traditions when making decisions about circumcision.

Robert M. Lembo
Alan L. Mendelsohn

References and further reading
American Academy of Pediatrics, Task Force on Circumcision. 1999. "Circumcision Policy Statement." *Pediatrics* 103:686–693.
Fetus and Newborn Committee, Canadian Pediatric Society. 1996. "Neonatal Circumcision Revisited." *Canadian Medical Association Journal* 154:769–780.
Maden, C. K., et al. 1993. "History of Circumcision, Medical Conditions, and Sexual Activity and Risk of Penile Cancer." *Journal of the National Cancer Institute* 85:19–24.
Parker, S. W., A. J. Stewart, and M. N. Wren. 1983. "Circumcision and Sexually Transmitted Diseases." *Medical Journal of Australia* 2:288–290.
Taddio, A., J. Katz, A. L. Ilersich, and G. Koren. 1997. "Effect of Neonatal Circumcision on Pain Responses during Subsequent Routine Vaccination." *Lancet* 349:599–603.
Williams, N., and L. Kapila. 1993. "Complications of Surgery." *British Journal of Surgery* 80:1231–1236.
Wiswell, T. E., F. R. Smith, and J. W. Bass. 1985. "Decreased Incidence of Urinary Tract Infections in Circumcised Male Infants." *Pediatrics* 75:901–903.

Communication, Parent-Child

Infants enter the world seemingly ready to communicate with their primary caregivers. Although they are not yet able to "talk" formally, babies use gestures, gaze, facial expressions, bodily movements, and nondistress as well as distress vocalizations to communicate with others. For their part, parents generally respond to their infants' communicative overtures in highly sensitive ways—for example, by using pauses, smiles, touches, and speech in ways that are temporally and emotionally contingent on their infants' initiatives and needs. These give-and-take exchanges between parents and infants set the stage for later, more mature forms of communication, like turn taking, in which formal language is used.

Newborns might be innately equipped to enter into "protoconversations" with their parents. Protoconversations are characterized by periods of turn taking and excitement; there is a building and waning of emotional intensities between partners as mothers and infants mimic and respond to the actions and vocalizations of each other. For example, a protoconversation between a six-week-old and her mother might be characterized by the infant's body movements, gazes, head turns, hand gestures, smiles, and pouts,

Give-and-take exchanges between parents and infants set the stage for later, more mature forms of communication. (Skjold Photographs)

all of which are met with gentle touches, smiles, and vocal ministrations by the mother. The sensitive and alert mother responds to the infant's actions in complementary and contingent ways—timing her own engagements so that they are in rhythm with those of her baby. Colwyn Trevarthen has compared this synchronized display between young infants and mothers to a musical duet in which two performers seek harmony and counterpoint with one another. (Trevarthen, 1993)

These protoconversations are enabled by the infant's seemingly innate motivations to engage the world socially. For example, some researchers have suggested that soon after birth infants realize that others are differentiated from themselves. With this realization comes the ability to begin to use the actions of others as models for their own actions. As an example, newborn infants are capable of imitating

the facial expressions of their mothers, if given time and patient exposure to them. Through tongue protrusions and exaggerated facial displays, infants mirror the expression of parents. These imitations are not merely reflexive, but rather occur after periods of seemingly intense observation. This tendency suggests an early, rapidly occurring inborn tendency to communicate with others.

An important quality of parent-infant protoconversations is emotional attunement. For their part, infants have been shown to be affected by and to mirror their mothers' mood. Similarly, parents demonstrate acute sensitivity to emotional changes in their infants. Parents soon distinguish among different types of infant cries (such as hunger versus pain), and consistently share in their infants' joys, sorrows, and frustrations. Parental attunement may be especially important to the infant's developing sense of inter-subjectivity or connection with others. Specifically, parents who key into their infants' emotional and affective experiences let their infants know that they understand and share their infants' feelings.

How do parents communicate and share feelings? A mother might "match" her infant's facial expression by smiling following an infant smile, or by frowning in response to the infant's expression of distress. Mothers might also tune into their infant's gestures or bodily movements, for example, by whispering "sweet dolly" after the infant gently pats a doll's hair. Theorists have viewed the onset of sharing emotions in experiences as a developmental moment for infants that lays a foundation for language. In support of this contention, studies show that mothers who more often share in their infant's emotions during communicative exchanges when their infants are nine months of age have infants who achieve important language milestones earlier.

In some instances, communication between infants and partners breaks down if one or the other partner is unable to sustain the mutuality and reciprocity of dyadic engagements. A mother who fails to approach her infant with attention and concern, who is not tuned into her infant's emotional expressions, or whose responses are ill timed with respect to her baby's signals will cause confusion, puzzlement, withdrawal, gaze aversion, and protest in her infant. For the infant's part, withdrawal from the mother's initiatives, detachment from the mother, and failure to smile or return gazes can lead to a mother's sense of confusion, concern, and unease. Some mothers react to this withdrawal of infant attention by increasing their own levels of stimulation in an anxious attempt to regain their infants' interest, which only serves to engender further withdrawal in their infants.

Once children begin to understand and produce language, typically at the start of the second year, parents and children can increasingly use language in the service of communication. Though children may initially produce few words, they are able to understand more than they say. This is particularly true when parents' verbal communications are accompanied by facial, gestural, and intonational cues. So, for example, a father who wishes to inhibit his child from touching the stove might say "No, (pause), Hot!" while holding up a finger, using a firm tone, and shaking his head. The child's understanding of this phrase is signaled both by the words themselves, as well as by these accompanying cues. Over time, as children become more proficient in understanding and producing language, such nonverbal cues may become less central to effective interpersonal communication and understanding, though they remain integral to ongoing conversations.

For their part, as children begin to produce words and phrases they are able to communicate complete ideas quite parsimoniously—supplementing with facial expressions and gestures to signal what they want and intend. So, for example, a child who wishes to communicate "Where are my blocks?" might point to an empty shelf and say "Blocks?" and then hold out her hands and shrug in confusion. Her intent is to communicate that the blocks are not where they typically are kept. Such an exchange is common in early stages of language development when children use single words to seemingly refer to complete sentences—a phenomenon referred to as *holophrases*. The parent who is sensitive to the child's communicative intent might pick up on the child's signals by responding: "Yes, the blocks are not there anymore. Remember we put them in your room yesterday?"

As children acquire more words in their lexicon, they eventually combine those words into phrases, but may express ideas in simplified formats—for example, saying "Mommy shoes" to indicate that Mommy bought new shoes at the store that day. In response to these syntactic limitations in children's language, parents themselves adjust the complexity of their own verbalizations to the limited verbal proficiency of their children. Thus, parents use relatively direct, brief sentences when addressing young children, rather than using sentences characterized by conjunctions or embedded clauses. Consequently, parents and children find ways to effectively communicate about events and experiences, even in light of children's still ever-changing communicative competencies. As such, the musical duet metaphor used to characterize parent-child interaction spans years of child development, though the nature and quality of the duet are ever changing.

Catherine S. Tamis-LeMonda
Marc H. Bornstein

References and further reading
Bloom, Lois. 1999. "Language Acquisition in Its Developmental Context." Pp. 309–370 in vol. 2 of *Handbook of Child Psychology*, 5th ed. Edited by William Damon (series), Deanna Kuhn, and Robert S. Siegler. New York: John Wiley and Sons.
Rochat, Phillippe. 1999. *Early Social Cognition: Understanding Others in the First Months of Life*. Mahwah, NJ: Lawrence Erlbaum Associates.
Stern, Daniel N. 1985. *The Interpersonal World of the Infant*. New York: Basic Books.
Trevarthen, Colwyn. 1993. "The Self Born in Intersubjectivity." Pp. 121–173 in *The Perceived Self: Ecological and Interpersonal Sources of Self-Knowledge*. Edited by Ulric Neisser. New York: Cambridge University Press.

Communication, Parent-Teen

Parent-child relations during adolescence have been traditionally characterized as strained and turbulent. Communication is believed to be infrequent and conflict laden. Current research, however, paints a calmer portrait of parent-child communication during this period, one in which communication patterns are not vastly different from previous ones and conflict peaks in mid-adolescence, dropping off in the late teens. Although communication problems are likely to arise during adolescence, they tend not to be extreme or long-lived in healthy families. Research also indicates that mothers are seen by teenagers as more approachable and involved than fathers, and daughters are more likely than sons to disclose information about their personal lives to parents. Conversations between parents and teenagers cover a broad range, from school and friendships to sexuality, career plans, and political opinions. The depth to which these matters are discussed varies by the gender of the adolescent as well as the gender of the parent.

Parent-adolescent communication can be most clearly understood when examined in the context of the overall relationship between parents and teenagers. Changes in communication are reflective of the transformation of the relationship. During adolescence, the parent-child relationship, which originally had a unilateral authority-based structure, begins to take on more elements of reciprocity. School-aged children see parents almost exclusively as authority figures, and the goals in their relations with parents are to please and to learn from them. Beginning in early adolescence, as children are exposed to a larger number of individuals outside the home and peers take on greater social significance, parents are no longer seen as the primary sources of knowledge about society. They are viewed by teens as flawed, and their opinions are recognized as one of many potential approaches to an issue. Parents can be questioned because they are just people. At the same time that their perspectives on parents change, teenagers are developing peer relationships characterized by

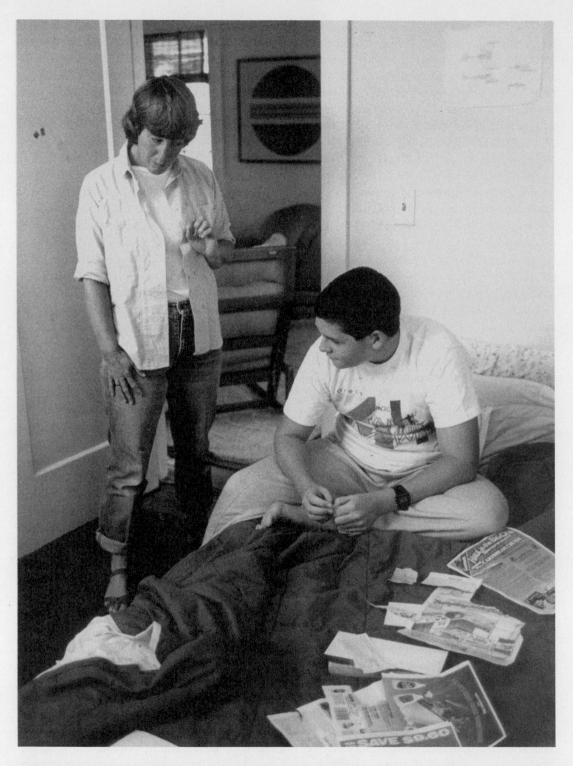

Although communication problems are likely to arise during adolescence, they tend not to be extreme or long-lived in healthy families. (Elizabeth Crews)

sharing and mutual respect, which they experience as very rewarding. The combination of developing reciprocal relationships with peers and the recognition that parenting is a role and not the whole of their parents' identities leads to a diminution of unilateral authority in the parent-child relationship.

This is a difficult change for both parents and children. There may be resistance from both sides because this new stage requires extensive renegotiation of boundaries and responsibilities. Disagreement often arises as to which areas of teenagers' lives should be under strict parental control and which of the decisions with which adolescents are faced should be decided by the teens alone. Adolescents spend the majority of their time outside of direct parental supervision. Parents who desire open communication with adolescents might feel dissatisfied with the amount of information they receive from their children. This frustration may stem in part from the fact that they cannot gain this information firsthand. Teenagers control the knowledge their parents have about their lives. That is not to say that teens typically fail to communicate to their parents about their daily activities, rather that the nature of the communication differs from that of younger children and their parents. Teenagers' relations with their parents have been described as voluntarily obedient. Adolescents are aware of their independence, while at the same time knowledgeable about what their parents expect of them. Most teenagers choose to abide by their parents' wishes in terms of both following rules of the household and acting in accordance with the moral guidelines their parents have instilled in them. Similarly, in families in which children have enjoyed a positive rapport with parents, they will continue to provide parents with information as teens.

It is well documented that adolescents communicate more frequently and on a greater number of topic areas with mothers than with fathers. Mothers tend to be more involved with their adolescent sons and daughters. Teenagers report that mothers initiate more discussions and are more accepting of their opinions than fathers are. Fathers are more likely to continue to be seen by adolescents as elusive and predominantly administrators of authority. There is often little casual conversation between fathers and teens, and fathers are not generally self-disclosing in discussions. Thus, the reciprocity that begins to develop between children and parents during adolescence is more characteristic of relationships with mothers. It is not uncommon for teens to view themselves as feeling capable of providing emotional support to their mothers in addition to being the recipients of such support. Communication with mothers serves a function beyond the simple approval teens sought at a younger age. It can serve as social validation because mothers are more likely to share their own experiences and tend to be more comfortable discussing the personal issues that arise during adolescence. Research indicates that not only do teens frequently solicit the opinions of their mothers, they are also motivated to communicate with their mothers to maintain healthy relationships with them.

There are, of course, heightened levels of parent-child conflict during adolescence. Although theorists suggest that the "storm and stress" model of adolescence is exaggerated in its depiction of the rebellious teenager, it is only natural for adolescents to clash more often with parents during this period, as both parents and children are trying to negotiate a balance between connectedness and independence. Ideally, parents remain available and involved with adolescents as they individuate and parents and teens agree on the appropriate levels of autonomy. The reality is far more complicated. Parents may have different expectations from their teens, and expectations for maturation and independence in decision making differ by area of the teen's life. It is important to note as well that in parent-teen conflict, what is not discussed or what is referred to only indirectly can be of even greater significance than what is discussed openly.

Research suggests that conflict with parents is often over daily activities as opposed to values and beliefs. Although children are exposed to a large variety of approaches to moral and social issues as they enter this exploratory period in development, teenagers are unlikely to fight with parents over their ideologies. This finding can be interpreted as meaning that teenagers are reluctant to give up the core values that they have grown up with because the values of their parents are integrated into their basic understanding of the world. Conflict over aspects of day-to-day life is therefore simply an exertion of independence, rather than an indication that teens are adopting vastly different worldviews from those of their parents. Another interpretation of this finding is that conflict over routine activities occurs because of what the daily decisions represent on a more abstract level. For example, an argument over what an adolescent daughter wears to school may be a source of conflict because her parents find her outfit to be too sexually provocative, in which case the true conflict is over the daughter's sexuality. It is easier, though, for them to argue over choice of clothes than to discuss sexuality issues. It has also been suggested that the most controversial issues are avoided because parents and teens are aware of their differences and they do not want to engage in conflict with little chance for resolution. Adolescents may be especially sensitive to recognizing such differences. Teenagers spend a large proportion of their time with peers with whom they feel comfortable sharing their ideas openly and who are frequently confronting the same issues, which can make their parents' perspectives seem distant. Research indicates that adolescents perceive their parents' views as more different from their own than they actually are. Believing that their opinions are even more distinct from those of their parents enhances the sense of establishing themselves as autonomous, at the same time limiting the potential for parent-teen communication on topics adolescents anticipate to be sources of conflict.

The openness and frequency with which topics of conversation are handled with parents differs by gender, especially when communicating with fathers. There is little difference between sons and daughters in terms of how approachable mothers are perceived in discussion of most issues, with the exception of sexuality, in which case girls are more comfortable than boys. Yet while both male and female adolescents describe their relationships with their fathers as relatively distant, daughter-father communication is clearly the poorest. Female adolescents are significantly less likely than males to talk to their fathers about such topics as career goals, their relationships with their mothers, plans for the future, views on sex, fears about life, and feelings about friends. Girls recognize the lack of reciprocity in the relationship, describing fathers as being unlikely to talk out differences and admit fears or doubts, to a greater degree than boys do. They also tend to have fewer activities, such as sports, in common with fathers than sons do, allowing them less opportunity for casual conversation. Despite such obstacles, many parents maintain positive communication with their teenagers as a continuation of healthy communication patterns laid down earlier in childhood, and adolescents reap the benefits in the form of more enhanced identity development and higher moral reasoning and self-esteem.

Carolyn E. Sartor

References and further reading
Ambert, Anne-Marie. 1997. *Parents, Children, and Adolescents: Interactive Relationships and Development in Context.* New York: Haworth Press.
Guerrero, Laura K., and Walid A. Afifi. 1995. "What Parents Don't Know: Topic Avoidance in Parent-Child Relationships." *Pp. 219–245 in Parents, Children, and Communication: Frontiers of Theory and Research,* LEA's Communication Series. Edited by Thomas J. Socha and Glen H. Stamp. Mahwah, NJ: Lawrence Erlbaum Associates.
Noller, Patricia, and Victor Callan. 1991. *The Adolescent in the Family.* New York: Routledge.
Youniss, James E. 1980. *Parents and Peers in Social Development: A Sullivan-Piaget Perspective.* Chicago: University of Chicago Press.
Youniss, James, and Jacqueline Smollar. 1985. *Adolescent Relations with Mothers, Fathers, and Friends.* Chicago: University of Chicago Press.

Contraception, History of

There's nothing new or modern about birth control. Since ancient times, women have sought to control their fertility using contraceptive methods ranging from magical charms to the latest medical advances reproductive technology can offer. These run the gamut from rudimentary barrier devices to concoctions seemingly limited only by human imagination.

Although it is commonly believed that the advent of the birth control pill in the 1960s launched the sexual revolution and women's demands for reproductive autonomy, this is not strictly true. Women have used every method possible (and some impossible methods) to control their fertility and better plan the frequency and timing of their pregnancies. Given today's injections and once-a-day pills, modern women may marvel at the primitive methods employed by their foremothers centuries ago, methods that involved more folklore and hope than actual understanding of how the body and reproduction work. However much they may marvel though, they can understand the desire for family planning.

Throughout the ages, abstinence has been the most common and most socially sanctioned form of birth control and remains one of the surest methods to this day. However, again just like today, abstinence has not always been the most practiced form of birth control. Through the ages, men and women have proven highly inventive in working out methods for preventing pregnancy.

The earliest known form of birth control was developed in Egypt between 2000 and 1000 B.C.E. and consisted of substances inserted in the vagina to block sperm. Ancient Greeks used olive oil as a spermicide, and an ancient intrauterine device, a very rudimentary predecessor to its modern descendant, was said to be found in the writings of Hippocrates. References in the Talmud describe an early barrier method—they advised using a vinegar-soaked sponge. Except for abstinence, no common device spanned countries or cultures, as birth control practitioners made use of materials and substances found in their environment. Numerous historic references to coitus interruptus exist in ancient texts, although the practice was frowned upon by the major religions: Jewish, Islamic, and Christian writers condemned wasting male seed. Because knowledge of the human body was primitive, many of these birth control methods seemingly stem from commonsense approaches. But potions relying more on divine intervention than on medical knowledge seemed equally appealing. In the sixth century C.E., Actios of Amida prescribed such preventatives as wearing cat testicles in a tube around the umbilicus while Islamic women of the thirteenth century were advised to urinate in wolf's urine.

Oral contraceptives were not an invention of the swinging sixties. They have been in use over the centuries as women mixed up concoctions designed to prevent pregnancy. The ingredients that were thought to have contraceptive qualities ranged from the benign, such as hawthorn and willow, to the lethal, including strychnine, arsenic, mercury, and lead. These latter ingredients killed many a woman in the Middle Ages.

While the Middle Ages did not prove a high point for oral contraception, the period did bring women a broader range of barrier methods. Barrier methods of birth control block the sperm from reaching the cervix, preventing it from reaching the uterus and the fallopian tubes, where fertilization takes place. In medieval times, the best-known barrier method was a process that involved covering the genitals with cedar gum or coating the uterus with alum. Early contraceptive sponges of that period consisted of a blend of elephant dung, pomegranate, and lime seeds inserted into the vagina; others involved wool tampons soaked in wine. Before the diaphragm was invented in the nineteenth century, women had to rely either on these unsophisticated barriers or on men's use of crude contraceptive devices to prevent pregnancy. A far cry from elephant dung, today's best-known barrier method is the diaphragm, a shallow, soft rubber cup that, when properly fitted, fits snugly over the cervix. It is used with a spermicide jelly and blocks the sperms' ascent into the vagina. In modern times, and until the 1960s, the diaphragm was the most popular method of birth control—studies show that at one time, as many as one-third of American couples practicing birth control used the diaphragm. By 1971, its use had diminished, in large part because of the development and distribution of the IUD and the pill.

Contraceptive devices were not for women alone. Some historians claim that a form of the modern-day condom was used by Egyptians as far back as 1000 B.C.E. Later, Casanova was said to be a regular user. What could be called the modern age of contraception—because it instituted a more scientific approach based on actual understanding of the reproductive process—began when a physician to King Charles II developed the condom in 1709. These early condoms were made of linen, as well as of animal intestines and fish bladders, and were used primarily to reduce the incidence of venereal disease. Because they were individually crafted, they were an expensive luxury, which meant that their use was confined to the upper classes. A rubber condom appeared in the 1840s, following the creation of vulcanized rubber, and in 1853 the discovery of liquid latex modernized the rubber condoms and made possible the development of cervical caps and diaphragms. Until the 1920s, condoms could be used only for prophylactic purposes, as state laws against contraception prohibited their use. Regardless, their quality continued to be poor and the rate of failure high until the federal Food and Drug Administration (FDA) brought condoms under its regulation. Today's condoms are effective in preventing the spread of sexually transmitted infections and, when combined with oral contraceptives or with a second barrier contraceptive, are highly effective as birth control devices.

Although more scientific in their approach, many of the methods used in this more modern period could be called primitive. By the 1800s, contraceptive sponges were in use as was a form of douche. The solution, a mixture of alum or zinc sulfate, was inserted into the vagina after intercourse. A quinine-based birth control suppository was manufactured in England in 1886 and was used by Englishwomen until World War II.

In 1846, the first American patent for a pessary was awarded to a curved hoop device that had a handle attached by a spring joint. It was not until 1909 that the first modern IUD became available. The device was a ring made of silkworm gut. The OTA ring and Graefenberg ring, the precursors to today's IUD, were developed in the 1930s and remained the only IUDs available until the Margulies Spiral and Lippes Loop were marketed in 1960. Drugstore and mail-order contraceptives— condoms, pessaries, and chemical douches —were in wide circulation throughout the nineteenth century. Except for the IUD, these early forms of contraception required strict compliance to instructions to be effective. Safety was an additional concern, as many of the chemicals and other materials placed into the vagina were toxic and the mechanical devices could cause injuries. Additionally, the failure rates for these forms of contraception were high, resulting in many unplanned pregnancies.

Because of these contraceptive failures through the ages, abortion has long been used to help women control family size. While not officially sanctioned by most societies, it has been allowed through the ages and was not officially outlawed until this century in such countries as the United States. It was not until the spread of agriculture and its growing importance to this nation's economic well-being that large families became desirable. At this time, both religious and secular law stepped in to promote fertility. Increasingly, laws were established to restrict contraception, although this did lead to an increase in abortion.

The history of contraception is not only a history of methods used, but of societal mores as well. Over the centuries, societal needs have affected the availability and acceptability of contraception. In ancient Greece, for example, Plato wrote, "if too many children are being born, there are measures to check propagation (and) a high birth-rate can be encouraged and stimulated by conferring marks of distinction or disgrace." (Connell, 1999) Religion, too, has had a strong role in the history of contraception, and still does to this day.

In the mid-nineteenth-century United States, some moralists began deploring "race suicide," deriding women who revolted against their "natural" role as mothers and helpmeets. This conservative reaction became extremely strong following the Civil War, leading to the adoption of the federal Comstock Law in the 1870s, an obscenity statute that criminalized contraception and abortion and prohibited the distribution and sale of information or products to promote their use. The law effectively blocked research, development, and distribution of birth control by criminalizing the mailing, importation, or transportation of "obscene, lewd, or lascivious matter." Local jurisdictions and states could enforce the law according to local standards, and it wasn't until the 1970s that the last of these laws were lifted. These laws were so far-reaching that in the United States, contraception was illegal in many states until 1965, when the Supreme Court heard *Griswold v. Connecticut*, and made birth control for married couples legal in all states.

The laws did not stop contraception and abortion, but did push them both underground. Indeed, very few American women, even during the height of the women's suffrage movement, publicly spoke out for a woman's right to control her own fertility. Some tried to get reproductive rights onto the party platforms of various political movements of the early twentieth century, but their efforts failed. Although without political and social support, women did their best to work around the restrictions imposed by the Comstock

Law. Although medical practitioners were prevented by law from providing their patients with contraceptives or information, women and their doctors could—and frequently did—turn to nineteenth-century marriage manuals for advice, should contraceptive techniques be "clinically indicated." These manuals described spermicidal douches, diaphragms (called "womb veils"), a "safe period" for sex, and condoms. Douches, containing such ingredients as Lysol, were sold to American women as feminine hygiene products up until the 1950s because the Comstock Law banned the advertising of contraceptives in general-interest magazines. During this time, menstrual clinics opened around the country to treat women for "dysmenor-rhea and irregular bleeding," all part of the effort to provide contraceptive counseling and family planning measures under the restrictions of the Comstock Law.

Birth control pioneer Margaret Sanger brought contraception and family planning to the forefront of the American social scene when she began advocating for contraception, not only for the wealthy but for the poor and immigrant women. Heeding these women's desires to know "the secret—what rich women use," she opened the first birth control clinic in New York in 1916, an action that landed her in jail under the Comstock Law. Undeterred, she pressed on. Because of her efforts, the definition of disease was broadened to include pregnancy. With this, it became legal to disseminate information about preventing disease from pregnancy.

The most significant advance, social and medical, in the history of birth control came about, very indirectly, because of International Harvester, the farm equipment manufacturer. Katharine McCormick, wife of the heir of International Harvester, met Margaret Sanger in 1917 and began lending her support in small ways. When McCormick's husband died in 1947, she was able to use her inheritance to support contraceptive research. By 1950, she and Sanger began a search for a scientist who could develop an oral contraceptive. Their quest brought them to Dr. Gregory Pincus, a reproductive biologist. His work, which began in 1951, and which involved several other scientists, culminated in the development of the birth control pill. This development of "a magic pellet," as Sanger called it, has revolutionized contraception. It was approved by the U.S. Food and Drug Administration in 1960. The pill was the first government-approved method of birth control. Within a year of its introduction, more than one million American women were "on the pill" because of its ease of use and high rate of effectiveness.

In the late 1960s, the women's liberation movement used the pill to reframe the reproduction debate, recasting it as part of an overall campaign for women's right to self-determination. The social advances this has brought to women's right to reproductive freedom have also brought many significant new medical advances, as reproductive technology has become an increasingly accepted form of scientific research. Since the introduction of the pill, science has increased women's birth control options. This has brought the introduction of modern vaginal sponges, which were first mentioned in the Talmud and were most recently reintroduced in the mid-1970s as a mushroom-shaped sponge saturated with spermicide. Progestin implants were approved by the FDA in 1991, and involve the release of small amounts of the hormone over three to five years delivered by capsules or rods that are surgically implanted under the skin on the inside of the upper or lower arm. And emergency contraceptives—a higher dose of birth control pills that, if taken within seventy-two hours of intercourse, can prevent pregnancy—have been introduced to the American market.

Sandra Jordan

References and further reading
Bullough, Vern L., and Bonnie Bullough, eds. 1994. *Human Sexuality: An Encyclopedia.* New York: Garland Publishing.
Connell, Elizabeth B. 1999. "Contraception in the Prepill Era." *Contraception* 59, no. 1:7S–10S.
Foner, Eric, and John A. Garraty, eds. 1991. *The Reader's Companion to American History.* Boston: Houghton Mifflin.
Planned Parenthood of America. 1991. *75 Years of Family Planning in America: A Chronology of Major Events.* New York: PPA.

Contraception, Methods of

Birth control of some form or another has been practiced in the world since the beginning of time. However, it was not until the contraceptive revolution of the 1960s and 1970s that many advances in contraceptive technology have been made, although none has yet been developed that is 100 percent effective and 100 percent safe. The most effective are oral contraceptives, intrauterine devices, sterilization, and abstinence, although barrier methods are gaining in popularity because they also can prevent sexually transmitted diseases.

History has seen men and women using many varied and inventive efforts to control fertility, most of which trusted to luck or relied on superstition or rudimentary knowledge of physiology. They also posed health hazards in and of themselves. In ancient China, women drank mercury to prevent pregnancy, while those in the Middle Ages consumed poisonous concoctions or used magic spells to combat fertility. Women have used plugs made of honey and crocodile dung, sipped teas brewed from dried beaver testicles, or used half a squeezed lemon as an early form of cervical cap. Victorian women endured painful douches, while American women in the 1950s used Lysol-based douches.

Contraceptive use has not been limited to women. Men, too, have long been involved in the effort to prevent pregnancy: ancient Egyptians painted their penises with pitch; Romans heated their testicles; and in parts of Australia today, men still cut openings in the base of their penises to spill semen outside of the vagina during ejaculation. Today, men and women do not have to risk their health or abstain from sex for fear of either having more children than they can afford or of endangering a woman's health with a high-risk pregnancy. And while the perfect contraceptive has yet to be developed, more than two out of eight American couples rely on modern methods of birth control to maintain the health and well-being of their families.

In the United States, once social and legal restrictions on contraceptives were lifted in the mid-1960s, science was not far behind. The modern age of contraception began in the 1960s, a decade that also saw the federal government beginning to support family planning initiatives. President Kennedy was the first U.S. president to endorse contraceptive research and to advocate the use of birth control as one of the remedies for the crisis of world population growth.

The contraceptive advances of the 1960s and 1970s launched an era of research that produced dramatic improvements in birth control methods. Spearheading many of these new developments has been private industry. As of 1999, more than 100 experimental contraceptive methods were currently being studied around the world. Developing new contraceptive products, however, requires enormous investments of time and money. It takes an estimated ten to fifteen years at a cost of approximately $20 million to $70 million to bring a new contraceptive method through research,

A teacher displays various forms of birth control to a student during sex education counseling, 1987. (Bernard Gotfryd/Archive Photos)

development, and final approval for marketing in the United States by the Food and Drug Administration (FDA). Contraceptive development is also affected by the growing risk of product liability litigation. In addition to private enterprise, the federal government has also played an important role in contraceptive research during the last thirty years, with the National Institutes of Health (NIH) holding claim to being the world's largest single source of funding for contraceptive research.

During the 1980s, cutbacks in government funding began discouraging researchers from entering the field of contraceptive research. Because of this slowdown, Americans have seen the number of available contraceptive options fall behind those that are available in other countries. By the time Norplant®, a progestin implant, was approved by the FDA in 1990, it had already been in use in twenty-two countries for nearly a decade. Depo-Provera®, which is medroxyprogesterone given in periodic injections to block menstruation, was not approved for use in the United States until 1992, but had already been used by more than 30 million women worldwide since 1969.

The need for contraceptive methods first came about because of individuals' desires to curb their fertility. In modern times, it is necessary for this purpose, as well as to provide protection against sexually transmitted diseases.

What follows is an overview of contraceptive methods currently available to Americans, followed by a brief glance at some of the methods that are being researched.

Hormonal Methods
The birth control pill, which was introduced in the 1960s, is one of the most effective methods of reversible contraception ever developed and is the most widely used of the hormonal contraceptives. The most common type of pill contains synthetic estrogen and progestin, similar to that produced by a woman's body, which alters a woman's hormonal balance so that ovulation does not occur.

Norplant®, a series of five matchstick-sized capsules that are implanted in the upper arm, release small amounts of progestin into the bloodstream and are effective for five to six years. A second generation product, Norplant II®, requiring only two implants, is being developed.

Depo-Provera® is delivered by a single injection of progestin that is usually effective for three months.

Intrauterine Devices
Intrauterine devices (IUDs) are coiled, looped, or T-shaped plastic or copper devices inserted into the uterus, where they prevent pregnancy by causing the uterine lining to reject the implantation of the fertilized egg. Older IUDs posed health risks, causing pelvic inflammatory disease, sterility, and other complications, leading to a significant decline in their use in this country. New IUDs on the market no longer pose health problems to women.

Emergency Contraception
Also called postcoital contraception, emergency contraception can prevent pregnancy after unprotected intercourse. It is provided in two ways: using increased dosages of hormonal contraceptive pills within seventy-two hours of unprotected intercourse, or insertion of a copper IUD (intrauterine device) within five days.

Barrier Methods
Condoms and other barrier methods have grown in popularity, particularly with the growing threat of infection with the human immunodeficiency virus (HIV) that causes AIDS. A more recent entry into the market, cervical caps, are essentially minidiaphragms. These devices aren't really so new—they were first manufactured from hard rubber in the early 1900s. Today's caps use flexible plastic and come in a variety of sizes.

Diaphragms and cervical caps are soft rubber barriers that cover the cervix and must be used with a spermicide cream or jelly. The diaphragm is a dome-shaped cup with a flexible rim that fits over the cervix. The smaller cervical cap is thimble shaped and fits snugly onto the cervix.

Female condoms are inserted deep into the vagina to keep sperm from joining the egg. They must be used with contraceptive foam, cream, jelly, film, or a suppository.

Spermicides are available in a variety of contraceptive preparations, including foams, creams, jellies, film, and suppositories. Their chemicals immobilize sperm.

Natural Methods
Continuous abstinence, because it involves no sex, will keep the sperm from joining the egg.

Withdrawal involves interruption of coitus to keep sperm from joining the egg.

Periodic abstinence involves learning how to chart the menstrual cycle to predict "unsafe" days when individuals should abstain from intercourse (periodic abstinence) or use condoms, diaphragms, cervical caps, or spermicide during the "unsafe" days.

Voluntary Sterilization
Tubal sterilization is a surgical operation that closes off the fallopian tubes, where eggs are fertilized by sperm. When the

tubes are closed, sperm cannot reach the egg, and pregnancy cannot happen.

Vasectomy is a simple operation that makes men sterile by keeping sperm out of the seminal fluids that form semen. After such surgery, the sperm are absorbed by the body instead of being ejaculated.

New Developments

After decades of few new choices in contraceptives, several new forms of birth control became available in the final decade of the twentieth century. Most of the contraceptive products for women that are expected to be available early in the twenty-first century are refinements of similar products that are already on the market.

Among these are barrier devices made of soft silicone that cover the cervix and are designed to last for at least three years.

A new vaginal sponge composed of spermicides and microbicides to protect against sexually transmitted diseases is under development and was expected to come to the U.S. market sometime in 2000.

A new birth control pill will employ a synthetic version of melatonin, a hormone found naturally in the body, instead of estrogen. Transdermal patches will gradually release the hormone into the body. The method works like the pill, but women need only remember to use it twice a month, not every day.

Oral or injectable vaccines to immunize women against pregnancy are being developed, with the possibility that they will use antibodies that attack eggs or sperm. Another vaccine would stimulate the immune system to create antibodies to a crucial type of protein molecule found on the head of sperm.

In addition, a single capsule that contains a more potent progestin that is designed to work for two or three years is in development.

Biodegradable implants containing progestin are implanted under the skin of the arm or hip and release the hormone gradually into the body for twelve to eighteen months.

A newly designed IUD shaped like a "T" contains a progestin that is released steadily into the uterus for up to seven years. Two "frameless" IUDs are being used in European clinical trials that it is hoped will cause less cramping because there is no rigid frame to press against the uterus.

Computerized fertility monitors are available that predict "safe" days for sexual intercourse by measuring daily changes in body temperature and cervical mucus. Another method monitors hormonal levels in urine. Other methods measure basal body temperature to determine fertility or hormones secreted in the saliva.

One of the methods of reversible contraception being developed may be appropriate for both women and men. A new group of drugs, gonadotropin-releasing hormone (GnRH) agonists, can prevent the release of follicle stimulating hormone (FSH) and luteinizing hormone (LH), which are crucial to the maturing of an egg in the ovaries, from the pituitary gland and temporarily suppress fertility in women.

And finally, oral contraception formulas for men are under development that could reduce sperm counts to levels that are unlikely to cause pregnancy. In Italy, a contraceptive pill containing synthetic hormones is being used by men in a clinical study. The men also receive testosterone injections to boost the effectiveness of the pill.

Sandra Jordan

See also Contraception, History of

References and further reading
Bullough, Vern L., and Bonnie Bullough, eds. 1994. *Human Sexuality: An Encyclopedia.* New York: Garland Publishing.

Connell, Elizabeth B. 1999. "Contraception in the Prepill Era." *Contraception* 59, no. 1:7S–10S.

Foner, Eric, and John A. Garraty, eds. 1991. *The Reader's Companion to American History.* Boston: Houghton Mifflin.

Harrison, Polly F., and Allan Rosenfield, eds. 1996. *Contraceptive Research and Development: Looking to the Future.* Washington, DC. Committee on Contraceptive Research and Development, Institute of Medicine, the National Academy Press.

Phillips, Susan P. 1999. "Contraceptive Technologies." Pp. 92–98 in *Encyclopedia of Reproductive Technologies.* Edited by Annette Burfoot. Boulder, CO, and Oxford, UK: Westview Press.

The Planned Parenthood Women's Health Encyclopedia. 1996. New York: Crown Trade Paperbacks.

Coparenting

The term *coparenting* refers to the coordinated parenting activities of two or more adults raising a child together. The concept of coparenting relationships within families (sometimes also referred to as the parental alliance) can be traced to the writings of a number of family therapists, including Virginia Satir, Theodore Lidz, and, most notably, Salvador Minuchin. According to structural family theory, in two-parent families the two adult partners assume mutual roles as architects and heads of the family. In effectively functioning partnerships, these individuals work collaboratively to provide for, care for, nurture, and socialize their offspring. In less effectively functioning partnerships, one of the adult partners may neglect his or her parenting role, or, alternatively, the two adults may work at cross-purposes. In the latter circumstance, the family environment is earmarked by a lack of consistency and coordination in the rules, expectations, and socialization climates the two adults provide for their children.

There are many potential eventualities of such family situations, which are frequently also characterized by overt or covert antagonism between the parenting partners. In some cases, according to Minuchin, one outcome can be the formation of maladaptive cross-generational power alliances between one of the two parents and one or more of the children, such that the other coparenting partner loses his or her share of the authority as family head. According to both structural family theory and to recent empirical research studies with both clinical and nonclinical populations, poorly coordinated coparenting partnerships within families place children at developmental risk not only for difficulties with shyness, anxiety, and social withdrawal, but also in many cases—especially among boys—for difficulties with comportment, aggression management, and impulse control.

The first empirical research studies to establish the importance of coparenting coordination in studies of child development were carried out with samples of divorced families. These investigations, which focused on the continuing coparental relationship in the postdivorce family environment, indicated that children from families in which this relationship was characterized by antagonism between the adults and by ill-coordinated sets of rules for the children across the two households demonstrated more problems with adjustment than did children whose parents shielded them from ongoing animosity and worked together to provide consistent sets of ground rules across the two households. In subsequent research with intact, two-parent families, the importance of coparenting cooperation has also been borne out. Children whose parents support one another's child-related interventions and avoid the temptation to oppose or undermine such interventions, speak affirmatively about the coparenting partner, and refrain from derogating the partner during conversations with the child are less likely to exhibit problems with adaptation than are children who come from families in which the coparenting relationship is antagonistic and contentious.

It is important to note that although the tangible division of labor in sharing child-related duties, such as feeding, diapering, chauffeuring, and disciplining children, has been identified as one important feature of coparenting relationships in many Western cultures, coparenting relationships can and do also exist in families and cultures in which just one parent shoulders virtually all of the child-related responsibilities. In many world cultures, the day-to-day ministrations to infants and young children are all performed by the child's mother and other (usually female) relatives from either the woman's extended family or from her husband's family. Far less is known about coparenting dynamics in these families. Preliminary findings from research on mother-grandmother coparenting partnerships among African American families in rural Georgia have paralleled those emanating from studies involving mother-father coparenting partnerships in both Anglo-American and African American families, indicating the benefits that a supportive and collaborative interadult relationship appear to have for promoting children's self-regulation. However, since very few studies of coparenting coordination have been carried out in cultures in which the child's family environment is constituted of a mother, father, and several cocaregiving relatives, the operation and meaning of coparenting dynamics in these families remain to be established. It seems likely that certain coparenting dynamics, such as pervasive contentiousness and oppositionality among the coparenting partners, may have disruptive effects for children regardless of the cultural context in which they occur, while other indicators of the coparental relationship, such as the relative balance of involvement with the child by the two parents, may have meaning

only within particular cultural contexts. For example, in studies of two-parent families in North America, research has indicated that minimal affectional contact by one of the two parents with the children is frequently a sign of distress in the coparental partnership. This same index may be less pertinent in cultures where fathers play less of an active role in the daily lives of their children. In such cultures, fathers' sensibilities concerning child rearing may or may not play an important role in child socialization.

Most of what is currently known about the operation of coparenting dynamics within families derives from either studies examining parents' self-reporting of coparenting-related activities or observational studies of mother-father-child family interaction.

Several different approaches to assessing the quality of the coparental relationship have been followed in studies employing self-reporting instruments. These studies have linked (1) greater discrepancies in parents' child-rearing ideologies; (2) more frequent weekly child-related conflicts; (3) lower perceived support from the coparenting partner in child-related affairs; and (4) propensities to speak disparagingly about the coparenting partner to the child to more adverse child outcomes, both concurrently and prospectively. Not surprisingly, within intact two-parent families these and other indicators of strained coparental relationships have been reliably linked to strains in the marriage. At the same time, it seems clear that problems with the coparenting relationship cannot simply be equated with marital discontent. Studies indicate that information concerning the extent of coparenting conflict within families enhances researchers' ability to predict which children will show problems with adjustment, when compared with information concerning the marriage alone. Parents' self-reports of their own coparenting conduct have also been linked to several features of the family group process, as observed during laboratory assessments.

By and large, most observational studies of coparenting dynamics have been conducted within laboratory settings. In such studies, families (the two coparenting partners, plus any children) take part in a series of tasks selected by researchers to maximize the likelihood of both parent-child and interadult involvement, coordination, and communication. These tasks vary by the children's ages and stage of development, and have involved such activities as face-to-face and object play for families of infants; challenging and cooperative educational, physical, and fantasy games, and cleanup tasks for families of toddlers and preschoolers; and family games and problem-solving discussions for families of latency-aged and adolescent children. Typically, the coparenting partners are briefed on what the activities will be, but are given no additional directions concerning how to structure the activities or appropriate rules of conduct or deportment for family members during the tasks. Researchers interested in interfamily differences later observe videotaped records of the family sessions and concentrate on such factors as levels of competitiveness, verbal sparring, cooperation, and warmth between the coparenting partners; whether the session contoured to the interests and initiatives of the children or the adults; whether there were roughly equal levels of engagement and participation by the two parents or, conversely, noteworthy disparities in parental involvement; overall levels of positive and negative emotions expressed within the family group; and quality of communication among the various family members. Converging findings suggest that coparenting exchanges that are poorly coordinated, negative in tone, and insensitive to child initiatives;

devoid of cooperation or positive affect; or severely skewed (with one parent showing excessive levels of involvement with the child and/or the other showing a paucity of involvement) are more common among married couples experiencing marital distress. Moreover, children from families demonstrating these disturbed coparenting dynamics are more likely to be rated on a variety of measures accessing behavioral and social adaptation as less well adjusted compared with children from families where coparental dynamics are coordinated, supportive, and balanced in terms of parental involvement.

Though there have been few naturalistic studies carried out in family homes, the data that do exist corroborate findings from laboratory-based studies. They indicate that coparenting partners who support one another's parenting interventions less frequently and undermine one another's interventions more frequently than is the case in other families are more likely than comparison couples to report distress in the marriage. Moreover, in families where there is more antagonistic behavior between coparenting partners, children show more disinhibition in their behavior over time than do children from families where the coparenting partners show low levels of hostile-competitive behavior. Home studies have also indicated a fair degree of stability in the quality of coparenting behavior, at least over short (six-month) time intervals.

Gender differences have occasionally been reported in studies linking coparenting to child adjustment, although there have not really been any robust, strongly replicable effects demonstrated in research to date. When gender differences are found, they tend to suggest that antagonistic coparenting has a particularly disruptive effect for young boys. Depending upon the study and age of the children involved, both externalizing- and internalizing-spectrum behavior problems have been reported as correlates of hostile-competitive coparenting in families of boys. It is important to emphasize, however, that other studies do not find gender differences, revealing detrimental effects for both male and female children. It is also important to note that antagonistic coparenting dynamics are not the only ones to show ties to child adjustment. Some studies have linked low levels of positive affect and comraderie in the family and low levels of mutuality in coparenting (i.e., imbalances in levels of parental involvement with the child) to child outcomes. There have been some indications that girls with parents experiencing marital distress are at greater risk for exposure to a coparenting dynamic marked by discrepant levels of parental involvement than boys with maritally distressed parents, and that these children may be more likely than girls from nondistressed homes to be rated as anxious by parents and teachers as they get older.

Evidence also suggests that the "spin" that children put on their family circumstances may play an important intermediary role in determining which children will and will not show the effects of coparenting difficulties. Preliminary studies suggest that this may be especially true for boys. Preschool boys who come from families where the coparenting partners demonstrate low levels of support and mutuality in family interaction are more likely than their peers to show difficulties in social interaction on the preschool playground—but this effect is mediated by how the boys make sense of family circumstances. It is those boys who show signs of discomfort when talking about families and/or who project aggression into their stories about families who exhibit the greatest peer problems. Boys from families whose coparenting interactions impress researchers as low in support, but whose views of the family tend to be positive nevertheless, tend to fare better during peer interactions.

Because empirical studies of coparenting dynamics within coresidential families only began in the mid- to late 1990s, there will undoubtedly be many new findings and perhaps also some refinements to the existing knowledge base in the years ahead. At present, however, it seems clear that coparenting dynamics are a unique family phenomenon and socialization force in young children's lives. While the quality of coparenting is related to both marital functioning and, to a lesser extent, to the quality of parenting that adults display when they are alone with their children (i.e., parenting outside the presence of their partners), the family's coparenting dynamic also helps to account for variability in child adaptation beyond that explained by marital or parenting information. To date, little is known about coparenting coordination, collaboration, and support in families beyond the nuclear, two-parent family unit, but research on diverse family systems is under way in the early twenty-first century in many parts of the world and can be expected to augment that which has been learned about mother-father-child dynamics in North American samples. Although very little information about how adults coparent multiple children in the same family is currently available, new studies are beginning to address this question and can be expected to provide some preliminary answers in the years ahead.

James P. McHale
Allison Lauretti
Jean Talbot
Regina Kuersten-Hogan

References and further reading
McHale, James, and Philip Cowan, eds. 1996. "Understanding How Family-Level Dynamics Affect Children's Development: Studies of Two-Parent Families." *New*

Directions for Child Development 74. San Francisco: Jossey-Bass.

McHale, James, Allison Lauretti, Jean Talbot, and Chris Pouquette. Forthcoming. "Coparenting and Family Group Dynamics." In *Retrospect and Prospect in the Psychological Study of Families.* Edited by James McHale and Wendy Grolnick. Mahwah, NJ: Lawrence Erlbaum Associates.

Corporal Punishment

Corporal punishment is defined as any disciplinary procedure designed to cause physical pain as a penalty for an offense. Methods of corporal punishment include slapping, punching, kicking, spanking, shaking, forcing uncomfortable body positions for long periods of time, and the use of extended "time-outs." In the home, spanking the buttocks with an open hand is the most frequently administered form of corporal punishment. Other methods of corporal punishment used by parents (in order of frequency) include slapping, hair and ear pulling, whipping, arm twisting, shaking, and kicking.

The definition of corporal punishment does not include the use of force to protect oneself, property, or others from injury. Likewise, the use of restraint procedures to protect a child from self-injury is not defined as corporal punishment.

Corporal punishment is a deeply rooted American tradition based upon religious ideology. The use of corporal punishment can be traced back to the Old Testament. In Proverbs (13:24), Solomon states, "he that spareth the rod hateth his son, he that loveth him, chasteneth him." Historically Judeo-Christian cultures believed that deviant behavior was the result of a youngster being possessed by an evil spirit. Corporal punishment was considered by many as an attempt to confront Satan by "beating the devil" out of children. This thought continues to be an important part of Christian fundamentalist or literalist belief.

One survey suggests 60 percent of American parents administer spankings as their primary form of discipline. (Straus, 1994) Ninety percent of parents have spanked their child at least once. One out of every five children is hit as a toddler. Often the spankings don't stop until the young adult leaves home.

Research has shown that the best predictor of a parent hitting his or her child is personal history. Parents that were spanked as children are likely to endorse and use corporal punishment. Likewise, parents that were either rarely or never hit as children usually do not spank their children. However, some parents who were spanked do not continue the cycle. These individuals tend to be educated at or above the master's level, hold liberal political and religious views, have a higher socioeconomic status, and live in suburbia.

Advocates of corporal punishment commonly respond to critics with "I was hit and I turned out OK." Furthermore, they say that children who are not spanked are less disciplined and exhibit worse behavior than children who are spanked. There is, however, no research supporting this statement. In fact, research consistently indicates that hitting children is a bad idea.

Spanking is nothing more than a short-term solution to improve behavior problems. While it may stop unwanted behaviors for a brief period of time, the long-term effects can be counterproductive and detrimental. The effects of corporal punishment vary from person to person and can range from feelings of hostility toward the parent to posttraumatic stress disorder. As spanking becomes more frequent and severe, the effects become increasingly negative. Frequent and severe spankings are associated with higher instances of delinquency, depression, and low self-esteem. These children grow up to believe that being spanked was good for them and that the only way for a parent to maintain discipline is through fear.

Corporal punishment may lead to inferior development of moral reasoning. Children who are physically punished may believe that using violence or force on another person to resolve conflict is acceptable. Studies have shown that children who are spanked are more likely to act aggressively toward peers. Even children who experienced "normal" spankings are almost three times as likely to assault a sibling as compared to children who are not physically punished.

Children who are spanked are more likely to approve of corporal punishment when they become adults. Corporal punishment can perpetuate the cycle of child abuse by teaching that it is justifiable to hit someone smaller and weaker when angry. Evidence strongly suggests that witnessing and/or experiencing corporal punishment results in the modeling of aggression.

If positive discipline methods are enforced, eliminating the use of corporal punishment does not increase misbehavior. However, the systematic use of positive alternatives and the prevention of misbehavior have been shown to significantly decrease the amount of misbehavior. Parents often fail to realize how much their approval motivates their children. Frequent encouragement, praise, and the judicious use of punishments such as "time-out" and withdrawal of privileges are the best formulas for effective parenting.

Some maintain that corporal punishment is necessary when children, especially toddlers, are in dangerous situations. Responsible parenting based on understanding developmental stages, childproofing homes, and teaching children to avoid danger via positive techniques is more effective.

To date, eight nations have banned the use of corporal punishment. Norway, Sweden, Denmark, Finland, Austria, Cyprus, Israel and Italy—either by legislation or court decree—prohibit parents from spanking and using other means of corporal punishment on their children. Currently, no state in the United States forbids a parent from spanking his or her child. Over half of the states now prohibit school officials from using corporal punishment on schoolchildren, and thirty-seven states prohibit foster parents from using corporal punishment. However, the struggle to ban the use of corporal punishment in American schools provides a good illustration of what may come if legislators attempt to ban the use of corporal punishment in the home. Before corporal punishment in the home will be banned, advocates will probably have to educate an entire generation of future parents about the adverse effects of physical punishment.

Irwin A. Hyman
Shannon Taich

See also Time-Out

References and further reading
Greven, Phillip. 1991. *Spare the Child: The Religious Roots of Punishment and the Psychological Impact of Physical Abuse.* New York: Knopf.
Hyman, Irwin A. 1997. *The Case against Spanking: How to Discipline Your Child without Hitting.* San Francisco: Jossey-Bass.
Straus, Murray A. 1994. *Beating the Devil Out of Them: Corporal Punishment in American Families.* San Francisco: New Lexington Press.

Cultural Influences on Parenting

Among other things, parenting entails preparing children for the physical, economic, and psychosocial situations that are characteristic of the culture in which they are to survive and thrive. Cross-cultural comparisons reveal that virtually all aspects of parenting—beliefs as well as behaviors—are shaped by culture. The origins of variation in maternal and paternal caregiving are extremely complex, but culture is among the factors of paramount importance. Cultural similarities and differences are always impressive, whether observed among different cultural groups in one society or among different cultures around the world, and cultural similarities and differences in parenting are no exception.

Culture influences parenting and child development in many basic ways, such as who normatively takes responsibility for parenting children, how parents conceive of childhood, and which paths parents follow in caring for children. In some cultures, children are reared in extended families in which care is provided by many individuals; in other cultures, parents and children are isolated from wider social contexts. Cultural differences can influence parental expectations of children as much or more than other factors, such as parents' experiences observing their own children, comparing them to other children, or receiving advice from friends and experts.

We can take the United States and Japan, two contrasting modern societies, to illustrate the case for cultural influences on parenting. These two countries maintain reasonably similar and high standards of living and both are child centered, but the two differ culturally in terms of history, beliefs, and child-rearing goals. Japanese mothers expect early mastery of emotional maturity, self-control, and social courtesy in their children; North American mothers promote autonomy and organize social interactions with children so as to foster physical and verbal assertiveness and independence in theirs. Japanese mothers consolidate and strengthen closeness and dependency within the dyad, and they are responsive to their children's social orientation; North American mothers respond more to their children's orienting outward from the dyad to the surrounding environment.

Japanese mothers foster children's pretend play in ways that encourage incorporation of a partner; North American mothers encourage exploratory and functional play. For North American mothers, toys used during play are frequently the topic or object of communication; for Japanese mothers, the play setting serves to mediate dyadic communication and interaction.

Parents in different cultures clearly behave in similar ways in some domains of parenting, but differently in others. A common core of primary family experience could underwrite shared kinds of parenting: certain beliefs and behaviors in parenting could recur across cultures due to factors indigenous to children and their biology. For example, helplessness or "babyish" characteristics, which are universal in infants, may elicit common patterns of caregiving. Alternatively, cross-culturally common characteristics of parenting could be instinctual to a parenting "stage" in the human life cycle: thus, it might be in the nature of being a parent to optimize the development and probability of success of one's offspring, possibly to ensure the success of one's own genes. A third set of explanations for cultural universals points to the environment: shared economic or ecological factors could shape parents to think and act in similar ways. The late twentieth century has witnessed changes in urbanization, modernization, media homogeneity, and Westernization that have combined to break down traditional cultural patterns.

Other attitudes and actions of parents are culturally specific. It could be that certain unique biological characteristics of children, such as constitutionally based features of temperament, promote parental attitudes and activities that typify different cultures. Adults in different cultures could parent differently because of their own differing biological characteristics (threshold sensitivity to child signals, loquaciousness). It could also be that ecological or economic conditions specific to a given cultural setting promote specific parental attitudes and actions, ones differentially geared to optimize adjustment and adaptation in offspring to the circumstances of the local situation.

In the end, parents in different cultures presumably wish to promote the development of similar general competencies in their young. Some do so in manifestly similar ways; others do so in different ways, where of course culture-specific patterns of child rearing are adapted to the specific society's settings and needs. Culture plays a large role in helping to shape parenting and the ecology of childhood. The child-rearing practices of one's own culture may seem "natural," but in actuality they may be unique in comparison with others. Moreover, few nations in the world are characterized by cultural homogeneity; therefore, cultural differences within a country color child-rearing practices just as surely as do larger cultural differences across countries. Cultural ideology makes for subtle, but meaningful, patterns of parent beliefs and behaviors.

Marc H. Bornstein

References and further reading
Bornstein, Marc H., ed. 1991. *Cultural Approaches to Parenting.* Hillsdale, NJ: Lawrence Erlbaum Associates.
LeVine, Robert A., Pamela M. Miller, and Mary M. West, eds. 1988. Parental *Behavior in Diverse Societies.* San Francisco: Jossey-Bass.
Munroe, Ruth H., Robert L. Munroe, and Beatrice Whiting, eds. 1981. *Handbook of Cross-Cultural Human Development.* New York: Garland STPM Press.
Stevenson, Harold W., Hiroshi Azuma, and Kenji Hakuta, eds. 1986. *Child Development and Education in Japan.* New York: W. H. Freeman.
Whiting, Beatrice. 1988. *Children of Different Worlds: The Formation of Social Behavior.* Cambridge, MA: Harvard University Press.

Custody Conflicts

Child custody conflicts in the court system involve determining what is best for children when their parents both seek custody through the court system. When parents go to court over custody of their children, the rule that drives the legal machinery is this: what custody arrangement would best serve their children's interests? While symbolically appealing, the implementation of this legal mandate creates unique challenges for parents and courts. One of the problems is the difficulty of applying this rule in a society that lacks any real consensus about what is best for children.

Rules that have guided courts throughout the history of judicial custody determinations include the paternal preference rule, which fundamentally granted children automatically to fathers, and the maternal preference rule, which presumed children of "tender years" belonged with their mothers. Historians trace the application of the best-interest-of-the-child standard in contemporary court proceedings from approximately 1960, depending on when various states implemented the rule. The best-interest standard has been implemented as a means to focus decision making on the children, rather than on parental rights.

A high divorce rate has contributed to an increase in legal conflicts over child custody. Divorce in the United States has increased steadily over the past century to a current rate of over one million divorces per year (Sweezy and Tiefenthaler, 1996). While custody conflicts are normally associated with divorce proceedings, there are many other kinds of situations that may require court intervention. For example, when one parent relocates to another state following a divorce, he or she may have to go to court to modify custody and/or visitation arrangements. A growing number of grandparents have filed for visitation rights, directing attention to the problems that arise when family relationships are dramatically altered. Parents who have never been married to one another often seek legal custody orders in order to establish their rights.

For legal purposes, the term *child custody* is divided among different categories according to parental rights and responsibilities. Courts distinguish between the custodial parent and noncustodial parent. These distinctions are important because the child's residence and school district remain with the custodial parent. The noncustodial parent generally pays child support and receives visitation on a weekly schedule. Physical custody refers to the child's residence, while legal custody means parents make joint decisions about medical, educational, and religious matters. Joint custody grants both parents the right to make such decisions together or "jointly." Parents may also share physical custody of their children by dividing the child's time equally between each parent. When both parents are willing to work together for their children's interests, these shared arrangements can benefit both parents and children by maintaining relationships. Research studies suggest that children who stay in close contact with both parents following divorce or separation adjust better than children who do not maintain contact with both parents.

One of the issues surrounding child custody conflicts in court is whether mental health professions should have a more prominent role in the decision-making process. This is due to the fact that judges often do not feel competent to make the necessary determinations. Truly determining what is in the best interest of each child in a custody dispute often requires time and resources that are in short supply for the legal system. In order to resolve these cases, courts have attempted to incorporate experts from both law and social science.

The best-interest-of-the-child standard has been the law guiding decisions for American courts since the 1970s. Social science, in particular psychology, has provided certain guidelines for this rule. *Best interest* is closely associated with the concept of psychological parenthood. This term arises from publications by the influential authors Goldstein, Freud, and Solnit. They have written three books on the best interest of the child, on which courts have relied in custody conflicts. These authors, among others, urged courts to focus on the psychological relationship between the parent and child. This theory essentially states that children belong with the parent who fulfills the child's psychological needs for a parent, as well as the child's physical needs, through interaction on a day-to-day basis.

In order to apply meaning to the term *best interest* and to resolve these disputes, courts both encourage parents to reach their own agreement and rely on a myriad of experts in law, psychology, and social services. Courts turn to law guardians, who are generally lawyers trained in child advocacy, to investigate children's homes and make recommendations to the judge concerning custody. The concerns for children and their rights in a divorce have helped to shape an increasing role for an independent lawyer for children. Social service agencies, along with private therapists, may be consulted to make recommendations about what is best for the children.

In addition, psychologists who specialize in custody conflicts often conduct custody evaluations. These evaluations are meant to evaluate the family, and to pay particular attention to relationships between parents and children. Once completed, a psychological report can provide valuable information to courts struggling to do what is best for the children who are subjects of the dispute. Although custody trials are rare, a psychologist may be asked to testify about his or her report if the case does reach the trial stage. Typically, parents reach their own accord in the course of the legal proceeding.

Resolving the case through negotiation is the most common way in which custody cases reach a conclusion. Many courts refer parents to mediation experts or invite alternative dispute resolution experts into the courthouse for the purpose of resolving custody conflicts. Experts believe that parents who can reach their own accord best serve their children's interests, both in the short and long term of the relationship. Going to court is a stressful event for parents and children, and negotiating an agreement can reduce the acrimonious nature of the procedure. Parents who can communicate with one another while under the pressure of a legal proceeding stand a better chance of continuing to communicate over issues involving their children and their interests.

Elizabeth Callaghan

References and further reading
Black, James C., and Donald J. Cantor. 1989. *Child Custody*. New York: Columbia University Press.
Coontz, Stephanie. 1997. *The Way We Really Are: Coming to Terms with America's Changing Families*. New York: Basic Books.
Goldstein, Joseph, Anna Freud, and Albert Solnit. 1973. *Beyond the Best Interest of the Child*. New York: Free Press.
———. 1979. *Before the Best Interest of the Child*. New York: Free Press.
———. 1986. *In the Best Interest of the Child*. New York: Free Press.
Guggenheim, Martin. 1998. "Reconsidering the Need for Counsel for Children in Custody, Visitation and Child Protection Proceedings." *Loyola University of Chicago Law Journal* 29, no. 2:299–352.
Maccoby, E., and Robert H. Mnookin. 1992. *Dividing the Child: Social and Legal Dilemmas of Custody*. Cambridge, MA: Harvard University Press.
Mason, Mary A. 1994. *From Father's Property to Children's Rights: The History of Child Custody in the United States*. New York: Columbia University Press.
Riessman, Katherine. 1990. *Divorce Talk: Women and Men Make Sense of Personal Relationships*. New Brunswick, NJ: Rutgers University Press.
Sweezy, Kate, and Jill Tiefenthaler. 1996. "Do State-Level Variables Affect Divorce Rates?" *Review of Social Economy* 54 no. 1.

D

Deafness and Parenting

Hearing impairments in parents and children range from mild to profound, but all can exert a substantial impact on parenting and family interactions. Three types of families are affected by deafness: deaf parents with deaf children, deaf parents with hearing children, and hearing parents with deaf children. In America, deaf parents and deaf children often subscribe to the same deaf culture; by contrast, in those families where hearing status differs between parents and children, parent-child dyads can be plunged into very different cultures. A defining feature of the deaf culture is its predominant use of American Sign Language (ASL). About 10 percent of all deaf children in the United States grow up in a bicultural/bilingual environment in which one parent speaks ASL and one parent speaks English.

Approximately 1 percent of live births in the United States result in a child with hearing impairment. Socioeconomic status (SES) plays a pervasive role in parenting and deafness. Parents of deaf children tend to be overrepresented in lower SES groups. In low-SES groups 49 percent of deaf children become deaf after birth, whereas in high-SES groups only 17 percent lose their hearing after birth. Such class differences could reflect different access to health care services and knowledge of child development. High-SES families tend to keep their deaf children at home, and their children attend local schools and are assisted by an interpreter or placed in special education classes. Low-SES deaf children are more likely to find themselves in state-funded residential schools and spend long periods of time away from their parents.

Cultural aspects of hearing loss and deafness play a large role in parenting. Identification with the deaf community and culture has more to do with how a person with hearing impairment feels than with the actual degree of hearing loss. Individuals who identify themselves as members of the deaf culture are more likely to use ASL as their main mode of communication than individuals who do not so self-identify; other deaf individuals tend to lip-read or use cued speech.

Relationships between parents and children vary across different hearing status groups. Hearing mothers have often been observed to be intrusive, tense, and directing in communications with their deaf children. Reciprocally, deaf children of hearing parents often have little exposure to first-language ASL use or to the deaf culture at large. Deaf mothers tend to engage in more touching of infants and young children than hearing mothers regardless of the hearing status of their children. Hearing mothers of deaf children also tend to report more stress and less satisfaction in parenting than do parents who share the same hearing status as their children. Social support is an important factor in the stress and adjustment of deaf families. Hearing parents benefit from extra nonfamilial support—extended family, friends, clergy, and therapists—for themselves and their deaf children.

Sara J. Salkind
Marc H. Bornstein

References and further reading
Marschark, Mark. 1993. *Psychological Development of Deaf Children.* New York: Oxford University Press.

Parasnis, Irene. 1996. *Cultural and Language Diversity and the Deaf Experience.* New York: Cambridge University Press.

Schlesinger, H. S., and Kathryn P. Meadow. 1972. *Sound and Sign.* Berkeley: University of California Press.

Volterra, Virginia, and Carol J. Erting, eds. 1994. *From Gesture to Language in Hearing and Deaf Children.* Washington, DC: Gallaudet University Press.

Death of a Child

The death of a child impacts parents on numerous levels, causing complex and unique grief responses, redefining their roles as parents, and adding stress to the marriage. While some theorists have outlined the prototypical stages of grief, experts in the field agree that there are a variety of common, healthy responses to the loss of a child. In addition to the anticipated feelings of distress and guilt after such a painful loss, many bereaved parents have reported personal growth as well. Parents who have experienced the death of a child consistently state, however, that there is no return to normal life because the loss marks a permanent change in their lives.

In order to understand why the loss of a child is qualitatively different than the loss of other loved ones, it is necessary to look at the unique aspects of parent-child relationships and to examine what it means to be a parent. Children have symbolic meaning to their parents. To some parents, their children are extensions of themselves: an opportunity to reexperience childhood vicariously, a chance to make right the mistakes of their youth, to live out their childhood dreams. A child may also give meaning to parents' lives, meet parental needs for love, or serve as proof to parents that they are competent, mature adults. Many adults define themselves through their parental role. The parenting role is extraordinarily demanding, with expectations and responsibilities well beyond those of any other relationship. Parenting requires constant empathy and awareness of the children's needs. The death of a child leaves many parents feeling as though they have failed in their parental duties. Parents' experiences of the death of a child are often described through an amputation metaphor. The loss of a child is like the loss of a part of the self. Parents learn to live with it; they don't "get over it."

For many parents, children provide the structure and self-regulation that keeps them going day to day. The loss of a child causes many grieving parents to experience mood swings, appetite loss, and difficulty sleeping, in addition to feelings of sadness and loneliness. Bereaved parents commonly experience some initial impairment in social and occupational functioning before they are able to develop a sense of meaning about their child's death and to restructure their daily lives. The time associated with this process varies by individual and may happen over a matter of months to a year or more. If one's reaction to the death of a loved one significantly interferes with personal, social, or occupational functioning, or if the event has overwhelmed one's ability to cope, then professional intervention may be in order.

Many factors influence parental grief responses. The characteristics of the death, such as whether or not it is viewed as having been preventable, the length of the illness, and the suddenness of the loss, may impact parental guilt feelings in particular. The question of what they could

Vonda and Michael Shoels weep after a video tribute to their son, eighteen-year-old Isaiah Shoels, at his funeral. Shoels was killed in the 1999 shootings at Columbine High School, Littleton, Colorado. (Reuters/Rick Wilking/Archive Photos)

have done to prevent the child's death is very powerful for parents. The personality and stability of parents, including maturity, coping skills, optimism, spiritual identity, and previous grief experiences, play a major role in terms of how the experience is construed. The parents' relationships with the deceased child and the meaning of the death are extremely influential in determining the grief response as well. Meaning-focused coping, which focuses on looking for some intrinsic value in an event, has been found to be adaptive over the long term. The answers to questions such as "What did the deceased child mean to the parents?," "What kind of terms were the parents on with the child when he or she died?," and "What was the

child's role in the family?" are influential in shaping parental grief. All of these issues contribute to parents' abilities to make meaning out of the loss, which will enable them to integrate this life change and adapt to their new circumstances—living without the deceased child.

There is no consensus among researchers as to whether it is more difficult to lose a very young child or an older one. Adaptation to the death of a child is seen instead as involving different developmental issues for the family depending on the child's age. Similarly, the pain of the death of an only child is not compared with the difficulty of grieving the death of a child while continuing to function as parents for the deceased child's siblings.

The two groups of parents have much in common, such as the tendency to track the age their deceased child would have been, "growing up with the loss," as they remember milestones such as birthdays and graduations. The loss of a child inevitably leads to the restructuring of the family, which brings up complex feelings in surviving children as well as parents.

Surviving siblings experience many of the same feelings parents do, including guilt and sadness, but on top of that, they carry the burden of being comforters to their grieving parents. Parents tend to be initially detached and unavailable to surviving children. Healthy children may serve as bittersweet reminders of the child they lost. Bereaved parents are often preoccupied with feelings of having failed in their protective roles and consider themselves to be bad parents. They may pull away from their other children, not only to grieve privately but out of fear of getting close to their other children and experiencing the devastating pain from the loss of those children. Parents may also become excessively protective of surviving children as a means of overcompensating for their perceived failure to protect the deceased child. In the wake of the child's death, parents may remember the deceased child as nearly perfect, their favorite child, which negatively impacts the other children in the family. Parents may unfairly impose the identity of the lost child onto the surviving children through expectations that they will take up the deceased child's hobbies, personality, or interests. The surviving children may feel like disappointments to their parents because they cannot compensate for the loss of their sibling by living up to the deceased child's idealized identity.

Though the death of a child places intense stress on a family, many families are able to find comfort from each other and avoid negative behavior patterns that lead to further strain. Although it is diffi-cult to act as a source of comfort to bereaved family members while trying to handle one's own grief, such an emotional challenge can bring families together. In fact, many parents report the desire to spend more time with their families after the loss of a child, as it has caused them to reevaluate their priorities and put family first.

The effect of parental bereavement on marriage is similarly complex. It is commonly believed that the death of a child leads to the disintegration of the marriage, but research has not consistently supported this notion. Just as in the case of the family, spouses can both increase stress and provide comfort during the grief process. It can be difficult to find support when one's best resource is also suffering. In general, women tend to be more outwardly distressed and have more difficulty with daily functioning. Differences in grief styles between spouses may cause tension in the marriage. For example, a wife who is very emotionally expressive may feel that her husband did not love the child as much as she did because he is more reserved in expressing his sorrow. Grief feelings tend to fluctuate and it may be difficult for one spouse who is having a "good day" to connect with the other, who is feeling particularly depressed at that time. Being out of synch may cause guilt feelings in the spouse who is feeling better and may make both feel detached from the other. The depressive feelings that are experienced during bereavement can also lead to a lack of communication between spouses, which may be interpreted as rejection. Acknowledging that one's spouse may grieve differently and making an effort to be available to him or her regardless of one's own mood can reduce the strain in this very delicate and painful experience. Studies have shown that bereaved individuals find contact with similar others, expressions of concern, opportunities to vent their feelings, involvement in social activities, and the presence of another person to be particularly helpful in coping with their loss. Bereaved parents may find that support groups and friends, as well as family, can be resources for such support.

Carolyn E. Sartor
Anthony Papa

References and further reading
Arnold, Joan Hagan, and Penelope Buschman Gemma. 1983. *A Child Dies: A Portrait of Family Grief.* Rockville, MD: Aspen Systems.
Finkbeiner, Ann K. 1996. *After the Death of a Child: Living with the Loss through the Years.* New York: Free Press.
Klass, Dennis. 1988. *Parental Grief: Solace and Resolution.* New York: Springer Publishing.
Leick, Nina, and Marianne Davidsen-Nielsen. 1991. *Healing Pain: Attachment, Loss, and Grief Therapy.* New York: Tavistock/Rutledge.
Nolen-Hoeksema, Susan, and Judith Larson. 1999. *Coping with Loss.* Mahwah, NJ: Lawrence Erlbaum Associates.
Rando, Therese A. 1986. *Parental Loss of a Child.* Champaign, IL: Research Press.
Shapiro, Ester R. 1994. *Grief as a Family Process.* New York: Guilford Press.
Stroebe, Margaret S., Wolfgang Stroebe, and Robert O. Hansson. 1993. *Handbook of Bereavement: Theory, Research, and Intervention.* New York: Cambridge University Press.

Death of a Parent

The death of a parent during childhood, though infrequent in the United States, is a very significant event in the lives of those children who do experience it. About 5 to 8 percent of children in the United States experience the death of a parent (Tennant, 1988), and the 1993 U.S. Census identified about 1.5 million children living with a widowed, single parent. The majority of cases have been of paternal death.

The death of a parent affects individual children very differently, as the effects depend on a variety of factors. Among these are the child's age, the social and eco-

When a parent dies, the surviving parent can help the children through the grieving process in a number of ways. (Skjold Photographs)

nomic context within which the child lives, and the way the deceased is mourned by the surviving parent. Death does not rupture the child's connection to the deceased parent but forces the child to construct a new relationship with his or her inner representation of that parent. The surviving parent can help the child through this grieving process in a number of ways, including and most importantly encouraging the child to express his or her feelings and thoughts about the death, rather than keep them private.

Most studies find that about half of all parental deaths occur suddenly, and slightly more than half occur after a prolonged illness. The varying circumstances of the death, including the social and economic context within which the child lives and the changes in that context following the death, can play a large part in how the child responds to and is affected by the death.

Researchers remain somewhat in disagreement on the question of what are the long-term effects on children's development after the death of a parent. Some studies have found that adults who lost a parent during childhood are more prone to depression and even to suicide, while other studies have found no differences between these adults and others who grew up with both parents in their home. These inconsistencies can be partly explained by methodological flaws in the research, and also by the abundance of factors that mediate the experience of parental death for children, summarized into the following four general categories.

Characteristics of the Child

A first group of factors that influence how the death of a parent is experienced by a child includes the unique characteristics of the child, such as his or her age at the time of the death, and the aspects of his or her personality, such as self-esteem level. As younger children think more concretely about things in general, they therefore understand death in a more concrete way and may ask questions about where the deceased parent has gone and how he or she may be rejoined. Older children are capable of understanding death at a more abstract level, and of experiencing more complex emotions surrounding the loss.

Nature of the Relationship

A second set of factors is the nature of the child's relationship with the deceased; this influences the way in which the child experiences and is affected by the death. The roles played by the deceased in the child's life differ among children, which will cause the grieving process to differ even among the children in the same family.

Circumstances of the Death

A third source of variation in how parental death affects children is the unique circumstances of the death. If the death was sudden and unexpected, then the child had no chance to say good-bye and may feel regret or self-blame. If the death was after a long, protracted illness, the child may have gone through an emotional roller-coaster ride and then may feel disbelief when death finally arrives, and subsequently guilt as a result of the disbelief. The child may also feel shame if the death is a result of a stigmatized cause, such as suicide, murder, or drug overdose.

Support from the Child's Familiars

Finally, the support received from the child's environment has an impact on how the death is experienced. A more supportive and stable environment with accessible adult caregivers and with few changes in the economic and living conditions of the family increases the chances that the bereaved child will be able to grieve effectively.

Research has proved inconclusive on the question of what long-term effects of parental death are on development. The main reason for this is that the studies have been methodologically flawed, confounding the effects of parental death with those of divorce, failing to control for factors such as socioeconomic status, or selecting inappropriate control groups. Among the few studies from which conclusions can be drawn, the findings are mixed. Several studies of exceptionally intelligent adults have found that a disproportionately high number of them had experienced the death of one of their parents during childhood. Yet a number of studies have also found links between early maternal death and later severe depression.

In the past, parents were advised to help bereaved children by teaching them to let go of the deceased parent. This was accomplished mainly by avoiding talking about the death and the deceased parent with the child. More recently, however, mental health experts have come to believe that talking about the deceased parent is in fact beneficial to grieving children, as it enables them to better understand the event and to construct a new relationship to the deceased parent.

The following suggestions have been made by mental health experts (Buchsbaum 1990): provide a stable environment for the family, or, if this is impossible, provide explanations, support, and sustained connections to familiar people, places, and events. Explain the facts and circumstances of a parent's death in a realistic, clear manner. Understand the child's developmental capacities for mourning with reference to both cognitive and affective aspects. Modulate tension and mood states and encourage the child to experience grief as well as foster progressive development. Finally, assist the child in dealing with new relationships that may occur at the end of the mourning period.

Marie-Anne Suizzo

References and further reading
Buchsbaum, B. 1990. "An Agenda for Treating Widowed Parents." *Psychotherapy Patient* 6, no. 3–4:113–130.
Finkelstein, H. 1988. "The Long-Term Effects of Early Parent Death: A Review." *Journal of Clinical Psychology* 44, no. 1:3–9.
Hatter, B. 1996. "Children and the Death of a Parent or Grandparent." In *Handbook of Childhood Death and Bereavement.* Edited by C. Corr and D. Corr. New York: Springer Publishing Company.
Tennant, Christopher. 1988. "Parental Loss in Childhood: Its Effects in Adult Life." *Archives of General Psychiatry* 45:1045–1050.

Demographic Transition

The demographic transition is the change from high fertility patterns to low fertility patterns that occurs in the context of modernization, industrialization, and economic development. In the United States, the demographic transition occurred from the mid-1800s until the 1960s at various times in different geographic regions and among different socioeconomic and cultural groups. In many ways, the changes in parenthood seen throughout American families this century are defined by the timing and intensity of local demographic change. At the turn of the twentieth century, total fertility rates were 3.56 for whites and 5.61 for African Americans (Haines, 2000), while in 1990 these were 1.89 for whites and 2.58 for African Americans (Clarke and Ventura, 1994), meaning that the number of children parented within a family decreased by about half during this century. An important consequence is that resources and time available per child within a family increased proportionately. Families with only one child can concentrate all their time and resources on that child. Each additional child requires parents to further divide their time and resources. This can have major ramifications in terms of children's educational and social attainment. Children from larger families have significantly lower completed educational levels than children from smaller families with the same socioeconomic status. Several studies have shown a strong link between educational level, lifetime income, and social achievement. The changes in labor markets that accompany modernization affect the opportunity structure within a society to a great extent. To successfully compete, parents must invest heavily in their children's educations. This is difficult to do in larger families, and a consequence of this may be the continuing reduction in fertility rates in the United States.

In the 1990s, large families are concentrated among people with low income levels. This may be due to the perceived benefits of large families in these socioeconomic strata. Alternatively, there may be high costs to large families in higher socioeconomic strata. If the latter is true, it helps to explain why the very rich are not having very large families. The very rich are competing with other extremely wealthy people in placing their children in positions of power and influence. Obtaining these positions requires high levels of education at the "right" institutions and also requires strong social connections. Both of these require the investment of high levels of resources, and the wealthy are competing against one another. This drives the cost of competition to dizzying heights, and limits the ability of wealthy parents to successfully raise more than a couple of children. The same processes may hold true for most Americans regardless of their socioeconomic level. For their children to successfully compete, parents are able to have no more than two children or the cost of education and social attainment are too high. In this scenario, the very poor are left out in the cold. Opportunities for their children are limited, and even if parents invested everything they had in one child it would have no effect. In this case, there is no cost to having large families and there may be significant benefits in terms of cooperation and sharing of resources.

The relationship of family size to income is by no means absolute. Some poor people have small families and some wealthy people large ones. Moreover, some groups are characterized by large families. Mormons, for instance, tend to have much larger families than non-Mormons of the same socioeconomic status. The Church of Latter-Day Saints has a religious philosophy that encourages large families. As a group, Mormons also have high educational and social attainment. How is this accomplished? In addition to encouraging large families, the Mormon Church also places very high emphasis on cooperative educational, health, and other institutional endeavors. In this way, members of this denomination are able to take advantage of what economists call an "economy of scale" and share the costs of large families. This cost is shared both within one generation of people all raising children but also intergenerationally. Older people who are no longer raising their own dependent children are helping to defray the younger generation's child-rearing costs. Similar kinds of cooperative arrangements may also characterize the ability of other groups of people to maintain large family sizes.

There are important implications of the continuing demographic transition for parenthood in America. Fertility is declining rapidly for all Americans and within the next twenty years will fall to what is called below-replacement fertility, meaning that the population will grow older and would eventually start to decline in the absence of immigration. This also means that the number of only children is growing at a high rate. The childhood experience of most people will be one without siblings. Will "spoiled child syndrome" become as common in the United States as it is in China, where a one-child-per-family policy was enforced for many years? Moreover, there will be more people who never have children and never experience parenthood. This speaks to major changes in the social structure and fabric. The conception of adulthood as bound up with parenthood in an important life stage and as a nearly universal experience will have to give way to one in which adulthood is defined by other characteristics. In the nineteenth and early twentieth centuries, the typical adult in the United States had four children, lived in the same community for his or her entire life, and lived a life centered around family and farm. In the twenty-first century, there may be a wide range of adult experiences. Some of these experiences may be family centered, others centered on other aspects of community, career, or interests. Perhaps the American penchant for work will take on even greater importance as a marker of adulthood. The consequences of parenthood for career advancement could cross gender divides.

In many places around the world, the demographic transition has resulted in social upheaval and a break from tradition. The social roles of parents and children have taken on new dimensions and forms. The same may be occurring in the United States now with major consequences for our conception of parenthood.

John Bock

References and further reading

Clarke, S. C. and S. J. Ventura. 1994. "Birth and Fertility Rates for States: United States 1990." *Vital Health Statistics* 21, no. 45.

Haines, M. 2000. "The Population of the United States, 1790–1920." In *The Cambridge Economic History of the United States.* Edited by Stanley Engerman and Robert Gallman. New York: Cambridge.

Development, Parental Beliefs about

In order to understand the role parents can play in their children's development one must consider not only what parents do, but also parents' beliefs both about development and about their role in their children's development. The beliefs that parents hold can have both direct and indirect influences on children's development. Beliefs can influence what opportunities parents make available to their children and how they interact with their children. Children can also be more directly influenced by their parents' beliefs by choosing to appropriate these beliefs as their own and then behaving in ways consistent with the beliefs. Parental beliefs and expectations are thought by many to originate in the parents' own cultural background, but are affected by other factors such as their children's characteristics and behaviors as well as their own current experiences.

Much is known about parental beliefs, especially cognitive ones, but far less is known about the influence of beliefs on development, and fairly little about the processes through which parental beliefs influence children's development. Regarding beliefs, it is important to realize that the term may encompass a variety of topics, such as goals, values, and expectations, as well as beliefs. Although the topic of parental beliefs has a fairly large empirical literature, only recently has research addressed the relation between parental beliefs and children's school success. Much current research illustrates how beliefs differ according to cultural group. However, what is called "culture" may also reflect educational and income differences among people rather than just ethnicity or racial differences.

There appear to be some documented differences in how parents conceptualize the developmental process. That is, parents differ in whether they view the child as an active participant in his or her development; they also differ in the complexity of their reasoning about the nature of development.

How might parents' conceptualization of the developmental process affect their children's development? Although there is no definitive answer to this question, there is some evidence that parents who take a more complex view of development interact with their children in a manner that may elicit more complex reasoning on the part of the child. Research has shown that a certain style of parental interaction that is labeled authoritative is beneficial for many children. This style includes both parental sensitivity to the needs and wants of the child, as well as parental demands for accountability. Such a style of parenting could be interpreted as consistent with a view that a child is an active participant in development.

Most parents when questioned express a range of goals for their children, including cognitive/academic and social/personal ones. Nevertheless, there appear to be some consistent differences across cultures, with Anglo-American parents emphasizing more of an individual orientation and non-Anglo-American parents expressing more of an interpersonal orientation. For example, a recent study found that mothers from Puerto Rico, when discussing goals for their children, emphasized the need to view oneself as a member of a group and behave in a manner consistent with the needs of others. Anglo mothers from the United States, on the other hand, emphasized more of a sense of independence. When mothers were observed interacting with their infant children, their behaviors were consistent with their goals.

The bulk of recent research on parental beliefs has focused on parents' beliefs about their children's cognitive and academic development. Although all parents may want their children to succeed academically, how parents view the road to success in school seems to vary based on sociocultural factors. Even how the construct of intelligence is defined seems to reflect cultural differences. One set of researchers questioned immigrant and native-born parents of first-grade children in the United States about what it means for a child to be intelligent and what types of behaviors they expect of their children in school. Anglo-American parents stressed cognitive factors as the sole component of intelligence much more than Hispanic and Asian parents, who also included various social aspects. Parents who had immigrated to the United States also emphasized the need for their children to conform to external standards of behavior much more than did native-born parents. Parents who emphasized conformity had children who did less well on scholastic tests.

A related line of research has explored parental expectations for their children's success in school. Harold Stevenson and his colleagues have worked with families in Japan, China, and the United States. Their findings consistently show that U.S. parents tend to view academic success as more influenced by their children's "native" ability and less influenced by effort expended studying than did Asian parents. Furthermore, parents in the United States appeared more satisfied with lower levels of performance than did parents in the Asian countries.

How might these beliefs influence children's performance in school? The evidence shows that children in Asian countries are more successful in school than are children in the United States. Although one might hypothesize that the differences in parental beliefs about the importance of effort plays a role, there is no direct evidence to support this. On the other hand, there is evidence from other studies to support the notion that parents may behave in ways consistent with their beliefs. The results of a study with Israeli families showed consistency between the age at which parents expected their children to display certain competencies and the age of their children when given materials relevant for such attainment. In a related vein, researchers in the United States have shown that parents choose preschools for their children that are consistent with whether they think there should be more of a social or academic emphasis during these years.

Another line of research has found differences in what are considered to be good educational practices among white, black, and Hispanic mothers in this country. There seems to be evidence across studies that parents of low-income African American and Hispanic families tend to believe in a more traditional, didactic method of educating their children than do middle-income white families. For example, one group of researchers found that low-income mothers stressed the importance of such methods at school, as well as emphasized the use of workbooks and flash cards at home. These mothers were more likely to instruct their children at home, or claim to, than other parents. A similar set of findings comes from a longitudinal investigation of children's reading development. When asked what is the best way to help young children learn to read, low-income families were more likely to emphasize a skills orientation, whereas middle-income families were more likely to emphasize the role of enjoyment as well as the child's engagement in an activity. Parents reported providing materials and opportunities consistent with their emphasis. When the children's early and subsequent reading development was assessed, it was found that parental emphasis on enjoyment was the better (and positive) predictor of subsequent reading development.

There are several recent literature reviews that stress the importance of consistency between parental beliefs and children's educational programs. A fairly large body of data now shows that many Hispanic or low-income families, although very much wanting their children to succeed in school, do not see themselves as participating in the process. Instead these parents do not contact teachers, do not assist the children, and do not come to school. What appears to be uninvolvement of parents is viewed negatively by teachers with the impact felt by the children. Part of parental uninvolvement may reflect families feeling incapable of assisting, but the issue is more complex than that. Clearly, some aspect of this is due to parental beliefs about their roles in their children's schooling.

Parental beliefs have proven to be quite firmly entrenched and not easily changeable. For example, a recent study attempted to provide a reading intervention for young children from low-income Hispanic families in California. Many of the families did not have any books at home. As reading storybooks has been considered an important means of fostering literacy development, the investigators sent home books in Spanish for the families to read together. Interestingly, the children made less progress when they were given books to take home than when they were given worksheets. In fact, it appeared that the families interacted with the books as if they were worksheets. The investigators concluded that materials need to be consistent with what parents believe about how children learn. Such a conclusion is consistent with the notion of a need for better understanding of parental beliefs in order to support children's educational success.

Susan Sonnenschein

References and further reading

Hoover-Dempsey, Katherine V., and Howard M. Sandler. 1997. "Why Do Parents Become Involved in Their Children's Education?" *Review of Educational Research* 67:3–42.

Murphey, David A. 1992. "Constructing the Child: Relations between Parents' Beliefs and Child Outcomes." *Developmental Review* 12:199–232.

Okagaki, Lynne, and Robert J. Sternberg. 1993. "Parental Beliefs and School Performance." *Child Development* 64:36–56.

Sonnenschein, Susan, Linda Baker, Robert Serpell, and Diane Schmidt. 2000. "Reading Is a Source of Entertainment: The Importance of the Home Perspective for Children's Literacy Development." In *Literacy and Play in the Early Years: Cognitive, Ecological, and Sociocultural Perspectives.* Edited by Kathy Roskos and Jim Christie. Mahwah, NJ: Lawrence Erlbaum Associates.

Development, Parental Knowledge about

Parental knowledge about child development refers to the extent to which parents are aware of the changing nature of children's abilities over the course of early childhood. Parents who are knowledgeable about child development are generally cognizant of the ages at which children acquire specific skills, as well as knowledgeable about the temporal ordering of specific developmental milestones relative to others. So, for example, knowledge that crawling occurs before walking; that toddlers play with objects concretely before using objects to pretend play; that first words appear somewhere around the start of the second year of life; that two-year-olds often say "no" out of a desire to express their autonomy; and that toddlers find it difficult to share their toys are all examples of parental knowledge.

Over the past two decades interest in parents' knowledge about child development has grown, particularly with respect to knowledge about children's abilities during the preschool years. Because this represents a relatively new area of research, most studies to date report on mothers' knowledge about child development, given that mothers continue to be the primary caregivers of children in most families. Some researchers have studied the phenomenon of maternal knowledge solely for descriptive purposes—that is, to better understand what mothers do and do not know about child development. In such studies, researchers might ask mothers to estimate when children first smile, walk, or say their first words. Others have explored the extent to which mothers' knowledge influences their actual interactions with their children. In such studies, researchers might ask mothers questions about child development and then observe mothers at play with their children. The ultimate goal is to see whether mothers' responses to questions about child development predict their sensitivity to children during interactions.

The burgeoning research in this area is driven by the notion that maternal knowledge about child development (or lack thereof) will influence a mother's interpretations of and reactions to her child's behaviors and competencies, as well as guide her own interactions with her child. Specifically, mothers who know more about children's current and future abilities are thought to be more likely to create optimally challenging environments for them and to offer their children age-appropriate experiences. As such, maternal knowledge about child development is hypothesized to indirectly affect children's developmental outcomes by exerting a more direct influence on the experiences that mothers provide to children.

To what extent are these ideas upheld in actual studies? In general, researchers have documented relations between maternal knowledge about child development and parenting, although associations tend to be modest in size. Specifically, studies show that mothers who are knowledgeable about child development are more likely to score higher on assessments of the quality of the home environment. Furthermore, mothers who are more accurate at estimating the timing or ordering of developmental milestones have been found to engage in more sensitive interactions with their children. For example, in one study, mothers of twenty-one-month-old toddlers who knew more about children's play development were found to engage in play that challenged their children to "make believe." Knowledgeable mothers were also less likely to prompt their children to engage in play that was too easy for them when compared to less knowledgeable mothers. In turn, the children of more knowledgeable mothers benefited from the more sensitive play interactions they experienced. In particular, they were found to engage in more sophisticated forms of play than other toddlers their age. Finally, the children of mothers who are more knowledgeable about child development have been shown to be developmentally competent. For example, in one study of mothers of preterm infants, the infants of mothers who were more knowledgeable about development scored higher on standardized tests of developmental status.

In families in which infants exhibit developmental delays, many researchers have observed less effective parenting. This less effective parenting has been attributed to both a lack of parenting skill as well as to a lack of knowledge about child development. Mothers who either overestimate or underestimate the timing of developmental milestones may have unrealistic expectations about what children should be doing at different ages, which may lead to poor parenting and further exacerbate developmental delay in children.

Several investigators have found that persistent underestimations of the timing of developmental milestones by a mother might reflect her inability to appreciate the protracted course of early development. Mothers who underestimate the age at which milestones occur expect children to walk, talk, share, listen, and pretend (for example) much sooner than children typically exhibit such skills. Such underestimation could set in place a pattern of maternal disappointment because children will be unable to live up to the inaccurate expectations that their mothers set. This might result in mothers becoming frustrated when their children do not perform as desired. In turn, a cycle of harsh, punitive, or prohibitive parenting may be set in motion.

On the other hand, mothers who overestimate the timing of developmental milestones may expect too little from their children and fail to challenge their children's thinking and behaviors in an age-appropriate way. As an example, a mother who overestimates when talking or understanding of language is likely to occur might insufficiently vocalize or respond to her child, potentially leading to an insufficiently stimulating language environment.

With respect to inaccurate expectations and knowledge, several studies have reported that adolescent mothers know less about child growth and development than do older mothers. Adolescent mothers' lack of information can lead to inappropriate interactions and unrealistic expectations about their children's abilities and behaviors. These unrealistic expectations may contribute to impatience in parenting, which has been linked in studies to the incidence of child abuse. Indeed, some abusive mothers have been found to engage in inadequate parenting in part because they misunderstand their children's behaviors. Studies indicate that adolescent mothers who are at risk for inappropriate parenting should be provided with emotional support and the information necessary to acquire competent caregiving skills. Knowing more about what to expect in children is one way of supporting sensitive and age-appropriate interactions in adolescent mothers, which in turn will help sustain healthy child development.

For the most part, research on maternal knowledge of child development has taken a generalized approach to mothers' knowledge. In such an approach, mothers are labeled as more or less knowledgeable across different areas of child development. More recently, it has been suggested that mothers' knowledge about children's development is specialized. That is, any given mother may know more about one area of child development than about another. Those areas in which a mother is more knowledgeable likely depends on the goals she has for her child. A mother who considers a particular area of child development to be highly important will be more likely to seek out information about that area than will a mother who does not deem it to be important. As an example, a mother who is highly concerned about preparing her child for school may focus her energy on obtaining information about school readiness and learning. As a result, she may be more aware about developments in children's literacy than she will developments in children's motor skills. A mother who is interested in promoting her child's creativity and imagination might seek out information about children's pretend play, and in turn will provide her child with a more flexible and creative environment.

In an effort to better prepare all mothers for the task of parenting, professionals engaged in early preventive interventions have also demonstrated an increased interest in the role of maternal knowledge in early parenting. Interventions aimed at modifying the sensitivity of maternal behavior have focused on links between maternal knowledge and maternal behavior. For example, teaching mothers more accurately to observe and understand their children's developmental abilities has been shown to help mothers appropriately engage and stimulate their children. Such interventions have enhanced both mothers' knowledge about child development as well as their ability to interact with their children in sensitive and nurturing ways. In turn, interventions aimed at teaching mothers more about children's development and needs have resulted in increased levels of interest in children and in decreased levels of boredom (from understimulation) and distress (from being confronted with exceedingly high expectations). However, preventive interventions that seek to teach mothers more about child development and parenting must be sensitive to the ways in which cultural views affect what mothers do and do not know about children's development. Professionals who attempt to understand relations between cultural ideologies and parenting knowledge are in a better position to effectively enhance the parent-child relationships of their clients.

Jacqueline D. Shannon
Catherine S. Tamis-LeMonda

References and further reading
Benasich, April Ann, and Jeanne Brooks-Gunn. 1996. "Maternal Attitudes and Knowledge of Child-Rearing: Associations with Family and Child Outcomes." *Child Development* 67:1186–1205.
Damast, Amy M., Catherine S. Tamis-LeMonda, and Marc H. Bornstein. 1996. "Mother-Child Play: Sequential Interactions and the Relation between Maternal Beliefs and Behaviors." *Child Development* 67:1752–1766.
Goodnow, Jacqueline J. 1995. "Parents' Knowledge and Expectations." Pp. 305–332 in vol. 3 of *Handbook of Parenting.* Edited by Marc H. Bornstein. Mahwah, NJ: Lawrence Erlbaum Associates.
Goodnow, Jacqueline J., and W. Andrew Collins. 1990. *Development According to Parents: The Nature, Sources, and Consequences of Parents' Ideas.* Hillsdale, NJ: Lawrence Erlbaum Associates.
Miller, Scott. 1988. "Parents Beliefs about Their Children's Cognitive Development." *Child Development* 59:259–285.
Sigel, Irving E., Ann V. McGillicuddy-DeLisi, and Jacqueline J. Goodnow. 1992. *Parental Belief Systems: The Psychological Consequences for Children,* 2d ed. Hillsdale, NJ: Lawrence Erlbaum Associates.

Disabilities, Parenting a Child with

Every child with a disability is different, and so the parenting of each child is a different experience. Disabilities can include cognitive problems (such as mental retardation, as well as more subtle learning disabilities), physical problems (such as cerebral palsy and spina bifida), or sensory problems (such as blindness, hearing loss, and problems with integrating sensory messages). Disabilities can also include chronic health issues (such as cystic fibrosis and seizure disorder). Some disabilities are due to genetic causes (such as Down

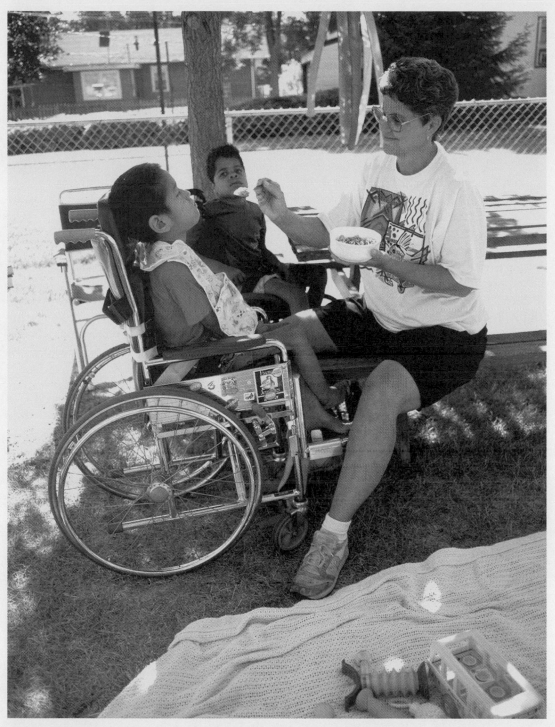

Children with special needs usually require extra time, effort, and resources from the whole family. (Skjold Photographs)

syndrome and Fragile X syndrome), while others come from environmental insults (fetal alcohol syndrome, HIV infection, anoxia). Some children have just one impairment. Other children have multiple disabilities, as for example a child who is born preterm and has cerebral palsy and mental retardation due to brain damage during the neonatal period.

Regardless of the physical or cognitive problems, a child with a disability is a child first, with a need for family, friends, silly stories, and outdoor play. Parenting children with disabilities is often a balancing act of meeting the child's medical and therapy needs, while also letting the child be a child and the family be a family.

Parents need to know the federal and state laws concerning children with disabilities, as these laws affect family life in a daily and tangible way. Changes in public laws have made educational and therapy services more available to children with disabilities than they were early on in this country. Prior to 1975, many children received no schooling and just stayed at home into adulthood, if their families could not afford private school. States were not required to provide education to children with disabilities, and so often they did not. Their parents taught them or cared for them as best they could. Other children were sent to state or private institutions, where they would spend their whole lives. In 1975, the Education for All Handicapped Children Act (P.L. 94–142) was passed that required states to provide "free and appropriate education" for all school-aged children. Suddenly, the child with mental retardation or the child who used braces and crutches could go to the public school with all the neighbor children. Not only did this give the child a better education, it freed parents up during the day to pursue their own career and family demands. In 1986, money was made available for states to develop services for children starting at birth. (P.L.

99–457, Part H) In 1991 and 1992, the act was amended and renamed the Individuals with Disabilities Education Act (IDEA).

Children with disabilities grow up and become adults with disabilities, and most want jobs and are capable of working. The important legislation for opening access to employment is the Americans with Disabilities Act (ADA), which recognizes people with disabilities as a special group and so gives a "national mandate for the elimination of discrimination against individuals with disabilities." (P.L. 104–327, 1990, with amendments that followed)

The 1986 legislation that brought infants with disabilities into consideration asked for development of a "statewide, comprehensive, coordinated, multidisciplinary, interagency program of early intervention services for handicapped infants and toddlers and their families." (Part H of P.L. 99-457, 1986) Each word of this act is important, as it shows a new approach to helping families. Most children with disabilities need attention from more than one professional to help them develop their full potential. This might include an occupational therapist, physical therapist, speech therapist, special educator, nurse, and social worker, as well as a pediatrician and specialty physicians. Before this legislation, a family had to find its way to new doctors or therapists or special programs on its own and start from the ground up in telling each professional about their child. This 1986 legislation required coordination among the professionals for the good of both the child and the family. Most locales now use a teamwork approach, in which a whole team meets together with the parents periodically to put together a service plan that suits both the child's and the family's needs. The family is always included as part of the team—that is required by law—because they are the most important people, the ones who will be with the child for life and not just for the school year or a shorter span. In short, the other family members are recognized as the experts on this particular child.

Before a child's birth, parents often say, "I don't care if it's a boy or a girl, so long as it's healthy." So, if the baby put in their arms is not so healthy, adjustments must be made. Some parents know from birth that their child has a disability. For others it may take months or even years before problems are noticed and diagnosed. Sometimes a mother senses that something is wrong—her child is not looking at her, or feels floppy in her arms, or isn't starting to talk—and asks her doctor again and again if anything is wrong. Diagnosis often is not possible early on, and professionals have to ask the family to "wait and see." This can be frustrating for parents who both want the problem to disappear but also want to get started with therapy if there is something wrong. Families can refer themselves to have a complete evaluation of their child by an interdisciplinary team (note the laws discussed above), and localities are required to perform the evaluation in a reasonable time. States have different agencies that handle this, and parents can usually find out from their hospital or their school district where to call to get started.

The news of a disability is not easy, even when it is a relief to finally know the truth. The most common initial response when a child has a significant disability is shock, disbelief, guilt, and an overwhelming feeling of loss. Families must grieve the loss of the "perfect" child they expected. The model of the stages of grieving described by Elizabeth Kubler-Ross in her work on dying applies to many families. They may go through stages as they adjust to this new reality. If they follow the described order (and they often do not), parents may go through denial ("it cannot be true; let's see another specialist"); depression (sadness, insomnia, fatigue,

and irritability); anger and guilt ("Why did God do this to me? What stupid mistake did the hospital make at birth? Or, "What did I do wrong?"); bargaining (including desperate efforts at nonconventional therapies in hopes of finding a magical cure); and finally, acceptance. Research has shown that acceptance comes more easily in families with a strong marital bond, supportive social networks, strong religious faith, and effective early interventions for the child in the home.

Children with special needs usually take extra time, effort, and resources on the part of the whole family. Relationships can be strained. Some families fall apart. Divorces happen. Other families become closer and feel more connected with each other as they pull together around this child. If all the family's energy is directed to the special needs child, siblings may feel neglected and resentful. Parents have to make efforts for the brother or sister to have a significant place in the family and not be overshadowed by the needs of the child with a disability. When they are appreciated for their own qualities and are allowed to help, these siblings often develop more maturity, sense of responsibility, and tolerance for others who are different. The extra work and stress of raising a child who has a disability in the midst of an already full and busy life can crush some families. Alternately, these same stressors prompt other families to find coping strategies and personal resources they did not know they had. Research shows that children with disabilities—like all other children—do better developmentally when they are in a well-functioning family, so it serves everyone's interests for a family to seek help if members find themselves caught in depression or conflict.

Babies and toddlers with disabilities benefit from early intervention. This does not mean that with intervention the disability will go away, but it has been proven that intervention improves the functioning of these children. It should start as early as possible. The brain is developing rapidly in the first months and years of life. That does not mean that it stops developing after age three, as some mistakenly believe, but the rapid growth and flexibility of the brain in the early months permits new connections and new pathways to develop. This is true for all babies and toddlers, not just those with disabilities, but it takes on special significance for a child who has a disorder that alters or delays the usual patterns in development. Intervention may be provided in the home or at a center; transportation may or may not be available; financial arrangements vary from place to place. The early intervention team is mandated to develop, along with the parents, an Individualized Family Services Plan (IFSP). Early intervention is always specialized to the child and the family—it is not a set of services that is the same for everyone. This plan should say clearly what the infant's level of functioning is at the present, what goals will be worked on, what services will be provided to help reach the goals (including teaching the family to provide certain services), what professional(s) will treat the child, how often, and the date at which the next evaluation will take place. Families are expected to do a lot and are taught how to incorporate "therapy" into daily life. For example, a father can stretch his baby's leg muscles as he changes a diaper, or use a sign for "ball" as he holds out a ball and also says the word "ball." Much early intervention takes place during play. In play, infants and toddlers learn to move their bodies, locomote and get around the room, stack and build with blocks, learn cause-effect relations, learn to pretend and imagine, develop language, and learn social skills with other children.

By age two and a half or three, early intervention often moves from home-based services to school-based services. These transitions can be stressful for the parents and the child, as they each must get used to a new routine of care and new professionals with which to relate. It is part of the early intervention team's job to help with this transition (this again is part of the law!), and so parents should expect and ask for this help in meeting new people and getting the paperwork set up. School starts younger for these children, as many get used to traveling on a school bus and wearing a little backpack. Once adjusted to the new routine, young children usually love to go to their classrooms and see their teacher and the other children. It is important to remember again that children with disabilities are children first (and not a "case" of Down syndrome or deafness) and much of what they "need" is the play and friendships and daily responsibilities that make up childhood. Before age five or six, many children with disabilities do not know that they are different. This awareness usually comes when they start regular school.

School-aged children with disabilities may have their schooling in a self-contained classroom, or they may be in an inclusive setting that has children with typical abilities, or they may spend part of the day in each setting. An advantage of inclusion is social contact with typically developing children. This often helps with social skills and is more fun for the child. For this to work, the school needs to provide enough teachers and aides so that all the children's educational needs are met. The school also needs to provide sensitivity training and enforcement of a "politeness policy" for the other children so that they will understand disabilities and not engage in teasing or bullying. Some training or education can be provided more directly for the special needs child in a self-contained classroom, or there may be parts of the regular curriculum that the special needs child is not able to master. Having both options available is a big help.

The school team must develop, with the parents, an Individualized Educational Plan (IEP). Like the IFSP, the IEP spells out in detail the goals and means to meet the goals of the individual child. Each child is an individual, and so there is not one "special education curriculum" that is applied to all children. One child may be doing math and French, another may be using a computer to write simple sentences, while another may be working on self-help skills with feeding and zippers. Any and all of this can be included in a child's IEP.

As a child grows older and moves into middle and high school, the IEP must realistically evaluate adulthood possibilities. If cognitive development is typical, a child with physical impairments can go to college and develop a desired career. (The ADA protects those rights.) Or, if the child will need to work, perhaps a setting with a job coach to help him or her master the appropriate job skills will be necessary. Vocational education and independent living skills are part of many adolescents' individualized educational plans—teaching them, for example, how to fix breakfast and lock the apartment door before leaving.

Educational supports continue until the child is twenty-one years old. Unfortunately, at this point there are fewer mandated services and opportunities for adults with disabilities. What is available varies across communities and is probably the next area of greatest need. Housing, employment, transportation, recreation—all of these are areas of life that adult children usually take on for themselves. Parents whose adult child has a disability and who cannot provide self-care face uncertainties about the future.

Although a great deal is guaranteed to individuals with disabilities by law, parents often find they must be advocates for their children and push the system to give the services they want. This advocacy may be at an individual level ("I want Charlotte to have three hours each week with the speech therapist this year") or it may involve coming together with other parents to get services or programs set up in their communities. Parents of children with disabilities have learned the power of support groups and of advocacy. There are support and advocacy groups for individual disabilities of all kinds, as well as for the larger disabled community. (Parents can check their yellow pages or search the Internet to find them.) One unexpected advantage of having a child with special needs is meeting and getting support from parents who have experienced the same thing.

Barbara J. Myers

References and further reading
Batshaw, Mark L. 1997. *Children with Disabilities: A Medical Primer.* Baltimore, MD: Paul H. Brookes.
———. 1998. *Your Child Has a Disability.* Baltimore, MD: Paul H. Brookes.
Bulletin of Zero to Three: National Center for Infants, Toddlers, and Families. Subscription available by writing to this organization at 734 15th Street, N.W., 10th Floor, Washington, DC 20005, calling (800) 899–4301, or at www.zerotothree.org.
National Information Center for Children and Youth with Disabilities (NICHCY). Write to P.O. Box 1492, Washington, DC 20013, call (800) 695–0285, or visit www.nichcy.org.

Discipline in the Home
What Is Discipline?
Ask any American to define discipline and the most likely response will be that it is punishment. For many, punishment means spanking, the most common form of punishment of children in America. Yet the term discipline comes from the Latin word *disciplina*, which had to do

with learning and teaching. It is also rooted in the concept of the disciple. Disciples
are those who willingly and without coercion follow and emulate their mentors,
teachers, or gurus. Neither term implies
coercion, force, or punishment.

Discipline in America: A Brief History
From its inception, American society has
been uniquely child centered. Colonial
success depended on every child being
kept alive. Also, the American colonists
had a patriotic desire to produce offspring
superior to their European ancestors. Two
attitudes concerning child rearing
emerged during colonial times. The first
was that children of the New World were
viewed as different from and more difficult to handle than their European counterparts. This view is reiterated through
generations of parents who view their
children as more challenging than children of previous generations. Second, historical accounts suggest that the early set-
tlers devoted a great deal of attention to
the early socialization of children. This
attitude, demonstrating a concern about
the relationship between early child experience and adult character, is paramount
today.

The seventeenth-century parent strictly
regulated the child. Obedience to parents
was emphasized and enforced with physical beatings. Children were viewed as
miniature adults and were expected to
emulate the hardworking behavior of
adults. These expectations of children
continued through the eighteenth century.
Children were often compared to plants,
in that they would grow wild if not properly cultivated. Physical beatings, forced
ingestion of urine, and the use of shame
and fear were popular discipline tactics.

A change in discipline tactics began to
take place during the latter eighteenth
century. Just as the American Revolution
replaced hierarchy with egalitarian relationships, a shift in parental attitudes

concerning the independence of children
was apparent. Children, for the first time,
were instructed to look adults in the face
when speaking and advised to speak freely
as opposed to merely speaking when spoken to. Also, less severe disciplinary
methods were utilized, and individual
needs of children were considered.

Several events in the nineteenth century had a profound impact upon child-rearing attitudes in America. The increasing
urbanization of American society, resulting in the isolation of parents from rural
communities and the extended family, led
to the creation of an industry dedicated to
the distribution of products and advice
regarding child care. During the latter part
of the century, the advice introduced a
more benevolent attitude toward children. Childhood began to be understood
as a period of growth and development
that precluded the assumption of adult
responsibility. By the end of the nineteenth century, American parents were
urged to believe that the good and inno-
cent qualities of children required less
stringent discipline and more understanding. Instead of conquering their children's
will, parents focused on training their
children to conform to social expectations.

In the twentieth century, science infil-
trated the growing social concern for children. The traditional American belief that
linked early childhood experience with
later adult behavior received scientific
support. Psychologist John Watson professed that a parent could shape a child's
character and vocational interests. He
also warned that inept parenting could
spoil a child's character. American parents were being convinced that one false
step could doom them and their children
forever.

This parental burden was compounded
by Freud and later psychodynamic theorists who maintained that a person's personality is set following a series of stages

during the first five years of life. The message again was that parental training has tremendous impact on the later values and traits of their children.

Emergence of Discipline Styles

There are many types of discipline, but they all have the purpose to persuade or force someone to behave in a particular way. As one can see from the historical account above, much of a person's approach to discipline is shaped by national and cultural beliefs. Also, personal experiences as a child influence a person's approach to discipline. For example, a person who was hit as a child is more likely to hit his or her own child than a person who was not hit. This is because children learn through modeling, through imitating the behavior of others. Albert Bandura's 1961 landmark study illustrates how a child learns aggressive behavior from an adult. This study exposed nursery school children to aggressive and nonaggressive behavior, using adults as models. One group of children watched an adult hit, kick, punch, and yell at a plastic Bobo doll, another group watched nonaggressive play with the doll, and a third group of children did not view play with the doll at all. Of the three groups, only those who viewed aggression against the doll became aggressive themselves when placed in a playroom with Bobo dolls.

Differences in Disciplinary Style

Psychologist Diana Baumrind delineates three different parenting styles: authoritarian or autocratic, permissive, and authoritative. Authoritarian parents strictly control the child. This style emphases unquestioning loyalty to leaders and reflexive obedience to authority. Parents extolling this style are often harsh and punitive.

Permissive parenting is at the opposite extreme. Parents do not assert their authority and impose few, if any, restrictions and controls. They tend not to have set time schedules and do not use punishment. Also, they tend not to place any demands on children such as doing chores, putting away toys, or doing schoolwork. Permissiveness, at its extreme, borders on neglect.

The authoritative pattern falls in between these two extremes. Authoritative parents exercise their power, but do not abuse it. They respond to their child's point of view and his or her reasonable demands. They attempt to govern with the consent of the governed.

Research has demonstrated that children raised in an authoritarian manner tend to be more withdrawn, lack independence, and are more angry and defiant. Children at the opposite end of the spectrum, raised in a permissive style, have shown similar behaviors. By contrast, children raised in the authoritative style demonstrated more independence, self-reliance, and social responsibility.

The three styles discussed above assume that styles of parenting represent unchanging characteristics of parents and that a one-way transfer takes place from parent to child. However, many researchers believe that parenting styles are not fixed. Instead, parenting styles change or adapt to meet the requirements of each particular child. These researchers believe that a child's disposition or temperament influences the way in which the parent interacts with him or her, and that the parent's approach to discipline further shapes this disposition. Thus, there is a reciprocal interaction taking place between child behavior and parenting approach.

Disciplinary Tactics

Psychologist Nancy Eisenberg discusses two tactics that are widely used by parents to discipline children: inductive discipline and power-assertive discipline.

Induction, widely used by authoritative parents, means reasoning in the service of discipline. In this tactic, parents point out to the child the consequences of his or her behavior for other people or another person's emotional state. There are many benefits to the utilization of this approach. The use of induction, because it directs the child's attention to others' needs and emotional states, encourages the child to understand the perspective of others and to sympathize with them. Hence, empathy and altruism may be fostered. Inductions provide reasons for behaving, or not behaving, that children can remember and apply in new situations. Parents, by using inductive discipline, send the message that the child is responsible for his or her behavior. Also, because a parent is reasoning with the child rather than hitting or yelling, the child receives a controlled, caring model for imitation. Finally, because this approach does not employ yelling and hitting, the child is not too emotionally aroused to attend to what the parent is saying, and is more likely to learn from the encounter.

Power-assertive discipline includes physical punishment, privilege deprivation, and/or threats of either of these. Research has shown that the effectiveness of this type of discipline varies according to the quality of the parent-child relationship. Excessive use of power-assertive techniques is associated with lower levels of moral development of children. Power-assertive techniques administered by cold, punitive (authoritarian) parents are unlikely to have any positive effects. Indeed, many drawbacks arise from the utilization of this approach. One major drawback is that parents model aggressive behavior for their children to imitate. Also, children of parents who are harsh and punitive are less likely to attend to what their parents say, and are not motivated to please their parents. Fear is the main outcome of these tactics, causing the child to focus on his or her own needs rather than those of other people. Children disciplined in a punitive manner may learn that the purpose of behaving is solely to avoid punishment, as opposed to a desire to behave or help others. They may have no motivation to behave in a helpful manner when no threat of punishment exists.

Irwin A. Hyman
Caroline Monforte Tisot

References and further reading
Eisenberg, Nancy. 1992. *The Caring Child.* Cambridge, MA: Harvard University Press.
Faber, Adele, and Elaine Mazish. 1982. *How to Talk So Kids Will Listen and Listen So Kids Will Talk.* New York: Avon Books.
Hyman, Irwin A. 1997. *The Case against Spanking: How to Discipline Your Child without Hitting.* New York: Jossey-Bass.
Joslin, Karen Renshaw. 1994. *Positive Parenting from A to Z.* New York: Ballantine.

Divorce

Although there has been a modest decline in the divorce rate since the late 1970s, 43 percent of marriages currently end in divorce in the United States, and it is estimated that 50 percent to 60 percent of children born in the 1990s will live in single-parent families, typically headed by mothers, at some point in their lives. This is likely to be a temporary situation, because about 75 percent of men and 60 percent of women remarry; however, the divorce rate is over 60 percent in second marriages. Thus, many children undergo a series of family disruptions associated with their parents' marital rearrangements, and the frequency of these transitions is associated with increasing problems in child adjustment.

Rates of separation, divorce, cohabitation, and births to single mothers are higher for blacks than whites. Black couples are less likely to marry, more likely to separate, to remain separated longer before obtaining a divorce or to never legally divorce, and less likely to remarry. Thus, black children are more likely than white children to spend longer periods of time in a household with a single, separated, or divorced mother, and often live with a grandmother or other kin.

Following divorce, 80 percent of children reside in the custody of their mothers. Children in the custody of their fathers are more likely to be boys or to be older. Although custodial mothers and custodial fathers share many of the same concerns and problems following divorce, such as task overload, worries about their adequacy as a parent, feelings of isolation, distress often reflected in depression, and health problems related to a breakdown in the immune system, mothers and their children are much more likely to slip into poverty. Women's income often declines 30 percent following divorce and is associated with multiple shifts in residence and moves to areas with less desirable neighborhoods, schools, and peer groups, and fewer resources in general, which makes successful parenting and raising competent children more difficult.

As marriage has become a more optional, less permanent institution in contemporary American society, children in all ethnic groups are faced with the stresses and adaptive challenges that accompany the marital transitions of their parents, and there is considerable diversity in children's responses to parental divorce. On the average, children from divorced families, in comparison to children from two-parent, nondivorced families, exhibit more behavior problems and lower psychological well-being, with some children showing severe, enduring adjustment difficulties associated with divorce, and other children showing delayed effects, appearing to adapt well in the initial stages following divorce, but showing problems at a later time. However, in the absence of sustained or new stresses and adversity, the majority of children (75 to 80 percent) recover within two to three years following the divorce and emerge as reasonably competent individuals functioning within the normal range of adjustment.

It should be remembered that, although divorce presents many children and parents with more stressful life circumstances, it also can result in an escape from conflict, more harmonious and fulfilling family relations, and the opportunity for greater personal growth and the formation of new, more satisfying intimate relations.

In the period immediately following divorce, most children experience emotional distress and behavior problems in response to their separation or intermittent contact with one parent, the stresses associated with family conflict and family disorganization, and the confusion and apprehension stemming from changing relationships with parents and shifts in their life situation. Common responses to divorce include anger, resentment, demandingness, anxiety, depression, and guilt. In addition, children from divorced families, in contrast to children from nondivorced families, commonly show increases in behavior problems, including aggression, noncompliance, and acting-out behaviors, as well as decreases in social responsibility, social competence, self-esteem, and academic achievement. They also have problems in their relationships with parents, siblings, and peers. Although the intensity of adverse responses tends to diminish over time following divorce, even in adolescence and young adulthood the offspring of divorced couples function less well than those from nondivorced families.

It has been noted that children in divorced families grow up faster than children in nondivorced families, in part because of early assignment of responsibilities, more autonomous decision making, and lack of adult supervision. Although the assignment of responsibility may be associated with resiliency and unusual social competence among girls in divorced families, task demands that are beyond children's capabilities are associated with low self-esteem, anxiety, and depression. In addition, adolescents who perceive themselves as unfairly burdened with responsibilities that interfere with their other activities may respond with resentment, rebellion, and noncompliance.

Normative challenges of adolescence and young adulthood, such as attainment in school and the workplace, becoming more autonomous from the family while maintaining bonds of attachment, forming constructive, fulfilling intimate and sexual relationships, and becoming a self-regulated, socially responsible individual, are more difficult for the offspring of divorced parents. In adolescence, children of divorced parents are at increased risk for behavioral and psychological problems, including dropping out of school, early sexual activity, having children out of wedlock, unemployment, substance abuse and delinquent activities, and involvement with antisocial peers. Many of these problems continue into young adulthood. Offspring from divorced families, in comparison to those from nondivorced families, experience lower socioeconomic and educational attainment and are more likely to be on welfare. In addition, they have more problems with family members, in intimate relations, in marriage, and in the workplace. Their divorce rate is higher, and their reports of general well-being and life satisfaction are lower.

Individual characteristics of parents and children make them vulnerable or protect them from adverse consequences associated with parental divorce. Many of these characteristics antecede divorce and contribute to problems in family relationships. Parents who later divorce, in comparison to those who do not divorce, are more likely preceding divorce to be neurotic, depressed, and antisocial, to be alcoholics, and to have economic problems. They have dysfunctional beliefs about relationships and poor problem-solving skills. Thus, in their marital interactions, they exhibit escalation and reciprocation of negative affect, contempt, denial, withdrawal, and negative attributions about their spouses' behavior, which in turn significantly increase their risk for marital dissolution and multiple divorces. Sometimes these patterns are found later in the marital relationships of their adult offspring. In addition, in their relationships with children, parents whose marriages will be later disrupted are more irritable, erratic, and nonauthoritative as much as eight to twelve years prior to the divorce.

Children whose parents later divorce, in comparison to those whose parents remained married, also exhibit poorer adjustment before the breakup of the marriage. When levels of behavior problems prior to the divorce are screened out, differences in behavior problems between children from divorced and nondivorced families are greatly reduced. It could be that marital conflict, maladapted parents, dysfunctional relationships, and inept parenting already have taken their toll on children's adjustment before the divorce occurs, or that divorce may be, in part, a result of having to deal with a difficult child. In addition, personality problems in a parent, such as negative emotionality and lack of self-regulation that lead to both divorce and inept parenting practices, also may be genetically linked to behavior problems in children.

In spite of these differences in adjustment preceding divorce, marital dissolution does exacerbate problems in adjustment in both children and parents, although these effects vary widely. Children who have easy temperaments, who are intelligent, socially mature, and responsible, and who exhibit few behavior problems are better able to cope with parental divorce. Existing behavior problems in children are likely to be increased by the stresses associated with divorce. However, if divorce is associated with a marked decrease in conflict and diminished stress, adjustment often improves. Children with difficult temperaments and problem behaviors are likely to elicit negative responses from their parents who are stressed in coping with their marital transitions. These children also may be less able to adapt to parental negativity when it occurs and may be less adept at gaining the support of people around them. Competent, adaptable children with social skills and attractive personal characteristics, such as an easy temperament and a sense of humor, are more likely to evoke positive responses and support and to maximize the use of available resources that help them negotiate stressful experiences.

Although developmental status and gender characteristics of children have been extensively examined in relation to adaptation to divorce, the results from these studies have been largely inconsistent. Some research has suggested that preschool-age children whose parents divorce are at greater risk for enduring problems in social and emotional development than are older children. Younger children may lack the cognitive skills to realistically appraise the causes and consequences of divorce, be more anxious about the possibility of abandonment, be more likely to blame themselves for the divorce, and may be less able to utilize the protective resources outside of the family. Older children, especially adolescents, in contrast to younger children, have increased opportunities to escape a troubled family situation and seek support and gratification elsewhere. Supportive relations outside of the family with peers and with other adults, such as teachers, coaches, friends' parents, and extended family members, may protect the child from negative outcomes associated with divorce. Moreover, academic, social, artistic, athletic, and extracurricular attainments, activities, and skills may serve to buffer children from the adverse outcomes of divorce.

Early studies commonly reported more deleterious effects of divorce for boys than for girls. However, more recent studies have reported less pronounced and consistent gender differences, and these effects are usually found with younger children and not with adolescents. The decrease in gender effects may be partially attributable to the fact that father custody, joint custody, and the involvement of noncustodial fathers are increasing and that the involvement of fathers may be more important for boys than for girls. Both male and female adolescents from divorced families show higher rates of conduct disorders and depression than those from nondivorced families. However, female adolescents and young adults from divorced families are more likely than their male counterparts to drop out of high school and college. Although male and female adolescents are equally likely to become teenage parents, single parenthood has more adverse effects for the lives of female than male adolescents, including decreased economic standing later in adulthood due to the sequelae of teenage motherhood and not finishing school. However, some girls and mothers in divorced, mother-headed families emerge as exceptionally resilient individuals, enhanced by confronting challenges and responsibilities that follow divorce. Such enhancement is rarely found among boys or fathers following parental divorce.

The quality of parenting serves an important role in protecting children or making them more vulnerable to adverse consequences from the stresses associated with divorce. Although the experiences of children in mother custody, father custody, and joint custody families vary, there is little evidence of the superiority of any of these custodial arrangements. Children can develop well in any type of custodial arrangement with an involved, authoritative parent. There are strengths and weaknesses in the parenting of custodial mothers and custodial fathers. Although custodial mothers and custodial fathers are perceived to be similarly warm and nurturing with younger children, mothers have more problems with control and with the assignment of household tasks, whereas fathers have more problems with communication, self-disclosure, and monitoring of their children's activities, particularly those of daughters. Close relationships with supportive, authoritative mothers or fathers who are warm but exert firm, consistent control and supervision are generally associated with positive adjustment in children and adolescents following divorce.

In the immediate aftermath of divorce, there is a period of disrupted parenting characterized by irritability and coercion and diminished communication, affection, consistency, control, and monitoring, but the parenting of both custodial mothers and custodial fathers improves after the first year. Although the parenting of divorced mothers improves in the early years following divorce, problems in control and coercive exchanges between divorced mothers and sons may remain high. Preadolescent girls and their divorced mothers often have close, companionate, confiding relationships. However, in adolescence there is a notable increase in conflict in these relationships, particularly among early maturing daughters and their divorced mothers.

Contact with noncustodial mothers and fathers diminishes rapidly following divorce, and about 20 percent of children have no contact with their noncustodial

fathers or see them only a few times a year, and slightly over one-quarter of children have weekly visits with their divorced fathers. Decreased parental involvement is related to residential distance, low socioeconomic status, and parental remarriage. When the child is a boy, when there is low conflict between divorced spouses, when mediation is used, or when noncustodial fathers feel they have some control over decisions in the lives of their children, paternal contact and child support payments are more likely to be maintained. Noncustodial mothers are more likely than noncustodial fathers to sustain contact with their children and to rearrange living arrangements to facilitate children's visits, and less likely to completely drop out of their children's lives or to diminish contact when either parent remarries.

Under conditions of low spousal conflict, contact with competent, supportive, authoritative noncustodial parents can have beneficial effects for children, and these effects are most marked for noncustodial parents and children of the same sex. In addition, it is the quality of contact, rather than the frequency of contact with a noncustodial parent, that is important to children's adjustment.

The long-term effects of divorce on children's adjustment are related more to continued parental conflict, new stresses encountered, individual characteristics of the child, qualities of the parent-child relationship, and resources and support systems available to the adolescent or young adult rather than to the divorce per se. Children fare better in well-functioning, single-parent families than in conflict-ridden, two-parent families. Unfortunately, when parents divorce, children frequently are exposed to multiple stressors such as continued parental conflict, depressed economic resources, changes in the availability of the custodial parent as well as the noncustodial parent, alterations in parenting styles, and more chaotic household routines. However, there is great diversity in children's long-term adjustment to divorce. On the average, most children from divorced families show more problems than those in nondivorced families. However, these effects are modest. Although children may be distressed by their parents' divorce, most children demonstrate remarkable long-term resiliency in adjusting to their new life situation.

E. Mavis Hetherington
Anne S. Mitchell

References and further reading
Emery, Robert E. 1999. *Marriage, Divorce, and Children's Adjustment.* 2d ed. Newbury Park, CA: Sage Publications.
Hetherington, E. Mavis, ed. 1999. *Coping with Divorce, Single Parenting, and Remarriage: A Risk and Resiliency Perspective.* Mahwah, NJ: Lawrence Erlbaum Associates.
Hetherington, E. Mavis, Margaret Bridges, and Glendessa M. Insabella. 1998. "What Matters? What Does Not? Five Perspectives on the Association between Marital Transitions and Children's Adjustment." *American Psychologist* 53, no. 2:167–184.

Doula

A birth doula assists the mother-to-be and her partner in preparing for and carrying out their plans for the birth. She stays by the side of the woman throughout the entire labor and delivery, providing continuous emotional encouragement and physical comfort. She also assists the mother in gathering information throughout the course of labor by facilitating communication between the laboring woman, her partner, and her attending hospital staff. A doula understands the physiology of birth and the emotional needs of a woman in labor. She recognizes birth as a key life experience that the mother will remember all her life. A doula sees her role as nurturing and protects the woman's memory of her birth experience. At postpartum, the doula provides care to a family with a newborn baby.

Background

As the modern medical era emerged, women became isolated during labor and delivery from the social support of other women that was a feature of childbirth in preindustrialized societies. Women helping women in labor is an ancient and widespread practice. For instance, anthropological data about birthing practices in nonindustrialized societies show that in all but one, support was provided by a woman. The Greek word *doula* means "woman's servant." In labor support terminology doula refers to a supportive companion (not a friend or loved one) professionally trained to provide continuous emotional and physical support to the mother and her partner during labor and delivery. The term *doula* was first used to describe "one or more individuals, often female, who give psychological encouragement and physical assistance to the newly delivered mother." (Doulas of North America, 1992) The use of the word *doula* is now widely accepted in the sense of a trained laywoman labor companion who provides the woman and her partner with continuous uninterrupted emotional and physical support during the entire labor and delivery, and to some extent, prenatally and in the first weeks after the birth. It is important to understand the vital shared ingredient that makes this role of continuous labor companion so powerful and beneficial.

Role of a Doula

To understand the special role of a doula one must first distinguish it from that of the other caregivers involved in childbirth. A doula is not a nurse or midwife. A nurse or midwife can provide support in labor if she does not have other duties, time constraints, or other patients. Many nurses and midwives choose obstetric work because of their empathic interest in helping women during childbirth. But the demands of the labor and delivery service, hectic schedules, and the large number of laboring women make it unlikely that nurses or midwives can be totally and continuously available to any one laboring woman for her entire labor. A doula is not trained to make any medical decisions, although her training includes learning about the usual medical interventions so that she can explain procedures about labor and delivery to parents in order to relieve some of their anxieties. A doula is always accepting and nonjudgmental. This feeling of total acceptance will remain with the mother as she relates to her own baby.

Doula support is by definition personalized. Through interaction with the mother and the baby's father or another loved one, the doula adjusts her care to the individual mother's needs. She must be able to enter a mother's space and be highly responsive and aware of her needs, mood changes, and unspoken feelings. At the same time she needs to be flexible in this process. For example, when women experience back labor, a doula suggests a variety of methods to help relieve the discomfort—for example, breathing, relaxation, movement, positioning, massage, hot cloths, pressure against the back, or sometimes no touch whatsoever. As labor progresses, by her presence, manner, and comforting touch and reassurance, the doula creates calmness and the essence of relaxation. This encourages the mother to focus on her body. As labor becomes more intense, doulas frequently cradle or hold the woman in their arms. If a woman should cry, the doula may get a damp cloth and wipe her face. Regardless of the response of the mother to labor, a doula remains encouraging and reassuring. The doula stays focused on what is happening to the mother and explains her progression of labor, offering words of encouragement and praise about her excellent progress. For the actual delivery, the medical caregivers are in charge. The doula remains by the mother's side along with the father. The doula supports the couple's prenatal wishes, making certain, for example, that mother and father have time alone with the baby and the mother breast-feeds early.

When the doula visits with the family following delivery she asks what they remember about the birth and allows them to share all their positive feelings and, if appropriate, their negative feelings. Almost all mothers gain from hearing details from the doula that fill in many of the missing pieces of the birth experience for them. This retelling of the birth story is an opportunity to heighten the mother's self-image by pointing out the strength she showed and the way her body followed its age-old biological course.

In a real sense, the doula "mothers the mother" by creating an emotional "holding" environment. This feeling of safety and acceptance with another woman reduces her fear and creates an inner strength that enables a woman to begin to test the limits of her own capacities and to experience dimensions possibly not recognized before—or perhaps recognized but not risked. This continuous nurturant support sends an underlying message to the woman of her value as a person, and as a mother and future caregiver. In this way her belief in her own competence can be sustained and resonate throughout her whole life.

Benefits of Doula Support

Continuous doula support has highly significant obstetrical advantages. Since the original studies published in 1980 and 1986, numerous scientific trials have been conducted in many countries investigating the effects of doula support. In all studies the participating women were expecting their first baby, were healthy, and had normal term pregnancies. The continuous presence of a doula during labor has been found to reduce the duration of labor, the likelihood of medication for pain relief, oxytocin augmentation, and Cesarean section. Doula support also resulted in improved scores given to newborns to determine overall physical condition. Studies of fathers' presence during labor do not report a decrease in Cesarean delivery rates. However, a recent study found a decreased rate of Cesarean deliveries and need for epidural analgesia when women and their male partners were supported by a doula, compared to support by their partners alone.

Fathers provide support to about 80 percent of laboring women in the United States. Fathers report that they want to be present at the birth of their babies and mothers also want them there. Recognition and validation of the father's right and need to be present at the birth of his baby is not only compatible with but also enhanced by the presence of a doula. When fathers' behavior patterns are compared to those of doulas, significant differences are found. Fathers remained farther from mothers and touched them significantly less than the doulas. This was in contrast to the doulas' continuous uninterrupted physical and emotional support, consisting of maintaining close proximity and frequent touching, stroking, or holding, and verbal encouragement that increased during late labor. Fathers' participation was rated by mothers as increasing the meaning of the labor experience and by the couple as strengthening their relationship.

The doula and father may work together as a support team. The doula touches and holds the woman's trunk so that the father is freed to offer more personal support, and do more intimate touching of the mother's head and face, when com-pared to the father's care without a doula present. The doula does not take the father's place as the main labor companion, but frees him to take on a more personal, intimate role. The father's presence during labor and delivery is important to the mother and father, but it is the presence of the doula that results in significant benefits in outcome.

In addition to the direct effects of the doula on labor and delivery, favorable effects of doula support on the subsequent psychological health of the mothers have been found. One study revealed that at twenty-four hours following birth, the mothers in the doula group had significantly less anxiety compared with the nondoula group, and fewer doula-supported mothers considered the labor and delivery to have been difficult. At six weeks mothers in the doula-supported group remained significantly less anxious, had fewer symptoms of depression, and higher self-esteem than the mothers without doula support.

The doula also has long-term effects on the mother-infant relationship. Doula-assisted mothers shortly after birth showed more affectionate interaction with their infants—for example, more smiling, talking, and stroking—than the mothers who did not have a doula. Doula-supported mothers at two months postpartum were also found to display more nurturant behaviors.

At six weeks after birth doula support has also been found to increase breastfeeding and decrease feeding problems. In another study, doula-supported mothers were more positive on all dimensions describing the specialness of their babies than were the nonsupported mothers. The supported mothers found becoming a mother was easier than expected. They saw themselves as closer to their babies, as managing better, and as communicating better with their babies. In contrast, the nonsupported mothers saw their adaptation to motherhood as more difficult. This suggests that doula care may encourage feelings of maternal attachment and a readiness to fall in love with their babies. Doula-supported mothers also reported picking up their babies more frequently when they cried than did non-supported mothers.

An important aspect of emotional support in childbirth may be the most unexpected, internalized one—that of the calm, nurturing, accepting, and holding model provided for the parents. Maternal care needs modeling; each generation benefits from the care received by the earlier one. Emotional support is an essential ingredient for every laboring woman. It is needed to enhance not only the mother's physical and emotional health during childbirth, but also the special relationship that ties the parents to each other and to their infant. It is hoped that further studies will support these very beneficial effects of this powerful and humane intervention.

The acceptance of doulas in maternity care is growing rapidly with the recognition of their important contribution to the improved physical outcomes and emotional well-being of mothers and infants. They are found in many birth settings, from the home to the hospital, and work in cooperation with physicians, nurses, midwives, and the partners and families of laboring women.

Neena Roumell

References and further reading
Doulas of North America. 1992. *Code of Ethics and Standards of Practice.* Seattle, WA: DONA.
Hofmeyer, Justin, Cheryl Nikodem, Wendy Wolman, Beverly Chalmers, and Tami Kramer. 1991. "Companionship to Modify the Clinical Birth Environment: Effects on Progress and Perceptions of Labor and Breastfeeding." *British Journal of Obstetrics and Gynecology* 98:756–764.
Kennell, John, Marshall Klaus, Susan McGrath, Steven Robertson, and Clark Hinkley. 1991. "Continuous Emotional Support during Labor in a U.S. Hospital." *Journal of the American Medical Association* 265:2197–2201.
Klaus, Marshall, John Kennell, and Phyllis Klaus. 1993. *Mothering the Mother: How a Doula Can Help You Have a Shorter, Easier and Healthier Birth.* Reading, MA: Addison-Wesley.
———. 1995. *Bonding: Building the Foundations for Secure Attachment and Independence.* Reading, MA: Addison-Wesley.
Scott, Katherine, Gail Berkowitz, and Marshall Klaus. 1999. "A Comparison of Intermittent and Continuous Support during Labor: A Meta-Analysis." *American Journal of Obstetrical Gynecology* 3:1054–1058.
Sosa, Robert, John Kennell, and Marshall Klaus. 1980. "The Effect of a Supportive Companion on Perinatal Problems, Length of Labor and Mother-Infant Interaction." *New England Journal of Medicine* 303:587–600.
Wolman, Wendy, Beverly Chalmers, Justin Hofmeyr, and Cheryl Nikodem. 1993. "Postpartum Depression and Companionship in the Clinical Birth Environment: A Randomized Control Study." *American Journal of Obstetrics and Gynecology* 168:1388–1393.
Zhang, Jun, James Bernasko, Etel Leybovich, and Marianne Fahs. 1996. "Continuous Labor Support from Labor Attendant for Primiparous Women: A Meta-Analysis." *Obstetrics and Gynecology* 88, no. 4:739–744.

Dr. Seuss
See Geisel, Theodor Seuss

Dual-Career Families
The term *dual-career family* has typically been used to describe families in which both spouses are employed in upwardly mobile jobs, and both are psychologically committed to their work. Dual-career families are a relatively new phenomenon in family lifestyle in Western societies. Shifts in parental roles have occurred between married couples in the last few decades that are likely due to increased employment rates of mothers in Western societies. In the United States, increases in women's labor force participation in

the 1970s and 1980s were motivated by changes in the organization and functioning of the U.S. economy, as well as by higher education levels among women. Prior to 1940, the typical working woman was young and single. Between 1940 and 1960, older married women entered the workforce, while rates of participation for young women did not sharply increase until after 1960. In 1994, 75 percent of women between the ages of twenty-five and fifty-four were in the labor force. (U.S. Bureau of Labor Statistics, 1995) The most recent change has been the increased employment of mothers with babies and preschoolers.

It is useful to distinguish between three family structures that can be identified in terms of marital relationships and career involvement. These are "dual-career," "dual-earner," and "traditional" families. In the *dual-career family* both spouses are committed to their upwardly mobile careers and at the same time maintain a family life together. This lifestyle requires coordination, balance, and integration of career and family roles for each spouse individually and as a couple. Their occupations usually require extensive professional training and education and long working hours. Generally, these are couples who hold professional or managerial employment, with examples including the fields of medicine, business management, architecture, educational administration, university teaching, law, and accounting.

Dual-earner family is a more general term than *dual-career. Dual-earner* is frequently used to describe families in which both parents work outside of the home, but there is little psychological attachment to work and few expectations of upward mobility. In the dual-earner family, one of the spouses may be pursuing a career, whereas the other views his or her occupational involvement as simply a job. Or, both spouses may consider themselves simply to hold jobs. Although researchers have made this distinction between dual-career and dual-earner families, as is obvious the boundaries between a "career" and a "job" can be unclear, as a job for one may be a career for another.

The term *traditional family* is characterized by a division of roles in such a way that the husband is the "breadwinner" and the mother is responsible for maintaining a home and family. It should be pointed out that, although people often refer to this arrangement as traditional, historically both parents have typically always worked. The family organization whereby the mother stays home and the father works is a relatively recent, post–World War II phenomenon for the United States. Finally, it is worthwhile to note that the term *dual-career family* typically refers to a man and a woman working and rearing children. However, consistent with other recent changes in the nature and composition of the American family, this is not necessarily the case. Dual-career families can also consist of lesbian couples or gay male couples rearing children.

Dual-career families typically struggle with coordination, balance, and integration of career roles, family and parenting roles, and marital roles. Work-family conflict occurs when the individual has to perform multiple roles, such as being a worker, spouse, and parent, and the person is not satisfied with his or her balance and integration of roles. Each of these roles requires time, energy, and commitment, and the cumulative demands of multiple roles can result in what is sometimes called role overload, role interference, or role strain. When conditions in one role (e.g., work) begin to affect a person's functioning in another setting or role (e.g., family), then there is "spillover" or "crossover" from one role to another. Spillover can be positive or negative. Negative events, stress, and pressure from the workplace spill over into the home when they cause the parent to be grumpy and short-tempered with the children at home, but positive spillover effects are also observed (e.g., when high career satisfaction and pleasant working conditions lead a parent to be happy, thereby increasing the chance of pleasant parent-child interactions). Spillover can also occur from the family world to the work world as well, since positive and negative dynamics at home can also affect a parent's functioning at work.

One area of conflict experienced by many dual career couples is equity of domestic responsibilities. Women in dual career couples today appear to be in a particular bind because, although they are now working as much as and as long hours as men, it is still the woman who typically does the majority of the domestic duties in the household. This inequity understandably creates conflict for many couples. Couples who share more equal responsibility for domestic activities have less role strain, less work-family conflict, and higher marital satisfaction. Dual-career couples who do not have children appear to experience much less role strain and work-family conflict. Having children while both parents are pursuing a career significantly increases the role strain for both members of the couple. Moreover, the more children dual-career couples have, the more work-family conflict and role strain couples typically experience. It is interesting to note that men often report that career interests intrude on fathering roles, while women are more likely than men to state that parenting interferes with career roles. Women are also more likely than men to report that their parental and career roles conflict with their marital role.

Research on the effects of dual-career parental employment on children finds that there are both pros and cons to this type of family arrangement. The single clearest benefit of having both parents employed is economic—dual-career families typically have a higher family income than families in which only one parent is working. Socioeconomic status and family income continues to be one of the best predictors of many positive child outcomes, including cognitive development, intelligence, academic performance, educational attainment, behavioral adjustment/control (as opposed to behavior problems and antisocial behavior), and improved health and nutrition. Higher income also typically leads to better living conditions for children, more social and material resources, and better neighborhoods, day-care centers, and schools. Women in dual-career families typically report higher self-esteem, greater intellectual companionship, and more self-actualization than women who do not work outside the home. These benefits appear to trickle down to daughters in dual-career homes as well, as they often report higher career expectations, less stereotypical sex-role beliefs and behavior, and higher self-esteem themselves, compared to daughters of mothers who do not work outside the home. Maternal employment is especially beneficial for child outcomes when the mother values a career and actually wants to work. Mother-child interactions involving stay-at-home mothers who would rather work are of much poorer quality than both those involving stay-at-home mothers who are happy to stay at home and working mothers who would rather be at home. Men in dual-career families report benefits in the form of freedom from bearing total economic responsibility and opportunities to take a more active role in parenting.

In terms of the potential negative effects of dual-career families on children, researchers note that it depends on parents' marital satisfaction, job satisfaction, and parenting style and competence. Negative effects on children occur to the extent that parents' work arrangements, stress, and job dissatisfaction (and parents' marital stress, conflict, and dissatisfaction) lead to poorer quality parenting. That is, parental employment status, per se, does not have negative effects on children, but if the working situation contributes to marital disruption, poorer quality parent-child interactions, and/or poorer parental monitoring and less effective and consistent care and discipline, then negative behavioral effects on children will be observed. Thus, some dual-career couples are able to maintain family stability and effective, authoritative parenting if the job/career is good, the working hours are not too excessive, the stressors are not too great, and the parents are satisfied with their jobs and marriage. But this is not the case for many other dual-career families in which the stress of trying to balance work, family, and marriage leads to either harsh, punitive parenting or excessively permissive parenting that eventually leads to child behavior problems. However, it is the quality of parenting and parent-child interactions that counts, not the quantity. Thus, dual-career couples who are wondering whether their arrangement is harmful for their children should assess their parenting style and whether and how much it would likely change if one or more of the parents were working less.

One persistent challenge for dual-career families is finding appropriate, affordable, and high-quality child care. Although many families depend on informal support systems, particularly relatives and friends, for child care, the vast majority of dual-career families use some form of outside help for the care of their children. Research has shown that the quality of day care/child care is important for positive child outcomes, and that—again—quality rather than quantity of non-parental care is the more important variable. Of course, the more hours per day a child spends in child care, the harder it is to find and afford quality care—so quantity and quality of care are often correlated for many families with fewer resources and options.

Eirikur Thorvardarson
Adam Winsler

References and further reading

Aryee, S., and V. Luk. 1996. "Balancing Two Major Parts of Adult Life Experience: Work and Family Identity among Dual-Earner Couples." *Human Relations* 49:465–487.

Bowden, G. L., and J. F. Pittman, eds. 1995. *The Work and Family Interface: Toward a Contextual Effects Perspective.* Minneapolis, MN: National Council of Family Relations.

Gupta, N., and G. D. Jenkins. 1985. "Dual-Career Couples, Stress, Stressors, Strain, and Strategies." Pp. 141–175 in *Human Stress and Cognition in Organizations: An Integrated Perspective.* Edited by T. A. Beehr and R. S. Bhagat. New York: John Wiley and Sons.

Hammer, L. B., E. Allen, and T. D. Grigsby. 1997. "Work-Family Conflict in Dual-Earner Couples: Within-Individual and Crossover Effects of Work and Family." *Journal of Vocational Behavior* 50:185–203.

U.S. Bureau of Labor Statistics. 1995. *Women in the Workplace: An Overview.* Washington DC: Government Printing Office.

E

Emotion, Infants' Facial Expression of

In order to understand emotional expressions, Charles Darwin observed their development in infancy. Darwin kept a diary of his first child's expressive behavior and used this record in his essay, *A Biographical Sketch of an Infant* (1877). In this work, he describes facial expressions (e.g., joy, surprise, interest, anger, fear, sadness, distress, and disgust) and their signaling purpose to others about one's feelings and intended action. For example, a fearful face, which involves raised and knit eyebrows, raised upper eyelids, and stretched-back lip corners, serves to communicate a need for help from a caregiver. For young infants, these facial expressions are their language, and the feelings associated with the facial expressions gives direction to their behavior.

Biological Factors: The Universal Features

Facial expressions of newborns, even when born premature, are the same as adults. Newborns at birth have the basic neuromuscular equipment necessary to respond to emotional situations. Facial expressive patterns are the same all over the world. Parents use the emotion categories that adults label as emotion expressions and make caregiving inferences about infant state and vocal behaviors.

For example, certain infant facial and vocal behaviors are commonly interpreted by parents as signs of their infants' distress, and parents then make appropriate and effective interventions. Seven emotions that have been most widely studied during the first year of life are discussed in the following sections: interest, happiness, surprise, disgust, sadness, fear, distress/pain, and anger.

Interest

Several distinct facial patterns of interest have been studied: brows drawn together and slightly lowered or brows raised. These may be produced alone or in combination with lips pursed or mouth open and relaxed. Interest expressions occur in a wide range of circumstances during infancy. Infants have shown the interest expression as early as two to three days of age when presented with a sugar solution. Research has shown that infants find the human face particularly interesting. Interest expression patterns have also been found to occur during mother-infant interactions. Mothers attend to these raised-brow patterns, which affirms the message that their infant wants to continue the social exchange. The lowered brows interest pattern observed in four- and six-month-old infants during learning has been interpreted as excitement. In a study of facial responses to pain, interest expressions were observed during parental

Bright-eyed smiling in response to outside stimulation usually occurs in infants at around two months. (Elizabeth Crews)

soothing following inoculation. This message assures parents that their comforting behavior has reduced their baby's distress.

Happiness

Infant smiling can be observed at birth. It is unlikely that these early smiles, which occur during light sleep, relate to a feeling of happiness and are regarded as "reflexive" responses. The developmental relationship between smiling and happiness in newborns is unclear. By the second week of life, infant smiling sometimes occurs when the eyes are open, but the infant's gaze is glassy and unfocused. Bright-eyed smiling in response to outside stimulation delights parents at around two months. However, smiling at familiar people and during newly mastered activities may occur between six and twelve weeks of age. Researchers agree that smiling signals happiness for infants around three months of age. The emotional meaning of smiles is strengthened by looking at accompanying or subsequent infant nonfacial behaviors. Investigators have found a relationship between smiling and sustained social play in six-month-old infants. Genuine smiles of happiness in the adult involve eye muscle action, whereas nongenuine (e.g., deliberately produced) smiles do not. Other research has shown that ten-month-old infants produce more genuine smiles with mothers than with strangers.

Surprise

Surprise expression components are brows raised (which widen the eyes) and an open rounded or oval mouth. This is the same pattern described for adults. Studies have observed the facial expression of surprise in newborns and found surprise expressions in four- to six-month-olds while they were learning a new behavior. The surprise expression may therefore reflect intense visual attention to the environment. One study found that the surprise expression occurs when the infant encounters an unexpected event in the natural environment. Another study observed surprise expressions in eight- and ten-month-olds during a peek-a-boo hiding game in which the mothers unexpectedly put on a mask before reappearing before their infants. Two surprise circumstances, a vanishing object and a hidden toy switch, produced surprise expressions in ten- to twelve-month-olds. Infants visually searched for the vanishing object and hidden toy switch, indicating that they were surprised.

Disgust

The disgust expression in infants is lowered brows, wrinkled nose, and an open, angular mouth with slight protrusion of the lower lip and tongue protrusion. The typical adult disgust expression is a simple wrinkled nose and upper lip lifted and tongue protrusion only with extreme reactions. This signal prompts the attention of caregivers during feeding. One researcher reported that pleasant and unpleasant odors (e.g., vanilla vs. rotten eggs) regularly elicited the disgust expression in newborns, while another study found that newborns and eight-week-old infants show disgust expressions in response to lemon juice, and yet another observed the disgust configuration in response to a sour vitamin solution. It has also been demonstrated that newborn responses to sour, bitter, salty, and sweet tastes were like the adult expression, that is, wrinkled nose and/or a lifted upper lip. For the sweet solution, the disgust expression appeared briefly in response to the insertion of the liquid-delivering pipette and was quickly followed by facial relaxation. Bitter also produced a gaping mouth along with nose wrinkle and upper lip lifted. Pursed lips and wrinkled nose accompanied the sour taste. The disgust expression has also been observed during intrusive caregiving situations—for example, during face washing.

Three-month-old boy upset (Elizabeth Crews)

Sadness

The sadness facial pattern consists of the inner corners of the brows raised, drawn out and down, and the mouth corners drawn downward. The sad facial expression has been observed in newborns. The sad facial pattern has been observed in a number of studies involving negative situations. In one "strange situation" study, a small number of infants (those classified as insecure) showed substantial amounts of sadness, while another study reported sad expressions in infants during a brief separation procedure, although anger was dominant. Infant sadness was also observed during a stranger approach sequence. Infants look sad in situations that are unfamiliar to them. Sadness (with fussing and anger) was shown toward the end of a learning task, suggesting that the procedure had become stressful to the infants.

Fear

The fear expression—brows level, drawn in and up, eyelids lifted, and mouth drawn back—is the same in infants and adults. The fear expression has not often been observed because it is displayed very briefly and is difficult to elicit. Research has shown that ten- to twenty-four-week-old infants do show fear expressions during a learning task. This suggests that the learning situation was extremely strange and novel to them. In another study, seven- and thirteen-month-old infants showed the fear pattern (perception of strangeness) in response to three-dimensional clay masks. These facial displays of fear were often seen in combination with other negative emotions, for example, sadness with fear components or anger with fear components. Ten- to twelve-month-old infants presented with two fear situations (stranger approach and illusion of depth) displayed components of the fear face to both situations. Infants also displayed the behavioral indicators of fear (i.e., avoidance of the stranger and refusal to cross the illusional cliff). Researchers' understanding of the fear expression and the circumstances that produce the fear face remains incomplete.

Distress/Pain

The distress/pain expressive pattern is brows lowered, eyes tightly closed, mouth is squared and angular. This expressive pattern is identical to anger, except that for anger the eyes are narrowed but open. Pain expressions have been found in adults. It is generally agreed that this expression and the accompanying cries are signals for the attention of the caregiver. In newborns, facial responses to pain stimuli (e.g., a heel lance) have been shown to vary with the infants' initial behavioral state. Quiet and alert infants show the pain expression, whereas quiet and sleepy infants do not produce the squared, open-mouth component, perhaps due to less intense pain reaction. Facial reactions to pain stimuli were studied most thoroughly in response to diphtheria-pertussis-tetanus (DPT) inoculations. The predominant facial response at two months is the distress/pain facial pattern. From two to nineteen months the expression of anger increases due to pain and the distress expression decreases.

Anger

The anger facial expression pattern is brows drawn together and downward, eyes narrowed, mouth squarish. The anger expression in adults is similar. One study examined the facial responses of one-, four-, and seven-month-old infants to nonpainful arm restraint. At both four and seven months, complete anger expressions were found. The one-month-olds tended to keep their eyes closed, showing the distress/pain pattern. Older infants tended to keep their eyes open, showing anger. Seven-month-old infants in frustration situations involving the repeated presentation and removal of a teething biscuit showed anger. In older infants, at thirteen and eighteen months, anger expression has also been observed in several investigations using developmental psychologist Mary Ainsworth's strange situation procedure. In one such experiment, anger was the predominant negative facial expression at both ages in response to mother-infant separation.

Infants over two months of age display an anger pattern as the dominant facial response to a variety of negative circumstances: inoculation, arm restraint, and separation from mother. This suggests that the anger facial pattern in older infants replaces the distress pain pattern shown at younger ages. The developmental change in the decrease in the distress expression and increase in anger expression is due to a general development of alertness. As infants grow older, they learn to respond with anger during painful and distressing situations.

Neena Roumell

See also Emotional Development

References and further reading
Camras, Linda, Carol Malatesta, and Carroll Izard. 1985. "The Development of Infant Facial Expressions in Infancy." Pp. 73–105 in *The Development of Expressive Behavior: Biology-Environment Interactions.* Edited by Gail Zivin. New York: Academic Press.
Darwin, Charles. 1877. *The Autobiography of Charles Darwin.* London: John Murray. (Reprint, New York: Norton, 1969.)
Demos, Virginia. 1982. "Facial Expressions of Infants and Toddlers." Pp. 127–160 in *Emotion and Early Interaction.* Edited by Tiffany Field and Alan Fogel. Hillsdale, NJ: Lawrence Erlbaum Associates.
Fox, Nathan, and Richard Davidson. 1985. "Sweet/Sour-Interest/Disgust: The Role of Approach-Withdrawal in the Development of Emotions." In *Social Perception in Infants.* Edited by Tiffany Field and Nathan Fox. Norwood, NJ: Ablex.
Izard, Carroll, and Carol Malatesta. 1987. "Perspectives on Emotional Development I: Differential Emotions Theory of Early Emotional Development." Pp. 494–554 in *Handbook of Infant Development.* Edited by J. Osofsky. New York: John Wiley and Sons.
Malatesta, Carol. 1985. "The Development of Expressive Behavior." Pp. 183–219 in *The Development of Expressive Behavior: Biology-Environment Interactions.* Edited by Gail Zivin. New York: Academic Press.
Oster, Harriet. 1978. "Facial Expression and Affect Development." Pp. 43–76 in *The Development of Affect.* Edited by Michael Lewis and Louis Rosenblum. New York: Plenum Press.

Sullivan, Margaret, Michael Lewis, M. Brooks, and Jeanne Gunn. 1989. "Emotion and Cognition in Infancy: Facial Expressions during Contingency Learning." *International Journal of Behavioral Development* 12, no. 2:211–237.

Wolff, Peter. 1963. "Observations on the Early Development of Smiling." Pp. 113–118 in *Determinants of Infant Behavior.* Edited by Bernard Foss. New York: John Wiley and Sons.

Emotional Development

Newborn infants show few emotional behaviors. They cry and show distress when pained or lonely or in need of food and attention. They listen to sounds, look at objects, respond to tickle sensation, and show positive emotions, such as happiness and contentment. The set of discrete emotions that they exhibit is limited, yet in a few months and by their third year of life, these same children display a wide range of emotions. By three years, almost the full range of adult emotions can be said to exist. In order to understand this rapid development, it is necessary to consider what is meant by emotion, and then look at the developmental sequence over these three years.

The Topology of Emotion

In the study of emotion, it is important first to make clear what is meant by the term. *Emotion,* like the *cognition,* refers to a class of elicitors, behaviors, states, and experiences.

Emotional States. Emotional states are defined as a particular constellation of changes in somatic and/or neurophysiological activity. Emotional states occur without our being able to perceive them. Individuals can be angry as a consequence of a particular elicitor and yet not perceive the angry state that they are in. An emotional state may involve changes in neurophysiological and hormonal responses, as well as changes in facial, bodily, and vocal behavior.

Emotional Expressions. Emotional expressions make reference to observable surface changes in face, voice, body, and activity level. Emotional expressions are seen by some as the manifestation of internal emotional states. The problem with emotional expressions is that they soon are capable of being masked, dissembled, and, in general, controlled by the individual. Moreover, emotional expressions are subject to wide cultural and socialization experiences. Thus, the relationship between expressions and states remains somewhat vague.

Emotional Experiences. Emotional experience is the interpretation and evaluation by individuals of their perceived emotional state and expression. Emotional experience requires that individuals attend to their emotional states, that is, changes in their neurophysiological behavior, the situations in which it occurs, the behaviors of others, and their own expressions. The attending to these stimuli events is neither automatic nor necessarily conscious. Emotional experience may not occur because of competing stimuli to which the organism's attention is drawn. Consider the following: the car a woman is driving suddenly has a blowout in the front tire; the car skids across the road, but the woman succeeds in bringing it under control and stopping the car on the shoulder. Measurement of her physiological state as well as her facial expression might show that while bringing the car under control, her predominant emotional state was fear. Because her attention was directed toward controlling the car, she was not aware of her internal state or her expressions. She only experienced fear after she got out of the car to examine the tire. Without attention, emotional experiences may not occur, even though an emotional state may exist. From the clinical literature, a patient may be in a depressed state, but attend to select features of that

By the age of three years, almost the full range of adult emotions can be said to exist.
(Elizabeth Crews)

state, such as fatigue, and so only experience tiredness.

Emotional experiences are dependent on cognitive processes, involving interpretation and evaluation, which involve cognitive processes that enable organisms to act on information but are very much dependent on socialization. The development of emotional experiences is one of the least-understood aspects of emotion. Emotional experiences take the linguistic form, "I am frightened" or "I am happy." The statement, "I am happy," implies two things; first, that I have an internal state called happiness, and second, that I perceive that internal state of myself. Research has demonstrated that self-consciousness does not occur prior to fifteen

months of age and emerges in the second half of the second year of life. It is only then that children can be both in a particular emotional state and be said to experience that state.

Once self-consciousness emerges, children are capable of experiencing emotions. The rules that govern how humans experience our emotional states or create emotional experiences themselves are complex and varied. Clearly, socialization rules are involved, both on a cultural as well as on a familiar or individual level.

From an interpersonal and intrapersonal point of view, the socialization rules that act on the experiencing of emotion are somewhat better articulated. Freud's theory of the unconscious and of defense mechanisms addresses this point. Defense mechanisms have as their chief function the prevention of individuals experiencing emotions or, alternatively, having emotions that they would not likely have. For example, denial or repression serve the function of preventing the person from having particular emotional experiences that he or she deems unacceptable. The defense mechanism prevents this by not allowing the subject to become conscious or self-aware. Projection, on the other hand, allows for the experiencing of the emotion, not as the self experiencing it, however, but as the self experiencing it in another. Various defense mechanisms have in common that their major function is to provide means for altering emotional experience.

A Model of Emotional Development
Following is a model of the emergence of different emotions over the first three years of life. Three years has been chosen because it represents the major developmental leap of the majority of adult emotions in emotional development. This is not to say that past the age of three years other emotions do not emerge or that the emotions that have emerged are not elaborated upon more fully. Both are probably the case.

At birth, children show a bipolar emotional life. On one hand, there is general distress marked by crying and irritability. On the other hand, there is pleasure marked by satiation, attention, and responsiveness to the environment. Attention to the environment and interest in it appear from the beginning of life. This interest and attention can be placed either in the positive pole or it can be separated, thus suggesting a tripartite division with pleasure at one end, distress at the other, and interest as a separate dimension. By three months, joy emerges. Infants start to smile and appear to show

excitement/happiness when confronted with familiar events, such as faces of people they know or even unfamiliar faces. Also by three months, sadness emerges, especially around the withdrawal of positive stimulus events. Three-month-old children show sadness when their mothers stop interacting with them. Disgust also appears in its primitive form, a spitting out and getting rid of unpleasant tasting objects placed in the mouth. Thus, by three months, children are already showing interest, joy, sadness, and disgust, and exhibiting these expressions in appropriate contexts. Anger has been reported to emerge between four and six months. Anger is manifested when children are frustrated, in particular when their hands and arms are pinned down and they are prevented from moving. Anger is an interesting emotion because, from Darwin on, it has been associated with trying to overcome a barrier blocking a goal.

Fearfulness seems to emerge still later. Again, fearfulness reflects further cognitive development. Research has shown that in order for children to show fearfulness they have to be capable of comparing the event that causes them fearfulness with some other event, either internal or external. In stranger fear the infant has to compare the face of the stranger to that of its internal representation or memory of faces. Fear occurs when the face is found to be discrepant or unfamiliar relative to all other faces that the child remembers. Children's ability to show fearfulness, therefore, does not seem to emerge until this comparison ability emerges. Children, around seven to eight months, begin to show this behavior, although it has been reported by some to occur even earlier, especially in children who seem to be precocious. In the first eight or nine months of life, children's emotional behavior reflects the emergence of the six early emotions, called by some primary emotions or basic emotions.

Surprise also appears in the first six months of life. Children show surprise when there are violations of expected events; for example, when infants see a midget (a small adult) walking toward them, they are reported to show interest and surprise rather than fear or joy. Surprise can be seen when there is violation of expectancy or as a response to discovery as in an "aha" experience. Surprise can reflect both a violation, as well as a confirmation, of expectancy. Cognitive processes play an important role in the emergence of these early emotions, even though the cognitive processes are limited; not so for the next class of emotions.

A new cognitive capacity emerges somewhere in the second half of the second year of life. The emergence of consciousness (self-referential behavior) gives rise to a new class of emotions. These have been called *self-conscious emotions* and include embarrassment, empathy, and envy. Although little work exists in the development of these emotions, there are several studies that support the emergence of embarrassment at this point in development. It has been shown that the emergence of embarrassment only takes place after consciousness occurs. Empathy, too, emerges in relation to self-recognition. While no studies on envy have been conducted, observation of children between eighteen and twenty-four months reveals the appearance of envy. The emergence of these self-conscious emotions is related uniquely to the cognitive milestone of paying attention to the self.

A second cognitive milestone occurs sometime between two to three years of age. This ability is characterized by the child's capacity to evaluate its behavior against a standard that can either be external, as in the case of parental or teacher sanction or praise, or internal, as in the case of the child's developing its own standards. This capacity to evaluate one's behavior relative to a standard develops in the third year of life.

The ability to be able to compare one's behavior to a standard gives rise to another set of emotions, which can be called *self-conscious evaluative emotions.* They include pride, shame, and guilt, among others, and require that the child have a sense of self and be capable of comparing the self's behavior against standards. If children fail vis-à-vis the standard, they are likely to feel shame, guilt, or regret. If they succeed, they are likely to feel pride. It is important to note that pride and shame are quite different from happiness and sadness. For example, we can win a lottery and feel quite happy about winning the money; however, we would not feel pride because we would not view the winning of the lottery as having anything to do with our behavior. The same is true for failure; we might feel sad if we were not able to do something, but if it was not our fault, then we would not feel shame or guilt. These complex social evaluative emotions make their appearance at around three years of age. Thus, by three years of age, the emotional life of the child has become highly differentiated. From the original tripartite set of emotions, the child, within three years, comes to possess an elaborate and complex emotional system. Although the emotional life of the three-year-old will continue to be elaborated and will expand, the basic structure necessary for this expansion already has been formed. New experiences, additional meaning, and more elaborate cognitive capacities will all serve to enhance and elaborate the child's emotional life. However, by three years of age, the child already shows those emotions that Darwin characterized as unique to our species: the emotions of self-consciousness. With these, the major developmental activity has been achieved.

Michael Lewis

See also Emotion, Infants' Facial Expression of

References and further reading
Darwin, Charles. 1965. *The Expression of Emotion in Animals and Man.* Chicago: University of Chicago Press (rpt. of orig. ed. 1872).
Lewis, Michael. 1992. *Shame, the Exposed Self.* New York: Free Press.
Lewis, Michael, and L. Michalson. 1983. *Children's Emotions and Moods: Developmental Theory and Measurement.* New York: Plenum Press.

Employment, Maternal

Since World War II there has been a steady increase in the number of women who are in the workforce. Today, 60 percent of women with children under six years of age are in the workforce, and 76 percent of women with school-aged children are working. The largest increase in mothers working outside the home has occurred among mothers with infants under the age of one year. Today, over 50 percent of these mothers are employed outside of the home. (U.S. Bureau of Labor Statistics, 1995) Most of these mothers return to work before their infant is three months old.

Many mothers feel that their roles as employee and mother are in conflict. They feel as if they are being pulled in many different directions at the same time. Historically, women have always participated in productive labor at the same time they were rearing their children. It has only been in the last century that a booming economy has provided families with the means for some women to be full-time mothers. Today, women are receiving conflicting messages from society. Women feel pressure to stay at home and raise their children and at the same time to return to the labor force. Women are returning to work in order to provide needed financial support for their families.

Though employment may create role conflict, many mothers find that employment has positive benefits. Mothers who are employed outside the home report a higher level of personal life satisfaction than mothers who are not employed outside the home. This may be due to many different things. For example, employment has been found to act as a buffer against stress from family roles. Employment also offers the mother a greater variety of activities. Mothers sometimes report a monotony in the daily routines of child care and housework that leads to boredom. The mother working outside the home has many different activities to perform during the day and is less likely to feel boredom. Mothers who are employed outside the home also gain positive experiences and social support from interactions with other adults.

Some women do find the multiple roles of worker and mother to be stressful. However, this stress may be due less to role conflict than to role overload. Mothers feel as if they have too much to do taking care of the family and their professional obligations and not enough time in which to do it. These mothers may not be receiving assistance with housework and child care from the other members of the family. The increase in maternal employment has not been met with a similar increase in fathers' participation in child care and housework. Surveys of fathers suggest that they are beginning to feel the pressure of multiple roles and may be experiencing role conflict and role overload.

Due to this role overload mothers and fathers have been working with employers to create a work environment that is more family friendly. The advent of "flex" time, less restrictive sick leave and parental leave policies, and home-based work has helped some parents cope more effectively with their role overload.

However, these family-friendly policies are not in widespread use in the United States and may not be adaptable to some occupations.

Many women cope with the role conflict and role overload by prioritizing family over work. Instead of focusing on one occupation and steadily climbing the career ladder, mothers may shift from full-time to part-time work or take jobs that fit their families' schedules rather than those that may lead to successful careers. However, role conflict and role overload may not be the reason why working mothers may be finding their lives stressful. In interviews and surveys, mothers have reported that it is not the number of roles that is having a major impact, but rather the rewards and quality of the experiences within the roles that is influencing their feelings of well-being. Mothers who gain a sense of satisfaction and reward, whether it is from one role or multiple roles, and experience fewer problems report greater happiness and self-esteem.

One area in which work and family merge and potential problems may occur is child care. The majority of the responsibility for providing child care and transporting the child to and from the child care rests on the mother. When child care is reliable and simple, mothers are able to function better in the workplace.

The mother's role preference also has an influence on her well-being. Mothers who have congruent employment preference and employment (i.e., who want to be employed outside the home and are working or who do not want to be employed outside the home and are not working) show little or no depression. Mothers who want to be employed outside the home but are not working show significantly more depression. However, mothers who do not want to be employed outside the home and are working do not show this higher level of depression. For these mothers their employment experiences may buffer them from depression.

Mothers' employment and family may influence each other in many different ways. For example, events that happen in the family arena may influence the mother's ability to perform her job and vice versa. This spillover may be both positive and negative. The mother's job stress may be alleviated somewhat by a satisfying marriage and positive interactions with her children. A rewarding job may also have positive effects on family interaction. Mothers who gain positive rewards and satisfaction from their jobs interact more positively with their children and husbands. Negative spillover effects may also occur with job stress putting strain on family interactions or difficult family situations having a negative impact on the mother's ability to perform well in her job.

For mothers, employment has been found to have both positive and negative effects. Mothers may gain a sense of satisfaction and positive experiences and rewards from their employment. The negative effects of employment have been found to center upon role overload rather than role conflict. This role overload may be decreased by an increase in participation of the other members of the family in child care and housework. The satisfaction the mother gains from her roles, rather than employment per se, may have the greatest impact on her well-being.

Diane E. Wille

References and further reading
Barnett, Rosalind. 1994. "Home-to-Work Spillover Revisited: A Study of Full-Time Employed Women in Dual-Earner Couples." *Journal of Marriage and the Family* 56:143–154.
Baruch, Grace, Rosalind Barnett, and Caryl Rivers. 1983. *Lifeprints.* New York: McGraw-Hill.
Goldberg, Wendy, and M. Ann Easterbrooks. 1988. "Maternal Employment When Children Are Toddlers and

Kindergartners." Pp. 121–154 in *Maternal Employment and Children's Development: Longitudinal Research.* Edited by Adele Gottfried and Allen Gottfried. New York: Plenum Press.

Hock, Ellen, and Debra DeMeis. 1990. "Depression in Mothers of Infants: The Role of Maternal Employment." *Developmental Psychology* 26:285–291.

Hoffman, Lois. 1989. "Effects on Maternal Employment in the Two-Parent Family." *American Psychologist* 44:283–292.

Managhan, Elizabeth, and Toby Parcel. 1990. "Parental Employment and Family Life: Research in the 1980s." *Journal of Marriage and the Family* 52:1079–1098.

McCartney, Kathleen, and Deborah Phillips. 1988. "Motherhood and Child Care" in *The Different Faces of Motherhood.* Edited by Beverly Birns and Deborah Hay. New York: Plenum Press.

Owen, Margaret, and Martha Cox. 1988. "Maternal Employment and the Transition to Parenthood." Pp. 85–120 in *Maternal Employment and Children's Development: Longitudinal Research.* Edited by Adele Gottfried and Allen Gottfried. New York: Plenum Press.

U.S. Bureau of Labor Statistics. 1995. *Women in the Workplace: An Overview.* Washington DC: Government Printing Office.

Employment, Parental, Children's Views of

There has been a great deal of observational research on the impact of parental employment on children, but only one study that has directly asked children about their views (*Ask the Children* by Ellen Galinsky). The studies from these two vantage points ask similar questions.

Is Having a Working Mother Good or Bad for Children?

Observational studies have compared the children of employed and nonemployed mothers. Underlying these studies was the implicit or explicit assumption that maternal employment would be harmful to the mother-child attachment. The preponderance of studies of young children do not find differences in the security of attachment relationships for the children of employed and nonemployed mothers. When negative findings occur, other factors are significant. For example, children are found to develop more positively when both the mother and father believe that the mother should work and when both the mother and father support each other emotionally. The income that mothers and fathers contribute to the family tends to make a positive difference in children's development. Furthermore, the quality of child care also affects children. A pair of leading theorists on maternal employment sum it up this way: "The existing data . . . suggest that mothers' employment may have effects, both positive and negative, on the child's social and academic competence, but these effects are not direct ones." They further suggest that " . . . the father's role, the mother's sense of well being, and parental orientations toward independence and autonomy" all make a difference. (Hoffman and Youngblade, 1999, 26)

In the one study that asked the children about their views, a nationally representative group of children in the third through the twelfth grades assessed how they were being parented on twelve parenting skills that research indicates are linked to children's healthy development, school readiness, and school success. The children were asked to respond to statements about their parents, such as those following, with the degree to which the statement was true for them: is raising me with good values, is someone I can go to when I am upset, spends time talking with me, appreciates me for who I am, provides family traditions and rituals, encourages me to want to learn and to enjoy learning, is involved with my school or child care.

This study found no differences in the assessments given by children who had employed mothers and those with mothers at home. It was the way children were parented, not whether their mothers worked, that mattered most.

Is It Quality Time or Quantity Time?

Observational studies have also probed whether the amount of time mothers and fathers spend with or away from their children affects children's development. A review of these studies leads to the conclusion that simply looking at the amount of time does not present a complete picture of family relationships. The quality of parent-child interactions also plays a role in the overall effect on children's development. For example, one study that examined father-toddler interaction found that child outcomes such as attachment security, positive affect, and attention were more strongly related to qualitative aspects of fathering, such as sensitivity, than to measures of the amount of time fathers spend with toddlers. When parents were responsive and warm with their children, the children were more socially competent in kindergarten and performed better in school.

The study that investigated children's views of their parents' employment came to the same conclusion. Children who reported spending more time with their parents saw them in a more positive light. Likewise, children who reported that they engaged in activities with their parents, that the time with their parents was calm, not rushed, and felt that their parents could really focus on them when they were together, assessed their parents' parenting skills more positively. In sum, both the quality of time and the quantity of time spent together are important.

Furthermore, time with both mothers and fathers matters. In fact, when children were asked if they had too little, enough, or too much time with their mothers and fathers, they were more likely to say that they have too little time with their fathers (35 percent) than their mothers (28 percent).

Is Child Care Good or Bad for Children?

Observational studies on the impact of child care have compared children cared for in child-care settings with children who have not experienced nonparental care. Without examining the quality of the child care, there are no clear-cut results in these studies. Furthermore, community-based studies in the United States have found that the vast majority of child care was mediocre in quality.

The study that examined children's perceptions found that only 50 percent of children felt that the child care they had experienced was very positive for their development. When child care was seen as positive, the children tended to use "kith and kin" words to describe it— whether it was a teacher in a center, a family child-care provider in his or her home, or a neighbor or relative.

Taken together, these two stands of research reveal that good child care can be good for children, while poor-quality child care is not. However, most children do not experience good-quality child care.

How Do Parents' Jobs Affect Children?

Studies on adults have investigated the impact that work stress, work-family conflict, role strain, and job satisfaction have on children's development. They find that parents who experience higher levels of stress and strain have children who are developing less well than the children of parents with less stress and strain.

Recent studies are beginning to identify the personal, family, job, and workplace factors that contribute to stress or satisfaction. Four factors make a difference: having a reasonably demanding job; having a job that permits parents to focus on their work; having a job that is meaningful, challenging, provides opportunities to learn, and job autonomy; and having a workplace environment with good interpersonal and supportive relationships where parents don't feel they have to choose between having a job and parenting. Parents who work in these environment are in better moods and have more energy for parenting, which in turn affects their interactions with their children and their children's development. The chain of effects, however, doesn't stop with home life. Parents with good situations at work, who come home in better moods and with more energy for their children, and who have children who are developing well, reinvest this energy back at work.

Although having a reasonable, not overly demanding job affects how parents care for their children, work demands have escalated over the past twenty years, according to the Families and Work Institute's nationally representative 1997 study of the U.S. workforce. (Bond, Galinsky, and Swanberg, 1998) And children are very attuned to the resulting stress that their parents bring home every day. According to Ellen Galinsky's *Ask the Children* study, one-third of children (32 percent) reported worrying about their parents often or very often. If one includes the children who say they sometimes worry about their parents, the percent went up to two-thirds of children who worry. One of the major reasons that children worried about their parents was because they saw their parents feeling tired and stressed. And, if given one wish to change the way their mothers' or fathers' work affected them, the largest proportion of children wished that their parents would be less stressed and less tired. Interestingly, when asked what they think their children would wish for, only 2 percent of parents correctly guessed that parental work stress was on their children's minds.

How Do Parents' Jobs Affect Their Children's Development?
An important way that parental employment influences children's development

is by affecting parents' values and child-rearing styles. The nature of employment, and employment itself, may influence parents' ways of thinking and behaving, which may have an effect on how they socialize their children. Many researchers have examined the relationship between parents' education and job characteristics and their child-rearing practices and values orientations.

One characteristic of jobs—job complexity—has repeatedly been linked to the way that parents interact with their children. Researchers have found that parents whose jobs are highly complex are more likely to value self-direction in their children, to encourage autonomy and intellectual flexibility, and to provide cognitive stimulation and affective warmth.

The *Ask the Children* study found that parents were not very aware of how they were transmitting information about the world of work, but children were acute observers. This study found that while three in five parents liked their jobs a lot, only two in five children thought that their parents liked their jobs a lot. Many parents saw work as competitive with their children, so they didn't share very much about their jobs with them. In addition, parents often came home and complained about work, without realizing that their actions provided a living laboratory for children to learn about the world of work.

The fact that only one study has systematically investigated children's views of their parents' work is indicative of a larger societal issue: the lack of communication between adults and children. In the *Ask the Children* study, most children did not give their parents very high marks for knowing what was really going on in their lives. Thus, there is a need for more research on children's perceptions of their parents' employment.

Ellen Galinsky

References and further reading

Bond, James T., Ellen Galinsky, and Jennifer E. Swanberg. 1998. *The 1997 National Study of the Changing Workforce.* New York: Families and Work Institute.

Fuligni, Allison Sidle, Ellen Galinsky, and Michelle Poris. 1995. *The Impact of Parental Employment on Children.* New York: Families and Work Institute.

Galinsky, Ellen. 1999. *Ask the Children: What America's Children Really Think about Working Parents.* New York: Morrow.

Hoffman, Lois W., and Lise M. Youngblade. 1999. *Mothers at Work: Effects on Children's Well-Being.* New York: Cambridge University Press.

Kohn, Melvin L., and Carmi Schooler. 1983. *Work and Personality: An Inquiry into the Impact of Social Stratification.* Norwood, NJ: Ablex.

NICHD Early Child Care Research Network. 1997. "The Effects of Child Care on Infant-Mother Attachment Security: Results of the NICHD Study of Early Child Care." *Child Development* 68, no. 5:860–879.

Parcel, Toby L., and Elizabeth G. Meneghan. 1994. "Early Parental Work, Family Social Capital, and Early Childhood Outcomes." *American Journal of Sociology* 99, no. 4.

Erik Erikson (Camera Press Ltd./Archive Photos)

Erikson, Erik
(1902–1994)

Erik Homburger Erikson was the émigré psychoanalyst who profoundly altered concepts of human development. Analyzed by Anna Freud, the daughter of Sigmund Freud, Erikson and Anna Freud began child psychoanalysis as a separate field of study and therapy in Vienna in the early 1930s. Later, as a Freud revisionist, Erikson disputed that development is stable on the basis of its roots in early childhood. He converted Freud's psychosexual view to one with a basis in psychosocial foundations and claimed that development is anchored in three systems—the biological, the psychological, and the social. He was the first to show that the social world exists within the psychological apparatus as well as in the world that is external to the person. Reshaping Freudian thought, he changed Freud's five-stage model of psychosexual development that ends with genital development to an eight-stage model of psychosocial development that shows development extending throughout life. Erikson's model builds on healthy development, shows change and growth, and claims that the person can alter the course of his or her own development. The well-known terms *identity* and *identity crisis* are Erikson's. *Identity* references the development of a sense of personal coherence, authenticity, commanding ideology, and self in future vocation that is attained in some beginning way by the end of adolescence. *Identity crisis* describes the period during which identity is formed, as well as the struggles that occur during that period. Identity is the bridge to adulthood, and all of adulthood represents identity's elaboration.

Erikson's view of lifelong human development was a dramatic deviation from Freudian dogma. Erikson's theory states that each of the eight stages of life, from infancy through old age, embodies a specific psychosocial challenge. Together these build toward a cumulative set of strengths by the end of life. Each challenge hosts a dialectic struggle in which the mental health-affirming counterpart or positive pole engages the destructive counterpart or negative pole. In the best of developmental health, both the positive and the negative are included in the resolution of each stage, with the balance tilted toward the positive, health-affirming pole. The stages that build from early life onward are trust/mistrust (infancy), autonomy/shame and doubt (early childhood), initiative/guilt (play age), industry/inferiority (school age), identity/identity confusion (adolescence), intimacy/isolation (young adulthood), generativity/stagnation (adulthood), and integrity/despair (old age). In his later writings, believing that his readers saw his theory as an achievement plan that excluded the negatives, Erikson removed the "versus" that he had previously placed between the two polar terms for each stage.

Erikson's writings include seven original books, four edited compilations of essays, one book that records the text of an Erikson dialogue, and 109 articles. His most popular book was *Childhood and Society* (1950; 1963). He won both the Pulitzer Prize and the National Book Award in 1969 for his book *Gandhi's Truth*. In addition to those texts, his other books are *Young Man Luther* (1958), *Identity and the Life Cycle* (1959), *Insight and Responsibility* (1964), *Identity: Youth and Crisis* (1968), *In Search of Common Ground* (1973), *Dimensions of a New Identity* (1974), *Life History and the Historical Moment* (1975), *Toys and Reasons* (1977), and *The Life Cycle Completed* (1982). A selection of his previously unpublished papers, edited by Stephen Schlein, was published in 1987 as *A Way of Looking at Things.*

Erikson was born on 15 June 1902 in Frankfurt, Germany. He was the son of a Danish Jewess and a gentile Dane, a father he never knew and to whom his mother was not married. When young Erikson was three, his mother married his pediatrician, Dr. Theodor Homburger, who later adopted him. The family lived in Karlsruhe, Germany. Blond, tall, and Nordic looking, Erikson did not feel accepted in the synagogue, where his features stood out. Because he was Jewish, he was rejected as well by his anti-Semitic German middle-class schoolmates. Sensitive, feeling an outcast, Erikson kept alive his sense of not belonging and, throughout his psychoanalytic writing career, worked on the borders of thought instead of within any one established field. He believed that this advanced his originality and made him understand how others can feel disenfranchised or diffuse in their identities.

After graduating from the gymnasium (German high school), Erikson became an itinerant artist. He wandered the Black Forest, sketched children's portraits, and carved woodcuts. He lived for a time in Florence, Italy, where one exhibit of his work was held. He soon recognized that he was not an originating artist and would not have great artistic success. Despondent, he returned to his family in Karlsruhe. In 1927, his childhood friend Peter Blos invited him to Vienna to teach in the progressive school that had been established for children whose parents were undergoing psychoanalysis, some of whom were in analysis themselves. Erikson's sensitivity to children was noticed by Anna Freud, who invited him to begin training as a psychoanalyst. During the three-year period he was analyzed by Anna Freud, Erikson worked in the Vienna school and simultaneously earned a Montessori Diploma. That and his full membership in the International Psychoanalytic Association upon graduation from the Vienna Psychoanalytic Institute (1933) were his only credentials. He earned neither a college degree nor any other credentials.

In 1930, Erikson married Joan Serson, an artist and a dancer. In 1933, the couple and their two young children, Kai and Jon, immigrated to the United States. (Their third and fourth children, Susan and Neil, were born in the United States.) Erikson was Boston's first child psychoanalyst. In 1934, he was appointed to the faculty of the Harvard Medical School. He worked at Massachusetts General Hospital and in Harvard's Psychological Clinic. In 1936, he accepted a research position at Yale University's Institute of Human Relations. In 1939, he moved to Berkeley, California, where he worked in a longitudinal study of normal children. He established a private practice in San Francisco. Refusing on First Amendment grounds to sign a loyalty oath, in 1950 Erikson left what was by then a full-time professorship at the University of California. From 1950 to 1960, his principal association was with the Austen Riggs Center in Stockbridge, Massachusetts, where he was a member of the senior staff. In 1960, he accepted a position as professor of human development at Harvard University, remaining there until his retirement in 1970. He retired first to Tiburon, California, and later to Cambridge, Massachusetts. He died on Cape Cod, Massachusetts, on 12 May 1994.

Erikson was known for his studies of the Yurok and Sioux Native Americans in the 1930s and for the articles and chapters that came from those studies. In the 1940s Erikson worked with the Committee on National Morale, contributing

to understanding of German prisoners of war, Nazi propaganda, and submarine psychology. At the end of the war, he contributed to efforts of the Joint Committee on Postwar Planning and to efforts then under way to address needs of returning veterans with symptoms of instability. In 1962. Erikson and his wife, Joan, traveled to India to begin seven years of fieldwork in search of the history and presence of Mahatma Gandhi. The book that resulted, *Gandhi's Truth*, was his effort to show both a leader at work in the crises of his life and times and the potential role of militant nonviolence in a nuclear era.

Carol H. Hoare

References and further reading
Erikson, Erik H. 1950. *Childhood and Society.* New York: Norton.
———. 1958. *Young Man Luther.* New York: Norton.
———. 1959. *Identity and the Life Cycle.* New York: Norton.
———. 1963. *Childhood and Society.* 2d ed. New York: Norton.
———. 1964. *Insight and Responsibility.* New York: Norton.
———. 1968. *Identity: Youth and Crisis.* New York: Norton.
———. 1969. *Gandhi's Truth.* New York: Norton.
———. 1973. *In Search of Common Ground.* New York: Norton.
———. 1974. *Dimensions of a New Identity.* New York: Norton.
———. 1975. *Life History and the Historical Moment.* New York: Norton.
———. 1977. *Toys and Reasons.* New York: Norton.
———. 1982. *The Life Cycle Completed.* New York: Norton.
Schlein, Stephen, ed. 1987. *A Way of Looking at Things: Selected Papers from 1930 to 1980: Erik H. Erikson.* New York: Norton.

Ethnic Identity

Ethnic Identity is an element of the self-concept comprised of an individual's identification with a certain ethnic group. Its development is most prominent during adolescence. Ethnic identity components

Three generations of a family attend a St. Patrick's Day parade in St. Paul, Minnesota. Parents can help their children develop a strong ethnic identity. (Skjold Photographs)

include the feelings, significance, and comfort attributed to the defining elements (e.g., values, symbols, and common histories) of an individual's ethnic group membership. Many scales have been developed to classify an individual into various ethnic identity stages or to capture the multidimensional nature of ethnic identity attitudes. Although most ethnic identity models and theories describe the psychological processes of ethnic minorities, ethnic identity models have also emerged to describe the psychological processes of white mainstream youth. For ethnic minority youth, the development of a strong ethnic identity entails learning both negative and positive aspects of ethnic minority and mainstream culture, while being challenged to internalize and fuse only the positive elements of each

into one identity. Succeeding in this task is an important determinant of healthy psychosocial development because, by achieving an integrated sense of self, an individual finds that personal goals are more easily defined, and integration with mainstream society is facilitated.

History
The study of ethnic identity probably begins in the United States with the classic African American racial identity studies showing that African American children preferred lighter-skinned dolls over darker-skinned ones. Three decades later Erik Erikson published his identity theory in *Identity: Youth and Crisis* (1968), in which he assigned identity development as the primary adolescent task. Erikson never empirically investigated identity

formation processes among ethnic minorities, yet postulated from his examination of African American literature (i.e., W. E. B. DuBois, Ralph Ellison, and Thomas Pettigrew) that the ethnic minority is at risk of developing a diffuse identity by internalizing the negative views held by the dominant society. Erikson considered the optimal identity outcome possible for the oppressed individual to be one that somehow maintained ethnic origins, yet also was integrated within the dominant society.

Questions surrounding the validity of the doll preference studies and of Erikson's individual identity model led to the emergence of ethnic identity models to explain the group identity formation process. Researchers have developed a model to describe the stages African Americans traverse before coming to accept their racial identity. In the initial "crisis" stage, the person's values and attitudes were dominated by European American views. The individual then moved toward an increasing identification with his or her ethnic and racial heritage, until reaching a clear and proud commitment to an identity that both accepted mainstream values and attitudes and internalized positive ethnic attitudes and values.

In one study, a psychologist created an empirical ethnic identity model to explain and measure the process of ethnic identity development of all ethnic and racial youth and found that youth from varying ethnic groups (white, African American, Asian, and Hispanic) fell within three distinct ethnic identity stages or categories, ranging from a diffuse ethnic identity to a stronger, more integrated and achieved ethnic identity. Other researchers devised four category measures that captured the potential bicultural nature of ethnic identities. In contrast to prior ethnic identity studies and models, these more recent models found that most ethnic minority youth are very proud of their ethnicity, do

not go through a stage that is saturated with negative mainstream attitudes, and that their ethnic identity attitudes do not vary across gender and socioeconomic groups. Some small differences across ethnic groups emerged, with African Americans and Hispanics living in the United States having stronger ethnic identity attitudes than Asians or Native Americans. Whites had the weakest ethnic identity attitudes across U.S. racial groups. In fact, the ethnic identities of mainstream whites were so weak that it was difficult to reliably classify them within ethnic identity stages. However, for nonmainstream whites, ethnic identity attitudes comprised an important part of the self-concept.

Ethnic Exploration
Many adolescents explore their ethnicity in an attempt to understand the personal implications of their ethnic group membership. Participation in ethnic activities provides a source of social support, especially for ethnic minority youth exposed to predominately mainstream settings. The effects of engaging in an ethnic search on adolescent outcomes are relatively unclear. Some studies suggest that this behavior is related to elevated levels of self-esteem and self-actualization, improved grades in school, increased college aspirations, decreases in substance abuse, improved memory, and resiliency against discrimination, ethnic threats, and negative stereotypes. Other studies have found slight, insignificant, or even negative relationships between ethnic exploration and self-esteem. Studies across ethnic groups have also found that those engaging in an ethnic search had greater concerns about drugs, and adverse mental health outcomes.

Strong or Achieved Ethnic Identity
Following a period of ethnic exploration, adolescents may develop an integrated,

achieved, or simply strong ethnic identity, which is characterized by strong feelings of ethnic pride. A strong ethnic identity is related to positive outcomes such as higher levels of self-esteem, psychological adjustment and functioning, academic abilities, improved health, greater satisfaction with physical appearance, and greater feelings of self-efficacy. In addition, ethnic or race pride may protect the adolescent against the internalization of negative stereotypes, prejudice, and discrimination, and ultimately protect self-esteem and reinforce the self-concept.

Having a strong ethnic identity is also related to attitudes about other ethnic and racial groups. Mainstream adolescents with strong ethnic identity attitudes are more likely to have prejudicial attitudes toward outgroup members. In contrast, a strong ethnic identity is not related to negative outgroup feelings among ethnic minorities. In fact, ethnic minorities with a strong ethnic identity are less likely to perceive ethnic threats and discriminatory situations.

Predictors of Ethnic Identity
Adolescent behavior and development are the product of a variety of contextual and individual factors. For example, adolescents' social contexts, such as their family, peers, schools, and neighborhoods, as well as individual factors, such as their skin color, language abilities, and behavioral patterns, influence ethnic identity outcomes. The salience of ethnicity varies with each social context. Situations, such as ethnic festivities or moments of racial conflict, may stimulate or inhibit ethnic expression, as may the stage of cognitive maturity.

Characteristics such as language and skin color may be the most important traits that distinguish ethnic minority youth from the mainstream and play an important role in the patterned outcomes of disliked ethnic and racial groups. Skin color, color stereotyping, color bias, and language abilities might result in unique identity formation processes. Darker-skinned adolescents may have greater difficulty in adopting a bicultural or mainstream identity than lighter-skinned ethnic minorities. Also, for adolescent immigrants, language is often used to express their ethnic identity, to bond with ethnic group members, or to assimilate into the mainstream. In fact, bilingual adolescents have been known to interact better with members of both cultures, to have higher aspirations, and to be better adjusted than monolingual immigrants.

The family is another important element that influences adolescent ethnic identity outcomes. Parents play an important role in ensuring the healthy psychological development of the child and influencing their children's ethnic identity development, often teaching their children appropriate ethnic behaviors, language acquisition, and means of surviving in mainstream culture. Ethnic group values are often transmitted from family members to the child before these values have been confirmed by the outside world. Parents' ethnic identification and parental behaviors, such as community involvement, ethnic socialization, and preparing children for discriminatory experiences, are strongly related to their children's ethnic identity outcomes. The use of ethnic socialization strategies differs across ethnic groups. Also, the importance of family may be muted by peer influences as children grow older.

Other factors to consider when trying to understand ethnic identity correlates and processes are the impact of social support, the ethnic composition of adolescent contexts (e.g., schools, neighborhoods, peers), adolescents' cross-ethnic contact, and community involvement on adolescents' ethnic identity attitudes. These elements and others that have not yet been explored are fundamental in determining adolescent ethnic identity outcomes.

M. Antonia Biggs

References and further reading

Bankston, Carl, and Min Zhou. 1995. "Religious Participation, Ethnic Identification, and Adaptation of Vietnamese Adolescents in an Immigrant Community." *Sociological Quarterly* 36:523–534.

Bilides, D. 1991. "Race, Color, Ethnicity, and Class: Issues of Biculturalism in School-Based Adolescent Counseling Groups." *Social Work with Groups* 14:23–43.

Cross, William E. 1978. "The Thomas and Cross Models of Psychological Nigrescence: A Review." *Journal of Black Psychology* 5:13–31.

Erikson, Erik. 1968. *Identity: Youth and Crisis.* New York: Norton.

Félix-Ortiz, Maria, Michael D. Newcomb, and H. Myers. 1994. "A Multidimensional Measure of Cultural Identity for Latino and Latina Adolescents." *Hispanic Journal of Behavioral Sciences* 16:99–115.

Knight, George P., Martha E. Bernal, Camille A. Garza, Marya K. Cota, and Katheryn A. Ocampo. 1993. "Family Socialization and the Ethnic Identity of Mexican-American Children." *Journal of Cross-Cultural Psychology* 24: 99–114.

Martinez, Ruben O., and Richard L. Dukes. 1997. "The Effects of Ethnic Identity, Ethnicity, and Gender on Adolescent Well-Being." *Journal of Youth and Adolescence* 36:503–516.

Phinney, Jean S. 1989. "Stages of Ethnic Identity Development in Minority Adolescents." *Journal of Early Adolescence* 9:34–49.

Spencer, Margaret B., and Carol Markstrom-Adams. 1990. "Identity Processes among Racial and Ethnic Minority Children in America." *Child Development* 61:290–310.

F

Failure to Thrive

The condition known as *failure to thrive* describes a child whose growth in height or weight is consistently below the third percentile for children of his or her age group. The designation is also sometimes applied to children who fall below the fifth percentile or whose rate of growth, in comparison with same-age peers, becomes markedly slower. Failure to thrive is not a disease in and of itself, but instead a symptom for a potentially serious biological or psychological condition that interferes with adequate growth.

Children may exhibit failure to thrive for a variety of reasons. For example, some children will be given this label simply because they have inherited short stature or a pattern of delayed growth compared to other children of the same age; they are otherwise normal in their development. However, children often exhibit failure to thrive because of disease, a metabolic disorder, or some other medical condition that prevents absorption of adequate levels of nutrients or a sufficient amount of calories. These children are said to display *organic failure to thrive* because a physiological or biological explanation can be identified as the source of their very slow growth rate. A substantial number of children also display failure to thrive as a result of underlying social or psychological factors. When infants or children exhibit abnormally slow growth, but without any iden-

tifiable biological basis for it, they are said to display *nonorganic failure to thrive.* The label *psychosocial dwarfism* is sometimes applied to children who display nonorganic failure to thrive when they become older.

The distinction between biological and psychological causes of poor growth is often difficult to make, and researchers have yet to discover the range of social and psychological factors contributing to failure to thrive. Typical characteristics of children displaying nonorganic failure to thrive include a passive demeanor, relatively little responsiveness to environmental stimulation provided by caregivers, and a tendency to withdraw from the efforts of others to initiate contact. These children show lessened facial expressions, display frequent irritability, and in some cases may even engage in self-destructive behaviors such as head banging. Another common observation relates to their eating habits. Children displaying nonorganic failure to thrive tend to be fussy about what they eat, sometimes refuse to eat for a period of time, or exhibit other disturbances associated with the ingestion of food, including difficulties in chewing and swallowing. When combined with a high activity level, problems associated with feeding in infants and eating in older children can directly contribute to poor physical development.

The behaviors, emotional support, and responsiveness of caregivers can play a significant role in the rate of children's growth as well. Parents of infants and children who exhibit failure to thrive are somewhat more likely to interrupt or interfere with the eating habits of their offspring and they may inadvertently provide an unbalanced diet for their young, stemming from concerns about obesity or allergic reactions to particular foods. Other kinds of poor parenting practices also may be observed when children exhibit failure to thrive. Mothers, for example, express less pleasure and fewer positive responses in communicating with their infants and children. This configuration of interactions can arise from a wide variety of factors, such as feelings of disappointment if the infant does not look or act as imagined before birth or the child fails to behave in accord with parental expectations.

In addition, parent and child often demonstrate an insecure relationship with one another as evidenced by the kind of attachment the child forms. Several factors appear to inhibit the ability of the child to establish a secure attachment. For example, a mother may be anxious about caring for the child, perhaps because she is young and unprepared for the duties of parenting. Also, a mother may not have established a secure bond with her own parents or may have experienced trauma in childhood that, in turn, has left her unable to develop a stable relationship with her child. Infants and children readily recognize the anxiety and insecurity evident in such parenting. In general, reduction in stress and a supportive family environment are important elements in child rearing that can decrease the risk for failure to thrive.

If left untreated, failure to thrive can rapidly affect a child's overall health and development. However, because numerous factors can contribute to the condition, pinpointing a specific cause and treatment is difficult, despite the relative ease with which poor growth can be measured. Parents or others who suspect failure to thrive should seek medical attention to determine whether a biological or physiological basis for the condition exists. Children may need to be hospitalized for both diagnostic purposes and to provide them with adequate nutrients. Because social and psychological factors can play a role in a substantial proportion of cases of failure to thrive, some children and their parents may also need to obtain counseling and psychological assistance.

Marvin W. Daehler
Amy MacConnell

References and further reading
Drotar, Dennis, ed. 1985. *New Directions in Failure to Thrive: Implications for Research and Practice.* New York: Plenum Press.

Kessler, Daniel B., and Peter Dawson, eds. 1999. *Failure to Thrive and Pediatric Undernutrition: A Trandisciplinary Approach.* Baltimore, MD: Paul H. Brookes.

Family Leave

Family leave is designed to allow an individual time off work to care for oneself or an immediate family member; it encompasses—but is not restricted to—parental leave following the birth of a child. Recent family leave provisions represent key first steps in recognizing the importance of balancing family and work obligations. Current policies, although limited in scope, have been utilized extensively by American families. Expansion of family leave policies may be warranted on the basis of accumulating social scientific evidence.

On 5 February 1993, just two weeks after his inauguration, President Bill Clinton signed the first piece of legislation of his young administration: the Family and Medical Leave Act (FMLA). The signing ceremony in the White House Rose Garden marked the end of an eight-year struggle that included three

President Bill Clinton signs the Family and Medical Leave Act, 1993. (Official White House Photo)

major name changes (from "maternity" to "parental" to "family"), two vetoes by President George Bush, and eighteen specific compromises.

With the passage of the FMLA, employees in companies with fifty or more workers were given the right to unpaid leave for twelve weeks during any twelve-month period to care for a child, a spouse, an ailing parent, or oneself. It also guaranteed job security and required an employer to continue health-care benefits during the leave of absence. In order to qualify, a worker must be employed for at least a year and must have worked at least 1,250 hours (twenty-five hours a week). It does not apply to grandchildren who want to care for grandparents, to sons- or daughters-in-law who want to care for mothers- or fathers-in-law, to cohabiting heterosexual couples, or to same-sex couples. The law requires that the employee give

advanced notice prior to taking the leave, and it allows a company to deny leave to an employee who is within the highest paid 10 percent of its workforce.

Although the passage of the FMLA was hailed as a major legislative achievement, the concepts of family leave and maternity benefits are scarcely new. Bismarck, for example, first established maternity benefits in Germany in the late 1800s. Britain, France, and Italy adopted similar initiatives prior to 1919, and almost all Western industrialized nations had adopted such policies by World War II. In 1985, when the first family leave bill was introduced in the U.S. Congress by Patricia Schroeder (D-CO), 135 countries had already established maternity leave benefits and, of those, all but ten nations mandated paid maternity leave.

Why the United States has been slow in developing a leave policy is, of course, open to speculation. One can certainly point to differences in political culture and ideology between European nations and the United States, to the decentralization of the American political system that places greater responsibility on the states, and to the more powerful labor unions in Europe that have succeeded in securing such family-oriented benefits. But despite the states' slow start in this area, concerns about the changing American family and its needs have climbed high onto the legislative agendas during the past two decades. For example, when the FMLA was signed into law, twenty-seven states had already adopted their own versions of the law, and several surpassed the federal statute in terms of employee benefits.

A primary catalyst for the marked increase in family-oriented legislation can be traced to the major changes that have occurred in the American workforce. Today, more women, and particularly mothers, are entering the workforce on a full-time basis than at any time since World War II. Nearly half (42 percent) of all wage and salaried workers have children under eighteen years old living at home. More than 60 percent of women with children aged three to five years are employed, representing the fastest growing segment of the U.S. labor force. More than 80 percent of working women are in their childbearing years (eighteen to forty-four), 65 percent of all American women in this age group are employed, and nearly 50 percent of all mothers with children under the age of one year are working. (U.S. Department of Labor, 1996) Equally significant, research results continue to show that working women, in addition to meeting various family and job-related responsibilities, are also the primary caregivers for their elderly family members. And further, the demand for elder care will increase even more as the baby boomers age.

For working parents and their young children in particular, the FMLA is very important. Whereas studies have not found direct effects of maternal employment per se on child development or marital relationship quality, the availability of family leave has been implicated as a key predictor of these family outcomes. In addition to access to social supports and quality child care, medical care, or elder care (as applicable), family leave is viewed by social scientists as crucial for responding to the needs of family members during crises and developmental transitions.

According to the American Academy of Pediatrics, infants are extremely vulnerable during the first few months of life. They are highly dependent on a parent or caregiver's sensitive responses to their needs for the establishment of trusting (secure) attachment relationships and the stabilization of sleeping, waking, and feeding patterns. In order for parents to address infants' physical, cognitive, and social developmental needs for stimulation and regulation, time off from work is a necessity, not a luxury.

And for toddlers, preschoolers, and school-age children, it is certain that they will become ill at times and demand care. Research has consistently shown that a parent's presence and emotional support during a child's illness is often crucial to the child's healthy recovery and future well-being. Again, time off from work under such circumstances is a necessity.

The major social trends identified above, combined with the everyday caregiving demands of parents of young children, strike at the very heart of an important public policy question. That is, where do we draw the line between what the family is capable of doing and what the government should be expected to do? Clearly, the FMLA serves as one example of a response to this question. But is it supportive of parents and fair to corporations? To date, little research has been conducted to address this query. However, in 1996, three years after the FMLA was implemented, the bipartisan Commission on Leave issued a 300-page report, *A Workable Balance: Report to Congress on Family and Medical Leave Policies.*

The commission reported that the FMLA applied to only 6 percent of the nation's corporations and about 60 percent of the workforce. It also concluded that for most employers, compliance was easy, costs were minimal, and the administrative impact was small. For employees the leaves were short, most returned to work, and the overall turnover rate declined. In terms of utilization, 59 percent of all leaves taken during the first three years of the law's existence were because of the employee's own illness. Almost 15 percent of all leaves were taken to care for a newborn/adopted child, and about 20 percent of the leaves were taken to care for an ill child, parent, or spouse. A finding that was both surprising and significant concerned men's role in family caregiving activities. It was reported that across both categories of family leave (parental leave and leave to care for a seriously ill parent, child, or spouse), the role of men was comparable to that of women (excluding women's leave for maternity benefits).

A troubling finding by the commission, however, was that 64 percent of those who indicated that they were unable to take leave cited financial difficulties as their primary reason. Other studies of women returning to work after parental leave have found that a majority wished they had taken a longer leave; they report, however, that they could not afford a longer *unpaid* leave. These findings, among others, prompted President Clinton to announce during a commencement address at Grambling State University on 23 May 1999 that he would ask the Department of Labor to explore the feasibility of using state unemployment insurance surpluses to fund paid leave. By the end of 1999, at least ten states had put forth several types of legislative initiatives designed to provide some wage replacement for employees who utilize the FMLA.

Since its enactment in 1993, the Family and Medical Leave Act has enabled more than 24 million Americans to take up to twelve weeks of leave. But if the FMLA is to undergo a major face-lift in the years ahead and provide paid leave, it is also likely that reformers will reconsider the length of the leave. It is important to remember that setting it at twelve weeks was the result of political compromise, not the product of scientific research. In order to appeal to as many legislators as possible, particularly those who were sitting on the political "fence" when the FMLA was being debated, proponents of the bill compromised on weeks, bargaining down from thirty-six to twenty-four to eighteen to twelve. How many weeks does a parent need to bond with a child before going back to work, and to what extent should legislators encourage *both* mothers and fathers to share equally in the early years of child rearing? These are two questions that could be informed by referring to appropriate research findings.

What is an appropriate amount of leave? The amount of time required for full physical recovery from childbirth, for example, varies greatly, but may take up to six months or more for some women. Several studies have found shorter parental leaves to be associated with less sensitive parenting (including negative parental behavior and affect directed toward infants), higher stress, and a greater risk for parental depression in men and women. For this reason, many developmentalists have recommended parental leaves of three to six months, as well as family leaves in excess of the current twelve-week federal standard.

Should leave be encouraged and supported for both parents? Although there has been some change in fathers' utilization of leave since the passage of the FMLA, lags in workplace acceptance of men's leave and the lack of paid leave mean that fathers are unlikely to take longer leaves. Family science research suggests that the first few months after childbirth and instances of family medical crises are important family transition times. Men and women need time to adjust and to negotiate and redefine roles as parents, spouses, and workers. Adequate provisions for paid family leave may be crucial for the establishment of egalitarian division of responsibilities that benefit families and workplace productivity.

Steven K. Wisensale
Preston A. Britner

References and further reading
Clark, Roseanne, Janet S. Hyde, Marilyn J. Essex, and Marjorie H. Klein. 1997. "Length of Maternity Leave and Quality of Mother-Infant Interactions." *Child Development* 68:364–383.
Elving, Ronald D. 1995. *Conflict and Compromise: How Congress Makes the Law.* New York: Simon & Schuster.
Frank, Meryl, and Edward F. Zigler. 1996. "Family Leave: A Developmental Perspective." Pp. 117–131 in *Children, Families, and Government: Preparing for the Twenty-first Century.* Edited by Edward F. Zigler, Sharon L. Kagan, and Nancy W. Hall. New York: Cambridge University Press.
National Partnership for Women and Families. 1998. *Guide to the Family and Medical Leave Act: Questions and Answers.* Washington, DC: National Partnership for Women and Families.
U.S. Department of Labor, Women's Bureau. 1996. *A Workable Balance: Report to Congress on Family and Medical Leave Policies.* Washington, DC: U.S. Department of Labor.

Family Rituals

Family rituals are a symbolic form of communication that is predictable and experienced by the family members through repetition. Family rituals are a process that changes with the demands of family life. The practice of predictable and meaningful family rituals such as eating dinner together, as well as annual celebrations of birthdays and holidays, shape the family identity. Family rituals may be any event or activity as defined by a given family. Rituals that are predictable and meaningful are powerful organizers of family life.

The meaning that is attached to predictable family interactions is significant for the individual family members and the family as a whole. The practice of routines and the representations and beliefs of the family's identity give all members a shared and important sense of belonging. Specific family rituals may center around mealtimes, bedtime, weekend activities, vacations, or any family activity that is predictable and deemed special by the family members. The transition to parenthood is a great opportunity for couples to reflect upon family rituals that occurred while they were growing up. This reflection should include discussion of the predictability and meaning of the rituals, consideration of which rituals the prospective parents would like to preserve, and thoughts about new rituals that they would like to establish as they start a family of their own. Parenthood and becoming a family have been identified as a stressful period for adults and their marital relationships. The practice of meaningful and predictable rituals during early parenthood, such as regularly scheduled meals, may protect couples from increasing levels of marital discord as their children enter preschool.

Seven primary settings have been identified for family rituals including dinnertime, weekends, vacations, annual celebrations (birthday, anniversary, first day of school), special celebrations (wedding, graduation, family reunion), religious hol-

The practice of predictable and meaningful family rituals shape the family identity. (Skjold Photographs)

idays (Christmas, Hanukkah, or Kwaanza), and cultural and ethnic traditions (naming celebrations, wakes, funerals, or baking particular ethnic foods). For each of the settings, eight separate dimensions of family rituals can be observed including the frequency of the activity; the degree to which attendance is viewed as mandatory; the degree of emotional investment the family members have in the activity; the attachment of meaning to the activity; the continuity of the activity across generations; the degree of advance preparation and planning associated with the activity; the assignment of roles and duties during the activity; and the rigidity or flexibility associated with the activity.

The ritual of eating meals together can be established fairly easily within the daily routine. For example, a daily dinner hour can be set in a household. Each family member can be assigned a role during dinnertime, such as helping plan the meal or setting the table. The tasks can be adjusted as children mature. If the act of eating together is invested with meaning beyond the mere intake of food, a greater significance is attached to the activity for the individual family members and the family unit. For example, a family may establish a practice of checking in on each other's activities during the day, sharing thoughts around the table, or even participating in a game. Such practices can become something that the family members look forward to. Then dinnertime becomes more than just an opportunity to eat. It is a special and predictable activity with meaning attached to it. Just as dinnertime allows for routine and significance, so do weekend activities, vacations, and special celebrations. The predictability and the special meaning attached to these activities and other special family activities help shape individual and family identity.

Children can be instrumental in creating new rituals as they grow up. New rituals can be incorporated into family life in order to respond to transitions and challenges during different stages of child, adolescent, and adult development. Unique therapeutic rituals as prescribed in therapy including healing, identity definition, belief expression, and membership can be instrumental mechanisms to help family members respond to problems and transitions, to create a new family membership (to include new members through the birth of a child or adoption), and to help family members adjust to changing roles.

Assessment of Family Rituals
The Family Ritual Interview (FRI), which focused on the transmission of alcoholism in generations of families, is commonly used to assess the practice of rituals in families. This interview assesses the level of ritualization, the evidence of developmental changes, the comparison of the same events in the family of origin for each parent, and the role of drinking in family rituals. The Family Ritual Questionnaire (FRQ) is a fifty-six-item forced-choice self-report questionnaire based on the Wolin and Bennett Family Interview. This questionnaire is based on the seven settings for family rituals including dinnertime and weekends and the eight dimensions of rituals including the frequency of the activity and the assignment of roles and duties during the activity. A family ritual routine factor and a family ritual meaning factor have been identified in research with this assessment device.

Research on Family Rituals
Research using the FRI and the FRQ has demonstrated that the practice of routine and meaningful family rituals buffers against disorders such as depression and anxiety under normal and stressful conditions including internalizing disorders

such as depression and anxiety. Measures of adolescent adjustment including children of alcoholics have demonstrated the protective functions of practicing family rituals. Family rituals have been found to improve marital satisfaction in families adjusting to the early stages of parenthood. Family rituals have also played an important role in families with members suffering from chronic pain. Family rituals have been found to have differential effects depending if the respondent is the patient or the caregiver. Research has also demonstrated different perceptions of family rituals within a given family depending on which member's self-report and comparisons are under investigation.

Current research in the area of practicing family rituals is looking at families with children with pediatric disorders including populations with asthma and Attention Deficit Hyperactivity Disorder. This research is looking at disorder management and the potential protective role of family routines and rituals. Future work in this area should comprise multimethod data collection strategies including observational studies of family rituals.

Kimberly J. Josephs

References and further reading
Fiese, Barbara H. 1992. "Dimensions of Family Rituals across Two Generations: Relation to Adolescent Identity." *Family Process* 31:151–162.
Imber-Black, E. 1988. "Rituals in Families and Family Therapy." Edited by Evan Imber-Black, Janine Roberts, and Richard Whiting. New York: Norton.

Father-Adolescent Relationships
Father-adolescent relationships are unique relations that exist between a father and his daughter or son during the second decade of the child's life, typified by a variety of paternal care activities that affect daughters and sons somewhat differently.

During adolescence, both daughters and sons are striving to establish their independence and distinctive identities. The types of father-child relations that help adolescents fulfill these tasks differ for daughters and sons. For adolescent daughters, fathers' active, energetic involvement can promote their ability to achieve a significant degree of separation from their mothers and provide them with a bridge to the world beyond the family. A father can support his daughter in establishing an autonomous identity and provide her with opportunities for constructive, assertive interactions with males.

For adolescent sons, in contrast, their psychosocial task includes achieving a significant degree of separation from their fathers. Their fathers' support from the sidelines promotes their ability to achieve a significant degree of autonomy, while also providing them with an ongoing bridge back to the family. Thus, it is not surprising that fathering during adolescence has a somewhat weaker impact than fathering during childhood on sons' adulthood outcomes.

The unique contributions fathers make in the lives of both their adolescent daughters and sons, of course, are enhanced or diminished by the larger family system, which may enable or undermine the three basic types of father-child relations, including physical-athletic, intellectual-academic, and social-emotional.

Father-Adolescent Physical-Athletic Relations

A father's relationship with his adolescent in the area of physical-athletic activities may include helping a son or daughter improve a jump shot or batting stance, monitoring nutrition, observing for possible drug/alcohol abuse, teaching the adolescent how to parallel park, or accompanying him or her to a medical appointment.

There are several precursors to strong father-adolescent physical-athletic rela-

tions. The child's age is relevant; fathers tend to be more involved in physical-athletic child-rearing activities when their adolescents are eleven to fifteen years old. Analysis of the Glueck Four-Decade Study found that men whose fathers used physical punishment or threats of physical punishment that instilled fear in them as boys tended to try to provide their own children with better parenting than they themselves received by developing strong, positive physical-athletic relationships with their adolescents. Men whose wives are relatively well educated and employed outside of the home are also more likely to devote attention to physical-athletic relationships with their adolescent children.

Daughters appear to reap great rewards from athletic interactions with their fathers during their adolescent years. The Haverford Longitudinal Study suggested that fathers who urged daughters to participate in athletics contributed much to their daughters' subsequent adult success. The Glueck Four-Decade Study confirmed that daughters who had experienced a high level of physical-athletic interaction with their fathers were, years later, significantly more upwardly mobile in both educational and occupational levels. The ability of fathers' physical-athletic care to influence their daughters to become high achievers suggests that these father-daughter activities contributed to the daughters' ability to compete with men beyond the family sphere.

Sons receive more benefit from strong physical-athletic relations with their fathers during the childhood decade than during adolescence. There is little or no evidence, for instance, that father-son joint athletic activity during the teenage years predicts sons' educational or occupational success. Sports can still be important during adolescence, however, given that most sports also provide many opportunities for strengthening social-emotional and even intellectual-academic relations. Much of what goes on under the guise of adolescent and adult athletic activities may have more to do with social-emotional bonding and intellectual debating.

Father-Adolescent Intellectual-Academic Relations

A father's intellectual-academic relationship with his adolescent could include discussing or explaining baseball statistics, taking a duo trip to an art gallery or bookstore, giving feedback on a school term paper, or discussing newspaper headlines during breakfast.

Fathers, according to the Glueck Four-Decade Study, tend to develop stronger intellectual-academic relations with their adolescents when their own mothers had relatively low levels of formal education. Conversely, the more educated a father's wife is, the more care he provides for his adolescent's intellectual-academic development. This pattern suggests that men compensate for their mothers' educational deficits by marrying women with more education and by supporting their wives' educational ambitions for their children.

Daughters benefit, but somewhat inconsistently, from strong intellectual-academic relations with their fathers during adolescence. Daughters' social mobility, for instance, is not regularly predicted by strong intellectual-academic relations with their fathers during the adolescent years, although some retrospective studies do report that successful women often recall fathers who prized their intellectual growth and actively urged their academic achievement. Daughters' psychological maturity, however, does show significant benefits. A follow-up study of the Oakland Growth Study found a strong relationship between fathers' cognitive-moral reasoning and their daughters' moral reasoning years later during young adulthood.

When parents' style of interaction interweaves Socratic-style challenging questions and supportive encouragement, the moral development of both daughters and sons is enhanced, according to the Walker and Taylor Longitudinal Study. Similarly, the ego development of both daughters and sons is promoted, according to analyses of the adolescents in the Allen and Hauser Longitudinal Study, when fathers provide a challenging interaction style that encourages perspective taking within a context of intellectual support and encouragement.

Sons most consistently benefit from strong intellectual-academic relations with their fathers during adolescence. Fathers' recognizing of their sons' academic achievement, treating their thoughts and intellectual life with mutual respect, and helping with homework as needed are all predictive of sons' academic success. The Weinberger Longitudinal Study compared self-restraint behavior in fathers to sons' academic behavior at twelve years old and then again at sixteen. Fathers' self-restraint (impulse control, suppression of aggression, consideration of others) was associated with sons' academic achievement in terms of grades, effort, and attendance. The fathers' expectations also were associated with their sons' later academic behaviors. Further, in the Glueck Four-Decade Study, sons who had fathers who stayed involved with their intellectual-academic growth during adolescence were significantly more likely to go on to attain a relatively high level of education. The intellectual-academic relationship between father and son is also important in terms of supporting a son's personal development. Analysis of the boys and their parents in the Kohlberg Longitudinal Sample found that fathers' cognitive-moral reasoning and education became the strongest predictors of their sons' moral reasoning maturity years later as adults.

Father-Adolescent Social-
Emotional Relations

Examples of a father's social-emotional relationship with his adolescent include a duo camping trip, attending church or ball games together, discussing dating problems, giving advice on resolving a conflict, or generally talking about emotionally charged issues. More generally, it also includes paternal activities that less directly support the adolescent's developing social-emotional competence, such as chaperoning a dance or encouraging his son or daughter to invite friends over to the house.

The Glueck Four-Decade Study revealed several predictors of father-adolescent social-emotional relations. Men whose own fathers had been employed in relatively better or more complex jobs tended to develop strong social-emotional relations with their own adolescents. Similarly, men who had grown up in homes where their own fathers and mothers worked well together and provided a cohesive home atmosphere also tended to develop strong social-emotional relationships with their own adolescent sons and daughters. Furthermore, men whose relationships with their fathers had been distant or nonnurturant tended to strive to provide better paternal care than they themselves received by developing strong, positive social-emotional relationships with their own adolescents. Fathers who have a high level of marital affinity or commitment also tend to devote more attention to social-emotional relations with their adolescent offspring. The child's age is also relevant. Fathers tend to be somewhat more involved in social-emotional child-rearing activities when their adolescents are eleven to fifteen years old.

Daughters greatly benefit from strong social-emotional relations with their fathers during adolescence. Retrospective studies of unusually competent women (e.g., doctoral students, managers, leaders)

have found that they often recall their fathers as men who involved themselves in joint endeavors with their adolescent daughters. The fathers' social-emotional styles were often recalled as active and encouraging, playful and exciting, but also including a significant degree of father-daughter conflict. The Haverford Longitudinal Study, for instance, suggested that the women who succeeded in their work had been raised by fathers who were steady and firm, but not tender, in their social-emotional style. Similarly, daughters of the fathers in the Glueck Four-Decade Study who had experienced a high level of paternal social-emotional support were significantly more upwardly mobile in educational and occupational levels by early adulthood than those who had not. These social-emotional relations were described as challenging, affirming the daughters' ability to function autonomously and vigorously. Finally, several small studies suggest that fathers' social-moral maturity, warmth, affection, and lack of overprotectiveness are also related to their adolescent daughters' advanced moral development.

A son's social-emotional relationship with his father tends to weaken temporarily during adolescence as the young man seeks to define himself. Sons, nevertheless, need their fathers to keep in touch with them, and fathers do continue to serve as unacknowledged role models for their sons during adolescence. Analysis of the Career Pattern Longitudinal Sample, for instance, recorded the degree to which fathers, other adults, and siblings served as role models for boys when they were freshmen in high school. Of the occupational role models that boys reported as freshman, only fathers' role modeling was associated with their sons' vocational adjustment and behavior a decade later. Fathers who were the most positive role models were more likely to have sons who attained their occupational goals and showed clear job satisfaction. Another four-year longitudinal study also found that fathers high in self-restraint significantly predicted adolescent sons' positive peer relations and social-emotional adjustment four years later. The relationship between father and son is important in terms of male identity and moral development. Additional analysis of the Kohlberg Longitudinal Sample also found that the fathers' parenting involvement and identification with their adolescent sons, which he interpreted as supporting democratic family discussions, made a unique contribution to predicting the sons' future moral development during adulthood. This suggests that as fathers are able to establish strong relationships and democratic communication styles with their sons, moral reasoning is enhanced.

Future of Father-Adolescent Relations
A successful father, as defined in terms of his daughters' and sons' development, must be able to contribute to his children's formation in ways that also fit the sociocultural and historical context. Given the rapidly shifting context of parenting in twenty-first-century America, therefore, it is impossible to define ideal father-adolescent relations in absolute terms. What seems to hold constant, however, is that fathers who establish warm, nurturing relationships, support physically related competencies, and participate in the intellectual life of their sons and daughters will equip them, in turn, to care for the next generation with wisdom.

John Snarey
Carla Gober

See also Father-Child Relationships

References and further reading
Allen, Joseph, Stuart Hauser, Kathy Bell, and Thomas O'Connor. 1994. "Longitudinal Assessment of Autonomy and Relatedness in Adolescent-Family Interactions as Predictors of Adolescent Ego Development and Self-Esteem." *Child Development* 65:179–194.

Bell, Alan. 1969. "Role Modeling of Fathers in Adolescence and Young Adulthood." *Journal of Counseling Psychology* 16:30–35.

D'Angelo, Lori, Daniel Weinberger, and Shirley Feldman. 1995. "Like Father, Like Son? Predicting Male Adolescents' Adjustment from Parents' Distress and Self-Restraint." *Developmental Psychology* 31:883–896.

Hart, Daniel. 1992. *Becoming Men: The Development of Aspirations, Values, and Adaptational Styles.* New York: Plenum Press.

Hawkins, Alan, and David Dollahite. 1997. *Generative Fathering: Beyond Deficit Perspectives.* Thousand Oaks, CA: Sage Publications.

Heath, Douglas. 1991. *Fulfilling Lives: Paths to Maturity and Success.* San Francisco: Jossey-Bass.

Snarey, John. 1993. *How Fathers Care for the Next Generation: A Four-Decade Study.* Cambridge, MA: Harvard University Press.

Speicher, Betsy. 1994. "Family Patterns of Moral Judgment during Adolescence and Early Adulthood." *Developmental Psychology* 30:624–632.

Walker, Lawrence, and John Taylor. 1991. "Family Interactions and the Development of Moral Reasoning." *Child Development* 62:264–283.

Father-Child Relationships

Father-child relations are unique relationships that exist between a father and his child, characterized by a variety of paternal care activities during the first decade of a child's life, which influence daughters and sons somewhat differently.

During childhood, both daughters and sons need their fathers' support as they negotiate life's hurdles. Positive paternal influence is more likely to occur, of course, when positive family and marital relationships exist. Because daughters' primary identification ideally remains with their mothers, fathers' friendly, but not overly warm, child care is an important support that does not draw them away from their primary identification. Fathers'

During childhood, both daughters and sons need their fathers' support as they negotiate life's hurdles. (Skjold Photographs)

exciting and rigorous physical-athletic interaction, in particular, appears to help their daughters avoid an extremely traditional sex-role identification. In contrast, for boys, the early portion of the childhood decade requires them to separate from their mothers and identify with their fathers as part of their gender identity development. Fathers' warm, close, guiding support of their sons' physical-athletic, intellectual-academic, and social-emotional development promotes this transition.

Father-Child Physical-Athletic Relations

A father's physical-athletic relationship with his children is typically characterized by action-skill lessons and medical care activities. More generally, it includes father-child activities that care for the development of physical-athletic well-being. Specific examples include directly caring for minor medical problems or taking a child to the doctor, accompanying the child to gymnastics class or skating lessons, and teaching the child how to play soccer or other athletic games.

The precursors of strong father-child physical-athletic relations are found both in an apparent male affinity for such relationships and in men's boyhood relationships with their own fathers. Research reviews have shown that fathers from diverse racial groups and social classes have a special inclination for physical-athletic play activities with their children, both daughters and sons, and that their play is more tactile, physically demanding, and rough-and-tumble than that of mothers. An analysis of the 240 men in the Glueck Four-Decade Study found that men whose own fathers had inconsistently or inadequately participated in their physical well-being as boys are also more likely to redress this loss by developing strong, positive physical-athletic relationships with their own children, especially during the later childhood years when sons and daughters are more physically capable and interested in developing and demonstrating their competence.

Daughters' life outcomes are notably influenced by their fathers' support of their physical-athletic development during childhood. One researcher has shown that fathers who encourage their daughters to participate in athletic sports help alleviate sex bias and promote sex-role flexibility, while another reported that daughters whose fathers expose them to high levels of physical play that is characterized by mutuality or balance, rather than highly directive tactics, also tend to be considered more popular and assertive by peers and adults outside the family. The Glueck Four-Decade Study showed that daughters whose fathers promoted their physical-athletic competence during childhood

Father-daughter physical-athletic activities contribute to the daughters' ability to compete with men beyond the family sphere. (Elizabeth Crews)

were the most educationally successful as young adults. These daughters appeared to have experienced their fathers as challenging and affirming of their ability to function autonomously and vigorously.

Supporting a son's physical-athletic development is at the heart of many American fathers' ideal image of good father-son relations. Men's support of their son's physical-athletic development is higher during the later childhood years than at any other time. For the sons of the men in the Glueck Four-Decade Study, their later adulthood occupational mobility was predicted by their fathers' care for their sons' boyhood physical-athletic development. But it is seldom recognized that participation in athletic sports also provides fathers with opportunities to develop strong social-emotional relations

as well as intellectual-academic relations with their children.

Father-Child Intellectual-Academic Relations

Activities that support a child's intellectual-academic development, such as intellectual skill lessons and cognitive activities, characterize a father's intellectual-academic relationship with his child. Specific activities that support a child's intellectual-academic development include reading to a child, playing word games, consulting with the child's teacher and monitoring homework, providing music lessons, or teaching a child how to identify different bird species or star constellations.

The Glueck Four-Decade Study demonstrated that fathers with higher intelligence quotient (IQ) scores tended to build stronger intellectual-academic relations with their children. They built especially strong intellectual-academic relationships with their children when they were between five and ten years old and in elementary school.

For daughters, short-term research has suggested that paternal intellectual-academic care during the childhood years, such as the amount of time fathers spend reading to them, are related to their intellectual competence. Longitudinal research, however, has not confirmed the impact of father-child intellectual-academic relations upon later adulthood outcomes of daughters.

For sons, the impact of father-child intellectual-academic relations on their life outcomes is very clear. Analysis of the Haverford Longitudinal Study found that boys whose fathers had helped them with homework and otherwise developed a significant intellectual-academic relationship with them became men who succeeded in their work. Similarly, the fathers in the Glueck Four-Decade Study who provided high levels of care for their sons' intellectual-academic development forecast sons who later showed the highest levels of educational mobility. Fathers' intellectual restrictiveness and authoritarian behavior, in contrast, are associated with sons' educational underachievement.

Father-Child Social-Emotional Relations
A father's social-emotional relationship with his child is often exemplified by companion activities, but also includes any father-child activity that functions to care for a child's social-emotional maturity. Spending time talking with a child before bedtime, comforting a child afraid of the dark, or giving him or her a birthday party are all included in this category.

The Glueck Four-Decade Study showed that men whose own fathers had been relatively better educated tended to build strong social-emotional relations with their own children. Fathers who have a high level of marital commitment also tend to devote more attention to building good social-emotional relations with their children.

In contrast to the benefits of a father's support of his daughter's physical-athletic development during childhood, fathers' social-emotional nurturance during the childhood decade tends to produce less beneficial consequences. Several short-term studies suggest that unusually strong (smothering) father-daughter social-emotional relations during the childhood years may inhibit daughters' cognitive development and sex-role flexibility. The Glueck Four-Decade Study revealed that extremely high levels of paternal support for childhood social-emotional development predicted low levels of daughters' educational success. Girls who received abundant support for social-emotional development from their fathers during their first decade of life attained relatively lower levels of education in early adulthood than those who did not receive such support. But this seems to change once daughters reach adolescence.

For sons, several short-term studies have suggested that fathers' strong social-emotional relations positively predict boys' academic skills, school grades, level of cognitive development, IQ scores, and other standardized test scores. Importantly, these trends have been supported by long-term studies. Analysis of the Haverford study found that the men who had succeeded in their work during early adulthood or who were the most mentally healthy were also significantly more likely than the other men in the study to have reported that their fathers had been accessible, affectionate, helpful, and encouraging during their boyhood years.

The Glueck Four-Decade Study confirmed that sons' educational success and mobility were forecast years earlier by their fathers care for their childhood social-emotional development. Finally, examination of seventy-five subjects who had been included in the Sears, Maccoby, and Levin 26-Year Longitudinal Study confirmed that sons who received more paternal involvement as children were more likely to report high levels of empathic concern for others as adults.

Future of Father-Child Relations
Fatherhood is changing. Fathers are more involved in child care, and coparenting is a higher priority with both men and women. And among divorced couples, a steadily increasing number of households are being headed by fathers. Studies that showed the negative effects of father absence are being replaced by studies that show positive effects of father presence. These demographic and research changes reflect the current realization that father-child relations are unique relationships that predict a surprising amount of the variance in children's life outcomes.

John Snarey
Carla Gober

See also Father-Adolescent Relationships

References and further reading
Biller, Henry. 1993. *Fathers and Families.* Westport, CT: Auburn House.
Hawkins, Alan, and David Dollahite. 1997. *Generative Fathering: Beyond Deficit Perspectives.* Thousand Oaks, CA: Sage Publications.
Heath, Douglas. 1991. *Fulfilling Lives: Paths to Maturity and Success.* San Francisco: Jossey-Bass.
Koestner, Richard, Carol Franz, and Joel Weinberger. 1990. "The Family Origins of Empathic Concern: A 26-Year Longitudinal Study." *Journal of Personality and Social Psychology* 58:709–717.
Lamb, Michael, ed. 1997. *The Role of the Father in Child Development.* 3d ed. New York: John Wiley and Sons.
Parke, Ross. 1996. *Fatherhood.* Cambridge, MA: Harvard University Press.
Pruett, Kyle. 2000. *Fatherneed: Why Father Care Is as Essential as Mother Care for Your Child.* New York: Free Press.
Snarey, John. 1993. *How Fathers Care for the Next Generation: A Four-Decade Study.* Cambridge, MA: Harvard University Press.

Fatherhood, Transition to

A revolutionary change in childbirth occurred in the last third of the twentieth century. In the mid-1960s, approximately 15 percent of new fathers were present at the birth of their children. As the century drew to a close, fully 85 percent of men expected to be present.

Presence at the birth is a precursor and indicator of an increasing father involvement with children, reversing a trend that began with the advent of the Industrial Revolution in the late nineteenth century. When men had to leave the family to work at distant locations, they were necessarily less available to their children. A division of labor standard evolved: man as breadwinner, woman as child-care provider and homemaker. As fathers become more involved with the birth and early care of their children, they face multiple joys and challenges.

Many men have described having been invited into the pregnancy, birth, and child care as among the most important and powerful moments in their lives. The transition to fatherhood is a transforming event for most men. They feel a host of intense emotions for the first time, and many report being surprised by both the amount of love and of anxiety they experience. Of course, a man's connection to the infant both in the womb and later is often mediated by the new mother. Because he does not share her nurturing biological link to the baby growing in her womb, he is somewhat reliant on her to provide closer access to the child. In this way the mother is a gatekeeper for the father-baby

As fathers become more involved with the birth and early care of their children, they face multiple joys and challenges. (Spencer Grant/Photo Researchers)

connection. Often, she remains the gatekeeper, allocating time and space for the father and infant to bond. For many men, this maternal control mediates the intensity of their emotion and is symbolic of a more pervasive conflict.

An expectant father soon becomes aware that the extra support, understanding, and caring that rightfully is offered to his pregnant partner is unlikely to be extended to him as well. In fact, he may well become the butt of apparently good-natured jokes about his potential loss of freedom or about the paternity itself. In a very significant way, expectant fathers commonly experience a double bind: the confluence of two opposing messages.

Even as he is invited, encouraged, perhaps cajoled, into full participation into the pregnancy and birth of his children, he is clearly given to understand that he is to remain an outsider. The difference is between a verbal message, "Please be involved," "You must be involved," and the unspoken codicil, "Thou shalt not upset the pregnant woman with any negative feelings." It is quite acceptable to be supportive. It is unacceptable to express worry or anxiety.

This creates a dilemma for the expectant father. To be fully aware and involved, he must recognize and experience his personal feelings about the pregnancy and impending fatherhood. When he does, he soon realizes that the feelings embrace a wide realm. If he reverts to the strong, silent traditional male role, he denies himself the intense positive feelings of this act of creation and invites criticism for not sharing. However, if he does share his feelings, he will inevitably be discussing his anxieties, sadness, and other "negative" emotions, affect that falls into the realm of "politically incorrect."

This double bind underscores both a man's fear of rejection and provides fuel for a host of fears during this transition. The anxieties, fears, and concerns normally experienced by expectant and new fathers fall into four realms: performance fears, security fears, relationship fears, and existential fears.

Performance Fears
Queasiness in the delivery room. Desire to be a part of the pregnancy and childbirth does not reduce a man's anticipation of discomfort regarding an abundance of blood and other bodily fluids. An expectant father anticipating his first birth participation wonders about his ability to "keep it together" and truly help his wife, instead of fainting or "losing his cookies" during the delivery. The importance of this concern is revealed in recent fathers' accounts of the birth of their children. Immediately after describing the birth as "wonderful," and commenting on the courage of their wives, they described with pride how well they personally came through the pregnancy with the contents of their digestive tracts intact.

The reality that very few men actually have such trouble does not diminish the concern. What passes for humor by physicians contributes to men's fears of experiencing the birth of their children from a prone position, under the table on a delivery room floor. The popular media also regularly portray the pregnant woman, about to deliver her baby, wheeling her unconscious husband into the hospital.

Financial and emotional responsibility. Nowhere is the socioeconomic programming so "hardwired" as in the intense pressure fathers feel to provide financial support for their families. The new child demands financial, physical, and emotional adjustments in the relationship. For many couples, the first pregnancy brings with it a change from two salaries for two people to one salary for three.

Tradition and social expectations, as well as the inequity in male and female salaries, typically make it inevitable that the father bears the brunt of the enhanced financial burden. It is common during a pregnancy for men to "moonlight" or switch jobs to build a "nest egg"—a peculiarly appropriate term under the circumstances.

Security Fears
Dealing with the OB/GYN establishment. Medicine that deals with female reproductive anatomy remains mysterious and alien to many men. Expectant fathers often experience feelings of dehumanization and embarrassment during their initial contacts with obstetrics and gynecology staff. Often, expectant fathers report nonacceptance from the same obstetrical staff that had previously praised their involvement—their questions silenced with looks that imply, "only a fool would not know that."

Many expectant fathers reported feelings of "being treated like a child" or "being dismissed" in their contact with these professionals.

Doubts about paternity. A surprising concern for expectant fathers involves fleeting thoughts that they may not be the biological father of the child. This particular concern is not a new one. In the fourth century B.C., Aristotle wrote "the reason mothers are more devoted to their children is that they suffer more in birth, and are more certain that the child is their own." This discomfort, often exacerbated by unintentionally cruel jokes about the physical appearance of various service providers, is commonly based less on a belief of infidelity than on a general feeling of inadequacy to be part of anything so monumental as the creation of life. Related fears expressed by men and women is a concern that the hospital staff mixed up babies in the nursery or that the baby will be born with serious defects.

Health and safety of spouse and infant.
Usually arising during the second
trimester and progressing forward is a
powerful fear of tragic loss. This fear may
be based on dreams, refreshed family
memories, distressing stories, and personal fears of abandonment or of being
replaced. Because his pregnant spouse is
normally turning inward toward the
infant and away from him at a time when
he is feeling particularly insecure, it is
easy for the prospective father's unconscious mind to transform her temporary
emotional distance into a premonition of
permanent loss.

Relationship Fears
Being replaced. It is common and important for pregnant women to turn inward
and begin bonding with the life growing
inside their bodies. At such times, husbands may feel neglected.

It is not surprising that men fear the
loss of their most important relationship.
Many have survived periods of great turmoil in marriage, experienced firsthand
the pain of their parents' divorce, or the
loss of their own prior relationships. As
children, most men have experienced a
feeling of abandonment by a mother or
other women. Such experiences can affect
their expectations of how likely a marriage is to survive the additional stress of
a child.

If his own father was committed to the
"earning a living" division-of-labor standard and was somewhere in the background (at work or in the garage), the primary bond in the expectant father's
childhood home was between mother and
child. Can he not then expect that as a
father he will also be pushed aside?

Existential Fears
Mortality. Of all the changes, fears, and
novel experiences a wife's pregnancy
brings to men, none is so subtle and yet so
dramatic as a new consciousness of the

biological life cycle. Reflecting on their
intimate involvement with the beginnings of life, many men describe feeling
closer to their own deaths. They also
described an increased sense of connection to their own fathers.

Because death is so much avoided in
our youth- and action-centered culture,
most men are surprised by their sudden
feelings about the fragility of human existence and particularly with their own
mortality. Until a man is a father, he
remains identified as a member of the
younger generation. His living parents or
grandparents, whom he expects to out-
live, act as a psychological buffer against
death. When he becomes a father, there is
now a new younger generation, one he
expects to predecease. This concern over
life and death epitomizes all fears por-
tending loss, helplessness, inadequacy, or
limitations. As the ultimate limitation,
mortality colors the experience of expectant fathers.

Pregnancy and birth are only the origin
of a major transformation. Performance,
security, relationship, and existential
fears expand and grow as one's children
do. Unaddressed and unchecked, they
plague fathers with anxiety and push
them from fuller participation in their
families. Appropriately acknowledged and
shared, these insights can be part of the
process that transforms a man into a loving father.

The following advice is offered to help
men on that path. Expect, accept, and pay
attention to the emotional changes you
feel. Fears are natural, as is an emotional
reassessment of the fathering you received
as a child and a reliving of feelings from
boyhood. Expect to be confronted with
double messages from others indicating a
desire for your presence and a simultaneous discomfort with your true feelings.

Become aware of your feelings of fear
and, if possible, the meaning of the specific fears to your personal history and

lifestyle. Once you are aware of your concerns about the pregnancy, share them with your pregnant partner. It is wise to choose quiet, private times to do so. Talk to her about her concerns and joys about the pregnancy. Make an effort to understand her shifting moods, fatigue, and physical symptoms.

Personalize the birth experience. The fact that a father's presence is welcomed doesn't mean that the birthing facility will be "user friendly." With your partner, determine the optimal setting and ambience for the birth and early moments of your child's life. Work with the facility to make it as close to your ideal as possible.

Get to know and talk frankly with other expectant and recent fathers. They are potentially the most understanding and will be good resources. Get to know more about your own father. If possible, reconnect with him and find out what his life was like when you or your siblings were born. Finally, try to be prepared to experience the exquisite joys and the miracle of your child's birth.

Jerrold Lee Shapiro

References and further reading
Greenberg, M. 1985. *The Birth of a Father.* New York: Continuum.
Pollack, W. 1998. *Real Boys.* New York: Random House.
Shapiro, J. L. 1993. *When Men Are Pregnant: Needs and Concerns of Expectant Fathers.* New York: Delta.
———. 1993. *The Measure of a Man: Becoming the Father You Wish Your Father Had Been.* New York: Delacorte.
Shapiro, J. L., M. J. Diamond, and M. Greenberg. 1995. *Becoming a Father: Contemporary Social, Developmental and Clinical Perspectives.* New York: Springer.

Fathering

Fathering may be defined as parenting behaviors engaged in by males that are complex and multidimensional, and change as cultural understandings of gender roles and child development shift over time. It is important to immediately note that these behaviors may be filled by a variety of individuals, and not just by a biological parent. The generic (i.e., layperson's) understanding of fathers is that the role is fulfilled by a biological or adoptive parent, but fathering behavior can be from a variety of individuals, such as stepfathers, grandparents, uncles, or family friends. Fathering influences can be direct or indirect, such that fathering can be thought of as ranging from support for the child's mother to direct interaction with the child.

In the last two decades of the twentieth century, social scientists have shifted considerably in their understandings of fathering, now arguing for the importance of fathering for child development. Part of this shift in the scientific understanding may be linked to political changes in the understanding of the roles of men and women with the rise of feminism in the 1970s. Indeed, one can trace the development of conceptions of fathering in U.S. history through at least four distinct stages: fathers as moral teachers during the colonial period, fathers as providers during industrialization, fathers as same-sex role models during the Great Depression, and fathers as involved and nurturant parents during the 1970s with the rise of feminism. While modern conceptions of fathering are certainly dominated by the fourth view, it is evident that all of these notions are part of the contemporary understanding of fathering.

Just what are the particulars of fathering? It is useful to conceive of fathering as both indirect and direct. Indirect fathering is best conceptualized as support for the mother, particularly in the realms of emotional support and housework. Assistance in these areas can be seen as bolstering the mother's ability to perform her role optimally. Direct fathering falls into the realm of interaction and caretaking behaviors with children. This area of direct fathering has been studied most extensively by researchers.

Direct fathering falls into the realm of interaction and caretaking behaviors with children. (Elizabeth Crews)

Numerous researchers have documented that fathers spend less time overall interacting with their children than mothers in virtually all realms: child care, parent-child leisure, and teaching activities. However, some research has argued that it is important to bear in mind a competence versus performance distinction here: while fathers show less involvement in terms of amount of interaction, this does not necessarily mean they are less competent than mothers to perform these functions. In addition to this well-established difference in amount of involvement, striking differences have been noted in mothers' and fathers' interactional styles. Fathers have been found to spend more time proportionately in play activities with their children, though mothers still spend more time in absolute terms. In particular, fathers are observed to engage in a boisterous, emotional arousing form of play that is less typical of mother-child interaction. Because of the high salience of this form of play, some have proposed that fathers exert an influence on their children that may be greater than expected in terms of the amount of time spent with them. This sort of arousing, boisterous play may well be associated with development of peer skills, as children may learn the nuances of emotional "give-and-take" in their interactions with fathers. One suggestion has been that children who have fathers who are low in play directiveness teach their children valuable lessons in how to recognize and send emotional signals during social interactions and, in turn, these children later show better social adaptation to peers. Thus, it is evident that it is the qualitative, not the quantitative, aspects of fathering that matter most for children's developmental outcomes.

Fathering has always been thought of as particularly important for boys. There is some evidence for its importance, with indications that boys are more identified with the masculine role and show better psychosocial adjustment when fathers are warm and involved. However, despite all the emphasis on what distinguishes fathering from mothering and the attempts to determine the unique contribution of fathers, there is also converging evidence that there should be more similarity than difference in the definitions. In fact, over time (i.e., through infancy, toddlerhood, school age, etc.) fathering and mothering behaviors look more similar than different, and one researcher has concluded that ultimately, for either successful fathering or mothering, warmth, nurturance, and closeness matter the most. There is also no evidence for innate gender differences in the way that adults relate to young children or vice versa; social determinants instead seem to drive such differences when they are observed.

Given that fathering interaction may be conceived of as much like mothering with perhaps a greater amount of play, and given that fathering consists also of indirect contributions to the mother's well-being, what is a useful framework for gauging about what it means to engage in successful fathering? A quote from the work of Michael Lamb is most instructive here: "[A] successful father, as defined in terms of his children's development, is one whose role performance matches the demands and prescriptions of his sociocultural and family context." (Lamb, 1997a, 14) This notion is critical to our understanding of fathering. Its definition is, to some extent, a moving target. Depending on the particular cultural zeitgeist, as well as the demands of the more immediate social environment, what it means to engage in successful fathering may differ radically. The provider from the industrial period may no longer be thought of as an adequate father, but surely the warm and nurturant ideal of today's fathering would have had little meaning at the turn of the twentieth century. To a great extent, one should bear in mind that fathering remains a social construct, to be shaped and reshaped as societal and individual needs shift.

Benjamin J. Gorvine

References and further reading
Cummings, E. Mark, and Anne Watson O'Reilly. 1997. "Fathers in Family Context: Effects of Marital Quality on Child Adjustment." Pp. 49–65 in *The Role of the Father in Child Development*. 3d ed. Edited by Michael E. Lamb. New York: John Wiley and Sons.
Lamb, Michael E. 1997a. "Fathers and Child Development: An Introductory Overview and Guide." Pp. 1–18 in *The Role of the Father in Child Development*. 3d ed. Edited by Michael E. Lamb. New York: John Wiley and Sons.
———. 1997b. "The Development of Father-Infant Relationships." Pp. 104–120 in *The Role of the Father in Child Development*. 3d ed. Edited by Michael E. Lamb. New York: John Wiley and Sons.
Marsiglio, William. 1995. "Fatherhood Scholarship: An Overview and Agenda for the Future." Pp. 1–20 in *Fatherhood: Contemporary Theory, Research, and Social Policy*. Edited by William Marsiglio. Thousand Oaks, CA: Sage Publications.
Mosley, Jane, and Elizabeth Thomson. 1995. "Fathering Behavior and Child Outcomes: The Role of Race and Poverty." Pp. 148–165 in *Fatherhood: Contemporary Theory, Research, and Social Policy*. Edited by William Marsiglio. Thousand Oaks, CA: Sage Publications.
Parke, Ross D. 1995. "Fathers and Families." Pp. 27–63 in vol. 3 of *Handbook of Parenting*. Edited by Marc H. Bornstein. Mahwah, NJ: Lawrence Erlbaum Associates.
Parke, Ross D., and Raymond Buriel. 1997. "Socialization in the Family: Ethnic and Ecological Perspectives." Pp. 463–552 in vol. 3 of *Handbook of Child Psychology*. 5th ed. Edited by William Damon and Nancy Eisenberg. New York: John Wiley and Sons.
Phares, Vicky. 1996. *Fathers and Developmental Psychopathology*. New York: John Wiley and Sons.
Pleck, Elizabeth H., and Joseph H. Pleck. 1997. "Fatherhood Ideals in the United States: Historical Dimensions." Pp. 33–48 in *The Role of the Father in Child Development*. 3d ed. Edited by Michael E. Lamb. New York: John Wiley and Sons.
Pleck, Joseph H. 1997. "Paternal Involvement: Levels, Sources, and Consequences." Pp. 66–103 in *The Role of the Father in Child Development*. 3d ed. Edited by Michael E. Lamb. New York: John Wiley and Sons.

Fathers, Stay-at-Home

Difficult to define, especially in today's changing society, the stay-at-home father typically is the primary caregiver of his child and/or children, spending at least thirty hours per week, and quite often more, at home.

The stay-at-home father may work outside the home (in the evening hours), in a home business, or he may spend his days caring for his child and managing the household, performing the role traditionally assigned to mothers.

Experts estimate that as of 1996, there were approximately 2 million stay-at-home fathers at home with their children in the United States, although the U.S. Census Bureau cannot provide exact figures. Estimates are complicated by the fact that some fathers work evenings or weekends and may not consider themselves to be stay-at-home dads; yet, by definition, they are the primary caregivers for their children.

While American society has, for the most part, maintained the viewpoint that men should be the main breadwinners for the family and women the main caregivers for the children, various factors have contributed to changing roles. The number of women entering the workforce in the late 1980s and early 1990s, the subsequent move toward equality of pay for women, and the growing awareness that men can be nurturers all have influenced the move toward involved fatherhood and made the choice of stay-at-home father a viable alternative. Economic factors—many stay-at-home fathers earned less in their prior employment than their spouses—have prompted some men to make the decision to stay home with the

The stay-at-home father typically is the primary caregiver of his child and/or children. (Laura Dwight)

children while their wives become the main or sole breadwinners for the family. Many families also cite the wish not to use day care as a reason why the father has opted to stay home with the child.

While the nature/nurture debate continues in many arenas, most now agree that women are not exclusively biologically programmed to care for children, and that excluding childbearing and breast-feeding, males are fully capable of raising and caring for infants and children. Stay-at-home fathers, as evidence, perform the same duties as mothers who care for children—changing diapers, feeding, bathing, shopping, and nurturing their children on a daily basis. Although research has indicated that mothers and fathers have different play styles (fathers are more physical, mothers more gentle),

studies show that fathers who are around their children more actually begin to engage in varied play styles, including activities that are more gentle and quiet, such as reading, bathing, and cuddling. These changing gender roles reflect not only women's progress in the workplace, but men's progress in creating a more well-rounded, balanced life for themselves, in which personal goals and values—as well as economics—are factors to be considered when deciding who will care for children. Stay-at-home fathers recognize that caring for children and family is not emasculating; as their children become older, they are likely to remain intimately involved with their children, aware of their friends, schoolwork, and activities, and active as the "on-call" parent, who responds when the child is sick at school.

Nevertheless, some adjustments must be made for the father to become comfortable in his new role. Some stay-at-home fathers experience a sense of isolation, and express concern about reentering the workforce in the future. Many stay-at-home fathers must adapt to the shift from being in the corporate world or outside the home for forty to fifty hours a week to being inside the home all week. While stay-at-home fathers are becoming increasingly accepted, they are still not the norm in most neighborhoods, and fathers who choose to be the primary caregivers for their children must develop the social skills required to fit into a home culture largely populated by female caregivers. Many stay-at-home fathers reach out to others like themselves through the Internet, forming their own play groups for their children with other dads who are caring for their own offspring, and chatting on-line about their concerns and problems. A national At-Home Dads Convention, held annually at Oakton Community College in DesPlains, Illinois, brings stay-at-home fathers together from across the country to attend seminars and share information.

The wife of the stay-at-home father has chosen to work for personal and/or economic reasons, and on the whole feels relieved that her spouse has agreed to be the primary caregiver for the children. However, many of these women report feelings of jealousy and sadness because they are not at home with their children. For the most part, however, the wives of stay-at-home fathers are content with the arrangement, though some do feel the stress of stepping from their workday into the fray of home life. (Unlike the traditional working male, the working mother characteristically participates in domestic tasks and child care as soon as she gets home from her workplace.)

The outcome of this fathering movement is positive, offering families another option in addition to mother, day care, extended family, or other possibilities for early and later child care. Research has also shown that families in which fathers care for the children have a more equal balance of parenting, with women taking over at the end of their workday to read to the children, give them their baths, and put them to bed. In the stay-at-home-father family, the child benefits from secure attachments to more than one caregiver, and is likely to seek comfort from his father as well as his mother. Research shows that a child's attachment to more than one person is a positive factor; the older child, too, will benefit from having established close bonds with both parents.

Family structure in the stay-at-home-father family is different from—not the reverse of—the traditional family structure. While working mothers tend to know their child's daily schedule during their absence, traditional fathers may be unaware of their children's day-to-day activities. The stay-at-home father is not only intimately involved in the child's daily activities—preschool, play dates, homework, and so on—but often maintains a strong bond and active role as the child grows older, shepherding his child from school to after-school social and sports activities. In families in which the father stays at home, both parents are cognizant of the child's social activities and academic progress.

Although studies on the children of stay-at-home fathers are limited, researchers speculate that children whose fathers are actively involved will be more comfortable with the nurturing role in their own lives, and will be more flexible concerning gender role issues as they grow older. Fathers who play an integral role in the family model for children show that men can be nurturers, and reveal that masculinity and nurturing can coexist. Children whose fathers are actively involved have also been shown to be more empathetic.

Robert Frank
Kathryn E. Livingston

References and further reading
At-Home Dad. Quarterly newsletter. North Andover, MA.
Fox, Isabelle, and Norman M. Lobsenz. 1996. *Being There: The Benefits of a Stay at Home Parent.* Hauppauge, NY: Barron's.
Frank, Robert, and Kathryn E. Livingston. 1999. *The Involved Father.* New York: St. Martin's Press.
Lamb, Michael, ed. 1997. *The Role of the Father in Child Development.* 3d ed. New York: John Wiley and Sons.
Pruett, Kyle D. 1987. *The Nurturing Father.* New York: Warner Books.
Radin, Norma. 1988. "Primary Caregiving Fathers of Long Duration." Pp. 127–144 in *Fatherhood Today: Men's Changing Role in the Family.* Edited by P. Bronstein and C. Pape Cowan. New York: John Wiley and Sons.
Reszel, Barry, ed. 1998. *The At-Home Dad Handbook.* Self-published by Curtis Cooper, Apple Valley, MN.
Slowlane.com (an on-line resource for stay-at-home dads).
U.S. Department of Commerce. *My Daddy Takes Care of Me! Fathers as Care*

Providers. Current Population Reports. 1997. P70–59.

Father's Day

Father's Day is a day set aside each year on the third Sunday of June to honor all fathers. Not that long ago in the United States fathers were not considered major conveyors of warmth and nurture. They were acknowledged primarily as disciplinarians and breadwinners. "Wait till Daddy comes home" did not mean his arrival was something children anticipated eagerly. Fathers were expected to command respect and obedience. As heads of the household, fathers had all legal prerogatives over their children. They were unrecognized, however, as conveyers of emotional nurturance. Emphasizing that point, in the nineteenth century, to lessen the father's right to custody over a child, the "tender years" doctrine was evoked in favor of mothers as the preferable parent and caretaker for children until puberty. Nevertheless, fathers in many households were strong sources of kindness, care, and emotional support. In fact, they were often the unsung heroes in a child's life.

One child, Sonora Smart, who grew up without her mother, was particularly grateful to her father for this exact type of parenting. After her mother died giving birth to the family's sixth child, her father, William Smart, raised all six children by himself on their farm in rural eastern Washington.

When she reached adulthood, Mrs. Sonora Smart Dodd remembered her father's efforts. She realized the strength and selflessness her father had shown as a single parent. It was her father who had made all the parental sacrifices and who had been a loving, courageous parent. She proposed Father's Day in 1909, after hearing a sermon about Mother's Day. Because her father had been born in June, she worked to have officials declare the first Father's Day on 19 June 1910.

Apparently, many people felt similarly about their fathers. Around the same time, other Americans began to hold comparable "Father's Day" celebrations. West Virginia held one in 1908. The idea, probably without shared communication, was promoted in Chicago in 1911 and Vancouver, Washington, in 1912. In 1924, President Calvin Coolidge supported the idea of a national Father's Day. When, in 1966, President Lyndon Johnson signed a presidential proclamation declaring the third Sunday in June as Father's Day, opinions about fathers' relationships with their children were in a dramatic transition. Today's father unabashedly assumes an openly loving connection with his children, and need not hesitate to participate in any area of caretaking. As with the Mother's Day holiday, Father's Day was initially inspired by grateful children rather than by entrepreneurs.

Ester Schaler Buchholz

See also Mother's Day

References and further reading
Glennon, Will. 1995. *Fathering: Strengthening Your Connection with Your Children No Matter Where You Are.* New York: Conari Press.
Mead, Lucy, comp. 2000. *Fathers Are Special: A Tribute to Those Who Encourage, Support, and Inspire.* New York: Gramercy.

Feeding Problems, Prevention of

Feeding problems are very common during childhood, occurring in 25 to 35 percent of all children. (Linscheid, 1992) It is not uncommon for feeding problems to occur as children acquire new developmental skills and are challenged with new foods or mealtime expectations. Most feeding problems are temporary and resolved easily with little or no intervention. Feeding problems that persist can undermine children's growth, development, and relationships with their caregivers, which can lead to long-term health

When mealtimes become stressful or confrontational, infants may be denied both the nutrients that they require and healthy, responsive interactions with caregivers. (Laura Dwight)

problems, including diabetes, heart disease, and complications of undernutrition or obesity. In addition, many serious emotional disorders may present initially as feeding problems during infancy. Helping children learn to develop healthy eating habits by encouraging them to eat nutritious foods and to eat to satisfy hunger rather than to satisfy emotional needs can prevent subsequent health and developmental problems.

Feeding is a complex activity that reflects a young child's emerging developmental skills. Not only is feeding a time for meeting infants' nutritional needs, but it also is an important opportunity for social interaction. Caregivers help their infants build expectations around food and mealtimes. Infants learn that their cries for food will be answered and that feeding occurs according to a predictable schedule. Infants and caregivers establish a partnership in which they recognize and interpret communication signals from one another. This reciprocal process forms a basis for the emotional bonding or attachment between infants and caregivers that is essential to healthy functioning.

If there is a disruption in the communication between infants and caregivers, characterized by inconsistent, nonresponsive interactions, then feeding may become an occasion for unproductive, upsetting battles over food. When mealtimes become stressful or confrontational, infants may be denied both the nutrients that they require and healthy, responsive interactions with caregivers. Caregivers who are inexperienced or under stress and those who have poor eating habits themselves may be most in need of assistance to facilitate healthy, nutritious mealtime behavior with their children. Innovative strategies are needed to promote healthy eating habits and to prevent growth and developmental problems among young children.

In the past, feeding problems were sometimes conceptualized as child-related issues, with little attention directed to the role of the caregivers or to the social environment. However, with the recognition that feeding occurs within a social context, most clinicians incorporate perspectives from the child, caregivers, caregiver-child interactions, and culture into the evaluation and treatment of feeding problems.

Child

From a child's perspective, feeding requires the integration of multiple systems, including physical development, temperament, psychosocial development, and food preferences. Problems in any of these areas can undermine successful feeding.

Physical Development. Feeding progresses through increasingly complex stages as children acquire the skills to move food from the front of their mouth to the pharynx in preparation for swallowing. Many early feeding problems are related to neurological or anatomical impairments, but behavioral problems can emerge, especially when caregivers are not sensitive to their infants' needs. Caregivers can prevent feeding problems during the first few months of life by offering breast milk or formula frequently, at predictable intervals, and when the child exhibits signs of hunger; by holding the child during feeding in a comfortable, cradled position with the head and trunk well supported; and by responding to signals from the infant that indicate satiety, distress, or hunger.

Weaning occurs when children switch from a diet that is primarily breast milk or formula to solid food. When solid food is introduced too early, while feeding is still dominated by sucking, food is often pushed forward and out of the mouth. Caregivers should be careful not to misinterpret this action as a signal that the child is rejecting the food or rejecting the caregiver. Rather, it is a sign that the child is not ready for the feeding challenges of solid foods. If the caregiver responds to the perceived rejection with anger or by intensifying the pressure on the child to eat, then mealtime can become upsetting and stressful to both the child and the caregiver.

Delayed weaning may also be associated with feeding problems. Some children may become very comfortable with the ease of consuming liquids or soft foods and resist the challenges imposed by foods that require them to work harder by chewing. In addition, breast-feeding or bottle-feeding that persists into the second year of life *without adequate complementary feeding* may not provide children with the variety of nutrients that they require for healthy growth and may perpetuate infantile behavior. Semisolid and finger foods are generally introduced between six and twelve months, followed by more complex textures as the child's feeding skills improve. Parents need to guard against choking as their child learns to chew and is interested in a variety of foods.

Once children learn to sit, high chairs and booster seats should be used because they provide support and enable children to achieve a body position that facilitates feeding. High chairs also restrain children, thus ensuring that they remain seated throughout the meal. However, high chairs can also be aversive to children if they are introduced suddenly with little preparation, if children are confined for long periods, or if they are associated with negative aspects of feeding.

Temperament. Children who have feeding problems often display difficult behavior in other settings. For example, a child with a passive temperament who does not demand food may be forgotten or neglected and not fed, particularly in a chaotic family. Conversely, a child who has a very active temperament may be very reactive to environmental events and have difficulty maintaining the attention and focus that are necessary for successful feeding. Feeding children on a regular schedule and minimizing environmental distractions facilitates successful feeding.

Psychosocial Development. As children move through the stages of psychosocial development, they may also experience feeding difficulties. During the first few months of life, feeding is an organizational task that requires reciprocal coordination between caregivers and infants. Caregivers learn to interpret their infants' cries for food, to prepare them for feeding, to hold them to facilitate feeding, and to interpret their signs of satiety. Infants who do not provide clear signals to their caregivers or who do not respond to their caregivers' efforts to help them establish predictable routines of eating, sleeping, and playing are at risk for a range of adjustment problems, including feeding disorders.

From approximately three months of life through the first year, a child's wakeful periods are dominated by social exploration. Infants may interrupt their feeding for visual exploration or get distracted by external sights and sounds. If caregivers interpret these pauses as signals to stop feeding, then infants may not have met their nutritional requirements and may continue to be hungry. Conversely, if caregivers are persistent and force their infants to eat during brief exploratory pauses, then infants may associate feeding with frustration and a loss of control. Caregivers must be patient during this stage of development and not attempt to feed their infants quickly.

From approximately six months and through three years of age, children begin acquiring the physical and oral motor skills that enable them to handle a greater variety of textures and tastes. During this time they also acquire the verbal skills to express their pleasure or displeasure about food choices. Because feeding is so central to the development of young children, it often becomes the central arena for young children to practice their emerging independence. Caregivers who do not understand their toddler's need for control may respond with harsh reprisals, almost ensuring that mealtimes will become a source of conflict. Caregivers should provide opportunities for their toddlers to exercise some control over the feeding situation by allowing them to choose their own food and utensils, to self-feed, and to make messes while using bibs to protect clothing and floor coverings to facilitate cleanup.

Food Preferences. Children accept or reject food based on intrinsic qualities of the food (e.g., taste, texture) and extrinsic factors that may be unrelated to the specific food (i.e., anticipated consequences of eating or not eating). Consequences of eating may include relief from hunger, participation in a social function, or praise from caregivers. Consequences of not eating may include additional time to play, becoming the focus of attention, or getting snack food instead of the regular meal. Caregivers should eat with children in a pleasant setting to ensure that mealtime is a positive experience.

Preschool children's intake during individual meals often varies significantly. Low-energy intake in one meal is often followed by high-energy intake during the subsequent meal, resulting in remarkably constant energy intake over a twenty-four-hour period. Therefore, caregivers should focus on feeding their children a balanced diet within each twenty-four-hour period, rather than within each meal.

Food preferences are also influenced by experience. Although children often have an initial aversion to novel foods, this may be reversed following repeated exposure. Caregivers can facilitate the introduction of novel foods by presenting the foods repeatedly so that they become familiar, pairing the novel food with preferred food, and eating the novel food themselves and signaling enjoyment.

Food preferences are also influenced by associated conditions. Children are likely to avoid food that has been associated with nausea or pain and to enjoy food that has been associated with pleasure and satiety.

Caregivers
Parents may contribute to feeding problems in their children by the foods that they provide and the feeding atmosphere. Parents' mealtime behavior, especially harsh disciplinary practices, can be upsetting to children and affect the amount they eat. Mealtimes that consist of battles, forced feeding, and threats reinforce patterns of unpleasant struggles around food. Although children are responsible for learning to regulate their internal food requirements, they benefit from caregivers who eat with them and provide encouragement through modeling. In addition, caregivers should avoid giving infants and young children inappropriate foods, such as sweetened drinks that may satisfy hunger or thirst but provide minimal nutritional benefits, and low-fat or low-cholesterol foods that can result in inadequate intake of required nutrients.

Caregiver-Child Interactions
Interactions during mealtimes between caregivers and children with feeding problems are often characterized by unclear messages, premature termination of feeding, inconsistent mealtimes, and limited food availability. When parents do not structure mealtimes, children do not learn to anticipate when they will eat and may feel anxious and irritable.

Children are more likely to develop an expectation for being fed and an appetite when they are not permitted to graze or eat throughout the day and when mealtimes are structured. Mealtimes should be pleasant and family oriented, with the goal of eating in a social context. When mealtimes are too brief (less than ten minutes), children may not have enough time to eat, particularly when they are acquiring self-feeding skills and may eat slowly. Alternatively, sitting for more than twenty or thirty minutes may be difficult for a child, and mealtime may become aversive.

Culture

There is a wide cultural variation in the timing, type, and amounts of food offered, and beliefs about the appropriate styles of feeding. For example, in some Nigerian households children are force-fed so that caregivers can ensure that they have consumed enough food. In contrast, in some Nicaraguan households, caregivers take a rather passive role because they believe that children will eat as much food as they need. Each culture has a set of generalized traditions for feeding infants and for defining when more complex foods should be introduced. Although these cultural norms can change based on specific situations, they are passed down through subsequent generations and often retain at least some common features. Caregivers should consult their pediatrician regarding general strategies for providing their children with healthy, balanced meals rather than relying on norms that exist within their families. However, providing children with diverse foods remains the best method for encouraging them to enjoy a broad variety of tastes, flavors, aromas, and textures, and for meeting nutrient requirements.

Ultimately, the goal of feeding is to provide children with healthy meals in a pleasant setting so that battles are minimized and children learn to regulate their own food intake.

Tanya M. Morrel
Maureen M. Black

References and further reading

Black, Maureen M., Pam L. Cureton, and Julie Berenson-Howard. 1999. "Behavior Problems in Feeding: Individual, Family, and Cultural Influences." Pp. 151–169 in *Failure to Thrive and Pediatric Undernutrition: A Transdisciplinary Approach*. Baltimore, MD: Paul H. Brookes.

Linscheid, T. R. 1992. "Eating Problems in Children." Pp. 451–473 in *Handbook of Clinical Child Psychology*. 2d ed. New York: John Wiley and Sons.

Fetal Alcohol Syndrome (FAS)

Fetal alcohol syndrome (FAS) refers to a collection of symptoms observed in children born to mothers who drank alcohol during pregnancy. It is the most common known cause of mental retardation in the United States and European countries. FAS occurs mostly in the children of alcoholic mothers, although a precise relationship between the amount of alcohol consumed, the timing of ingestion, and severity of symptoms has never been established. Milder cases are referred to as fetal alcohol effects (FAE), in which symptoms are similar, but less severe. These may also be referred to as prenatal alcohol exposure (PAE), alcohol-related birth defects (ARBD), or alcohol-related neurodevelopmental defects (ARND).

Symptoms of FAS are extremely variable, and may include very small head size (microcephaly), short stature, low body weight, slow growth, facial anomalies (including a thin upper lip and wide-set eyes and other distinctive features), hyperactivity, irritability, difficulties with attention, learning disabilities (especially in mathematics and phonological processing), mental retardation, delayed development, poor social skills, and faulty judgment. In addition, other physiological

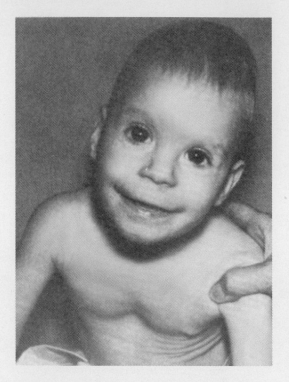

Symptoms of FAS include facial anomalies.
(James W. Hanson)

abnormalities such as heart and genital defects are found less often. Most of the time, symptoms are relatively subtle, and the severity of each one varies tremendously between individuals. Many physical symptoms tend to change with age, so FAS is rarely diagnosed at birth, usually being diagnosed later in infancy or early childhood. Facial anomalies tend to fade during late childhood, with faces becoming more normal looking by adolescence, but intellectual and behavior problems remain, often despite remediation. If the child remains in the custody of his or her alcoholic biological parents, abuse, neglect, and instability in the home often compound the child's problems. However, foster-care placement is often unsuccessful due to the child's behavior problems. Emotional problems, such as depression and anxiety, as well as intel-

lectual, behavioral, and social problems, often hinder the ability of those exposed to alcohol to live normal, independent lives in adulthood, and they have high rates of suicide and attempted suicide.

FAS was first described and named in France in 1968 and in the United States in 1972. The lateness of this discovery was due to the subtlety of symptoms and the tendency of facial anomalies to change with age. Anatomical studies have shown that alcohol causes neurons in the developing brain to fail to migrate to their intended destinations and impedes neural differentiation and myelination, and so causes a lack of development in many different brain areas, including the cerebral cortex, hippocampus, basal ganglia, cerebellum, and corpus callosum. These effects are caused by oxygen deprivation and formation of free radicals, as well as failure of transport of nutrients by the placenta. These widespread effects cause a high rate of stillbirths, complications of pregnancy and delivery (including miscarriage, premature birth, and respiratory distress at birth), and the wide array of symptoms described above. Alcohol may also impair neural plasticity, hindering the brain's ability to respond to environmental enrichment.

The correspondence between the amount of alcohol consumed and the severity of effects is not precise; studies on humans have been hampered by the tendency of problem drinkers to underestimate their consumption. However, both human and animal studies have indicated that binge drinking appears to have worse effects than similar amounts of alcohol consumed on a more regular basis, as binge drinking puts more alcohol into the mother's and therefore the child's blood. Alcohol exposure during the first trimester has the most devastating effects, but continuation of binge drinking into the second and third trimesters produces the most severe cases. Most cases of FAS occur in women who are at a late stage of alcoholism, and so affected children often have older siblings who are less affected and younger siblings who are more affected. Only about 2 to 10 percent of alcoholic pregnant women have babies with FAS, but about 40 percent have FAE. (Weiner and Morse, 1996)

Alcohol has been found to interact with some heartburn medications, causing worse effects than the simple combination of their effects. Although no specific interactions with poor nutrition or use of tobacco, caffeine, marijuana, cocaine, or other substances have been found, ill effects of these conditions coexist with those of alcohol. Research has found that most alcoholic women also smoke cigarettes, so reduced birth weight and other health problems associated with tobacco use are particularly common in children exposed to alcohol.

The most striking physical manifestation of prenatal alcohol exposure is small head circumference, or microcephaly, which usually continues to be evident in adulthood. Low birth weight and small size are common at birth and become small stature and underweight during childhood, continuing into adulthood, except that the weight of girls exposed to alcohol tends to become normal or above normal after puberty. Facial anomalies are less common and are particularly associated with exposure to alcohol during the first trimester. They often include a thin upper lip, wide-set eyes, a flattened midface, small and upturned nose, and a receding chin line. As mentioned above, most of these change are not evident by adolescence. The chin often becomes prominent; the nose and lips often become larger and more normal in appearance. Lack of muscle tone is common in infancy and early childhood. Many other physical effects occur less frequently, such as heart and urogenital defects, cleft palate and other defects of the palate, neurological prob-

lems such as spina bifida or hydrocephalus, eye problems such as strabismus or squint, and defects of the formation and movement of the hip, feet, and fingers. These often cause respiratory distress at birth, poor sucking, poor growth, and gross and fine motor delays during development. Failure to thrive is also frequently reported among alcohol-exposed children; this results from eating and neurological problems in early childhood that are a consequence of prenatal alcohol exposure, and also from maltreatment by alcoholic parents.

The most reported behavioral symptoms of FAS include hyperactivity, problems with social relations, and mental retardation and other learning difficulties, which also persist into adulthood. With increasing age, age-related developmental problems such as enuresis (bed-wetting), eating problems, and gross and fine motor delays tend to fade, but new ones, such as speech and language disorders, emerge when intellectual demands increase as children progress in school. Sleep disorders are common from infancy on. Children with FAS sleep more frequently, for a shorter time, and less well. They also are often drowsy when awake. Inability to switch tasks, or perseveration, as well as failure to inhibit responses, are particular problems in school, but persist and cause lifelong problems in social and intellectual functioning. Stereotyped behavior, such as rocking, is also sometimes present.

Delays in language development are common, as are problems in memory, reasoning, processing speed, phonological processing, problem solving, spatial relations, sensory integration, and perceptual motor skills. Standardized tests in school-aged children often show multiple difficulties, with scores in math, reading, and spelling below grade level, although arithmetic difficulties are particularly prevalent. Additional difficulties in school are caused by distractibility and lack of persistence on educational tasks. Those with milder symptoms are often placed into more restrictive educational settings as time goes on due to decreasing ability to keep up in regular classes. Placement into a new home and educational remediation often result in less improvement than would be expected for other disorders, especially for the most severely affected, and so many alcohol-exposed children require special education and fail to finish high school.

In adulthood, employment is often problematical, due to lack of ability to inhibit impulses, distractibility, restlessness, lack of persistence on tasks, and poor judgment, as well as low levels of academic skills.

Emotional difficulties also are often evident in FAS children from very early childhood on. Higher rates of insecure attachment to caregivers, particularly the pattern of disorganized attachment frequently seen among abused and neglected children, have been reported. An inability to trust others, irritability, and social withdrawal are also common. Hyperactivity and lack of communication skills often lead to aggressive behavior toward others. As mentioned previously, alcoholic parents often provide poor care, are not consistent in their own behavior, and have high rates of child maltreatment, which worsen the outlook for alcohol-exposed children. Family instability is a particular problem, with the stresses of poverty, unemployment, frequent moves, inconsistent discipline, having four or more children in the family, changes in caregivers as children spend time in the homes of people other than their biological parents, and changes in family constellation as parents die, divorce, desert their children, or acquire new partners, or children are removed from the parents' home due to maltreatment. Children in foster care may experience a number of short-term placements that do not work out, due to their

multiple behavior problems. These problems lead to a higher rate of emotional problems from childhood through adulthood, with low self-esteem, anxiety, and depression common, and a high rate of suicide and attempted suicide.

About 40 percent of children with FAS do not have any psychiatric symptoms, however, and are able to eventually lead relatively normal lives. (Steinhausen, 1996) Prevention and early intervention are likely to improve outcomes for children of alcoholic mothers, particularly if aimed at women before conception occurs. Education campaigns and warning labels on containers have helped increase awareness of the dangers of alcohol for most people, but often miss those most at risk who already drink heavily. Surveys have shown that only about half of doctors routinely screen patients for alcohol abuse; increasing screening and identification of alcohol problems by health-care providers, social services, and other agencies involved with the most at-risk women, with effective referrals to treatment programs, would help prevent many cases of FAS. The number of treatment slots, especially for pregnant women, should be increased. Effective treatments address the multiple problems alcoholic women often face, including use of other drugs or substances such as tobacco, partners who abuse substances, domestic abuse, poverty and unemployment, low self-esteem, past experiences of abuse or neglect by parents or partners, child care, poor nutrition, and low educational level, as well as alcohol abuse.

Treatment programs during pregnancy, although less effective, could also prevent many of the most severe cases of FAS. Improved screening and referral by health-care providers, along with an increase in the number of treatment slots and counseling, have helped many pregnant women reduce their alcohol consumption and improve the outcomes for their babies.

Early intervention for children is often hampered by the inability to diagnose fetal alcohol exposure at or shortly after birth; however, prompt referral to compensatory services, such as speech, occupational, and physical therapy, and follow-through to assure compliance, help ameliorate educational and developmental delays. Intensive educational interventions specifically targeted at each child's particular problems are most effective. Structured, nondistracting home and classroom environments have also been used, as well as consistent discipline and improved intellectual stimulation. In addition, social services need to be provided to help the parents stop drinking and improve family stability and child treatment, so as to prevent the compounding of the child's initial problems.

Although most research has focused on maternal drinking, paternal alcohol use may also have deleterious consequences, especially among male offspring. Inconsistent results have been reported, varying considerably by species, dose, and timing of alcohol exposure and testing, use of valid comparison groups, and other methodological details. Human studies have shown that biological sons of alcoholic fathers have a greater tendency to become alcoholics themselves than those of nonalcoholic fathers; however, no genes for alcoholism have been identified. These sons also tended to have more intellectual deficits, hyperactivity, and hormonal abnormalities than other men, although no facial anomalies were reported. Children of two alcoholic parents may be worse off, both socially and physically, than those of couples including only one alcoholic. When male rats were exposed to alcohol and mated with nonexposed females, lower numbers of pregnancies and surviving offspring resulted, and male offspring demonstrated impaired spatial

learning and lower levels of blood testosterone and fertility, compared to nonexposed controls. Alcohol-induced mutations in sperm DNA, causing lower sperm counts or reduced motility or viability, have been suggested as causes of these results, but these proposals have not been confirmed.

Shelley Mae Drazen

References and further reading
Cicero, Theodore. 1994. "Effects of Paternal Exposure to Alcohol on Offspring Development." *Alcohol Health and Research World* 18:37–41.

Dorris, Michael. 1989. *The Broken Cord.* New York: HarperPerennial.

Hannigan, John, Linda Spear, Norman Spear, and Charles Goodlett, eds. 1999. *Alcohol and Alcoholism: Effects on Brain and Development.* Mahwah, NJ: Lawrence Erlbaum Associates.

Spohr, Hans-Ludwig, and Hans-Christoph Steinhausen, eds. 1996. *Alcohol, Pregnancy and the Developing Child.* Cambridge, UK: Cambridge University Press.

Steinhausen, Hans-Christoph. 1996. "Psychopathology and Cognitive Functioning in Children with Fetal Alcohol Syndrome." Pp. 227–246 in *Alcohol, Pregnancy and the Developing Child.* Edited by Hans-Ludwig Spohr and Hans-Christoph Steinhausen. Cambridge, UK: Cambridge University Press.

Streissguth, Ann P., Jon M. Aase, Sterling K. Clarren, Sandra P. Randels, Robin A. LaDue, and David F. Smith. 1991. "Fetal Alcohol Syndrome in Adolescents and Adults." *Journal of the American Medical Association (JAMA)* 265, no. 15:1961–1967.

Streissguth, Ann P., Paul D. Sampson, Heather C. Olson, Fred L. Bookstein, Helen M. Barr, Mike Scott, Julie Feldman, and Allan F. Mirsky. 1994. "Maternal Drinking during Pregnancy: Attention and Short-Term Memory in 14-Year-Old Offspring: A Longitudinal Prospective Study." *Alcoholism: Clinical and Experimental Research* 18:202–218.

Weiner, Lyn, and Barbara Morse. 1996. "Fetal Alcohol Syndrome: A Framework for Successful Prevention." Pp. 269–288 in *Alcohol, Pregnancy and the Developing Child.* Edited by Hans-Ludwig Spohr and Hans-Christoph Steinhausen. Cambridge, UK: Cambridge University Press.

Foster Parents

Foster parents are adults who are given temporary legal guardianship of a minor who is a ward of the state. Although the term *foster care* is used to describe a variety of situations in which a minor is not living with his or her legal parents (e.g., foster family homes, preadoptive homes, group homes, institutions, supervised independent living), foster family care comprises about 80 percent of all foster-care placements. In 1999, it was estimated there were approximately 410,800 children under the age of eighteen living in foster family care, which is defined as temporary, noninstitutional family care by a relative or nonrelative. (U.S. Department of Health and Human Services, 1999) Today, children are primarily placed in foster family care when state social service agencies obtain custody of the child because the child's health or life is endangered; that is, the child is neglected or abused. Although reports of child abuse are more sensational than reports of child neglect, most of the children in foster care are there due to severe physical or medical neglect, and not abuse.

Foster family care in the United States has its origins in the "placing out" system of the New York Children's Aid Society. The placing out system, founded by Charles Loring Brace in the 1850s, was modeled after the indenture system of colonial times. New York City's most impoverished, homeless, and neglected children were placed in midwestern farm families, where they were expected to participate in chores in exchange for food and shelter until they reached adulthood. The goal of this system was to prevent the spread of delinquency among poor urban children. Foster care developed into what it is today largely through the work of Charles Birtwell, a social reformer active in the late 1800s who believed the goal of foster care should be to restore the child to his or her biological parents. The belief that the bond between biological mother and child is important and therefore worth preserving is widely held in popular culture, but not supported by psychological research with humans. Social policy advocates beginning with Brace and Birtwell have long believed that family care is inherently superior to institutional care for children undergoing crises, and psychological theories and research support this view. For example, research on attachment indicates that if children are to develop normal social and emotional functioning in adulthood, they must develop a secure attachment with a caregiver. Psychoanalytic theory suggests that the early caregiver-child relationship sets a pattern for other relationships throughout one's life. Therefore, especially for those children in foster care who have little or no hope of being reunited with their families, foster family care provides the opportunity to develop secure attachments to adult caregivers and thereby a chance to develop normal social, emotional, and intellectual functioning. Today, foster care is seen as a temporary solution for families in crisis, families in which the child has been subjected to neglect (e.g., the child is malnourished) or abuse (physical, sexual).

Prospective foster parents go through an extensive application process to become licensed foster parents. Although the particulars of licensing vary by state, child welfare agencies prefer heterosexual couples who are healthy and have no criminal record, have sufficient income to meet their needs and space for an additional child, and whose home meets sanitary and safety standards and is located in an area with adequate community (e.g., educational, religious, medical, recreational) facilities. Agency representatives also assess the emotional well-being and suitability of the prospective foster family (e.g., their discipline strategies, the flexibility of their beliefs, and their ability to work with the agency). Child welfare agencies reimburse foster parents for the child's basic needs (food, clothing, shelter), but foster parents are not paid. The role of foster parents is to care for their foster children as if they were their own, and part with them for the sake of family reunification.

Linda R. Cote

References and further reading

Bowlby, John. 1982. *Attachment and Loss.* Vol. 1 of *Attachment.* New York: Basic Books.

Kadushin, Alfred. 1967. *Child Welfare Services.* 3d ed. New York: Macmillan.

Rutter, Michael. 1979. "Maternal Deprivation 1972–1978: New Findings, New Concepts, New Approaches." *Child Development* 50:283–305.

Tiffin, Susan. 1982. *In Whose Best Interest? Child Welfare Reform in the Progressive Era.* Westport, CT: Greenwood Press.

U.S. Department of Health and Human Services, Administration for Children and Families, Administration on Children, Youth and Families, Children's Bureau. 1999. *The AFCARS Report.* Vol. 1. (Online). Available at: www.acf.dhhs.gov/programs/cb/stats/afcars/rpt0199/ar0199.htm.

Anna Freud with father, Sigmund Freud. (Collections of the Library of Congress)

Freud, Anna (1895–1982)

Anna Freud was a pioneer in applying psychoanalytic principles to the treatment and study of children. As an ego psychologist, she was primarily concerned with how children adapt to the realities of the external world. Her most famous work, *The Ego and the Mechanisms of Defense,* written in 1936, explains the use of defense mechanisms as an attempt to adapt to environmental stresses. Defense mechanisms are strategies used by people to help them deal with difficult situations and information. The exploration of defense mechanisms was a continuation and elaboration of the work of her father, Sigmund Freud, the founder of psychoanalysis. Anna recognized the important role played by the family in the development of children; she was one of the first psychoanalysts to include parents in the treatment process. In addition, she studied the infant-mother relationship and the negative effects of maternal separation. In her later work, she created a developmental framework based on different aspects of psychoanalytic theory. She used this to distinguish "normal" development from "abnormal" processes that might lead to psychopathology. Despite living in her father's shadow, Anna Freud made great contributions to the psychological treatment of children and to human development. Her influence today can be seen in the work continued by the Hampstead Center for the Psychoanalytical Study and Treatment of Children in London, as well as in her many books and publications.

Anna Freud was born in Vienna, Austria, on 3 December 1895, the youngest child of Sigmund and Martha Freud. As early as 1913, Anna became her father's personal secretary and he became her most important professional influence. However, Anna did not begin her career as a psychoanalyst. After completing her secondary education at the Cottage Lyceum, she trained to become an elementary school teacher, a career she continued until 1920. Teaching gave her the opportunity to collect information about children that she later used to develop her theories of child psychotherapy and development. She did, however, begin a training analysis with her father in which she received psychoanalytic psychotherapy from him. She never received an academic or medical degree.

Anna's interest in becoming an analyst was apparent by 1920 and may have been solidified after attending a lecture given by Hermine von Hug-Hellmuth that same year. Hug-Hellmuth is little known, but is considered by many to be the first child psychoanalyst. She was the first to apply Sigmund Freud's principles to children and tried to incorporate his teachings into the educational environment. Although she did not practice psychoanalysis as it is known today, she counseled parents, children, and school personnel using psychoanalytic methods. She is considered to be the first person to use play therapy with children. As a fellow educator, Anna was heavily influenced and inspired by Hug-Hellmuth's work.

In 1922, Anna gave her first lecture at the Vienna Psychoanalytic Society, and her professional career as a psychoanalyst officially began. A year later Sigmund Freud developed cancer of the palate, the disease that led to his death seventeen years later. Anna served as her father's nurse during these years and spent much of her time tending to her father. Although her father's sickness was undoubtedly a great burden, Anna continued to be productive professionally during this period.

In 1926, her book *Introduction to the Technique of Child Analysis* was pub-

lished and was both influential and controversial. In it Anna introduced a theory to apply psychoanalytic principles to therapy with children. She also created some novel techniques. These included the use of picture drawing, working with the parents in treatment, and the use of a preparatory phase (to make the children feel more comfortable) before beginning analysis. The book was considered controversial because Anna disagreed with another noted analyst, Melanie Klein, who, along with Anna Freud, was a pioneer of child psychoanalysis. Klein expanded on Hermine von Hug-Hellmuth's use of play with children and popularized its use as a psychoanalytic technique. Anna Freud disagreed with some of Klein's beliefs, however, and a lifelong rivalry developed between the two. One of their greatest disagreements regarded the role of "transference." Transference is a process involving the unconscious thoughts the patient has about the analyst during the therapeutic process. For instance, a patient may unconsciously see the therapist as a father or mother figure. Klein believed that children could engage in transference with the therapist, but Anna Freud believed that children could not engage in true transference because they were too involved with their parents during childhood. Despite their differences, there is no doubt that Anna Freud respected Klein's work and was heavily influenced by her over her lifetime.

In 1925, Anna Freud met her lifelong friend and colleague, Dorothy Burlingham. After leaving her mentally ill husband in America, Burlingham came to Vienna with her four children and received psychoanalytic training from Sigmund Freud. In 1928, she moved in with the Freuds and, after Sigmund Freud's death, continued to live in the house with Anna until her own death. Burlingham took up the teachings of the Freuds, became a child psychoanalyst, and was a supporter as well as a contributor to Anna Freud's professional accomplishments.

In 1936, Anna Freud's classic work, *The Ego and the Mechanisms of Defense* was published. This book was a comprehensive study of the ego and examined the defenses used by the ego to protect the psychological self in the face of stresses. Sigmund Freud had done some of the original work in this area, but Anna's book was a more thorough exploration that attributed a greater role to the ego than to other parts of the personality. It included new defense mechanisms, as well as those posited by other theorists. The book was a tremendous critical success and is considered Anna Freud's greatest contribution to psychoanalytic theory.

When the National Socialists rose to power in Germany and annexed Austria, the Freuds were in great personal danger, not only because they were Jewish, but also because their psychoanalytic writings were looked upon with disfavor. Sigmund Freud, however, was reluctant to leave Austria. After Anna was arrested and interrogated by the Nazis, her father was finally convinced that they should leave. They arrived in England in June 1938, where Anna would live for the rest of her life. It is believed that Anna Freud's efforts were instrumental in getting many psychoanalysts and their families out of Austria.

World War II brought about many changes for Anna Freud, both personally and professionally. Soon after arriving in England, the Freuds moved to Hampstead in greater London, where Sigmund Freud died on 23 September 1939. Despite their closeness, Anna Freud displayed no public emotion regarding his death. Instead, she immersed herself in her work. She and Dorothy Burlingham established the Hampstead Wartime Nursery for Homeless Children in 1940 near their home. The nursery served as a home and school for war orphans, as well as a research and training institute.

During her wartime work at the Hampstead Nursery, Anna Freud made an important observation. She realized that children in the nursery were not traumatized so much by the war itself, but by the abrupt separation from their parents. In particular, she concentrated on the negative effects of separation from the mother, labeled maternal deprivation syndrome. This work led her to examine the developmental importance of mother-child interaction using a psychoanalytic framework.

The Hampstead Nursery expanded during the postwar years and continues today as the Hampstead Center for the Psychoanalytical Study and Treatment of Children. It is a school based on psychoanalytic and Montessori principles that provides psychoanalytic counseling for children and mothers, and also serves as a research and training institute.

The postwar years marked Anna Freud's increasing international prominence. She helped found *The Psychoanalytic Study of the Child*, a publication dedicated to psychoanalytic issues with children. She served as an officer of the International Psychoanalytic Association and gave frequent lectures, including many in the United States. She was given the first of ten honorary doctorates when she visited Clark University in Massachusetts in 1950.

After a decade of lecturing, private practice, and work at the Hampstead clinic, Anna Freud began to formulate her ideas on normal development and psychopathology. In 1960, she presented a series of lectures in New York City that formed the basis for her later book, *Normality and Pathology in Childhood*. In this work, Anna Freud synthesized decades of psychoanalytic theory into a comprehensive developmental framework. She introduced the concept of "developmental lines" or sequences of normal development based on different aspects of psychoanalytic theory. Based on her theory of normal development, Anna Freud described the way in which psychopathology would develop if normal development were obstructed. Although not her most famous work, this book was the culmination of years of experience with children and their families in different settings and situations.

In the 1960s, Anna Freud took an active interest in the legal rights of children, sparked by her concern that their best interests were often ignored by the legal system. She was especially concerned with the psychological plight of adopted and foster-care children. As a visiting professor at Yale Law School in 1963 and 1964, she gave a seminar on these issues and eventually wrote a book, *Beyond the Best Interests of the Child*, with professors from the Yale University Child Study Center. Partially through her efforts, children have gained greater legal rights, independent of parental figures.

The later years of Anna Freud's life were spent primarily lecturing and gathering honors from around the world. In 1975, she was named honorary president of the International Psychoanalytic Association. A few years later she helped launch the *Bulletin of the Hampstead Clinic*, a quarterly journal based on research occurring at the clinic she founded. On 9 October 1982, Anna Freud died in her London home at the age of eighty-six.

Anna Freud is best remembered for her contributions to child psychoanalysis, human development, and ego psychology. Many of her pioneering theories and techniques continue to be influential today, and her legacy also endures through the work of the Hampstead clinic. Although her work is well respected, she has had her critics. Those that adhere to Klein's beliefs have disagreed with many of Anna Freud's conceptualizations regarding child

psychoanalysis. As beliefs in psychoanalytic principles seem to be on the decline, it is unclear how the general public will view her contributions in future years. Among her peers, however, Anna Freud was undoubtedly well respected. In 1971, psychiatrists and psychoanalysts were surveyed in order to find out whom they regarded as their most outstanding colleague. Anna Freud was voted most outstanding by both groups.

John D. Hogan
Matthew S. Broudy

References and further reading
Dyer, Raymond. 1983. *Her Father's Daughter: The Works of Anna Freud.* New York: Aronson.
Fine, Reuben. 1990. "Anna Freud." Pp. 96–103 in *Women in Psychology: A Bio-Bibliographic Sourcebook.* Edited by Agnes N. O'Connell and Nancy F. Russo. New York: Greenwood Press.
Peters, Uwe H. 1985. *Anna Freud: A Life Dedicated to Children.* New York: Schocken Books.

Friendship, Adolescent

Friendship takes on particular importance as a child enters adolescence. There are a number of reasons. First, adolescence is a time of biological change. Sexual maturation brings changes not only in appearance but also in physical drives and social interests. Friendships provide support and security as the child matures physically. For example, by talking with friends the child may learn that what he or she is experiencing is typical, that others also are dealing with these new sensations and experiences. Second, adolescence is a time of separation from parents. With adolescence, children generally try to distance themselves from parental viewpoints and sometimes challenge parental control. But as the child tries to exert his or her own autonomy, there is also a fear of separation, a wish that parents will remain in control. Friends help adolescents in dealing with this separation conflict. Friends

Friendships provide support and security as children mature physically. (Skjold Photographs)

provide support as the child attempts to achieve new levels of responsibility and also (under ideal circumstances) alert the child to the dangers of outright rejection of parental values. A final reason for the importance of friendship is that the adolescent has reached an intellectual level at which he or she has a desire to think about his or her life more analytically, more philosophically, and to talk with others about these new understandings. Adolescence can be a time of isolation, a time when one feels alone with one's thoughts. Friends bring a sense of belonging and acceptance, and thus provide protection against feelings of alienation.

Friends are important before adolescence, but the meaning of friendship is very different before and after adolescence. Young children think of friendship pragmatically. When children in the early elementary grades are asked to explain what makes someone a friend, their first responses are usually that a friend is someone they play with or that a friend is someone who is "nice." As children approach adolescence, loyalty emerges as another criterion for friendship. Now friends are distinguished from nonfriends, not only on the basis of how much time is spent together but on the basis of whether the person can be trusted. Interestingly, preadolescents and young adolescents tend to have a different definition of trust than do older adolescents. Younger adolescents tend to think of trust in terms of what a friend will not do to them. For example, a middle school child may define a friend as someone who will not "stab you in the back" or "laugh at you." Older adolescents think of trust as involving personal understanding and acceptance. Thus, a friend to a high school senior is someone "who understands you," someone "with whom you are comfortable," and someone with whom "you can be yourself."

As age influences the meaning of friendship among adolescents, so does gender in defining the nature and functions of friendship. It is often said that girls' friendships with other girls are more restrictive and more exclusive than are boys' friendships with other boys. Restrictiveness refers to the guardedness with which girls hold their friendships and the rigor with which groups of friends screen newcomers as potential friends. Exclusiveness refers to the small size of friendship groups. Compared to those of girls, boys' friendship groups tend to be loose, open to newcomers, and extensive. This difference in restrictiveness and exclusiveness leads to the common observation that boys' friendships seem less intense and less serious than those of girls. Boys, for example, appear more forgiving of friends following disagreements and less jealous of other relationships.

An important question is why boys' and girls' friendships have these differing qualities. The answer lies in the different functions that friends serve for boys and girls. Girls' friendships place a premium on talk and, in particular, on self-disclosure. The function of such intimate relationships is to provide emotional support, security, and help in problem solving. Boys' friendships also involve talk and self-disclosure. But they tend to be more playful than those of girls and more frankly competitive. Boys rely on friends to help prepare them for independence and to help "toughen them up" for dealing with a competitive world. Thus, while friendships for both genders provide association, positive experiences of camaraderie, and security, boys' and girls' friendships do have different qualities. It will be interesting to see, as more young women play competitive sports and compete in the world of business, whether adolescent friendships continue to differ as a function of gender. It has been observed, for example, that friendships among college women who play on the same varsity athletic team resemble the friendships of men in their playfulness, competitiveness, and "rough-and-tumble" character.

How are adolescent friendships established? While some adolescent friendships exist in relative isolation from other adolescents, other friendships occur in the context of larger networks, usually called cliques. Thus, in looking at the process of friendship formation, one must distinguish between isolated pairs of friends and those friendships that are embedded in larger networks. In general, the most healthy adolescent friendships are those in which each person in a friendship has other friends and where some of these other friendships overlap.

Friends generally select one another and respond to one another's overtures for friendship on the basis of common interests and activities. For boys, the dynamics of friendship establishment are subtle and the process can appear unsystematic. Boys often initiate friendship through sports, shared involvement in school (e.g., clubs or extracurricular activities), and social activities, some of which may be considered deviant (e.g., going out drinking). It is usually important for potential friends to relate easily to current members of the clique or friendship group, although occasionally a best friendship exists outside of a friendship group. Girls tend to be more explicit in initiating their friendships, often offering the newcomer an invitation to an event or gathering. Girls also make overtures toward friendship by sharing personal information, and in this way signal the wish for a friendship. As is the case with boys, it may be difficult for a girl to sustain a friendship with a newcomer if she is not accepted by current friends. In fact, girls are usually less willing than boys to tolerate a group member who is not uniformly welcomed. One reason for this may be that boys' cliques are hierarchical by nature, and thus there is always room for someone lower in the hierarchy.

While it has long been assumed that friendships promote healthy social and emotional development, it is only more recently that the question has been empirically investigated. Studies show that the way in which friends influence later development is complex. The effects of friendship depend on the personality characteristics of the friends. They also depend on whether the friendship is truly reciprocal or whether it is unbalanced.

Among children of normal mental health, having positive, reciprocated friendships is associated with generosity, empathy, social confidence, and better psychological adjustment. Absence of supportive friendships is associated with loneliness and psychological distress. Sometimes an adolescent attempts to form a friendship with someone who is only mildly supportive, or is conditional in his or her acceptance of the person wanting to be friends. For example, an adolescent wishing to be friends may be "allowed" to associate with members of a friendship group, but may be treated as inferior to the other members. While such relationships may meet temporarily the adolescent's need for companionship, the long-term effects may be damaging. Possible negative outcomes include learning to assume the role of "fall guy" or "clown" as a means of acceptance, or engaging in antisocial behaviors to earn respect.

When children are known to have serious behavior problems, such as delinquency, friendships with similar children often exacerbate the behavior problems. There is much evidence that antisocial children reinforce one another positively for antisocial activities, including inappropriate language, disrespectful behavior, and aggression. Clinicians recognize the importance of discouraging rather than encouraging such friendships, even if the adolescents themselves seem satisfied with them. In fact, mental health interventions designed to improve the social adjustment of aggressive adolescents are likely to fail if they do not separate the aggressive youngsters from antisocial peers.

It is important to recognize the role that parents have in influencing adolescents' selections of friends and in influencing the impact of adolescent friendships. First, the kind of person an adolescent chooses as a friend is likely to depend on parental values. Adolescents tend to have similar views as their parents on such matters as the importance of education and achievement, tolerance for deviant behaviors, and appropriateness of adult behaviors—in particular, early sexual activity. Further, adolescents tend to choose friends who are similar to themselves in their feelings and viewpoints about these activities. In addition, whether children engage in healthy friendships well integrated into their home and school relationships or whether they engage in friendships in which they are isolated from home and school is very dependent on the quality of the children's home life. Parents who get along with one another, are firm, clear, and consistent in their disciplinary practices, and spend time with their children in frequent and warm interactions have a positive influence on adolescent friendships. Such parents are encouraging their children to form close attachments with others, but also to continue to trust the parents as the people who will provide security, protection, and guidance. When home life is chaotic or conflictful, adolescents may turn to friends for the security and clarity they do not have in the home. In such cases, friendships may be undesirably close and influential, and may lead the child to antisocial and even self-destructive behaviors.

David E. Barrett

References and further reading

Berndt, Thomas J. 1982. "The Features and Effects of Friendship in Early Adolescence." *Child Development* 53:1447–1460.

Dishion, Thomas J., Joan McCord, and Francois Poulin. 1999. "When Interventions Harm: Peer Groups and Problem Behavior." *American Psychologist* 55:755–764.

Hartup, Willard W. 1996. "The Company They Keep: Friendships and Their Developmental Significance." *Child Development* 67:1–13.

Froebel, Frederick (1782–1852)

Frederick Froebel might well be regarded as the father of modern early childhood education. He was one of the first to emphasize the educational importance of the early years of life. Although trained as a crystallographer, he left his chosen profession to become a teacher. To this end he studied with the Swiss educator Frederick Pestalozzi. Pestalozzi was the first educator to translate Rousseau's radical educational philosophy—that children had their own ways of learning and knowing—into practice. From Pestalozzi and Rousseau, Froebel inherited a distrust of formal education and a faith in children's ability to learn from their own, self-initiated and -directed activity. But he was unique in believing that young children can and should be educated before they enter school. The name for the early educational program he invented, kindergarten ("children's garden"), came to him during a walk in the woods.

Froebel was a deeply religious man who believed in the essential goodness of children. The educational program he created was moral and philosophical as well as instructional. In his view the aim of education was to enable young people to realize all the dimensions of their personality fully and totally. Froebel believed that evil and wickedness did not exist separately but rather, were manifestations of incomplete, interrupted, or stunted devel-

Frederick Froebel (1782–1852) (Collections of the Library of Congress)

opment. In this respect he anticipated the Freudian view that neuroses were the result of deviations from the normal course of psychosexual development. For Froebel, education had to provide for the child's moral and physical growth, as well as for his or her intellectual progress.

At the heart of the kindergarten philosophy was Froebel's conviction that young children learn through play. To encourage this activity he created songs and games for mothers to use with their infants. Games like "This Little Piggy Goes to Market" and songs like "Happy Birthday" have a Froebelian ancestry. In his own school Froebel offered no formal instruction in morals and character. He thought these qualities were naturally acquired as children learned to care for living things. Plants and animals, therefore, became a fixture of most kindergartens. In looking after plants and animals, children learned not only about the natural world but also about responsibility and caring for living things.

One of Froebel's major contributions was his conception of the child's developmental stages and their relation to learning. Froebel recognized that children learn differently at different stages of their growth. Although the stages he described are relatively simplistic by today's standards, they nonetheless foreshadowed a number of contemporary ideas. For example, he suggested that the preschool child seeks to make his or her internal world external through the use of language, whereas the school-age child seeks to make the external world internal through the incorporation of rules, facts, and values. This distinction between early childhood education and elementary education has been reintroduced today under the rubric of "developmentally appropriate practice."

Among Froebel's most important contributions to early childhood education were what he called his "gifts" (the play materials themselves) and "occupations" (the ways the materials could be used). There were twenty gifts. These ranged from simple forms (sphere, square, and cylinder) to entire sets of wooden geometric shapes of many different sizes and painted a variety of colors. There were colored paper geometric figures with adhesive backs so that they could be pasted together into different shapes. One gift included a wooden pin with which children could create patterns by punching small holes into sheets of paper. Another gift was a set of sticks and dried peas that could be put together into various shapes (the forerunner of today's Tinker Toys™).

The principle that motivated these gifts was Froebel's belief that children could be taught universal ideas from a particular one. He felt that one could start with something simple like a coin or simple

geometric form and move from that to more general ideas about man and the world. Not surprisingly, Froebel illustrated this pedagogical principle with the use of crystals. The formation of crystals, he believed, reflected the operation of a crystallogic force that represented all of the many and varied forces of nature. Crystals, moreover, were a general manifestation of the unity, individuality, and diversity, as well as the harmony and union to be found throughout nature. His first gift to a child was a ball that represented not only a simple geometric form but also the earth, continuity, unity, and diversity.

What Froebel hoped to achieve with these gifts and occupations, and with the kindergarten experience in general, was to create a sensitive, inquisitive child with an unbounded curiosity and a true respect for nature, family, and community. Clearly, Froebel regarded early childhood education as providing children with a positive orientation toward life and learning, not an inert collection of facts and skills.

Perhaps Froebel's greatest contributions to early childhood education were his humanism and his holism. He regarded all children as valuable, regardless of their social status or background. He firmly believed that all children had the potential to lead creative, productive lives. He was, moreover, opposed to the compartmentalization and drill employed by Pestalozzi and argued instead for an educational program that recognized that young children are not fragmented, but learn with their entire beings. Early childhood education, he urged, should offer children a setting in which to experience a full life, rich in opportunities for work and play, for leisure and recreation, for art, and for spiritual renewal. Early childhood, for Froebel, was an important stage of life valuable in its own right and not simply as a preparation for what is to come later.

The kindergarten idea caught on quickly in all parts of the world, and thousands of kindergartens were part of the educational landscape by the turn of the century. Indeed it may well have played an important role in the art and architecture of the beginning of the twentieth century. Frank Lloyd Wright attended a Froebelian kindergarten, as did artists Paul Klee and Georges Braque. There is a startling resemblance between their buildings and paintings and some of the products of children in Froebel's kindergartens. Kindergarten can certainly cannot explain genius, but it is important to recognize that early childhood experience may, nonetheless, affect the manner in which genius is realized and expressed.

David Elkind

References and further reading
Brosterman, Norman. 1997. *Inventing Kindergarten*, New York: Henry A. Abrams.
Froebel, Friedrich. 1893. *The Education of Man*. New York: D. Appleton.

G

Gay and Lesbian Children

Many gay and lesbian children, children who will grow up to love others of the same sex, become aware that they feel "different" very early on, although they may not fully understand what the difference means. Others may not become aware until puberty that they are attracted to those of the same sex. Other children may be bisexual, feeling attraction to both males and females. And some children may not be sure what their final orientation will be. The causes of sexual orientation are not completely clear, although current researchers suggest that a combination of biology and early environmental factors may be involved. Sexual orientation is not the result of poor parenting or lax adherence to traditional sex roles. This is not a "choice" or preference but an essential part of the person's nature. Although there is nothing wrong with being gay or lesbian, society's reactions may put these children at risk because of harassment or intolerance.

The assumption in our society is that everyone is heterosexual. This pervades the media, education, and everyday conversation so completely that children may grow up not knowing that there is anything else. Sexual minority youth (the general term used for children and adolescents who are anything but heterosexual) may think there is something wrong with them because they don't fit the mold. Role models who are openly gay and lesbian can go a long way toward decreasing their feelings of isolation and difference.

Unfortunately, sexual minority youth may be punished or stigmatized for their actions. Behaviors that would be acceptable from a heterosexual child (hugging or kissing someone, holding hands) may be discouraged by adults or mocked by peers. Behaviors that would be acceptable from a heterosexual adolescent (experimenting with sexuality) may be viewed by adults as deliberately "flaunting" their sexuality and may lead to severe peer harassment. These exploratory behaviors are a natural, developmentally appropriate part of growing up and ideally would be treated as such.

This ideal reaction seldom occurs. American society subscribes to many myths about homosexuality. Contrary to those myths, however, tomboys don't necessarily grow up to be lesbians; boys who are artistic, play with dolls, dress up, or do not play sports don't necessarily grow up to be gay; and mothers who have a close relationship with their sons don't make them gay.

Further, homosexuality is not a disease, and a person can't "catch" it. Gay people are not destined to get AIDS, nor is being gay or lesbian a mental illness. Homosexuality can't be "cured" by way of therapy or prayer. A person can't change

Anti-gay sentiment puts gay and lesbian children at risk of harassment. (Skjold Photographs)

another person's sexual orientation, only their overt behavior, nor will finding the "right person" change sexual orientation. A gay or lesbian person can indeed choose parenthood. In short, a gay or lesbian person can have a happy life and be a productive member of society.

Because of social stigma, intolerance, and harassment, sexual minority youth are at risk in a number of ways. Rates of depression, suicide, and drug use or abuse are higher, especially in adolescence, where the desire to fit in is so strong. Sexual minority youth suffer more harassment and violence at school, and consequently are more likely to drop out. Some parents, due to religious beliefs or a lack of information about sexual minorities, have even responded by subjecting their children to abuse or kicking them out of the house. This may lead to homelessness, and life on the street may lead to prostitution, drug use, and AIDS or other sexually transmitted infections.

Parents should not overreact if they discover that their child is gay or lesbian. Even parents who don't completely accept the child's sexual orientation should keep an open mind and seek support. Parents, Family, and Friends of Lesbians and Gays (P-FLAG) is a support group that can be helpful. Parents should not rush to judgment and shouldn't listen to those who would demonize their child. Parents should keep the lines of communication open and make sure that home is a safe place for their child.

Even parents who may be comfortable with and accepting of their child's sexual orientation may worry about telling others. Parents need to make decisions with their child about whom to tell. A balance should be maintained between the negative effects of keeping a secret and the legitimate safety and social needs of the child. There is no set formula for deciding how, when, and to whom to disclose. This is a complicated issue, and requires more discussion than space here allows. Many of the resources listed below can be helpful for parents in this decision-making process.

School plays a major role in a child's life, so how the school handles this issue can make a big difference in the child's well-being. It's important, not just for the gay or lesbian child, but for any child who is perceived as different, that school be an accepting, tolerant, and safe place. Once again, this is a complicated issue, and space allows only brief mention of some strategies that might be helpful. The resources listed below provide further information about this topic. To begin with, it is not necessary to disclose a child's sexual orientation in order to make a difference at the school. Being involved in encouraging programs that value diversity and stop harassment and bullying can do a lot toward making school a safe place. In addition, parent support groups such as P-FLAG and educational organizations such as Gay, Lesbian, and Straight Education Network (GLSEN) can help with resources, advice, and support for starting specific programs at a school, such as a gay-straight alliance. Children who are harassed verbally or physically at school can't handle it alone. School counselors, social workers, or psychologists are the school personnel most likely to be of help for a child who is being harassed.

In addition to family and school, there are other situations in a child's life in which parents may need to intervene. All professionals are not equally knowledgeable about sexual minority youth, and may inadvertently make the gay or lesbian child feel misunderstood or not supported. These professionals may need to be educated. Once again, organizations such as P-FLAG can be a tremendous resource and source of referrals.

Parents who suspect that their child may be gay or lesbian and want to talk about it may wish to start with a general discussion of current events, or watch a movie or read a book with a sympathetic gay or lesbian character and discuss it with the child.

Catherine A. Fiorello
Julie Agresta

See also Gay Fathers; Lesbian Mothers, Children of

References and further reading
Bernstein, Robert A. 1995. *Straight Parents, Gay Children: Keeping Families Together.* New York: Thunder's Mouth Press.
Fairchild, Betty, and Nancy Hayward. 1998. *Now That You Know: A Parents' Guide to Understanding Their Gay and Lesbian Children.* New York: Harcourt Brace.
Parents, Family, and Friends of Lesbians and Gays (P-FLAG), 1101 14th St., NW, Suite 1030, Washington, DC 20005, (202) 638-4200; fax: (202) 638-0243; E-mail: pflagntl@aol.com.

Gay Fathers

Gay parenting is an underresearched yet much debated topic. Several common misconceptions about gay parenting prevail: for example, that few gay men are involved in parenting; that gay men are not fit parents; and that compared with children of heterosexual men, the sons and daughters of gay fathers might be more vulnerable to various psychological difficulties. Despite the methodological difficulties in this area, researchers have begun to appraise the role that gay parents play in their children's lives and systematically reexamine and refute these widespread misconceptions.

It is difficult to accurately estimate how many gay men are involved in parenting. Given the prejudice (homophobia) that is regularly encountered by lesbians and gay men, many are reluctant to disclose their sexual identity. Estimates of the number of lesbian and gay parents in the United States range from 6 to 14 million (American Civil Liberties Union, 1999), with large-scale surveys conducted within the lesbian and gay communities across the United States finding that about 10 percent of gay men reported having children. (Bryant and Demian, 1994) However, many other gay men may be involved in parenting in some capacity, for example, through parenting their partner's children.

The largest group of gay parents appears to be those who had children through a previous heterosexual relationship and have subsequently identified as gay. Most of these men then move out of the marital home, but some continue their relationship with the child's mother. An important issue for gay and bisexual men who have had children in the context of heterosexual relationships is whether to "come out" as gay or bisexual to their ex-partner and their children. Coming out may be easier both for the gay parent and other family members if it is carefully planned and the disclosure is not made in the context of a crisis. Disclosure may be more difficult if it coincides with other events such as divorce, the start of a new relationship, the results of a positive HIV test, or illness.

Divorced or separated gay fathers may find that their relationship with the children is heavily dependent on how the child's mother responds to their sexual orientation and the particular judicial jurisdiction in which they live. Courts vary in how they decide to award custody and access and what "the best interests of the child" are. Those that adhere to the "nexus test" will not allow the sexual orientation of a parent to be used as a basis for refusing custody or access, unless it is shown to cause harm to the child. Other jurisdictions invoke the "per se rule" and allow decisions to be made on the presumption that gay men are automatically unfit to continue with their parental responsibilities. Therefore, if the child's mother contests the case, the court may dismiss the gay father's previous parenting involvement and he is unlikely to win custody rights. It is also not unknown for courts to place conditional restrictions on the gay parent's access to his child that have no parallels in court orders issued to heterosexual fathers, for example, prohibiting the child from meeting their father's new partner. Access and visitation issues consequently may play a large part in shaping the type of postdivorce relationship fathers are able to form with their children. Little is known about the likely distress felt by both children and fathers if a previously close relationship is lost after parental separation.

A growing group of gay parents are men who have children after coming out as gay. This may be through adopting or fostering a child, through a surrogacy arrangement, or through a formal or informal agreement to share parenting with a single lesbian mother or a lesbian couple. Although many gay couples decide to bring up children together with an equal commitment to parenting, the law is sometimes such that only one partner can receive public recognition as the child's legal parent.

Can gay men be effective parents? Research at the closing of the twentieth century was limited to the reports of gay men who had children from previous heterosexual relationships who have volunteered to participate in studies. Most of these studies focus on the reported experiences of gay fathers and few collect data from children. Some of the studies lack comparisons with appropriate control groups, consequently it is difficult to disentangle specific influences of paternal sexual identity from the particular circumstances of parenting. Despite these methodological limitations, the available research evidence suggests that gay men's parenting is in many respects similar to the parenting of heterosexual fathers in equivalent situations. One study found that divorced gay and heterosexual nonresident fathers reported similar relationships with their children in terms of level of involvement and intimacy, except that gay fathers tended to report a more authoritative parenting style in terms of being less indulgent in their parenting, setting consistent standards for behavior, and giving explanations. Gay fathers in the study were also less likely than the heterosexual fathers surveyed to report showing physical affection to their partner in front of their son or daughter. Two studies that have interviewed the children of gay fathers found that the majority of sons and daughters reported close relationships with their gay parent.

Research has addressed key aspects affecting the satisfaction with family life for the members of gay stepfamilies. For the divorced gay father, his male partner, and the adolescent children, the factor most associated with family satisfaction was the degree to which the new gay partner had become integrated into family life. However, research has so far not detailed how integration can be achieved, and gay partners often lack legal and public recognition of their parenting role.

It is often thought that the children of gay fathers will encounter various problems in their psychological development. As yet no published research has systematically evaluated the mental health of the children of gay fathers. However, indications from existing qualitative accounts given by gay fathers and their children are that both sons and daughters generally enjoy good mental health. The authors of one qualitative study examining the reflections of children of gay fathers on their lives concluded that: "They are like all kids. Some do well in just about all activities; some have problems, and some are well adjusted." (Barret and Robinson, 1994, 168)

The gender development of the children of gay fathers also has been neglected as a topic for systematic research. However, various studies have considered other aspects of the psychosexual development of the children of gay fathers. Detailed research conducted with the sons of gay fathers concluded that the large majority of sons were heterosexual with only 9 percent identifying as gay or bisexual, a percentage that the authors suggest is compatible with a low rate of genetic inheritance. (Bailey, Bobrow, Wolfe, and Mikach, 1995) Other, smaller investigations including both the sons and the daughters of gay fathers have concluded that most children of gay fathers grow up to identify as heterosexual.

Another issue that is commonly raised in debates about gay parenting is that children may be stigmatized because of their gay parent. Gay parents themselves often voice this concern. One survey found that many gay fathers were worried that their child could be stigmatized at school because of having a gay father; however, only a fifth of fathers reported that any of their children had actually experienced any problems. (Wyers, 1987) It seems likely that gay fathers and their children are mostly successful in using a variety of strategies to deal with or avoid the possibility of homophobia.

One aspect that gay parents are likely to have in common is the shared challenge of parenting in the context of prejudice. One source of prejudice may arise from the common gender role stereotypes suggesting that men are less suited than women to care for children. Prejudice directed at gay men's parenting may also arise from the confusion of pedophilia and homosexuality—a fallacy unsupported by legal or research evidence. Gay fathers have to successfully deal with a double dose of marginalization. They may feel stigmatized because of their sexual identity in mainstream society, yet through their parental responsibilities feel different from other gay men and sometimes excluded within the gay community.

Openly gay parenting is a relatively recent phenomenon, although historical documentation exists to show many examples of fathers who had homosexual relationships. Gay parenting is often viewed with suspicion, but the available empirical evidence leads to the conclusion that gay men can be effective parents. This new area of research is less developed than research into lesbian parenting, and systematic investigations have only just begun to explore the variation in experiences of gay parents and their children.

Fiona Tasker

See also Gay and Lesbian Children; Lesbian Mothers, Children of

References and further reading
American Civil Liberties Union. 1999. "ACLU Fact Sheet: Overview of Lesbian and Gay Parenting, Adoption and Foster Care." <http://www.aclu.org/issues/gay/parent.html>.
Bailey, J. Michael, David Bobrow, Marilyn Wolfe, and Sarah Mikach. 1995. "Sexual Orientation of Adult Sons of Gay Fathers." *Developmental Psychology* 31:124–129.
Barret, Robert L., and Bryan E. Robinson. 1994. "Gay Dads." Pp. 157–170 in *Redefining Families: Implications for Children's Development.* Edited by Adele Eskeles Gottfried and Allen W. Gottfried. New York: Plenum Press.
Bigner, Jerry J., and R. Brooke Jacobsen. 1989. "Parenting Behaviors of Homosexual and Heterosexual Fathers." Pp. 173–186 in *Homosexuality and the Family.* Edited by Frederick W. Bozett. New York: Harrington Park Press.
Bozett, Frederick W. 1987. "Children of Gay Fathers." Pp. 39–57 in *Gay and Lesbian Parents.* Edited by Frederick W. Bozett. New York: Praeger.
Bryant, A. Steven, and Demian. 1994. "Relationship Characteristics of American Gay and Lesbian Couples: Findings from a National Survey." *Journal of Gay & Lesbian Social Services* 1:101–117.
Dunne, Edward J. 1987. "Helping Gay Fathers Come Out to Their Children." *Journal of Homosexuality* 13:213–222.
Miller, Brian. 1979. "Gay Fathers and Their Children." *Family Coordinator* 28:544–552.
Patterson, Charlotte J., and Raymond W. Chan. 1996. "Gay Fathers and Their

Children." Pp. 371–393 in *Textbook of Homosexuality and Mental Health*. Edited by Robert P. Cabaj and Terry S. Stein. Washington, DC: American Psychiatric Press.

Strasser, Mark. 1997. "Fit to Be Tied: On Custody, Discretion, and Sexual Orientation. *American University Law Review* 46:841–895.

Wyers, Norman L. 1987. "Homosexuality in the Family: Lesbian and Gay Spouses." *Social Work* 32:143–148.

Geisel, Theodor Seuss (1904–1991)

Theodor "Dr. Seuss" Geisel was an author and illustrator of children's books whose name is immediately recognized for his lifelong contribution to the literary education of children. A self-taught illustrator, Theodor Geisel earned a living for almost a decade as a cartoonist, until in 1937, using the pen name Dr. Seuss, he wrote and illustrated his first children's book, *And to Think That I Saw It on Mulberry Street*. That book, and the many that would follow in the years to come, would forever change the appearance and content of children's books.

Theodor Seuss Geisel was born in Springfield, Massachusetts, on 2 March 1904 to Theodor Robert Geisel and Henrietta Seuss. Theodor grew up in Springfield with his sister, Margaretha Christine Geisel, who was two years his senior. He entered Dartmouth College in 1921, planning to study German literature, and worked as a cartoonist and humor writer for the Dartmouth humor magazine, the *Jack-O-Lantern*. By his senior year at Dartmouth, Geisel was appointed editor in chief of the *Jack-O-Lantern* and graduated later that year on 23 June 1925 as a student of English literature. In October 1925, Geisel sailed to Oxford to attend Lincoln College. He intended to acquire a doctorate in English literature in the hopes of later becoming an English professor.

While at Oxford, Geisel met Helen Palmer and became engaged to her. After two years at Oxford, Geisel grew disenchanted with the teaching at Lincoln College and decided to abandon his plans for a doctorate degree. Geisel returned home to Springfield with his new fiancée and began submitting cartoons to various magazines including *Life* and *The New Yorker*. One of his first published cartoons appeared in the *Saturday Evening Post* and earned him the then impressive pay of $25. This first taste of success inspired Geisel and Palmer to move to Manhattan, New York, where Geisel planned to pursue a full-time career in writing and cartooning.

Geisel was offered a job as a writer and cartoonist at one of the leading humor magazines in America at the time, *Judge* magazine. The *Judge* paid Geisel a salary of $75 a week, which allowed Geisel to feel confident enough to marry Helen Palmer on 29 November 1927. Ted Geisel's debut cartoon in the *Judge* was published on 22 October 1927 and was signed by Geisel using only his middle name, "Seuss." A few weeks later, he added "Dr." to the "Seuss" in one of his cartoons and used the pseudonym of "Dr. Seuss" thereafter. The name "Dr. Seuss" was Geisel's way of poking fun at the Oxford doctorate he had never completed. While working for the *Judge*, Geisel continued to submit cartoons to other well-known magazines, such as *Life*, *Vanity Fair*, and *Liberty*, which earned him the then tidy sum of $300 per cartoon.

In many of his *Judge* cartoons, Geisel's characters made references to an insecticide called Flit. These references to Flit were so prevalent that a commonly used catchphrase of the time, "Quick Henry, the Flit," was taken from one of Geisel's cartoons. Such frequent referrals grabbed the attention of the makers of Flit insecticide and eventually led to a contract between Flit insecticide and Geisel that earned him $12,000 a year. Geisel's ads for Flit insecticide brought his talent to a

Theodor Geisel (1904–1991) (Collections of the Library of Congress)

wider audience and helped to gain him national recognition. The pairing of Geisel and Flit created one of the most successful marketing campaigns of that time and forged a relationship between them that lasted over seventeen years.

In 1936, on the way home from a European vacation, Geisel was struck by the sounds of the ship's engines. The unique cadence of the *Kungsholum*'s engines inspired him to write rhyming prose that ultimately became his first children's book, *And to Think That I Saw It on Mulberry Street.* Geisel's initial title for the book was "A Story That No One Can Beat." This first attempt at writing children's books was not an instant success; the first twenty-seven publishers to whom he showed it rejected Geisel's book. A year later, in 1937, while returning home after a disappointing meeting with a publisher, Geisel decided to abandon his dream of publishing a children's book and resolved to burn the book immediately upon arriving. As luck would have it, he ran into an old Dartmouth friend named Mike McClintock who read it and decided to help Geisel publish and distribute the book. *And to Think That I Saw It on Mulberry Street* was released September 1937 and went on to become moderately successful.

In the three years that followed the publishing of *And to Think That I Saw It on Mulberry Street,* Geisel continued to write and released four other books: *The 500 Hats of Bartholomew Cubbins* (1938); *The Seven Lady Godivas* (1939); *The King's Stilts* (1939); and *Horton Hatches the Egg* (1940). On 30 January

1941, *PM Magazine* published an anti-Hitler cartoon drawn by Geisel. This cartoon caught the attention of both the U.S. Treasury Department and the War Production Board. Soon after, Geisel was contacted by both agencies and was hired to draw posters and ads in support of war bonds and to rally the nation against Hitler and the Axis powers. In 1942, Geisel was offered an army commission to join Frank Capra's Signal Corps unit in Hollywood, California. Geisel's position within the army was made official on 7 January 1943, when he was given the rank of captain and was assigned to the army's Information and Education Division. The army made the most of Geisel's talents and sent to him Hollywood to work with Frank Capra to create war propaganda documentaries, biweekly newsreels, and animated war-related cartoons. Captain Geisel wrote for Frank Capra's Signal Corps unit (for which he won the Legion of Merit) and did two documentaries, *Hitler Lives* (1946) and *Design for Death* (1947), for which he later won Academy Awards. Geisel also won an Academy Award in 1951 for an animated cartoon he created called *Gerald McBoing-Boing.*

In 1947, Geisel returned to writing and illustrating children's books with the release of *McElligot's Pool.* Geisel continued to create children's books and released the following books at an average of one book per year: *Thidwick the Big Hearted Moose* (1948); *Bartholomew and the Oobleck* (1949); *If I Ran the Zoo* (1950); *Scrambled Eggs Super!* (1953); *Horton Hears a Who* (1954); *On beyond Zebra* (1955); and *If I Ran the Circus* (1955). In 1957, Geisel's fame was about to skyrocket after agreeing to write a book for William Spauling. Spauling had asked Geisel to create a children's book that contained 225 words Spauling felt were essential to the vocabulary of first-grade children. Geisel worked hard on the book

and the end result was *The Cat in the Hat.* After its official release in 1947, *The Cat in the Hat* became one of Geisel's most successful books and was later translated into dozens of different languages. Later that year, Geisel published the Christmas classic, *How the Grinch Stole Christmas,* and in 1958 he released two more books that would soon become classics, *Yertle the Turtle* and *The Cat in the Hat Comes Back.* During a 1960 meeting with his friend Bennett Cerf, Geisel was talked into taking an odd bet. Cerf bet Geisel that he could not write a book using only fifty words that he had selected. Geisel accepted the bet and wrote the immensely successful book, *Green Eggs and Ham.*

Geisel continued to write children's books and is often remembered for his lifetime contribution to the literacy of children. The popularity of Geisel's artwork and rhythmic prose work together to keep the young reader interested in the contents of a Dr. Seuss book. Geisel died on 24 September 1991 in his La Jolla, California, home.

José Antonio Maradiaga

References and further reading
Geisel, Theodor Seuss. 1995. *The Secret Art of Dr. Seuss.* New York: Random House.
Greene, Carol. 1993. *Dr. Seuss: Writer and Artist for Children.* Chicago: Children's Press.
Lystad, Mary. 1980. *From Dr. Mather to Dr. Seuss: 200 Years of American Books for Children.* Boston: G. K. Hall.
Martin, Patricia Stone. 1987. *Dr. Seuss, We Love You.* Vero Beach, FL: Rourke Enterprises.
Morgan, Judith, and Neil Morgan. 1995. *Dr. Seuss and Mr. Geisel.* New York: Da Capo Press.
Weidt, Maryann N., and Kerry Maguire. 1995. *Oh, the Places He Went: A Story about Dr. Seuss—Theodor Seuss Geisel.* Minneapolis, MN: Carolrhoda Books.

Gender Stereotyping

Gender stereotypes are broadly shared beliefs about the characteristics that are

Children themselves learn gender stereotypes very early, beginning by about two and one-half to three years of age. (Laura Dwight)

typically associated with being male or female within a particular culture. For example, the beliefs that most boys are active and like to play with guns and trucks, whereas most girls are quiet and like to play with dolls and dress in pink clothing are gender stereotypes. These beliefs can influence the ways parents and other adults perceive and treat children. In addition, children themselves learn gender stereotypes very early, beginning by about two and one-half to three years of age. Gender stereotyping reaches a peak around five to seven years of age, when children hold very rigid beliefs about what behaviors, clothes, toys, and occupations are acceptable for boys and girls or men and women. As children get older, they learn more about gender stereotypes, but also learn that these stereotypes are not necessarily always true or useful.

In adolescence, gender stereotyping again strengthens, as children strive to conform with their peers and to clarify their sex-role identity. Children learn gender stereotypes from many sources, including parents, peers, children's literature, and television. Although all children appear to go through periods of strong gender stereotyping, parents and the media can influence individual children's stereotyping.

A common first question asked of parents following the birth of an infant is, "Is it a boy or a girl?" The answer to this question influences the parents' and others' perceptions of and expectations for the baby. For example, parents in one study rated newborn girls as softer, finer featured, littler, and more inattentive than boys, and in another, more recent study rated newborn girls as finer featured, less strong, more delicate, and more feminine than newborn boys. Fathers in the older study differentiated between boys and girls more than the mothers did, but in the more recent study the mothers and fathers showed the same amount of stereotyping. Fathers of older children also are sometimes found to show more gender stereotyping than mothers.

Another recent study found that gender stereotyping affected mothers' perceptions of their infants even before the infants were born. Mothers who knew their baby's gender prenatally (as a result of prenatal testing) perceived the movements of boys as strong and of girls as gentle, even though other studies have found no actual differences in the prenatal activities of male and female fetuses.

After the baby is born, parents show gender stereotyping in their choices of clothing, room decor, and toys for the baby. Items for girls are typically pink and items for boys are typically blue. Girls are given more dolls and boys are given more sports toys. Parents also interact differently with girls and boys, but it is difficult to determine if the parents are acting on the basis of stereotypes or responding to actual differences between the sexes. This question has been addressed in a series of studies in which adults observe or interact with an unfamiliar baby who is dressed in gender-neutral clothing and described as a boy for some participants and as a girl for other participants. This procedure ensures that any differences in the adults' behavior are related to the adult's knowledge of the infant's gender rather than any differences in the baby's behavior. These studies, when taken as a whole, suggest that adults' toy choices, interpretations of ambiguous infant behavior, and beliefs about appropriate infant activities are affected by gender stereotypes. For example, labeled girls

were more likely to be given a doll to play with, and a crying infant was more likely to be described as "angry" when labeled a boy and "fearful" when labeled a girl.

Parents of older children and teachers also have gender stereotyped perceptions and expectations for children. Both believe that boys are more aggressive and better at math and science and that girls are more nurturing and better at verbal skills. For example, adults are more likely to notice and react to physical aggression in girls, presumably because adults do not expect girls to be aggressive. Similarly, aggression in boys may often be overlooked, because it is expected—"Boys will be boys!" Male teachers and teachers with less experience are more likely to be influenced by gender stereotyping, and adults with less formal education in general hold stronger gender stereotypes. Adults can convey their stereotypes to children in very subtle ways. For example, when the gender of a character in a storybook is unclear, parents label the character a male 90 percent of the time. (De Loache, Cassidy, and Carpenter, 1987, cited by Golombok and Fivush, 1994)

Most children begin to consistently label themselves and others as male and female by about two years of age. Clear evidence of gender stereotypes can be observed by about two and a half years. These young children are quite confident about such beliefs as: only girls wear pink; men and boys don't wear dresses; boys don't play with dolls; only women are nurses; only men are truck drivers; hammers are for men and boys; sewing is for women and girls, and so on. Children rapidly acquire more of these beliefs during the preschool years, and generally enter school with very strong and rigid ideas about gender-appropriate traits, activities, occupations, appearance, and possessions. During the preschool and early elementary school years, children may insist on the truth of gender stereotypes even in the face of obvious exceptions. For example, a child whose mother is a doctor may insist that only men can be doctors. During this time children may even have difficulty remembering events that don't fit their stereotypes: children show better memory for pictures of adults engaged in gender-stereotypic activities than for pictures of adults engaging in activities that children consider more appropriate for the other gender. Children may even remember an event incorrectly, reporting that they saw a female nurse and male doctor at the health clinic, when in fact the opposite occurred.

Most children learn the basic components of the gender stereotypes that exist in their culture by about seven years, although more complex learning about gender-typical personality characteristics, sports, school tasks, and occupations continues into adolescence. Most children also learn about the stereotype for their own gender earlier than they learn about the stereotype for the other gender. Girls often know more about male stereotypes than boys know about female stereotypes. Children of both genders typically consider their own gender to be better and to have more positive characteristics (i.e., "boys are loud and messy," from a girl, and "girls are silly and dumb," from a boy). However, when girls discover after about age ten that females are often devalued in our culture, their stereotypes of males may become more positive than their stereotypes of females.

After about age seven, children become more tolerant of gender-role violations and become better able to make decisions about people based on characteristics other than gender. Girls on average become more flexible in their applications of gender stereotypes earlier than boys do. However, the male stereotype continues to be applied more rigidly than the female stereotype. Thus, a boy who shows "feminine" behavior will suffer more peer rejection, especially from other boys, than will a girl who shows "masculine" behavior. In fact, "tomboyish" behavior in girls is often evaluated positively. By the time children reach adolescence, gender stereotyping again increases, as pressure to conform to peer standards and the need to establish a more elaborate gender-role identity become important.

Children learn gender stereotypes from their parents, other adults, peers, and the media. Parents with stronger gender stereotypes typically have children with stronger gender stereotypes. Children raised in more traditional homes also learn gender stereotypes more quickly. Children whose mothers are employed, especially girls, show less stereotyped beliefs. Children probably learn some of the content of their gender stereotypes by simply observing the behaviors of the people around them and figuring out which activities, occupations, characteristics, and so on, are associated with people of each gender. Parents and others may reward children for gender stereotyping, although in general parents seem to treat their male and female children fairly similarly. One notable exception to this finding is that fathers often discourage boys from engaging in opposite-gender behavior.

Books and television provide children with a great deal of information about gender-typical behavior. Male characters outnumber female characters in both children's literature and television programs, and male characters are much more likely to play the lead and to be active and adventurous. Female characters are more likely to be victims. Although the degree of gender (and other) stereotyping in children's literature has been declining during the past two decades, much of it remains, and children continue to read (or have read to them) classic stories such as fairy tales that are highly gender stereotyped.

Both contemporary and classic television programs, as well as television commercials, also portray a high level of gender stereotyping. Children who watch more television have been found to hold stronger gender stereotypes, and when communities acquire television access, the degree of gender stereotyping in their populations increases.

Children's gender stereotyping is only one aspect of their gender-role development. For example, a child can have a great deal of knowledge about gender stereotypes and yet perceive him- or herself to behave in ways that are not strongly related to those stereotypes. Preferences for playing with children of the same gender also are unrelated to the strength of a child's gender stereotyping. During the time when children's gender stereotyping is particularly strong and inflexible, these stereotypes do seem to guide some of their behavior. For example, children show much greater interest in playing with toys that are packaged in boxes with pictures of same-gendered children than with toys that are in boxes with pictures of opposite-gendered children. Knowledge of gender stereotypes probably is most important in guiding children's expectations for, and interpretations of, other people's behavior. For example, when a new child moves into the neighborhood, the gender of that child helps determine other children's assumptions about what types of toys, games, and activities the new child will enjoy.

Parents vary in the extent to which they want their children to learn about gender stereotypes and acquire gender-typed behavior patterns. Those who try to raise their children without these stereotypes are often amazed by the degree to which young children learn and are influenced by these stereotypes, despite parents' best efforts to prevent exposure to or discount stereotyping. Although parents are a potent influence on their young children's development, children are also influenced by other adults, peers, and the media, and children seem to be highly motivated to learn gender rules. Parents can be assured that the extreme gender stereotyping seen in preschool and early elementary-aged children typically does not last. Nonetheless, exposing children to counterstereotypic information can reduce the degree of stereotyping shown by children. Parents can also assist children in understanding the importance of gender equity, the idea that individuals of both genders should be treated fairly. Parents of older children and adolescents can help to ensure that their children do not constrain their own or others' opportunities through excessive adherence to gender stereotypes. Girls can be encouraged to take math classes and participate in sports; boys can be encouraged to take art classes and learn about child development. Despite children's tendency to divide the world according to gender, all children can be encouraged to develop to their full potential.

Katherine Hildebrandt Karraker

References and further reading
Beal, Carole R. 1994. *Boys and Girls: The Development of Gender Roles.* New York: McGraw-Hill.
Golombok, Susan, and Robyn Fivush. 1994. *Gender Development.* Cambridge, UK: University of Cambridge Press.

Generativity

Generativity is the term Erik Erikson coined for the care of progeny, products, and ideas, the central concerns of middle adulthood. Based on the accumulated strengths derived from the challenges and resolutions of earlier life stages, the individual is ready at last to generate and care for offspring and ideas and to play a decisive role in the ongoing cycle of generations. Generativity, with its negative pole of stagnation, is the psychosocial strength that occurs as a result of the central stage of adulthood, Erikson's seventh stage. This stage occurs between his intimacy stage of young adulthood and his final integrity stage of older adulthood. In this period, adults are invested in parenting and teaching children, in sustaining the work of their lives, in ethical role modeling, and in their concerns for preserving the species. Erikson chose the word *generativity* because it focuses attention on fostering, supporting, and guiding the generation that will succeed the adult. Lest readers understand his stage theory as an achievement model, he drew attention to the fact that every positive resolution contains elements of the negative. In the case of generativity, some stagnation and rejection take up residence in even the most generative of adults.

According to Erikson, the generative person is ready to care for offspring and ideas and to play a decisive role in the ongoing interlocking and unfolding of generational cohorts. As a result of having worked through a diverse set of challenges and stage-specific tensions, the adult now operates within a wide set of roles and social responsibilities. In full psychosocial maturity, the focus of psychological energy is now directed toward the care of children and products in service to the current world and to the world that will survive one. One learns, through the requirements of the generativity stage, what one can do to care for others. This includes guiding children, mentoring younger adults, and producing and sustaining creative works and useful ideas.

In this stage, the adult's energy shifts from the genitality of young adulthood to productive generativity, grounded in intimacy, but with more expansive interests. "Care," Erikson wrote, "is the widening concern for what has been generated by love, necessity, or accident; it overcomes the ambivalence adhering to irreversible obligation." (Erikson, 1964, 131) Erikson meant that the care for others is now an extended care. His principal interest was to show that parenthood is of generativity's essence, that of bringing along the next generation.

Among the contributions Erikson made to our understandings about the broad span of adulthood called middle life, two stand out. First, he showed that through active involvement, the person moves toward greater ethical functioning and eventual completion as an integrated human. The adult has put his or her own desires and needs aside to invest in the care of others. Second, Erikson showed that generative adults are integral to the cycle of generations. As linchpins, they maintain generational continuity and, through their investments, provide the first gifts of trust, hope, and other vital strengths to children.

In Erikson's generativity concept, adults' lives and those of their children are interdependent, for "the generational cycle links life cycles together by confronting the older generation's generativity with the younger one's readiness to grow." (Erikson and Erikson, 1981, 269) Accumulated strengths cultivate strength in the next generation and provide a reciprocal arena for the development of the strengths of caring among those who so invest themselves.

Generativity is the core of Erikson's ground plan of adulthood. It represents the mature obligations of "householding" or "maintenance of the world," the altruistic gift of self. (Erikson, 1976, 16) The mature adult gives freely to the young without the promise of anything in return. However, such care is itself the self-verification of such labor. Generativity is an extended form of identity, an identity now derived through adults' interests in "what and whom they have come to care for, what they care to do well, and how they plan to take care of what they have started and created." (Erikson, 1969, 395) Thus, identity is now derived through the adult's definitions of, and concerns for, those dependent upon him or her and the key products of one personal life.

It is in the generative stage that one finds Erikson's most complete expression of Freud's purported, but unverified, claim that adulthood means "lieben und arbeiten," to love and to work. Erikson held that attending to the young requires solicitude, teaching, and transmitting facts, logic, and the principles of one's version of humanity. This extended love keeps traditions alive, thus extending one's own identity. As a result, although generativity is outer- and other-directed, it aids the synthesis of earlier accumulated strengths, gives meaning to the adult life, and ensures the continuity of the species.

The basis for the ability to function as a generative adult occurs as a result of all earlier strengths. Special contributions arise from the care one has received early in life and from the love and care accepted and reciprocated in the prior intimacy stage. Erikson wrote that "love in the evolutionary and generational sense is . . . the transformation of the love received throughout the pre-adolescent stage of life into the care given to others during adult life." (Erikson, 1964, 127–128)

Erikson was concerned about those who chose not to have children, believing that such repression of instinctual drives could lead to difficulties for the person, for the culture, and for the species. And, he called those without children to care for the next generation in other ways. They were expected to guide, sponsor, and feel responsible for all children among us.

Among those who are nongenerative, Erikson held that some had experienced "faulty identifications with parents," were narcissistic, or lacked "some belief in the species . . . which would make a child appear to be a welcome trust." (Erikson, 1968, 138) Frequently Erikson found that such persons were self-indulgent. They had regressed to "stagnation, boredom, and interpersonal impoverishment." (Erikson, 1968, 138) Psychological or physical invalidism often resulted due to egocentrism and an overemphasis on self-care. Failing to develop the capacity to care, such adults tended to reject others. Eventually they turned on themselves to become self-rejecting.

Erikson's concept of generativity carries ethical requirements. His work defines what one must do to ensure an adulthood of meaning, service, and continuity. This requires sublimated work, investment in the development of others, and a love for others that eventually permits the adult to transcend one life. Through caring for others, through finding joy in the growth of the young, such adults find deep meaning in life, knowing all the while that it must end.

Carol H. Hoare

See also Erikson, Erik

References and further reading
Erikson, Erik H. 1964. *Insight and Responsibility.* New York: Norton.
———. 1968. *Identity: Youth and Crisis.* New York: Norton.
———. 1969. *Gandhi's Truth.* New York: Norton.
———. 1976. "Reflections on Dr. Borg's Life Cycle." *Daedalus* 2:1–28.
Erikson, Erik, and Joan M. Erikson. 1981. "On Generativity and Identity." *Harvard Educational Review* 51, no. 2:249–269.

Genetic Counseling

Genetic counseling focuses on helping people deal with issues relating to inherited disorders. Inherited disorders are the result of inheriting genes causing a particular disorder from one or both parents. By undergoing genetic counseling, prospective parents can be warned of the chances of passing these potentially harmful genes to their children. However, genes being passed to a child can also be damaged by environmental factors or by chance events

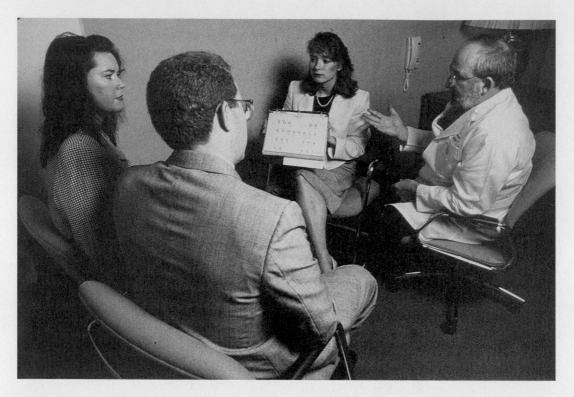

Due to advances in behavioral genetics, genetic difficulties increasingly can be forecast, anticipated, and planned for before a child's birth. (Will and Deni McIntyre)

during cell division, and this can also lead to serious developmental problems.

Due to advances in behavioral genetics, genetic difficulties increasingly can be forecast, anticipated, and planned for before a child's birth. In fact, as scientists' knowledge regarding the specific location of particular genes expands, predictions of what the genetic future may hold are becoming increasingly exact.

Genetic counselors use a variety of data in their work to make people aware of the possible risks involved in a future pregnancy. Typically, a counselor takes a thorough family history, seeking any familial incidence of birth defects that might indicate a pattern of recessive genes or defects linked to the X chromosome. The counselor also takes into account factors such as the age of the mother and father and any previous abnormalities in other children they may have already.

Genetic counselors generally suggest a thorough physical examination. Such an exam may identify physical abnormalities that potential parents may have, but of which they are not aware. In addition, samples of blood, skin, and urine may be used to isolate and examine specific chromosomes. (The table on page 273 shows specific tests now available.) Assembling a karyotype, a chart containing enlarged photos of each of the chromosomes, can identify possible genetic defects, such as the presence of an extra sex chromosome.

If a woman is already pregnant, testing of the unborn child itself is possible. A variety of testing methods is available. In amniocentesis, a small sample of fetal cells is drawn by a tiny needle inserted into the amniotic fluid surrounding the unborn fetus. By analyzing the fetal cells, technicians can identify a variety of genetic defects. Although there is always

Diseases with Genetic Tests Available

Disease	Description	Incidence
Adult polycystic kidney disease	Multiple kidney growths	1 in 1,000
Alpha-l-antitrypsin deficiency	Can cause hepatitis, cirrhosis of the liver, emphysema	1 in 2,000 to 1 in 4,000
Familial adenomatous polyposis	Colon polyps by age 35, often leading to cancer	1 in 5,000
Cystic fibrosis	Lungs clog with mucus; usually fatal by age 40	1 in 2,500 Caucasians
Duchenne/Becker muscular dystrophy	Progressive degeneration of muscles	1 in 3,000 males
Hemophilia	Blood fails to clot properly	1 in 10,000
Fragile X syndrome	Most common cause of inherited mental retardation	1 in 1,250 males; 1 in 2,500 females
Gaucher's disease	Mild to deadly enzyme deficiency	1 in 400 Ashkenazic Jews
Huntington's disease	Lethal neurological deterioration	1 in 10,000 Caucasians
"Lou Gehrig's disease" (ALS)	Fatal degeneration of the nervous system	1 in 50,000, 10% familial
Myotonic dystrophy	Progressive degeneration of muscles	1 in 8,000
Multiple endocrine neoplasia	Endocrine gland tumors	1 in 50,000
Neurofibromatosis	Light brown spots to large tumors	1 in 3,000
Retinoblastoma	Blindness; potentially fatal eye tumors	1 in 20,000
Spinal muscular atrophy	Progressive degeneration of muscles	7 in 100,000
Tay-Sachs disease	Lethal childhood neurological disorder	1 in 3,600 Ashkenazic Jews
Thalassemia	Mild to fatal anemia	1 in 100,000

a danger to the fetus in such an invasive procedure (e.g., risk of infection), amniocentesis is generally safe when carried out between the twelfth and sixteenth weeks of pregnancy.

An additional test, chorionic villus sampling (CVS), can be employed even earlier. The test involves taking small samples of hairlike material that surrounds the embryo. CVS can be done between the eighth and eleventh week of pregnancy. However, because it is riskier than amniocentesis and can identify fewer genetic problems, its use is relatively infrequent.

Other tests that are less invasive and therefore less risky are also possible. For instance, the unborn child may be examined through ultrasound sonography, in which high-frequency sound waves are used to bombard the mother's womb. These waves produce a rather indistinct, but useful, image of the unborn baby, whose size and shape can then be assessed. By using ultrasound sonography repeatedly, developmental patterns can be determined and physical defects can be revealed.

After the various tests are complete and all possible information is available, the parents meet with the genetic counselor again. Typically, counselors avoid giving specific recommendations. Instead, they lay out the facts and present various options, ranging from doing nothing to taking more drastic steps, such as terminating the pregnancy through abortion. Ultimately, it is the parents who must decide what course of action to follow.

The newest role of genetic counselors involves testing to identify whether an individual is susceptible to disorders that emerge later in life because of genetic abnormalities. For instance, Huntington's disease, a devastating, always fatal disorder marked by tremors and intellectual deterioration, typically does not appear until people reach their early forties. However, genetic testing can identify much earlier, even prenatally, whether a person carries the flawed gene that produces Huntington's disease. Presumably, people's knowledge that they carry the gene can help them prepare themselves for the future.

There is an ever-increasing number of other disorders that can be predicted on the basis of genetic testing (see the table that accompanies this article). Although such testing may bring welcome relief from future worries, positive results may produce just the opposite effect. In fact, genetic testing raises difficult practical and ethical questions. Furthermore, genetic testing is a complicated issue. It rarely provides a simple "yes" or "no" answer. Typically, it presents a range of probabilities, which many people find difficult to comprehend. In addition, people are increasingly demanding the latest genetic test, even if evidence is scanty that they are at appreciable medical risk of having a particular disease.

Christopher R. Poirier
Robert S. Feldman

See also Genetic Disorders

References and further reading
Baker, Diane Lynn, Jane L. Schuette, and Wendy R. Uhlmann, eds. 1998. *A Guide to Genetic Counseling.* New York: Wiley-Liss.

Genetic Disorders
More than 200 genes have been identified as the cause of hereditary diseases. Many of these disorders are associated with either a defective gene that has been passed down from parent to child or conditions caused by a combination of multiple effects. Abnormal and/or missing proteins or enzymes may cause a defect on one or more genes. A genetic disorder or disease is the result of such a defect.

Abnormal and/or missing proteins or enzymes may cause a defect on one or more genes. A genetic disorder or disease is the result of such a defect. (Laura Dwight)

teins or enzymes may cause a defect on one or more genes. A genetic disorder or disease is the result of such a defect.

Chromosomes are the packages of hereditary information that are passed down from one generation to the next. There are forty-six chromosomes in each cell in our bodies. These chromosomes come in twenty-three pairs, with one member of each pair donated by each parent via the sperm or egg cell. One of the twenty-three pairs of chromosomes differs in males and females. These are the sex chromosomes. Males have an "X" and a "Y" chromosome, while females have two "X" chromosomes. Chromosomes, in turn, are made of genes, the individual units of hereditary material. Genes come in pairs, with one member of each pair also coming from either parent. Genes provide the cells with a set of instructions that interact with the child's experiences to cause growth and development.

Genetic conditions are typically categorized into three major groups: single gene disorders, chromosomal aberrations, and multifactorial conditions. Single gene disorders include autosomal dominant, autosomal recessive, and X-linked conditions. Autosomal dominant conditions are expressed in the presence of one abnormal gene, despite the presence of one normal gene. Autosomal recessive conditions are caused by a mutation that inactivates a gene. Because humans have two copies of each gene, losing one copy does not matter. The autosomal recessive problem arises when someone receives two copies of the mutant gene. X-linked conditions involve genes located along the X chromosome. An X-linked recessive condition will be expressed in a male because he has no normal partner gene, while a female will usually be a carrier, i.e., unaffected but able to pass on the mutant gene to a child.

Chromosomal abnormalities are not typically inherited. They occur when there are either too few or too many chromosomes with a piece missing or an extra piece attached. Multifactorial conditions result from the interaction of genetic predispositions and environmental factors.

Children with genetic disorders often require considerable specialized care throughout their lives. These children and their families face many obstacles in their day-to-day activities. Parents and prospective parents may be unaware that they carry a defective gene and that their child may be born with a genetic disorder. Parents may feel guilt for transmitting these diseases or disorders to their children. When faced with the reality of their child's condition, parents and family members may experience a sense of loss, resentment, and denial. Such feelings and reactions are not uncommon. Parents and family members need to be thoroughly informed about a child's specific needs, development, and the nature of the genetic disorder. The following is a brief description of a few common genetic disorders and diseases affecting children.

Cystic Fibrosis
Cystic fibrosis (CF) is both a lifelong and life-threatening genetic disease caused by an abnormality on Chromosome 7. This abnormality is passed down from parent to child and, although a person may carry the trait, they may not have CF (autosomal recessive). When two trait carriers (parents) have a child, there is a one in four chance that their child will have CF. Overall incidence of CF is approximately 1 in 2,000 births. (Stark, Jelalian, and Miller, 1995; Batsche and Tunnicliffe, 1998)

CF affects the way the body absorbs and secretes salts and water. The lungs and digestive system produce too much mucus as part of an effort to counteract this malabsorption and secretion. Persons with CF have chronic respiratory and breathing problems, most noticeably chronic coughing and shortness of breath, in addition to nutritional deficiencies, liver and pancreatic problems, and recurrent infections. This disease is taxing on the child and the family; constant medical therapies, special diets, physical exhaustion, and stress are part of the everyday life of these individuals. Generally, individuals with CF are not compromised cognitively.

Historically, CF was considered a childhood disease, as only within the last decade has the life expectancy of persons with CF been extended beyond adolescence. Medical and technological advancements have raised the life expectancy of many persons with CF to approximately age thirty.

Down's Syndrome

Down's syndrome is the most common form of mental retardation. This disorder appears in all races and nationalities and can be detected through amniocentesis of the mother's intrauterine fluid. Although the overall incidence of Down's syndrome is approximately 1 in 900 births, as maternal age increases, so too does the likelihood of having a child with this syndrome. Mothers over the age of forty-five have a one in twenty chance of giving birth to a child with Down's syndrome. (Trimble and Baird, 1978) Nearly all cases are due to an extra copy of Chromosome 21. Normally, a human cell has forty-six chromosomes (two of each), but in these cases each cell has forty-seven chromosomes, due to an extra copy of Chromosome 21. This chromosomal abnormality causes changes in the way the brain and the body develop. Down's syndrome is associated with mental retardation, health-related problems, and a distinct physical appearance. Most persons with this disorder are well developed socially, but have poorly developed communication skills. Health-related problems often include heart defects, increased susceptibility to respiratory infections such as pneumonia, increased risk of leukemia, vision concerns, digestive tract problems, skin conditions, and oral/dental difficulties.

Distinctive physical features make the person with this syndrome more easily identified. Those affected often have eyes with a characteristic upward slant and an extra eyelid fold, a short and stocky build, straight fine hair, broad hands with short fingers, a disproportionately large tongue, and decreased muscle tone.

Most individuals with Down's syndrome require some supportive care and guidance throughout their lives; social support and assistance needs to provide the least restrictive environment possible and focus on the role of these persons as productive members of society.

Fragile X Syndrome

Fragile X syndrome is one of the leading inherited causes of mental retardation, affecting approximately 1 in 750 males and 1 in 1,250 females. (Batshaw, 1997) The condition results from the presence of an abnormal or defective gene (the fMR-1 gene) on the child's X chromosome. This abnormal gene leads to a weakness of the structures of the X chromosomes, which can be seen as a "break" or fragile site under the microscope. Because the defective gene is on the X chromosome, the condition predominately affects males. Because females have two X chromosomes, one from each parent, their normal chromosome can compensate for the effects of the abnormal one. Girls are therefore usually unaffected or mildly affected by the fragile X gene (X-linked). In contrast, males who have one X and one Y chromosome, have no backup for the affected X chromosome, and are therefore more susceptible to the effects of the abnormal gene.

The majority of affected males have some degree of mental impairment, ranging from mild learning disabilities to severe mental retardation. Most tend to cluster in the mild to moderate range of mental retardation. About one-third of females affected by the abnormal gene have learning disabilities or mild mental retardation. Other commonly seen problems include sensory impairments, hyperactivity, attention problems, self-stimulating behaviors, and difficulties with social interaction. Delayed speech and language development also occur frequently and are often the first indication of a problem that leads to a diagnosis.

Children with fragile X syndrome can have a number of distinctive physical characteristics. These include a large head, prominent forehead, large testicles, tall face, large ears, and prominent chin. Physical problems may include double-jointedness, low muscle tone, flat feet, and occasionally heart murmur. Ear infections (otitis media) are also common.

Klinefelter Syndrome

Klinefelter syndrome only occurs in males (1 in 500). (Cody and Hynd, 1999) These individuals have an extra X chromosome (XXY). The syndrome is frequently not recognized before puberty. After puberty the chief characteristic is small testicles. Usually the secondary sexual characteristics (e.g., body hair and deepening of voice) are poorly developed and males may develop feminine breasts. Many individuals are very tall with disproportionately long legs. Learning disabilities are common, particularly language-based disabilities and difficulties in reading and writing.

Males with XXY chromosomes have few behavioral problems during childhood and tend to be passive. However, a higher incidence of psychotic behavior (unpredictable behavior that includes both unusual thoughts and actions, such as hearing voices), neuroses, and deviation of personality have been reported in adult males with XXY. Many males with this disorder are not identified until they seek treatment for infertility. These individuals may benefit from counseling (couple and individual), and innovative treatments provide hope that these men can become parents themselves.

Sickle Cell Disease

This disorder occurs most frequently in individuals of African heritage, but also occurs in Italians, Sicilians, Turks, and East Indians. Eight percent of African Americans are carriers of the sickle cell trait. (Smith, 1999) This disorder's name derives from the shape of the red blood cells, which resemble a sickle or a crescent moon. People with sickle cell disease (SCD) are at high risk for stroke and bleeding in the brain, especially during childhood. Neurological injury following such brain trauma may have long-term cognitive and behavioral consequences. Recurrent pain is commonplace in SCD and often requires lengthy hospitalization. SCD places children at great risk for academic difficulties. The life expectancy of individuals with SCD varies greatly, from premature death during infancy to normal age expectations.

Spina Bifida

This disorder occurs in approximately 1 in 1,000 births, with girls being more susceptible. (Shine, 1998) The spine of children with spina bifida fails to fuse during the first trimester of pregnancy. Spina bifida may be detected prenatally through the use of a sonogram and/or ultrasound. The defect may occur in any part of the spine, but most frequently the involvement is in the lower region. As a result, there may be complete or partial paralysis of the lower extremities, loss of sensation, and loss of bowel and bladder control. Approximately 80 to 90 percent of the children born with spina bifida develop hydrocephalus (a buildup of fluid in and around the brain). (Fletcher, Dennis, and Northrup, 2000) Cognitive skills vary in persons with spina bifida; however, most individuals have normal intelligence and abilities. The lack of understanding of this disorder both by individuals with this disorder and by persons close to them presents the greatest challenge in their day-to-day routine.

A promising new treatment for spina bifida is corrective surgery on the developing fetus to cover the still-developing spinal nerves and spinal cord before damage occurs. This surgery is generally performed during the third trimester of pregnancy. Intrauterine closure of the exposed spinal cord has been found to significantly decrease the debilitating effects of spina bifida. Although there are risks associated with fetal surgery (including premature delivery and loss of fetus), this procedure holds much promise.

Turner's Syndrome

This rare genetic syndrome is the result of a child being born with only a single sex chromosome, an X chromosome (XO). Occurring in 1 out of 2,500 female births, this disorder results in the underdevelopment of ovaries and poor bone growth. (Powell and Schulte, 1999) As a result, this chromosomal disorder causes short stature with normal body proportions and inadequate sexual maturation. Treatment with growth hormones extends the life expectancy of girls and women with this disorder. In addition to the use of growth hormones, estrogen replacement therapy is a common medical intervention. Females who receive estrogen therapy may develop normal menses during the course of hormone therapy.

Girls with Turner's syndrome are frequently identified as having learning disabilities and social-emotional difficulties. It is important that these girls receive intervention and support from an early age that will enable them to experience long and productive lives.

Gregory L. Wallace
Cheryl A. Nolte

See also Genetic Counseling

References and further reading
Adzick, N. Scott. 1998. "Successful Fetal Surgery for Spina Bifida." *Lancet* 352:1675–1676.
Batsche, George, and Hope Tunnicliffe. 1998. "Cystic Fibrosis." In *Health-Related Disorders in Children and Adolescents.* Edited by LeAdelle Phelps. Washington, DC: American Psychological Association.
Batshaw, Mark L., ed. 1997. *Children with Disabilities.* 4th ed. Baltimore, MD: Paul H. Brookes.
Bruner, Joseph P., et al. 1999. "Fetal Surgery for Myelomeningocele and the Incidence of Shunt-Dependent Hydrocephalus." *Journal of the American Medical Association* 282: 1819–1825.
Cody, Heather, and George Hynd. 1999. "Klinefelter Syndrome." In *Handbook of Neurodevelopmental and Genetic Disorders in Children.* Edited by Sam Goldstein and Cecil R. Reynolds. New York: Guilford Press.
Fletcher, Jack, Maureen Dennis, and Hope Northrup. 2000. "Hydrocephalus." In *Pediatric Neuropsychology.* Edited by Keith Yeates, M. Douglas Reiss, and H. Gerry Taylor. New York: Guilford Press.
Powell, M. Paige, and Timothy Schulte. 1999. "Turner Syndrome." In *Handbook of Neurodevelopmental and Genetic Disorders in Children.* Edited by Sam Goldstein and Cecil R. Reynolds. New York: Guilford Press.
Shine, Agnes E. 1998. "Spina Bifida." In *Health-Related Disorders in Children and Adolescents.* Edited by LeAdelle Phelps. Washington, DC: American Psychological Association.
Smith, Julien T. 1999. "Sickle Cell Disease." In *Handbook of Neurodevelopmental and Genetic Disorders in Children.* Edited by Sam Goldstein and Cecil R. Reynolds. New York: Guilford Press.
Stark, Lori, Elissa Jelalian, and Deborah Miller. 1995. "Cystic Fibrosis." In *Handbook of Pediatric Psychology.* Edited by Michael C. Roberts. New York: Guilford Press.
Trimble, B. I., and P. A. Baird. 1978. "Maternal Age and Down Syndrome: Age-Specific Incidence Rates by Single-Year Intervals." *American Journal of Medical Genetics* 2:1–5.
For additional information on genetic disorders, see Genetic Alliance (www.geneticalliance.org) and March of Dimes (www.modimes.org).

Gesell, Arnold L. (1880–1961)

Arnold L. Gesell was a pioneer of child development research. Trained as both a psychologist and pediatrician, he helped to establish developmental norms for infants and children, particularly in the areas of physical and motor development. Many of those norms remain in use today. He created one of the earliest measures of infant intelligence and later extended his research to include adolescent development. His work was innovative, including the use of film records, an unusual methodology for the time. He wrote many scholarly articles, but also published a

Arnold L. Gesell (Gesell Institute)

series of books that were aimed at parents and made him the best-known child-care consultant in the country. His approach was "child-centered" and emphasized the role of maturation in development. He was active for more than four decades and his writings influenced innumerable psychologists, educators, pediatricians, and policymakers. His influence continues today, although it is not always recognized. He paved the way for many of the child-care experts who followed, including Benjamin Spock.

Gesell was born in Alma, Wisconsin, on 21 June 1880, the oldest of five children in a close-knit family. He attended Stevens Point Normal School in north-central Wisconsin and after graduation taught high school for two years. He continued his education at the University of Wisconsin, and later at Clark University in Worcester, Massachusetts. There he came into contact with G. Stanley Hall, one of the pioneers of developmental psychology. Hall was both president of Clark University and a professor of psychology.

Hall's attempts to establish a scientific foundation for human development, although flawed, gave birth to a new branch of psychology. A central part of Hall's approach was his belief in evolution as a unifying explanation in human development. This was an emphasis that Gesell accepted, though in a modified form. Gesell became one of Hall's most important students and always spoke of Hall with reverence, calling him a genius.

Gesell graduated from Clark University in 1906 with a Ph.D. degree in psychology. His doctoral dissertation was on jealousy in animals and humans. After a succession of brief jobs, he accepted an offer to teach psychology at the Los Angeles State Normal School in 1908. The offer had come from Lewis Terman, who had been a fellow student at Clark and would later become renowned for his work in intelligence testing. While in Los Angeles, Gesell met and married a fellow teacher, Beatrice Chandler. They soon collaborated on a book, *The Normal Child and Primary Education* (1912). Eventually, they had two children—a daughter, Katherine, who later assisted her father in compiling a pictorial volume, *How a Child Grows* (1945), and a son, Gerhard, who became a successful attorney in Washington, D.C., and played an important role in the Watergate hearings in the 1970s.

Although he was successful as a teacher, Gesell became increasingly interested in pursuing clinical work with children. In the summer of 1909, he visited two of the most important clinical sites of the time—Lightner Witmer's clinic at the University of Pennsylvania and Henry Goddard's laboratory at the Vineland School in New Jersey. In 1911, Gesell entered Yale Medical School to study for a medical degree, in part so that he could understand better the biological basis of behavior. While in medical school, he received an appointment from Yale and established a psychological clinic there. A few years later, while continuing his work at the clinic, he also became a school psychologist for the state of Connecticut, the first school psychologist in the nation to use that title officially. On receiving his M.D. degree in 1915, he became a professor of mental hygiene at Yale and the director of the Clinic of Child Development.

Gesell is best known for his emphasis on maturation in development. Although he maintained that heredity and environment each contributed to development, his work stressed the natural unfolding of the body's blueprint according to an inner timetable. Clearly, he was influenced by the work of Charles Darwin, but he also was influenced by the research of G. E. Coghill, an embryologist. Coghill demonstrated that behavior was closely linked to neural development, a position that was at the heart of the maturationist argument.

Gesell and his associates conducted extensive observations of infants and children, and kept highly detailed accounts of the results. Many of these observations were recorded on film. They maintained that although development proceeds at different rates, the sequence is always the same. Rates of development, they argued, were one of the chief causes of individual differences, and an important item to consider when evaluating children. In addition, Gesell pointed to the existence of patterns in development, and described a number of them in great detail.

His research, and that of his associates, had obvious implications for parents. Gesell believed in the "wisdom of the body," which manifested itself in a variety of self-regulatory behaviors in children. For instance, when infants are left to their own inclinations, they develop appropriate patterns for many of their basic functions, including sleeping and eating. The role of the parent is to provide a supportive environment, appropriate to the developmental level of the child. Often this means that the parent must learn to sit back and enjoy the process of development, rather than try to interfere with it. Consistent with this emphasis on maturation, Gesell believed that children should not be hurried. Training that is not appropriate to the level of the child will result only in temporary benefits and may do some psychological harm. He maintained that parents should always take their cues from the child. In a larger sense, he suggested that parents were not as responsible for children's behavior as they usually believe.

Most of Gesell's work consisted of observation, although he also conducted a few studies. Among the most famous of these was his twin research. For example, one member of a twin set was given training in walking. At the end of the experimental period, when the twins were compared, it was clear that the twin with the training was walking at a more advanced level. However, after a brief passage of time, both twins were walking at the same level. In other words, it was not the training that made a difference, it was the maturation of the child. Although Gesell conducted most of his research on physical and motor activities, he believed his principles held for all levels of psychological development.

Gesell's work was criticized for its insularity. He appeared not to recognize the contribution of other important theories as explanations for development. For instance, he virtually ignored the contributions of learning theory and psychoanalysis, except to condemn them. His work was also criticized because it did not place enough emphasis on cultural and individual differences. Most of the children in his studies were from white, middle-class, intact homes. More-over, his writing emphasized group norms rather than the individual child. By the late 1940s, his approach had begun to fall out of favor. His work was still considered accurate and useful, but many experts concluded that there were more important ways to learn about infants and children. Nonetheless, Gesell's normative data remained the standard for many psychologists and pediatricians.

During his lifetime, Gesell saw his institute grow from a single room, with himself as the only staff member, to a thriving organization covering five floors of the Yale Human Relations Institute, with a staff of thirty-one. In its heyday, the institute had literally hundreds of visitors each year, eager to learn the latest techniques of research in child development. On his retirement in 1948, Gesell and several of his colleagues established the Gesell Institute of Child Development in New Haven, Connecticut, an institution that continued to function after his death.

John D. Hogan

See also Hall, G. Stanley

References and further reading
Ames, Louise Bates 1989. *Arnold Gesell: Themes of His Work*. New York: Human Sciences Press.
Gesell, Arnold. 1952. "Arnold Gesell." Pp. 123–142 in vol. 4 of *A History of Psychology in Autobiography*. Edited by Edwin G. Boring, Herbert S. Langfeld, Heinz Werner, and Robert M. Yerkes. Worcester, MA: Clark University Press.
Thelen, Esther, and Karen E. Adolph. 1992. "Arnold L. Gesell: The Paradox of Nature and Nurture." *Developmental Psychology* 28:368–380.

Gifted Children

Children who are extremely advanced in the intellectual, academic, creative, artistic, or leadership areas for whom special educational supports are required are often labeled gifted. However, most public school systems focus solely on intellectual and academic giftedness in their programming.

Common Characteristics of Gifted Children

Whether they would be described as globally or unevenly gifted in an academic or aesthetic area, research studies have consistently revealed the following three characteristics of gifted children. First, they tend to be *precocious*, in that they take the first steps toward mastery of some area or skill earlier than average. For example, a child may be able to identify all the letters and associate the sounds with some of them by age two. Second, gifted children are typically *intrinsically motivated*. They have an intense interest in the area in which they are focusing and do not need the support or involvement of a parent to motivate them to pursue their learning. Finally, gifted children have been found to *learn in qualitatively different ways* than typical children. They are often self-taught with very little instruction and are more likely to be creative and possess strong problem-solving abilities and advanced higher-order thinking skills that allow them to identify patterns, perceive relations, work with abstractions, and develop generalizations. For example, a young gifted child with an interest in dinosaurs may independently seek out books above his or her expected age level that provide detailed information about dinosaurs and be able to appropriately identify similarities and differences among the different types of dinosaurs and categorize them according to particular attributes. He or she may also be able to place dinosaurs within the evolutionary progression and understand their relationship to earlier and later life forms, demonstrating an insight into complex concepts far greater than would be expected of a child that age.

Evaluation of Giftedness

The current trend in the identification of gifted children views giftedness as a multidimensional trait that includes superior abilities in one or more intellectual, academic, creative, artistic, athletic, or leadership areas, as well as elements of creativity, self-motivation, and special talent. Earlier evaluative criteria of giftedness focused more exclusively on academic and intellectual abilities, and for the most part, public education systems have maintained this focus.

Parents or teachers who suspect that a child may be gifted can request, in writing, a multidisciplinary evaluation through the child's school. Federal law requires states to serve gifted children, but procedures for identification vary by state. The determination of giftedness within schools is typically made based on the findings from the administration of an individualized intelligence test (see entry on Intelligence Testing) and measures of other variables. Other measures may include rating scales, achievement tests, and tests of creativity. Although the criteria for designation as "gifted" vary across school districts, one commonly employed requirement is that a child score in the top 2 percent on the intelligence test (equivalent to an IQ score of 130 or higher).

Children who score overall in the top 2 percent and are also achieving at a high level may be described as *globally gifted*. Some common characteristics of globally gifted children that usually emerge before age five have been identified. These children typically speak early, progress quickly to the use of complex sentences, and are frequently precocious in their physical development as well, reaching developmental milestones for sitting, crawling, and walking several months ahead of their peers. Globally gifted children often learn to read by age four and are fascinated with numbers and number relations.

They are very alert as infants and are able to maintain this attention for extended periods of time. While engaged, they prefer novel experiences and can exhibit an almost obsessive interest in a specific area. They are curious self-starters who generally require little direct instruction to learn. Gifted children typically have high energy levels that can often be mistaken for hyperactivity, especially when they are not sufficiently challenged. Socially, globally gifted children tend toward solitary play, either as a result of personal preference or because there are few children who share their interests. They tend to be philosophically astute from an early age and think or worry about moral, political, and philosophical dilemmas. One of the most consistent findings of globally gifted children is that they possess a highly developed sense of humor that emerges from their strong language skills.

It is important to note, however, that globally gifted children are the exception rather than the rule. More commonly, gifted children have unique patterns of abilities and exhibit particular strength in one or more areas. These children could be described as *unevenly gifted.* One commonly noted difference is that some children may have much higher verbal than mathematical abilities, or the reverse. Superior mathematical abilities are typically associated with excellent visual and spatial thinking and nonverbal reasoning, while strengths in verbal areas are associated with knowledge of general information and abstract verbal reasoning. Gifted programs that rely on high overall scores may overlook these children. Gender differences have been identified here, with more highly mathematically gifted males and more highly verbally gifted females.

An extreme unevenness in the ability profile for a child who is believed to be gifted may suggest the presence of a learning disability. It is estimated that about 10 percent of high-IQ children exhibit language-based learning disabilities. They may be reading significantly below grade level or have spelling problems, dyslexia, or spatial difficulties. If a parent or teacher has concerns about this area, he or she would be advised to seek consultation with a psychologist specializing in the diagnosis of learning disabilities. The accurate diagnosis of a learning disability is a complex one and is best made by a professional experienced in this highly specialized area.

Gifted children can also be identified in nonacademically focused areas. Early talents in music, visual arts, dance, athletics, and leadership ability can emerge in very young children. Children gifted in these areas appear to intuitively understand, create, and process aesthetic, athletic, and dynamic information without the benefit of direct instruction. More frequently, these children would be described as "talented" versus gifted; however, research has found very little support for a distinction between these two categories.

The Origins of Giftedness

Giftedness in children has been a controversial subject. Some argue that all children are, or could be, gifted if provided with the right environmental stimulation or exposure. Others argue that giftedness is purely biologically based and is, therefore, determined before the child is born. The recent research on giftedness suggests a combination of the two. Studies of gifted children typically reveal that there are some biological, mostly brain-based neurological and genetic differences noted in children who have been identified as gifted. It is difficult to determine, however, whether the differences in the brains of these individuals are the *cause* of their giftedness or a *result* of the often rigorous and challenging intellectual activities in which they engage. Environmental differences are also noted for gifted children. They tend to come from families in which they are either the eldest or only child, and live in homes that provide an enriched environment. Parents of gifted children appear to model and set high standards for achievement, yet provide independence, nurturance, and support for their children's endeavors. The research suggests, therefore, that there is a biological basis for giftedness, but how this is manifested is affected by the degree to which the family and environment are able to support the child's talents and abilities.

Social Implications of Giftedness

Gifted children have unique intellectual and personality attributes that can place them at risk for difficult social relationships. Their intrinsic motivation and intense pursuit of their area(s) of interest can often set them apart from other children their ages and cause them to feel "different" from their peers. This can lead to feelings of isolation and loneliness, which can be particularly troublesome for children during adolescence when the need to fit in with peers is typically very strong. Gifted children often place unrealistically high expectations for performance on themselves that can lead to anxiety, depression, and feelings of inadequacy when faced with challenge or failure. Gifted children are sometimes singled out and provided extra attention by adults because of their strengths or talents, and this can lead to strained peer and sibling relationships.

Adults can guard against these difficulties by recognizing that the gifted child's emotional and social development does not always keep pace with his or her intellectual development. Being sensitive to children's need for developmentally appropriate play and social contact, as well as providing them with opportunities to express their feelings, will support them through these potential trouble spots. In addition, contact with gifted peers through appropriate educational programming can provide role models and support.

Educating the Gifted Child

Historically, parents of bright children who have excelled early in school have sought to have their children identified and placed in a program for gifted children through their local school district. It is important to recognize, however, that not all "bright" children are gifted, and placement in a program for gifted children should not be viewed as a reward for excellent academic achievement. Many children achieve well but are appropriately served in regular classes. Programs for gifted children are designed to assist children who require specially designed instructional programs that are tailored to support their unique pattern of talents and abilities. Just as children with learning difficulties require individualized educational planning to support their academic progress, so, too, do gifted children.

Underidentified Populations of Gifted Children

Within certain groups of children there are those who may be gifted, yet are particularly at risk for being underidentified for a variety of reasons. Specifically, racial, ethnic, or language minority children may often be overlooked because their early experiences may not fit the pattern of what is typically expected of a gifted child or because of English-language delays associated with second-language learning. Children with disabilities, most often those with physical, emotional, or communication issues, may not be considered gifted because of barriers presented by their specific disabling conditions. Personality factors may also play a role in the underidentification of gifted children. Conforming girls who may have difficulty asserting themselves or actively demonstrating their talents or abilities may not present as gifted. Conversely, active boys who move rapidly from task to task may not be thought to be gifted, despite a pattern of abilities that suggest the contrary. In the absence of appropriate levels of challenge and stimulation, gifted children may act out, become hyperactive, or exhibit other patterns of behavior that interfere with their identification.

Catherine A. Fiorello
Annemarie F. Clarke

See also Intelligence Testing

References and further reading
Alvino, James. 1996. *Parents' Guide to Raising a Gifted Child.* New York: Ballantine Books.
Galbraith, Judy, and James R. Delisle. 1996. *The Gifted Kids' Survival Guide: A Teen Handbook.* Minneapolis, MN: Free Spirit.
Galbraith, Judy, and Pamela Espeland. 1998. *The Gifted Kids' Survival Guide: For Ages 10 and Under.* Minneapolis, MN: Free Spirit.
Webb, James T., Elizabeth A. Meckstroth, and Stephanie S. Tolan. 1989. *Guiding the Gifted Child: A Practical Source for Parents and Teachers.* Scottsdale, AZ: Gifted Psychology Press.
Winner, Ellen. (1996). *Gifted Children: Myths and Realities.* New York: Basic Books.

Ginott, Haim (1922–1973)

Haim Ginott was a clinical psychologist, child therapist, and parent educator whose books, *Group Psychotherapy with Children* (1961), *Between Parent and Child* (1965), *Between Parent and Teenager* (1969), and *Teacher and Child* (1972), revolutionized the way child therapists, parents, and teachers relate to children. The books were best-sellers for over a year and were translated into thirty languages.

Ginott was the first resident psychologist on the *Today Show* and wrote a weekly column, syndicated by King Features, and a monthly column for *McCall's*

Magazine. He also served as adjunct professor of psychology at New York University Graduate School of Arts and Sciences and at Adelphi University Institute of Advanced Psychological Studies Postdoctoral Program in Psychotherapy, where he conducted courses in play therapy and served as therapy supervisor.

The communication skills that Ginott advocated in his books help adults enter into the world of children in a compassionate and caring way and teach them how to become aware of and respond to feelings. As Ginott said:

I'm a child psychotherapist, I treat disturbed children. Suppose I see children in therapy one hour a week for a year. Their symptoms disappear, they feel better about themselves, they get along with others, they even stop fidgeting in school. What is it that I do that helps? I communicate with them in a unique way. I use every opportunity to enhance their feelings about themselves. If caring communication can drive sick children sane, its principles and practices belong to parents and teachers. While psychotherapists may be able to cure, only those in daily contact with children can help them to become psychologically healthy.

Before he became a psychologist, Ginott was an elementary school teacher in Israel. He was a graduate of the David Yellin Teachers College in Jerusalem (1942), but after teaching for a few years, he realized that he was not sufficiently prepared to deal with children in the classroom. As he said, "I tried to teach them to be polite and they were rude; to be neat and they were messy; to be cooperative and they were disruptive." It was then that he decided to come to Columbia University Teachers College, where he received his doctorate of education degree in 1952. However, the education courses there were also not helpful, in Ginott's opinion. Like most teachers, he came to the profession with the best of intentions, but what he lacked were the skills to fulfill those intentions, to be able to function in the classroom humanely, as well as effectively. He wanted to learn how to discipline without humiliating; how to criticize without destroying self-worth; how to praise without judging; how to express anger without hurting; how to acknowledge, not argue, with feelings; how to respond so that children would learn to trust their inner reality and develop self-confidence.

"What is the goal of education? What is the goal of parenting?" he would ask. "We want our children to grow up to be decent human beings, a 'mensch,' a person with compassion, commitment, and caring." How does one go about humanizing a child, making a "mensch" out of him? Only by using "menschy" methods; by recognizing that the process is the method, that ends do not justify the means, and that in our attempt to get children to behave we do not damage them psychologically. Thus, we must be careful not to talk to children in a way that will enrage them, diminish their self-confidence, inflict hurt, or cause them to lose faith in their competence or ability. Children learn what they experience. They are like wet cement: any word that falls on them makes an impact.

It was as a child psychotherapist that Ginott developed the communication skills that enabled him to listen and to talk to children in a special way and then to share this knowledge with parents and teachers. They welcomed the idea that finding it difficult to bring up children and not always knowing what to say and do did not mean that they needed psychological help to become more caring and effective parents. At the time Ginott's

books were published, most psychologists felt that poor parenting was the result of parents' psychological problems, rather than lack of parenting skills, misinformation, or poor parental models.

After receiving his doctorate in clinical psychology from Columbia University, Ginott took an internship with the Jewish Board of Guardians under Sam Slavson, whose teaching influenced his use of groups in child psychotherapy.

As chief psychologist at the Sacksonville, Florida, Guidance Clinic, Ginott treated emotionally disturbed children and adolescents. This intensive experience with troubled children sensitized him to children's emotional needs and to the needs of their parents. He came to realize that the traditional model of offering psychological treatment to these parents may help them personally, but did not necessarily teach them how to relate to their children in a more compassionate way. Thus, in the early 1950s, Ginott began experimenting with parent education and guidance groups as an alternative to psychotherapy for parents. Eventually, he expanded his parent guidance groups to include parents of healthy children who wanted to learn how to be more caring and effective with their children, to become aware of how they felt about their own feelings, and thus become more understanding of their children's anger and hurt.

Ginott's development as a clinical psychologist and child therapist was influenced by his teacher, Virginia Axline, who had been a student of Carl Rogers. As a graduate student assistant to Axline he learned the Rogerian technique of how to communicate empathy by acknowledging and reflecting feelings. It was a skill that he used with children who were in treatment with him and he also taught the skill to parents. Acknowledging and reflecting feelings was the primary tool that both Axline and Rogers used in treating children and adults. But Haim Ginott realized soon after he started treating disturbed children that he needed to develop a more varied set of tools for communicating with his young patients. The children would get angry and he had to respond to their anger; he got angry and he had to learn how to express his anger; how to criticize, praise, and say "no" without inflicting hurt or doing damage to the child's emotional well-being. As a result, he experimented until he came up with specific communication skills that he found therapeutic in treating disturbed children and that he shared in his books with parents and teachers.

The philosophy that guided Ginott was partly the Hippocratic oath: *Primum, non nocere* ("At first, do no damage"), and the dictum "Deal with the situation, not the person." When things go wrong, do not blame the child, but look for a solution. State the problem and possible solutions. By concentrating on the mishap and not on the perpetrator, the parent protects the child from feeling guilty and from developing a negative self-image.

Parents, Ginott felt, need to discard their language of rejection and learn a language of acceptance. They even know the words. They heard their own parents use them with guests and strangers. It was a language that was protective of feelings, not critical of behavior. He tried to encourage parents and teachers to treat children as guests, to be as aware as they are of hurting their guests' feelings when they respond to children.

Ginott's approach to parent education involved understanding for parents, as well as children. His books show the compassion he felt for the challenged parents even as he showed compassion and understanding for their children.

Ginott's process of parent guidance or education follows three steps: the parent educator responds to parent complaints with attention, understanding, and accept-

ance; the parents are "sensitized" by directing their attention toward the distress that the children may be feeling; and the educator helps parents become comfortable with their new communication skills. The group leader supports parent participants with the healing empathy that they will be encouraged to provide for their children.

Many parents and teachers were confused when they listened to Haim Ginott or read his books. They could not decide whether he was strict or permissive. They were concerned that if they started to relate to children in a caring way they would have to sacrifice setting limits and setting standards, that the children would become undisciplined.

Ginott was both strict and permissive. He encouraged teachers and parents to be strict when it came to behavior. There was acceptable and unacceptable behavior. Parents and teachers had to decide for themselves what behavior they would or would not tolerate, and act accordingly. But he encouraged permissiveness when it came to feelings, because neither children nor adults can help how they feel. He said: "Birds fly, fish swim, and people feel." That is how we are. It is therefore not in anyone's best interest to make children feel uncomfortable or, even more serious, guilty for the way they feel.

Over the years, many parents and teachers studied with Ginott. They contributed to his understanding, providing many of the anecdotes in his books that illustrate his principles of communication. They, on the other hand, benefited from his wisdom, his warmth, and his humor. Although English was not his native tongue, he loved the English language. He loved it as a poet, using it sparingly and with precision. Raised in a verbal Jewish tradition, Ginott often made his points through jokes, parables, and anecdotes. He was in great demand as a speaker in person and on television, where his message, expressed with caring, humor, and enthusiasm, easily seduced his audience.

Even though Ginott died at the young age of fifty-one, he enjoyed an exciting, creative, and accomplished intellectual life. His innovative ideas of communicating with children that he disseminated in his books, lectures, and columns reverberated not only in the United States but all over the world. He influenced the development of parenting workshops, where parents and teachers who learned his communication skills, which were caring as well as effective, not only enriched their lives but helped their children develop self-respect, confidence, and compassion.

Alice Ginott

References and further reading
Ginott, Haim G. 1961. *Group Psychotherapy with Children.* New York: McGraw-Hill.
———. 1965. *Between Parent and Child.* New York: Macmillan.
———. 1969. *Between Parent and Teenager.* New York: Macmillan.
———. 1972. *Teacher and Child.* New York: Macmillan.
Orgel, A. R. 1980. "Haim Ginott's Approach to Parent Education." Pp. 75–100 in *Handbook on Parent Education.* Edited by M. J. Fine. Orlando, FL: Academic Press.
Santrock, J. W., A. M. Minnett, and B. D. Campbell. 1994. *The Authoritative Guide to Self-Help Books.* New York: Guilford Press.

Grandfatherhood

Grandfatherhood, which begins when a man's child becomes a parent, has been traditionally regarded as the last period of a man's family life cycle, but it is no longer typically limited to the last decade of a man's life. Yet, becoming a grandfather is not under a father's control or otherwise inevitable; his children may or may not "make" him a grandfather, regardless of whether or not he desires the position. Once a grandchild is born, however, a man can choose to assume the "role" of a grandfather, and in the United States there is considerable flexibility in how this role is performed.

In the most general terms, grandfathers seek to find a balance between doing things for their grandchildren and being emotionally available to them. Still, emotional distance between grandfathers and grandchildren may widen as those grandchildren get older. Currently grandfathers, along with grandmothers, are becoming more involved in being parental surrogates for their grandchildren, which has raised the issue of grandparents' legal rights. Finally, grandfathers deserve more attention in social scientific research, with particular emphasis needed on the grandfathering experience within American ethnic populations.

Demographics of Grandfatherhood

Because Americans' life expectancies and general health have improved over the past century, more people than ever before are living long enough to become grandparents. Men generally become grandfathers during the middle-adulthood years among Euro-Americans and even earlier among many ethnic subgroups. Thus, many men spend two to four decades in the grandfather role.

According to the National Survey of Families and Households, more than 50 million Americans are grandparents, but given men's shorter life expectancy and older age at marriage compared to women, fewer than half of that number are grandfathers. Men are less likely than women to survive into their grandchildren's adult lives or to witness the birth of their first great-grandchild. Yet more precise population estimates of grandfathers in America, Maximiliane Szinovacz notes, are difficult to calculate with confidence because complex intergenerational and intrafamilial patterns cannot be summarized easily by census data.

Ken Bryson and Lynne Casper of the U.S. Census Bureau have clearly docu-

One study on grandfathers revealed that they tend to underestimate the strong attachment they come to feel for their grandchildren. (Elizabeth Crews)

mented one dramatic statistical increase in the experience of grandfathers: many now share their homes with grandchildren, usually serving as one of the children's primary caregivers or as a parental surrogate. They report that in 1997, 3.9 million children (5.5 percent of all children under age eighteen) were living in homes maintained by grandparents, with 57 percent of those households having a grandfather present—over 1.7 million grandfathers. Kathleen Roe and Meredith Minkler also have estimated that more than 10 percent of all grandparents raise a grandchild for six months or more, generally for much longer, and that 23 percent of those caregiver grandparents are grandfathers. Most positively, this situation allows grandfathers to rework their parenting skills and to build upon the many

lessons they learned while rearing their own children. Yet the task of raising a second generation also threatens grandfathers with potential negative consequences, such as social isolation, physical and emotional exhaustion, financial problems, and the difficulty of ensuring adequate health care for both themselves and their grandchildren. In light of such examples of caregiver stress, it is clear that the folk wisdom—that grandfathering conveys the benefits, but not the responsibilities, of parenthood—is quickly becoming a myth and that it is more important now than ever before to understand grandfathers.

Dynamics of Grandfatherhood
Research on grandfathers has painted a complex, if somewhat limited, portrait.

The consensus of the research literature suggests that same-gender relationships between generations are closer, that is, grandfathers tend to be closer and more involved with their grandsons than with their granddaughters, although it also has been found that both grandfathers and grandmothers tend to invest more strongly in the children of their daughters than in the children of their sons. Consequently, boys and girls in the United States tend to have somewhat different experiences of their maternal and paternal grandfathers. And, as Helen Kivnick also has shown, a man's relationship with his own grandfathers, particularly his closest grandfather, provides him with his principal role model as he begins defining himself as a grandfather.

The concept of grandfathering "styles" has been used by researchers to succinctly describe complex variations. A classic study conducted by Bernice Neugarten and Karol Weinstein, for instance, documented five different grandparenting styles. Most of the grandfathers (36 percent) primarily used a "formal" style, which was characterized by providing occasional services and special treats. This was followed by the "distant figure" grandfather (31 percent), who was a benevolent figure usually seen on only holidays, and the "fun seeking" grandfather (27 percent), who indulged his grandchildren and enjoyed doing fun activities with them. The two least common styles were the "reservoir of family wisdom" and the "parent surrogate" styles. As has been noted, however, the current demographic trends indicate a significant increase in the grandfathering style of assuming the role of the parent, as when both parents work or are otherwise absent.

More recently, a study by Karen Somary and George Stricker has further explored the meaning of grandparenthood for grandparents by comparing their expectations before their first grandchild's birth with their actual experiences one to two years later. They noted that grandfathers tended to underestimate the strong attachment they would feel toward a grandchild, as well as how important it would be to them for the grandchild to be able to turn to them for support. Grandfathers, however, were more accurate when predicting how open they would be to caretaking and the emphasis they would place on being wise teachers for their grandchildren.

Exploring similar territory, Jeanne Thomas interviewed grandparents regarding the meaning of grandparenthood. She learned that grandfathers emphasized the importance of grandchildren for generationally extending the family and indulged grandchildren more than did grandmothers, but that they also reported somewhat lower satisfaction with grandparenting than did grandmothers. This lower satisfaction rate seems related to the way that grandfathers are perceived by their grandchildren. Several studies have shown that the maternal grandmother tends to be more frequently favored by grandchildren of all ages, while the paternal grandfather tends to be the least frequently named as a favorite grandparent. A classic study by Boaz Kahana and Eva Kahana, however, showed that this picture is actually more complex because what is valued by grandchildren changes over time: younger children (ages four and five) tend to prefer indulgent grandfathers bearing gifts, whereas eight- and nine-year-olds tend to want active, fun-sharing grandfathers, and eleven- and twelve-year-old children tend to want more distant, less mutual grandfathers. This variance suggests that grandfathers' relational styles, such as those originally identified by Neugarten and Weinstein, must be flexible and nuanced in order to optimally match their grandchildren's developmental needs, as well as to increase the likelihood that both grandfathers and grandchildren will derive fulfillment from their interactions.

Grandfathers' interactions with infants follow patterns similar to those found among fathers and infants (e.g., robust physical play) just as grandmother-infant interactions show many of the patterns characteristic of mother-infant relations (e.g., verbalizations). Grandfathers also have been shown to be more responsive to (e.g., approaching, touching) unfamiliar infants than other men. Yet, when observing infant-grandparent play interactions in white middle-class families, Barbara Tinsley and Ross Parke found that when infants were with their grandfathers, the infants demonstrated fewer positive behaviors than when they were with their parents or grandmothers. But they also found that "middle-aged" grandfathers (aged fifty to fifty-seven years) were more playful, involved, and affectionate with their infant grandchildren than either younger (aged thirty-six to forty-nine) or older (aged fifty-eight to sixty-eight) grandfathers, and, on some measures of interactive behavior, these infants also interacted more positively with middle-aged grandfathers than they had with either their grandmothers or parents. Further, infants who had highly responsive and playful grandfathers also had higher scores in cognitive, social, and motor interactions using the Bayley Scales of Infant Development. Intriguingly, however, other studies have reported that relatively older grandfathers who felt a high level of responsibility for helping and caring for their young grandchildren also felt higher levels of grandparenting satisfaction than did younger grandfathers. Also, grandfathers as a whole were less reluctant than grandmothers to offer child-rearing advice to their own children or educational-career advice to their adolescent grandchildren. This readiness to give advice is connected, Gunhild Hagestad believes, to grand-

fathers' felt responsibility to "be there" as a helper and economic support to their children and grandchildren in times of need. In other words, as Marc Baranowski has noted, grandfathers tend to focus more on what they can *do* for their grandchildren instrumentally than on how they can *be* with them emotionally, and so they concentrate on the giving of tangibles to their grandchildren and on the receiving of intangibles from their grandchildren.

Challenges to Grandfatherhood
The growing number of American grandfathers involved in direct parental care of their grandchildren and the complex dynamics of such paternal care, which have been described above, underscore two major challenges to understanding grandfatherhood in the United States. One is legal and the other is empirical.

The legal challenge involves several related issues. One such issue is the need for legislative action in support of funding for caregiving grandparents who are supporting their grandchildren. The National Family Caregiver Support Act, introduced in Congress during 1999 by Senator Michael DeWine (R-Ohio), is a federal effort meant to amend the Older Americans Act of 1965 (42 U.S.C. 3001 et seq.), and several states have instituted programs that provide subsidy payments to grandparents (or other relatives) who have obtained legal guardianship of the children they are raising. A related issue involves allowing grandparents without formal legal custody or guardianship to enroll their grandchildren in school or to grant permission for medical treatment; at least five states have instituted consent laws that allow for these situations. Another issue that involves grandfathers is the matter of access to and visitations with grandchildren, particularly after a divorce or a parental death. All fifty states recognize the prerogative of grandparents to petition the courts for visitation rights, but as Ross Thompson and his colleagues have noted, a key issue in the legal process is determining what is in the "best interest" of the grandchild—specifically, how that interest is met or contested by the interests of parents, grandparents, and other parties to the dispute. Because intergenerational interests and conflicts are here entangled with legal interests and decisions, the process is complex, and the potential for lasting psychological damage to children and adults is high.

The second major challenge to strengthening grandfatherhood in America is simply recognizing that what is known about this period of a man's life is limited. This empirical challenge primarily involves two research biases: gender and ethnic. The gender bias becomes clear when one realizes that most studies of grandparents have overwhelmingly focused on grandmothers, particularly maternal grandmothers. In contrast, grandfathers, especially paternal ones, have been overlooked in the research literature, which can reinforce the caricature that they are less accessible, less influential, or less involved in the lives of their grandchildren.

Ethnic favoritism is the other major research bias that needs to be rectified. This bias can be seen clearly when one realizes that studies to date have more often focused on middle-class Anglo-American or Caucasian grandfathers. Some notable exceptions are Jeffrey Watson and Sally Koblinsky's study of working-class African American grandparents and Linda Burton's study of African American grandparents raising grandchildren. But, in general, few scholars have paid attention to grandfathers among minority populations, and, again, those studies that do exist have generally focused on grandmothers rather than grandfathers. To gain a more complete picture of grandfatherhood in the American experience, more research must be done on the experience of men becoming grandparents and assuming that role within America's diverse ethnic groups.

John Snarey
Peter Yuichi Clark

See also Grandparenthood; Grandparents as Primary Caregivers

References and further reading
Bryson, Ken, and Lynne M. Casper. 1999. *Coresident Grandparents and Grandchildren.* Washington, DC: U.S. Department of Commerce, Economics and Statistics Administration, Bureau of the Census.
Burton, Linda M. 1992. "Black Grandparents Rearing Children of Drug-Addicted Parents: Stressors, Outcomes, and Social Service Needs." *Gerontologist* 32, no. 6:744–751.
Neugarten, Dail A. 1996. *The Meanings of Age: Selected Papers of Bernice L. Neugarten.* Chicago: University of Chicago Press.
Roe, Kathleen M., and Meredith Minkler. 1999. "Grandparents Raising Grandchildren: Challenges and Responses." *Generations* 22, no. 4:25–32.
Somary, Karen, and George Stricker. 1998. "Becoming a Grandparent: A Longitudinal Study of Expectations and Early Experiences as a Function of Sex and Lineage." *Gerontologist* 38, no. 1:53–61.
Strom, Robert D., and Shirley K. Strom. 1990. "Raising Expectations for Grandparents: A Three Generational Study." *International Journal of Aging and Human Development* 31, no. 3:161–167.
Szinovacz, Maximiliane E. 1998. "Grandparents Today: A Demographic Profile." *Gerontologist* 38, no. 1:37–52.
Tinsley, Barbara, and Ross Parke. 1988. "The Role of Grandfathers in the Context of the Family." Pp. 236–250 in *Fatherhood Today: Men's Changing Role in the Family.* Edited by Phyllis Bronstein and Carolyn P. Cowan. New York: John Wiley and Sons.
Watson, Jeffrey A., and Sally A. Koblinsky. 1997. "Strengths and Needs of Working-Class African-American and Anglo-American Grandparents." *International Journal of Aging and Human Development* 44, no. 2:149–165.

Grandparenthood

The stereotype of grandparents depicts white-haired seniors who stay home, knitting, baking, gardening, and reading the paper. The reality is that the majority of adults become grandparents when they are middle-aged and still active. In fact, most grandparents are likely still to be involved with careers, community activities, and leisure pursuits.

Several grandparenting styles have been identified. Some styles seem to be more prevalent in some subcultures than others. Regardless of style, grandparents are likely to become more involved with their grandchildren when their children's lives change dramatically. While parenthood is often voluntarily chosen, grandparenthood is not, but for most grandparents it is a rewarding relationship.

A national survey of grandparents of teenagers conducted in the mid-1980s identified three major styles of grandparenting. *Companionate* grandparents was the most common style. These grandparents saw their grandchildren frequently, enjoyed sharing activities with them, and hesitated to interfere with their children's child-rearing rules. This group was the most satisfied with their role. *Remote* grandparents rarely saw their grandchildren, usually because they lived far from them. Most felt emotionally distant as well. This group was the least satisfied with their role.

Involved grandparents saw their grandchildren frequently and helped with child care, gave advice, and played other practical roles in their grandchildren's lives. A subset of these involved grandparents were substitute or custodial parents who lived with their grandchildren because their children (usually daughters) were unmarried, recently divorced, worked outside the home, or unable to raise their own children. Others lived with their grandchildren or played a large day-care role.

Relationship strength is often tied to the number of activities that grandchildren can do with their grandparents and how often they see their grandparents. (Skjold Photographs)

When both parents and grandparents are highly involved in child rearing, additional stress can arise for all as well as some irritation and jealousy between grandparents and their adult children. Especially in single-parent homes, grandparents may face a double bind: parents may expect grandparents to be supportive without interfering.

The roles of companionate and remote grandparents may change if their children face a crisis, such as a divorce, job change, health problem, or death. Grandparents have been called "the family national guard," because they often have to come to the rescue if their children are in crisis.

In American culture generally the relationships between grandchildren and their maternal grandmothers are closest. In Native American and African American subcultures, grandmothers may have special significance. These grandmothers are often involved with their grandchildren, and are regarded as cultural teachers and tradition bearers.

The age at which people become grandparents can impact how they feel about the role. People who become grandparents very young, in their late twenties or thirties, or very old may feel less enthusiastic about the role than those becoming grandparents "on time," that is, in middle-age. Women who become grandmothers in middle-age or later in life see themselves as having more information about grandchildren, as being stronger teachers of their grandchildren, and as being less frustrated with the grandparent role.

Several factors have been found to be operating in close grandparent-grandchild relationships. Relationships with younger grandparents and grandparents in better health may be perceived as stronger than relationships with older and/or less vigorous grandparents because relationship strength is often tied to the amount of activities that grandchildren can do with their grandparents and how often they can see their grandparents. Other reasons for grandchildren feeling close to their grandparents include enjoying the personality of the grandparent, enjoying the activities they share, receiving individual attention and support from the grandparent, and being able to relate to the grandparent as a role model.

The frequency of contact between grandparents and grandchildren is related to geographical distance, quality of the relationship between the grandparent and the parent, number of grandchildren, gender of the grandparent, lineage of the grandchildren, and marital status of the grandparent. The grandparent-grandchild relationship is likely to be closest when they live near each other and when the grandparent had a close relationship with his or her own grandparents. In rural populations, the relationships between grandchildren and grandparents are closer when the relationships between parents and grandparents are close. Grandchildren view their grandparents as important and influential figures in their lives, and they benefit when they have frequent contact with them. Of course, the grandparental role changes as grandparents and grandchildren age.

Unfortunately, not all grandparent-grandchild relationships are close, or can remain close. Four circumstances are associated with grandparent loss of contact with live grandchildren: parental divorce, conflict with both parents, death of an adult child, and stepparent adoption following remarriage. When a grandchild dies, grandparents often grieve both for the lost grandchild and for the pain their children are facing. Grandparents may feel guilty for having survived their grandchild, and also helpless about the pain their children are feeling. Many grandparents report emotional rupturing and physical health problems when they lose contact with a grandchild.

Joyce Prigot

See also Grandfatherhood; Grandparents as Primary Caregivers

References and further reading
Berman, Ellen. 1998. *Grandparenting ABC's: A Beginner's Handbook.* New York: Berkley Publishing Group.
Drew, Linda, and Peter Smith. 1999. "The Impact of Parental Separation/Divorce on Grandparent-Grandchild Relationships." *International Journal of Aging & Human Development* 48, no. 3:191–216.
King, Valarie, and Glen Elder. 1997. "The Legacy of Grandparenting: Childhood Experiences with Grandparents and Current Involvement with Grandchildren." *Journal of Marriage and the Family* 59:848–859.
Kruk, Edward. 1995. "Grandparent-Grandchild Contact Loss: Findings from a Study of 'Grandparents Rights' Members."

Canadian Journal on Aging 14, no. 4:737–754.

Uhlenberg, Peter, and Bradley Hammill. 1998. "Frequency of Grandparent Contact with Grandchild Sets: Six Factors That Make a Difference." *Gerontologist* 30, no. 3:276–285.

Watson, Jeffrey. 1997. "Grandmothering across the Lifespan." *Journal of Gerontological Social Work* 28, no. 4:45–62.

Watson, Jeffrey, and Sally Koblinsky. 1997. "Strengths and Needs of Working-Class African-American and Anglo-American Grandparents." *International Journal of Aging and Human Development* 44, no. 2:149–165.

Grandparents as Primary Caregivers

More grandparents are assuming or being given the primary care of their grandchildren than in previous generations. The U.S. Bureau of the Census estimates that approximately 3.3 million children in the United States lived with grandparents in 1991. In 1991, black children (12.3 percent) were much more likely to live with grandparents than white (3.7 percent) or Hispanic (5.6 percent) children. The greatest percentage increase, however, has been in white families. The increase in the numbers from 1980 to 1991 was 54 percent for white children, 40 percent for Hispanic children, and 24 percent for black children. Although African American grandparents are four times as likely as white grandparents to have primary care and twice as likely as Latino grandparents, the child-care arrangements are often very fluid or cyclical in nature.

Grandparents are providing primary care to children for a variety of reasons. Increasingly, the reasons are drug related (45 percent); most common is alcohol followed by cocaine (crack or powder). Other causes are increased incarceration of women, increased maternal death from AIDS, and the unraveling of social safety nets. Additionally, more child protective agencies are choosing to place children with relatives, especially grandparents, which accounts for about 22 percent of children. Other causes include abandonment (6 percent), teenage pregnancy (6 percent), parent unable (5 percent), and death of parent (5 percent). (Woodworth, 1996)

Many grandparents speak of "the living dead; their sons and daughters who are lost as if dead to them and their children." (Woodworth, 1996) These families have no grieving process with which to resolve their loss. They continue to hope that one day their adult child, the parent, will return to the family, but they have few they can turn to for support and understanding as they try to begin their lives again. This is also a difficult time for the grandchildren, as they grieve the loss of parent and try to adjust to new surroundings, rules, and roles.

Studies suggest that caregiving grandparents are at an increased risk for emotional and physical health problems, social isolation, family conflict, as well as legal and financial problems. Socially, grandparents may feel left out of their peer group because they have the routine demands of child rearing to consider. When their peers are spending more time in leisure and recreational activities including travel, child-rearing grandparents may lack the time, energy, and/or financial resources for these activities.

Grandparents who feel they "failed" with their own children may fear they will "fail" with their grandchildren. They may also fear that what was acceptable when their children were young may not be the right thing for their grandchildren. The grandchild's actions and previous experience may be foreign to the grandparents' own experiences as parents or children. These grandparents are often in search of help in their new role and could be more successful if they were well informed about current parenting goals and child-rearing practices.

In addition to the basic concepts of child growth and development, child guidance, nutrition, health, and safety, parenting curricula should be designed to meet specific needs of these grandparents. The following are topics that should be included in a parent education curriculum for grandparents who are providing primary care for grandchildren: (1) legal issues, including medical insurance, ex parte orders/orders of protection, stalking statutes, custody, child protective/foster-care system rules, social security, and wills; (2) substance abuse, addiction, and codependency, including substance abuse prevention and positive stress management strategies; (3) strategies to help grandparents cope with the nonnormative task of parenting again, including fears of failure, anxiety about their new roles, and living with chronic illnesses and/or financial problems; (4) resources in the school and community available to assist with specific issuesl (5) support groups and counseling for both grandparents and children as they experience the normal stages of grief related to the different issues of loss and separation each experiences, including blame, anger, guilt, and denial; (6) general information about heredity and transmission of predispositions for certain conditions, mental and physical illnesses, as well as developmental delays; and (7) advocacy skills to empower grandparents to work on behalf of themselves and their grandchildren within the legal, protective services, educational, and medical systems.

In addition to parent education classes specifically designed for these grandparents, schools should consider various adjustments, including modifying language as they request signatures, send notes home, or arrange parent conferences. Teachers should know who the primary caregivers of their students are—whether it be "Grandmother," "Papa," or "Granddad"—so that they can accurately acknowledge these important relationships in their students' lives. Teachers may wish to allow extra time for parent conferences with caregiving grandparents to discuss how the school can help the grandparents be successful in their new (old) role. Teachers and other school staff may wish to provide information for grandparents to help them arrange short-term relief from their child-rearing responsibilities, perhaps through after-school programs or baby-sitting "co-ops" with other grandparents. Finally, those working with grandparents serving as primary caregivers must be aware of the potential for role reversal, as children may need to provide assistance to grandparents as the households learn to live together.

Peggy Tuter Pearl

See also Grandfatherhood; Grandparenthood

References and further reading
de Toledo, S., and D. E. Brown. 1995. *Grandparents as Parents: A Survival Guide for Raising a Second Family.* New York: Guilford Press.
Grandparent and Relative Caregivers. Selected Internet resources available under "Articles" link at www.fosterparents.com.
Woodworth, Renee S. 1996. "You're Not Alone . . . You're One in a Million." *Child Welfare* 75, no. 5:619–635.

Growth, Patterns of

The measurement of growth is used around the world as an early, objective method to assess a child's developmental well-being, particularly during the early years of life. Growth during infancy and toddlerhood is very rapid. In healthy newborns, birth weight doubles by five months of age, triples by the end of the first year of life, and quadruples by the end of the second year of life. Birth length increases by 50 percent over the first year of life and doubles by four years of age.

The potential to measure and chart infants' growth trajectories provides parents and clinicians with the opportunity to assess for healthy growth, as well as screen for the possibility of growth problems, such as failure to thrive or obesity. Detecting abnormalities in growth early in life allows for the prompt initiation of treatment, which reduces the health and developmental risks that may accompany growth problems.

For the evaluation of growth, infants and children should be weighed and measured using standard procedures (e.g., from the National Health and Nutrition Examination Surveys I, II, and III) by trained personnel. Weight is measured without clothes on a scale that is calibrated regularly. For children less than two years of age, height is measured in a recumbent position, and in a standing position for children older than two years of age. Weight and height are plotted on gender-specific growth charts, acquired through the National Center for Health Statistics (NCHS) (see sample chart, showing NCHS growth percentiles for boys from birth to thirty-six months). Growth charts represent normal growth from infancy to early adulthood. They are color coded (pink for girls and blue for boys) and include separate charts for the first three years of life when growth is rapid, and for two to eighteen years of age when growth proceeds at a slower rate. Growth charts not only allow for the comparison of an individual child's current growth status in relation to other children in the same age group, they also allow predictions to be made of the child's future growth.

Growth charts allow for repeated plotting of children's weight and height (on the vertical axis) by age (on the horizontal axis) on gender-specific charts. There are three indices (frequently expressed as percentiles from 5 percent to 95 percent) derived from these charts that are commonly used to describe children's growth: weight-for-age, height-for-age, and weight-for-height. Weight-for-age represents a child's weight in comparison with the weight of other children of the same age.

For example, a six-month-old child who weighs sixteen pounds falls on the twenty-fifth percentile line. This means that out of 100 six-month-old children, approximately 75 percent weigh more and 25 percent weigh less than this child. Weight-for-age is commonly used in pediatric clinics to track a child's growth and is an excellent indicator of changes in weight over time. However, weight-for-age does not account for variations in height. When a child's weight-for-age is low, it is unclear if the primary problem is low weight, short stature, or a combination of the two.

Height-for-age represents a child's height in comparison with the height of other children of the same age. Children's height reflects the genetic contributions from their parents. Thus, children's height-for-age is sometimes adjusted by a formula using the mean height of their parents. However, if the parents themselves were malnourished or experienced growth failure as children, their stature may underestimate their children's genetic growth potential. Low height-for-age (short stature) is sometimes a sign of chronic undernutrition.

Weight-for-height (weight plotted by height, regardless of age) reflects body proportionality and is an indicator of body fat. Low weight-for-height (less than fifth percentile) is often a sign of malnutrition and may reflect low caloric intake. On the other hand, high weight-for-height (greater than ninety-fifth percentile) is often a sign of obesity and may reflect high caloric intake.

Body mass index (BMI) is an alternative measure that may be used to assess body proportionality. BMI, which is weight in kilograms divided by the square of height in meters (BMI = $weight/height^2$), is a useful way to compare body stature. However, BMI changes with age, reflecting the classic chubbiness of infancy, followed by the slimming of the preschool

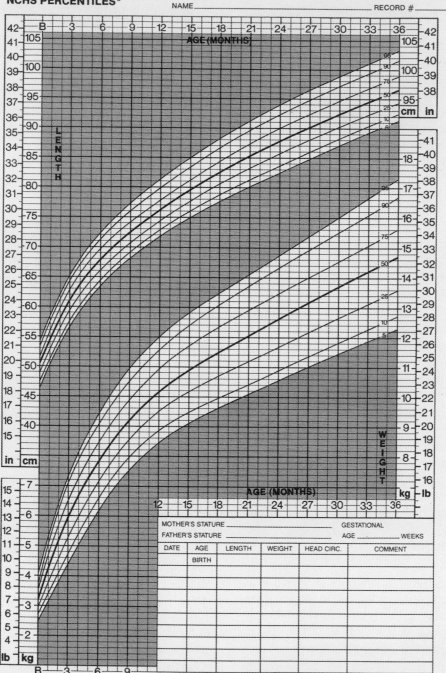

BOYS: BIRTH TO 36 MONTHS
PHYSICAL GROWTH
NCHS PERCENTILES*

The potential to measure and chart growth trajectories provides parents and clinicians with the opportunity to assess for healthy growth, as well as screen for the possibility of growth problems. (Adapted from P. V. V. Hamill, T. A. Drizd, C. L. Johnson, R. B. Reed, A. F. Roche, and W. M. Moore. 1979. "Physical Growth: National Center for Health Statistics Percentiles." AMJ CLIN NUTR 32:607–629. Data from the Fels Longitudinal Study, Wright State University School of Medicine, Yellow Springs, Ohio) years. Thus, BMI cannot be evaluated independent of age. The newly revised growth charts from the NCHS utilize the BMI norms, which can be plotted over time in addition to height and weight.

Growth-Related Issues to Consider
During the first two years of life, children's weight-for-age, height-for-age, and weight-for-height vary as they move closer to the average, or mean. Beyond two years of age, there are fewer shifts, and children tend to follow their genetically determined growth curve. Therefore, examining rate of change for an individual child should always account for a child's position on the growth distribution. For example, a child who drops fifteen points in weight from the seventy-fifth to the sixtieth percentile may be moving closer to the average in weight for children of the same age. Whereas a child who drops fifteen points in weight from the twentieth to the fifth percentile may be experiencing a failure in growth. If there are instances of concern with respect to a child's rate of growth, parents are encouraged to consult their health-care provider.

When measuring growth, a single measure provides little information regarding the developmental health status of a child. Growth assessments should be plotted over time. In addition, growth occurs in intermittent, steplike spurts. If children's measurements of growth are taken frequently and within close proximity, there may be periods of no growth, leading to false conclusions regarding growth failure. Thus, children should not be measured daily. For most children, monthly growth checks are adequate.

Children with Growth-Related Health-Care Risks
There are certain instances when children's rate of growth may be appropriate, yet plot below NCHS standards. For example, children with a history of low birth weight or prematurity may gain weight at an expected rate, yet plot below the fifth percentile. There are specific growth charts available through NCHS for children born below 1,500 grams or children born prematurely. In addition, clinicians often calculate children's estimated weight gain per day (see table).

Median Daily Weight Gain	
Age	*Grams*
0–3 months	26–31 grams
3–6 months	17–18 grams
6–9 months	12–13 grams
9–12 months	9 grams
1–3 years	7–9 grams
4–6 years	6 grams

During illnesses, children may eat less food and may lose weight or gain weight at a slow rate, thereby experiencing a decrease in weight-for-age and/or weight-for-height percentile. Following recovery from the illness, children often undergo a period of catch-up growth during which they "attempt" physiologically to return to their previous growth percentile. Factors that determine the catch-up growth potential include, but are not limited to, the severity and duration of the illness and the developmental stage of the infant.

Children who fail to grow according to age and gender expectations or experience a deceleration in expected weight gain may be classified by clinicians as having failure to thrive (FTT), a relatively serious pediatric problem. On the other extreme, children with accelerated weight gain (weight-for-height above the ninety-fifth percentile) may be experiencing obesity. Both conditions can have serious health consequences. Children with either decelerated or accelerated growth should be evaluated by their primary health provider and referred to treatment programs.

Angelo Ponirakis
Maureen M. Black

References and further reading
Berhane, Rahel, and William H. Dietz. 1999.
"Clinical Assessment of Growth." Pp.
195–214 in *Failure to Thrive and Pediatric
Undernutrition: A Transdisciplinary
Approach*. Edited by Daniel B. Kessler and
Peter Dawson. Baltimore, MD: Paul H.
Brooks.

Ulijaszek, Stanley J., Francis E. Johnston, and
Michael A. Preece, eds. 1998. *The
Cambridge Encyclopedia of Human
Growth and Development*. Cambridge,
UK: Cambridge University Press.

H

Hall, G. Stanley (1844–1924)

G. Stanley Hall was a pioneer psychologist in the United States, and is considered the father of "developmental psychology," the study of normal development from conception to death. Early in his career, he was a leader of the child study movement, a social movement that led to a changing view of the child, as well as to many practical outcomes such as compulsory education and child labor laws. Hall was one of the first researchers to use scientific methods to study children and, although his research was largely unsuccessful, it laid the foundation for important contributions from others. In addition to his work as a developmental psychologist, he was the first president of Clark University, in Worcester, Massachusetts, where he created one of the earliest and strongest psychology departments in the world. He founded the American Psychological Association and served as its president twice. He was one of the first American psychologists to recognize the importance of Sigmund Freud's work, and in 1909 he invited Freud to give several lectures at Clark University, where Freud received his only honorary degree. Hall was also the founder of several important psychological journals that continue to be published today.

Granville Stanley Hall was born on 1 February 1844 in Ashfield, Massachusetts, a farming community in the western part of the state. After graduating from

G. Stanley Hall (Collections of the Library of Congress)

Williams College, he entered Union Theological Seminary in New York City. One of the professors there encouraged him to study in Germany, a center of philosophical thinking at the time. With the help of Henry Ward Beecher, an influential minister, Hall received the money necessary to finance the trip. Hall was strongly influenced by German philosophers, and was introduced by them to the importance of developmental and historical processes. He wanted to stay in Germany to continue his studies, but he ran out of money and was forced to return to the United States. After completing his studies at Union Theological Seminary, he took a position at Antioch College in Ohio teaching English literature and modern languages.

During his stay at Antioch College, Hall became interested in the controversial evolutionary theory of Charles Darwin and the work of Darwin's disciple, Herbert Spencer, who took Darwin's evolutionary ideas a step further, theorizing that human consciousness was the result of evolution. During this period, Hall read the work of Wilhelm Wundt for the first time. Wundt, a professor at the University of Leipzig in Germany, had proposed founding a new science based on the questions of philosophy and the experimental methods recently developed in physiology. Wundt's work is considered the foundation for modern experimental psychology.

When the curriculum at Antioch College was restructured, Hall left to find a new position. He finally decided to pursue a doctorate degree in philosophy at Harvard University, where he came under the influence of William James, one of America's first psychologists. Hall took most of his courses under James, and in 1878, two years after enrolling at Harvard, Hall was awarded a Ph.D. Because his dissertation used a problem typical of the "new" experimental psychology, it was decided to award his degree in psychology. His degree is considered to be the first Ph.D. in psychology awarded in the United States, perhaps the world.

After completing his degree, Hall returned to Germany, where he studied briefly under Wundt, as well as with several other prominent scientists of the day. During this period, he was exposed to the recapitulation theory of Ernst Haeckel, a disciple of Darwin, who believed that individual development mirrored the evolution of the species. Haeckel's theory integrated evolutionary principles and developmental processes, two areas in which Hall had great interest. Haeckel's theory had a great influence on Hall's later developmental beliefs.

Hall's second trip to Germany marked an important personal event. In 1879, he married Cornelia Fisher, an art student he had first met while at Antioch College. Hall then applied to several U.S. universities in the hope of securing a job teaching philosophy or psychology. He was not successful. Fearing he would never make money working in these areas, he turned to the subject of teaching and education, or pedagogy, which had become popular in Germany. He believed that psychology and evolutionary biology had important implications for education, and he hoped he could apply his psychological beliefs to educational reform in the United States. After his return to the United States, Hall was given the opportunity to lecture on philosophy and pedagogy in the Boston area, and his lectures proved to be very popular, especially with teachers.

In 1882, in a speech to the superintendents of the National Education Association, Hall called for child study to become the focus of the profession of pedagogy. He believed that child study would help teachers become enthusiastic in their teaching and sensitive to the needs of their students. Using questionnaires as a scientific method, he contributed to the child study movement by conducting one of the first empirical studies of children, entitled *The Contents of Children's Minds on Entering Schools* in 1883. The study was a popular success and gave him a great deal of visibility among educators. However, Hall wanted to explore a career in scientific psychology rather than in pedagogy, and, in the early 1880s, he accepted a position at Johns Hopkins

University as a professor of psychology and pedagogy.

At Johns Hopkins, Hall was finally in a financially secure position. This was especially important since, in addition to his wife, he now had two children. He proceeded to create the first experimental psychology laboratory in the United States. In addition, his interest in the biological determinants of development deepened. In 1887, Hall founded *The American Journal of Psychology*, a journal dedicated solely to the scientific study of psychology. Although it was eventually successful, the journal was a risky venture because psychology had not been widely accepted as a new science. He bankrolled the publication of the journal himself and this led to financial difficulties. In 1888, Hall left the university to become the founding president of Clark University in Worcester, Massachusetts.

Clark University was important for the emergence of psychology as an accepted discipline in the United States. Hall worked closely with Jonas Clark, the university's founder, in establishing its priorities. A graduate institution, Clark University eventually would boast one of the strongest psychology departments in America, thanks to Hall's resources and influence. Despite Hall's initial success at Clark, hard times were about to befall him. In 1890, while he was away from Worcester recovering from diphtheria, his wife and daughter were accidentally asphyxiated. Hall's parents had died a few years before and Hall was left alone with his nine-year-old son. His professional ambitions began to suffer as well. Jonas Clark, the university's benefactor, began to withdraw his emotional and financial support from the university. Despite Hall's efforts and the success of his second journal, *Pedagogical Seminary* (currently published as the *Journal of Genetic Psychology*), the university began to decline. When the school proved unable

to pay the professors a suitable salary, two-thirds left to join the faculty of the newly formed University of Chicago, taking 70 percent of the student body with them. This was a major blow to Hall, and left his professional reputation tarnished.

In 1892, worried that psychology was splitting into factions, Hall invited a group of influential psychologists to Clark University in hopes of unifying the discipline. This meeting resulted in the formation of the American Psychological Association, and Hall was named its first president. The association continues today as the largest and most influential organization of psychologists in the world. Despite the formation of the organization, Hall's influence in the psychological community continued to decrease. His criticism of the work of other influential psychologists led him to be perceived as egotistical and abrasive. Ironically, it was his return to the study of children that helped him to regain his prominent status.

Progress in the field of child study had slowed since Hall left it almost two decades before. Based on his physiological and evolutionary background, Hall maintained that heredity was primarily responsible for human development. Because genetics propelled development, he believed it was important for education and parenting to be adapted to the individual development of the child. He emphasized the importance of physical health and providing an environment that would allow for the expression of children's individual interests. Hall supported the use of drawings and play as a form of expression, predating their popularization as a therapy technique.

In 1904, Hall published *Adolescence: Its Psychology and Its Relations to Physiology, Anthropology, Sociology, Sex, Crime, Religion, and Education*. This book was the culmination of his years of research in the field of child study.

Adolescence reiterated Hall's belief in developmental psychology and implied that the job of parents and teachers was to cultivate an optimal environment that would maximize a child's natural development. Although the book was criticized by several colleagues (they found Hall's focus on sexual topics to be overdone), *Adolescence* was very popular and influential among both parents and teachers. Hall's work in the child study movement also influenced many of his students. One student, Lewis Terman, became a leader in the testing movement, and developed the most influential early intelligence test, the Stanford-Binet Intelligence Scale. Another student, Henry H. Goddard, worked with the disabled and was important in disseminating information about intelligence testing throughout the United States. A third student, Arnold Gesell, established norms for child development that are still in use today.

In 1909, Hall established the Children's Institute of Clark University, the first of its kind. The institute served as a center for child research, and contained a clinic and experimental school. Hall saw the institute as an opportunity to coordinate efforts among child welfare workers and scientists. Also in 1909, Hall invited Sigmund Freud to speak at the twentieth anniversary celebration of the founding of Clark University. Hall had become interested in Freud's work in child development, psychopathology, and sexuality, and was one of the first psychologists to offer courses on his writings in the United States. When Freud accepted, it marked his only visit to the United States and the beginning of worldwide recognition for his work in psychoanalysis.

Hall had spent his middle age studying child development. He spent the last years of his life dedicated to the study of aging. In 1920, he resigned as president of Clark University after thirty years, leaving a huge void at the university. In 1922,

he published *Senescence*, an examination of old age and death. Having studied both child development and the aging process, Hall was one of the first psychologists to study development over the life span. In 1923, he published his autobiography and was elected president of the American Psychological Association for the second time. He did not live to finish his term. G. Stanley Hall died on 24 April 1924 in Worcester, Massachusetts.

Matthew S. Broudy
John D. Hogan

References and further reading
Hall, G. Stanley. 1923. *Life and Confessions of a Psychologist.* New York: D. Appleton.
Hogan, John D. 1991. "G. Stanley Hall: The Founder of the Journal of Genetic Psychology." *Journal of Genetic Psychology* 152:397–403.
Ross, Dorothy. 1972. *G. Stanley Hall: The Psychologist as Prophet.* Chicago: University of Chicago Press.
Sanford, Edmund C. 1924. "Granville Stanley Hall." *American Journal of Psychology* 35:313–321.

Head Start, Early

Early Head Start (EHS) is a comprehensive preventive intervention program for low-income families and their children, prenatally to age three. Early Head Start was established through the Head Start Reauthorization Act of 1994, which designated funds to provide services to families and children for the developmental period prior to Head Start eligibility (Head Start targets families of preschoolers). The program, which began in 1995, is administered by the Administration on Children, Youth and Families of the U.S. Department of Health and Human Services.

Like Head Start, Early Head Start is a child development program designed to affect child, family, staff, and community development. The program takes a multidisciplinary approach toward intervention by incorporating health care, education, mental health, and social services into its activities.

Early Head Start is a child development program designed to affect child, family, staff, and community development. (Shirley Zeiberg/Photo Researchers)

Because Early Head Start is a downward extension of Head Start, background information on Head Start provides a useful context for understanding the philosophy and mission of Early Head Start. Funding for Head Start evolved out of the Economic Opportunity Act of 1964 in which Congress proclaimed a "war on poverty." Sargent Shriver, director of the Office of Economic Opportunity, launched the idea of a program that would improve the cognitive abilities and school readiness of preschool children from low-income households. The Head Start Planning Committee was thus formed in 1964. Its membership included physicians, a nurse, educators, clinical psychologists, and research psychologists.

Initially conceived as a summer program, Head Start became a nine-month, half-day program in 1966. By 1972, most Head Start programs adopted this schedule. Today, 80 percent of Head Start funding comes from the federal government; the remaining funding comes from local resources. (Zigler, Styfco, and Gilman)

Early Head Start was developed in part out of a concern that Head Start services began too late in children's lives—that is, already by three years of age, many children entering Head Start were found to be at a developmental disadvantage, partly due to new information from brain development research. In response to these developments, 3 percent of Head Start funds were set aside in 1995 to finance the first sixty-eight Early Head Start programs. In 1997, 4 percent of the Head Start budget was designated for Early Head Start, and 5 percent was earmarked in 1998. To date, funding for Early Head Start services has continued to grow.

The emphasis of Head Start on preschoolers rather than on infants and toddlers was somewhat explained by the social climate that existed at its conception over thirty years ago. In the 1960s, there existed widespread prejudice against out-of-home care for young infants. At that time, few programs existed for children younger than three years of age. Over the past several decades, several factors have conjoined that have firmly established the need for services for infants and toddlers: the increasing number of women with very young children who were entering the workforce; the growing recognition of the importance of experiences during children's first three years, as well as a greater acceptance of formal day care for infants and toddlers; the political shift in welfare policies, in which parents are mandated to work or enter training programs in order to receive benefits. These factors helped drive a need for programs to support parents with very young children. Under current policies in some states, parents are required to begin working when their children are as young as three years old.

Early Head Start enables programs to reach parents and provides the necessary support to lead them to self-sufficiency, when they may be more likely and able to involve themselves in program activities. Parents of very young children may greatly benefit from home visits and parent education during their children's early development, as parenting styles and routines are still in flux and less likely to be firmly established. Thus, Early Head Start provides a window of opportunity for low-income families to receive the services necessary to enable them to competently support their infants' emerging achievements.

Early Head Start is founded on the same guiding principles as Head Start, five of which are particularly noteworthy. First, Early Head Start asserts that in order to be most effective, early interventions must be aimed at the "whole child," incorporating children's nutrition, physical health, mental health, cognitive, and social-emotional needs in their design. To do so, Early Head Start programs provide a variety of services such as educational experiences for very young children, health screening and referrals, social services, mental health services, hot meals, nutrition education, and parental involvement.

Second, Early Head Start recognizes the importance of establishing *both* the child and the parents as foci of program intervention. Parents are provided guidance and information about competent parenting, early childhood education, social services, and the opportunity to be actively involved in the program through planning, administration, and engagement in daily activities. This emphasis on parent involvement in preschool programs had been unprecedented at the time of Head Start's conception and continues to be essential to the success of Head Start as well as Early Head Start.

Third, Early Head Start recognizes the various environmental influences that together contribute to infants' and toddlers' development. It is believed that in order to enhance children's developmental outcomes, parents, staff, neighborhoods, and communities must share and support the goals of the program.

Fourth, the philosophy of Early Head Start is "strength based"—emphasizing the many attributes and resources that children, families, and communities offer, rather than emphasizing their potential deficits. The program is designed to encourage successful experiences by maximizing opportunities for success; the aim is to empower families and children and to strengthen their motivation to succeed. This strength-based approach is reflected in the goals of center-based Early Head Start classrooms, as one example. Classroom goals include providing a flexible schedule to meet the needs of individual infants and toddlers, encouraging exploration of the environment, supporting creative and dramatic play, and providing maximum opportunities for the development of verbal skills and conversation.

Finally, Early Head Start is not a nationally standardized service program. Like Head Start, Early Head Start follows performance standards, but does so in a way that uniquely addresses the needs of its local community. Some sites offer center-based care. Other sites offer home-based intervention, particularly those in rural locations in which individuals live far apart and do not have ready access to transportation. Other sites combine a mixture of the two approaches, offering both center-based and home-based interventions. Still others offer group meetings at rotating locations, such as a neighbor's house or town hall. This type of grassroots approach to intervention allows individual communities to determine how to best meet the needs of their families. Again, however, regardless of the type of program, the goals and principles of all Early Head Starts remain the same: to provide comprehensive services to families in the areas of health, early education, mental health, and social services.

As yet the effectiveness of Early Head Start has not been systematically evaluated, although the effectiveness of Head Start has been demonstrated. Volumes of studies have documented the short-term benefits of Head Start, which include short-term gains on intelligence and achievement tests, improvements to the physical health of children, better school

adjustment for recent graduates, increased parental involvement and self-esteem, and increased motivation in both parents and children. In addition, teachers view children who have graduated from Head Start as more competent and their parents as more interested in their children's education. However, the long-term benefits of Head Start have not received the attention necessary to draw any firm conclusions about the program's continued effectiveness.

To what extent do benefits identified in Head Start programs extend downward to children and families enrolled in Early Head Start? Because it is such a new program, the answer to this question is not yet known. However, the effectiveness of Early Head Start is currently under investigation in an ongoing research and evaluation project. This Early Head Start Research and Evaluation Project represents a joint effort and partnership among members from the Administration on Children, Youth and Families (ACYF), seventeen local Early Head Start programs and their local researchers at neighboring universities, and the Early Head Start national evaluation contractor. The program evaluation involves approximately 3,000 children from seventeen diverse communities across the United States. The selected communities are meant to reflect the ethnic and geographic diversity of low-income families living in the United States. The EHS evaluation project has several goals, including: evaluation of program implementation; the assessment of effectiveness of the intervention; an understanding of the pathways that lead to desired outcomes in children; and provision of feedback to programs to help improve the quality of their services. Through the inclusion of diverse populations, locations, and community structures, the EHS research consortium will be able to explore variations across sites in the four areas of inquiry listed above. The hope is that the Early Head Start Research Evaluation will lead to quality improvements in EHS programs, as well as to a greater understanding of program practices that are most effective in benefiting families and children between birth and three years of age.

Joanne Roberts
Catherine S. Tamis-LeMonda
Esther Kresh

References and further reading
Zigler, E., and S. Muenchow. 1992. *Head Start: The Inside Story of America's Most Successful Educational Experiment.* New York: Basic Books.
Zigler, E., S. J. Styfco, and E. Gilman. 1993. "The National Head Start Program for Disadvantaged Preschoolers." In *Head Start and Beyond.* Edited by E. Zigler and S. J. Styfco. New Haven, CT: Yale University Press.

Home Schooling

Many parents choose to teach their children at home rather than send them to public or private schools. Some do so because they feel that schools undermine their religious faith, some (unschoolers) do so because they feel that the rigid academic and social structures of schools are harmful, and some do so because they perceive home schooling as the best way to educate a child with special needs.

There are two broad approaches to home schooling: curriculum based and child led. A parent can develop or buy a curriculum to follow at home. This type of home schooling may resemble traditional schooling based in the home. The children may follow a set schedule for doing schoolwork in different curriculum areas, and may participate in scheduled extracurricular activities. In the second approach, the parent implements child-led learning. This type of "unschooling" uses the child's natural curiosity and learning ability to direct daily activities. It assumes that children are naturally motivated to learn, and respects their

When implementing any type of home schooling, parents make individual decisions about the academic and social aspects of their child's schooling. (Laura Dwight)

judgment about what is important for them to learn at any given time. Parents serve as facilitators who provide materials, activities, and guidance, while following the child's interests. When the child is interested in learning something in an area in which the parent does not have expertise, the parent may arrange for classes, tutoring, or an apprenticeship.

When implementing any type of home schooling, parents make individual decisions about the academic and social aspects of their child's schooling, in contrast to traditional schooling, in which experts decide on these aspects, aimed at the "average" child. This individualization makes it possible for parents to meet the unique needs of their children. On the other hand, this necessitates parents educating themselves about academic and social needs and the means of meeting them.

Many people who are not familiar with home schooling are concerned that the children will not be appropriately socialized. However, the majority of parents who home school do so in order to provide social benefits to their children. Many religious parents, for example, are concerned about exposing their children to a variety of moral approaches that may contradict their church's teachings. In this case, they prefer that their children socialize with others of the same religious faith. Unschoolers, on the other hand, are often concerned about the coercive social practices of the public schools. They prefer that their children socialize with others of various ages and backgrounds, and avoid an emphasis on conformity. Overall, home-schooled children fare at least as well as traditionally schooled children in social skills.

In the academic arena home-schooled children, on average, perform better on standardized achievement tests than traditionally schooled children. Of course, this above-average performance may not be entirely due to the home schooling itself. Parents who have the motivation and ability to home school are different in many ways from the "average" parent. Their children might have done well anyway. But research clearly shows that small class sizes allow for individualized instruction and lead to higher achievement, and home schools typically have extremely small class sizes.

Although schools systems are not obligated to provide materials and supports for home schoolers, many do. And there are many resources available in communities to support parents who wish to home school. Local public school districts, public libraries, and community colleges and universities are all excellent starting points. Material costs of home schooling are generally significantly below what either a private school or a public school spends per child. However, the home-schooling family must also consider the cost of one or both parents giving up paid work to educate the children. This can be a considerable cost, both financially and professionally.

States vary widely in their requirements for home schoolers. Some states simply require parents to notify the state department of education that they intend to home school their children, while others require curriculum approval, standardized achievement testing, and/or parents who are certified teachers. Outcomes for children who are home schooled do not appear to vary depending on the level of state regulation. Parents who are interested in home schooling would be well advised to contact both their state's department of education and a local support group to find out the requirements.

Catherine A. Fiorello

References and further reading
Bell, Debra. 1997. *The Ultimate Guide to Homeschooling.* La Lergne, TN: Word Books, distrib. by Ingram.
Griffith, Mary. 1998. *The Unschooling Handbook: How to Use the Whole World as Your Child's Classroom.* 2d ed. Rocklin, CA: Prima Publishers.
Growing without Schooling (magazine), 2269 Massachusetts Ave., Cambridge, MA 02140.
Moore, Raymond S., and Dorothy N. Moore. 1994. *The Successful Homeschool Family Handbook: A Creative and Stress-Free Approach to Homeschooling.* Surrey, UK: Thomas Nelson.
National Home Education Research Institute, P.O. Box 13939, Salem, OR 97309.

I

Immigrant Families

Immigrant families, in which one or more parents were born outside of the United States, represent one of the fastest growing groups of families in this country. In 1997, the children from immigrant families represented almost one-fifth of the total population of American children. Today's immigrant families exhibit greater ethnic, socioeconomic, and linguistic diversity than ever before in American history. Unlike the European-dominated immigration in the early 1900s, the majority of recent immigrant families come from Asian and Latin American countries such as Mexico, the Philippines, El Salvador, Vietnam, Cuba, and Korea. Though diverse in their backgrounds, most immigrant parents share an emphasis on the following themes in their child-rearing practices: a strong value placed on education, a sense of duty and obligation to the family, and the importance of maintaining the family's cultural identity.

Ethnic, Socioeconomic, and Linguistic Backgrounds

Today's immigrant families hail from 170 different nations. Nevertheless, the immigrant population is not equally distributed according to national origin. In recent decades, the number of immigrants from more-developed countries has declined, while the number from developing countries has risen. In addition, the sending countries' geographical proximity and historical relationship with the United States influence the likelihood and ease of immigration. The new immigrants tend to be dominated by those from Latin America and Asia, with these regions accounting for over two-thirds of the foreign born. Mexico is by far the country of origin for the largest number of immigrants, representing over 25 percent of the foreign-born population. The largest Asian group consists of immigrants from the Philippines, followed by those from China, India, and Vietnam. Recent years have also witnessed an increase in immigration from countries in the Caribbean, which now contribute one-tenth of the current foreign-born population. (U.S. Bureau of the Census, 1997)

Contrary to popular conception, great socioeconomic diversity exists among immigrant families. On the one hand, more than one-third of the foreign-born population has not completed high school, as compared to only one-sixth of the American-born population. On the other hand, immigrants are as equally likely as American-born adults to have received bachelor's and graduate or professional degrees. This apparent contradiction is due to the differences that exist among the foreign-born according to their national origin. Immigrants from Asia tend to be more educated and occupationally skilled than those from Latin America and the Caribbean. Dramatic

311

Most immigrant parents place an emphasis on education in their child-rearing practices.
(Skjold Photographs)

exceptions to these regional differences can be found in the difficult economic situations of the refugees from Southeast Asia that were admitted to the United States under special humanitarian provisions. Only one-half of the immigrants from Laos and Cambodia were in the labor force in 1990. Each group had a poverty rate of approximately 40 percent, and almost half received some form of public assistance. (U.S. Bureau of the Census, 1997)

In terms of language use, almost 80 percent of the foreign-born speak a language other than English at home. Even so, only one-quarter of those who speak a foreign language at home report being poor English speakers. The rate of English proficiency can vary dramatically according to the immigrants' national origin. Almost one-half of those from Mexico, China, and El Salvador indicate a poor

knowledge of the English language. The corresponding rates for India and the Philippines, former colonies of Britain and the United States, are less than 10 percent. (Stevens, 1994) Proficiency is also associated with socioeconomic background, as immigrants with more years of education tend to possess a greater command of English.

Child-Rearing Practices

Like most parents, those from immigrant families place the health and well-being of their children as the primary focus of their child rearing. In addition, the parents tend to emphasize goals that appear to be characteristic of immigrant families. First, regardless of their socioeconomic or ethnic background, many immigrant children find themselves in a family environment that is strongly supportive of education. Parents as diverse as those from Central America, Indochina, the Caribbean, and India place a great importance on the academic success of their children. Immigrant parents believe education to be the most significant way for their children to improve their status in life. Many parents encourage their children to overcome any setbacks they might face in school because their educational opportunities in the United States are superior to those available in their home countries. The encouragement and aspirations of immigrant parents may be the most important ways they can influence their children's education. Because of their long work schedules or discomfort with speaking English, foreign-born parents are less likely to become involved in their children's school lives through more formal mechanisms such as volunteering at school.

Second, many immigrant families come from cultural traditions that emphasize family members' responsibilities and obligations to one another. These traditions of family support and assistance take on an immediate and practical importance for immigrant families. Parents and other adult family members often know very little about the workings of their new societies. Some of the new arrivals can join existing immigrant communities, but many others have left behind extended family and friends in their native countries. Foreign-born parents often must take on low-level occupations because of a lack of education or a reluctance of American employers to recognize the training that the parents received in their native countries. These limitations present immigrant families with the very real need for their children to contribute to the support and maintenance of the household. Attending American schools, children tend to assimilate to American society more quickly than their parents. As a result, children often help their families with negotiating the official tasks

and more informal demands of the new country. The children from immigrant families feel a profound sense of duty and obligation to their families, both in the present and in the future. For example, they are more likely than those from American-born families to believe that they should help their parents financially and have their parents live with them when the children become adults.

Children from immigrant families view school success as one of the most important ways that they can assist their families. Parent often emigrate to the United States in order to provide their children with better opportunities, including the chance to pursue education through and even beyond secondary school. Some students say that they would feel guilty about not trying hard in school, given the many personal and professional sacrifices their parents made to come of this country. Other children believe that their educational attainment will help them to secure employment and support the family in the future. Students from immigrant families often cite such indebtedness and responsibility as their primary motivations to do well in school. In addition, the obligations associated with immigrant families provide children with integral roles within the family. These roles delineate a set of expectations, such as supporting the family's reputation and well-being, that may keep immigrant children from engaging in activities that would disappoint or embarrass the family in the larger immigrant community.

Finally, parents from immigrant families encourage their children to maintain their cultural identities at the same time they are becoming full members of American society. Virtually all immigrant parents emphasize the need for their children to become fluent in English, but they also encourage their children to retain the family's native language. Despite the pressure to conform to Americanized ethnic and racial categories, immigrant families and their children tend to avoid such labels and instead retain their original cultural identities. Immigrant families relate more to nationalistic identities, such as Mexican or Chinese, than to pan-ethnic or hyphenated labels such as Latino or Asian American. Such cultural identifications have important implications for children's adjustment, and a bicultural orientation of maintaining cultural traditions while adopting specific American norms may be associated with positive developmental outcomes. Some observers have suggested that children with a strong identification with their family's cultural traditions tend to do better in school and are less likely to become involved in risky behavior.

Andrew Fuligni

References and further reading

Booth, Alan, Ann C. Crouter, and Nancy Landale, eds. 1997. *Immigration and the Family: Research and Policy on U.S. Immigrants.* Mahwah, NJ: Lawrence Earlbaum Associates.

Stevens, G. 1994. "Immigration, Emigration, Language Acquisition, and the English Proficiency of Immigrants in the United States." In *Immigration and Ethnicity: The Integration of America's Newest Immigrants.* Edited by B. Edmonston and J. S. Passel. Washington D.C.: Urban Institute Press.

U.S. Bureau of the Census. 1997. *Current Population Reports: The Foreign-Born Population: 1996.* Washington D.C.: Government Printing Office.

Zhou, Min, and Carl L. Bankston. 1998. *Growing Up American: How Vietnamese Children Adapt to Life in the United States.* New York: Russell Sage Foundation.

In Vitro Fertilization (IVF)

In vitro fertilization (IVF)—fertilization that takes place outside of the mother's body—is one of several forms of assisted reproductive technology (ART) that is used by fewer than 5 percent of contem-

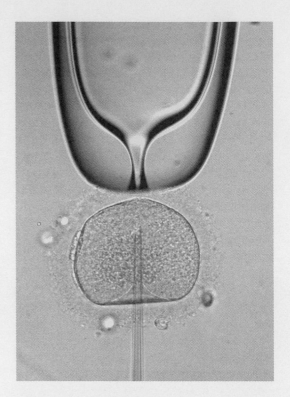

Light micrograph showing a needle injecting the DNA of a sperm into a human egg during in vitro fertilization (CC Studio/Science Photo Library)

porary infertile couples in the United States. (Komaroff, 1999) This technique has become increasingly common for women with blocked or damaged Fallopian tubes and for men with sperm problems. The "test-tube baby" (as the first of these, Louise Brown, was called in 1978) is technically a misnomer because the fertilization is seldom performed in either a test tube or in vitro (in glass). Specifically, male sperm is added to a plastic dish containing the female egg and the dish is placed in an incubator (observed at twelve- and twenty-four-hour intervals to assess how many eggs have been fertilized and whether the embryos are dividing normally). Usually two to four embryos are used in one treatment cycle (to increase the chances of success); if more have been fertilized, they are often frozen for later use. A catheter (thin plastic tube) is then placed inside the uterus and the embryos are placed through the catheter into the uterus. To help an embryo implant and grow in the lining of the uterus, the female is prescribed progesterone for several weeks or months. Pregnancy cannot be determined conclusively for about ten days, at which point a developing placenta secretes human chorionic gonadotropin (hCG) into the female's bloodstream.

Conception and live birth rates through IVF compare favorably with those for spontaneous conception, but decline with the mother's age. Although children conceived through IVF tend to be smaller than average, their mental development is within the normal range and their head circumference is normal. Further, recent research has documented no subsequent differences in children's emotions, behavior, and relationships with parents related to family types that included children conceived naturally, through IVF, through donor insemination (DI), or adopted. However, the quality of parenting in families with a child conceived by assisted conception (IVF, DI, adoption) was shown to be superior to that of parents with naturally conceived children.

IVF is extremely expensive, with an average cost of $72,000 per successful pregnancy. (Neumann, Gharib, and Weinstein, 1994) A single attempt—covered by some, but not all, insurance companies—costs approximately $8,000 and usually does not produce a child (the success rate is about one birth in seven attempts). (Tan, Royston, Campbell, Jacobs, Betts, Mason, and Edwards, 1992) Related to this, as well as to the risks of miscarriage (22 percent) and multiple births (30 to 50 percent) that are increased

when using IVF, psychological intervention (e.g., therapy, group support) is often helpful for couples undergoing this procedure and thereafter.

In addition to IVF, other assisted reproductive technologies include: zygote intrafallopian transfer (ZIFT), which is similar to IVF except that the embryos are transferred into the Fallopian tubes through laparoscopic surgery; gamete intrafallopian transfer (GIFT), which is similar to IVF and ZIFT except that mature eggs are not fertilized by sperm in a laboratory dish, but immediately placed by laparoscopy into the Fallopian tubes; and intracytoplasmic sperm injection (ICSI), which uses micromanipulation techniques to insert a single sperm directly into an egg (that was induced and retrieved as in IVF), and any fertilized eggs that grow into embryos are then placed in the uterus. Approximately 16,000 babies are born each year in the United States from some form of ART. Success rates are higher for ZIFT, GIFT, and ICSI (each results in about one birth in five pregnancy attempts) than they are for IVF (one in seven). (Komaroff, 1999)

Complementing these assisted reproductive technologies are other alternative modes of conception. These include: artificial insemination by a donor (AID, injection of sperm into a woman's cervix, accounting for 65,000 births per year); ovum transfer (implantation of a fertilized donor egg from another woman in the recipient mother's uterus); and surrogate motherhood (by mutual agreement before conception, a pregnancy carried to term by a woman impregnated by the prospective father—usually through AID—who then gives the infant to the father and his wife).

ART as well as these other forms of conception have raised many personal and ethical questions that must be addressed by both the individuals involved and society at large. Some of these questions include: What happens to embryos conceived in vitro and frozen indefinitely when a couple divorces? Do embryos conceived in vitro have the right to be implanted rather than kept frozen indefinitely or destroyed after a time limit? Is surrogate motherhood analogous to baby selling? Should all forms of alternative conception be available to everyone, regardless of marital status, socioeconomic status, sexual orientation, age, and/or motives for wanting a child? We, as a society, will probably struggle with such issues for some time to come because, as long as there are people who want children but are unable to conceive them, human ingenuity and technology will most probably refine these techniques and develop even more.

Jack Demick

See also Infertility

References and further reading
Brandes, Joseph M., Anat Scher, Judy Itzkovitz, Israel Thaler, Miriam Sarid, and Ruth Gershoni-Baruch. 1992. "Growth and Development of Children Conceived by In Vitro Fertilization. *Pediatrics* 90:424–429.
Crockin, Susan L. 1993. "The Legal Response to the New Reproductive Technologies." Pp. 407–411 in *Technology and Infertility: Clinical, Psychosocial, Legal and Ethical Aspects.* Edited by Machelle M. Seibel, Ann A. Kiesling, Joseph Bernstein, and Seymour R. Levin. New York: Springer-Verlag.
Golombok, Susan, R. Cook, Alison Bish, and Clare Murray. 1995. "Families Created by the New Reproductive Technologies: Quality of Parenting and Social and Emotional Development of the Children." *Child Development* 66:285–298.
Komaroff, Anthony L. 1999. *Harvard Medical School Family Health Guide.* New York: Simon & Schuster.
Neumann, Peter J., Soheyla D. Gharib, and Milton D. Weinstein. 1994. "The Cost of a Successful Delivery with In Vitro Fertilization." *New England Journal of Medicine* 331:239–243.
Tan, Sean L., Patrick Royston, Simon Campbell, Howard S. Jacobs, June Betts, Brendan Mason, and Robert G. Edwards. 1992. "Cumulative Conception and Live Birth after In Vitro Fertilization. *Lancet* 339:1090–1094.

Incarcerated Parents

Incarcerated parents are those parents who are in prison and have children under eighteen years of age. The large, and growing, population of incarcerated parents in the United States is faced with a set of concerns above and beyond those of other prisoners and parents. As parents, they worry about the effect their incarceration will have on their children and their relationship with their children. In addition, incarcerated parents are confronted with the challenge of negotiating between their dual identity as prisoner and parent and proving to society that they have the right and ability to care for their children. Due to parental incarceration, children of incarcerated parents struggle with a number of challenges and have been found to have problems in school and in their emotional reactions to their parents' incarceration.

Incarcerated Parents

It is difficult to accurately determine the number of incarcerated parents in the United States. Estimates have been made: in 1992, there were approximately 690,000 incarcerated fathers (56 percent of incarcerated males), and in 1993 there were approximately 67,500 incarcerated mothers (75 percent of incarcerated females). (U.S. Department of Justice, 1993) These numbers do not include the number of mothers and fathers who had been previously incarcerated.

The demographic profile of incarcerated parents is similar to the general incarcerated population: they have lower levels of education, job skills, and incomes; are predominantly single parents; many have histories of substance abuse and addiction, have been victims of physical and/or sexual abuse, and have had childhoods filled with instability and trauma.

Despite numerous shared characteristics between male and female prisoners, gender differences do exist. Incarcerated mothers are less likely to be married, more likely to be the primary caregivers for their children prior to incarceration, and are usually arrested for less-violent crimes than incarcerated fathers. They are also more concerned with maintaining personal relationships both inside and outside of prison and about long-term damage to outside relationships. This concern is exacerbated for incarcerated mothers, whose primary relationships in jeopardy are those with their children. Even though differences exist, men and women prisoners (both parents and non-parents) have historically been treated alike. Fortunately, new programs and legislation aimed at addressing the special needs of incarcerated men, women, fathers, and mothers have initiated change in these trends.

Prisons vary enormously in the programs and services offered to incarcerated parents. Some prisons offer services aimed at strengthening family relationships, such as parent education and support groups, on-site nurseries for newborn babies, child-oriented visiting facilities, and half-way houses where infants and mothers may live for the first few months after birth. On the other hand, some prisons offer no services for incarcerated parents and/or have policies that hinder the maintenance of relationships. For example, physical contact during visits may not be allowed, time allowed for visitation may be limited, visiting rooms may be uninviting for children, prenatal care allowed may be minimal, and newborn babies may be removed from mothers directly after birth.

Maintaining an adequate relationship with their children is one of the primary concerns facing incarcerated parents. Visitation and other forms of communication are central to maintaining relationships while in prison. However, many obstacles stand in the way of routine visitation, such as loss of custody, geographic location of the prison, lack of transportation, and prison policies that hinder the quality and amount of time allowed for visitation. Incarcerated parents' dependence on other people to maintain a relationship with their children often compounds these problems. A child's current caregiver may not want to bring the child to visit a parent for any number of reasons, including not wanting to upset the child, being angry at the parent for his/her behavior, or seeing visits as inconvenient.

It has been found that the amount of involvement parents have with their children during incarceration corresponds, in part, to the amount of involvement in the children's life prior to incarceration. Increased involvement prior to incarceration has been associated with increased number of visits, more involvement in decision making, and the maintenance of stronger relationships. Fathers are usually less involved, if at all, with their children's lives before incarceration, and as a result typically have less contact and less involvement with their children during and after incarceration.

Where, and with whom, their children will live during parental incarceration forms another major concern of incarcerated parents. In addition, permanent custody of children is often threatened during incarceration. In many states, parental rights can be lost if a parent fails to sustain an "adequate" relationship with his or her children. However, "adequate" relationships are difficult to maintain while in prison due to the numerous forces intentionally or unintentionally hindering relationships. In addition, parents may lack the material resources required to regain custody of their children when first released from prison, such as a job, money, and a home.

The tangible worries of maintaining relationships with, and custody of, one's children is further compounded by the constant battle incarcerated parents face in having to prove their competency as parents. Undeniably, incarceration is usually the result of participating in behaviors that do not fit the ideal image of a parent, such as drug addiction, theft, or prostitution. However, participation in such activities does not necessarily equate with such sentiments as "bad parent," "lacking concern about children," and "children are better off without them." Holding incarcerated parents to middle-class standards of good parenting is unreasonable. Furthermore, there is no evidence that incarcerated parents are worse caregivers than other parents of similar race and socioeconomic status and/or exposed to similar traumatic experiences. In addition, loss of a primary caregiver or salient adult role model is always disruptive to children's lives. Though children may feel confused, or even resentful, about their parent's incarceration and subsequent separation, they have been found to experience loss and sadness. Moreover, incarcerated parents may be aware of their children's needs and have appropriate concerns about their children's welfare, but may lack the material and/or emotional resources necessary to provide for them.

Using the incarcerated parent's desire to be a good parent is one method of having an impact on the rehabilitation process. Many times, the hope of regaining the parental role and responsibilities serves as an impetus for change. Instead of making incarcerated parents feel as though their parental identity is being taken away, perhaps emphasizing training in good parenting skills, the development of a parental identity, and the means for obtaining the material and emotional resources needed to be "good parents" would benefit both parents and children.

Children of Incarcerated Parents

It has been estimated that there are approximately 1.53 million minor children with incarcerated parents in the United States. (Gabel and Johnston, 1995) Parental criminal involvement and forced parent-child separation is surrounded by a myriad of other risk factors (e.g., parental substance abuse, single parenthood, low socioeconomic status) that combine to form one of the highest multiple risk contexts conceivable for children of all ages. Exposure to this high-risk environment may not foster healthy development in children and may instead result in behaviors similar to those of their parents, helping continue a cycle of low socioeconomic status, violence, drug addiction, and incarceration. As a result, it is important for researchers and policymakers to focus on better understanding the effect of parental incarceration on children in order to implement effective prevention and intervention programs.

Like their parents, children of incarcerated parents face a unique set of circumstances and subsequent issues. Namely, children of incarcerated parents confront any or all of the following: numerous living placements (including foster care); separation from siblings; exposure to crime and the law from an early age; the stigma and shame of having a parent who has been incarcerated; deception about the facts of their parents' incarceration; and trauma caused by witnessing their parents' incarceration, separation from their parents, or any of the behaviors stemming from their parents' illegal activity. These variables, in addition to the risk factors present in their lives irrespective of the incarceration, affect children of different ages in different and complex ways.

The research available about the behavioral, emotional, and psychological outcomes of children of incarcerated parents is sparse. However, it has been found that children of incarcerated parents exhibit a variety of problems related to school, such as decreased achievement and increased behavior problems. It has also been illustrated that children of incarcerated parents show some degree of sadness, confusion, and anxiety regarding their parents' incarceration.

A developmental analysis has been proposed by researchers to hypothesize the potential effects of parental incarceration on children. The risk to child development may begin before birth with prenatal stresses related to incarceration and criminal activity, such as exposure to drugs. In addition, mothers could be exposed to inadequate prenatal care while in prison and perhaps worse care if not incarcerated. During the first two years of life, separation from parents potentially places both the formation of attachment bonds and the development of trust at risk in children of incarcerated parents. However, few direct effects of incarceration per se have been found on infants' physical and intellectual development.

During early childhood, the development of increased autonomy and a sense of initiative are the primary developmental tasks. However, the traumatic experiences of parental criminal activity, incarceration, and parent-child separation may inhibit this development. Because the child does not yet view himself or herself as a separate entity from the parent, he or she may experience the trauma of his or her parent as his or her own and/or feel guilty and responsible for the parent's problems. Furthermore, the long-term effects of traumatic experiences may be more enduring when they occur during this stage because young children perceive and remember traumatic events, but are unable to process and adjust to the trauma without adult assistance.

The primary developmental tasks of middle childhood center around preparing to work with peers, becoming more

socially aware, and succeeding in school. In addition, children's self-esteem and approval of peers gain more importance. As a result, the stigma and shame associated with parental incarceration may become more salient. In addition, the effects of parental separation could be critical at this age because children potentially experience multiple living placements outside of their homes and lack the consistent parental role models necessary for modeling socially appropriate behaviors. As children navigate school, behavioral reactions to trauma and/or separation from parents may begin to interfere with school-related behaviors and outcomes.

By early adolescence, children of incarcerated parents potentially have had many experiences with crime, arrest, and incarceration. During this period, the development of behavior patterns oriented toward achieving long-term goals could be disrupted in a variety of ways. First, normal adolescent limit testing may become exaggerated because adolescents can begin to understand their parents' behaviors leading to their incarceration, resulting in decreased respect for their parental authority. Second, parent-child separation is suspected to bring about role reversal during parental absence. Third, adolescents may begin to engage in antisocial behaviors to satisfy their need for risk taking, to reduce anxiety, and to gain peer acceptance. These antisocial patterns potentially emerge because traumatized adolescents may lack the organized behavioral and social skills, and communities may lack the resources, to constructively structure their time.

In late adolescence, the cumulative effects of repeated exposure to crime and trauma might begin to appear and affect the developmental tasks of identity formation, transition into adult work, and the development of successful relationships. As in early adolescence, antisocial behavior patterns possibly emerge as traumatized children try to organize their emotions and behaviors. When good outlets for these emotions/behaviors do not exist, they may be channeled into maladaptive coping strategies such as illegal and/or gang activity. These could follow directly into adult crime and incarceration, continuing or beginning the intergenerational cycle of crime, drug abuse, and incarceration.

Rebecca B. Silver
Cynthia García Coll

References and further reading
Baunich, Phyllis Jo. 1985. *Mothers in Prison.* New Brunswick, NJ: Transaction Books.
Bloom, Barbara, and David Steinhart. 1993. *Why Punish the Children?: A Reappraisal of the Children of Incarcerated Mothers in America.* San Francisco: National Council on Crime and Delinquency.
Gabel, Katherine, and Denise Johnston. 1995. *Children of Incarcerated Parents.* New York: Lexington Books.
Garcia Coll, Cynthia, Jean Baker Miller, Jacqueline P. Fields, and Betsy Matthews. 1997. "The Experiences of Women in Prison: Implications for Services and Prevention." Pp. 11–28 in *Breaking the Rules: Women in Prison and Feminist Therapy, Women and Therapy Special Edition.* Haworth Press.
U.S. Department of Justice. 1993. *Prisoners in 1992.* Report No. NCJ-141874. Washington, DC: Bureau of Justice Statistics.

Infanticide

Literally, *infanticide* means the killing of an infant, but the word is used with different interpretations among academic disciplines and among criminal codes of different places. In certain countries such as Canada and England, although not in the United States, "infanticide" is a crime distinguished in law from other homicides. In Canada, the Criminal Code limits the crime of infanticide to the killing of a newborn infant by the mother if "she is not fully recovered from the effects of giving birth to the child and by reason thereof or of the effect of lactation consequent on the birth of the child her mind is then disturbed." (Martin's Annual Criminal Code § 216, Canada Law Book, Inc.) The special category of homicides for mothers who have killed their infants bespeaks a moral sentiment that such crimes should be distinguished from killings of infants by others.

Maternally perpetrated infanticide is not universally criminalized. In traditional nonstate societies it is widely considered an unfortunate but understandable recourse in some circumstances. The ethnographic reports of a worldwide probability sample of societies in the *Human Relations Area Files* indicate reasons or circumstances for infanticide. In a tabulation of all professed rationales for infanticide that were described in thirty-nine of sixty societies, half of the 112 reasons could be categorized as maternal incapacity to cope with the demands of child rearing because of illness, famine, lack of paternal assistance, a still-nursing older sibling, or the birth of twins. (Daly and Wilson, 1988) The remaining reasons covered inappropriate paternity and low probability of the infant surviving because of illness or deformity. The expressed rationales represent "rational reproductive decisions" even when buttressed with superstitious justifications. The pragmatic element in these neonaticidal decisions is illustrated by the cross-cultural correlates of the practice of infanticide after the birth of twins: killing of both twins is extremely rare, and the routine killing of one is virtually confined to societies in which the burden of maternity is unrelieved by accessible female relatives or other social supports.

Maternal youth is another risk factor in traditional and modern societies. A very detailed anthropological study of the incidence and determinants of infanticide in a population of South American natives during a period of adverse social and economic circumstances revealed that older Ayoreo mothers were less likely to dispose of newborns than younger mothers. In modern industrialized nations, like the United States, Canada, and England, mothers are also less likely to commit infanticide with increasing age. The decreased risk with older mothers has been interpreted as reflecting a life-span developmental change in women's emotional commitment to their newborns as their capacity to produce additional future children diminishes.

Female-selective infanticide has been the object of considerable study and debate, although it is by no means typical of societies in which infanticide occurs. In complex, stratified societies, the practice is status graded, with the upper classes more likely to eliminate daughters, while concentrating investments in sons. In many societies, there is a general tendency to favor sons over daughters.

In some nonhuman animals, such as group-living lions and Hanuman langur monkeys, nursing infants are routinely killed by the adult male upon defeating and usurping the resident male, who presumably was the sire of those infants. This has been called sexually selected infanticide because of the reproductive benefits accruing to the new male. These benefits derive from destroying the offspring of a rival and from the fact that the lactating females of the group he has taken over will be able to conceive sooner than if the females had continued nursing. Similarly, in several biparental bird species, new mates are likely to kill the dependent young of the female's prior mate; however, tolerance and care of these "step-offspring" are more common outcomes. Various combinations of factors such as sex ratio imbalances in the population, multiple nestings in a breeding season, and season-to-season persistence of pair bonds affect the probability of a new mate killing or investing in a female's dependent young.

Human infants, like many other species, do not commonly reside with a stepparent, but when they do the risk of being killed is much higher. Homicides of infants and toddlers perpetrated by men in the role of stepfather do not exhibit the hallmark features of sexually selected infanticide observed in lions and langurs. The human cases are much more likely to be the culmination of a pattern of episodic neglect and abuse interspersed with periods of adequate care.

Rates of maternally perpetrated infanticide in modern nation-states are extremely low. Data collected by the FBI indicate that about two babies were killed by their mothers within the first year of life for every 100,000 born in 1990 in the United States. However, such estimates are questionable for a number of reasons, most notably because an unknown proportion of such infanticides are successfully disguised as natural deaths.

Margo Wilson
Martin Daly

References and further reading
Blaffer Hrdy, S. 1999. *Mother Nature.* New York: Pantheon Books.
Daly, M., and M. Wilson. 1988. *Homicide.* New York: Aldine de Gruyter.
———. 1999. *The Truth about Cinderella.* New Haven, CT: Yale University Press.
Dickemann, M. 1979. "Female Infanticide, Reproductive Strategies, and Social Stratification: A Preliminary Model." Pp. in *Evolutionary Biology and Human Social Behavior.* Edited by N. A. Chagnon and W. Irons. North Scituate, MA: Duxbury Press.
Granzberg, G. 1973. "Twin Infanticide—A Cross-Cultural Test of a Materialistic Explanation." *Ethos* 1:405–412.
Hausfater, G., and S. B. Hrdy, eds. 1984. *Infanticide.* New York: Aldine de Gruyter.
Parmigiani, S., and F. S. vom Saal, eds. 1994. *Infanticide and Parental Care.* Chur, Switzerland: Harwood Academic Publishers.
Rohwer, S., J. C. Herron, and M. Daly. 1999. "Stepparental Behavior as Mating Effort in Birds and Other Animals." *Evolution & Human Behavior* 20:367–390.
Scheper-Hughes, N. 1985. "Culture, Scarcity, and Maternal Thinking: Maternal

Detachment and Infant Survival in a Brazilian Shantytown." *Ethos* 13:291–317.

Infants, Parenting of

During infancy, children change dramatically, going from helpless and totally dependent beings to being able to move around, communicate some of their needs, make things happen, and recognize and seek out their primary caregivers. Development can be divided into a number of areas: fine motor (what the child can so with small muscle groups including picking up and banging things together); cognitive (such as understanding object permanence and how to make things happen); language and communication (including receptive language or what the child understands, and expressive communication or how the infant gestures); emotional development (emotions and their regulation) and social development (attachment and relatedness). Knowing what infants need to learn in these areas of development can inform parents of toys to buy and games to play with their infants, but even more useful is knowledge of the major overall gains that infants need to make in the first year for development to progress optimally. These qualitative shifts or reorganizations allow for increasing adaptation to the environment and can be helped to develop significantly by the experiences that parents provide for their infants. In the first year there are five major achievements that occur.

First, infants establish a predictable eating and sleeping schedule and begin gradually to be able to calm themselves or self-quiet for brief periods. Second, infants have periods of interest and responsiveness in the world, particularly with parents who respond to their social overtures. Third, an attachment is developed with primary caregivers. Fourth, the infant explores the world with curiosity and excitement and is more alert and goal directed. Fifth, the infant enjoys "making things happen" and moving around in the world.

For these developmental gains to happen, infants need a number of types of responses from their parents, and certain critical parenting principles are important to practice in the infancy period. First, parents need to get to know their infant's temperament or behavioral style and learn to adapt to it. For example, some infants may be hypersensitive to touch, loud noises, or bright lights, and the environment should be adjusted to protect infants from excessive stimulation. Some infants may be more intense than others and need more soothing and calming. Finding the best way to calm an infant is critical. Second, parents need to provide infants with plenty of experiences of touch and physical contact. Touch and physical contact can enhance the development of infants. In fact, touch in the form of massage improves weight gain in premature infants and holding upright can encourage alertness in young infants. Of course, if an infant, is hypersensitive to touch, a special type of deep pressure may be necessary. Holding and rocking are also important means of soothing and calming, particularly if the infant is fussy and crying. Third, infants need toys and activities to encourage gross and fine motor control. From very early it is important that infants are provided with toys and activities that give them a chance to learn new skills and practice them. Fourth, infants need to receive comforting when they are hurting, ill, or upset. When infants are responded to predictably they learn that they are safe and become secure in knowing that parents will be there when they are needed. After about eight weeks of age infants can begin to learn to self-calm or to self-regulate. Waiting for a few minutes when an infant begins to fuss and possibly rubbing his or her back or talking calmly

Parents interacting with their infant son (Laura Dwight)

or watching to see if he or she self-calms by sucking a hand or finger or gazing at an object can sometimes delay the need for feeding, especially if the infant was only just fed. Responding to and noticing infants is crucial. It is important that babies are attended to when they just need attention, are bored, or need someone to share a moment with. With this kind of sharing of interactions, as well as being responded to when upset, a secure attachment relationship can be established. It is important to use activities and games that both infant and parent enjoy. These times can be brief, but they need to be warm, intimate, and to allow the infant to take the lead sometimes to be meaningful. Fifth, it is important to provide infants with a sense of predictability and safety. Gradually beginning to establish a predictable routine of eating and sleeping for baby is important. While not insisting on a rigid schedule, providing a calm and consistent routine of bathing and feeding will gradually help the baby learn to self-calm and eventually to establish a regular schedule. This will give the baby a sense of consistency and safety. Equally important is the need to provide infants with a safe environment including adequate food and housing. Infants also need to be protected from excessive noise and stimulation and especially from any violence between parent and from abuse, sexual, physical, or emotional.

If parents are depressed, angry, or overwhelmed or if it is very difficult for an infant to settle or alternatively to engage in periods of responsiveness, parents should seek help from their physician, public health unit, or mental health center.

In providing these types of interactions, parents fill a number of roles. First, a parent is a comforter and nurturer, comforting

Parenting Infants from Birth to Twelve Months

Development

Birth to seven months
- Infants establish a predictable eating and sleeping schedule and self-calm for brief periods
- Infants have periods of interest and responsiveness in the world

Seven to twelve months
- An attachment is developed with primary caregivers
- Explores the world with curiosity and excitement and is increasingly goal directed
- Enjoys "making things happen" and moving around in the world

Parenting

Principle 1: Get to know baby's temperament and behavioral style and adapt to it.
Principle 2: Provide baby with lots of experiences of touch and physical contact.
Principle 3: Provide toys and activities to encourage gross and fine motor control.
Principle 4: Provide baby with comforting when baby is hurting, ill, or upset.
Principle 5: Respond to and notice infants.
Principle 6: Provide predictability and let baby know she will be safe.

Toys

Birth to seven months
- Mobiles
- Musical box
- Foot finders of foot socks
- Mirror
- Squeezy toys and rattles
- Ball

Seven to twelve months
- Board and cloth books
- Activity centers
- Pop-up toys
- Suction toys
- Roly-poly toys
- Stacking rings
- Shape sorters
- Large peg-boards
- Toy telephone

Games and Activities

Birth to seven months
- "Ride a horse"
- "Row, row , row your boat" with baby on your knee
- Massage baby
- Put toy in her hand and encourage her to reach
- Singing and talking during dressing and diapering
- Tummy kisses

Seven to twelve months
- "Itsy bitsy spider" with actions
- "This little piggy went to market"
- Peekaboo
- Hiding objects for baby to find
- "I'm going to get you"
- "Pat-a-cake"
- Dance with baby in your arms
- "I'm a little teapot"
- Play with baby in front of the mirror

the infant so that he or she is not overwhelmed by intense emotions. Second, as a playmate the parent provides games and activities and positive, joyful, free, and spontaneous moments of fun. Third, as a teacher the parent teaches about the world. Fourth, as limit setter the parent begins to establish routines, a predictable schedule, and—as the infant becomes a toddler—rules and standards.

See chart above for a summary of development and optimal parenting in the infancy period.

Sarah Landy
Rosanne Menna

References and further reading
Ainsworth, Mary D. Salter, Mary C. Blehar, Everett Waters, and Sally Wall. 1978. *Patterns of Attachment: A Psychological Study of the Strange Situation.* Hillsdale, N.J.: Lawrence Erlbaum Associates.
Bornstein, Marc H., ed. 1995. Vol. 1 of *Handbook of Parenting.* Mahwah, NJ: Lawrence Erlbaum Associates.
Brazelton, Terry. B. 1983. *Infants and Mothers: Differences in Development.* New York: Delacorte.
Greenspan, Stanley I. 1995. *The Challenging Child.* Reading, MA: Addison-Wesley.
Stern, Daniel N. 1985. *The Interpersonal World of the Infant: A View from Psychoanalysis and Developmental Psychology.* New York: Basic Books.

Infertility

Infertility, defined as the inability to conceive a child after one year or more of regular intercourse without contraception, affects approximately 15 percent (6 million) of all American couples. Until middle adulthood, men and women are equal contributors to fertility problems: in 40 percent of the cases, the man is the primary source, in another 40 percent the woman is the primary source, and in the remaining 20 percent both partners are responsible or the source is unknown. (Seibel, Kiessling, Bernstein, and Levin, 1993) In both men and women physical causes of infertility predominate, although psychological factors may be related. For women, causes of infertility include: problems with the Fallopian tubes, which transport the egg from the ovary to the uterus and where egg and sperm meet (e.g., the tubes may be blocked or pulled away from the ovaries due to scar tissue related to pelvic surgery, pelvic inflammatory disease, endometriosis, or a prior ectopic pregnancy); infrequent ovulation (i.e., related to being overweight, underweight, and/or having hormone problems); and disorders of the uterus that prevent eggs from implanting in the uterine wall and/or lead to a miscarriage (e.g., fibroids, noncancerous tumors, ovarian cysts). Respectively, these contribute to 30 percent, 20 percent, and 20 percent of female-related infertility problems. The remaining 30 percent of problems are age related: after middle adulthood, ovulation becomes less regular so that a woman may experience some cycles with no ovulation and others in which several eggs are released; as a result, older women take longer to conceive and are also more likely to experience multiple births when they do. (Seibel, Kiessling, Bernstein, and Levin, 1993) For men, causes of infertility include: abnormal numbers of sperm; abnormal movement (motility) of sperm (to travel into the uterus and Fallopian tubes); and abnormal shape (morphology) of sperm (to fertilize an egg). While the exact causes are unknown, contributing factors are thought to include: cystic fibrosis; impotence; inflammation of the testicles; hormonal disorders (e.g., diabetes) causing nerve damage and impotence; sexually transmitted diseases (e.g., gonorrhea) prohibiting the passage of sperm to the urethra; retrograde ejaculation (sperm traveling backward into the bladder); use of alcohol, marijuana, and/or tobacco (reducing the number and motility of sperm); surgery (e.g., for prostate cancer) leading to scarring, nerve damage, and/or blockage of the sperm to the urethra; and varicose veins in the scrotum.

Infertility must be distinguished from sterility, being incapable of reproducing, for which there is no remedy. However, because of both increased knowledge concerning the ways in which lifestyle changes can improve fertility and improvements in infertility testing and treatment for both men and women, 50 percent of previously infertile couples ultimately achieve a pregnancy. (Komaroff, 1999) Recommended lifestyle changes include: moderate exercise; a healthy diet (including vitamins); weight loss or weight gain; stress reduction; and avoidance of alcohol, coffee, smoking, herbal supplements, and certain prescription and non-prescription drugs. In fact, there is a clear association between infertility and cigarette smoking for both men (see above) and women; women who smoke heavily have been shown to be less fertile than light smokers.

Infertility testing for women includes: blood tests; endometrial biopsy (uterus lining removed and examined under a microscope); hysterosalpingogram or hysteroscopy (dye techniques for viewing the uterine cavity); laparoscopy (a lighted tube is inserted through the abdomen to examine pelvic organs on a monitor); and ultrasound (to detect abnormalities in the ovaries and uterus). Treatment typically includes drugs (e.g., clomiphene citrate, bromocriptine) to induce ovulation; laparoscopic surgery (e.g., to open blocked Fallopian tubes); and assisted reproductive technology. For men, infertility testing typically includes semen analysis; blood tests; and/or urethral cultures; while treatment includes sperm washing (the most rapidly moving sperm are collected and stimulated to fertilize the egg); treatment of infections (e.g., sexually transmitted diseases, prostate infections) with antibiotics; and surgery.

Infertile couples seeking medical help should check their medical insurance coverage early on in the process. There is wide variation in the amount and extent of insurance coverage for fertility testing and/or treatment. In addition, infertility may burden a marriage emotionally, and, thus, the individuals involved may benefit from professional counseling and/or group support. For example, infertile individuals often have difficulty accepting their infertility, which may lead to feelings of depression and self-blame. Spouses also often become angry with each other, and their sexual relationship may suffer as sex becomes a matter of "making babies, not love." (Sabatelli, Meth, and Gavazzi, 1998) RESOLVE, a national nonprofit organization based in Boston, is an example of an organization that offers professional counseling and group support specifically for such couples. In addition, the infertility literature contains much data attesting to the negative impact of infertility on women's and men's well-being. However, recent research has suggested that having a child has the potential to mitigate these negative effects. That is, becoming a parent—especially for infertile women—can lead to increases in global well-being as manifest by less stress, less negative affect, and more personal control.

Jack Demick

See also In Vitro Fertilization (IVF)

References and further reading
Abbey, Antonia, Frank M. Andrews, and L. Jill Halman. 1992. "Infertility and Subjective Well-Being: The Mediating Roles of Self-Esteem, Internal Control, and Interpersonal Conflict." *Journal of Marriage and the Family* 54:405–417.
———. 1994. "Infertility and Parenthood: Does Becoming a Parent Increase Well-Being?" *Journal of Consulting and Clinical Psychology* 62, no. 2:398–403.
Baird, Donna D., and Allen J. Wilcox. 1985. "Cigarette Smoking Associated with Delayed Contraception." *Journal of the American Medical Association* 253:2979–2983.
Komaroff, Anthony L., ed. 1999. *Harvard Medical School Family Health Guide.* New York: Simon & Schuster.
Sabatelli, Ronald M., Richard L. Meth, and Stephen M. Gavazzi. 1988. "Factors Mediating the Adjustment to Involuntary Childlessness." *Family Relations* 37:338–343.
Seibel, Machelle M., Ann A. Kiessling, Joseph Bernstein, and Seymour R. Levin, eds. 1993. *Technology and Infertility: Clinical, Psychosocial, Legal, and Ethical Aspects.* New York: Springer-Verlag.

Intelligence Testing

Intelligence testing of children is generally done in order to identify the need for special educational services, either because of intellectual giftedness or a disability. Every child has a pattern of intellectual abilities that is unique to the individual. While some children may have specific areas of strength and weakness, others have abilities that are more evenly displayed across many areas. Intelligence testing is a vehicle for obtaining a clearer picture of the pattern of the child's intellectual abilities so that appropriate decisions can be made regarding educational placement and instructional methods.

Intelligence testing is a vehicle for obtaining a clearer picture of the pattern of the child's intellectual abilities so that appropriate decisions can be made regarding educational placement and instructional methods. (Laura Dwight)

What Is Intelligence?

Intelligence is a concept that was first put forward early in the 1900s as a way to explain apparent differences in levels of functioning among individuals. Both the concept of intelligence and how best to measure it have received a great deal of study within the educational and psychological communities for nearly 100 years. From the beginning, and to this day, competing theories about the origins and nature of intelligence have been proposed.

As it was originally conceived, intelligence was best understood as an overall general ability ("g") that enabled the individual to function equally at a particular level in all areas. In this regard, the individual would possess a certain level of intelligence, known for some time as the "Intelligence Quotient," or IQ, that

existed on a continuum spanning levels of functioning ranging from mental retardation to giftedness. An individual's IQ would create a certain expectation of how he or she would function in all areas. IQ scores are computed compared to others of the same age. An IQ score on a modern test generally has an average (mean) of 100 and a spread (standard deviation) of 15 or 16 points. This means that a score between 85 and 115 on an intelligence test would generally be considered average.

While the term *IQ* is still widely used, its meaning has evolved. As the concept of intelligence underwent extensive study throughout the twentieth century, support for different ideas of intelligence emerged. Research began to suggest that intelligence is not only a single overall ability, but also includes many different abilities that determine how the individual will function in the world. Researchers differ in their views about general ability, with some still claiming that it is the only important intellectual factor, some claiming that it is important but that specific abilities are also important, and some claiming that there is no such thing as general ability and that only specific abilities are important. There are also a number of different theories about what intellectual abilities are important and to what extent current intelligence tests measure these abilities. Some specific intellectual abilities include verbal ability and knowledge (crystallized ability), ability to reason and solve novel problems (fluid ability), perceptual-motor and visual organization ability, auditory processing abilities, mathematical computation and reasoning abilities, speed of processing information, short-term and long-term memory, and metacognitive or planning abilities. One researcher, Howard Gardner, also includes inter- and intrapersonal abilities, musical and artistic abilities, and bodily-kinesthetic abilities in his theory of multiple intelligences. Although there may be some differences among professionals regarding which specific grouping of abilities best captures one's intelligence, within the psychological and educational communities there is currently wide acceptance of intelligence as a multidimensional construct. Understanding how one conceptualizes intelligence is critical because this will determine how one measures it. There is not currently a single test that assesses all of the intellectual abilities that are seen as important.

Testing of Intelligence

Testing of intelligence can be approached in two major ways. In group testing, many children are evaluated at one time utilizing an objective paper and pencil test that is administered under standardized condi-

tions. These tests typically sample a variety of abilities thought important for school learning, such as verbal knowledge and reasoning and perceptual-motor organization and reasoning. These tests are economical because they permit the evaluation of many children at once. They are often used as screening tools to quickly identify children within a classroom who may have intellectual abilities, either high or low, who may require specialized educational intervention and for whom more extensive testing may be conducted. Examples of group-administered intelligence tests are the Otis-Lennon School Ability Test (OLSAT) and the Comprehensive Test of Basic Skills Test of Cognitive Skills (TCS).

Individualized testing is often conducted as a follow-up to group testing or because of a parent or teacher referral. In this type of testing, a child meets one-on-one with a psychologist who administers one of the many individual standardized intelligence tests currently available. The child is presented with different types of questions of increasing difficulty aimed toward assessing his or her abilities in a variety of areas. In individual testing, however, the child also often is presented with materials such as puzzles, blocks, story cards, beads, pegs, and figures with which to work to complete the question. The child is generally not asked to write his or her answers, but rather to respond verbally or manually to the psychologist's questions. Individual intelligence tests are available for all ages from two to adult, although scores obtained on children younger than about six are not as stable or meaningful as those obtained when they are older. Intelligence tests for children under two do not currently exist, although their overall development can be assessed to see if there are delays.

One of the most valuable aspects of individual testing is the opportunity to observe the child work. Through observation, the psychologist gains important information about the child's approach to the task, problem-solving strategies, motivation, language use, and any emotional variables that may have an impact on the outcome of the testing (i.e., fatigue, anxiety, confusion). The depth and breadth of information gained during individual testing helps create a context within which to understand the scores obtained by the child. In addition, because of the greater flexibility of individual testing, it is recommended over group testing for the assessment of young children or children with sensory impairments, physical or emotional disabilities, or language or cultural differences. This can enable the psychologist to more thoroughly determine the child's level of functioning, as well as better identify the optimal educational placement and/or instructional strategies to employ. Although individual testing is more time consuming and often more expensive, the quality of information obtained may offset these potential negatives.

There are many individually administered intelligence tests for children. Two of the most commonly used instruments are the Wechsler Intelligence Scale for Children—Third Edition (WISC-III) and the Stanford-Binet Intelligence Scale—Fourth Edition (SB-IV).

*Use of Testing to Identify
Children with Special Needs*
Individual intelligence testing is usually used as part of the process to diagnose giftedness, mental retardation, and learning disabilities. Much of this testing occurs because of a referral from a parent or teacher concerned that a child has special learning needs. Children are eligible for evaluation services through the public school district in which they live, even if they attend private, parochial, or home school. Parents can make a written referral for evaluation, detailing the concerns

they have about their child's learning. A committee, which includes the parents, then decides whether individual testing is called for.

Programs for gifted children often require individual intelligence testing for entrance. Other information is also taken into account, but programs often rely heavily on the results of intelligence testing. Often, guidelines exist requiring that children score in the top 2 to 10 percent of overall ability to be eligible. Programs for gifted children should not be seen as a reward or privilege, but as a necessary service for children whose needs cannot be met through traditional classroom instruction.

Part of the process of identifying mental retardation involves individual intelligence testing. Mental retardation is a condition that involves intellectual functioning that is well below the average range (generally the bottom 2 percent of overall ability) and functioning in daily life (adaptive behavior) that is also significantly below average. Children with mental retardation learn at a much slower rate than their peers, and generally require special education services to meet their needs.

Part of the process of identifying a learning disability also involves individual intelligence testing. A learning disability is a condition that involves a child not achieving up to expected levels based on his or her overall ability because of a presumed neurological deficit (also called a processing disorder). Other terms for a learning disability include dyslexia and dysgraphia. To test for a learning disability, the overall ability of the child is tested with an intelligence test. Evidence of specific processing deficits are sought through the intelligence test and other tests. The child's achievement is then compared to the level expected based on his or her ability. If the child is not achieving up to the expected level (this is called having a "severe discrepancy" between ability and achievement), there is evidence of a processing deficit, and there is no other reason for the underachievement (such as lack of adequate education, being a second-language learner, or a physical or sensory disability), the child is labeled learning disabled. Children with learning disabilities generally require special education services to meet their needs.

Individual intelligence testing is also part of a neuropsychological evaluation, which might be done in case of a traumatic brain injury or disease that causes brain damage. Discussion of neuropsychological assessment is beyond the scope of this entry, but the intelligence test is used to evaluate current intellectual functioning level and strengths and weaknesses just as it is with any other child.

Intelligence Testing with Minority Populations

All types of tests are developed for use within a particular cultural context. The content and format of the questions assumes that the child has had exposure to the dominant culture. Although some minority children are included in the development and standardization of intelligence tests, concern has been raised that the tests might not be measuring the same thing for these children. For example, for second-language learners, an intelligence test might actually be measuring their proficiency in English rather than their intellectual ability. Similarly, for culturally different children, an intelligence test might actually be measuring their acculturation to middle-class values rather than their intellectual ability. Because of this, questions have been raised about the ethical use of intelligence tests with ethnic or language minority children. (In some cases, there have been legal challenges to their use as well. For example, intelligence tests cannot be used on minority children in California for special education place-

ment.) This is even more of a concern with group tests when the psychologist has no opportunity to fully evaluate the child's English-language fluency and his or her degree of prior exposure to the type of content and task demands, so it is preferable to use an individually administered intelligence test. An instrument should be selected that closely reflects the child's cultural upbringing, and a bilingual assessment of bilingual children is preferable. Consideration may be given to the use of a nonverbal intelligence test such as the Universal Nonverbal Intelligence Test (UNIT) that minimizes the impact of language or cultural differences on the child's performance.

Catherine A. Fiorello
Annemarie F. Clarke

References and further reading

Cookson, Peter W., and Joshua Halberstam. 1998. *A Parent's Guide to Standardized Tests in School: How to Improve Your Child's Chances for Success.* New York: Learning Express.

Gardner, Howard. 1993. *Multiple Intelligences: The Theory in Practice: A Reader.* New York: Basic Books.

McNamara, Barry F., and Francine J. McNamara. 1995. *Keys to Parenting a Child with a Learning Disability.* Hauppauge, NY: Barron's.

Interracial Families

Interracial families, once illegal, are now increasingly common in the United States. They are formed by the marriage of partners from different races, or by transracial adoption. Even though American culture is highly conscious of race, there is no scientific definition of race or ethnic group. Because interracial families challenge stereotypes based on race and color, they sometimes provoke opposition from their extended families, friends, and the larger community. Parents in interracial families may be concerned that their children will be less well adjusted than other children, but

Psychological research does not support the idea that children in interracial families will be less well adjusted than other children. (Laura Dwight)

psychological research does not support this. The children might have a more difficult transition to adolescence, however, as they work to incorporate two or more racial or cultural identities. Interracial families' strengths lie in their efforts to embody social equality and color blindness, and in their efforts to create a community of similar families.

When Richard Loving brought his bride home in 1958, he was promptly arrested. The crime: he was white, she was black, and they lived in Virginia. He could have spent five years in prison, but since he had been a good citizen, he received a suspended sentence with exile—the Lovings were ordered to stay out of the state for at least twenty-five years. Instead, they sued. *Loving v. Virginia* wended its way up to the U.S. Supreme Court, which ruled in 1967 that all state laws against intermarriage, also called miscegenation,

were unconstitutional. The Lovings' union was finally legal. (*Loving v. Virginia*, 388 U.S. 1, 1967)

Since 1958, interracial marriage has become more common, even if not more accepted, in the United States. Well-documented statistics are scarce, but according to the U.S. Bureau of the Census, there are about 1.2 million interracial married couples in America today. Approximately 20 percent of those are black-white marriages, and the rest are all other ethnic group mixes. (Jacobson, 1995) African Americans have the lowest rate of marriage outside their ethnic group, with only about 3 to 5 percent married to someone who is not African American. In addition, an unknown number of transracial families have been formed when parents of one or more racial groups adopted a child or children from one or more different ethnic groups, or mixed-race children. There have been about 15,000 intercountry adoptions to the United States each year since 1990, and between 9,000 to 11,000 of those were transracial, according to the Joint Council on International Children's Services. (Joint Council website)

Even though "race" or "ethnic group" appear often as boxes to check on survey forms, the terms have no scientific definition. Race and ethnicity are determined more by social prescription than genetic composition. One researcher estimates that race accounts for only about 0.01 percent of the genetic variations between people, and the black U.S. gene pool has about 20 to 30 percent originally white genetic material. But American society is highly conscious of race, even if that consciousness is unspoken, and American culture imposes an all-or-nothing definition of race. As researcher Yanick St. Jean says, "One is either Black or White, even when Black and White." (St. Jean, 1998, 3) Interracial families challenge this all-or-nothing view. Challenges to stereotypes can make some people very uncomfortable, so interracial families face difficulties as trivial as intrusive questions in the supermarket and as serious as discrimination against both parents and children.

Parents of children adopted from another ethnic group may be concerned that their children will not be as well adjusted as children adopted by parents of their own race. The small amount of research in this area is based on families in which black or mixed-race infants or children were adopted by white parents in Great Britain and the United States, even though recent patterns in transracial adoption include children from Asia and Latin America.

In the United States transracial adoption rarely occurred before World War II. After 1945, U.S. couples began adopting orphaned children from Germany,

Austria, Japan, and Greece. Intercountry adoptions by American couples increased steadily from about 1,500 per year in the 1960s to 15,040 in 1999, according to the Joint Council on International Children's Services. The pattern is similar in Western Europe, where about 10,000 children are adopted from other countries every year. (Joint Council website) Transnational adoption is a worldwide phenomenon.

In the 1960s, liberal child welfare organizations promoted transracial placement to give African American orphans an alternative to long-term foster care. However, the African American community had little involvement in these decisions, which contributed to the opposition to transracial placement by the National Association of Black Social Workers (NABSW) in 1972. The NABSW continued its opposition to placement of African American children with Caucasian families, and that opposition, coupled with social work policies favoring family preservation, kept many African American and mixed-race children in foster care for years. By 1987, thirty-five states prohibited the adoption of African American children by Caucasian families, and in 1989 the NABSW formally reaffirmed its opposition to transracial adoption. The national Multiethnic Placement Act of 1994 and its 1996 amendment required states to stop using race as a criterion for foster or adoptive parents.

Ethnic identity has been a major issue in political debates about transracial adoption and in judicial decisions about custody. Opponents argue that minority children placed with nonminority parents cannot develop a positive ethnic identity or learn to deal with racial discrimination. Parents of multiracial children may have similar concerns. However, the concept of ethnic identity has been poorly defined and is only now being scientifically measured. The link between a "positive ethnic identity" and mental health has also not been adequately tested, and the research findings on transracial adoption or on children of an interracial marriage do not lead to firm conclusions about its negative effect on ethnic identity formation.

Parents are often concerned that their transracially adopted children will not do as well in school as other children. Some school systems, teachers, and social workers also promote this view. However, the few researchers who have studied transracially adopted children found that the majority are well adjusted, when measured by school achievement and peer relationships. A Norwegian study found that teachers rated transracially adopted children has having more problems with math, but there were no differences in reading or writing. The country of origin did make a difference, probably because most of the children adopted from Korea to Norway were younger when they were adopted. Still, none of the adopted children were judged to have problems so severe that they could be classified as maladjusted.

At adolescence multiracial children are most likely to have difficulty, because their primary psychological task is to forge a unique identity. If their parents are of different races, the children must integrate two racial and cultural identities. Some clinical psychologists report that multiracial children sometimes identify with one parent and reject the other, as a way out of this difficulty. Minority children lose their birth culture and possibly language in transracial or intercountry adoption. The loss may be a special problem during the transition to adolescence.

As long as human rights and privileges are distributed according to color, its dilution in interracial families can threaten the status quo and create opposition. Families can encounter opposition at many levels. Within the extended family, the parents of interracial couples might be hostile to a partner of a different race. The grandparents of children from a different or mixed race also might be hostile, especially to an adopted child who is not a "blood relative." A major concern of white future in-laws in an interracial marriage often focuses on the skin color of their children's offspring, or on mixed facial features. Mixed-race children are living manifestations of intermarriage, and may be a visible threat to existing cultural definitions of race.

Friends and the larger community can support or undermine an interracial family. Research shows that white people tend to disapprove of black-white marriages, whereas African Americans usually approve, but African American women are less tolerant of the unions than African American men or white women. Partners who grew up in a mixed neighborhood reported that the experience helped them develop positive attitudes toward racial issues and toward intermarriage. Some small-scale research has suggested that neighborhood is important to a child's developing racial identity, consistent with the few other studies that have found significant effects of neighborhood on other child outcomes. Researchers have found that transracially adopted African American children who lived in racially integrated neighborhoods and attended integrated schools felt "positive" about themselves as African Americans.

In many communities, discrimination in housing is still practiced. In others, a warm welcome by other interracial families can support an interracial family. In neighborhoods with other interracial families, social support in the larger community of schools, informal parent groups, and churches can further support the family. But communities with racist attitudes may intensify the negative effects of social isolation. The lack of peer families further isolates interracial families. One study found that some of the people who grew up in mixed neighborhoods and had an interracial marriage approved of it for others, while others disapproved because of their own experience with the stress of growing up in an interracial family.

Besides their potential difficulties, however, interracial families share strengths. Some scholars emphasize that interracial families symbolize social equality and color blindness. They challenge racism and learn to cope with it in unique ways. A study of interracial couples reported that the couples' notion of color changed; they talked of "marriage" and objected to the term "intermarriage." After their marriage, couples said color meant little, if anything. Parents of children from a different race also say that they are often unaware of their child's "differentness" and see only the child. They can help their children benefit from the best of two or more cultures; in fact, the parents themselves change as they incorporate aspects of their child's birth culture and country into their own lives.

Interracial families can build on their strengths by finding a mixed group of friends to socialize with, a group that includes all types of mixed families, not just families similar to theirs. They discover environments for their children to show them that people come together for reasons other than race. Children will be successful at finding their own niches, and friendships with children of other races, if parents take the first step and find the group. Parents in interracial families are challenged to examine the neighborhoods in which they live and the groups they join to find ideal environments for their children.

Kathleen Whitten
Melvin N. Wilson

References and further reading

Also-known-as website: http://www.akaworld.org.

Altstein, Howard, and Rita J. Simon, eds. 1991. *Intercountry Adoption: A Multinational Perspective.* New York: Praeger.

Andresen, Inger-Lise K. 1992. "Behavioral and School Adjustment of 12– and 13-Year-Old Internationally Adopted Children in Norway: A Research Note." *Journal of Child Psychology and Psychiatry* 33, no. 2:427–439.

Garbarino, James. 1992. *Children and Families in the Social Environment.* New York: Aldine de Gruyter.

Jacobson, Cardell K. 1995. *American Families: Issues in Race and Ethnicity.* New York: Garland Publishing.

Joint Council on International Children's Services website: http://www.jcics.org.

Kaeser, Gigi, and Peggy Gillespie. 1997. *Of Many Colors: Portraits of Multiracial Families.* Amherst: University of Massachusetts Press.

Rainbowkids website: http://www. rainbowkids.com.

Rushton, Alan, and Helen Minnis. 1997. "Annotation: Transracial Family Placements." *Journal of Child Psychology and Psychiatry* 38, no. 2:147–159.

Sellers, Robert M., Mia A. Smith, J. Nicole Shelton, Stephanie J. Rowley, and Tabbye M. Chavous. 1999. "Multidimensional Inventory of Black Identity: A Reconceptualization of African-American Racial Identity." *Personality and Social Psychology Review* 2, no. 1:18–39.

Simon, Rita J., and Howard Altstein. 1987. *Transracial Adoptees and Their Families: A Study of Identity and Commitment.* New York: Praeger.

St. Jean, Yanick. 1998. "Let People Speak for Themselves: Interracial Unions and the General Social Survey." *Journal of Black Studies* 28, no. 3:398–409.

L

Labor, Division of

The division of labor in parenting refers to the partition and distribution of caregiving responsibilities between the child's parents or between the child's parent(s) and other family or nonfamilial caregivers. Parenting activities range from nurturing to emotional exchange to management of social relations to cognitive stimulation. These diverse responsibilities are apportioned among the various members of the child's social network—mothers and fathers, grandmothers and aunts, and nurses, day-care providers, and others, whether in the family at home, in day-care facilities, in village centers, or in fields. When two or more caregivers are involved with a child, they may share identical responsibilities in identical ways, or caregivers may specialize in different activities. For example, a baby-sitter may take primary responsibility for baths, walks, and management of peer play, freeing the mother to focus on reading, one-on-one play, and emotional exchange. In the prevailing Western view, responsibilities for caregiving fall primarily to mother and father in the nuclear family, but in practice child-care responsibilities are often shared with other nonparental figures. In many nonindustrial and rural societies, caregiving responsibilities are commonly divided among parents and the young child's older sibling(s) or other relative(s).

Children normally have many people invested in them. Most people agree that mothers traditionally play a central role in children's development. Cross-cultural surveys attest to the primacy of biological mothers in caregiving, and theorists, researchers, and clinicians have long been concerned with mothering, rather than parenting, in recognition of this fact. Mothers in many cultures spend more time than fathers do in direct one-on-one interaction with young children, for example.

Fathers are neither uninterested nor inept in parenting. Although fathers are capable of parenting sensitively, they often yield responsibility for child tending to their wives when not called upon to demonstrate their competence. Females and males have divergent interests in reproduction and rearing, however, which in turn translate into conflicts of interest in parental investment and time budget constraints. Natural variation in parental interests and abilities may also cause mothers and fathers to devote different amounts of time and resources to different domains of child rearing, such as school, sports, or household responsibilities. Thus, both mothers and fathers are clearly capable of, and often engage in, the full range of child-rearing activities; however, they often stress different responsibilities when with their children, and engage children emphasizing different

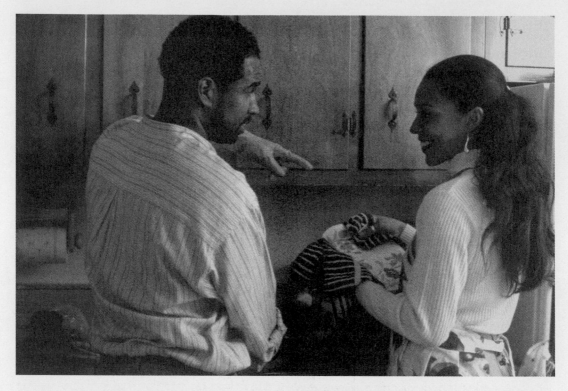

In the prevailing Western view, responsibilities for caregiving fall primarily to mother and father in the nuclear family. (Laura Dwight)

types of interactions. In short, mothers and fathers interact with and care for children in seemingly complementary ways, dividing the labors of parenting.

In general, mothering is associated with caregiving, and fathering with playful interaction. Mothers are more likely than fathers to kiss, hug, talk to, smile at, tend, and hold their infants, for example, and fathers are more likely than mothers to engage in physically stimulating, unpredictable, and arousing play.

At one time in America, perhaps most children were reared by at-home mothers; today, however, those children are parents themselves, and many employ child-care providers. Indeed, historically, direct child care by a biological parent may be more the exception than the rule. Thus, individuals other than mother and father also "parent" young children. Siblings often

care for younger children. In Western and industrialized societies, siblings are seldom entrusted with much responsibility for parenting, as they are themselves engaged in activities preparatory for maturity, but in other societies siblings can play a substantive role in child caregiving. When parenting, siblings display features of both adult-child and peer systems of parenting. Sibling pairs resemble adult-child pairs to the extent that they differ in experience and levels of cognitive and social ability, and siblings typically spend most of their child-tending time in nurturant caregiving. However, sibling dyads share common interests and have more similar behavioral repertoires than do adult-child dyads.

Children commonly encounter a caregiving world that extends beyond the nuclear family as well. In some societies, multiple caregiving is the norm. Grandparents and various nonparents play salient roles in child care, offering caregiving that varies depending on a variety of factors, including age, gender, age gap, quality of attachment, and personality. Children's parents and children's other caregivers also behave in complementary fashions to one another, dividing the full labor of child caregiving by emphasizing different parenting responsibilities and functions. Thus, different caregivers tend to exhibit somewhat different interaction styles and emphasize somewhat different competencies when with children.

No value judgment can be made or implied about equivalence or nonequivalence of care in exclusive versus shared caregiving. It could be that, for some child-care responsibilities, exclusive care of a child is "just right" and the "more or less" provided in shared care situations is not; or, it could be that exclusive care is inappropriate for some sorts of caregiving, but that shared caregiving results in more appropriate balances for the child. The social contract established between parents and their child's other care providers is usually implicit rather than explicit. Many parents have no cultural role model for how the responsibilities of child care are to be distributed between themselves and their children's other caregivers. Still unclear, too, are the implications of diverse patterns of "parenting" relationships and divisions of child care for child development.

The family is the child's primary "social system," and family members adopt interdependent and collaborative roles and functions in child rearing. With the addition of extrafamilial child care, these several responsibilities are further shared among members of a wider social network. Thus, various divisions of labor in parenting and child care actually obtain

widely. To understand the behaviors of any one member of a family or child's extended social network in parenting therefore necessitates understanding the collaboration that exists among all significant others in the child's life.

Marc H. Bornstein

See also Child Care

References and further reading
Barnard, Katherine E., and Louise K. Martell. 1995. "Mothering." In vol. 3 of *Handbook of Parenting.* Edited by Marc H. Bornstein. Mahwah, NJ: Lawrence Erlbaum Associates.
Bornstein, Marc H., and Michael E. Lamb, eds. 1992. *Development in Infancy: An Introduction.* New York: McGraw-Hill.
Clarke-Stewart, K. Alison, Virginia D. Allhusen, and Dorothy C. Clements. 1995. "Nonparental Caregiving." In vol. 3 of *Handbook of Parenting.* Edited by Marc H. Bornstein. Mahwah, NJ: Lawrence Erlbaum Associates.
Honig, Alice S. 1995. "Choosing Child Care for Young Children." In vol. 3 of *Handbook of Parenting.* Edited by Marc H. Bornstein. Mahwah, NJ: Lawrence Erlbaum Associates.
Parke, Ross D. 1995. "Fathers and Families." In vol. 3 of *Handbook of Parenting.* Edited by Marc H. Bornstein. Mahwah, NJ: Lawrence Erlbaum Associates.
Smith, Peter K. 1995. "Grandparenthood." In vol. 3 of *Handbook of Parenting.* Edited by Marc H. Bornstein. Mahwah, NJ: Lawrence Erlbaum Associates.
Zukow-Goldring, Patricia. 1995. "Sibling Caregiving." In vol. 3 of *Handbook of Parenting.* Edited by Marc H. Bornstein. Mahwah, NJ: Lawrence Erlbaum Associates.

Labor and Delivery, Complications of

Potential problems can arise during labor and delivery. Several types of complications are described below.

Fetal distress is indicated when the baby's heart rate drops from the normal 120 to 160 beats per minute to below 100 beats and is persistently at this level. When fetal distress persists in spite of giving the mother oxygen or turning her on one side, immediate delivery of the baby may be necessary. In the first stage of labor this would be by Cesarean section, and in the second stage possibly by forceps delivery.

Cephalopelvic disproportion (CPD) occurs when the head of the baby is too big to pass through the mother's pelvis, and it is necessary to do a Cesarean section.

Prolapsed cord results when the umbilical cord comes down in front of the baby and becomes compressed by it. This rare abnormality calls for immediate delivery.

Breech presentation is a situation in which the baby is in a feet-first or buttocks-first position in the uterus. From conception and up until about thirty-two to thirty-four weeks into the pregnancy, most babies (approximately 85 percent) present in this position. It is normal for the presentation to change spontaneously to a head-first position *(cephalic)* between the thirty-second and thirty-fourth weeks. In some cases, this does not happen and at term a breech presentation persists. Because breech presentation presents more hazards for the fetus and possibly the mother, an attempt may be made to correct the presentation by abdominal manipulation in the doctor's office or in the clinic. If that is not possible, the decision is often made to deliver breech babies by Cesarean section to avoid potential difficulties, especially if it is a first pregnancy.

Shoulder presentation is a rare complication seen most often in women who have had children before. It is usually incompatible with a vaginal delivery and necessitates a Cesarean section.

Occipito-posterior position results when the baby is facing forward toward the mother's abdomen as it comes through the birth canal. In most cases babies are delivered with the back of the baby's head (the *occiput*) facing forward toward the mother's abdomen *(occipito-anterior)*. When the occiput is toward the back *(occipito-posterior)*, the labor may be prolonged and mostly felt in the back, and it may be necessary for the doctor to turn the baby's head on the delivery table in order to deliver it. This is one of the most common causes of a prolonged and difficult labor with a first baby.

Forceps delivery is the use of a grasping-type instrument to help maneuver and extract the baby. This may be necessary when the mother is unable to push the baby out with her own expulsive efforts, either because it is too large, or it is in the *occipito-posterior* position, or because the mother is too tired. In order for this procedure to be done, the cervix should be fully dilated and the head fully "engaged" in the pelvic cavity; otherwise it may cause too much trauma for both the mother and the baby.

Vacuum extraction is performed when a suction cup is attached to the scalp of the baby, and with gentle traction delivery is effected. This may be used as a substitute for forceps delivery in some centers.

Cesarean section is delivery of the baby through the mother's abdominal wall. It is indicated in cases of placenta previa, abruptio placentae, fetal distress, cephalopelvic disproportion, and also in "failure to progress" in labor. The incidence of Cesarean section has risen steadily and dramatically in recent years, so that in some institutions it may be as high as 25 to 30 percent of all deliveries. (American College of Obstetricians and Gynecology, 2000) Anesthesia for Cesarean section may be general (patient asleep), spinal, or most optimally, epidural. Usually the abdominal incision is made transversely just above the hairline and the uterine incision is also transverse, the so-called lower segment operation. In subsequent pregnancies delivery may be by the vaginal route in many cases (VBAC). When the incision in the uterus is vertical, it is always safer to do a repeat Cesarean section for subsequent deliveries for fear of rupture of the uterine scar.

Postmaturity or *postdatism* are terms for the condition that results when a pregnancy extends beyond forty-two weeks. In many of these cases, the assumed date of conception may have been later than was thought, so there is no problem. However, there are some cases of true postmaturity, and in a proportion of these, the baby may suffer from some lack of oxygen in the uterus. For this reason tests are often carried out when the baby is more than one week overdue to check its well-being. These tests include a sonogram to assess the amount of amniotic fluid around the baby (the fluid will gradually reduce after term) and fetal monitoring to evaluate the fetus's condition.

Induction of labor may be necessary to bring on labor that has not occurred spontaneously. These cases might include postmaturity when the baby is one to two weeks overdue, uncontrolled toxemia of pregnancy, and for ruptured membranes without labor. Some doctors induce labor because the baby is getting too big, although this indication is controversial. The method of induction is to give the patient a drug containing a synthetic form of oxytocin, which is the hormone that stimulates labor. This is usually administered intravenously in very small doses, usually controlled by computer, and gradually increasing until regular contractions are established. Sometimes a vaginal suppository of hormonelike substances *(prostaglandin)* is used to soften the cervix before the induction.

Post-partum hemorrhage is the primary complication during the third stage of labor. This has been one of the most common causes of maternal morbidity. It may be prevented and often controlled by the use of various drugs that cause contraction of the uterus, but should never be used until after the baby has been delivered. If the placenta has not been delivered spontaneously, a manual removal may be necessary.

Leonard Wolf

References and further reading
Cunningham, F. Gary, ed. 1997. *Williams Obstetrics.* 20th ed. Stamford, CT: Appleton and Lange.

Labor and Delivery, Stages of

Labor is the term used to describe rhythmic contractions of a mother's uterus during birth. It is not known what causes labor to begin, but it usually does so one to two weeks either before or after the baby's due date. Labor can be divided into three stages: the first stage extends from the onset of labor to the full dilatation or opening of the cervix. The second stage lasts from full dilation to the delivery of the baby. And the third stage continues from delivery of the baby to delivery of the placenta and membranes (afterbirth).

First Stage
Often, but not always, before labor starts there may be a vaginal discharge of mucus tinged with blood, often referred to as the "bloody show." This may precede the actual labor by a day or two, or may not occur until well into the first stage of labor. It need not occur at all. Most often labor begins on or about the due date with the onset of uterine contractions, which will be felt in the lower abdomen or lower back as pressure, and ultimately as painful. At first these are irregular but eventually become regular. There are intervals between these contractions when the expectant mother is quite comfortable. Ultimately, they occur as often as one to two minutes apart. By this time the expectant mother should be where she intends to give birth.

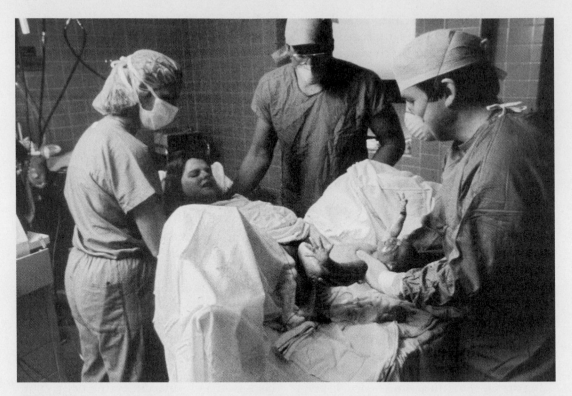

Most babies are delivered head first (cephalic), and once the head is delivered the rest of the baby follows rapidly. (SIU)

Another mode of onset of labor is that the "bag of waters" may burst (ruptured membranes). This can occur without contractions. Under these circumstances it may be necessary to admit the mother to the hospital to induce labor in order to avoid infection. In many cases this condition can be observed without interference for twenty-four hours.

Progress in Labor. Progress in labor is measured by descent of the baby's head into the pelvis and by the opening of the cervix. At term, the cervix is usually long and closed in a first-time mother *(primigravid)*, but may be shorter in women who have given birth before *(multipara).* In some cases the cervix may become shorter in the weeks before labor, but opening does not usually occur until labor starts. When the cervix is 10 cm dilated it is said to be fully dilated. An

average duration for the first stage of labor is twelve hours for a first baby and six to eight hours for a subsequent baby, but there is great variation in these figures.

In many cases the mother, especially if trained, will not require any pain medication ("natural childbirth") until the cervix is 5 or 6 cm dilated. In these cases, in modern obstetrics, if pain relief is required, an epidural anesthetic is the method of choice (see below). However, in some cases the pain may be severe before it is possible to give an epidural anesthetic, and in these cases a drug, such as "Demerol," administered intramuscularly or intravenously may be used.

Fetal Monitoring. In recent years it has become commonplace to monitor the fetal heart rate electronically during labor and particularly in the first stage. This method gives a readout of the fetal heart rate at all times by placing a belt on the mother's abdomen. By placing a second belt, the uterine contractions can be picked up also. In many hospitals this is carried out continuously throughout the labor after admission, and in some it is done intermittently at selected intervals depending on the stage of labor. A rise or fall in fetal heart rate may be significant, the normal range being between 120 and 160 beats per minute. Particularly significant is a drop in the fetal heart rate late during a contraction that does not immediately return to normal after a contraction (late deceleration). These are signs of possible fetal distress, and require attention by the obstetrician. Often turning the patient on her left side to take the pressure of the uterus off the large blood vessels in the mother's abdomen is sufficient, together with administering some oxygen to restore the fetal heart rate to normal.

Second Stage
The second stage of labor occurs from the full opening of the cervix until the baby is delivered. This is the expulsive stage, and here the mother's cooperation is important. This stage lasts up to two hours in a first-time mother, but often is much more rapid with subsequent pregnancies. The patient is encouraged to bear down with each contraction, and to relax between them.

Most babies are delivered head first *(cephalic)* and once the head is delivered, this being the greatest diameter, the rest of the baby follows rapidly. Delivery is carried out in most cases with the mother on her back with her legs in stirrups, *(lithotomy position)*, but sometimes delivery takes place with the mother on her left side *(left lateral position)*. Labor and delivery may be entirely natural, and training in childbirth education classes in the prenatal period and the learning of breathing techniques may help avoid the

need for pain medication. In the past, when pain relief has been required, drugs have been used in the first stage, and when anesthesia has been required for delivery, general anesthesia (mother asleep) has been employed. While these methods are still used in some centers, they have become supplanted by epidural anesthesia, in which a local anesthetic is introduced into the space around the spinal cord, causing the mother to feel numb in the pelvis and lower part of her body. By leaving a plastic catheter in this space, additional doses of medication may be administered throughout the labor and delivery *(continuous epidural)*. This may be introduced in the first stage as early as 4 to 5 cm dilatation, but can slow the labor and can sometimes prevent the mother from exerting her best expulsive efforts, and therefore should be allowed to wear off just before the delivery. For mothers who are not anesthetized, but require an episiotomy (see below) at the time of delivery, a local anesthetic or a *pudendal* block (injection of anesthetic through the vaginal wall) may be introduced. This blocks the nerves supplying the perineum, which is where the episiotomy is made.

An episiotomy is an incision that is made in the perineum (between the vagina and toward the rectum) to make it easier for the baby's head to be delivered and to prevent overstretching and tearing of these tissues. An episiotomy may or may not be necessary, and it is often not predictable until the actual time of delivery.

After the baby is born the umbilical cord is tied and then cut, and the baby is handed to the mother after its airways have been cleared by the doctor or nurse.

Third Stage
This is the period from the delivery of the baby until the passage of the placenta and membranes. This stage may last from a few minutes to half an hour in normal

cases. After the baby has been delivered there is usually a latent interval until the uterus resumes contractions and expels the placenta into the vagina. The delivery is aided either by pressure on the top of the uterus or by gentle traction on the umbilical cord. This is accompanied by a gush of blood. Average blood loss at delivery is 10 to 20 ounces. If the placenta is not delivered in a short time, then it should be removed manually by the midwife or obstetrician. This is done to prevent blood loss, and also to prevent the cervix from clamping down and trapping the placenta. After the placenta is delivered, inspection is made to see that there have been no portions of it remaining in the uterus, and also the patient is examined for possible damage to the cervix, vagina, and surrounding tissues.

Leonard Wolf

References and further reading
Cunningham, F. Gary, ed. 1997. *Williams Obstetrics*. 20th ed. Stamford, CT: Appleton and Lange.

Language Acquisition

Acquiring language is unquestionably one of children's most remarkable achievements. In a span of two years, the cooing and babbling infant develops into a relatively competent communicative partner, able to express thoughts, intentions, and wishes in simple sentences and to understand the speech of others. This journey into the world of language begins at birth, if not before, and its course is marked by a number of noteworthy milestones, including the emergence of receptive language, first words in production, a spurt of rapid vocabulary expansion, and the combination of words into sentences. Though there tends to be consistency in the developmental ordering of these language firsts, there exists enormous variation among children in the developmental timing of language abilities as well as in children's sophistication in language at any given age. Individual differences in language acquisition are explained by many factors, including but not limited to gender, temperament, affect, motivation, articulatory control, cognition, and variation in environments that children experience, notably those produced by parents.

In early infancy, babies appear to be equipped with basic capacities that suitably predispose them to learning a language. In the first months of life, babies seek out the sources of sounds around them, discriminate among different sounds in language (such as consonants and vowels), and express their own emotions through whining, crying, cooing, and babbling. Over the course of the first six months, babies' vocalizations, gestures, and expressions all become increasingly purposeful and focused. Early random and reflexive actions evolve into more intentional and communicative ones. The seemingly arbitrary nature of babies' first vocalizations changes, as they increasingly respond to and direct their vocalizations toward familiar persons, such as mothers, fathers, siblings, and other caregivers. In just a few months, babies are better able to initiate interactions with others through smiles, gazes, and targeted vocalizations.

By around nine months of age, babies demonstrate rudimentary understanding of simple words and phrases. This early understanding also depends on the facial and gestural cues that accompany parents' speech. For example, a nine month old might gleefully clap hands in response to a parent saying "clap hands," but this routine expression is just as likely signaled to the baby by the "sing-song" nature of the parent's voice, eager expression of anticipation, and/or the parent's own clapping. Over the next several months, as the baby's familiarity with specific words and phrases grows, the baby comes to under-

In just a few months, babies are better able to initiate interactions with others through smiles, gazes, and targeted vocalizations. (Elizabeth Crews)

stand the same word or phrase in the absence of these nonverbal cues. At this point, comprehension of a word or phrase is considered to be firmly established.

During the last quarter of the first year babies begin to imitate the sounds and words they hear around them (e.g., imitating "ba" to a parent saying "ball"). However, it is unclear whether infants' first imitative expressions actually indicate an understanding that words can refer to referents. For example, if a baby imitates an adult saying "ball" it is not certain that the baby appreciates the fact that his or her own "ba" refers to the object "ball" or is instead a mimic of the sound just heard.

In contrast to earlier imitations, the start of the second year is a time when spontaneous production of words first occurs. For many children, the first words produced are "mama" or "dada," followed by labels for common and easily pronounceable objects, such as ball or dog. Words used in simple routines, such as "bye-bye," "up," "down," and "more," also tend to emerge somewhat early in the child's vocabulary.

From the time of their first spontaneous words through the next several months the expansion of children's vocabulary is slow and almost effortful. Each week the child adds one or a few words to her or his verbal repertoire, sometimes leaving old words behind. However, during this period, babies' language comprehension improves at a much quicker rate. In short, children understand much more than they can say. In fact, a child might be able to carry through with a verbal request as complex as "get your doll and bring it to grandpa in the bedroom," even if the child is unable to actually *produce* any of the words herself.

By the middle of the second year, around the time when children have acquired fifty words in their productive vocabulary, there is a marked change in the rate of language production, termed the *vocabulary spurt* or *vocabulary explosion*. Children are suddenly able to produce a new word upon hearing it only once or a few times. The growth in the child's vocabulary at this time is so rapid that it is even difficult for parents to keep track of their children's new learning. During this vocabulary spurt, children add many verbs or action words to their vocabulary as well as adjectives, or words that describe the attributes of objects (e.g., red, soft). Thus, rather than being limited to labeling objects or people, children are now able to refer to parts and characteristics of objects and events, as well as to the actions that they carry out. This linguistic phenomenon might indicate an important underlying change in children's cognitive competencies.

By the end of the second year, children begin to combine words into rudimentary sentences. These first sentences tend to be very simple, parsimonious versions of adult sentences in that they contain only the essential information that needs to be communicated. Thus, a child might say "get ball" rather than "get me the ball," or "Mommy house" rather than "Mommy went into the house," leaving out smaller prepositions and markers of verb tense. These early sentences have been referred to as *telegraphic speech* in that they mimic the nature of messages that were once contained in telegrams. Afterward sentence complexity advances as children become increasingly proficient in the syntactic or grammatical structure of their native language. Prepositions, prefixes and suffixes, verb inflections (-ing, -s, -ed), plurals, and conjunctions all begin to appear in children's speech, leading to growth in the average length of children's sentences.

Although the developmental ordering of most of these language achievements is virtually universal (single word expressions always precede the combination of words into sentences), the actual ages that children achieve each of these early linguistic milestones vary tremendously. Thus, parents need to be aware of the great range that exists around these average ages. Some children might utter their first words at nine months of age, others not until twenty months; some children might combine words into sentences at fifteen months, others not until two years of age.

What might explain the impressive variability among children in early language acquisition? The answer to this question is not simple, and has been the focus of a vast amount of research for decades. Many factors play a role in the language learning process, and it is the combination of those factors that best explains when a child achieves a particular milestone and how capable a child will be in language at any given period in development. Aspects of both child and social context feed into language acquisition. For example, a child's gender, motivation to talk, articulatory abilities, emotion regulation or affect, and cognitive development all contribute to language acquisition. Specifically, girls tend to be more advanced in early language abilities than boys; children with greater articulatory control tend to produce more words at earlier points in development than children who are less able to clearly pronounce sounds; children exhibiting poor regulation of their emotions tend to be slower at language early on; and some children appear more motivated to talk or express their intents than others. However, the extent to which these early differences affect the course of later language growth remains unclear. Many children who appear slower in learning language early on soon catch up with their more precocious peers.

Germane to parenting and environmental predictors of language variation, children from low-income families are at a disadvantage in language when compared to children from middle-class backgrounds, most likely due to the fact that they are exposed to less language at home. In fact, the effects of poverty on young children's language growth are greatly attenuated if differences in parenting interactions are controlled.

Indeed, parenting has been found to be one of the most robust predictors of children's language abilities across income groups and cultures. Research on the topic of "joint attention" suggests that optimum occasions for language learning occur when adult speech is focused on and relevant to children's attention. Empirical studies show that children best acquire new pieces of linguistic information when parents share in their topic of focus. Parents who are verbally responsive to their infants' bids for attention, vocalizations, emotional expressions, and exploratory initiatives tend to have children who achieve language milestones earlier in development, and who are more proficient at language within a given age. Conversely, intrusiveness in parenting—interrupting the child's focus, overstimulating children, or frequent reprimanding and prohibiting—is found to be either unrelated or inversely related to gains in children's language. Thus, it is the *quality* and *timing* of verbal input rather than the sheer amount that appears most important for children's language growth.

Some studies have suggested that the precise nature of *what* parents say when responding to their children is also important for children's language. In early stages of language acquisition parents tend to simplify the complexity of the information they communicate to infants and toddlers—both grammatically and semantically. This simplification of verbal messages to match the level of children's emerging abilities facilitates the language learning task by making the most salient information in a message more readily available. In addition, parents who respond to their children's communicative and exploratory initiatives by labeling and describing objects and events in the environment and by imitating and expanding on their children's own attempts at verbalizing support their children's acquisition of language, as well as their motivation to use language to communicate with others. As an example, in the early stages of language acquisition, saying "That's a blue ball" to a child who picks up a ball is more conducive to language growth than is the response "Oh yes!" Similarly, saying "ball" in response to a child saying "bah" reinforces the child's attempts at communication and teaches the child how to put words in the service of communication. Later on, when children are increasingly competent in their use of language, asking questions about prior experiences feeds into continued language growth and the development of children's autobiographical memories. Thus, asking questions such as "What happened when we went to the zoo yesterday?" of two- and three-year-olds encourages them to mentally reflect on the prior day, and to translate memories of past events into meaningful language.

Catherine S. Tamis-LeMonda
Marc H. Bornstein

References and further reading
Bates, Elizabeth, Inge Bretherton, and L. Snyder. 1988. *From First Words to*

Grammar: Individual Differences and Dissociable Mechanisms. Cambridge, UK: Cambridge University Press.

Bloom, Lois. 1993. *The Transition from Infancy to Language.* New York: Cambridge University Press.

Bornstein, Marc H. 1989. *Maternal Responsiveness: Characteristics and Consequences.* San Francisco: Jossey-Bass.

Tamis-LeMonda, Catherine S., Marc H. Bornstein, Ronit Kahana-Kalman, Lisa Baumwell, and Lisa Cyphers. 1998. "Predicting Variation in the Timing of Linguistic Milestones in the Second Year: An Events-History Approach." *Journal of Child Language* 25:675–700.

Latino Parenting

At the start of the twenty-first century Latinos make up 11 percent of the population of the United States (U.S. Bureau of the Census, 1997), yet they differ from one another in terms of country of origin, race, social class, educational level, length of time in the United States, and home language use. Despite this variation, Latino families share adherence to a central core of family values, which include respect for parents and elders and mutual aid and support among extended, as well as nuclear, family members. Although characterized in past social science research as authoritarian and male dominated, Latino families today are more likely to exhibit shared decision making. Supported in part by continuing large-scale immigration from Latin America, many Latinos continue to express loyalty toward the culture of their home country, even after several generations in the United States.

A discussion of Latino families must take into account the extraordinary variety that exists within the Latino population. The U.S. Bureau of the Census uses the term "Hispanic-origin" to refer to those of any race whose origin is Mexican, Puerto Rican, Cuban, Central or South American, or some other Hispanic origin. As a group and compared with the non-Hispanic population of the country, Hispanics tend to be younger, more likely to live in poverty, and have less education, as shown in Table 1. At the same time, Hispanics are more likely to live in households with children than are non-Hispanics.

Tremendous variation characterizes the population (see Table 2). Mexican Americans make up the largest group within the Latino population. Although continuing to be concentrated in the American Southwest in lands formerly part of Mexico, Mexican Americans can increasingly be found throughout the country and, today, mainly in urban centers. Cuban Americans, originally refugees from the communist takeover of their country in 1959, continue to be concentrated in Florida and have higher levels of education and income than other Latino groups in the United States.

Familism, the set of shared values of family allegiance, mutual support, and respect for elders, continues to be central to the Latino family. In the past, researchers often associated familism with traditional values and practices that were perceived to keep immigrant families from full acculturation to American norms. In addition, children's collective rather than individualistic values were believed to prevent Latino children from achieving in American schools at levels comparable to their non-Latino peers. Latino parents, however, see the upbringing *(educación)* that they are providing their children as providing the moral foundation on which schooling and formal education are built. Current studies increasingly demonstrate that Latinos' strong family orientation is supportive of, and complementary to, academic attainment values.

Allegiance to and support of extended family, in addition to nuclear family members, form part of core Latino values. However, extended family households

TABLE 1   Selected Demographic Characteristics

Characteristics	Hispanic	Non-Hispanic
Median age	26.1 yrs.	35.5 yrs.
% of population under age 10	21.7%	14.2%
% 25 years or older high school graduates or beyond	54.7%	84.8%
% 25 years or older with B.A. or more	10.3%	25.2%
% of households below poverty level	26.4%	9.4%
Median annual household income	$24,906	$36,542
% of family households (parents, either married or single, with children)	80.6%	68.5%
% of households w/ single female head of family	19.7%	12.0%

Source: U.S. Bureau of the Census, *Current Population Survey* (March 1997).

TABLE 2   Comparative Characteristics of Latino Populations

Characteristics	Mexican origin	Puerto Rican origin	Cuban origin
Median age	24.3	27.0	40.8
% 25 years or older h.s. graduates or beyond	48.6%	61.1%	65.2%
% 25 years or older with B.A. or more	7.5%	10.7%	19.7%
% of households below poverty level	27.7%	33.1%	12.5%
Annual household income	$24,368	$21,908	$28,413
% of households w/ single female head	16.7%	29.5%	12.5%

Source: U.S. Bureau of the Census, *Current Population Survey* (March 1997).

have never been the norm for Latino families in the United States. More common is for the nuclear family of parents and children to live in one household, with aunts, uncles, and grandparents living in close proximity. Extended family provides networks for finding jobs and housing for recent migrants, financial assistance in times of need, moral support in crisis situations, and social ties that are reinforced through visits and celebrations such as weddings and *quinceañeras* (girls' fifteenth birthday celebrations). Family members also provide a major source of information and "social capital" for Latino families.

In addition to familism and a collectivist orientation, Latino culture has been characterized by machismo, or a cult of male superiority, and it has been pointed out that among Mexican scholars, Octavio Paz has been the most eloquent proponent of this perspective. However, there are few current empirical findings that support the view of Latino families in the United States as rigidly patriarchal and male dominated. On the contrary, Latino families emerge in several recent studies as being egalitarian in decision making and task allocation. Although most of the child care and household tasks continue to be carried out by mothers, fathers are responsible for an increasing portion of the care and supervision of children. Indeed, single father families are more than twice as likely to be found among Latino families as among non-Latinos.

In what has been termed the "social science myth" of the Latino family, parenting practices were assumed to be authoritarian and restrictive. Fathers were assumed to be distant and mothers more accessible, yet submissive. Current studies indicate that there is considerable variation in practices among Latino families. Some follow more traditional patterns in which the father, as head of household, is responsible for major family descisions, and children are expected to show respect for elders and live at home until they form their own families. Other families, while also maintaining values of respect and family unity, are more egalitarian in descision making, activities, and gender roles. This is associated for Latino families, as it is for American families in general, with a rise in the past two decades in participation of mothers in work outside the home.

As indicated in the census data in the figures above, Latino families are more likely to be living in poverty than are non-Latino families. Lower rates of family income are associated with lower educational attainment levels. First-generation immigrants, born outside of the United States, typically enter the country with considerably lower education levels than the mainstream population. However, of greater concern is the persisting underachievement of Latino students of succeeding generations. One study used cross-national data to demonstrate a marked decline in achievement orientation between Mexican students in Mexico and Mexican American students in the United States. Other researchers have attributed persistent underachievement to Latinos' minority status in American society; they argue that lack of opportunities to compete for jobs and lower pay for similar work contribute to students' low motivation to do well in school. Still other scholars look to discrimination and tracking within the schools themselves as reproducing cycles of academic failure for Latino youth.

Conditions of poverty, family breakdown, and low levels of education are also associated with gang activity on the part of Latino youth. Contrary to stereotypes perpetuated by the media, most Latino youth are not *cholos*, or gang members. However, researchers investigating Mexican American gang activity in the Los Angeles area over time have shown that the gangs have become increasingly marginalized and violent and gang members increasingly older. With economic restructuring in the 1980s, more stable and better-paying unionized jobs in industry and larger firms are giving way to lower-paying, unstable jobs in the service sector and increasing competition from recent immigrants. Increased job instability has led to prolonged gang involvement, and members today are less likely to be in school than they were two decades ago.

U.S. census figures indicate the Latino population is presently growing at a rate five times faster than the rest of the U.S. population, and Latinos are the focus of increasing scholarly as well as popular attention. Older views of immigrant assimilation into American society based on models of turn-of-the-century European immigration patterns are inadequate to explain the diversity of, and continued involvement with, the native culture among Latinos. Increasingly, perspectives that emphasize biculturalism and ethnic identity maintenance are used. For example, one researcher described language and cultural maintenance among "border balanced" Mexican American families who maintain social and economic ties on both sides of the Mexico-Arizona border. Another study found that ethnic loyalty persisted for several generations, while Mexican American families on the whole shifted dramatically from Spanish to English-language use within two generations.

Leslie Reese

References and further reading

Delgado-Gaitan, Concha. 1992. "School Matters in the Mexican-American Home: Socializing Children to Education." *American Educational Research Journal* 29, no. 3:495–513.

Griswold del Castillo, Richard. 1984. *La Familia: Chicano Families in the Urban Southwest, 1848 to the Present.* Notre Dame, IN: University of Notre Dame Press.

Mirandé, Alfredo. 1988. "Chicano Fathers: Traditional Perceptions and Current Realities." Pp. 93–106 of *Fatherhood Today: Men's Changing Role in the Family.* Edited by P. Bronstein and C. P. Cowan. New York: John Wiley and Sons.

Reese, Leslie, Silvia Balzano, Ronald Gallimore, and Claude Goldenberg. 1995. "The Concept of Educación: Latino Family Values and American Schooling." *International Journal of Education Research* 23, no. 1:57–81.

U.S. Bureau of the Census. 1997. *Current Population Survey: 1997.* Washington D.C.: Government Printing Office.

Valdés, Guadalupe. 1996. *Con Respeto: Bridging the Distances between Culturally Diverse Families and Schools.* New York: Teachers College Press.

Vélez-Ibáñez, Carlos. 1996. *Border Visions.* Tucson, AZ: University of Tucson Press.

Lesbian Mothers, Children of

Lesbian mothers first became a focus of public attention in the 1970s when lesbian women began to fight for custody of their children when they divorced. At that time, lesbian mothers almost always lost custody on the grounds that it would not be in the children's best interests to remain with their mother. Specifically, it was argued that the children would be teased and ostracized by their peers, and would develop behavioral and emotional problems as a result, and that they would show atypical gender development—that is, that boys would be less masculine in their identity and behavior, and girls less feminine than their counterparts from heterosexual homes.

The early studies of the outcomes for children growing up in a lesbian-mother family adopted a similar design in that they compared children in lesbian-mother families with children raised in families headed by a single heterosexual mother, and focused on the two main areas of concern in child custody cases—the children's socioemotional development and their gender development. The rationale for the choice of single heterosexual mothers as a comparison group was that the two types of family were alike in that the children were being raised by women without the presence of a father, but differed in the sexual orientation of the mother. This allowed the effects of the mothers' sexual orientation on children's development to be examined without the confounding presence of a father in the family home.

The findings of these investigations were strikingly consistent. In terms of the children's socioemotional development, children from lesbian-mother families did not show a higher incidence of psychological disorder or of difficulties in peer relationships than their counterparts from heterosexual homes. With respect to gender development, there was no evidence of gender identity confusion for any of the children studied, and no differences in gender role behavior were found between children in lesbian and heterosexual families for either boys or girls—that is, daughters of lesbian mothers were no less feminine, and sons no less masculine, than the daughters and sons of heterosexual mothers.

A limitation of these early studies is that only school-age children were studied, and it has been argued that children raised in lesbian families may experience emotional and relationship difficulties when they grow up. It has also been suggested that children from lesbian homes will be more likely than those from heterosexual backgrounds to themselves adopt a lesbian or gay sexual orientation in adulthood—an outcome that is considered undesirable by courts of law. In an

In studies, daughters of lesbian mothers were no less feminine, and sons no less masculine, than the daughters and sons of heterosexual mothers. (Hella Hammid/Photo Researchers)

investigation that followed up children raised in lesbian-mother households to adulthood it was found that young adults from lesbian backgrounds did not differ from their counterparts from heterosexual homes in terms of psychological well-being or the quality of family relationships, and the large majority identified as heterosexual. Thus, the commonly held assumption that lesbian mothers will have lesbian daughters and gay sons was not supported by the findings of the study.

In recent years, studies of lesbian families with children conceived by donor insemination have begun to be published. Unlike lesbian women who had their children while married, these couples planned their family together after coming out as lesbian, and the children have been raised in lesbian families with no father present right from the start. Although the children were still young when the findings were reported (around six years on average), the evidence so far suggests that they do not differ from children in two-parent heterosexual families in terms of either emotional well-being or gender development. However, co-mothers in two-parent lesbian families were found to be more involved with their children than fathers in two-parent heterosexual families.

Susan Golombok

References and further reading

Patterson, Charlotte J. 1992. "Children of Lesbian and Gay Parents." *Child Development* 63:1025–1042.

Tasker, Fiona, and Susan Golombok. 1997. *Growing Up in a Lesbian Family*. New York: Guilford Press.

Literacy

Derived from litteratus (L.) "lettered" or "learned" and littera "letter," pl. "learning," the term literacy refers to a condition of education, especially the ability to read and write, or the condition of being literate. According to the *Oxford English Dictionary* (1970) the term was formed as the antithesis of illiteracy. During the 1930s, often only illiteracy was listed as a term. But as illiteracy steadily decreased worldwide and literacy has become the norm, there was a need to define what literacy meant in more detail.

Literacy has been consistently correlated with education, knowledge, and the predominant culture in industrialized nations. Yet the standard has been elusive. As literacy tasks in education, work, recreation, religion, and communication changed to meet society's demands, and literature expanded to include the writings of many cultural groups, the definition of what it meant to be literate changed as well. At one point it took only a signature to prove literate status. Literacy also primarily referred to reading, but now includes writing as well. One newer use of the term *literacy* specifies the domain of literate endeavor, such as computer literacy, musical literacy, or scientific literacy, emphasizing specialized knowledge needed to be called literate in one of these domains. Currently literacy, measured in different ways, is used as the measure of success in the world of work, in education, in government, and in many countries is one of the requirements to become a citizen.

The spread of literacy over time has featured a complex interaction of a number of variables: social class, language, ethnicity, culture, gender, age, and even geographic regions and economic conditions. However, when technological change occurs in combination with other social and economic factors, making the printed texts accessible to more people and the need to read and/or write more relevant, the level and incidence of literate behavior also potentially changes.

Gutenberg's invention of the printing press in the fifteenth century sparked a literacy revolution, as printed texts became more readily available. This continued as texts were translated into multiple languages. With mass-production printing and the movement to provide schooling for all children in the 1800s, the number of literate people again increased substantially.

It is important to note that in the past the emphasis has been on reading and somewhat less on writing. This, too, is changing. With the growing need for global communication and the prevalence of computers, a new demand for written communication has redefined literacy to include a new emphasis on writing as well as reading.

How does one measure literacy or the rate of literacy? The assessment of literacy still is not an exact science, nor are literacy rates easily compared among countries, due to different educational systems, goals, and requirements. Methods of assessment range from examining the level of education attained to skills- or standards-based assessment. The important questions to ask about the latter are: What is the purpose of the assessment? Which literacy tasks are being measured? Is the test designed to assess whether individuals have met certain criteria on particular tasks, a criterion-referenced measure? Or is it a norm-referenced test designed to compare individual performance to a comparable population? This is similar to the norm-referenced testing that most school districts use in the United States. Parents need to understand that these tests are actually designed (and will be redesigned) to insure that 50 percent of the students on whom the test is based fall below average (i.e., grade level) on the test. Two other important

The new literacy research stresses the importance of immersing young children in an environment rich in oral and print language. (Laura Dwight)

questions for parents to ask are does the literacy assessment measure what is being taught in the schools, and are the literacy tasks in the curriculum and on the test "real" tasks, representative of the literacy tasks required of a literate citizen?

Another important issue for parents to understand is the process of becoming literate. How does a child learn to read and write? In the past, a belief in readiness for reading at an arbitrary age guided educational policy. This policy has been modified in light of new research on the precursors for, and development of, early literate behavior, or *emergent literacy* (see Clay, 1975, 1991, 1993). The new research stresses the importance of immersing young children (ages birth through school age) in an oral language-rich and print-rich environment. They need to verbalize and understand their experiences in activities such as dramatic play, being read to,

"reading" environmental print or simple illustrated books using the pictures, drawing, painting, and writing, which might look more like scribbling and letterlike figures. Also, a mind-set for literacy develops when preschool and school-age children observe adults as models engaged in a wide variety of reading and writing tasks, especially if some of these are enjoyable, interactive activities, such as reading a favorite book aloud together.

Learning to read and write has been plagued by the swinging pendulum between various methodologies, such as phonics (i.e., linking letters and sounds) versus sight words (automatic, visual recognition of words) or phonics versus whole language (a philosophy of stressing all the language arts—listening, speaking, reading, and writing—and using complete texts through which skills are taught). Research shows that a balanced approach including strategies for word recognition and spelling as well as for comprehending and composing is most effective. Ensuring that children engage in as much reading and writing as possible is also critical for the development of fluency and competence.

Comprehension and Composition
The main reason and motivation for reading, no matter what the purpose, is understanding what has been read. For composing, it is to communicate meaningfully and clearly. Both comprehension and composing are affected by the purpose, topic, and genre or structure of the text. Without experience with and background knowledge of topic and genre, comprehension and composing are unlikely to be successful. The purpose for reading or writing also determines the cognitive strategies and the way language is used. Consequently, it is very important for school literacy programs to provide a wide variety of texts, on a variety of topics written in a variety of genres, and read for many different purposes. Students need to have the opportunities to enjoy reading, as well as to focus on learning particular strategies such as retelling or summarizing, responding, analyzing, synthesizing, and critically evaluating the text. Learning the strategy of "reading like a writer" helps children understand how an author composes a particular kind of text for a particular purpose.

Concurrently the school program, particularly from third grade and through the higher grades, needs to provide real communicative reasons for children to write a similar variety of texts, handing in multiple drafts after receiving teacher or peer feedback, revising, and editing them. The role of the teacher is critical in fostering the motivation, coordination, and integration of comprehending and composing for real communicative purposes, which all too often is lacking in commercial reading programs.

Word Recognition and Spelling
One method to assist children in learning to recognize or decode words is phonics, or learning the connection of letters and letter clusters (e.g., /ch/ /au/) with sounds. While simple symbol-sound relationships are important to learn, this is only part of what is involved in learning to read. A child must learn when to use a particular symbol-sound relationship and how to apply decoding in continuous text when encountering an unknown word or correcting an error. To see the complexity of decoding, consider the pronunciation of the vowel "o" in the following words: open, ox, lemon, through, book, loose, boy, coin, or, snow, ouch, towel. In addition, there are many words that require visually recognizing longer spelling patterns and attaching sounds to them. Some include patterns with silent letters (e.g., "night," "knock") or unusual pronunciations (e.g., "was," "thorough"), or longer words with prefixes, suffixes, and roots from other languages such as Greek, Latin, German, and French (e.g., "pseudonym," "apotheosis"). Eventually, children need to build a reading vocabulary of sight words, words that are recognized automatically without reference to letter sounds, and continue to add to it.

Often voracious, good readers who read a wide variety of genres become good spellers due to their growing awareness of the printed representations of the many words they read. Consequently, children need to read many kinds of texts (e.g., stories, poems, informational texts, etc.) about many different topics in order to learn to integrate the use of the meaning and language patterns of the text with the application of decoding skills. Strategic use of the meaning and language in a story to assist in figuring out the pronunciation of a particular word and its meaning are often referred to as using context clues, another important part of word recognition.

Spelling involves the cognitive strategy of linking sounds to letters, the reverse of the strategy used in recognizing words. Research by linguist Charles Read in the seventies documented the power of children's slow articulation of words and then writing down what they heard—what Read called invented spelling. Research describes four stages in learning to spell. Writing in the prephonetic stage has no resemblance to the sound-letter correspondence and may include letterlike symbols. The semiphonetic stage includes some regular sound-letter correspondences. The phonetic stage includes representation of all sounds in a word, but does not necessarily include accurate spelling, and the transitional stage includes not only phonetic spelling, but also the eventual learning of visual spelling patterns that are not regular in their sound-letter correspondences. These four stages lead to accurate spelling of words, or writing vocabulary, which increases over time if children are held accountable.

Many children learn sound-letter correspondences through initial writing when allowed to use invented spelling, moving with teacher expectation to adult spelling. Marie Clay, a well-known literacy researcher, makes a cogent argument that beginning writing causes a child to attend closely to the features of print and how words are put together in ways that supplement reading. (Clay, 1991) However, she points out that some children go more easily from sound to letter, others from letter to sound, but that some children in both groups fail to see the connection between the two and need the teacher to facilitate the awareness that what is learned in writing can be used in reading and vice versa. (Clay, 1993) Many school beginning-reading programs do not truly integrate the teaching of reading and writing, a needed change for future literacy instruction.

M. Trika Smith-Burke

References and further reading
Atwell, Nancie. 1998. *In the Middle: New Understandings about Writing, Reading, and Learning.* 2d ed. Portsmouth, NH: Boyton Cook/Heinemann.
Bolton, Faye, and Diane Snowball. 1993. *Teaching Spelling: A Practical Resource.* Portsmouth, NH: Heinemann.
Clay, Marie M. 1975. *What Did I Write?* Portsmouth, NH: Heinemann.
———. 1991. *Becoming Literate: The Construction of Inner Control.* Portsmouth, NH: Heinemann.
———. 1993. *An Observation Survey of Early Literacy Achievement.* Portsmouth, NH: Heinemann.
Griffin, Peg, Catherine E. Snow, and M. Susan Burns. 1998. *Preventing of Reading Difficulties in Young Children.* Washington, DC: National Academy Press.
Holdaway, Donald. 1969. *Foundations of Literacy.* London: Ashton Scholastic.
Oxford English Dictionary, L–M Volume 6, Oxford, UK: Clarendon Press. Reprint 1970 (orig. 1933).
Trelease, Jim. 1995. *The Read Aloud Handbook.* New York: Viking Penguin.
Webster's New Twentieth Century Dictionary, Unabridged 2d ed. 1978. New York: Collins World.

Locomotor Development

Locomotor development refers to changes in children's mastery of mobility. The developmental progression begins with spontaneous arm and leg movements during the fetal and newborn periods, followed by rolling, crawling, and other idiosyncratic forms of prone progression midway through the first year, then pulling to a stand and balancing upright, then walking at the end of the first year, and finally, running, jumping, and more sophisticated forms of mobility during the second year. For nearly 100 years, the popular belief was that locomotor development is a chronological and hierarchical process: each stage builds on the previous one in a strict and orderly march toward erect locomotion. However, researchers now believe that normative data (milestone charts that tell when the "typical baby" achieves each milestone)

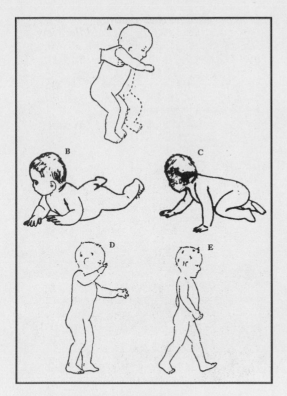

When held under the arms in an upright position, newborns reflexively move their legs in a stepping pattern (A). Most Western babies crawl, on bellies (B) or on hands/knees (C), before they walk (D). By age seven, they walk like adults (E).
(Ludovic Marin)

and aroused, but without any noticeable prompt. Flailing and kicking movements are important for development because they help to build and strengthen muscles necessary for later locomotion and they provide a way for infants to discover the limits of their body space. However, infants are still a long way from achieving true mobility.

Everyone knows that newborn babies cannot walk. There are two biomechanical reasons for this. First, infants' leg muscles are too weak relative to their leg fat for them to lift one leg while supporting the body's weight on the other leg. Second, newborns cannot keep balance in an upright position. They do not yet use stimulation from their visual system, inner ear, and muscle senses to control balance. Furthermore, the problem of keeping balance is exacerbated by infants' top-heavy body proportions. With more weight in their head and chest, newborns have a higher center of gravity and, like a top-heavy bookcase, are prone to tipping. Surprisingly, when constraints of muscle strength and balance control are eliminated, newborns can do something that looks like walking. When held under the arms in an upright position, newborns spontaneously move their legs in an alternating pattern—the stepping reflex. A few months later, when babies' legs are too fat for them to march along the tabletop, the stifled alternating leg movements reappear when they are held over a motorized treadmill. In both cases, the adult provides the missing balance control and leg strength by holding infants upright and by partially supporting their body weight. In addition, the treadmill compensates for leg strength by stretching one leg backward and allowing it to pop forward like a spring. However, in newborn stepping and treadmill walking, the adult does not provide a key ingredient of real walking—the motivation to go somewhere.

may not accurately reflect individual infants. In fact, the order and appearance of each form of locomotion stems from parents' child-rearing practices unique to each culture, infants' body proportions and muscle strength, and their temperament and motivation to go somewhere.

The earliest precursors of locomotion are the spontaneous arm flails and leg kicks of babies in the womb. Such fetal movements may be masked at the end of gestation because babies' limbs are so tightly packed into the womb. After infants are born, again they display spontaneous rhythmical arm and leg movements. They make these movements when they are lying on their back, awake

Once babies achieve independent mobility and travel from place to place on their own, they begin to actively explore their environment. (Laura Dwight)

Prelocomotor infants experience displacement of their bodies when their caregivers carry them from place to place. Such passive movements provide visual stimulation and activation of the vestibular system of the inner ear. Although babies enjoy being carried and often look out at the world, there is no evidence that infants learn about balance control or places to go from passive locomotion. Once babies achieve independent mobility and travel from place to place on their own, they begin to actively explore their environment. Now they can go see what is around the corner or behind the door. They can learn about surfaces, places, and paths between them and they can discover various methods of locomotion for going somewhere. Independent locomotion is certainly important for babies, but also for parents who view infants' first

steps as a marker of emotional independence and maturity.

Self-initiated locomotion often begins with idiosyncratic solutions. Some babies begin moving long distances by rolling, others by bum-shuffling in a sitting position, others by pushing backward in a prone position, and still others by lying on their backs and arching like a wrestler. Most babies, however, discover some form of prone progression. The crawling posture is not rigidly structured; there are at least twenty-five different kinds of crawls and creeps documented in the literature. Approximately half of crawlers begin by dragging themselves forward with their abdomen on the ground in some form of belly crawling. These babies later crawl on hands and knees with their abdomen suspended in the air. The other half of crawlers skip the belly-crawling period completely and go straight to hands and knees. Belly crawlers tend to move their arms and legs in a variety of combinations and permutations, even from cycle to cycle. Hands-and-knees crawlers, in contrast, all move their limbs in a trotting pattern with limbs on diagonal sides of the body moving together. Some hands-and-knees crawlers also discover that they can move forward on hands and feet.

Most Western babies (around 85 percent) crawl at some point before they begin walking. (Adolph, 1997) Exceptions to this rule exist, however. Cultural expectations and practices, as well as a babies' individual skills and temperament, influence whether they will crawl and the type of crawling strategy they will select. For example, in the Bombara culture of Mali, babies rarely crawl before walking. They are jounced up and down in a sling by their mother's side, exposed to rigorous exercise and massage during daily baths, and are rarely put down in a prone position. In contrast to crawling, which is not obligatory, in all documented instances, infants experience some sort of upright skills prior to independent walking. For example, babies pull to a stand, let go and balance, "cruise" sideways holding onto a couch or low table for support, walk frontward pushing a cart, or walk frontward holding a caregiver's hands. In this transitional stage, to locomote without falling over, infants require some sort of manual support.

Independent walking is heralded by parents as the most exciting and important stage in locomotor development. It typically appears around twelve months but varies widely between individual babies. Because walking involves only two limbs over a smaller base of support, it requires more balance control than crawling or cruising. Unlike crawling, the body is far away from the floor, and unlike cruising,

a walking infant does not use any manual support. Although minor falls and tumbles are experienced by all new walkers, walking is more risky than crawling or cruising because walking mistakes can have more serious consequences.

Beginning walkers have a long way to go before they become proficient masters of their newly acquired skill. There is a dramatic change in walking gait from babies' first steps to the toddler years and beyond. New walkers take small steps with their feet spread wide apart. They walk on their toes or plant their whole foot down rather than walking in a heel-toe progression like adults. Like Charlie Chaplin, some babies keep their toes pointed outward and their legs almost straight with their elbows bent upward and their palms facing the ceiling. Others charge along headlong with toes pointed straight ahead and swinging their arms wildly. New walkers' gait appears drunken because they lack coordination between arms and legs, and they must recover balance from step to step as they weave and lurch along. This strange and funny walk progressively improves so that by the time children reach seven years of age they walk like adults. The rate of walking improvement is exponential but varies across individual babies.

Walking is certainly not the final stage of locomotor development. In the second year of life, toddlers acquire other locomotor skills such as running, jumping, turning, walking backward, and walking up and down stairs while holding a rail. As their environments expand, they discover innovative strategies for locomoting down hills, over and under barriers, and over varied terrain. As they become more social, they use locomotion playfully to dance and to learn athletic skills. While locomotor milestones (balancing, sitting, crawling, and walking) develop most rapidly in the first two years of life, the development of locomotor skills never actually stops. From manual tasks that require fine motor coordination to learning how to play a new sport, humans are constantly faced with new tasks that require new locomotor abilities.

Ludovic Marin
Idell B. Weise
Karen E. Adolph

References and further reading

Adolph, Karen E. 1997. "Learning in the Development of Infant Locomotion." *Monographs of the Society for Research in Child Development* 62, no. 251:1–140.
Adolph, Karen E., Beatrix Vereijken, and Mark A. Denny. 1998. "Learning to Crawl." *Child Development* 69:1299–1312.
Thelen, Esther, and Beverley D. Ulrich. 1991. "Hidden Skills: A Dynamic Systems Analysis of Treadmill Stepping during the First Year." *Monographs of the Society for Research in Child Development* 56, no. 223:1–98.

Low Birth Weight Infants

In the past, the term *premature* was applied to any infant who weighed less than five and one-half pounds at birth. The term *premature* is no longer used; infants who weigh less than five and one-half pounds at birth are now referred to as low birth weight infants. Low birth weight infants can be divided into two categories: preterm and small for date. Preterm infants are born three weeks or more before the due date. How low their weight is may depend upon how well they were nourished in the womb. Some preterm infants who were well nourished in the womb may be small at birth, but not low birth weight. Infants born at term, but who weigh five and one-half pounds or less are referred to as small for date (or small for gestational age) infants. Infants who are small for date tend to have more serious problems than do preterm infants. Studies have identified the factors that most commonly contribute to infants being small for date.

These factors include smoking during pregnancy, malnutrition of the mother, exposure to high levels of pollution, and either not receiving prenatal care or not receiving it until late in the pregnancy. Small for date infants can experience long-term problems. The lower the birth weight, the more serious the consequences generally are. Physical problems can include vulnerability to infections, cerebral brain hemorrhages, respiratory distress syndrome, developing cerebral palsy, and damage to the eyes (retinopathy of prematurity). Intellectual problems may include experiencing language problems, such as being slow in starting to talk, and learning difficulties due to being distractible, scoring low on intelligence tests, and not achieving well in school.

However, interventions can help small for date infants to overcome some of the intellectual problems that can occur. Providing support to the parents so that they can be responsive to the special needs of these children and high-quality day care starting at around one year of age are examples of such interventions.

Low birth weight is a preventable complication of pregnancy that can be caused by a number of environmental factors. One of the most common reasons that infants are small for date is maternal cigarette smoking. Tobacco can be identified as a factor in 25 percent of all low birth weight births in the United States. (Berger, 1998) Therefore, women who find out that they are pregnant should attempt to stop smoking. Psychoactive drugs, such as cocaine, also slow the growth of the fetus in the womb. Also, a malnourished mother is likely to deliver a low birth weight infant. Women who live below the poverty level are more likely to be malnourished than middle- or upper-class women. They are also more likely to be ill, because they often live in crowded environments where they are exposed to more illnesses, and to receive late prenatal care. It appears

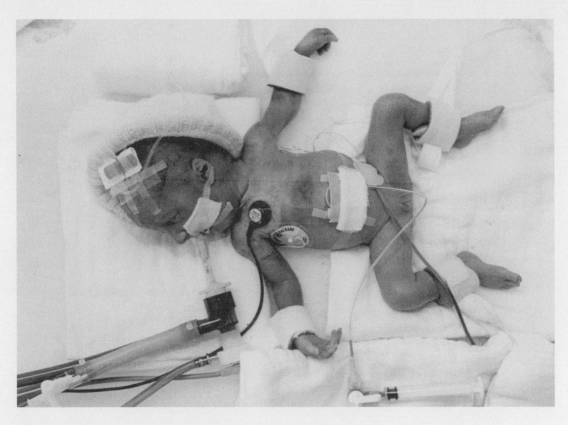

Two-pound premature baby on life support (Elizabeth Crews)

that living in poverty can put a woman at risk for delivering a low birth weight infant. Programs that provide adequate nutrition and prenatal care for pregnant women who live in poverty may help to prevent them from delivering low birth weight infants.

Because of the serious problems that occur in low birth weight infants, many of them are likely to spend some time in a neonatal intensive care unit (NICU), a hospital unit that specializes in the care of seriously ill newborns. They may be placed in isolettes, plexiglass boxes that control body temperature, because they may have difficulty maintaining enough body heat. They may be fed intravenously or through nasogastric tubes (tubes that are inserted through the nose and passed into the stomach). These infants, especially those born more than six weeks

early, often develop respiratory distress syndrome. Their lungs have not fully developed and the air sacs in them may collapse. They may also not have enough surfactant, a substance that helps to keep the air sacs expanded. Therefore, many of these infants have to be intubated and placed on respirators to assist their breathing.

Another problem that may affect low birth weight infants in the NICU is retinopathy of prematurity (ROP). In this disorder the growth of the blood vessels in the retina of the eye is disrupted and visual impairment results. Factors that have been implicated in causing ROP are the high oxygen concentrations in isolettes and the fluorescent lights that are often used in neonatal intensive units. Lowering oxygen concentrations in the isolettes has helped to decrease the incidence of ROP.

Current research is continuing to investigate whether or not the fluorescent lights actually cause ROP.

The staff in the NICU makes it a priority to involve parents in the care of their low birth weight infant. They share information about the infant's condition with the parents, involve them in making decisions about the care their infant receives, and prepare them to provide care to the infant at home. One important aspect of providing care for the low birth weight infant is making sure that he or she receives adequate stimulation.

Because low birth weight infants are often placed in isolettes, they may be touched or held less often than normal infants. This lack of touch can affect both their physical and emotional development. It may be more difficult for these infants to form an attachment bond with their parents. Regular touch can help low birth weight infants to gain weight. In a 1998 study, it was found that preterm infants who were massaged for fifteen minutes three times a day through the portholes in their isolettes gained 47 percent more weight and were hospitalized for six days less than preterm infants who did not receive the massage treatment. (Field, 1998). Other methods of stimulation may include the use of waterbeds, mobiles, and tapes of soft music or caregivers' voices.

Michele V. Karpathian

References and further reading
Berger, Kathleen Stassen. 1998. *The Developing Person through the Life Span.* New York: Worth Publishers.

Berk, Laura E. 1993. *Infants, Children and Adolescents.* Boston: Allyn & Bacon.

Field, Tiffany. 1998. "Massage Therapy Effects." *American Psychologist* 53, no. 12:1270–1281.

Kaplan, Paul S. 1998. *The Human Odyssey: Lifespan Development.* 3d ed. Pacific Grove, CA: Brooks/Cole Publishing.

Klein, Alan H., and Jill Alison Ganon. 1998. *Caring for Your Premature Baby.* New York: HarperPerennial.

M

Malnutrition

We commonly think of nutritional deficiencies as occurring primarily in less developed, non-Western countries. However, evidence indicates that even in developed societies, such as our own, significant numbers of children and their parents have diets that place them at nutritional risk. For example, in low-income groups in the United States survey data indicates that up to 10 percent of young children may show stunted physical growth as a result of an inadequate diet, while between 20 and 30 percent of such children may have nutritionally related iron deficiency anemia. (Cook and Martin, 1995) While nutritional deficiencies are more likely to be found in low-income populations, economic factors in and of themselves are not the sole cause of malnutrition. Even after family economic circumstances are taken into account, children of more educated or more intelligent parents are found to have a better diet than children of less educated or less intelligent parents. In addition, culturally based parental beliefs about appropriate feeding practices have also been shown to have a major effect upon the quality of children's diet. Many studies have shown the adverse developmental consequences associated with malnutrition, chronic undernutrition, or inadequate levels of trace minerals or vitamins in the diet. While the adverse developmental consequences associated with nutritional deficits are primarily viewed as due to the impact of inadequate nutrition upon brain development, there is an increasing interest on the role played by parent-child relationship patterns as well. Of particular importance is what has been called the "functional isolation hypothesis." This hypothesis is based on evidence indicating that children who are malnourished or who have micronutrient deficits such as iron deficiency anemia are more likely to be physically smaller and to show lower activity levels and greater fearfulness. When children are physically smaller, parents are more likely to treat them as if they were younger than their actual chronological age, as well as how the behavior patterns of malnourished children act to reduce parental encouragement for children's active exploration of their environment. The adverse consequences of nutritional deficits upon children's brain development are accentuated by parental behavior patterns that reduce the child's ability to explore and learn from their environment (functional isolation). The link of child malnutrition to parental behavior patterns is likely to be further increased if the parents themselves are undernourished, which means that they have less available energy to provide their children with developmentally appropriate stimulation. In terms of designing intervention strategies to reduce the developmental consequences of malnutrition, it seems clear that efforts to ensure that children are adequately nourished must be combined with training parents to provide a more developmentally stimulating environment for their children, if maximal child development is to occur.

Theodore D. Wachs

References and further reading

Cook, J., and K. Martin. 1995. "Differences in Nutrient Adequacy among Poor and Non-Poor Children." *Center on Hunger, Poverty and Nutrition Policy Monograph.* Medford, MA: Tufts University School of Nutrition.

Engle, P., and L. Lhotska. 1999. "The Role of Care in Programmatic Actions for Nutrition." *Food and Nutrition Bulletin* 20:121–135.

Pollitt, E., M. Golub, K. Gorman, S. Grantham-McGregor, D. Levitsky, B. Schurch, B. Strupp, T. D. Wachs. 1996. "A Reconceptualization of the Effects of Undernutrition on Children's Biological, Psychosocial, and Behavioral Development." *Society for Research in Child Development Social Policy Reports* 10, no. 5.

Maternal Depression and Parenting

Depression is an emotional and physical state that involves feelings of unhappiness and despair, a sense of rejection and negative self-image, and a lack of bodily energy and vigor. Because depression affects both one's internal feelings and moods and one's outward behavior, it is important to understand the causes of maternal depression and the ways in which it affects children's development.

Women with children are particularly susceptible to the development of depressive symptoms, such as negative mood, sleep difficulties, and feelings of low self-worth. Most women who suffer from depressive symptoms have only minor, or passing, symptoms. Sometimes these symptoms become severe enough to be called a depressive episode, of which there are several types. Approximately 10 to 20 percent of all mothers experience "postpartum blues," a mood disorder that occurs during the period of time immediately following childbirth. (O'Hara, Zekoski, Philipps, and Wright, 1990) Mothers of young children are also prone to developing depression; estimates of the disorder among this population range from 12 to 50 percent, depending on how depression is measured. (Garrison and Earls, 1986) Depressive episodes may be recurrent; women with a history of depression are twice as likely to suffer from future episodes than are women without a history of depression. This means that a mother may experience two or more depressive episodes over the course of her child's life.

A depressive disorder can affect a mother's ability to rear and care for her child in many ways. Though not all depressed mothers exhibit the same pattern of behaviors, most mothers who are clinically depressed find it difficult to provide the type of responsive, sensitive care that children need in order to thrive. Children need caregivers who are emotionally and physically available to them and provide consistent care. Depressed caregivers often are emotionally withdrawn and distant, with low energy and affect. Depression may also cause caregivers to be irritable and hostile. Both of these patterns prevent a mother from being "tuned in" to the needs of her child, able to respond predictably and with empathy. In addition, children need to be able to develop a sense of their own agency, or power, in affecting their environments. Children whose caregivers are unresponsive to them may find it difficult to develop these feelings of efficacy or competence.

Maternal depression has been found to have an adverse effect on children's functioning in a number of areas of development, including social, emotional, linguistic, and cognitive. The types of problems a child manifests in response to maternal depression depend upon factors in the child (such as age, temperament, gender), the family situation (such as the availability of other nondepressed caregivers), and the disorder itself (for example, the length of the depressive episode and whether the mother is hospitalized). Child age is an important factor, because children of different ages spend varying amounts of time with their mothers, face different developmental issues, vary in their physical and psychological maturity, and differ in their exposure and ability to utilize other coping resources. While children are not "immune" to the effects of maternal depression at any age, early exposure may have a greater impact on children than exposure in later childhood. Recent research on infant brain development and the role of early experiences shows that the brain continues to develop throughout the first years of life and that social experiences affect the way in which it is organized and functions.

One of the most prominent effects of maternal depression is on children's emotional development, beginning in infancy. Emotions have been called the "language of infancy," a vehicle for communication between parents and children. Infants of depressed women have been found to mirror their mothers' negative and "flat" affect. Toddlers of depressed mothers show more negative and less positive affect than do toddlers of nondepressed mothers. At older ages, children of depressed mothers have greater difficulty regulating their emotions in response to events in the environment, and have more problems with impulse control and reactivity to stress.

For infants and toddlers, a salient developmental task is forming attachment relationships. Children with secure attachments use their parent as a "safe haven" in times of stress, and are better able effectively to explore their world. This task is difficult for infants of depressed mothers, and there is a greater likelihood that they will form insecure attachments in response to a caregiver who is insensitive to infant cues, inconsistent or unresponsive in caregiving, or who interacts in a hostile or intrusive fashion.

Toddlers and preschoolers of depressed mothers may show language delays. This is in part because depressed mothers talk less to their children and are slower to respond to their children's utterances. Most mothers use "motherese," or child-directed speech, with very young children. This type of language interaction, characterized by high pitch and exaggerated affect, is believed to promote linguistic development. The use of "motherese" is not common among depressed mothers.

School-aged children may suffer in social and cognitive realms, because this is a period in which academic achievement and peer interaction are important developmental issues. School-aged children of depressed mothers exhibit more attention deficits and impairments in intellectual functioning than their peers. They may also be less competent in peer relations, have greater behavioral problems, and have difficulty with conflict and empathy.

Not all children of depressed mothers show the effects mentioned here. While maternal depression is a "risk factor" for children's healthy development, there are "protective factors" that may help compensate. Some of these protective factors lie within the child (for example, having an easy temperament or native intelligence). Others are part of the child's social environment (such as the presence of a sensitive, available father or teacher) or community resources (such as the availability of therapeutic resources or good after-school programs). In part, children's adaptation to maternal depression depends upon the severity of the mother's symptoms, the timing of the depressive episode(s), and whether the mother's depression occurs once or repeatedly during the child's lifetime. Depressive episodes may be short-lived, though some mothers continue to express some of the symptoms of depression (such as low self-esteem) after their episodes have ended. As a result, children may be exposed to stressful home environments for extended periods of time, and may continue to exhibit signs of stress or maladjustment when parents think that everything should be "back to normal."

While there has been a great deal of research on the effects of maternal depression on children, the effects of depression among fathers are less well known. This "bias" in research has several roots: mothers typically are their children's primary caregivers; additionally, men with affective disorders often do not marry or father children; finally, the research suggests that mothers' mental health has a more pronounced effect on children's development than does fathers' mental health.

Research shows that depressive disorders tend to aggregate in families, meaning that the children of depressed mothers show higher rates of clinical depression than do the children of nondepressed women. The reasons for depression "running in families" are complex, and involve both biological (genetic) and psychosocial factors. One important factor in the transmission of depression is maternal child-rearing style. For example, depressed mothers are often highly unstable in their disciplinary practices and may be withdrawn and unavailable to their children. Hostility, criticism, and aggression also may characterize interactions. These factors may lead to feelings of helplessness and negative self-concept in children, feelings that are associated with depression. In addition, children may model the behaviors of their parents by observing them. Children of depressed mothers are likely to observe patterns of emotional regulation that include flat or negative affect, pessimism about the future, and other symptoms of depression. Because children mirror their mothers' emotional states, this is one way in which depression may be transmitted across generations.

Christine A. Graham
M. Ann Easterbrooks

References and further reading
American Psychiatric Association. 1994. *Diagnostic and Statistical Manual of Mental Disorders.* Rev., 4th ed. Washington, DC: American Psychiatric Association.

Cohler, Bertram J., and Judith S. Musick. 1983. "Psychopathology and Parenthood: Implications for Mental Health of Children." *Infant Mental Health Journal* 4:140–164.

Field, Tiffany. 1995. "Psychologically Depressed Parents." Pp. 85–99 in *Handbook of Parenting.* Edited by Marc Bornstein. Mahwah, NJ: Lawrence Erlbaum Associates.

Garrison, William T., and Felton J. Earls. 1986. "Epidemiological Perspectives on Maternal Depression and the Young Child." Pages 13–30 in *Maternal Depression and Infant Disturbance. New Directions for Child Development*, no. 34. San Francisco: Jossey-Bass.

Gelfand, Donna M., and Douglas M. Teti. 1990. "The Effects of Maternal Depression on Children." *Clinical Psychological Review* 10:329–353.

O'Hara, Michael W., Ellen M. Zekoski, Laurie H. Philipps, and Ellen J. Wright. 1990. "Controlled Prospective Study on Postpartum Mood Disorders: Comparison of Childbearing and Nonchildbearing Women." *Journal of Abnormal Psychology* 99:3–15.

Tronick, Edward Z., and Tiffany Field, eds. 1986. *Maternal Depression and Infant Disturbance: New Directions for Child Development*, no. 34. San Francisco, CA: Jossey-Bass.

Maternal Guilt

Maternal guilt is a pervasive emotional state characterized by a mother feeling that she is not doing the right thing for her child. Such guilt feelings may consist of concern, anxiety, and sorrow, and may be caused by the conflict women experience in balancing their roles of mother, wife, and employee in today's society. In particular, mothers who return to work after the birth of a child may experience guilt as a result of leaving their child in the care of others. A majority of mothers with young children work. For example, in 1998, 65 percent of women with children under age six were in the labor force as compared to just 39 percent in 1975. (Children's Defense Fund, 1999) This increase in working women can be attributed to many factors, including the rising educational levels of women, the need to develop some occupational competence due to the instability of marriage, a desire for personal satisfaction, and economic needs. An additional factor is that women currently on welfare roles are required to find employment. For these reasons, the number of women in the labor force is unlikely to decline. Further, more mothers continue to work up to the child's birth, and return to work sooner, than was previously the case. As a result, more than half of infants under one year spend some time in the care of someone other than their parents on a regular basis.

Why Working Women Experience Guilt Feelings

Working mothers may experience maternal guilt for a variety of reasons. Mothers may feel guilt due to the social admonishment that "good mothers stay home with their children." Other sources of guilt for the working mother may stem from concerns about the effects maternal employment has on children. For example, a mother may feel that her employment negatively impacts her relationship with her child, or that placing her child in the care of others may result in negative outcomes. While negative outcomes, such as an increase in aggressiveness and illnesses, are sometimes reported, placement in quality child care—especially

after age three—may have benefits. For example, as children progress through each developmental stage, at some point the child's autonomy emerges. Separation from the mother can actually enhance social competence and foster independence in young children.

Further, mothers may feel guilt regarding their decision to return to work, particularly when that decision was made for personal satisfaction rather than economic necessity. In light of the recent research on the importance of stimulation during the first three years for brain development, these feelings of guilt may be exacerbated.

Suggestions for Reducing Guilt Feelings

First of all, mothers must realize that some degree of maternal concern, anxiety, and guilt are actually quite normal and healthy! Such feelings cause parents to make proactive decisions with their children's best interest in mind. Nevertheless, feelings of maternal guilt may be unnecessarily overwhelming for some. The following suggestions may help reduce inappropriate feelings of maternal guilt.

Become knowledgeable about high-quality child care. Research has suggested that those who felt satisfied with their child-care arrangements were less likely to feel guilt. Information about child care may be obtained from child-care licensing agencies, early childhood accreditation programs, or the local library. University extension services also provide information about selecting quality child care. In addition, an Internet search using keywords such as "child care" or "high-quality child care" may yield useful information. Checklists on quality child care are often available through the above-named sources, and serve as an efficient means of evaluating child-care programs. For comparison purposes, checklists should be completed on each program visited.

Consider parental needs. In addition to seeking a quality child-care setting, parents should consider their needs when selecting child-care arrangements. For example, parents who wish to enhance specific developmental areas might choose a different program than those parents stressing the social aspects of the child-care provider relationship. Parents should tour several programs prior to making a placement decision, and understand that a good match involves balancing their needs, those of the child, and the center's philosophy.

Visit and gain information. At each program, parents should obtain and read the center's written program philosophy and other printed materials. In addition to the printed material, and prior to enrollment, parents should schedule an orientation meeting. At that meeting, orientation materials can be reviewed and questions answered. A clear understanding of the program—its philosophy, mission, and goals—is important. Initial parental awareness of program philosophy and teaching style can help parents make informed decisions that best meet their needs.

Foster good communication. Effective communication is a key ingredient to the successful home-school partnership. Individuals working with young children tend to focus upon the well-being of the child, but the focus must be broadened to encompass both the child and parent to assuage maternal guilt. Mutual trust and rapport are necessary for developing a positive relationship between the family and the program for effective communication to take place. In particular, mothers must feel comfortable about asking questions about their child's care.

Become involved. Another strategy for promoting effective communication, and hopefully reducing maternal guilt, is for the parent to become involved with a program's parent advisory board. Such involvement allows the parent to have a voice in program decisions that might affect the child. The resulting sense of empowerment should help to reduce guilt.

As the number of women entering the workforce continues to rise, maternal guilt will remain an issue. Families must make well-informed choices in choosing the best setting for their children's care. In so doing, maternal guilt feelings will be lessened.

Mary Beth Mann

References and further reading
Caine, Lynn. 1985. *What Did I Do Wrong?: Mothers, Children, Guilt.* New York: Arbor House.
Children's Defense Fund. 1999. *The State of America's Children Yearbook.* Washington, DC: Children's Defense Fund.
Hickey, Mary C., and Sandra Salmans. 1992. *The Working Mother's Guilt Guide: Whatever You're Doing, It Isn't Enough.* New York: Penguin Books.
Hilton, Joni. 1996. *Guilt-Free Motherhood: How to Raise Great Kids and Have Fun Doing It.* American Fork, UT: Covenant Communication.
Mann, Mary Beth, and Kathy R. Thornburgh. 1998. "Maternal Guilt: Helping Mothers of Infants and Toddlers in Child Care." *Child Care Information Exchange* (July/August):26–29.

Memory in Infancy

Parents are often amazed at how long infants can concentrate, how fast they learn, and what they remember. Infants seem to have the capacity for long-term memory even at birth. As the weeks progress, they remember for longer periods of time and they become less context dependent. It is important for parents to realize that alert infants explore their worlds with all their senses, learn associations, form concepts, and develop expectations of how the world works. Parents need to provide age-appropriate stimulation for their ever-changing infants. Despite the considerable cognitive activity during infancy and toddlerhood, people do not recall much of their lives before the age of three or four. This phenomenon is called childhood amnesia. However,

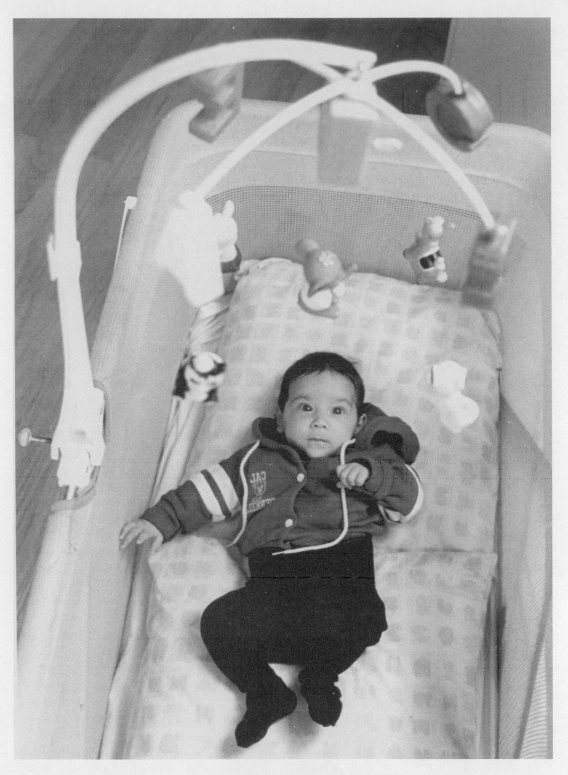

Cues in the environment can help infants remember a learned task. (Elizabeth Crews)

the experiences that infants and toddlers have form the basis for their understanding and their expectations of their social and physical environments.

It has been shown that even newborns have long-term memories. In a well-known early study, research psychologists DeCasper and Fifer published their account of a novel demonstration of memory in newborns. They played a song to a fetus during its last month in the uterus. Later, they showed that as a newborn it calmed down more quickly to that song than to an unfamiliar one. Since that time, many studies have shown that newborns are capable of learning and remembering. It has also been shown that newborns can remember a specific sound for one day. Within the first few days, newborns distinguish the odor of their mother's breast from odors belonging to other women. Also, they show a preference for their mother's voice compared to the voice of a female stranger.

Much of what is known about young infant memory has come from research studies that employ an operant conditioning task. In operant conditioning, an infant learns that some of its actions can bring about desired results. One such task, the Conjugate Reinforcement Mobile Task, was used by Rovee-Collier and her colleagues. In this unique situation, an infant is placed on its back in the middle of its crib to which mobile stands have been attached. One end of a ribbon is attached to a stand and the other end is tied around one of the infant's ankles. Then, an unfamiliar mobile is placed on the stand to which the ribbon is attached. When the infant kicks, the mobile moves, and the infant has the opportunity to learn that his/her kicks are moving the mobile. Infants as young as two months of age tend to learn this quickly, within about five minutes, and can remember it for up to three days; three-month-old infants can remember the task for over one week; and six-month-olds can remember it for about two weeks.

Once the memory for the mobile task has become inaccessible, and infants seem to have forgotten the task, that is, they do not kick in the presence of the mobile to make it move, they can be reminded how to do it if the mobile is again placed over their cribs and moved by the researcher for several minutes. The day after such a reminder, their memory for the task is accessible and they once again kick to make the mobile move. Thus, being prompted helps bring back inaccessible memories.

Before infants are about seven or eight months of age, their ability to remember improves if there are many cues that match those present when they initially learned the task. For example, it is more likely that infants will remember the mobile task if they are tested in the same environmental context (in the same crib or with the same music playing) as when they first learned the task. It seems that infants have to be over seven or eight months of age before they can recall memories, on their own, without the help of environmental cues. It is around eight months of age that infants can search for objects that have disappeared.

By the time they are twelve months old, it has been demonstrated that infants can recall a sequence of specific events. By the time they are about twenty-four months old, infants can recall events that happened several months earlier, and can relate them verbally in story form. However, events experienced before the age of about eighteen months are not remembered verbally; events experienced between about eighteen months and two and one-half years are reported verbally in fragmentary fashion and may be prone to error. From about three years of age, children can give reasonably coherent verbal accounts of their past experiences, and remember them for long periods of time.

Generally, young children's ability to remember is determined by what they are asked to remember, the number of exposures to the event, and the availability of reminders of the event. With age, there is an increase in the range of effective reminders for a particular memory. Once information is no longer tied to a small number of specific reminders, the range of situations in which learned information can be retrieved increases. This may contribute to the decline of childhood amnesia in the third year of life.

Joyce Prigot

References and further reading
Amabile, Toni, and Carolyn Rovee-Collier. 1991. "Contextual Variation and Memory Retrieval at Six Months." *Child Development* 62:1155–1166.
Bauer, Patricia. 1996. "What Do Infants Recall of Their Lives? Memory for Specific Events by One- to Two-Year-Olds." *American Psychologist* 51, no. 1:29–41.
DeCasper, Anthony, and William Fifer. 1980. "Of Human Bonding: Newborns Prefer Their Mothers' Voices." *Science* 208:1174–1176.
Fagan, Jeffrey. 1984. "Infant Memory: History, Current Trends, Relations to Cognitive Psychology." In *Infant Memory: Its Relation to Normal and Pathological Memory in Humans and Other Animals.* Edited by M. Moscovitch. New York: Plenum Press.
Fivush, Robyn. 1998. "Children's Recollections of Traumatic and Nontraumatic Events." *Development and Psychopathology* 10, no. 4:699–716.
Hayne, Harlene, Shelley MacDonald, and Rachel Barr. 1997. "Developmental Changes in the Specificity of Memory over the Second Year of Life." *Infant Behavior and Development* 20, no. 2:233–245.
Howe, Maria, and Mary Courage. 1993. "On Resolving the Enigma of Infantile Amnesia." *Psychological Bulletin* 113, no. 2:305–326.
Newcombe, Nora, Anna Drummey, and Eunhui Lie. 1995. "Children's Memory for Early Experience." *Journal of Experimental Child Psychology* 59, no. 3:337–342.
Rovee-Collier, Carolyn. 1987. "Learning and Memory in Infancy." In *Handbook of Infant Development.* 2d ed. Edited by J. D. Osofsky. New York: John Wiley and Sons.

Menopause

Menopause is the complete stopping of a woman's monthly menstrual periods. This stopping of periods may occur gradually over a couple of years, with periods first becoming irregular. For example, a woman may have a menstrual period for one month and then not have another for two or three months. When the menstrual periods stop completely, women are no longer fertile and are no longer able to bear children. It is important for women who want to have children to know about menopause so that they can plan to have children before they lose their fertility. This is especially important in our current culture because many women today prefer to establish careers before they begin to have families. Some are having a first child in their late thirties or even early forties. Although most women experience menopause between the ages of forty-two and fifty-two years of age, about 10 percent of all women experience it before forty years of age. (Kaplan,1998; Santrock,1999) The age of onset of menopause may be determined in part by heredity. What this means is that a woman can get some idea of when it might occur for her by asking her mother at what age she experienced menopause.

During menopause the amount of the hormone estrogen that is produced by a woman's ovaries decreases greatly. This decrease in estrogen production can cause some uncomfortable symptoms. Women who are experiencing other life stresses, such as a divorce or death of a loved one, may have higher rates of symptoms. One of those symptoms is hot flashes. Some women may feel exceedingly hot at times due to the hormonal changes that are taking place. They may experience flushing of the skin on the head and neck and perspiration. Hot flashes may last from several seconds to several minutes. Hot flashes may continue for up to five years in about 25 percent of women who experience them. More commonly they last about one to two years. However, some women never experience them. Other symptoms can include nausea, fatigue, rapid heartbeat, irritability, and depression. Estrogen decline may also cause the membranes of the vagina to become thin. If this happens, a woman may experience painful intercourse. The majority of women experiencing menopause do not report symptoms serious enough to require medical care. However, since postmenopausal women are at greater risk for heart disease and osteoporosis, a condition that causes bone loss and makes a woman more susceptible to fractures, many visit their gynecologists to discuss whether or not hormone replacement therapy is appropriate for them. In addition, for those women who do experience more serious symptoms, hormone replacement therapy often provides relief from them.

Hormone replacement therapy usually consists of taking two hormones: estrogen and progesterone. Taking estrogen by itself can increase a woman's risk of getting uterine cancer. Taking progesterone along with it protects the woman from developing uterine cancer. The hormones are usually taken every day. Hormone replacement therapy is generally not recommended for women who are at increased risk for breast cancer, for example, those with a family history of breast cancer. One concern that has been raised is whether women using estrogen are at increased risk for breast cancer. Although most research studies have found that the use of estrogen does not increase a woman's risk of breast cancer, a few have found a very slight increase in the incidence of breast cancer in women taking estrogen. Gynecologists usually discuss the risk factors and benefits of hormone replacement therapy openly and in depth with their postmenopausal patients. The patients can then make an informed choice about whether or not to receive hormone replacement therapy.

Some women who choose not to take hormone replacement therapy may choose to eat certain foods that mimic the effects of estrogen. Foods such as tofu, miso (soybean paste), soybeans, cashew nuts, peanuts, oats, corn, wheat, apples, almonds, and alfalfa contain compounds that are known as phytoestrogens (plant estrogens). Phytoestrogens may help to relieve hot flashes and other menopausal symptoms. What is not yet known is if these compounds are effective in preventing osteoporosis.

Postmenopausal women can also help to decrease symptoms and protect themselves against heart disease and osteoporosis by eating a diet low in fat and high in calcium. Their physicians may also recommend taking a calcium supplement. Starting an aerobic exercise program may also help to decrease menopausal symptoms, increase emotional well-being, and offer some protection against heart disease. The exercise program is very important because after menopause and during middle age, coronary arteries (the arteries that supply blood to the heart tissue) narrow, and blood pressure and "bad" cholesterol rise. Engaging in an exercise program can lower blood pressure and "bad" cholesterol while raising "good" cholesterol, which helps to prevent narrowing of the coronary arteries due to fatty deposits.

The attitudes that women have about menopause vary. Most women neither have negative attitudes about it, nor do they regret having reached it. Women who have negative expectations or make incorrect assumptions about menopause may have negative experiences with it once they reach it. However, many women view it as a positive experience because they no longer have to worry about having menstrual periods or getting pregnant. The negative attitudes that some women have about menopause may be precipitated by our culture's emphasis on youth and fear of growing old. In China where old age and older individuals are respected, there is no word or term for hot flashes. Differences in symptoms among cultures have also been discovered. In one study Japanese women were found to have a lower occurrence of hot flashes and depression than were women in the United States and Canada.

Michele V. Karpathian

References and further reading
Cabot, Sandra. 1995. *Smart Medicine for Menopause.* Garden City, NY: Avery Publishing Group.
Gaby, Alan R. 1994. *Preventing and Reversing Osteoporosis.* Rocklin, CA: Prima Publishers.
Kaplan, Paul S. 1998. Pp. 369–371 in *The Human Odyssey: Lifespan Development.* 3d ed. Pacific Grove, CA: Brooks/Cole Publishing.
Santrock, John W. 1999. Pp. 444–445 in *Life-Span Development.* 7th ed. Dubuque, IA: McGraw-Hill College.

Mental Retardation, Parenting a Child with

Mental retardation is a condition that has a range of causes, as well as a variety of effects. Individuals with mental retardation exist in all cultures and economic, educational, racial, and ethnic groups.

An individual with mental retardation is a person whose ability to learn and to function is slower and more limited than those of others the same age. The American Association on Mental Retardation (AAMR, 1992) has outlined three criteria for diagnosing an individual with mental retardation: first, the individual has a score below 70 to 75 on an individually administered intelligence test (where 100 points is considered the average score of the population). Second, the individual has significant limitations in two or more adaptive areas (such as communication, self-care, social skills, health and safety, and community functioning). Third, this condition is present before eighteen years of age.

The age of diagnosis varies depending on the cause. Some children, such as those with Down syndrome, can be identified at birth. Others, including those for whom there is no known cause, are often not diagnosed until they approach school age and have not attained the same skills as other children the same age.

It is estimated that approximately 1 to 3 percent of the population in the United States is mentally retarded. (Watson and Gross, 1997) A slightly higher proportion of boys than girls is diagnosed with this condition. About two-thirds of those with mental retardation have known causes. Although there are more than 750 known organic causes of mental retardation, the most prevalent of these (32 percent) is early alteration of embryonic development, such as the chromosomal changes that occur in Down syndrome. Environmental hazards, such as exposure to lead paint or inadequate nutrition, are the next most frequent cause (18 percent). Problems associated with pregnancy (such as placental insufficiency) or problems occurring around birth, such as prematurity, are the third most frequent cause of mental retardation (11 percent). Hereditary disorders (such as fragile X syndrome or Tay-Sachs disease) and acquired childhood diseases (such as encephalitis or meningitis) are less frequent causes of mental retardation. (Crocker, 1989)

Mental retardation has a range of effects. The majority of children diagnosed with mental retardation (87 percent) are mildly affected by this condition. These children learn more slowly than their classmates, may have slower motor and language development, and tend to have difficulty in maintaining attention and in developing short-term memory function. Most, however, will be able to live and work in the community with minimal assistance when they

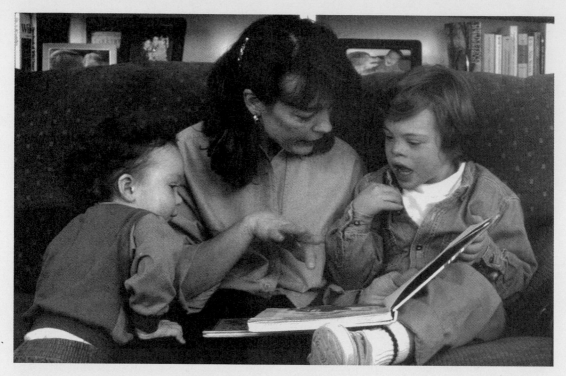

Raising a child with mental retardation can be challenging, but for most families, levels of stress are within the normative range. (Laura Dwight)

become adults. The other 13 percent (generally those with intelligence quotients under fifty) are likely to experience significant limits in their functioning and independence, but they demonstrate a capacity to learn and benefit from educational interventions.

Although in the past many professionals believed that parents who raise a child with mental retardation experience pathological levels of stress and are more likely to have their marriage dissolve, current data do not support either of these assumptions. Parents with mentally retarded children are no more likely to divorce than are other parents. Raising a child with mental retardation can be challenging, but for most families, levels of stress are within the normative range. The greatest stressors reported by parents of children with mental retardation are those due to children's health conditions

and to behavior problems rather than to cognitive impairment per se.

Differences between fathers and mothers in parenting a child with mental retardation have been reported. During the early childhood years mothers report more stress related to social isolation and the demands of parenting, whereas fathers report more stress related to the child's temperament. Gender of the child may also be important as fathers with sons, in comparison to those with daughters, report higher levels of stress. Similar gender differences have not been found consistently for mothers. Helpful networks of social support composed of family, friends, and professionals reduce stress for mothers; this finding has not been replicated for fathers. Both mothers and fathers who cope with stress by using strategies that aim at problem solving (rather than rely only on emotional support) report reduced stress over the early and middle childhood period.

Although many parenting challenges are similar for parents of children with mental retardation to those experienced in the general population, research studies have noted some potential distinctions. During the infant and toddler years, children with mental retardation tend to show less distinct cues about their needs and display somewhat diminished responses to caregivers. They also may take somewhat longer to respond to parents' initiations. Research has also demonstrated that parents of very young children with mental retardation tend to be highly directive of children in their interactions when playing together. Although a few children respond well to the high level of direction, those who experience the highest levels of parent direction during playful situations tend to become less self-motivated over time. The challenge for parents thus becomes how to encourage children in their play and make sure that children have a chance to initiate, as well as respond, when interacting with parents and others.

Parents of children with mental retardation have reported that certain points during the life cycle are particularly challenging. The extent of challenge depends on the child's functional skills, communication skills, and whether he or she exhibits many problem behaviors, such as tantrums or excessive stubbornness. Traditional points of transition, such as entry into preschool, middle, or high school, and the termination of schooling often require careful planning. The involvement of parents in collaboration with schools and other community agencies is necessary to make the transition beneficial for the child. During the school years, parents have reported that children with mental retardation often have a range of friends, but may have a smaller network of close friends. Their networks

also tend to be more highly reliant on family members than on peers. Parents also report, however, less concern about the typically high-risk behaviors of many adolescents, such as substance abuse, although these risky behaviors are more likely to occur for adolescents with a network of typically developing friends. At age twenty-two, or when the young adult leaves the school system, is often a difficult time for parents, especially if the young adult is not able to live somewhat independently. During the adolescent and young adult years parents often become increasingly involved in planning for their child's future financial resources and living situation.

The federal Individuals with Disabilities Education Act of 1990 (IDEA), reauthorized in 1997, mandates that all children, including those with disabilities, are entitled to an education that is both "free" and "appropriate." Children with disabilities are entitled to receive publicly funded education from the age of three until age twenty-two. By law, parents have many rights regarding the assessment of children and the type of school placement recommended for their child. Schools are required to provide parents with information about their rights. One right is that the child be educated in the "least restrictive environment." This is often interpreted as a right to attend general education classes to the maximum extent possible. Many students with mental retardation attend only general education classes, possibly with an aide for part or all of the school day. Others attend a mix of general and special education classes; a smaller number attend only special education classes or special schools. There is much variation in placement options from state to state and from district to district within states. During the adolescent years, schools are required to initiate transition planning with the student and parents to make sure plans are made about the student's transition from the school system into vocational or further educational endeavors. Schools are also required to offer students with disabilities a vocational assessment during the high school years.

From birth to age three, mentally retarded children and their families are entitled to early intervention services. Each state has a designated state agency, typically education, public health, or mental health, which offers early intervention services. Early intervention services also vary from state to state, but usually involve home visits by educators, physical therapists, occupational therapists, speech and language therapists, or social workers. These individuals work with the child and the parents to provide necessary therapeutic interventions or recommended practices that fit with the family's values and perspectives on child rearing. Therapeutic interventions for the child may also occur in day care or other community services in consultation with parents.

Many organizations exist to assist parents in their task of parenting a child with mental retardation. National and state advocacy organizations often provide parents with information, resources, and links to other parents. Long-standing examples of national organizations are the National Down Syndrome Congress, the American Association on Mental Retardation, and The Arc (formerly Association for Retarded Citizens).

Penny Hauser-Cram
Ann Steele

References and further reading
American Association on Mental Retardation. 1992. *Mental Retardation: Definition, Classification, and Systems of Support.* 9th ed. Washington, DC: AAMR.
The Arc of the United States website: *http://thearc.org.*
Burack, Jacob A., Robert M. Hodapp, and Edward Zigler, eds. 1998. *Handbook of Mental Retardation and Development.* New York: Cambridge University Press.
Crocker, A. C. 1989. "The Causes of Mental Retardation." *Pediatric Annals* 18:623–635.
Hodapp, Robert M. 1998. *Development and Disabilities.* New York: Cambridge University Press.
Kingsley, Jason, and Mitchell Levitz. 1994. *Count Us In: Growing Up with Down's Syndrome.* New York: Harcourt Brace.
Rowitz, Louis, ed. 1992. *Mental Retardation in the Year 2000.* New York: Springer-Verlag.
Watson, G. S., and A. M. Gross. 1997. "Mental Retardation and Developmental Disorders." Pp. 495–520 in *Handbook of Prevention and Treatment with Children and Adolescents: Intervention in the Real World Context.* New York: John Wiley and Sons.

Montessori, Maria (1870–1952)

Maria Montessori originated an educational method that is used for both mentally impaired and normal children. Encouraged by worldwide enthusiasm for her work, she organized a network of schools and societies devoted to the Montessori method, an approach that was developed from observation of children's interactions with the environment. Montessori's prime educational objective was to foster personality development in children by allowing students to work at their own pace, within a carefully prepared environment. Many elements of the modern education system have their origin in Montessori's theories. The development of such key educational concepts as the open classroom, individualized education, manipulative learning materials, and combined age groups have been credited to her.

Maria Montessori was born 31 August 1870 in Chiaravalle, Italy, the only child of middle-class, educated parents. Despite opposition from her father and teachers, she enrolled at the University of Rome as a student of mathematics, physics, and the natural sciences, intending to become an engineer. However, she soon changed her focus to medicine. In 1896, she gradu-

Maria Montessori (1870–1952) (Popperfoto/Archive Photos)

ated from the University of Rome Medical School at the top of her class, earning the first medical degree granted to a woman in Italy.

In 1895, Montessori obtained a competitive post as an assistant doctor, specializing in pediatrics and psychiatry. As part of her work, she visited various insane asylums in order to select patients for treatment. There she saw mentally handicapped children confined to empty rooms without any social or educational provisions. Recognizing the need of these children for stimulation and interaction, Montessori initiated a wave of reform within the asylums. She implemented programs to teach the youngsters how to care for themselves and their environment, used manipulative perceptual puzzles to provide the children direct experience with concrete objects, and insisted that staff interact with children in a respectful manner. Montessori's work with this population led her to conceptualize mental deficiency as an educational problem, rather than a medical one.

Fueled by her growing interest in education, Montessori undertook a study of all previous research on the education of the mentally handicapped. Her search led her to the contributions of two Frenchmen, Jean Marc Itard and Eduoard Seguin. Itard had become famous for his work with "Victor, the Wild Boy of Aveyron," a young man who—it was believed—had been raised in the wild. Itard attempted to educate Victor, hoping that this experiment would shed light on the relative contributions of heredity and environment to human development. Itard quickly noted that this "wild boy," who lacked all language and social skills, was unwilling or unable to learn most things. From his observations, Itard theorized that normal development is marked by a sequence of "sensitive periods" during which a child is particularly receptive to development in a particular domain. If the child does not experience stimulation in that area during the appropriate period, that skill may be lost forever. The notion of "sensitive periods" later became an integral component of Montessori's educational theory. Both Itard and Seguin believed in a scientific approach to education, based on thorough observation and experimentation. This perspective appealed to Montessori and later became the cornerstone of her educational method. She was also influenced by the educational theories of Jean-Jacques Rousseau, Johann Pestalozzi, and Friedrich Froebel, to whom she owed her focus on self-discovery through sense training.

Montessori's work in the insane asylums gained public acclaim when many of the mentally deficient adolescents under her care were able to pass standard public school sixth-grade tests. Responding to this attention, Montessori maintained that her success demonstrated that public schools were doing a poor job educating normal children. The Italian Ministry of Education did not welcome this idea and denied Montessori access to public school children. Montessori's chance to offer her educational methods to normal children came in 1907 when a real estate group, renovating a housing project for the poor, invited her to establish a day-care center for preschool children.

Montessori's first Children's House (Casa dei Bambini) was a single room in an apartment building located in one of the worst slum districts in Rome. The class consisted of about fifty preschoolers who were taught by one untrained caregiver. The children entered the class withdrawn, impulsive, and often aggressive. Montessori began by teaching the older children to help with everyday tasks and chores. The children swept and dusted the classroom, and organized the materials. Within weeks, a surprised Montessori noted that the children were becoming more verbal and sociable, and that they worked diligently in the absence of obvious rewards. The children showed an immediate interest in the puzzles and perceptual training devices. They also enjoyed learning practical living skills, which Montessori believed fostered their self-esteem and independence. The children showed a spontaneous interest in writing and reading, which led Montessori to develop new materials and strategies for the acquisition of early reading and writing skills that normally were taught four years later in Italian public schools.

Montessori's success at the Children's House earned her international acclaim and a lifelong reputation as an educational wonder worker. Educators and students from all over the world traveled to Rome in order to be trained by her. In 1909, Montessori held a training course, culminating in the first formal statement of her educational method. This statement was later translated into English as *The Montessori Method*, the first of many books describing her educational approach. The period between the opening of her Children's House in 1907 until the 1930s was the most productive in Montessori's career. She continued her study of children, expanded the preschool curriculum, and developed an educational system for the elementary school level. By 1910, she had created an international franchise system, allowing only those teachers trained by her to oversee Montessori classrooms. Montessori schools were formed throughout Europe, North America, and Asia. Governments in some countries officially adopted the Montessori method in their school systems. In 1929, she organized the Association Montessori Internationale (AMI), headquartered in Amsterdam. This organization, which institutionalized Montessori's approach, aimed to oversee the schools and societies that she helped to develop.

The Montessori method was not built upon systematic research, but evolved gradually through careful observation and impromptu experimentation. Montessori conceived of the first six years of life as the period of the "absorbent mind," during which the child assimilates the external world involuntarily. She believed that the absorbent mind functioned through time-bound, irreversible "sensitive periods," when children are particularly receptive to development in certain areas. She hypothesized that "sensitive periods" exist for order, motor development, language, writing, interest in small objects, morality, socialization, and reading.

Montessori developed many of the materials used in her classrooms, and she regularly reworked them to fit the needs of her students. These self-correcting materials allowed children to explore the world through their senses and increase self-confidence by gaining mastery over the external world. Many of the perceptual puzzles and educational toys that are commonly used in today's larger educational community are based on Montessori's materials. She believed that education should be child focused rather than teacher focused. In the Montessori classroom, the role of the teacher is to provide an enriched environment that minimizes the need for direct instruction. The teacher determines what each child needs for optimal development and facilitates learning by guiding the child toward that goal. Montessori believed that allowing children to choose materials at their own pace nurtured their independence.

Her focus on the optimal learning environment is evident throughout her method. She was the first to acknowledge the frustration children experience operating in an adult-size world. She furnished her classrooms with child-size furniture and objects, enabling the children to do for themselves what others previously had to do. Montessori made certain that the tables were light enough for the children to lift. She obtained plates and utensils that fit the small hands of a child. Materials were stored in low, easily accessible shelves so children could pick out materials at will. Montessori's innovative environmental engineering has found its way into the educational mainstream.

Maria Montessori first visited the United States in 1912, amid a great outpouring of enthusiasm and support. By the following year, approximately 100 Montessori schools were operating in the United States. It was not long, however, before the Montessori method met with harsh criticism. The criticism stemmed primarily from a group of educators and psychologists, the most influential of whom was William Kilpatrick, a respected professor at Teachers College, Columbia University, who dismissed Montessori's work as outdated. Kilpatrick asserted that the Montessori method failed to provide enough emphasis on social development and interaction among students. He was also highly critical of Montessori's teaching materials, which he believed did not allow for social interaction and failed to foster imaginative thinking and creative play. Spurred by such criticism, the Montessori method faded from the educational scene in the United States as abruptly as it had entered. Despite

Montessori's tremendous success in other parts of the world, Kilpatrick's dismissal of the Montessori method stood largely unchallenged in the United States until the 1960s.

Child development research over the past several decades has shown that Montessori's educational theory anticipated many current psychological and educational notions, suggesting that her ideas were decades ahead of her time. For example, her method of breaking down complex tasks into smaller, manageable components parallels modern-day behavior modification procedures. Her view that motor skills precede symbolic aspects of learning is consistent with the work of the eminent child psychologist, Jean Piaget. Key concepts in Montessori's educational theory, such as the importance of early environmental conditions in child development, sensitive periods, intrinsic motivation, and the role of cognitive development in the social and creative abilities, are now widely recognized by the scientific establishment. The 1960s saw a resurgence of interest in Montessori education that has continued to the present day. At the close of the twentieth century, there are more than three thousand Montessori schools in the United States.

Maria Montessori spent most of her adult life developing, teaching, lecturing, and writing about her educational method. She never married, although she had one child, Mario Montessori, with Guiseppe Montesano, her codirector at the Orthophrenic School in Rome. The existence of her son was kept secret for many years, particularly early in her career. Montessori's contributions to education have received numerous awards and honors. She was nominated three times for the Nobel Peace Prize and was an Italian delegate to the UNESCO conference in 1950. She died on 6 May 1952 of a cerebral hemorrhage, shortly before her eighty-second birthday. Her last home in Noordwijk aan Zee, the Netherlands, became the headquarters for the AMI, which was headed by her son, Mario, until his death in 1982.

John D. Hogan
Lorissa Byely

References and further reading
Kramer, Rita. 1976. *Maria Montessori: A Biography.* New York: G. P. Putnam's Sons.
Montessori, Maria. 1964. *The Montessori Method.* New York: Schocken Books.
Rambusch, Nancy McCormick. 1962. *Learning How to Learn: An American Approach to Montessori.* Baltimore, MD: Helicon Press.
Standing, E. M. 1962. *Maria Montessori: Her Life and Work.* New York: Mentor Omega.

Moral Development

Morality refers to the idea that some things are right and others wrong, independent of whether they bring reward or punishment. It includes *proscribed* behaviors, which are usually obligatory, such as not lying, cheating, or breaking a trust, and *prescribed* behaviors, which may be discretionary, such as helping others who are in need. These are usually called *prosocial morality* or *altruism.* A third domain is *distributive justice,* which pertains to how rewards are allocated in groups or society. All three domains of morality have three aspects: moral conduct or behavior that is consistent with some standard of conduct; moral emotions and feelings, such as guilt and shame, which occur when one has failed to live up to one's (society's) standards; and knowledge of right and wrong as expressed in evaluative judgments and reasoning about moral choices. All three facets of morality (judgment and reasoning, emotions, and overt conduct) are important for a complete understanding of moral development.

However, investigators have adopted different strategies, giving greater emphasis to one or another aspect of morality.

As children get older, they begin to base moral decisions on the effect of their actions on others. (Laura Dwight)

The argument against focusing on overt behavior has been that without knowing the meaning of the behavior for the individual one cannot evaluate its moral significance. And, moral emotions, such as guilt and shame, are often so disproportionate to any rational or reasonable moral standard that their moral significance becomes suspect.

The argument for not focusing on moral judgments and reasoning is that they may simply reflect cognitive sophistication. Nevertheless, in the past three decades most researchers interested in the development of morality have chosen to emphasize moral judgments and justifying reasoning, in part because of the convenience of studying them and in part because of the assumption that judgments of right and wrong lie at the heart of morality. Although there is considerable difference of opinion concerning the

processes by which morality develops, there is substantial agreement that certain changes regularly occur.

The first developmental change noted in children's moral reasoning is from emphasis on the more surface, concrete to the more inferential and psychological aspects of a moral act. For example, young children sometimes focus on the concrete outcome of the act (e.g., the amount of damage done) rather than the intentions behind it (whether the outcome was intended or accidental), whereas older children tend to pay more attention to the intentions behind the act.

The second change is from more self-centered to more general and disinterested moral criteria. Thus, young children often judge an act as wrong only if it negatively impinges on them, whereas older children, adolescents, and adults judge acts to be wrong if they harm others or violate ideas of fairness regardless of the consequences for self.

A related third change has been posited: *from* a morality based on the assumption that one's moral duty is to obey/defer to authority and avoid punishment *to* a morality based on the idea that one's duty is to act in accord with basic notions of justice and fairness, and to help and not harm others. This shift in the fundamental concept of morality, which was hypothesized by the Swiss developmental psychologist Jean Piaget and later elaborated by the American psychologist Lawrence Kohlberg, is based on the idea that moral judgments develop by a series of differentiations and reorganizations of thinking about right and wrong. According to this theory, young children first fail to differentiate physical events (e.g., glass breaking) from moral/social events (e.g., dishonesty), then later begin to differentiate issues of right and wrong from simple social conventions, and still later from particular social norms, when those norms violate fundamental ethical principles such as the injunction to treat individuals as ends and not as means. The development of moral thinking is thus seen as a successive "purifying" of moral concepts, differentiating genuine moral concerns from those irrelevant to morality, such as punishment and reward.

Elliot Turiel, a developmental psychologist at Berkeley, and his colleagues have recently challenged this conceptualization of morality and claim that even young children (age four or five) intuitively know that the moral domain is fundamentally different from practical and social conventions and do not confuse the two. For example, young children understand that while the conventions in their own school may be that teachers must be addressed by their last name and children must eat sitting down at snack time, in another school it might be agreed that all children may call teachers by the first name or eat standing up. However, children understand that it would not be morally legitimate to agree that it was all right to harm someone without provocation or to break a promise without some compelling *moral* reason. While they have mustered considerable evidence in support of this idea of separate moral and social-conventional domains of judgment, the controversy about the nature of development of moral thinking is far from settled.

The fundamental change in children's/adolescents' thinking about morality appears to proceed from a concrete, particularistic, and perhaps obedience-oriented mode to a more symbolic, universal, and autonomous mode of moral thinking.

There is also much controversy concerning whether the above fundamental developments in moral thinking also occur in different cultures, subgroups within society, and males and females. Some theorists have argued that when the superficial content of moral judgments (roughly, "what" is right and wrong) is stripped away from the underlying structure ("why" it is right or wrong), the inner "logic" of the thought is revealed. These theorists have posited that this underlying structure of moral reasoning consists of an ever-increasing ability to take and to integrate diverse moral perspectives in a situation. Moral reasoning is then seen to proceed along similar lines, although the rate of that development will, of course, vary according to social and cultural circumstances.

Another approach to explaining cultural differences in morality is that the differences do not reflect differences in moral values but in the interpretations of the situation. For example, the fact that the Inuit (Eskimos) place the elderly out to die does *not* mean that they do not value human life or the elderly, but rather reflects their religious beliefs concerning the afterlife, in which one's condition reflects the physical condition at the end of one's life. Therefore, to let someone deteriorate physically is inhuman, because it compromises the afterlife. Other more anthropologically oriented scholars, like Richard Shweder at the University of Chicago, have argued, in part based on interviews with Brahmins in India, that cultures fundamentally differ in their moral values, and that the Western distinction between social conventions and moral values is just that, a Western—not a universal—distinction. Others have pointed out the need to avoid the danger of stereotyping cultures with labels such as "collectivist," "individualistic," "rights-based," "duty-based," and the like, and recognize that other cultures like our own are not monoliths but different according to particular roles, social relationships, and the like.

Kohlberg and other theorists believe that this development has an ultimate end and that that end is justice, or fairness to all. Others deny the idea of one end to the development of moral thought. Foremost among these critics is Carol Gilligan of Harvard Graduate School of Education, who has concluded that justice is only one framework for moral reasoning, and that caring is another equally valid framework, in which responsibility and empathy for others, rather than impartiality and universality are the guiding criteria. According to Gilligan and her coworkers, people decide moral dilemmas less in terms of abstract ethical principles and more in terms of the particular social context in which the dilemma is embedded. For example, they found that the decision of whether or not to abort an unwanted pregnancy was typically made in the context of particular social relations and not in terms of abstract principles. Further, many of these writers on morality have claimed that while all moral persons may be guided by justice

and caring, females give special emphasis to the caring criterion. Again, there is much dispute around this issue, and many researchers have reported both orientations, towards justice and toward caring, equally to characterize moral thinking by both sexes.

Another controversy concerns the relationship among the three facets of morality discussed above, and especially between moral conduct and moral judgment. Early research had indicated that the relationships between moral judgment and conduct are weak and inconsistent, and some critics concluded that "talk is cheap" and that therefore moral judgment reflects cognitive sophistication, not moral commitment. This pessimistic conclusion has been tempered by later research showing weak but relatively consistent relationships between moral conduct and moral thought. This issue of consistency between moral judgment and conduct is a complicated one, but inconsistency may be due, in part, to the kinds of measures used to assess moral judgment and conduct, and the perspective from which the decision to judge and to act are made. Here it is important to distinguish between straightforward moral conflicts, in which a moral duty or right is in conflict with a nonmoral need or desire, and complex moral dilemmas, in which two moral duties or rights are in conflict. In the first case, it is not hard to know *what* is the right thing to do although it may be hard to *do* it. In the second case, it may be difficult even to know what to do because two rights are involved.

Much of the research on children's and adolescents' moral reasoning has focused on children's reasoning about moral dilemmas, whereas measures of their overt behavior usually involve the cognitively "simpler" but nonetheless emotionally difficult moral conflicts. Another explanation for the oft-noted divergence between how children reason about hypothetical moral situations and how they behave overtly is that the situation may be interpreted differently when serving as an observing judge of a past action and as the self facing the need to make a moral decision in a complex situation. For example, one's understanding of how much freedom of choice one has in a moral situation is very different when one is the actor facing the decision to be made and the observer on the sidelines looking at a decision already made. Thus, explanations of the disparity between moral thought and action must go beyond the simplified conclusion that "talk is cheap."

How does the environment affect moral development? Two factors in the environment have been shown to be important. The first is how parents rear children and especially the kinds of discipline they use. Research studies by developmental psychologists Martin Hoffman, Herbert D. Saltzstein, and by Diana Baumrind, among others, have found the use of more coercive discipline, such as physical punishment, is associated with lower scores on verbal measures of moral development, while more psychological and less coercive methods, such as pointing out the consequences of one's acts for others, is associated with higher scores. The evidence seems fairly clear. How to interpret these findings is less clear, because children may influence parents just as parents surely influence children. Therefore, the above noted correlations may reflect the fact that parents are more likely to punish difficult children, who are difficult at least in part because of other influences, such as temperament or peers. Also complicating matters is the fact that children may misinterpret what parents do and what they believe. So, for example, research by Saltzstein and his coworkers demonstrate that children appear to attribute judgments to parents or adults that are harsher and more primitive than the parents' actual beliefs and (perhaps) their practices.

This question of causal direction has not been resolved, but no doubt some of the correlation between child-rearing practices and children's morality is due to children's influence on parents more than the reverse. That said, surely parenting does influence how the child develops morally. The questions are *when, to what extent,* and *how?*

The other factor, which has been hypothesized to promote moral development, is perspective taking. This refers to the ability to look at a moral situation from different points of view and to integrate these different perspectives. According to this view, anything that promotes the development of this ability to take and integrate diverse perspectives promotes moral development, especially morality conceived of as fairness or justice. Some of the effect of discipline may be understood in these terms. However, other kinds of social experience, such as how much children are permitted to participate in decisions in the family and school, in peer groups, and so on, may also be important for the development of that part of personality that makes us distinctly human.

Herbert D. Saltzstein

References and further reading
Damon, William. 1988. *The Moral Child: Nurturing Children's Moral Growth.* New York: Free Press.
Grusec, Joan E., and Jacqueline J. Goodnow. 1994. "Impact of Parental Discipline Methods on the Child's Internalization of Values: A Reconceptualization of Current Points of View." *Developmental Psychology* 30:4–19.
Haidt, Jon, Silvia H. Koller, and Maria G. Dias. 1994. "Affect, Culture and the Morality of Harmless Offenses." *Journal of Personality and Social Psychology* 65:613–629.
Kohlberg, Lawrence. 1981. *The Psychology of Moral Development.* New York: HarperCollins.
Saltzstein, Herbert D., ed. 1997. *Culture as a Context for Moral Development: New Perspectives on the Particular and the*

Universal, New Directions for Child Development, no. 76. San Francisco: Jossey-Bass.

Schweder, Richard A., M. Mahapatra, and Joan G. Miller. 1987. "Culture and Moral Development." In *The Emergence of Morality in Young Children*. Chicago: University of Chicago Press.

Mother's Day

Mother's Day is a day set aside each year on the second Sunday in May to honor all mothers. Particular celebrations for motherhood have a long history, dating back to antiquity. Fertility rights and rituals, while directed to the goddesses, also offer special recognition of maternity. Perhaps we can trace back the earliest Mother's Day celebrations to the spring festivals of ancient Greece in honor of Rhea, the Mother of God. Much later, during the 1600s, England celebrated a day called Mothering Sunday on the fourth Sunday of Lent. Mothering Sunday honored the mothers of England. On this day, servants were given the day off and were encouraged to return home to spend the day with their mothers. A distinctive cake, baked for the occasion, called the mothering cake, was often purchased to add a festive touch.

Honoring the Virgin Mary as Supreme Mother might be considered yet another way of sanctifying motherhood. In fact, when Christianity spread throughout Europe, those celebrations changed to include the Mother Church—the spiritual power that gave people life and protected them from harm. Over time, the church festival blended with the Mothering Sunday celebration. People began to commemorate their actual mothers, as well as the church. Bear in mind, however, that these historical happenings, though related to the concept, are not necessarily connected to the holiday as celebrated today.

Many people believe that people interested in commercial profit invented modern Mother's Day (and Father's Day, celebrated in June). Certainly, businesses use both holidays to gain customers. Shopkeepers at the given times organize their merchandize, and restaurants their advertising, in keeping with the events. Yet, these holidays have more specific origins. In the United States, Julia Ward Howe (who wrote the words to the "Battle Hymn of the Republic") first suggested Mother's Day in 1872 as a day dedicated to peace. She held formal Mother's Day meetings in Boston, Massachusetts, every year.

In 1907, one Ana Jarvis from Philadelphia began a campaign to establish a national Mother's Day. She persuaded the church in Grafton, West Virginia, to celebrate Mother's Day on the second anniversary of her mother's death, the second Sunday of May. By the next year, that same unique day for mothers was celebrated in Philadelphia.

No absolutely clear record of how the holiday took hold nationally and internationally exists. Nevertheless, many peoples of the world, from countries such as Denmark, Finland, Italy, Turkey, Australia, and Belgium, simultaneously celebrate Mother's Day on the second Sunday in May. But while different nationalities honor mothers with a special time, many celebrate on different dates throughout the year.

Ester Schaler Buchholz

See also Father's Day

Mr. Rogers
See Rogers, Fred McFeely

Multiple Births
See In Vitro Fertilization (IVF); Twins and Multiples

Munchausen Syndrome by Proxy

Munchausen syndrome by proxy, also known as factitious disorder by proxy

(FDP), is a form of abuse in which a perpetrator intentionally and secretively fabricates a medical history or symptoms or induces illness in an individual under his or her care and then persistently presents the victim to an unsuspecting physician for medical treatment. The diagnosis is given to the perpetrator, who engages in this behavior in order to assume the patient's role vicariously and enjoy the ensuing attention, admiration, and support from friends, family, and the medical community. Typically, FDP is expressed as child abuse and directed by a parent, predominantly the mother, toward one or more of her children in order to fulfill a pathological emotional need. It represents a physically and psychologically damaging form of aberrant parenting that is a challenge to diagnose, prove, treat, or comprehend.

Factitious disorder by proxy is a variant of factitious disorder (FD), described in the *Diagnostic and Statistical Manual of Mental Disorder* of the American Psychiatric Association (4th ed., 1994) as the intentional fabrication of illness in oneself, without secondary gain, in order to assume the sick role. The original nomenclature, Munchausen syndrome or Munchausen syndrome by proxy, was derived from a Baron von Munchausen, an eighteenth-century raconteur who told fanciful tales.

Perpetrators of FDP are likely to have a family history of FD. Both FD and FDP are diagnosed in many cultures, and case studies appear in medical journals throughout the world.

By reporting a false medical history or secretively simulating or inducing fever, apnea, bleeding, seizures, infection, vomiting, diarrhea, rashes, behavioral abnormalities, developmental delay, or other compelling symptoms, the parent elicits medical attention from physicians and nurses who become "unwitting accomplices." (Ostfeld and Feldman, 1996, 84)

Invariably, their diagnostic and treatment efforts are doomed to end in failure, thus intensifying the physician's concern. In response to these medical challenges, physicians may extend hospital stays so that the patient may undergo medical tests, including unnecessary exposure to radiation and even exploratory surgery. These futile evaluations or interventions are not without risks and can lead to additional health problems that further gratify the parent's intense and complex emotional needs.

In 9 percent of all cases (Rosenberg, 1987), the parent's efforts to induce or feign illness result in the child's death. Most typically, the death occurs because the parent has overestimated the child's capacity to endure the harmful procedures used to induce symptoms (i.e., suffocation, salt poisoning, bloodletting, contamination of blood samples, imposition of dietary restrictions, or withholding of necessary medication). In families in which more than one child has been the victim of FDP, the mortality rate increases significantly. For survivors, there is a high rate of physical and psychological morbidity. Reported one adult survivor, "I go through . . . mourning for a childhood lost. . . . I am disfigured with permanent physical scars. Because of distorted motherly love, I continue to battle deep emotional wounds." (Byrk and Siegel, 1997) FDP is costly to society in additional ways. There is a risk that these children will grow into adults who fabricate their own illnesses or become factitious abusers of their offspring. FDP cases place a heavy burden on medical resources and raise the cost of medical care for all.

"[FDP] presents a haunting paradox (in that) two of society's most intensely heartfelt yet diametrically opposed states, 'good mothering' and 'callous child endangerment,' occur simultaneously." (Schreier and Libow, 1993) This paradox is underscored in published excerpts from thirty-three videotaped recordings in which perpetrators belie their public personas as nurturing parents by privately inflicting pain and suffering while showing either great anger or no emotion at all. (Southhall et al., 1997) Under a facade of normalcy sustained by superficial social skills frequently seethes a significantly disordered personality, variously described as antisocial and narcissistic. While not all individuals with FDP meet the criteria for a personality disorder, case reviews or evaluations generally report the perpetrators to be emotionally immature, lacking in empathy, excessively needy of attention and admiration, self-centered, manipulative, shallow, and exploitative. Case studies provide evidence of perpetrators given to pathological lying and denial, detached from their emotions, and impaired in the ability to acknowledge wrongdoing or express remorse or guilt, even in the face of objective proof and successful legal prosecution. Yet the ability of these parents to convince providers of their devotion to the very children they are abusing indicates how successful they are in "(fabricating) not only illness but also empathy." (Rosenberg 1997)

A number of psychological, social, and biological theories have been advanced concerning the etiology of this disorder. However, the perpetrator's tendency to provide a false family history of dramatic childhood events, including sexual abuse, makes it difficult to evaluate some of the hypotheses under study. Further limiting the study of etiology, identified cases are often the most severe and therefore may not be representative of milder cases. It does appear, however, that factors that increase the risk for developing FDP include victimization of the perpetrator in childhood by FDP, a history of FD, a personality disorder, and an early pathological relationship between the perpetrator and his or her parents. However, risk factors alone do not constitute proof, nor does their absence preclude a diagnosis of FDP.

By 1994, more than 250 cases of FDP were reported in medical literature. (Rosenberg,1994) However, the incidence rate for this form of abusive parenting remains difficult to establish. Until recently, the disorder was not well known and therefore rarely considered as a possible diagnosis. Moreover, even when physicians do suspect that it is taking place, they encounter difficulty in accepting the prospect or proving it to a judicial system that lacks knowledge of this form of child abuse and therefore reacts with disbelief. After all, FDP perpetrators appear highly respectful to, and appreciative of, medical personnel and health-care systems, making them well liked by staff and contributing to the difficulty providers have in imagining them as child abusers. They have been described as perfect parents who selflessly tend to their sick children, often to the exclusion of their other family members, and occasionally receive publicity for their courage in the face of seemingly insurmountable adversity. So compelling was the endurance and devotion of one such parent that in 1994 she was selected to present her child's medical history at a highly publicized Washington, D.C., health-care reform conference and was featured in publicity with First Lady Hillary Rodham Clinton. Ultimately, this mother was found to have FDP and convicted of causing the complex and seemingly untreatable medical problems her daughter endured, including seizures, an impaired immune response, and digestive problems so severe that they required the use of feeding tubes. Once removed from her mother's care, the child recovered—a classic outcome. Consistent with other types of abuse, FDP ultimately involves the collusion of the victim, who trades safety for a sustained—although troubled relationship—with the parent.

Physicians are also reluctant to pursue an FDP diagnosis because of their fears that they simply might have failed to diagnose or properly treat a seemingly obscure but genuine illness. But perhaps the most compelling source of ambivalence in confronting a parent is that, without adequate evidence, the physician may be unable to activate protective services or prevent a suspicious parent from removing his or her child against medical advice and pursuing care from a new and unsuspecting physician and hospital system, thus prolonging the duration of the abuse the child will suffer. A 1987 report estimated that an average of 14.9 months elapsed between the presentation of symptoms suggestive of FDP and the rendering of a diagnosis. (Rosenberg, 1987) Since then, many medical systems have attempted to improve the diagnostic process by using multidisciplinary medical teams to work collaboratively on cases, enhancing medical and legal education, and creating new protocols for gathering proof, including covert video surveillance, a controversial but highly effective intervention in which suspected parents are videotaped during hospital stays as they induce the symptoms that justify the prolongation of the hospitalization.

In several countries, covert surveillance has been used to obtain objective proof in cases with strong circumstantial evidence. Procedures for this type of documentation must address ethical, medical, and legal issues, and are generally developed collaboratively by child protection agencies and risk management and health-care systems. Documentation of an episode of symptom induction tends to occur swiftly, within a median of twenty-nine hours, reflecting the continual need for perpetrators to sustain the symptoms that justify continued hospitalization.

The high rate of video corroboration in cases that have been published or prosecuted indicates that the markers of suspicion that are used to alert physicians are valuable. Warning signs in the child have been compiled in numerous sources and may include: highly unusual symptoms that are beyond the experience of multiple primary-care physicians and specialists and that make no sense physiologically and defy diagnosis; too robust a picture of health in contrast to what the symptoms would suggest; failure to respond to all standard treatments; and a disappearance or resolution of all symptoms when the parent is absent. In addition, the parent is always alone with the child when symptoms emerge. Although the medical and nursing staff may witness the continuation of symptoms, such as fainting or a seizure, the parent is the only one to witness their onset.

Simultaneously, there are aspects of the parent's behavior that raise concerns. The physician may note that he or she is often more distressed than the parent that a cause cannot be found. The parent grows distressed when the child appears to recover or approach discharge. Medical tests are welcomed even if they are painful or invasive. The parent insists on giving all medications and feedings to the child. The parent is deemed to be a poor reporter, presenting information that is inconsistent with what had been observed by others or recorded in tests. When the child's medical history is questioned or supporting documentation is requested, the parent appears defensive and often reports that records have been lost. Other dramatic and unsubstantiated health episodes are described by the parent in their own medical history or in the history of their other children. It is important to note, however, that warning signs merely raise suspicion and suggest that further investigation is required. Apart from covert surveillance, investigatory procedures may include temporary separation of parent and child or the collection of the child's biological specimens for tox-icologic analysis.

Physicians are mindful of the harm that could be caused by an incorrect diagnosis of FDP. Therefore, they are careful to distinguish several types of parental behavior or illnesses that should not be confused with it. Some legitimate illnesses have a great variability in the severity of their symptoms over the course of time. An alarming symptom first noted at home may be milder by the time the patient has been brought to the emergency room. However, the parent will not refute the change in severity. Some parents may appear overanxious, more concerned about a symptom than a physician feels is warranted. However, in these instances, the parent is seeking reassurance and is receptive to the physician's information. Occasionally, an older child may be a malingerer, falsely describing alarming symptoms that the parent feels compelled to report. A secondary gain for the child can usually be identified when malingering is suspected. Of greatest concern are cases in which a legitimate medical illness, syndrome, or disorder, such as sudden infant death syndrome (SIDS), lacks a specific anatomical or biochemical marker that irrefutably defines the diagnosis. Although SIDS is one of the most common causes of infant mortality, a unique diagnostic marker has not yet been identified. Therefore, SIDS is diagnosed only after a death-scene investigation and an autopsy are conducted and all known causes of sudden death in a seemingly healthy infant are ruled out. Even though SIDS has clearly defined epidemiological characteristics, "and is significantly more common than infanticide, the absence of a clear-cut marker renders parents vulnerable to charges of abuse . . . [producing] additional distress for legitimately bereaved parents. Mindful of their suffering, the Committee on Child Abuse and Neglect of the American Academy of Pediatrics has endorsed guidelines that . . . enhance the recognition of infanticide without stigmatizing SIDS families." (Ostfeld and Feldman, 1996, 101) Finally, there are instances in which FDP has been charged in custody cases between divorcing parents. Each case must be carefully evaluated on its merits.

Perpetrators of FDP are not psychotic and are able to distinguish right from wrong. Therefore, they are not excused from criminal prosecution and imprisonment, even in instances when a personality disorder may be identified. In addition to prosecuting the parent, the court issues recommendations to ensure the safety of the child. The child is separated from the parent and is placed in foster care or in the care of relatives who can assure his or her safety. A psychological evaluation and therapy is also often recommended for the child. Before the family can be reunited, the parent is required to undergo therapy. To date, however, therapeutic interventions have not been highly effective, particularly in cases in which the parent attempts to manipulate the therapist by denying the abuse or participates without investment, doing so only because it is required by the court. However, as milder cases become identified, these may prove more responsive. If supervised visits begin, the court requires careful monitoring of the child's medical status. Reunions require active participation by reliable family members to prevent the family from disappearing from supervision and resuming the abuse.

Barbara M. Ostfeld

References and further reading
American Psychiatric Association. 1994. *Diagnostic and Statistical Manual of Mental Disorders.* 4th ed. Washington, DC: American Psychiatric Association.
Byrk, Mary, and Patricia T. Siegel. 1997. "My Mother Caused My Illness: The Story of a Survivor of Munchausen by Proxy Syndrome." *Pediatrics* 100:1–7.

Ostfeld, Barbara M., and Marc D. Feldman. 1996. "Factitious Disorder by Proxy: Clinical Features, Detection and Management." Pp. 83–108 in *The Spectrum of Factitious Disorders* (Clinical Practice Series, no. 40). Edited by Marc D. Feldman and Stuart J. Eisendrath. Washington, DC: American Psychiatric Press.

Rosenberg, Donna A. 1987. "Web of Deceit: A Literature Review of Munchausen Syndrome by Proxy." *Child Abuse & Neglect* 11:547–563.

———. 1994. "Munchausen Syndrome by Proxy." Pp. 226–278 in *Child Abuse: Medical Diagnosis and Management.* Edited by Robert M. Reece. Philadelphia: Lea & Febiger.

———. 1997. "Munchausen Syndrome by Proxy: Currency in Counterfeit Illnesses." Pp. 413–430 in *The Battered Child.* 5th ed. Edited by Mary E. Helfer, Ruth S. Kempe, and Richard D. Krugman. Chicago: University of Chicago Press.

Schreier, Herbert A., and Judith A. Libow. 1993. *Hurting for Love: Munchausen Syndrome by Proxy.* New York: Guilford Press.

Southall, David P., Michael C. B. Plunkett, Martin W. Banks, Adrian F. Falkov, and Martin P. Samuels. 1997. "Covert Video Recordings of Life-Threatening Child Abuse: Lessons for Child Protection." *Pediatrics* 100:735–760.